American Ambassador

American Ambassador

JOSEPH C. GREW and the Development of the United States Diplomatic Tradition

---

BY WALDO H. HEINRICHS, JR.

with photographs

OXFORD UNIVERSITY PRESS
New York Oxford

Oxford University Press
Oxford New York Toronto
Delhi Bombay Calcutta Madras Karachi
Petaling Jaya Singapore Hong Kong Tokyo
Nairobi Dar es Salaam Cape Town
Melbourne Auckland

and associated companies in
Beirut Berlin Ibadan Nicosia

First published in 1966 by Little, Brown and Company, Boston
First issued in paperback in 1986 by Oxford University Press, Inc.
200 Madison Avenue, New York, New York 10016

Library of Congress Cataloging-in-Publication Data

Heinrichs, Waldo H.
American ambassador.

Reprint. Originally published: Boston : Little,
Brown, 1966.
Bibliography: p.
Includes index.
1. Grew, Joseph C. (Joseph Clark), 1880–1965.
2. Ambassadors—United States—Biography.
3. United States—Foreign relations—20th century.
4. United States—Foreign relations—Japan.
5. Japan—Foreign relations—United States.
6. United States—Diplomatic and consular service.
I. Title.
E748.G835H4 1986 327.2'092'4 [B] 86-16184
ISBN 0-19-504159-3 (pbk.)

Printing (last digit): 9 8 7 6 5 4 3 2 1

Printed in the United States of America

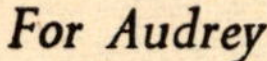

For Audrey

Preface

DURING most of their past Americans have barely tolerated diplomats. The art is a mysterious one and its practice tends to set the diplomat apart from his country. Diplomacy was alien to the American experience and contradictory to the national virtues of democratic simplicity and non-entanglement abroad. American diplomats have received more than their share of criticism, being described from time to time as soft, snobbish, subversive, or simply inept. The only diplomat who has always been acceptable was the most guileful of them all, Benjamin Franklin.

However alien, diplomacy and diplomats have been increasingly important to the United States. Rise to world power and the growing complexity of the nation's interests abroad have required expert conduct of relations with foreign nations. The United States dispensed with the idea of amateur representation, became more amenable to European diplomatic practice, and provided various inducements to retain a corps of experienced diplomatic officers. In time the nation established a full-fledged diplomatic career. The officers retained and promoted developed a sense of professionalism about diplomacy.

American professional diplomacy is perhaps best understood as a disagreeable necessity. Because they were necessary, the diplomats were in a strategic position to define their role. Up to a point, they could establish their own criteria of performance, develop an independent perspective in keeping with their role as middlemen, adopt European practice, and relate themselves in their own way to American values. However, the American public and government were bound to take a hand in defining the role of the diplomat. They would seek to housebreak diplomacy, determining the values to be represented, setting the style, describing the functions, and deciding what degree of independence was tolerable. The nature of American professional diplomacy was defined by the interaction resulting from these different perspectives.

The process of definition began at the turn of the century and has proceeded ever since, though with lessening intensity in recent years. A crucial point in the process was the passage of the Rogers Act in 1924, which created a single American Foreign Service from the old Diplomatic and Consular Services. In my brief career in the Foreign Service I became interested in the nature of American professional diplomacy, and later, as a graduate student at Harvard, I took advantage of Professor Oscar Handlin's seminar to start an investigation of its origins. It seemed that 1924 was a strategic point of attack. In a sense then, I began this book with Chapter 7, which is about the establishment of the American Foreign Service.

Research introduced me to the papers of Joseph C. Grew, who as Under Secretary of State figured prominently in the establishment and early administration of the new Service. This collection, conveniently located at Harvard's Houghton Library, proved astonishingly rich. It consisted mainly of well over a hundred typed, neatly ordered, leatherbound volumes. Included were Grew's correspondence, memoranda of official conversations, newspaper clippings, and most important, the huge diary, which runs to some six thousand pages for the Japan mission alone.

Grew started his extraordinary collection in 1909 when he was a junior Secretary in the American Embassy at St. Petersburg. Like anyone abroad, he wanted to keep in touch with his family and friends and to describe his travels and exotic experiences. He wrote his letters on a typewriter and kept copies of all his correspondence. By 1911 he saw the advantage of a diary. One account and extra carbons would provide a record for his own family as well as his wife's. Ultimately it provided for intimate friends, daughters, and sons-in-law as well. As Grew's career and responsibilities advanced, the diary became more historical. With a keen sense of history, he determined to enlarge the record from his vantage point inside events. It also served as a record for himself, to which he would refer for what he had thought or heard or said on any particular diplomatic event or subject. He found the diary a useful way of mulling over ideas and problems. Given some success in diplomacy, he might also use the diary as a basis for publishing his memoirs.

Any daily record with so many addressees cannot be entirely candid or intimate. The value of his diary, together with his other papers, lies mostly in the sheer bulk and detail. Grew provided sufficient information to reconstruct not only the manner and substance of his diplomacy over large parts of his career but also for certain periods the day-to-day framework of assumption, knowledge, and belief with which he viewed events.

The more familiar I became with Grew's career, the more interesting it seemed as the basis for a study of American professional diplomacy. He started out at the turn of the century, when American diplomacy was an episodic, amateurish affair, and saw it develop into a fully established and accepted career. Indeed, he was one of the first Americans to achieve a full career in diplomacy. He not only figured prominently in setting up the Foreign Service in 1924 but had already developed a strong sense of professionalism that animated the rest of his career. He was the model professional diplomat of his generation.

His career spanned most of the modern age of American diplomacy, from Theodore Roosevelt to Harry Truman. He attended two major international conferences and held two ambassadorships, two Under Secretaryships, two ministerships, and every junior rank in the Service. He was at Berlin when the United States went to war with Germany in 1917 and at Tokyo when Japan went to war with the United States in 1941. He was Ambassador to Japan from Manchuria to Pearl Harbor and played a part in Japan's surrender in 1945. If anyone was likely to reveal what American professional diplomacy was really like, it would be Joseph C. Grew.

I decided to make a full-scale study of Grew's career. It would be a biography, but one concerned with his life mostly for the way it revealed him as a diplomat. It would be diplomatic history insofar as the context of Grew's diplomacy contributed to an understanding of his diplomacy. Grew's career up to 1925 was the subject of my doctoral dissertation, and since then I have carried the study forward to completion. This book is the result.

In the course of this study I met Mr. Grew several times. He was invariably kind and helpful. He gave me permission to use his papers and was always available when I wished to consult him. At no point did he interfere or comment, either adversely or favorably. He was content to let his records speak for themselves. I could not have asked for more. After Mr. Grew's death, his daughter, Mrs. Albert Lévitt, assumed the responsibility for giving permission to publish from the Grew Papers, as well as from the papers of her former husband, Jay Pierrepont Moffat, who died in 1943. She read the entire manuscript and pointed out a few minor inaccuracies but in no case asked for a deletion or change. For her gracious assistance I am deeply grateful.

This study would have been impossible without the time, effort, and expert advice of many people. Professor Frank Freidel and Professor Ernest R. May of Harvard directed the dissertation and have continued to assist me far beyond the call of duty. Professor Keith M. Greenwood and several of his colleagues at Robert College, Istanbul, read the chapters on the mission to Turkey and offered valuable comments and corrections. Professor Akira Iriye of Harvard read most of the chapters on the Japan mission and Mr. Ikuhiko Hata the early chapters. If I have erred in describing Japanese politics and policies, it is not for want of effort on their part to explain. The chapters on the Japan mission would have been hopelessly difficult without their advice and encouragement. Dr. Kent Roberts Greenfield gave me the benefit of his wisdom and precise criticism on a number of chapters. I am grateful to Professor Oscar Handlin for setting me on my way in the Grew study and to Miss Winifred Levey for her expert stylistic criticism. To Professor Otis A. Pease of Stanford I owe more than I can say, not only for his professional assistance in this study but for his constant encouragement of my historical pursuits. Professor Charles A. Barker, my colleague at The Johns Hopkins University, has sustained me in many ways.

I wish to thank Dr. E. Taylor Parks of the Department of State Historical Office and Miss Patricia Dowling of the National Archives for their help in locating and providing records of the State Department. I am grateful to the staff of the Houghton Library, the Minnesota State Historical Society Library, St. Paul, Minnesota, and the Library of Congress for assistance in research. The East Asian Institute at Harvard University made possible a year of study and writing there that was crucial in forwarding the chapters on the Japan mission. I am also grateful for a travel grant from the Ford Foundation.

No one can undertake such a study without a deep sense of gratitude for the craftsmanship of Walter Johnson in editing the Grew Papers. Encompassed within the two volumes of *Turbulent Era*[1] are the essential elements of Grew's career, selected in a manner to provide a smooth and fascinating autobiography. That there is much, much more in the treasure of the Grew Papers, Professor Johnson would, I am sure, agree.

Family assists in ways impossible to relate. My mother, and before his death my father, helped as only parents can. My wife, Audrey S. Heinrichs, was my best critic. If writing a book is suffering, as it is, mine was shared six ways, by Peter, Tim, Ricky, Mark, and above all by Audrey.

WALDO H. HEINRICHS, JR.

Knoxville, Tennessee
July 1966

Contents

Illustrations

(*between pages 216 and 217*)

PART ONE

Background and Early Career

(1880 – 1922)

ONE

The Making of a Diplomat

BOSTON'S Back Bay still looks respectable. An occasional brisk, clean-lined building jostles its ponderous neighbors, but most of the way up Marlborough Street the drab brick front remains unbroken, frowning down on rows of parked cars, between which an occasional cart horse clip-clops along swishing his tail as if to flick away the glittering anachronisms. Between Exeter and Dartmouth streets is a two-family structure only slightly more impressive than the rest. Number 185 differs from its other half only in having rounded instead of angular window bays. It was here that Joseph Clark Grew, who was born on May 27, 1880, spent his boyhood.

Joseph Grew's great-grandfather John Grew was born in Boston exactly a century before him during the Revolution, and this ancestor's father was born in Birmingham, England, in 1752. By Joseph's time the Grews had established a solid reputation and modest fortune in Boston business. While not one of Boston's first families, the Grews were socially among them. Joseph was related directly or indirectly to Parkmans, Sturgises, and Wigglesworths. His father, Edward Sturgis Grew, was a successful wool merchant; his uncle, Henry Sturgis Grew, was a partner in Russell & Company, famous China traders. Grew's mother, Annie Crawford Clark Grew, had been born in nearby Milton, the daughter of Joseph Clark, a prominent Boston businessman with Western mining interests. Her mother, Eleanor Arnold Clark, came from a well-known Quaker family of Providence.[1]

There are few children in Back Bay now. Not so in the 1880's. Then the Charles River, the Fens, Beacon Hill, and Copley Square bounded a small world of prosperous young families. Within these strict boundaries, the atmosphere was small town rather than urban or cosmopolitan. William Phillips, who lived a few blocks down Marlborough Street, recalls what a pleasant world it was. Cousins or family friends lived on every street. Gangs of Phillipses and Motleys waged merciless small-boy war, carrying the advantage even up the enemy's back stairs, to the outrage of cooks and maids. Grew suggests that "Coppie" Doyle's beat past 185 Marlborough was no sinecure either.[2]

Joseph was the youngest of three boys. His older brothers Randolph and Henry followed the appointed path to Harvard and State Street, Randolph in real estate and Henry in banking. There was also a sister, Eleanor.

Grew was always very close to his mother. His relations with his father are hard to assess. They were severely strained later over his choice of career, and thereafter their correspondence was most perfunctory. How far back there was tension between the ultra-conservative businessman and his high-spirited son remains a question. Two facts about their early relationship are suggestive but inconclusive: the father insisted that the boy switch from left-handed to right-handed writing, with a resulting cramped scrawl, and used to "drum" multiplication tables into the lad.[3]

Back Bay was a self-contained and satisfying world to grow up in, but there was a wider world as well: open country at his father's estate in nearby Hyde Park, and the seashore at All Oaks, the family summer home in Manchester on the North Shore. When he was seven Grew went to Europe with his parents for the customary tour of sights and watering places. Like countless other small boys, he dutifully accosted the wax policeman at Madame Tussaud's. Boston-bound, the small boy's mind could wander the world with Kipling or ply the China trade aboard one of his Uncle Henry's tea clippers.[4]

In the fall of 1892 when Joseph Grew was twelve he was sent to Groton, then in existence only eight years. The purpose of the school was "to cultivate manly Christian character, having regard to moral and physical, as well as intellectual development." To that end the boys were assigned dormitory cubicles with only a modicum of privacy and comfort, parents were warned not to send food, and a rigorous program of studies and sports was arranged to fill every waking moment from early morning cold shower to evening study hall. Spare time, the boys were admonished, should not be spent indoors where "the clear, cold air of heaven cannot penetrate." [5]

Grew's Groton career was unexceptional, but the school had a penetrating influence on his character. He won no prizes, but was "retained" while six of the ten boys in his entering form failed to graduate with him. Although he undoubtedly formed deep friendships among his classmates, none were significant to his later career. He was acquainted with Franklin D. Roosevelt, two years behind, but friendship between boys of different forms was frowned on.

Groton's formal education was successful more in rigorous discipline than in imaginative content. If a boy interspersed his Latin scanning with hesitant er's or ah's, he was told to be seated until he could rise to recite clearly. This cured Grew of slurred speech forever. The boys toiled through traditional texts in Latin, Greek, and French, learned their Catechism and Bible, practiced interest, algebra, and geometry, and dabbled in German and science. They read the usual classics of English literature and a few in history such as Lord Bryce's *American Commonwealth.* Daily themes, translations, and recitations coddled no self-expression, but forged a disciplined, precise style of writing and what Grew would call a "well-ordered mind." This did not necessarily imply a creative or imaginative mind. George Santayana wrote that Groton was "nicer" than Eton in everything but the result. "Tap an Eton mind," says Oliver Alden in *The Last Puritan,* "and you find the Odes of Horace; tap a Groton mind, and you find the last number of an illustrated magazine." The product of this rigorous apprenticeship in manly Christian character was "nicely groomed to run in harness." [6]

However, the purpose of Groton was not to produce an intellectual élite but to increase the social utility of the rich and wellborn. Most Grotonian consciences never twinged properly, but Reverend Endicott Peabody's ideal of public service pervaded the impressionable years of Franklin D. Roosevelt, Averell Harriman, Dean Acheson, and Joseph C. Grew; who can say it failed?

The Rector's influence worked in slow, mysterious ways. There were his sermons which Roosevelt remembered so vividly. There were heart-to-heart talks with Mr. Beebs, as Grew's housemaster Reverend Sherrard Billings was known. But it was more than words or events. Purposeful living was in every gulp of Groton air a boy breathed. It seeped in for five years, said Grew, during which he was a thoroughly inconsequential boy, and then one day in May of his fifth year it suddenly took hold. He never forgot that day. He had been despondent about his lack of academic and athletic success and rose early for a walk in a countryside bursting with spring. As he walked he suddenly perceived "the astounding truth that the only way to get your teeth into life is to bite hard." Grew bit. He studied hard and passed all his college examinations that summer. The following year, his last, he managed the sixth form play, successfully advocated a restriction of immigration before the Senior Debating Society, rowed on the second Squannacooks crew, and secured a place on the board of editors of the *Grotonian.*[7]

Grew's canoe, as he put it, would no longer drift aimlessly with the current. There is no evidence of immediate dedication to a career of public service, but such a dedication was persistently suggested by the school during Grew's years. A lecturer advised the boys that every man must make himself felt in the government of his country. Mr. Billings spoke of the need for the ablest men to serve as missionaries in Asia. *Grotonian* editorials warned of a degeneration in American public life and rang with assurances that "bossism" and Tammany Hall would fall as soon as citizens awoke to their duty. Captain Alfred Thayer Mahan stirred the boys with the thesis that war as well as peace had its virtues. Jacob Riis showed stereopticon slides of how the other half lived in New York slums. "We saw several pictures of quaint ragamuffins," the *Grotonian* primly reported.[8]

Just a month after Grew's awakening, Theodore Roosevelt arrived to describe his police reform in New York. He left the boys with the promise that success was born of failure and the challenge that it was every American's duty to be a "worker and not a looker-on in life." Finally, in Grew's last spring, war with Spain broke out. The *Grotonian,* of which he was now an editor, deplored American isolation from world affairs and advised the school not to limit horizons to studies and sports but to be aware of "the great affairs of the greater world." [9]

Grew emerged from Groton at eighteen, a handsome, well-built young man though still in knickers. He sat stiffly for school pictures, slicked-down hair parted squarely in the middle, eying the camera with cool condescension. He weighed 167 pounds, slightly heavier than his weight in 1911. The following fall of 1898 he entered Harvard.

Addressing the Harvard freshman class many years later, Grew suggested that the greatest asset gained in a college education was an analytical, disciplined, well-ordered mind. Intellectual brilliance, he felt, was not enough in the "practical rough-and-tumble of life." A further asset was intellectual "background" or "culture." This could be obtained from history, which acted like a compass in shaping the nation's course, and from experience in diversified fields of knowledge.[10]

On this occasion Grew was in effect describing his own experience. If the first and greatest asset, that of a well-ordered mind, he owed more to Groton than to Harvard, the second, his broad liberal education, was peculiarly the product of the Harvard of his day, the Harvard of Josiah Royce, William James, Archibald Cary Coolidge, and Charles Townsend Copeland. Under such intellectual inspiration, the well-prepared, well-groomed, well-heeled young aristocrats of Harvard's Gold Coast acquired their "gentlemanly C" with no great effort, and some enjoyment and profit, without risking deliberate commitment to the mastery of any particular subject. They would have been intellectual dilettantes if they had chosen to show off their smattering of culture, and they wore it discreetly.

Far more important was extracurricular life in which Grew was strenuously active. He became president of the *Advocate* and a senior editor of the *Crimson,* which gave him opportunities to develop literary and managerial talents. Franklin D. Roosevelt was with him on the *Crimson* staff, and Richard Washburn Child, later his colleague at Lausanne, was a contributor of local-color stories to the *Advocate.*

Grew tried hard in sports but experienced only modest success and a great deal of bad luck. As first substitute tackle on the freshman football team he journeyed to New Haven, and was about to enter the game when the final whistle blew. He also went to New Haven as first alternate for the crew, and was just stepping into the shell to replace a varsity oarsman who was stale, when a telegram from the head coach ordered the crew to race with the original line-up. He was on the second team in varsity football until his senior year when he was dropped. He then commenced Spartan conditioning for track by cross-country running over the snow. He made the team as a miler and was the first Harvard man to finish against Yale, but three New Haven milers beat him, the last by inches, and he missed his "H," thereby to his disappointment never qualifying as a member of the Varsity Club.[11]

Grew with his Boston and Groton background was inevitably a club man, following the usual path from the Hasty Pudding to the "Dickie" and finally the Fly or Alpha Delta Phi as it was then called. He was pledged to Fly in his bathtub by later Secretary of War Dwight Davis. He chose Fly rather than the more exclusive Porcellian or AD Clubs, he explained, because he and six of his friends vowed to stick together in one club and because Fly was more "democratic" in taking men on the basis of their "personal merits and popularity rather than on their family connections." Thirty years later he described his clubs and friends as the highlight of his college experience, followed in order by athletics, the *Advocate* and *Crimson*, and last the "lecture rooms." [12]

Summers from the age of fifteen Grew roamed further and further developing his love for the deep woods and the sea. He camped and sailed in Maine where once a seal surfaced in Northeast Harbor to hear him play the mandolin. In 1899 he shot elk at Jackson's Hole in Wyoming; in 1901 he hunted moose in the wild interior of New Brunswick. By graduation, Grew, sporting a pipe and bristling mustache, was a dedicated hunter-explorer and determined to prove himself. This was the age of Rooseveltian strenuosity, of man, vigorously disciplined in moral and muscle fiber, venturing into the unknown to tame the forces of nature. After graduation in 1902 he set off for an eighteen-month round-the-world trip.[13]

The most ardent disciple of Rudyard Kipling and Theodore Roosevelt could not have wished for a more romantic and adventurous *Wanderjahr*. As his ship neared Sicily on a moonlit night, "a great round mass of what seemed like molten gold" erupted from the dim shape of the volcano Stromboli. Then Suez, Colombo, with its first heady fragrance of the East, Penang, Singapore, and into the Malay jungle for a drenching, fruitless tiger hunt. He emerged with malaria and spent the following months convalescing and sight-seeing in northern India and New Zealand. At Lahore he reverently straddled Kim's gun. In New Zealand he had the luck to leave the brink of a great geyser five minutes before it erupted "with the hissing of a thousand rockets and the roar of a thousand cannon." Fit again, Grew retraced his course to India for better hunting, this time wild goat in the high Pamirs. He was triumphantly successful, bagging the limit including a magnificent ibex whose horns measured forty-four inches. It was here he met his greatest mountain, Nanga Parbat, sixteen thousand feet of which hung like a glistening cathedral above his tents.

Bear hunting in Kashmir followed, and then Grew sailed for China to seek the Amoy tiger. This was the climax of his expedition and a hunting experience which Theodore Roosevelt himself described as among the most thrilling and sportsmanlike imaginable. The Amoy tiger inhabited caves in the barren hills behind the port of Amoy. Here beaters cornered a ten-foot beast in its lair, and Grew, dragging his .450 Holland and Holland express, squirmed through a narrow passage to the inmost recess where the tiger lay, "his green eyes shining and blinking sleepily in the light, his great striped back moving up and down as he panted from fright and anger." The hunter lay five minutes watching, then moved his rifle slowly into position, and though unable to see the sights fired. The report extinguished the torches and left Grew in darkness, wedged in his tiny crevice with the wounded tiger leaping about the cave. Two more shots fired blindly killed the animal. On this exploit Grew rested his laurels as a big-game hunter. By Christmas 1903 he was back in Boston with twenty-two pieces of baggage, a Japanese valet, and an unconquerable desire to serve his country abroad.

Why this career? As with any man, the reasons were numerous and their relative weights hard to assess. He listed the call of the sea and the woods as preeminent in luring him from the prosaic life of State Street. "I developed the 'wanderlust' — which Kipling calls 'the old spring fret' — on that trip around the world and there was no settling down thereafter," he wrote in 1931.[14] Government service abroad would satisfy his yen for travel. An alternative for rebellious young Bostonians had been a tour abroad with one of the city's famous trading firms. Grew's uncle had spent several years in Shanghai for Russell & Company before settling down in Boston. But the China trade had dwindled, and the firm foundered in the nineties, so this avenue was closed.

The pull of the world, however, was accompanied by the push of Boston, Groton, and Harvard. Grew and his father were not of the same mold. The prospect of following a career so closely associated with a man so different in temperament could not have been attractive to the sensitive, "headstrong" son. Hugh Wilson, later Ambassador to Germany, and a close friend of Grew, spoke for this first generation of diplomats when he said that they rejected the way of their fathers because ease and education had made it difficult for them to understand the grimness with which their fathers faced life and pursued the amassing of fortunes. There must be a wider scope for life than business, they felt.[15]

Harvard added its influence as well. A notable line of diplomats emerged from Harvard of that day, among them Edwin Morgan '90, Phelps Dodge '92, Charles S. Wilson and Franklin Mott Gunther '97, Frederick Sterling '98, Robert Woods Bliss, William R. Castle, Jr., and William Phillips '00, and Grew '02. Upon many of these, Grew among them, the pioneering courses in Middle Eastern and Russian History of Professor Archibald Cary Coolidge exerted a powerful influence in the direction of international affairs.[16]

Grew felt a call to public service too. The chemistry of Groton catalyzed by Theodore Roosevelt had done its work. Many young men of "seasoned wealth and seasoned conscience" were joining the Progressive movement, but politics held no appeal for Grew. It meant coming to terms with the State Street of his father or the South End of the Irish immigrant. He rebelled against the former and had no inclination to rub shoulders with the latter. He heard Roosevelt's appeal as a call to adventure in his country's service abroad. Cutting oneself off from Boston was, as Phillips said, "doubtful business." In diplomacy he could explain it as duty. Furthermore in diplomacy he could retain his Back Bay values in a more exotic setting. He was not yet fully committed to public service. Diplomacy was an escape into the world beyond, but one carefully rationalized with the world he left behind. For Grew and others of his generation it was an adventure that only later became a career.[17]

During the eight months following his return from the Far East, Grew occupied himself so energetically in such diverse activities that it is little wonder his father lost hope of him settling down to be a Boston banker. First the young man compromised with his father, agreeing to try publishing, but there were no openings. Meanwhile, he enrolled in a commercial school to learn touch typing. Then he left for France to polish up his French, but not before he had met and fallen in love with his future wife.[18]

Alice de Vermandois Perry was all an aspiring diplomat could wish for in a wife. Her beauty and charm became an important asset in his career. She was a direct descendant of America's first diplomat, Benjamin Franklin, and of Commodore Oliver Perry. Her father, Thomas Sergeant Perry, scholar, critic, and one of the last of the "Boston Brahmins," became a dearly loved father-in-law whose correspondence crackled with wit and sense. Her mother was a Boston Cabot. Furthermore, Alice Perry had lived in Japan with her family and spoke the language, to the delight of Suzuki, Grew's valet, who delivered her admirer's notes and flowers.[19]

Grew missed his first chance for a Foreign Service appointment on account of a physical defect that handicapped him throughout his career. Edwin V. Morgan, Consul General in Korea, sought Grew for his private secretary, but was advised by Professor Archie Coolidge, who inquired at Grew's club, that the young man was deaf. Grew's deafness was apparently due to a defect in the vibratory bones of the middle ear on both sides, the result of scarlet fever at the age of seven. While he could hear well enough in face-to-face conversation, provided the speaker enunciated clearly, he lost most general conversation, speeches, and pianissimo music. Frequent treatments brought only slight, temporary improvement. "I almost committed suicide upon losing the Korean assignment," he recalled, but in fact he was fortunate, for the position never materialized.[20]

Coolidge's misunderstanding of the extent of Grew's deafness was corrected, and soon another opportunity came. He was living with a French family at Tours when a telegram arrived from Coolidge offering him a clerkship with Edwin Morgan's brother Fred at Cairo. Grew sent two telegrams, the first asking for time to consider, the second four hours later with his unconditional acceptance. He returned hastily to Boston, became engaged to Alice Perry, made peace with his father, and left for Cairo. He arrived at his first post on July 19, 1904, with the temperature 118 degrees in the shade.

What sort of "service" had Joseph Grew embarked on so impetuously? Service is hardly the word to describe the aggregation of consuls and diplomats which represented the United States abroad at that time. None of the characteristics of a professional civil service organization were present: no entrance by examination, no tenure, no system of promotion for merit. The diplomats consisted of ambassadors, ministers, and secretaries. Ambassadors and ministers were generally important politicians, temporarily unemployed, or heavy contributors to political campaigns. There had also been a few literary lights such as James Russell Lowell, who "covered our nakedness in the eyes of foreigners." There had even been a few, like Charles Francis Adams, of exceptional diplomatic talent. These amateur diplomats took secretaries with them, young men of independent means seeking a few years in world affairs and European society before settling down to serious occupations. Few of these remained in diplomacy longer than their chiefs; only a handful succeeded in making it anything approaching a career.[21]

Consular appointments were small coin by comparison. They served as rewards and incomes for minor politicians. The pittance of a salary (Grew's was six hundred dollars) was augmented by private business ventures, consular fees, and often by swindling. In quality of service the government got what it paid for In 1906 an inspector of American consulates in the Orient found two consuls who were decrepit, two otherwise unfit for duty, one morally suspect, one charged with coercing a sultan into paying a debt for which he, the consul, was collector, one charged with drunkenness and the issuance of fraudulent papers, and one, "a coarse and brutal type," against whom eighty-two complaints had been registered.[22]

The prospects for Grew's career were not as dark as the record indicated, however. In fact, they were just beginning to brighten. The expansion of American political and economic interest in world affairs toward the end of the nineteenth century, sharpened and symbolized by the Spanish-American War, gave new national importance to the work of diplomats and consuls. The glare of public interest revealed them as hopelessly inadequate. Businessmen seeking new markets received little helpful information. American travelers were rebuffed or ignored by officials in dingy consulates and embassies located on back streets. Abroad this powerful nation appeared weak, inefficient, and corrupt. What looked to the muckraker like corruption looked to the businessman like inefficiency, and for both the solution was civil service reform. Articles in *Harper's, Outlook, Century, North American Review* and *Nation* called the attention of the educated Eastern middle class to the imperative need for reform, while businessmen engaged in foreign trade brought powerful pressure to bear through chambers of commerce and the National Board of Trade.[23]

The reform movement was at its height when Theodore Roosevelt succeeded to the Presidency during Grew's senior year at Harvard. It was particularly congenial to Roosevelt, for here was an opportunity for improving the civil service as well as for increasing American influence in world affairs. In 1906 pressure for reform culminated in a bill opening the way for a professional Consular Service. Roosevelt promptly installed it by executive order, and his successor President Taft applied the same principle to the diplomats in 1909. Deficiencies of scope, organization, and pay remained, but the 1906 and 1909 reforms were the first important steps in American Foreign Service development. Furthermore, the size of the American diplomatic establishment was growing by leaps and bounds, the number of choice European secretaryships more than doubling between 1899 and 1906.[24] Judging by the past, Grew never could have hoped for a Foreign Service career, but looking forward it would seem like a reasonable gamble, and in Cairo, Grew was learning the fine art of poker.

Poker at the officers' mess of the King's Royal Rifles, pigeon shoots, tennis in the burning afternoons at Gezireh, cool nights on a camp cot at the edge of the desert, clawing barefoot up the smooth, overhanging casing at the top of the second pyramid of Gizeh: these experiences in the "perpetually romantic" Egypt of Lord Cromer, Grew remembered fondly. But he did not neglect the duties of a lowly consular clerk. Indeed he was overzealous. Long ago, diplomacy involved the indexing, deciphering, and preservation of ancient documents called "diplomas." Grew took this traditional archivist approach to his consular duties, indexing ten years of Cairo correspondence with the loving care of a twelfth-century Papal Chancery clerk. It took him three months of night work. When completed the index was promptly consigned to the cellar by his chief, who thought it too cumbersome. It was a significant effort, however, for a consulate is like a law office in that it deals with an infinite variety of individual cases involving regulations and laws of the United States. Archives, as Grew instinctively perceived, are indispensable for local precedents and case histories. Besides, he was orderly by nature. His office always had to be up to date and efficient and his desk clean of back work.

A consulate is also a shipping company, public relations agency, research organization, and travelers' aid society. Grew learned how to certify invoices and write trade reports. Consul General Lewis Iddings, a former reporter, blue-penciled ponderous Grotonian prose into a light, conversational style. As Deputy Consul General, a title without salary, Grew made his first diplomatic bows and friendships. Obtaining the personal confidence of diplomatic colleagues upon whom he would depend for vital information was costly in time. Friendships such as those in Cairo with Horace Rumbold and Francis Lindley were pleasantly renewed at later posts, and quickly eased Grew into unfamiliar surroundings.

In the fall of 1905 Grew went home to marry Alice Perry. After a honeymoon in the Maine woods he returned to Egypt with his wife, but all their wedding presents were lost when the ship transporting their goods sank off the Barbary Coast.

Happily and vigorously Grew learned the routine of consular work. He felt "part of the big machine" at last. But though he never regretted this, his only consular assignment, he wanted to be a diplomat. Grew's family made his wishes known to their friend Bellamy Storer, Ambassador to Austria-Hungary. Mrs. Storer wrote to Mrs. Theodore Roosevelt asking for Grew as Third Secretary in Vienna. The President answered coolly that he had made his own opportunities in public life by proving himself better able to do the job than anyone else, that he had never heard of Grew, and that he had other young men of eminent fitness in mind.[25]

Finally in March 1906 the Amoy tiger did its greatest service in securing Grew the appointment as Third Secretary of Embassy in Mexico City. Alford W. Cooley, Roosevelt's Assistant Attorney General, was a Harvard classmate of Randolph Grew. As Cooley scrambled along with the President on a hike one day, he related Grew's adventure in China and his desire for a diplomatic appointment. Roosevelt, who regarded diplomats as "stuffed dolls,"[26] probably saw sturdier stuff in the young man and promised to help him. Despite a recently issued order requiring examinations for appointment, transfers were still possible, and a secretaryship was found. Grew entered as one of the last under the old system.

The year from April 1906 to June 1907 was one of the most hectic and frustrating of Grew's career. His wife was expecting a baby and he felt compelled to leave her in France with her parents while he took up his new post in Mexico. He crossed the Atlantic only to return to his wife's side, with the blessing of the Department of State. After Edith Grew was born in September 1906 the little family had such a rough Atlantic crossing that it seemed as if only the baby and captain were not seasick. Their belongings were further depleted when Mexican customs officials roughly unpacked them and delivered them to a carter who took them to his own home for a thorough ransacking. The Grews had just settled in Mexico when Mrs. Grew became dangerously ill, apparently from the altitude. She was completely paralyzed and had to be carried out of Mexico on a stretcher. Grew hurried his wife to Boston in November 1906, where she was for a time near death but gradually recovered. A new post was arranged for him at St. Petersburg, Russia, where he arrived on May 31, 1907. On this move all their furniture was lost.

At one time diplomatic secretaries were nothing but secretaries, who wrote the minister's letters, kept his papers, and left his cards. Gradually, as is the tendency in governmental development, the position of secretary of legation evolved, with a small stipend and diplomatic status.[27] By 1907 a ladderlike hierarchy of First, Second, and Third Secretaries existed in larger embassies. At St. Petersburg, Grew was the junior Secretary, and upon him devolved strictly secretarial duties such as laboriously transcribing typed dispatches into permanent record books. This left his betters, the First and Second Secretaries, free to circulate in society gathering political news and gossip. However, this Third Secretary, with his love of efficiency, saw a better way. Why not use carbons? The Ambassador was willing but the First Secretary, whom Grew in his ardor had bypassed, promptly quashed the reform. Undoubtedly more than a violation of the chain of command was involved, since embassies in those days, with a precariously small amount of required routine work, could scarcely afford to be efficient.

It was an enjoyable year at St. Petersburg. Where George Kennan might be impressed with the coldness of the River Neva, moving "silently and swiftly, like a slab of smooth grey metal," Grew, in prerevolutionary days, found the colors on the river at twilight "superb, sometimes a pink and sometimes a delicate blue haze covering it. . . ." Czarist Russia provided handsome spectacles, though an American diplomat had to worry about tripping over his sword as he crossed the polished floor to make his first bows to royalty. But the court functions were infrequent and Embassy hours short, so there was plenty of time to study Russian and German, and to sport with diplomatic colleagues such as Nevile Henderson, later ambassador to Germany, and Count Leopold Berchtold, later Foreign Minister of Austria-Hungary. The Grews toured only once, to Moscow.[28]

At the end of the year Grew was transferred to Berlin and promoted to Second Secretary. After six years of world wandering at a frantic pace, he settled down to what would be, with a hiatus of eighteen months, sixteen years of continuous service at posts in western Europe.

With the exception of a short term in 1911 and 1912 in Vienna, Grew served in Berlin from 1908 until America entered the war in 1917. This was the twilight of the Victorian era, a period Herbert Hoover called the happiest of all humanity in ten centuries. Society seemed immutable to those it favored and insulated by wealth or social position. Joseph Grew moved in just such a "fool's paradise," to use his words, where the illusion was heightened by a glittering court society.[29]

Although Grew found Berlin society stiff and rank-conscious, he took his entertaining duties very seriously. During the season, the Grews' social calendar was booked solid with luncheons, teas, dinners and dances. Mrs. Grew with her "gleaming black hair, a flashing smile, a slender and beautifully clothed figure," was an indefatigable hostess, much sought after in society. Because they both spoke fluent German they were occasionally invited to houses where they were the only diplomats, but generally from one affair to the next they saw the same faces: diplomats, particularly from the British and Italian embassies, Foreign Office officials and a sprinkling of nobility. An occasional royal prince, businessman, professor, musician or traveling American was added for seasoning. One searches in vain for significant acquaintanceships among intellectuals, business leaders, politicians, and "second class Germans." These were not in the "best crowd." However, Grew made a practice of getting to know newspaper correspondents, whom, one suspects, diplomats used for collecting information which did not penetrate the drawing rooms.[30]

Grew's social circle was aristocratic, but this was still the era of courtier diplomacy. As he said, in explaining why they had not gone into mourning for the death of a relative: "We had engagements booked ahead nearly every single evening, most of them dinners. An Embassy's standing and prestige depends largely on its personnel and this also largely determines its usefulness." [31]

Furthermore, the United States at this time, contrary to its traditional adherence to "Jeffersonian simplicity" in representation abroad, was particularly sensitive to its prestige in European capitals. John Bassett Moore, an authority on international law, noted in 1905 a recent "visible tendency toward conformity to customs elsewhere established . . . accelerated by the natural drift of a great and powerful nation toward participation in world affairs." The rank of ambassador was created in 1893, he felt, not from need but from a dislike of eccentricity. In Vienna, Mark Twain derided the small salaries paid our diplomats. The United States was a young woman in society now who "stops sleeping with her little sister, has a room of her own, and becomes in many ways a thundering expense." [32]

The predecessor of Grew's chief at Berlin was Charlemagne Tower, whose lavish entertainment had created a position for his wife as the "von Moltke of German society." When the Kaiser intimated that Tower's successor, Dr. David Jayne Hill, might not be able to afford to maintain the Embassy's prestige, and word leaked to the press, there was a public outcry in the United States. But the protest was directed not so much against spending money to win prestige as it was against the fact that the government did not provide sufficient salary so that any American could afford to serve. "If we are going into the game, we must play it according to the rules," said the *Nation*.[33]

But even granting the pressure for conformity, Grew was more sympathetic than critical toward the customs of Berlin society. He felt that a uniform such as European diplomats wore was just as appropriate for his service as it was for the Army and Navy. When an ambassador set the example, Grew arrayed himself in striped pants, gold-laced coat, sword, and fore-and-aft hat with red, white, and blue cockade. In 1913 he urged the new Ambassador, James W. Gerard, to buy a uniform. Failure to wear one would be regarded as a "distinct lack of courtesy and deference to the well-known wishes of the German court." The Tammany chief agreed, but word leaked back to America and the Democratic Administration ordered Berlin back to white tie and tails.[34]

Grew's letters home contain a minute account of parties and court functions, with repeated admonitions that all this "hobnobbing with royalty" had left his "American simplicity" unaffected. "I only put everything down for your own interest," he wrote his mother, "and not because we attach any importance to the fact that royalty seems to smile on us." [35]

It is hard to understand how Grew could sincerely and persistently proclaim his democratic instincts and yet obviously enjoy aristocratic society. The apparent ambivalence is explained by his definition of the word "democratic." What he meant was that people should be treated according to their merit and not their rank. He was critical of Berlin society as being too rank-conscious, preferring Vienna society where admission to the inner circle depended on personal merit alone. This had been his reason for favoring the Fly Club at Harvard. But what were the merits Grew judged men by? He admired qualities of character such as sincerity, loyalty, and integrity wherever he found them, but almost invariably the outward man was judged along with the inward. Thus he would describe a colleague as pleasant, able and genuine, but "none too presentable," and "a little common." For Grew and others of his social position in America, there was a harmony assumed in the word "gentleman" between the outward and inward man. Being a gentleman implied qualities of character but also had outward manifestations in tact, taste, and manners.[36]

Thus the people Grew found congenial had a similarity of background and social position; his democratic criterion was applied within upper-class society. To most Americans he and his friends would appear exclusive, aristocratic, and often snobbish.

If Grew's usefulness as a diplomat is judged by the company he kept, it appears limited. He circulated in court society; his close friends were only a tighter circle within that society. He himself admits as much. He wished he could give a colleague in Berlin some letters to "nice Germans," he wrote from Vienna, "but as a matter of fact our good friends in Berlin were almost entirely among the diplomats." It should be added that his friendships among the diplomats were warm and useful and that this type of social life was typical of diplomats at that time.[37]

The Grews lived comfortably and fashionably in the manner of diplomatic secretaries of that day and post. His salary, from two to three thousand dollars, was supplemented by private income and allowances from his mother to a total of approximately fifteen thousand dollars, a substantial income in those days. The Grew ménage in 1912 consisted of a two-floor apartment in a fashionable quarter of Berlin. Downstairs were four rooms for entertaining. Upstairs were rooms for the four little girls: Edith, Lilla, born in St. Petersburg in 1907, Anita in Berlin in 1909, and Elizabeth or Elsie in Vienna in 1912. There was a big staff of servants consisting of governess, nurse, cook, valet, chauffeur, and maids, but wages were low.[38]

Except for occasional spurts of activity, Grew spent only a few morning hours at the Chancery. He rose early to practice the piano for two hours before walking down the Tiergarten to his office. During the season the Grews attended opera and symphony assiduously, even though he had difficulty hearing the pianissimo parts. On winter afternoons he took the children skating, in the summer on family picnics by the Wannsee. Evenings at home, when work permitted and the entertaining season was over, he could relax by the fire, his faithful bulldog snoring noisily in his lap.[39]

In the "old days of diplomatic serenity," as Grew described them, Embassy business, as distinct from social life, was a leisurely affair of regular reports and news summaries with an occasional "case" or negotiation to spell the routine. Grew was no slacker. He worked at home regularly, studying international law and perfecting his German and French. When the situation required, he remained at the Chancery as late as 2 A.M., but the situation seldom required it.[40]

Some idea can be gained of the trivial nature of diplomatic business in those days from *Foreign Relations of the United States*. In this official series, the sections on American relations with Germany from 1908 to 1914 and with Austria-Hungary in 1911 and 1912 contain only six subjects in which these embassies played a part. Two were citizenship cases, two extradition cases, one a potash negotiation, and one a case involving the expulsion of Mormon missionaries.[41]

Grew participated in several of these cases, and many unpublished ones. He was particularly successful in arranging the extradition from Austria-Hungary of Boston diamond thieves whose crime was not covered by treaty. He succeded in this case by inviting his friend Count Berchtold, the Foreign Minister, to dinner, where he made a forceful plea. The food was undoubtedly delicious, the wines and cigars select, and the friendship from St.

Petersburg days warm. No word passed in writing, but the prisoners were delivered to American detectives at the ship the next day. It was humdrum diplomacy mostly, but valuable experience nevertheless, involving painstaking search for precedent, frequent trips to the Foreign Office, careful composition of notes and dispatches, and repeated drill in enciphering and deciphering.[42]

As a diplomatic secretary he had a variety of duties. An American businessman selling cavalry remounts wrote the Secretary of State a note of appreciation for Grew's services in opening the right doors for him at Vienna. Grew did more than his share of translating from the German newspapers and interpreting for the Ambassador. He was always available to seat a table or arrange a dance for the Ambassadress or even to shop for an Ambassador's toasted corn flakes and sarsaparilla! By willingly and thoroughly accomplishing any task, he was convincing his superiors that he was a capable and useful officer, and upon that conviction rested his surest hope of being retained in the Service.[43]

In 1911 when he went to Vienna as First Secretary, Grew had his first responsibility for running the Chancery, or Embassy office. Now he could satisfy his passion for orderliness and efficiency, and get "the reins . . . in my own grip." A dusty safe was cleaned out; correspondence was brought up to date. Soon the Department of State was ranking Vienna first among the embassies in the value and extent of its reports and clipping service. It was not long before the Ambassador complacently allowed his First Secretary to draft all diplomatic notes. During his tour in Vienna, Grew was left in charge while the Ambassador went on vacation for the summer. This, his first experience as chief of mission, came when he had just turned thirty-one.[44]

During these learning years at Berlin and Vienna, Grew became fully committed to a career in diplomacy. His position was still protected by executive order and not by law, but there were hopeful signs that the career principle had been accepted. Three successive Republican Administrations permitted some continuity in personnel. An increasing number of secretaries were settling down in diplomacy with the hope of eventually becoming ambassadors as Henry White had done. Their hopes were fed by administrative reorganization under Secretaries of State Elihu Root and Philander Knox that resulted in closer supervision, promotion for merit, and new posts to fill. These innovations received nearly unanimous support from those Americans, particularly among the Eastern, educated middle class, who gave any thought to foreign affairs. Consequently Grew could argue with good reason in a letter of 1913 to the Harvard *Crimson* that great progress had recently been made in establishing diplomacy on a professional basis, affording a career incentive to young men.[45]

This favorable climate fostered the growth of an *esprit de corps* among the diplomatic secretaries. Grew began collecting photographs of the previous incumbents of his Berlin position to hang on the wall of his office, and urged a friend at Constantinople to set up a similar "Rogues' Gallery." In 1910 he noted with pride that twenty-seven of ninety-five diplomatic officers were Harvard graduates. Common background and experience inspired a growing network of friendships among the secretaries, formed as they crisscrossed Europe on assignments or vacations, and strengthened by intimate correspondence.[46]

A diplomatic career was still a precarious occupation, however, as Grew was well aware. He took every precaution to protect his position by entertaining visiting American officials. He preferred Berlin to Vienna, he wrote, because at a larger post a secretary "is continually being brought in touch with important men who go back to Washington and talk about him." In this way he made the acquaintance of Brigadier General John J. Pershing in 1908.[47]

The most important dignitary he entertained was Theodore Roosevelt. When it became known that the ex-President would visit Berlin after his hunting expedition in 1910, Grew conceived the happy idea of inviting him to lunch to meet Professor Carl Schillings, the big-game photographer. Roosevelt was delighted. He wrote Ambassador David Jayne Hill to arrange the schedule as he wished, "but be sure to allow me to have that luncheon with Grew. . . ." Relations between the Ambassador and his First Secretary became "extremely tenuous," but Grew played his "trump card" for all it was worth. He planned every detail, even ordering Roosevelt's books from London and providing his guest with a copy of his own *Sport and Travel in the Far East*, an account of his trip in 1902-03. The luncheon was a splendid success, the guest of honor relishing the champagne with small strawberries and hugely enjoying Schillings's stereopticon slides. "I never had a pleasanter experience," Roosevelt wrote G. O. Trevelyan. The Grews triumphantly returned to the United States on home leave with the Roosevelt party.[48]

The only clear gain, however, turned out to be nomination by Roosevelt to the Boone and Crockett Club. The Democrats finally returned to power in 1912 and Grew, Republican to the core, was faced with his first career crisis.[49]

With the office-hungry Democrats threatening to turn out all diplomatic secretaries as well as chiefs of mission, Grew's recess appointment as First Secretary in Berlin was held up in the Senate. He responded by an active campaign for political support. He advised his family not to approach Henry Cabot Lodge as the Department of State was not on good terms with the Senate, but Representative Andrew Peters, Democrat of Boston, a classmate of Randolph Grew at Harvard, and Franklin D. Roosevelt were approached by the family, as were other friends such as Moorfield Storey,

Perry Belmont, and Henry White. Also active in Grew's behalf was Norman Armour, a recent graduate of Princeton, who had served one summer as Grew's private secretary. All these efforts succeeded when, on the last day before he would automatically have ceased to be a member of the Diplomatic Service, the Senate confirmed his appointment. Uncertainty remained until the war in 1914, but President Wilson resisted pressure to rescind his predecessor's executive order protecting diplomatic secretaries, and in 1915 an act of Congress finally provided an ironclad guarantee of tenure for diplomatic secretaries.[50]

In March 1914, in response to his father-in-law's advice that he abandon diplomacy for law, Grew politely demurred. He had risen at thirty-three as far as most men did at forty, and could well afford to wait a few years for a ministership.[51]

That spring the Grews went home for vacation. Word of the assassination of Archduke Franz Ferdinand reached him on the golf course at Manchester. He returned to Europe leisurely, stopping in London to test his guns on the Holland and Holland range, and finding "no news of interest." By July 27 he was back in Berlin, "glad to resume a normal and peaceful life." That day Ambassador Gerard informed his government that he had good reason to believe war would be avoided. The following day Austria-Hungary declared war on Serbia.[52]

TWO

Wartime Berlin

IT was August 1914, and the troop trains, jammed with cheering soldiers, moved through Berlin toward the frontiers with mathematical precision. The city seethed with rumor, breast-thumping patriotism, and xenophobia. In the Wilhelm-Platz, across the park from the Chancellery and Foreign Office, a crowd of stranded Americans pressed toward the massive door of the old Hatzfeld Palace, over which the Stars and Stripes lazily slapped in the summer breeze. Straw hats shaded anxious frowns and handkerchiefs fluttered to the eye as people waited to pass the restraining arm of the Embassy porter.

Inside there was no more pushing. A line moved along the corridor, each person clutching his number, to a barricade where troubles were sorted. Relief cases went upstairs to the ballroom where, under the massive chandelier, Embassy wives registered, assisted, and comforted those in need. Weeping was limited to ten minutes. The more fortunate ones were sent to the ticket office to purchase steerage berths home, or to the passport office to acquire that precious identification. Clerks, attachés, volunteers, and diplomatic secretaries, with little American flags in their buttonholes, bustled about with piles of letters, telegrams, and forms, converging on one office, beyond the murmuring and weeping, but not the hammering of typewriters and insistent peal of phones. Here, behind a battery of eighteen in-and-out boxes, working at "steam heat," sat the Embassy's executive officer, Joseph Grew.[1]

He had never been happier. The atmosphere of crisis was exhilarating. War was a storybook affair of brief, heroic encounters little affecting civilians. The German Army would soon be "jumping through the British and French armies much as a poodle jumps through a paper hoop at the circus." [2] On September 2, four days before the German offensive staggered to a halt in the Battle of the Marne and the agony of the trenches began, Grew wrote his mother:

> Isn't it wonderful what successes the Germans are having? I suppose that you and nearly everyone at home is [sic] very anti-German, for the American press has not played them fair, all the reports having come through from England, but my sympathies are mostly all on this side, though they are perhaps founded more on admiration of their marvelous organization and the fact that they are fighting against enormous odds than anything else.

He correctly ascertained the pro-British bias of American war news, but he completely failed to realize that he himself had swallowed German propaganda, "hook, bait and sinker," as he later admitted. His views on the causes of the war were no more sophisticated than those of the man in the street. Russia, England, and France, jealous of Germany's success and prosperity, "carefully cooked up" the war. Germany could expand no further, "and something had to give." He spoke of the "inherent hostility of Slav to Teuton and Teuton to Latin," and saw Europe, weakened by war, a prey to the "Yellow Peril." [3]

Grew was still an innocent abroad. He had paid little attention to the political intelligence side of diplomacy. In 1912 he found nothing in American relations with Austria-Hungary "worth humming about," and in March 1914 "few important matters . . . pending" at the Berlin Embassy. The best source of information from Vienna was the correspondent of the London *Times*. Reporting the press was a chore; when pressed for time he skipped articles dealing with European affairs in general. By comparison, Grew's opposite number in the British Embassy at Berlin, Sir Horace Rumbold, took his intelligence duties very seriously. During the war crisis his dispatches to London showed a discriminating knowledge of German public and government-inspired opinion. The comparison is not entirely fair, since the State Department pursued a traditional American policy of non-entanglement in Europe and did not encourage comprehensive political reporting. Nevertheless, in May 1914 Colonel Edward M. House, after only a brief immersion in the European scene, reported to President Wilson from Berlin: "The situation is extraordinary. It is militarism run stark mad. Unless some one acting for you can bring about a different understanding, there is some day to be an awful cataclysm." Unquestionably, six years of leisurely, cocoon-like existence in court society had left Grew complacent, uninformed, and lacking a critical and objective point of view.[4]

Boston soon brought him about. Letters from the family came back taunting him for his "easy gullibility." Pained at being an "outcast from the family circle" and sobered by the deepening horror of the war, he protested his absolute neutrality. He had taken the German side, he now claimed, only for the love of argument and in common fairness; his position as a neutral diplomat required him to avoid all moral, ethical, or political judgments. This was not enough for Boston where his pro-German reputation was spreading. By December he had swung fully into line. "Whatever may be our sympathy for individual Germans and our admiration for the great fighting machine they have built up . . . we are, at heart, entirely pro-Ally," he now wrote to his father-in-law. "We are opposed to the German cause, and all it stands for, the origin of the war, the method of conducting it." Though the rôle of the aloof neutral diplomat appealed to him, it was not worth the sacrifice of his ties with home.[5]

During the first two years of war Grew had little to do with diplomacy, so his attitudes toward Germany were mostly his own concern. On the great issues involving American neutrality Ambassador James W. Gerard played a lone role, to the extent that Washington allowed him any role. He was content to leave supervision of all Embassy work to his First Secretary, who with a flair for organization and detail found it "bully fun." "I have to be regarded," Grew wrote exuberantly, "as the one person who carries all the threads in his own brain." [6]

This indispensable position was his own creation. He arranged for all incoming and outgoing mail to funnel through his office. Each of his assistants was assigned an area of responsibility: British interests in Germany, British prisoners of war, American citizens, transfer of private funds, and so forth. He read the mail, ascertained the action required, and sent it to the officer responsible. He then let the assistant "go ahead unhampered by close supervision, which only dampens ardor." But, since he read all outgoing mail too, he was able to catch mistakes. This gave him a perilously heavy work load, but kept the Embassy's widely scattered activities integrated under an experienced officer.[7]

Thanks to Grew, the quality of Embassy personnel, both regular and temporary, was exceptionally good. In regular staff appointments, William Phillips, Third Assistant Secretary of State, was careful to consult his friend Grew in order not to "spoil the machinery" Grew had developed. In temporary appointments, Grew consulted his brother Randolph and Professor Archie Coolidge. Harvard, as a result, was well represented, with nine graduates serving at various times on the wartime staff, four of whom were also Grotonians. Grew felt this hand-picked staff "leavened" the Diplomatic Service, as indeed their subsequent records prove. Ellis Loring Dresel became High Commissioner in Germany, Lithgow Osborne Minister to Norway, Robert M. Scotten Ambassador to New Zealand, Hugh Wilson Ambassador to Germany, and Alexander Kirk Ambassador to Italy. Christian Herter left diplomacy but ultimately returned and became Secretary of State.[8]

Efficiency was Grew's pervading purpose. It meant creating a close-knit organization of capable men working long hours together during the week and then relaxing together Saturday nights at poker. It also meant developing quicker, surer ways of doing the job. Typewriters were a particularly congenial method, and he soon had them in every room, "banging away so fast that you don't know whether you are in the accounting room of Jordan Marsh & Co., or under machine gun fire in the trenches." Mimeographed circulars, rubber stamps, a numbering system for telegrams, and indexes galore were introduced. Grew, said the Ambassador, was "the best organizer he had seen in any walk of life." [9]

Grew's administrative role in the Embassy was significant for his developing sense of professionalism. In the first place, the regular staff of the Embassy, through Grew, retained control over all American wartime activities in Germany. This was unusual in the "heyday of irregular diplomacy." Elsewhere in Europe, Herbert Hoover's relief organization ranged freely outside diplomatic control, while in Russia divided control resulted in a bewildering confusion of policy. The task was undoubtedly easier in Germany where relief activities were few and hostility to Americans made it more convenient to work through diplomatic channels. In any case, Grew's ability to retain control of irregular diplomatic activities undoubtedly increased his sense of the adaptability and efficiency of a fully professional Foreign Service.[10]

In the second place, he was developing a case for a career service. He saw the Embassy as "simply a large business organization," with diplomacy manufactured in Washington and sent out ready-made. However, like business, it required training, he wrote in 1916, recalling no doubt the hours he had spent breaking in new staff members. Therefore, he concluded, some assurance of promotion to the rank of ambassador or minister was necessary to provide a career incentive to young men.[11]

And finally, the experience was significant in developing *esprit de corps* in the Diplomatic Service. Morale could have been a serious problem. The atmosphere of Berlin was intensely hostile and the pressure of work brought several men to the verge of breakdown. Yet Grew and Wilson remember the Embassy staff as a happy group. Seeing so much of each other in work and play, they became closely bound together by common interests and affections. To Grew it was more closely knit than any fraternity. The experience was repeated during the war and postwar years at other posts. New chapters in the fraternity appeared and new faces in every chapter, but a comfortable stratum of intimate friends remained.[12]

As First Secretary and from July 1916 with the newly adopted rank of Counselor of Embassy, Grew was preoccupied with running the Embassy, but he stayed abreast of diplomatic developments, both because this was his duty in case of the absence of the Ambassador, and because steadily deteriorating German-American relations were an absorbing test of his profession. He loyally supported his chief, but found himself increasingly estranged from him, both personally and in the objectives and techniques of diplomacy. Though their relationship became painful, Grew learned a lot in watching and judging Gerard, and emerged with a far more mature and well-articulated conception of his profession.

The relationship between an ambassador and his principal assistant has traditionally been a delicate one, as George Kennan has pointed out with the authority of experience. The two offices are essentially competitive, being "in tandem" both as to function and responsibility. Where the Ambassador is an amateur and the Counselor of Embassy a professional, the situation is even more delicate, for the latter tends to "hover nervously" around his inexperienced chief to prevent embarrassing blunders.[13]

The differing personalities of Grew and Gerard exacerbated the built-in strain of their official relationship. As a boy, the intense, wiry, sharp-faced New Yorker had set off for prep school with two sets of boxing gloves. He still prided himself on his pugnacity. In contrast to the pleasant and accommodating Counselor, the Ambassador had an unbridled temper with which he belabored officials of all ranks and persons of all estates with democratic even-handedness. While Grew was being lectured at Groton on the evils of city politics, the young Tammany lawyer James Gerard was defending loyal Tammany voters accused of illegal registration. As a final strain on their relations, as if the two were not already far enough apart, their wives were barely on speaking terms.[14]

Grew's criticism of Gerard was always circumspect and was balanced with sincere praise of his virtues. He stressed two basic faults of the Ambassador, his "slap-dash" methods, and his tactlessness. By slap-dash methods, Grew meant the Ambassador's tendency to make snap judgments, based on intuition rather than careful analysis and weighing of evidence. He would dash off important telegrams in seconds, handing them over unread to be enciphered. A perusal of Gerard's communications substantiates this criticism. His personal letters to Secretary of State Robert Lansing are a hodgepodge of unrelated facts and desultory opinions. One of Gerard's reports moved the President to comment, "Who can fathom this? I wish they would hand this idiot his passports." [15]

Grew felt Gerard's second basic fault, tactlessness, explained the Ambassador's anti-German reputation. Gerard had no confirmed prejudice against Germans. It was more a question of hypersensitive patriotism. His knight-champion view of American representation abroad, combined with his temper and aggressiveness, led to unnecessary incidents. According to Grew, visitors came from the Ambassador's office cowed to tears by his insults and curses, or worse still for the Embassy, eyes ablaze with anger. At the Foreign Office, Under Secretary Arthur Zimmermann "wished that Mr. Gerard would not lose his temper so often," while at the Kaiser's headquarters there was an embarrassed hush at the mention of the Ambassador's name. German hostility to the United States found a convenient focus in Gerard, and he was subject to periodic attacks in the press. The result,

Grew felt, was added harassment to the severe strain German-American relations were already undergoing, and a diminution of the Embassy's influence with the German government.[16]

Despite Gerard's obvious weaknesses, Grew learned from him how vital it was for an ambassador on occasion to present his government's views bluntly and forcefully. During the *Sussex* crisis in the spring of 1916 Gerard was invited to the Kaiser's headquarters at Charleville, France, and took Grew with him. There every effort was made to persuade the Ambassador to soften the American demand for public disavowal of indiscriminate submarine warfare. But Gerard warned the Germans that only complete acceptance would satisfy the United States, thereby giving the Chancellor the necessary push to fight for public disavowal and win it. Grew concluded in admiration:

> Mr. Gerard was the right man in the right place at this important juncture. He does not mince words, he speaks with force and directness — which is sometimes the only method that carries weight here — and once he sees an issue clearly he rams it home straight from the shoulder. . . . Had he given the least loophole of hope for further temporizing or discussion, the German answer would in all probability have dodged the issue, would have been unsatisfactory to our Government and would have resulted in a severance of diplomatic relations, which would almost certainly have eventually led to war.[17]

As Grew's concept of diplomacy matured, a picture of the ideal diplomat was gradually forming which borrowed qualities associated with both the professional and the amateur. Only a well-trained mind, uncommon in politically bred ambassadors, could provide the necessary comprehensive, analytical reporting. Only experience could teach "certain finesses, certain little ways of expressing, writing and doing things, certain little necessary discriminations" that smoothed relations between countries.[18] Indefinable but vital qualities like tact, moderation, adaptability, foresight, and poise might by luck be found in an amateur, but were best sought in young career applicants and carefully nurtured. On the other hand, there were critical junctures when a diplomat had to speak with elemental forcefulness and bluntness, gauging his words of warning by the extent of his people's indignation, thereby preventing mistaken judgments. But peace, always, was the diplomat's objective. War, if it came, would be the deliberate act of the governments involved. The diplomat's job was to prevent any faulty communication or minor irritant from beclouding fundamental issues, by establishing close and if possible sympathetic relations with the government to which he was accredited.

In spite of the opportunities for valuable experience, Grew's strained relations with his chief made these unhappy years. Furthermore, he longed to see his little daughters who stayed in America with their grandparents. He was missing their charming years of babyhood. In January 1916 his father died leaving family affairs to be attended to. But even temporary relief was hard to obtain. Gerard, suffering from rheumatism and overwork himself, clung tenaciously to his efficient "organizer," endeavoring to block Grew's Italian vacation in 1915 and home leave in the spring of 1916. On the latter occasion Gerard complained to Colonel House of Grew's "deserting" him, this in spite of the Ambassador's official report that Grew was "out of touch with American affairs." "Grew is a nice fellow and competent worker," Gerard wrote House, "but is entirely under his wife's influence, and she affects his judgment." Grew was not one to shirk duty, however. His anxiety for home leave in 1916 is explained by, and is a measure of, how deeply unhappy he was under Gerard. Imprisoned with this personal animosity in the wider hostility of wartime Berlin, it is not surprising that he sought permanent relief from an atmosphere which had "long ceased to be sympathetic."[19]

For relief he turned to William Phillips and Colonel House. Phillips was Grew's close friend and a faithful mentor of the career principle in diplomacy and Grew's interests in particular. But it was House who had the final say on all personnel shifts. Grew had met House in 1914 and his mother was acquainted with Mrs. House in North Shore summer society. In March 1915 Grew had approached House for a transfer and the Colonel had been sympathetic, but nothing came of it. In January 1916 he mentioned it again to House during the latter's visit to Berlin. On this occasion House asked him about his political affiliations. As months passed with no word of transfer, Grew, Republican by conviction, worried that this might be the obstacle, and therefore with great care composed a letter to House denying any political survival as sincerely admiring the President's policies, he wrote a "rests upon the fact that it is the duty of the diplomat to conscientiously represent the Government to the best of his ability, whatever party happens to be in power. . . ." However, perhaps as aware of the exigencies of political survival as sincerely admiring the President's policies, he wrote a friend in June 1916 that he was "quietly" supporting Wilson's re-election.[20]

But House finally decided that it would be an "unnecessary worry" to Gerard to upset his staff, so Grew's transfer was again postponed. He did get home leave in the late spring of 1916 and spoke of his hopes again to Phillips and House. This time, though he was considered too junior for a ministership, he was promised the position of Chief of Western European Affairs in the Department of State, but again he was disappointed. Gerard demanded his return by July 1, and Grew dutifully agreed. As there had been talk in May of Gerard coming home himself, the prospect of being left in charge at Berlin undoubtedly sweetened Grew's decision to return. Two months after his return to Berlin, Gerard was finally persuaded to come home on leave, and the Counselor became Chargé d'Affaires for a crucial three-month period preceding Germany's decision for unrestricted submarine warfare. In considering the recall of the Ambassador, House and Lansing agreed that Grew was "perfectly competent" to handle the situation.[21]

Grew's chargéship lasted from late September to late December 1916. American-German relations had been relatively calm during the summer, but the day Ambassador Gerard sailed for home a virulent anti-American campaign broke out in the German press. From that day to the day Gerard returned, the Chargé d'Affaires, to use his nautical analogy, was on the bridge constantly.[22]

By this time Grew's attitude toward Germany had hardened. Before, his pro-Ally sentiment had been somewhat impersonal and in part designed to please Boston. Now, seeing "incontrovertible" evidence of German brutality and sensing the growing hatred for Americans, his feelings were more subjective: he became angry, insulted, aggrieved. The turning point in his attitude appears to have been the sinking of the *Lusitania* in May 1915. "The dreadfulness of this calamity struck us with full force at once," he said. It came as a great shock to the Americans, the English-born Princess Blücher noted. At the Esplanade they had always been cordial toward the Germans:

> But a sudden change now took place. The Americans openly avoided the Germans, almost cutting their friends of the day before. . . . Their rage and horror at the idea that Americans had been killed knew no bounds. . . .

Grew shared the rage and horror, but according to Princess Blücher never betrayed his feelings by word or deed.[23]

When Grew became Chargé, the United States and Germany were entering a twilight period in relations resembling the atmosphere exactly twenty-five years later between Japan and the United States, when Grew was Ambassador at Tokyo. The accommodation of differences became more and more difficult as the war presented increasingly grim threats to the national survival of Germany. He saw perilous navigating ahead as Chargé, "reefs on both sides . . . and storms hovering along the horizon." [24]

On October 10, 1916, two weeks after Gerard's departure, Grew was informed by the American Legation at Brussels that German military authorities had begun deporting able-bodied Belgians for work in German factories. Relief authorities, fearing that the British would now have grounds for halting their supplies passing into Belgium, asked that the matter be brought to the attention of the German Foreign Office. Grew acted promptly and energetically. He was aware of the "far-reaching results of these new measures and their ultimate effect on the world's opinion." He was also aware, undoubtedly, that this issue offered a challenging opportunity to try his diplomatic skills. Had he foreseen the dangerous waters into which Belgian deportations would lead him, he might have been far less eager to take the initiative.[25]

Grew asked for and received authorization to make informal representations at the Foreign Office on humanitarian grounds. This he did twice, receiving no satisfaction. He then requested authority to take up the matter informally with the Chancellor, which was also granted. Now deeply committed, Grew spent three weeks formulating his case. He sought detailed information and recommendations from Brussels and prepared the way for a wider appeal by consulting diplomats of other neutral countries. After collecting all available evidence and carefully preparing his arguments, he applied for an interview with Chancellor von Bethmann-Hollweg and on November 22 stepped across the Wilhelm-Platz to the Chancellory for his first diplomatic *démarche*.

At the interview Grew described the deportations in detail and their effect on world opinion, and then offered six points of possible amelioration. The Chancellor listened patiently and at the end of Grew's presentation turned abruptly and deliberately to the subject of peace, waving aside deportations as the inevitable result of failure abroad to act on Germany's oft-expressed desires for peace. The tall, bearded Chancellor, who had lost a wife and son in the war, spoke in a way "impressive beyond description, . . . sitting at his desk, speaking slowly, deliberately and sadly of the horrors of war. He seemed to me like a man broken in spirit, his face deeply furrowed, his manner sad beyond words." Grew immediately cabled Washington a description of the interview, concluding, "I could not fail to feel, although not directly expressed, his clearly intimated disappointment that the United States had not taken steps leading toward peace." [26]

Meanwhile in Washington, President Wilson was formulating his famous peace note offering United States mediation in the European conflict. On November 15 the newspapers announced that Grew had received authority to make a formal protest on Belgian deportations. The President, ignorant of Secretary of State Robert Lansing's more limited authorization, and determined not to let this new issue interfere with his peace move, was furious. Lansing hastened to reassure him and inform the press that Grew was not making a formal protest, while House, in his words, "used this action of the Germans as an argument against making a peace move at the present." Lansing several days later echoed the argument, advising the President that the risk of Allied rejection was greater while Germany "persisted in enslaving the civilian subjects of enemies who have fallen into her hands." [27]

The President himself was keenly sensitive to the swelling public protest. On November 26 he informed Lansing that grounds existed for a "very solemn protest," which should point out, among other things, that deportations had placed "a very serious obstacle in the way of efforts toward peace . . . which I was anxiously seeking an opportunity to make." This observation, the President continued, would "from Mr. Grew's recent despatches . . . be the most persuasive part of the protest." [28] What Wilson meant was that if the Chancellor was sincere in his desire for peace, as Grew reported he seemed to be, he should discontinue deportations so that American peace efforts could move ahead. This was made clear to Grew in an instruction of November 29. He was to make a formal protest and was authorized to inform von Bethmann-Hollweg:

> . . . that the President has noted with the deepest interest your report . . . of the evident distress and disappointment of the Chancellor that nothing had come of his intimations about peace, and that what the President is so earnestly desiring is practical cooperation on the part of the German authorities in creating a favorable opportunity for some affirmative action by him in the interest of an early restoration of peace.[29]

Grew received this instruction with dismay. A subjective impression drawn not from words but from manner and tone was now to be reconveyed to the Chancellor not only as a communication from the President, but also in the context of a stiff protest. In his anxiety, Grew even read "evident distress and disappointment" to mean that the President assumed the Chancellor had voiced these feelings. He saw two possibilities of "ruin" for him:

> . . . first I might have mistaken the Chancellor's intentions in speaking to me as he did; perhaps he had merely wished to tell me that he personally hoped for peace overtures from the belligerents themselves, not that he had any intention whatever of asking the President to intercede; he might resent the President's message as uncalled for. Second, even if he wished the President to intercede, he might resent the tone of the latter's message, which was distinctly sharp in wording. He might make a scapegoat of me and say: "Who asked the President to intercede anyway? Young man, you have misunderstood me." I would have to report his reply, of course, and then it would be all over with me for having led the President into an impasse, a rebuff to his overtures and an indignity to the United States. Agreeable prospects.[30]

After sleepless nights waiting for an interview, Grew screwed up his courage and presented the message as directed, word for word.[31] The Chancellor received it in silence, stroking his beard, and promised an early reply. The next day, after another sleepless night, Grew spoke to his friend Zimmermann, now the Foreign Secretary, and warned him that repudiation could ruin his, Grew's, career and would do no good for German-American relations.[32] Zimmermann, to the young Chargé's immense relief, promised that the reply would be friendly. What the Germans then did was to give their reply in two installments. The first, on December 7, was a vague, friendly acknowledgment of the President's interest in peace. The second, December 11, amounted to a rejection of the American protest on deportations, though Zimmermann promised amelioration of conditions. Little more could be done. Later reports from friends in Brussels led Grew to believe his representations might have resulted in an easing of the practice.

His fear of repudiation had been unfounded. November 22 Bethmann certainly had intended his concern to reach the President and it is to Grew's credit that he used him as a medium of communication. It is true that by December 5 Bethmann was less interested in a Wilson peace move and he could hardly have been encouraged by the deportations protest which accompanied Wilson's reply. But he was not prepared to discourage an American initiative, as he would have by treating the American Chargé brusquely. Nevertheless, Grew could only speculate what went on in the minds of the German Chancellor and his own President and live with his anxieties. For the career diplomat such experiences breed caution.

Grew's main preoccupation as Chargé was reporting political developments bearing on the crucial issue of peace or war. His dispatches excelled in clarity, completeness, and frequency. The historian Charles Seymour judged them among the best coming out of Europe. In addition to brief reports of events as they happened, he provided regular press summaries, special background analyses on such subjects as the political complexion of the Reichstag, and detailed résumés of developments over a period of time. He had the incentive of knowing that what he wrote would be of immediate interest to the President, Lansing, and Colonel House, as indeed it was. But he was also motivated by a keen sense of the historical importance of the events he was witnessing. Furthermore, one gains the impression, particularly in reading the exhaustive description of his chargéship in his report of December 21, that Grew sought to convince his superiors of the efficacy of professional diplomacy.[33]

In political reporting Grew depended heavily on his staff, acting more as the editor and arbiter of ideas than as the originator. Particularly valuable was Captain Walter Gherardi, the Naval Attaché, whose sources of information at the Admiralty provided a sure gauge of the pressure there for unrestricted submarine war. But Grew considered Gherardi radically pro-Ally. At the other extreme, the prisoner-of-war Attaché, John B. Jackson, was radically pro-German. Diplomatic secretaries Hugh Wilson and Alexander Kirk, both graduates of the École des Sciences Politiques, provided the "mean," to which Grew himself adhered.[34]

The question agitating the Berlin mission most persistently was how to weigh the threat of submarine war against the Chancellor's peace offensive. Grew's prognostications on this crucial issue were guarded, but over the months he became more preoccupied with the possibilities of peace and less with those of war. In October the Chancellor faced a crucial battle in the Reichstag on the submarine question, during which Grew repeatedly warned of the danger of a decision for unrestricted warfare, concluding on October 17 that, though the Chancellor had weathered the crisis, no permanent security for the United States was to be looked for. However, he did see temporary relief, and when German peace feelers came out in November, he became convinced that shortage of food and war weariness were driving Germany "to make great sacrifices at the present time in order to try to secure peace." Of the receptivity of the Allies he was much less hopeful.[35]

In reality peace and war were two faces of the same German policy. The Chancellor sincerely hoped for a compromise peace, but he also regarded his peace efforts as a means of uniting the German people and ensuring continued American neutrality in case pressure for unrestricted submarine warfare from the Army and Navy became irresistible. That pressure steadily increased. Bethmann won a Pyrrhic victory in October, since the Reichstag left the power of decision for unrestricted submarine war with Field Marshal Paul von Hindenburg, the new army commander. Grew recognized von Hindenburg's decisive position but believed he stood with the Chancellor on the submarine issue. On the contrary, the Field Marshal only awaited the right strategic moment to press for unrestricted warfare. The intensification of peace sentiment which impressed Grew therefore developed within the context of intensified pressure for extending the war under the seas. It was not a question of one pressure diminishing as the other increased, the way Grew reflected the situation, but of both pressures increasing simultaneously. Paradoxically, Grew's judgment of temporary relief from the submarine danger introduced a degree of complacency in the American government, contributing to the postponement of Wilson's own peace move until it was too late. Cautiously adhering to the mean of opinion in the Embassy, and underestimating the weight of military imperatives in the decision-making process, Grew failed to provide an entirely accurate representation of the forces determining German policy. It should be added, of course, that the task of probing the intentions of a government at war is speculative at best.[36]

Ambassador Gerard returned on December 21. Immensely relieved not to have committed any blunders, Grew felt as if he had just completed a college examination. Gratifying compliments came in from the Department of State and from Colonel House who wrote: "You have won the respect and confidence of all of us. . . ." His reputation was spreading even beyond official circles, the Paris *Temps* characterizing him as a diplomat of high quality.[37]

Events moved swiftly to a break with Germany, the pronouncement of unrestricted submarine warfare occurring on January 31, 1917, and the rupture of diplomatic relations by the United States four days later. When news of the break came, Grew took charge of closing the Embassy, arranging seating on the train, getting work up to date, transferring archives to the Spanish Embassy, and attending to all the personal distresses and complaints with that "quiet force, tact and personal magnetism" which his staff so much admired.[38]

Grew bid polite adieux to his friends at the Foreign Office. "The duty of a diplomat," he wrote, "is to cultivate friendly relations. . . . I had cultivated those personal relations and could not break them, whatever political events had intervened." [39] On February 10 at 8:10 P.M. the Embassy train pulled out and headed southward through the night toward Switzerland, the passengers liberally toasting the ill-fortunes of Germany in champagne.

After seeing the American party safely to Paris, Grew was ordered to Vienna as Counselor. "Vesuvius having erupted successfully, I am transferred to Stromboli and await events. . . ." He did not have to wait long. American policy of trying to prevent Austria-Hungary following Germany into war had little hope, and considering the Ambassador, it had none at all. Grew was guarded in personal criticisms, but about Frederick C. Penfield he lost all reserve, describing him as one of the most "irrational, selfish, conceited, heartless" men he had ever met, and a "positive danger to the service." Grew did what he could to restore sympathetic relations by renewing old friendships, but Germany forced a decision and on April 14 he closed another Embassy and headed at last for the United States.[40]

The Grews sailed from Spain on April 21, 1917. After seven months of intense strain he could relax and record it all in his diary during the sunny crossing. He found the United States wonderfully comfortable and unchanged. It was late spring and Boston was fresh and green. He spent happy days getting reacquainted with his daughters, now ten, nine, eight, and five. He arrived in time for Anita's eighth birthday, and for Fifteenth Reunion festivities at Harvard. After a few weeks' rest he reported for duty at the Department of State where he was given a vague position charged with miscellaneous but familiar tasks such as compiling a summary of Central Powers intelligence, receiving diplomats, making arrangements for German and American prisoners of war, and coordinating relief for peoples in enemy-occupied territories.[41]

In January 1918 Grew was sent on a propaganda mission to the Midwest to spark lagging Liberty Bond sales. He was accompanied by his good friend Hugh Gibson, who, as Secretary of Legation in Brussels, had started Grew along the thorny path of Belgian deportations. During an eleven-day swing through Illinois, Wisconsin, Minnesota, Iowa, and Missouri, they spoke before twenty-four thousand people on twenty-three occasions, including six speeches in one day in Minneapolis. A second trip during the late winter took them deeper into the West to counter Non-Partisan League sentiment in North and South Dakota.[42]

Propaganda was an unfamiliar experience for Grew, but he entered upon his assignment with gusto. His lecture was entitled, "Why We Must Defeat Germany." German culture, he told the Westerners, was skin-deep, with "barbarism, license and international faithlessness" underneath. Germans were humorless, intemperate, and narrow-minded. They were guilty, the *Milwaukee Journal* quoted Grew as saying, of "the most shameless and almost incredible trickery, deception, and bad faith." He spared no details of German atrocities and assured his listeners that he emerged from that "unenlightened" land as Stanley had emerged from Darkest Africa. It was a "terrific arraignment," the Milwaukee paper commented, yet "calm, judicial, dispassionate. These earnest, conscientious, high-minded gentlemen simply told what they knew." [43]

Whether Grew's severe indictment of German character moved Milwaukee German-Americans to buy bonds is questionable. But he spoke from the heart. He undoubtedly exaggerated somewhat, but in letters home and in his diary he neither qualified nor minimized what he said publicly. The contrast with his sentiment in 1915, just before the sinking of the *Lusitania,* could not be more striking. Then he had written: ". . . there is something about Germany, with its wonderful system, organization and sympathetic people which grows on one more than any other country saving our own. . . ." [44] Since then he had experienced the shock and horror of all-out war, but this still fails to account for the vehemence of his denunciation. One cannot avoid the feeling that he looked on his earlier idealization of Germany as not only wrong but also un-American, and that he was now determined to prove his patriotism. Significantly, he delivered a speech with the same title in Boston.

George Kennan writes that most of what was said about the war came from the educated upper class who felt called upon to set the tone for public discussion. Failing to discover any tradition in America that could explain a foreign war, they depicted the German threat as something inhuman, external and inexplicable, personified by the "beast-like Hun." Within the protective cover of their "noble indignation," they felt safe against dangerous doubt and moral isolation. Fear of moral isolation could not have been negligible to Grew who had lived apart from his people for fifteen years and returned to them in the midst of crisis. Having escaped State Street, he found himself needing Main Street. Consequently, he relished the opportunity to establish a rapport. Though he found the farmers close-fisted, selfish, "all to the bad," the rest of "the great American peepul [sic] are all right." "I never before realized," he wrote back to Boston, "what a splendid person the average rough-edged American citizen is." Grew gave it to his fellow Americans "straight from the shoulder" in the snow-driven wilderness of Spearfish, South Dakota, and felt at home again.[45]

Grew was different from the diplomat he had been four years earlier—more sober and industrious, more broadly proficient, more attuned to internal and international politics, more sensitive to public opinion at home. Retrospectively the change was an improvement. Yet his competence before the war had been unquestioned. Then, his government, prompted by the momentarily influential minority of citizens in overseas trade and genteel society, had been primarily concerned with winning markets and prestige abroad. These values, to which Grew had responded and which he found congenial, diminished with the coming of Wilson and war, and others arose. Grew responded again, developing new style and capacities, and once again gained recognition for competence. Ambitious for a career and distinction in diplomacy, adaptable, possessed of a keen instinct for survival, he made himself the instrument of the new diplomacy as he had of the old.

THREE

The Paris Peace Conference

WAR meant the end of diplomacy, but it meant the beginning too. Grew, one of the last to leave Germany before the outbreak of hostilities, was one of the first to participate in peace planning. In August 1917 Secretary of State Robert Lansing asked him with several others to prepare secret memoranda for use at a peace conference whenever one should be held. Grew's share was to trace the war aims of all the major belligerents, a "seemingly colossal task." He wrote his father-in-law, Thomas Perry, for the name of someone qualified to compile the necessary documents and public statements, who would be paid privately for the work. Otherwise, he saw himself devoting a week's vacation to it. On September 2, the President, who had in mind something far more comprehensive than Lansing or Grew envisioned, assigned the task to Colonel House with authority to organize a group of experts. Thus The Inquiry was born.[1]

Though excluded from the team of experts, Grew remained in close touch with diplomatic developments. With his experience in Berlin and Vienna and his talent for thorough reporting, he was assigned the task of compiling summaries of enemy intelligence. Assisted by a "breezy" correspondent whom he had met in Berlin, William Bullitt, he gradually expanded these to include economic as well as political and military information. After his second trip West he welcomed the opportunity of a regular position in the Department of State, that of Chief of Western European Affairs. He was still excluded from policy-making, which for the most part the White House reserved to itself. Nevertheless, when House went to Europe for armistice deliberations in October 1918 he needed an experienced diplomatic secretary, and Grew, the only official exclusively concerned with the powers involved, was the logical choice. Furthermore, he was well and favorably known to House.[2]

Gordon Auchincloss, House's son-in-law and secretary, advised Grew of his new mission on October 13 and recorded that Grew was "pleased as he could be." After hurried packing the party secretly boarded the U.S.S. *Northern Pacific* in New York harbor on the night of October 17. At 4 A.M. as the fog lifted, she weighed anchor, slipped quietly out to sea and joined by two destroyers set course for France.[3]

Aboard ship Grew was very close to Colonel House. The Colonel spoke with him intimately for hours explaining his objectives and methods and asking Grew's advice. Prospects for Paris were exhilarating. Upon arrival, however, they quickly soured with the realization that he was useless as an interpreter-secretary at Supreme War Council meetings on account of his deafness. Grew's replacement was Arthur Frazier, Counselor of Embassy in Paris and a former colleague at Berlin. House naturally came to depend on Frazier and Auchincloss, leaving Grew with routine matters of code work, written translation, and liaison. However, House did make every effort to find a rewarding assignment for Grew, recommending on November 8 that he be sent to the new states of Central Europe to organize a system of reliable political intelligence. This tantalizing opportunity, which Grew saw as "one of the biggest jobs of the war," also passed him by. House's cable crossed one appointing Herbert Hoover to investigate conditions in that area, leaving Grew's status uncertain. Finally Grew's fortunes brightened with his designation on November 13 as Secretary of the United States Commission to the Peace Conference.[4]

As Secretary, Grew would be responsible for the functioning of the entire delegation and would rank next to the Commissioners themselves. It looked like a magnificent opportunity. Yet a year later when the conference was all over and the last crates of documents were shipped off for burial in archives, the experience seemed like a nightmare. It was "the most discouraging, unsatisfactory and regrettable" assignment of his career. Great hopes ending in bitter disillusion were the theme in Paris that year.[5]

Grew's troubles began, earlier than most, on the very day of his appointment as Secretary of the Commission. This appointment came as an unwelcome surprise to Colonel House who expected to organize the delegation himself and secretly hoped to be chairman. He had already been planning accommodations, personnel, and communications. With the arrival of The Inquiry, directed by his brother-in-law, Dr. Sidney Mezes, the peace commission would have been under his personal control. Now he learned that Grew, an officer responsible to Lansing, was to be in charge, and furthermore that the Secretary of State was unwilling to hasten the departure of The Inquiry. House suspected that Lansing was trying to snatch away the organization designed to support the crowning achievement of his life. Lansing thenceforth could "carry his own fortune without help or hindrance from me," he bitterly concluded. "He has not been entirely considerate after all I have done for him." [6]

Grew was caught in the middle of this tug-of-war. He constantly needed

House's advice in setting up the delegation, but the Colonel's animosity toward Lansing inevitably cooled his relations with Grew. Reflecting House's disappointment, Auchincloss wrote that what they needed were more "hard-headed business men" like Herbert Hoover, "who could really get to the bottom of the problems," instead of diplomats, too many of whom were "hanging around." [7]

House was correct toward Grew, however, assigning Major Willard Straight of his staff to help in planning. If Grew would only leave most of this work to Straight, Auchincloss commented, he would "do all right." "Joe hasn't much executive ability," he added, "but he is a terribly nice fellow. . . ." They would do their best to "push him through the job." Grew and Straight had no sooner started to work when they both came down with the influenza then raging in Europe. Straight died and Grew was in bed for a week, only slowly gaining his strength thereafter.[8]

In spite of his weakness, Grew worked desperately to ready the organization for the arrival of the President and the delegation as a whole on December 14, only weeks away. Perhaps remembering his Berlin experience, he favored an organizational plan in which, as he said in 1914, he was the one person who carried all the threads in his own brain, an arrangement he was soon to regret. All service staffs were to report to Grew. All communication between the President and the Commissioners on the one hand and the experts on the other was to pass through Grew's office. He was to be the indispensable link.[9]

As soon as his plan was ready Grew turned to the staggering problem of housing and servicing the delegation. This involved not only leasing a hotel but also, for security reasons, staffing it mostly with Americans. Furthermore, it meant establishing a complete communications system. In addition to round-the-clock code and cable facilities, a large staff of couriers and messengers had to be maintained and a complete American telephone exchange installed. Reproduction of a vast amount of paper work required scores of stenographers, mimeograph operators, and even a special printing plant.

He saw only one way to meet his need for personnel: draw upon the Army in France. Actually it was not Grew but House who brought the Army into the peace conference organization. On November 11 and 12, before Grew's appointment, House had cabled urging the use of specially qualified military personnel for intelligence, counterespionage, stenography, and coding. Wilson and Lansing approved, and General John J. Pershing, whose troops were marking time waiting for ships, was only too happy to cooperate. Grew drew from this source his able executive officer, Captain Richard Patterson, former assistant to the Mayor of New York, and Lieutenant W. L. Black, former manager of the Hotel Vanderbilt, who became manager of the Hotel Crillon where most of the delegation was housed.

These officers and others brought assistants and the assistants brought assistants.

Soldiers came by the truckload to man elevators, drive cars, make beds, haul coal, carry bags, and run errands. And they brought in tow nearly an equal number to care for their records, cut their hair, cook their food, and censor their mail. Since soldiers out of the trenches were not the world's most willing workers, even generous Army personnel requirements had to be increased. Grew, with no time to quibble about how many bedmakers he needed, simply kept drawing on the ever brimming supply. The total personnel, as a consequence, rose alarmingly, reaching proportions that would make efficiency-minded business executives purple with rage. The maximum reached approximately 1300 of whom only 191 were civilians.

But Grew had his organization ready by December 14 when the *George Washington* steamed into Brest through solid lines of French and American warships, each saluting as the President passed.

With the delegation's arrival Grew's troubles really began. House records that Wilson came in an "ugly mood" toward Lansing. The President disclaimed knowledge of Grew's appointment, though the evidence indicates he had approved it. He told House to start over and build a new organization. His rancor seems to have arisen from Lansing's selection of Grew's assistants, Philip Patchin and Leland Harrison. Both these State Department officials were *persona non grata* to the President. Harrison, the very image of the dandified diplomat Wilson disliked intensely, had gained the enmity of Inquiry professors aboard ship by assigning them four to a cabin like steerage passengers. Grew apparently caught the backlash of the President's wrath.[10]

The President was ready to chuck all Lansing's men, including Grew. House pleaded for Grew as being, though unsuited for the position, "a gentleman, . . . honest and trustworthy," and Grew loyally pleaded with House for Patchin and Harrison. Finally all three were saved, but the President was left hostile to the regular organization and was the more inclined to ignore it.[11]

This suited House perfectly, for the Colonel had been quietly building up his own organization for the President's use. Though he transferred some of his staff to Grew, he kept about a dozen officials and twice as many stenographers. These, with his carefully nurtured Inquiry, would be a fully sufficient private secretariat for the President, completely separate from the regular organization.[12]

Wilson was prepared to use it. He gave his private secretarial work to Auchincloss and Frazier, as well as to George Creel. Furthermore, he gave Patchin's press assignment to Ray Stannard Baker. Thus important segments of Grew's command were withdrawn from his control and his position was weakened even before the conference opened. Later, when the question arose of an American secretary to the Peace Conference Secretariat, a position which normally would have been Grew's, Wilson preferred Frazier. Auchincloss, aware that Grew wanted the post "as a matter of pride," advised the President it was a "rotten" assignment, and suggested Grew, leaving Frazier free for more important work. Wilson agreed.[13]

Grew's difficulties with House and Wilson were only the beginning. The cohort of Inquiry professors was ready for battle as soon as they stepped off the gangplank. Convinced that demography, geography, and history could clear up the mess the diplomats had made of the world, and furbished with a tweedy scorn for protocol and red tape, they immediately charged Grew's position. All access to Commissioners House, Lansing, General Tasker Bliss, and Henry White was supposed to be through Grew's office. This arrangement lasted only three days before The Inquiry's young, blunt, aggressive executive officer, Isaiah Bowman, had secured direct access to the top.[14]

The Inquiry took over other functions. The political intelligence work Grew had originally been assigned was transferred to The Inquiry, together with the field agents who were to provide the information. The office of Current Intelligence Summaries also went under Bowman's wing, with its chief, William Bullitt, whom Grew had brought to Paris to continue his admirable intelligence epitomes. And finally, Bowman arranged for members of The Inquiry to see leaders of various nationality groups without referring first to Grew's Liaison Office. The Inquiry was soon well launched on its own career and henceforth would refer to Grew only for service or complaints about poor service.[15]

No sooner had The Inquiry won its independence, when the Army launched an attack upon Grew's somewhat battered position. Brigadier General William T. Harts, Chief of the Paris District, made repeated attempts to take over command of all military personnel and thus, in effect, command of the organization. Grew met this challenge by securing the backing of Colonel House, Secretary Lansing, and the President, thus preventing a command structure based on military rank rather than special abilities. But the Army, one offensive halted, launched another under Brigadier General Marlborough Churchill, Chief of Military Intelligence, who had collected a staff of twenty officers to accompany Secretary of War Newton Baker to Paris. Baker remained in Washington, but sent his staff anyway. Churchill sought command of military personnel as General Harts had done. Grew met this thrust rather skillfully. First he secured the backing of the Commissioners and then tactfully assigned Churchill the job of surveying his organization to weed out inefficient and useless men. Churchill, mollified, turned in two favorable reports and went home.[16]

When General Marlborough Churchill gracefully retired from the field, it was the turn of the Peace Commissioners. Since they were given little to do,

Lansing filling his time buying Dutch silver, they found ample opportunity for a full agenda in Grew's bailiwick. They even began to pass on the use of automobiles. In one day Grew sent them twenty-one memoranda for consideration.

It was not long before they suspected dead timber in the delegation and, with the willing assistance of Bowman, whose organizational talents appear still to have found too little scope, they conducted several personnel forays. As a result of these investigations Grew's organization was in worse repute than ever. House characterized it as "wretched," with Grew's position "far beyond his capacity," while Bowman confidently predicted he could cut personnel in half, mostly by depleting service troops. Bliss, who had insisted that General Churchill be taken care of, now complained of "a tendency to overload the Commission with unnecessary assistant-personnel." [17]

As a result of Bowman's recommendations some cuts in personnel were effected. For example, the Ceremonial and Liaison Offices, with twenty-two officers, were abolished. Grew had already been subjected to some long-range sniping about these offices. William Phillips had sent him a friendly warning that Congressmen were complaining that their constituents were being ignored in favor of sons of Social Register families. Grew replied that "socially prominent" was in any case a relative term, and that what few he had were in the Ceremonial and Liaison Offices because of their social affiliations with important people and knowledge of French. He had been under considerable pressure from socially prominent families to take in their sons. Occasionally it had been prudent to accept them, as in the case of Grafton Winthrop Minot, grandson of Senator Henry Cabot Lodge. Others, Grew undoubtedly felt, could do little harm, and be of some use handling details of protocol. Most of these officers were now released, but this was about the extent of Bowman's success in reorganization.[18]

While Grew was dealing with these successive frontal assaults by The Inquiry, the Army, and the Commissioners, he was fighting continual skirmishes with nine technical advisory staffs headed by such individualists as Herbert Hoover, Samuel Gompers, Edward Hurley, and Bernard Baruch. Hoover brought on a crisis by insisting on extra rooms in the Crillon, threatening to go home if not satisfied. Gompers demanded two limousines for a trip to Belgium. Baruch had to have a telephone in his quarters at the Ritz. Lesser lights had no hesitation in complaining about poor service and asking for additional rooms, messengers, and bookcases. Someone even sent around for a razor strop! [19]

Grew was thus buffeted from all sides. The Peace Commission turned out to be a loose federation of staffs led by powerful, strong-willed men, who were able on all matters of policy to ignore this relatively minor bureaucrat, yet bore heavily on him for the satisfaction of routine and material needs and the airing of every grievance, legitimate or not. He was reduced to the oppressive and humiliating paper work of passes, procedures, and personnel, and to the intensely tiring task of placating and cajoling, of oiling the machinery, as he put it. Instead of being intimately associated with the high policy-making for a new world order, he became a "combined department store manager, director of traffic and floor sweeper of the Hotel Crillon."[20]

If his disappointment in being excluded from important work was the same as that of many others in Paris, it was no less real. He, at least, had a final satisfaction. Regular diplomatic officials attended the signing ceremony at Versailles, "distinguished at last from their professorial colleagues by silk hats and full diplomatic regalia." Grew, the foremost, affixed the President's signet to the molten wax of the peace parchment. He sat right next to the signing table. It was "impressive beyond description. . . ."[21]

The question remains whether he was a failure as Secretary of the Peace Commission. In Berlin he had acquired the reputation of being a good organizer, yet it was precisely the lack of this quality that House and Auchincloss deplored. The contradiction is explained by the fact that there are different kinds of good organizers. In Berlin responsibilities were clear, lines of authority dircct, and activity mostly familiar and routine. Berlin was a tidy walled compound compared to the administrative jungle he entered at Paris. To make order out of this chaos required someone with more than bureaucratic experience; it needed a person of great forcefulness and shrewd political talent. It called for a man able to resist to the utmost any challenge to his authority and, at the least doubt of support from above, willing to threaten resignation. Grew simply could not do this. Not only was he by nature and experience given to accomplishing his ends by tact and persuasion, but also he could not take the ultimate step of resignation without ruining a career which he had carefully husbanded through crises for fifteen years. He now ranked as a minister and was due for a legation if he could survive the ordeal of Paris.

A man like Hoover might have created a more efficient organization and successfully resisted encroachments, but it is still doubtful that the delegation would have been homogeneous. The relations between the President and his advisers, House and Lansing, were more than anything responsible for the divisiveness of the American establishment, and no one but the principals involved could have solved that problem. Considering this basic condition, there is something to be said for a tactful, hard-working diplomat introducing what little harmony and unity he could, and this in effect is what Grew did.

As a result of Grew's heavy use of army personnel, his organization was undoubtedly inefficient compared to business practices. But their services cost the American taxpayer nothing extra. They were more efficiently employed at the Peace Commission than sitting in camp waiting for ships.

They were mostly wounded or gassed men, poorly housed at first, and not anxious for work in any form, but they provided the essential services in their heavy-footed way. Professor James Shotwell and the rest had an American breakfast every morning, and lived, as he admitted, "with absolutely no privations." [22] Delay and inconvenience there were, but what is surprising is that in the space of those feverish December weeks Grew created an organization which performed many of the principal operations of the United States government. If the peace delegation was an aggregation of autonomous groups, this was only because it faithfully reflected the nature of the Executive at Washington, of which it was a cross-section.

Despite his distressing position, Grew was not completely a cipher in the conference proceedings, for he did make a significant contribution in personnel, in particular an extremely able group of diplomatic secretaries for whom he arranged positions in the delegation. He placed Ellis Dresel in charge of the Division of Current, Diplomatic and Political Correspondence. Dresel later took an important investigatory mission to Berlin and ultimately became High Commissioner in Germany. Under Dresel, Grew placed Allen Dulles, who had come to Paris as a statistician, Frederick Dolbeare, from the Legation at Berne, and Lithgow Osborne. This unit was gradually built up with men from the State Department into an organization designed to keep that Department informed of Paris developments and, one suspects, to reinstitute its influence at Paris. When The Inquiry was dissolving in the spring of 1919, Dresel's men took over its work.[23]

In addition, Grew was influential in selecting secretaries for the Commissioners. Christian Herter, whom he recommended to Henry White, subsequently acted as secretary to the Commission as a whole. Grew probably was influential in bringing Alexander Kirk from The Hague to act as secretary to Lansing, while Hugh Wilson from Berne briefly acted as secretary to the Commissioners in the absence of Herter. Thus from Berlin and Vienna days, Dresel, Dulles, Dolbeare, Kirk, Wilson, Herter, and Osborne all were attached to the peace delegation by Grew. If influence depended on loyal assistants, Grew was not to be outdone by the rest.[24]

For the Department of State the organization of the conference was a great challenge. Paris showed how far removed from the requirements of the twentieth century Old State with its pigeonholes and sealing wax had been. The gap was filled by a magnificent amateur effort on the part of The Inquiry. The State Department changed, glacially, but one wonders if there would have been any change at all if Grew had not exposed his group of young and able diplomatic colleagues to the full force of the "heyday of irregular diplomacy."

By the end of the Peace Conference, Grew had reached a crucial turning point in his career. Behind him were fifteen years of assiduous and loyal service in the secretarial ranks, including periods of critical responsibility.

Ahead of him, with a favoring fortune, would be ministerships, even ambassadorships. But the difference between a counselor of embassy and a minister was wholly unlike that between a first secretary and counselor. To become a chief of mission was more like vaulting from captain to general, for while the Army, Navy, and Consular Service provided a gradation of lesser commands, in the Diplomatic Service there were only ministers and ambassadors and their staffs. The chief staff member might occupy a key position and even function as ambassador for extended periods, but to the outside world he was only an assistant enjoying reflected prestige and authority. Thus to become a chief of mission was in no sense to climb another rung up the ladder, but rather to be raised into another world far above the arduous trails and terraces of secretarial purgatory. In this small paradise the elect, each in his private domain of legation or embassy, held the substance of prestige and authority. This ascension alone could make worthwhile the years of waiting, the years of covering up and smoothing out for bungling superiors, the years of plodding details and humble chores, of fetching the corn flakes and sarsaparilla.

Yet what made Grew's career so uncertain and difficult was that he had no right to expect this reward. He moved just ahead of the tide of professionalization creeping up the hierarchy with guarantees of tenure and merit promotion. Today the qualified diplomat can count on a system of promotion boards eventually granting him access to the chief of mission ranks. Then it depended entirely on the judgment of highly placed individuals subject to political pressure and the uncertainty of party fortunes.

Therefore, it could only have been with great anxiety that Grew began his bid for a legation as soon as the Treaty of Versailles was signed. He was in the further dilemma of already ranking as minister before the assembled diplomats of the world. A prolonged assignment at his old rank, he was well aware, would publicly imply his failure at Paris. But, though Grew was repeatedly criticized as Secretary General, his critics retained a warm personal regard for him and a deep confidence that he was entirely trustworthy and reliable. Indeed, Grew's character was his greatest asset. In addition, his critics readily recognized what a thankless task he had at Paris. Consequently, Henry White, Colonel House, and Frank Polk, who was head of the American delegation in Paris after June 1919, all recommended him for promotion, Polk praising in particular Grew's rare tact and judgment. Polk and William Phillips were concerned about resignations from the Service at the end of the war. Many of the younger diplomats preferred the alluring prospects of making money in business to the uncertainties of career diplomacy. Without some promotions to ministerial rank, the Diplomatic Service would be chaotically depleted.[25]

Though Grew had many conditions in his favor, it was many months before his reward came. Brussels was a hope until it was made an embassy.

He sought Berne, but the incumbent declined to vacate the post. With no post in sight by the time the Peace Conference ended, he moved over to the Embassy in Paris as Counselor, a convenient perch while the quest continued. Finally, through the influence of his friends, the legation in Copenhagen was offered him in April 1920, and he accepted immediately.

On May 22 six Grews, two servants, seven suitcases, picnic boxes, typewriters, golf clubs, guns, gasoline cans, and tires were fitted into the Cadillac and its trailer like the works of a watch into its case, and Minister Grew with enormous relief and zest for the new adventure set out on the first diplomatic mission he could call his own.

FOUR

Minister Grew

TIME stood still in Denmark. Insulated from the tragic and bitter turmoil of postwar Europe, the placid Danes tended their cows, thronged to the beaches for ritual suntanning, and scrubbed their tidy kingdom aseptically clean. The race, the language, the stratified society, and the court paraphernalia must have strongly reminded Grew of prewar Germany. The past five years had been only a troubled dream and he was back again among the trappings of courtier diplomacy.[1]

Danish-American relations presented no problems to disturb a calm and sunny mission. His one important assignment, that of gathering information about Bolshevik Russia, was unfruitful. Such information as he could obtain was indirect, scanty, and repetitive compared to information provided by the American Legation at Riga, Latvia. Therefore, he had little to report to Washington, just as the Department of State, in a fit of postwar economy, desired. "Don't send in too much stuff," he was advised. His small staff of two secretaries, a naval attaché, and a commercial attaché was ample for routine work. Following his principle of delegation of authority, he allowed his First Secretary to run the Chancery and visit the Foreign Office, leaving himself free to "buzz here and there, like the little busy bee, gathering honeyed information from the choicest flowers." [2]

The center of Grew's activity was the Raben House, a stately mansion built in 1754, only a short distance from the royal palace and across the street from the Legation. His study in the blue room on the main floor served as his office. There, with a direct wire to the Legation, and surrounded once again by his books, papers, and fine furniture, he could receive visitors in quiet, comfort, and dignity.

The Raben House was well suited for the entertaining Grew had in mind when he wrote his brother for more money, "in order to put the Legation . . . on a footing it has not had for years. . . ." [3] During the season the Grews gave large formal dinners for court society and the diplomatic corps in their spacious ballroom. There, in soft light playing on gleaming silver, wild duck or pheasant was the high point of a six-course dinner, each course accompanied by a fine wine. Wines, Grew mused half-seriously, were the backbone of diplomacy. His favorite, Rüdesheimer 1897, roused even the dour Foreign Minister, Harald Scavenius. After dinner the guests were entertained by classical music: an orchestra, a singer, or Grew himself at his Bechstein piano. As a result of a season of such entertainment, Grew concluded:

> . . . we now know everybody in the Copenhagen blue book more or less intimately, have entertained everybody we had to, and a lot more, have eaten enough to ruin any less cast-iron constitutions, and haven't assimilated a new idea or thought worth having. That is Copenhagen — at least blue book Copenhagen. If Denmark has a soul, it is to be found elsewhere, and I hope now to have time to go in search of it.[4]

His search was only halfhearted. He met some prominent Danish businessmen and inspected their plants, but he never became intimate with them. He attended one dinner of Danish merchants but found the protocol of *skaaling* severe, the food heavy, and the conversation dull. He took lessons in Danish and soon could read the newspapers, but he seldom spoke the language, undoubtedly because most prominent Danes spoke English. William Phillips was facing the same problem of broadening his circle of acquaintances at the same time as Minister in The Hague, but he took a bolder approach. In order to break out of the womb of courtly life in the capital and meet the "actual" leaders of the country in Amsterdam, he made a yearly pilgrimage there to give large receptions and dinners for noted lawyers, industrialists, bankers, and professors. The response was "almost impulsive." He was enthusiastically received and made many fresh acquaintances. Such an approach never occured to Grew.[5]

Grew's one major effort to get in touch with the general public was a speech he delivered at an open air Fourth of July celebration before fifteen thousand Danes. He praised Denmark and its contribution through men like Jacob Riis to the development of the United States. The speech was interesting, apropos, and skillfully delivered. "I laid it on with a trowel," he wrote home in exuberantly mixed metaphors, "and the Danes lapped it up and wagged all over." Mr. Grew had been little known or talked about by the general public, wrote a local paper, but now it would be different. Yet this lone effort at people-to-people diplomacy cost Grew dearly in labor and anxiety. He could not speak from notes and hated to read a speech, so he memorized it word for word, perhaps, as in later years, a paragraph at a time while shaving. He memorized easily and loved to cap verses thanks to his Groton experience, but he abhorred the prospect of public speaking and lived for the day each year, marked in red on his calendar, when his speech-making was over.[6]

Neither did Grew care for casual contacts with the general public. Trips to the fair and the beach with the children were occasionally cut short because of "the dirty, smelly crowd of all the rabble of Copenhagen." He feared diphtheria and scarlet fever, but social discrimination influenced him too. He noted that a group of Danish-American singers whom he entertained were listed as carpenters, plumbers, house-painters, and gardeners, and bluntly commented in his diary, "They look it." [7]

In diplomacy Grew adapted himself to new conditions as necessary and as best he could. Socially he changed least of all. What characterized his mission to Denmark was the lack of any imperative need for change. At home the Republicans and "normalcy" were back. Prewar life and diplomacy could never be recaptured, but they might be approximated. He was only too glad to "make hay in the sunshine" after five years of grim war work and sixteen years of "sweeping out" for others. He worried that his diary was giving his family in Boston the impression that "our life is simply a round of society," but in fact this was mostly what it was. Those with whom he relaxed were, as in prewar Germany, only a congenial segment of the diplomatic and court sets. This was the easy, familiar way to gain the repose he felt he had earned.[8]

Recreation, purposeful recreation, was the theme of Grew's Danish mission. He played the piano beautifully, practicing daily at least one hour. Piano and poker each in its own absorbing way refreshed his mind and outlook. He played tennis several times a week with a strong competitive urge and zest for physical activity. But the greatest happiness of Copenhagen was the time he could spend with his family: strolls with Mrs. Grew along wooded paths by mossy moats in Citadel Park; a game of Blindman's Buff with the children on the grassy slopes above the seaside resort of Hornboek, delicious swims in the ocean with young Elsie riding the waves on her daddy's back; a rollicking reading of *Pickwick Papers* during a picnic in the deep woods near Roskilde; or the quiet teatime hours with his daughters, helping them with their Latin and piano. In bad weather they all went to the movies and laughed to tears watching Harold Lloyd, or, by himself, he might burrow deep in a chair by the fire to read *The Scarlet Pimpernel* from cover to cover. These were the ingredients of that fullness of life he sought and cherished.

This placid period in Copenhagen, when Grew's diplomatic activity was relatively unimportant, offers an opportunity for a closer look at Grew himself. The Danish and Swiss missions in the years 1920 to 1924 marked the midpassage of his career. At Copenhagen he turned forty, having completed, as he said, twenty years of preparation and nearly twenty years of experience. He was now "swinging down the course at the height of . . .

[his] strength." Contemplating the lengthening row of leatherbound volumes containing his papers, he saw unfolding a career which already contained historic value. With secret joy he wrote, "Woe to my biographer!" [9]

He made a striking impression. His height, powerful shoulders, trim waist, erect carriage, bushy brows, bristling mustache, dark hair parted in the middle and slicked down, and jaunty Savile Row clothing gave the appearance of a British Guards officer. In fact, he was mistaken for an Englishman several times. He was reserved but neither aloof nor haughty. That "inborn suavity, gracefulness of movement and lightness of touch," with which he characterized members of Boston's exclusive Somerset Club, were his in full measure. There was no affectation, no fake dignity, no hurry. Here, as a European newspaper reported, was the "perfect Anglo-Saxon gentleman." [10]

His library provides evidence of his interests and tastes at this period in his life. His consuming interest was diplomacy, and with the practical American how-to-do-it approach he studied texts on diplomacy by John Foster and Sir Ernest Satow as well as books on writing and public speaking. Diplomatic memoirs with their intimate glimpses of the ways of his art always interested him. As the participants in the diplomacy of the World War and the Peace Conference began publishing their reminiscences and diatribes, he avidly bought them to test and enlarge upon his own experience. Aside from his library of diplomacy, his tastes were more recreational than intellectual. He enjoyed P. G. Wodehouse, Mary Roberts Rinehart, Maurice Maeterlinck, O Henry, and, of course, Rudyard Kipling. His lifelong love of travel led him to acquire books on exploration, mountain-climbing and the *Boys' Book of Steamships*.[11]

Grew's library suggests a rather satisfied, practical mind without any restless intellectual curiosity or speculative depths. A further and more striking characteristic suggested by his papers is a pervading conservatism. He was conservative by nature. When the Gillette safety razor was introduced, he hoped it would be made to last because, "the older a possession became, the more I liked it." He treasured his battered bedroom slippers. Increasingly he became committed to his own social and cultural heritage, less than ever the rebel who ran away from State Street. If he had had a son, the boy would have gone to Groton, or possibly St. Mark's or St. Paul's. He worried that his children's French accent would not be as perfect as his wife's because they had learned English first. And in 1920 he decided to join the Somerset Club as a non-resident member.[12]

Politically he was back in the Republican fold. During a visit home in the midst of the presidential campaign of 1920 he politely declined to meet Franklin D. Roosevelt and soon after wrote his friend Dresel: "Frank Roosevelt got right down into the gutter and trotted out all the usual catch phrases, mud-slinging and campaign slogans that one associates with the lowest form of ward politics." The Democratic campaign was a "farce." Although he found a good deal of common sense in John Maynard Keynes's *Economic Consequences of the Peace*, he supposed it was "heresy" to say so and judged the author "somewhat of a radical." His greatest concern was Bolshevism.[13]

There was nothing peculiar in Grew's reaction to Bolshevism. It was undoubtedly inspired by antipathy for the dogma, fear of the threat to property, stability, and duly constituted authority, revulsion at its murderous rise to power, and sense of betrayal in the separate peace with Germany. The peace of Brest-Litovsk, remarked Hugh Wilson, who viewed things the way his friend Grew did, marked the end of the era of "scrupulous courtesy" and "good manners" in international dealings and the beginning of the era of "diplomacy by vituperation." This manifestation of the threatening new Russia struck home most forcibly to a diplomat of the old school like Grew. Bolshevists were not gentlemen. It would be foolhardy to recognize a nation which had no intention of keeping faith in international relations. Western negotiations with Russia at Genoa and Rapallo in 1922 were "profoundly disgusting," resembling nothing so much as, significantly, "a ward political meeting at home." [14]

Typically, too, he argued that food would bring the Russians to their senses. But by 1921 it was obvious that the Reds were firmly in power, and that "the old halcyon days, when we worried profoundly over trifles, are gone, and we may now worry over things really worth worrying about." Bolshevism was not confined to Russia, and that was "item number 1." The danger of Communism in Germany led him to deplore the French *revanchiste* policy. In 1922 he argued for a financially solvent Germany as essential for the political health of Europe, to be accomplished by a moratorium on reparations payments and by loans. But Grew's anxiety for the weakened bastions of civilization in Europe turned to horror at the news of the Boston Police Strike. "Bolshevism and anarchy are pretty near our gates," he exclaimed, "when that sort of thing can happen." In Denmark he praised members of the nobility and others, "clearly gentlemen," who successfully broke a dock strike by loading ships themselves. It was the story of the Boston strike all over again, and "the one and only answer to the Unions." [15]

Grew's placid mission to Denmark was badly jolted in August 1921 by an incident at Nimb's Restaurant in Copenhagen.[16] He had gone there to a luncheon in honor of the American delegation returning from the Interparliamentary Congress at Stockholm. For a variety of reasons he arrived without having met the senators and representatives of the delegation before. He was precisely on time, easily distinguishable from the crowd of guests in the anteroom by his lordly presence and debonair English claw-hammer coat and yellow waistcoat. The legislators, on the contrary, were indistinguishable in plebeian business suits. There was no one at hand who knew the Americans and the host was busy receiving, so Grew had to find his way alone in a hum of conversation particularly confusing to a person hard of hearing. He had barely spoken to two out of eight members of the delegation when Foreign Minister Scavenius, in accordance with Danish custom and diplomatic protocol, offered his arm to Grew and the two stalked in to lunch leaving the members of Congress, open-mouthed, to trail humbly behind.

They were furious. They felt they had been deliberately snubbed by their own diplomatic representative. The key members, whom Grew unfortunately had not met, were a powerful, aggressive pair whose enmity no diplomat could afford. Heavy-set, fiery-eyed Senator Joseph T. Robinson, soon to be Democratic Minority Leader, was subject to "fits of rage so intense that his whole frame shakes, and his face purples visibly." Representative Fred A. Britten, an ex-pugilist from Chicago with a keen sense for publicity and a "Peter Pan-ish" approach to protocol, was sufficiently influential to have the Army-Navy football game moved to Illinois. Repercussions were quick. In the wake of the delegation touring Europe, American missions buzzed with Britten's and Robinson's biting comments. Grew was a "pink tea diplomat" unfit to represent the United States and never again to be confirmed in a diplomatic appointment.[17]

The worst of the affair was that by coincidence Grew was transferred to Switzerland as Minister only a few days later to make way for a political appointee in Copenhagen. Failure to obtain Senate confirmation would kill his career. Senator Henry Cabot Lodge and Under Secretary of State Henry Fletcher between them secured the confirmation by sneaking it through on a day Senator Robinson was out playing golf. But before that success Grew spent many sleepless nights and was moved in despair to write that the episode made him want to "chuck the whole ——— [sic] job." On his next trip home he made his Canossa to Capitol Hill and succeeded in restoring relations with all his enemies except the most important one, Robinson, who clung to his grudge. As a result Grew lived in doubt of senatorial confirmations for ten long years, until on his way to Japan as Ambassador in 1932 he met Robinson, then Majority Leader, on the floor of the Senate for an affable chat which healed the breach. As Grew himself had said in 1916 of a colleague who lost his promotion on account of a tiff with a senator, "It is a great pity, but the moral is evident." [18]

There is no question of Grew's intentions in the Copenhagen Incident. He obviously desired to meet the delegation, and in fact hoped for an "historic love feast" with the Congressmen, at which he might convince them of the need for a professional Foreign Service. To rebuff anyone was so completely foreign to Grew's character as to be unthinkable. What had happened was due mostly to bad luck. He learned of the visit officially from

Washington only after it had occurred, and unofficially only two days before they arrived. His town house was closed, Copenhagen was deep in summer slumber, and he had weekend guests at the seashore. Nevertheless, he invited the delegation out for a swim and "tea," which could be variously defined according to their prohibition proclivities. As the train was uncertainly late and it was Sunday morning, he sent his Third Secretary with the invitation, reserved hotel rooms, and placed the secretary at their service for the day. The delegation declined the invitation because of previous engagements. Yet with all he tried to do, Grew failed to do the essential, that is, to meet the delegates at the train himself, thereby allowing proper, leisurely introductions before he stood alone and deaf in the anteroom at Nimb's. Such foresight may be expecting too much, but the impression remains that Grew was slow to realize the possibilities of the situation, somewhat out of contact with affairs in Copenhagen that summer, and reluctant to miss several delicious swims in the Oresund that unlucky Sunday morning. Maybe after all he was treating senators and representatives as mere mortals!

The Grews moved to Switzerland in October 1921. As a comfortable, carefree post, Berne was like Copenhagen. Though occasionally Grew was so busy he took a sandwich lunch at his desk, there were relatively undisturbed months when he could practice the piano as much as three hours a day and slip away with his daughter Anita to Wengen for breathtaking ski runs in the shadow of the Jungfrau. They had the added advantage of excellent schools for the girls nearby. As in Copenhagen the Grews mixed assiduously in Swiss society. They felt it their duty, they enjoyed it, and, in Grew's judgment, members of Swiss society kept their ears to the ground and provided valuable information. Since most diplomats sought "a peaceful period" in Switzerland and paid little attention to the Swiss, the Grews' efforts were warmly received. Word passed that the Legation was "perfect, different from ever before; . . . that it is wonderful to have a Minister who speaks the languages of the country." On the whole, Grew had an excellent staff that included such later lights of American diplomacy as Arthur Bliss Lane, and Herschel V. Johnson. It was a "congenial shop," establishing under Grew's close supervision a reputation in the Department of State for good reporting, both in content and English. He would see to the latter! [19]

Grew's managerial tasks at Paris and his isolation in Denmark had left him on the fringes of the central problems agitating European affairs. Now, as Minister to Switzerland, he gradually became enmeshed in them. His introduction was given him by President and later Federal Councillor Edmund Schulthess. Grew had met Schulthess, "the uncrowned King of Switzerland," in 1917 after the exodus from Germany, and had carefully recorded their conversation on Swiss water power. Thus when he presented his credentials to President Schulthess on November 1, 1921, he was able to recall, after reference to his papers, the details of that first meeting. Much gratified, Schulthess became extraordinarily cordial and the two formed a close friendship. With complete confidence in Grew's discretion, Schulthess provided him with confidential information on European developments. After some important international conference he would stop in at Grew's home, and in the intimacy of Grew's study, settled in a comfortable chair by the fire with one of Grew's cigars, would unburden his heart for the American Minister's willing ears. In this way Grew became so well informed on the basic economic and political problems of Europe that he was able to make a speech on the subject to a Berlin conference of American chiefs of mission which made a deep impression on them all.[20]

As Minister in Switzerland, Grew could do more than hear about postwar international affairs; the League of Nations gave him an opportunity for an active role. In his first instruction as Minister he was directed to obtain all League of Nations printed material affecting directly or indirectly the interests of the United States and its citizens. Very little indeed could not be included under such a sweeping category.[21]

This surprising interest by the new Republican Administration in an institution which it had repudiated was due to several reasons. In the first place the Republican triumph of 1920, though inconclusive as a mandate for repudiation, had eased the deadlock between the executive and legislature, removed the League from the arena of intense political controversy, and opened a tiny space for maneuver by the Secretary of State.[22] In the second place, by rejecting the League, the United States had placed itself in the ridiculous position of excluding itself from prewar humanitarian organizations now under League aegis. No reasonable man, no matter how bitterly anti-League, could object to some degree of international cooperation against anthrax, opium, and white slavery. In the third place, the League, contrary to expectations, was very much alive, and was busily making decisions touching the interests of the United States and of American citizens. The terms of the British mandate in Palestine, for example, threatened American oil interests in the area. The United States could not afford to be ignorant of what was happening at Geneva. Finally, the attitude of Secretary of State Charles Evans Hughes was a factor. Though sternly realistic about the impossibility of political connection with the League, Hughes had a broad humanitarian and internationalist point of view, an attachment to most League principles, a lawyer-like hunger for pertinent documents, and sensitivity to the interests of his client, the United States. He would not, could not, ignore the League. Consequently, there was better reason than one might expect for Grew's instruction to get in touch with the League.

So hypnotized was the Administration by the irreconcilables in the Senate, however, that Grew's contact with the League had to be practically on the level of espionage. His instruction was confidential. He was to send documents under cover of a confidential dispatch for the eyes only of the Secretary and Under Secretary. In fact, so secretive was his mission that Grew felt obliged to conceal from the State Department's own Bureau of Accounts the fact that he had hired extra clerks to handle League material.[23]

Grew lost no time getting in touch with the League. In the Section of Administrative Commissions of the League Secretariat was a Bostonian whom he had known in the American delegation at Paris, Huntington Gilchrist. Grew wrote him asking for a meeting at some "quiet and unobtrusive place." Gilchrist replied with an invitation to lunch at his little cottage on the lake a few miles north of Geneva. Grew drove down from Berne on November 26, had a pleasant renewal of old acquaintance, and incidentally asked for copies of League documents, which Gilchrist willingly provided. Thereafter League publications found their way to the Legation at Berne in swelling volume, whence they were forwarded to interested American missions and to Washington.[24]

This first slender connection brought after it, like the heaving line its hawser, increasingly complex and important relationships during the next ten years, which, though never consummating in formal participation, involved the United States in many League activities. Grew worked hard to broaden the connection during his mission. His Christmas holidays in 1921 were spent at the ski resort of Gstaad, whether by design or coincidence in the same hotel as Sir Eric Drummond, Secretary General of the League. The two diplomats had pleasant conversations during the festivities, for they also had in common the hectic months of the Paris Conference. Another Paris colleague at Geneva was Arthur Sweetser, assistant director of the League information service. Grew would meet Sweetser at Geneva either in the privacy of Princess Ella Radziwill's apartment, which he called his "League of Nation's Office," or for walks along the Quai Mont Blanc where Sweetser "crammed" him full of the latest League news.[25]

In this way Grew established himself as an effective "subterranean channel of communication" between the League and the Department of State. When the United States wished to inform the League discreetly of its position in the Palestine Mandate controversy, Grew was able to convey the information to Sweetser by telephone. When the Chilean Ambassador in London, also president of the Third Assembly of the League, met Grew at a dinner party and intimated a desire to meet Secretary Hughes privately to discuss the League, Grew was able to advise him how to proceed. When the League offered, informally, a secretarial staff for the Pan American Conference, Grew forwarded the offer and the American declination, again informally. On August 10, 1922, Grew notified the Department of State by personal letter to Leland Harrison that the League was anxious for American participation in the work of the Opium Commission. Subsequent invitations for participation in humanitarian activities and an encouraging number of acceptances passed back and forth through Grew's office. In September 1922 he began conveying American economic statistics to the League by personal letter to Drummond.[26]

He did all this with at least the tacit approval of Hughes, of course. However, there were rigid limitations to Grew's activities. When he was so bold as to drive to the door of League headquarters in the Hotel National to pick up Sweetser one day, he was recognized to his dismay by a famous correspondent of the *Chicago Tribune*, whom he begged to keep silent. Fortunately, the correspondent cooperated, but Grew never dared enter the League offices, or visit Geneva except briefly and, according to the gentle Sir Eric Drummond, the American Minister always turned up his collar when they passed on the street. Grew even felt he was taking a risk in extending Arthur Sweetser's passport. He was well aware that if just one newspaper clipping dwelling on his intimacy with League officials reached Senator William Borah's desk, all his work would be undone. Besides, his relations with the Senate were already tenuous enough, thanks to the Copenhagen Incident.[27]

On the basis of Grew's activities and repeated suggestions for enlarged American participation in the League, one might gain the impression he was an ardent advocate of it. But his letters can also give the opposite impression. He disavowed any inclination for formal commitments in Europe. "Let the others fight it out on the scrimmage line," he wrote with typical American interwar smugness,

> while we stand well back with our eye on the ball and an unclouded view of the field. Forward passes and drop kicks, which have nothing whatever to do with the scrimmagers, are frequently the plays that score.[28]

Grew at least was on the playing field, but he felt that the League as an instrument for peace was "spineless and impotent," a vehicle for "cutthroat European politics," and the United States "well out of it." Despite his sour comments during these years, Grew confided to his diary in 1924, after his appointment as Under Secretary of State, that the League, if imperfect, was the only step yet taken in the right direction and a welcome one. He did not believe the United States should join, he continued,

> . . . for we have different problems from those of Europe. But I do hold that we should cooperate with the League to the greatest possible extent and give it all encouragement, support and approval. Our opposition to it is 90% domestic politics. . . .[29]

Making due allowance for prudent trimming on such an explosive issue, one can conclude that Grew was slightly ahead of American official opinion regarding the League. More energetically and more insistently he advocated participation in its humanitarian organizations, and other non-political activities, though never putting to the most private paper any commitment to formal membership. He sharply distinguished between diplomatic intercourse and membership, and would have pursued the former, if for no other reason, because it was the life and breath of a diplomat. Geneva at Assembly time was like a reunion. There he could meet colleagues from every former post and gather pouchfuls of information. He must have felt like a star salesman excluded from his industry's annual national convention held at the hotel next door.[30]

Grew finally obtained an opportunity to come officially and openly to Geneva in February 1924, when he was appointed observer at a session of the Temporary Mixed Commission dealing with the regulation of international traffic in arms. Grew's mission was apparently inconclusive, but actually it was a failure.

This unhopefully titled commission was one of several established by the League in its first decade to thrash out informally the problems of disarmament. Traffic in arms was one aspect of disarmament which could at least proceed from a prepared text. The Convention of St. Germain, concluded during the Peace Conference at Paris and signed by the United States, proposed a detailed system of arms categories, prohibitions, government licensing, and publicity, but the Convention had been thrown out by the Senate along with the peace treaties. Progress was halted until the world's largest armaments producer could be persuaded to cooperate.[31]

During the next four years the United States played ostrich. Requests for ratification were at first not even answered. However, it became increasingly difficult for the United States to ignore the League on this issue. On the one hand, the problem grew more acute in 1922 as war surplus arms cut a bloody swath in Turkey and posed a threat to international peace. On the other hand, the United States took a leading role in disarmament at the Washington Conference, began participation in League humanitarian activities, and stood publicly committed by November 1923 to cooperation in international conferences promising "useful conventions."[32] Thus the United States was in the invidious position of apparently obstructing international peace in one phase of disarmament while advancing it in others, simply because the forum for discussion happened to be the League of Nations. To escape this position and clarify American policy, Hughes accepted an invitation to send a representative to Geneva and appointed Grew.

The Secretary of State had strong objections to the St. Germain Convention quite apart from the League issue. It left the major arms-producing countries of Europe free to trade among themselves and supply their colonies and mandates exclusively, thereby securing them a monopoly of arms traffic. Furthermore, prohibition of arms shipments to non-signatory powers would prevent the United States from supporting oppressed peoples seeking to overthrow their governments and, perhaps more to the point, from supporting governments such as those in Latin America where it might be to the interest of the United States to maintain order. His government would be weakening its arms-manufacturing industry in order to protect the armaments industries of Europe. This would be an exceedingly bad bargain.[33]

Of course the "intertwining" of the League and the Convention was a major objection of the United States, but not an insuperable one, with proper reservations, Hughes believed. In his instruction to Grew, he listed the League objection last and least emphatically. Grew was discreetly to make the point that the convention was not a sincere attempt at disarmament but rather "a political arrangement for the protection of existing governments." With typical ingenuity Hughes was trying to shake off the stultifying League issue with its burden of responsibility for obstructing peace endeavors. However, he did not dare propose a set of controls that would be acceptable to the United States, and Grew was left in the awkward position of having to place the European powers on the defensive or represent the same old hopelessly negative American policy.[34]

The fact that Grew, in attending the Temporary Mixed Commission meeting on February 4, 1924, was the first American diplomat to appear at a League function was occasion enough to send a flutter of excitement through Geneva. But what made the occasion historic was that Woodrow Wilson had died only the day before and his Under Secretary of State, John Davis, like a guardian angel, appeared among the distinguished visitors and correspondents in the audience. It seemed like an act of divine redemption. Ecstatic, Arthur Sweetser called it "one of the greatest moments in history." [35]

To his relief Grew could look around the table on familiar faces. Five of the members had been at Paris and two more were colleagues at Berne. He even knew slightly the most important of them all, Viscount Cecil of Chelwood, that tireless League worker whose sharp countenance so belied his gentle manner that he reminded someone of a vulture chasing butterflies.[36] Grew was called upon to respond to the eulogies paid the League's founder and did so gracefully, despite his horror of "off-the-cuff" speeches. When the meeting adjourned for the day and Grew repaired to his friend's apartment for a much-needed drink, John Davis told him he had never seen a person so much "on the spot."

Grew's appearance was highly newsworthy. Paris afternoon papers featured it and the *New York Times* gave page one prominence the following day to the headline AMERICAN MINISTER AT LEAGUE SESSION. Momentarily transfixed by the glare of public interest, Grew cautiously kept quiet after briefly stating the limitations of his instructions, waiting for proposals requiring his comment.

On February 6, a draft convention came under consideration article by article. One of the first articles, hopefully designed to meet American objections, created an international office the power of which extended only to the collection of information on the trade in arms. There was no mention of the League, but the United States would be required to furnish information. Grew now felt compelled to rise and draw the Commission's attention to the American objection to the Convention of St. Germain that its provisions were "intertwined" with the League, an objection applicable, he felt, to the point under discussion.[37]

It was soon apparent that he had blundered. Members of the Commission eagerly grasped this first lengthy comment by the American observer as his major objection to the proposed convention and in a winningly conciliatory vein stated their earnest desire to redraft the objectionable article to suit the United States. Grew quickly rose again to warn that this point did not exhaust American objections, but it was too late. The impression was firmly established by Cecil that if only the United States could be placated over the details of administration, the rest of the draft would be acceptable. The press followed his lead, with the *New York Times* reporting that the League issue was the "principal" one standing in the way of agreement. Hughes was distinctly displeased and cabled Grew that such an impression was incorrect. While we must reserve our attitude on the administration question, the Secretary of State observed, "we do not want a mere question of administration given chief attention as if that were the difficulty in the way." Our basic objections, he repeated, were with respect to "the freedom of the parties of the convention to sell to each other and the prohibition against selling to others." He also criticized Grew for declining to discuss control of arms manufacture.[38]

Hughes's cable arrived after the close of the session. Grew had catalogued the full list of objections by then but they were lost in the wake of the first. To the public the United States still appeared to be governed by its negative policy toward the League. Hughes's effort to escape the miasma and re-establish this phase of disarmament negotiation on the plane of national self-interest within the larger framework of international cooperation had failed.

A weak convention devoted merely to arms trade publicity finally emerged from League deliberations in 1926, was signed by the United States, and went to a lingering death in the Senate. If the Senate could not even stomach this much, it seems hardly likely that it would have accepted a rigorous disarmament convention such as Hughes felt should be given most careful consideration. Therefore, Grew's caution on the League issue was in tune with Congress. Added reason for caution might have been the knowledge, received most confidentially a few days earlier, that he was under consideration for the post of Under Secretary of State. Nevertheless, Grew's mission was not to secure proposals that might be acceptable to the Senate. Rather it was to demonstrate publicly that the United States was not opposed to arms trade control but to control proposals that perverted the disarmament ideal. His failure lay in not perceiving this, or if he perceived it, in allowing himself to be maneuvered into a position where his objections had to be along outworn lines. He seemed insensitive to the publicity opportunities of international conferences and hypersensitive to the dangers. He was distressed with the way his objection had been highlighted as the principal one, yet he remained unaware that he might have used the opportunity to emphasize more important objections.[39]

It should be added that Grew's position was an awkward one to begin with and that he made a good impression on diplomats present. Sweetser noted the "tact, and, if I may use the word, charm with which Grew met a situation which might have been rather difficult." [40]

The open diplomacy of Paris and Geneva did not suit Grew. Where his position was poorly defined, where the public spotlight was on him, where the situation was unfamiliar, tangled, or shifting, he was at a disadvantage. He lacked the necessary forcefulness, boldness, quick reaction, and capacity for political maneuver. On the other hand, where guidelines were clear, where the forum was restricted and shielded from the public, where he had time to grasp the situation and size up personalities, where he could proceed methodically and quietly, then he shone. The previous year, in 1922 and 1923, he had been given the opportunity of demonstrating his abilities in circumstances that suited him at the Lausanne Conference and he had turned in a polished performance.

PART TWO

Diplomacy as a Profession

(1922 – 1927)

FIVE

The Lausanne Conference

ON October 28, 1922, one year after his arrival in Switzerland, Grew was assigned to the Conference on Near Eastern Affairs at nearby Lausanne. The conference was held for the purpose of ending an old war and averting a new one. Technically it was the final stage of the Paris Peace Conference for settling accounts with Germany's ally Turkey. But three years had worked a vast change in the Near East.

At the end of the World War, the victorious Allies assumed the Ottoman Empire to be entirely at their disposal. They proceeded energetically to dismember it and divide Asia Minor into zones of influence. The Greeks, supported by the Allies and inspired by Pan-Hellenic visions, occupied the port of Izmir (Smyrna) and drove inland. The Treaty of Sèvres imposed military, economic, and financial terms on the supine Sultanate that deeply impaired Turkish sovereignty. However, invasion by the despised Greeks and a humiliating peace stirred profound Turkish resistance. Nationalists found their leader in a former Ottoman general, Mustafa Kemal, who organized an army and a *de facto* government in the interior. Brilliantly playing off the Soviet Union against the West and the Allies against each other, he gained strength and his movement assumed increasing legitimacy. Finally, in September 1922, he crushed the Greeks and reoccupied Izmir. Now Britain stood alone at the Straits, barring the way to Istanbul and European Turkey. For a moment war seemed imminent, but the British commander concluded an armistice and his government gave way, in effect accepting Kemalist Turkey. A peace conference was called at Lausanne to arrange a comprehensive settlement. Turkey came absolutely determined to gain acceptance of her territorial integrity and unimpaired sovereignty. The other powers hoped to recover most of their former rights and secure their current interests under the new regime.[1]

The United States had not been at war with Turkey but felt its interests deeply involved in the settlement and accordingly sent a delegation of observers to Lausanne, one of which was Grew, an obvious choice with his experience, particularly in Paris, and his proximity.

The conference opened November 20, broke up in failure on February 4, 1923, reconvened on April 23, and concluded with the signing of the Treaty of Lausanne on July 24, 1923. Grew was one of three delegates at the first phase, and was the sole delegate at the second, during which he was also entrusted with separate negotiations with the Turks which concluded with a treaty on August 6, 1923.

Lausanne was a major event in Grew's career. The first phase introduced him to the broader aspects of European diplomacy. At the same time it widened his diplomatic horizon to include hitherto "backward" people who were insisting on being treated as players rather than pawns in the game. Conditions at Lausanne favored diplomats of the old school. The important work took place in private conversations where hardness of hearing was not a severe handicap and where reporters could be kept at bay. His position was greatly strengthened by the Chief of the Near Eastern Division, his old friend Allen Dulles, and by Secretary Hughes. He received the constant support of their trenchant realism, legal precision, and long-range view of American interests. During the second phase these conditions and his enjoyment of sole responsibility brought to their fullest effectiveness Grew's charm, candor, integrity, and well-seasoned diplomatic skills. The combination produced a classic performance of American diplomacy. It established Grew's reputation and led directly to his appointment as Under Secretary of State and later as Ambassador to Turkey.

Grew drove down to Lausanne several days before the conference opened to set up offices for the American delegation. He chose the Hotel Beau-Rivage, a quiet resort situated in a private park by the lake shore. The splendid panorama of lake and mountain was now wasted on a deserted waterfront where rows of plane trees, once pools of deep, cool shade, stood bare like bristly, gnarled fists. With tourists gone, the Beau-Rivage was fortunate to be host to several delegations at the conference. Its creaky lifts and plush period furniture were reassuringly familiar. Black-frocked, bespatted diplomats were already gathering in buzzing knots or whispered tête-à-têtes behind potted palms, gossiping, gesticulating, thrusting, and parrying in the time-honored fashion of their art. Grew saw familiar faces: the impish Harold Nicolson, fellow sufferer at Paris; Sir Horace Rumbold, monocled sphinx from Cairo and Berlin days; Maurice Bompard, colleague at St. Petersburg; and many others. But he had little time for fraternization until he had properly housed and organized the delegation. The job was finally completed by the evening of the conference and he paused to enjoy the view from his window. In the clear sky a thin crescent moon rose above the building where the conference was to open the following day. Was it an omen? he asked himself.[2]

Grew would have few such tranquil moments of reflection during the coming months. His instructions demanded a role far more active than his title "observer" indicated. "In view of our direct interests," the Department of State explained, "it would expose us to serious criticism were we to keep aloof from the sessions. . . ." Grew must remain keenly aware of the course of negotiations. He must be ready at any time to interpose the American view on issues of special concern, and even on occasion be prepared to throw the full weight of American influence into the balance. And all this must be done without engaging the United States too closely in European diplomacy. "No point of advantage should be forfeited, no just influence lost, no injurious commitments made." A startling diplomatic assignment for the isolationist era! [3]

Furthermore, the American interests he was to protect were extraordinarily complex and diverse. To have a sure grasp of the positions of the other powers and of his own would have required thorough schooling in Near Eastern history and extended diplomatic experience in the area, neither of which he had. Inevitably then the Lausanne Conference, at least its first phase, was a learning experience for Grew, involving hesitancy, doubt, and changes of mind.

Grew was far less an amateur than his American colleagues. Rear Admiral Mark Bristol, United States High Commissioner in Constantinople, had the advantage of four years' experience in Turkey. He was bluff, loyal, and shrewd, but he was first-to-last a sailor, impatient with diplomatic niceties, ignorant of Europe and imbued with a typical American sea-dog Anglophobia.[4]

Grew already knew the leader of the delegation, Richard Washburn Child, Ambassador to Italy. As president of the *Advocate* at Harvard he had published some of the latter's stories. Child was a political appointee with the familiar prejudices and naïveté of the American amateur diplomat. Gnawing suspicion of European diplomacy, what Grew called an overdevelopment of the poker sense, was combined with an oversimplified view of American foreign policy, which he suggested could be encompassed by this maxim:

> We will steal nothing from others.
> We will allow no others to steal from us.
> We are against others who steal from others.[5]

Exhilarated by the new Fascism in Italy, ambitious to make a name in diplomacy, vain yet engaging, and according to Grew, "no fool — not by a long shot," Child was determined to be leader of the delegation in fact as well as in name.

The American interests which Child, Grew, and Bristol were directed to protect were set forth in an instruction of October 27, 1922. This was a bare outline which was heavily modified and amplified during the course of negotiations. Nevertheless, it was something for Grew to begin his schooling with.[6]

The first interest in order was "Capitulations." These were legal and economic privileges originally granted freely to foreigners residing in Turkey to facilitate their trade and ease their residence in a land whose culture was so radically different. The enjoyment of these privileges by American businessmen and missionaries in Turkey depended on a treaty with Turkey, which in turn depended on treaties with European powers which had been abrogated by Turkey in 1914. It was obvious to all that the aggressively nationalistic Turkey of Mustafa Kemal would never restore capitulations completely. The extent to which they could be restored in any form would depend on the terms of the Allied treaty with Turkey. Grew was instructed therefore to urge restoration of those capitulations "essential to the protection of American citizens," meaning the judicial safeguards.[7]

Grew's second task was "The Protection of American Educational, Philanthropic and Religious Institutions." He was later to become intimately acquainted with American missionaries in Turkey. In 1914 they had been operating seventeen missions, over two hundred substations, and six hundred schools. This painfully knit fabric of Christian influence had been almost completely destroyed in the chaotic interval. Now Grew was to seek Turkish guarantees permitting the missionaries to rebuild. The difficulty was that the missionaries were repugnant to the highly secular, xenophobic Kemalist regime, particularly since they had worked much among the Armenians who were regarded as a threat to the new government.[8]

The third assignment given the mission was the "Protection of American Commercial Interests," in effect maintenance of the Open Door policy. Lausanne was Grew's first exposure to Open Door diplomacy. The reaffirmation of this traditional American policy may have appeared perfectly natural and straightforward to him at first, but he discovered it to be the most tortuous of his assignments. The basic difficulty was that the United States was seeking equality of opportunity for exploitation of a resource in which powerful strategic and commercial interests were deeply concerned. That resource was oil.[9]

Grew's information about the struggle for Near Eastern oil was very scanty. Later as Ambassador to Turkey he was able to learn more from the files of the Embassy. But even today an air of mystery and intrigue surrounds the controversy. Grew did know, as was generally known, that a consortium of the most important American oil companies was seeking, with State Department support, access to oil-rich areas of the former Ottoman Empire which Britain was jealously guarding to fuel her fleet. One of the best of these was Mosul which the British wanted to incorporate in their Iraq Mandate. Mosul oil was controlled by the British-owned Turkish Petroleum Company from which American interests were excluded. The United States had protested against this "sphere of influence" as contrary to the Open Door policy and the principles of Versailles. The State Department also contended that the original Ottoman grant to the Turkish Petroleum Company was invalid because it was incomplete on the outbreak of war in 1914.

This controversy would inevitably be affected by the Lausanne Conference. The future status of Mosul itself was in doubt since this was one segment of the old Ottoman Empire the new Turkey claimed for itself. Regardless of the outcome, American interests would be endangered. The British would certainly be tempted to improve their position by bargaining for a new concession if Mosul went to Turkey or a validation of their old title if it went to Iraq. It was Grew's job to block either move.[10]

The next important interest was "Protection of Minorities." No issue at Lausanne was of greater concern to the American people. Successive massacres of the Armenians had hammered out an indelible popular image of the Terrible Turk, and the pillaging and burning of Izmir only weeks before Lausanne had struck a familiar note of horror. The State Department was receiving a "flood of letters" demanding protection of minorities. Americans were determined that the new Turkey should not enjoy the comity of nations without guarantees of good behavior.[11]

Representatives of American relief and Armenian organizations, who besieged the delegation headquarters at the Beau-Rivage, continually reminded Grew of this sentiment. But he also had Admiral Bristol to tell him that there was no hope of obtaining such guarantees. Only the threat of war backed by military force would induce the Turks to concede, the Admiral believed, and Allen Dulles in Washington fully agreed. War would result in the extermination of the Armenians anyway, Dulles pointed out, a case of the means to an end defeating the end itself. Force being out of the question, Grew was left with the task of making demands strong enough to satisfy the American public but not so strong as to defeat the accomplishment of other objectives with the Turks.[12]

The last important interest of the United States at Lausanne was "Freedom of the Straits," which depended entirely on the British Navy. Even now fifty British destroyers and seven battleships stood between the victorious Turks and Europe. With Russia weak, British strategy called for free transit of the Straits in peace and war under international control. The United States was not prepared to share control but it was anxious to support the British at least in keeping the Straits open for merchant ships and warships in peacetime. Later Grew received instructions to support the British for free transit of neutral merchant ships and warships in time of war as well.[13]

In addition to these specific interests, there were two dominant objectives for Grew and his fellow observers at Lausanne, objectives on which the protection of all other interests depended. The first was the obvious necessity of a settlement between the Allies and Turkey which would restore peace and settle boundaries in the Near East. The second was the need for an American treaty with Turkey. The old treaty basis was hopelessly outdated by the Kemalist revolution. The new treaty would embody, hopefully, many concessions won by the Allies in their treaty, would settle the claims and grievances of the war years, and would encompass the host of minor, detailed agreements on which normal relations between nations depend. Grew was directed to grasp the "first appropriate opportunity" of undertaking treaty negotiations with the Turks.[14]

As Grew revolved these various interests in his mind during the opening days he could not fail to have been struck with the delicacy of his position. There were certain American interests such as capitulations, the Straits, and minorities, which were identical with the Allies'. Obviously these would best be served by supporting the Allies against the Turks, but only at the risk of incurring Turkish ill-will and endangering the success of the missionary guarantees and the separate treaty. On the other hand the Open Door would best be maintained by standing with the Turks against the Allies at the risk of endangering the peace settlement. It was a situation calling for tact and skill.

Since Child was determined to play the leading role in the delegation, Grew had the advantage of being able to remain passive for a while, accustoming himself to issues and personalities. The conference met in a stuffy, dreary, Victorian hotel dining room. The delegates were seated around an immense U-shaped table at the head of which bulked the dominating figure of Lord Curzon, the British Foreign Secretary. Curzon fascinated Grew. The cold stare of that "proconsular mask," the imperious rigidity of that tremendous barrel chest were impressive. But what really captured Grew was Curzon's dazzling display of diplomatic expertise: his monumental knowledge, his viceregal perspective of Near Eastern affairs, his mastery of facts, arguments, words, men and moods, from the tenderest to the most frigid. Grew's diary is sprinkled with bouquets: "marvelous suavity," "a purist and speaks delightfully," "remarkably clever and amusing," "never at a loss."[15]

On Curzon's right sat a grizzled veteran of diplomacy, the seventy-one-year-old Camille Barrère. The "superb" Barrère, a man of great intelligence and honesty, had served as French Ambassador at Rome for twenty-five years. On Curzon's left, reminding the Foreign Secretary of a turtle, sat Marchese Camillo Garroni of Italy. Grew, always kinder, thought Garroni a nice old man, but a tag-along among the Allies. Observers and minor powers, the Americans, Japanese, Rumanians, and Yugoslavs occupied most of the verticals of the U, but confronting each other across the center were the immediate belligerents, Greece and Turkey. Eleutherios Venizelos of Greece was next to the Americans and when the formidable Cretan spoke the blood rose in his throat like a thermometer and Grew had to shift his position to avoid the flailing arms.[16]

Opposite sat the leader of the Turkish delegation, Ismet Inönü. Ismet was a little birdlike man with delicate fingers, flowing black hair, neat mustache and "charming little head." Such an appearance hardly fitted the general who had twice defeated the Greeks at Inönü and thereby saved Ankara and the Turkish nationalist movement. Still less did he bear any resemblance to the popular image of the Terrible Turk.[17]

Grew's first impression of Ismet was unfavorable. He noted the "small, hard face, perpetual frown, and baneful staring eyes." The dislike may have been partly due to his difficulty in hearing Ismet, who was deaf himself and spoke halting French in a low, indistinct voice. Also he was irritated at the Turk's amateurishness as a diplomat. Ismet's graceless tactics, poor French, and rude remarks marked him as a stranger in this club of professionals. Had he not risen during the welcoming session to harangue the European powers? "Most tactless," commented Grew. The Turkish delegation, he quickly concluded, had no experience or skill in international conferences.[18]

However, a more profound prejudice than professionalism affected Grew's attitude toward Ismet. This was his assumption, common among Americans and Europeans, that the Turk was an Oriental and thereby essentially different from and inferior to the Westerner. With Grew's background of Roosevelt, Kipling, and Cromer, this feeling was perhaps inevitable. Nevertheless, his image of the Turk contained a hopeful ambivalence. He shared the view of those diplomats, particularly the British with their colonial experience, who felt the Turk should be treated like a rug dealer. The tactic indicated was to force the bargaining highhandedly, confident the slippery fellow was asking twice the value and would bluff until the last minute and then capitulate. Grew would occasionally speak of the "wily" Turk. On the other hand, he also shared Admiral Bristol's view that the Turk should be treated like a child. Patience was called for; trust and affection should be cultivated. Frequent repetition was necessary to turn the young mind in the right direction. Solicitous attention should be given to preventing hurt feelings and loss of face. The very contradiction of these views forced Grew to keep an open mind. He continued to ponder the "inherent nature of the Turk" until the end of the conference when he arrived at the conclusion that Ismet was, after all, honest, straightforward, and a superb diplomatist.[19]

Actually very little more than ruminations such as these was required of the Americans during the first weeks of the conference. The British were cooperative. Lord Curzon was well aware of the weakness of his position.

Britain's Allies were content to let her suffer the consequences of her original support of Greece's reckless attempt to expand into Asiatic Turkey. France seemed fickle and opportunistic in the Near East, already having secured an understanding with Kemal in order to protect Syria. In Europe, President Raymond Poincaré's *revanchiste* policy toward Germany had led to further deterioration in Anglo-French solidarity. Mussolini, newly arrived in power, was a mystery. Meanwhile, the British Empire from the Khyber to the Nile was twitching with nationalist movements, British oil policy in the Near East had elicited distant rumblings from across the Atlantic, and the British people were profoundly weary of their world-wide burdens. The feet of Prime Minister Bonar Law became "positively glacial," Curzon said, at the thought of taking any risks. In this vulnerable position the Foreign Secretary thought the best defense was attack. By wresting control of conference proceedings, by rebuilding the Alliance, and by winning the neutrals, he might bring relentless pressure to bear on an isolated Turkey, secure England's most vital interests, and restore her diplomatic prestige.[20]

Therefore the British were cordial to the American delegation. Rumbold informed Grew before the conference opened that territorial and military questions, in which the United States had little interest, would be considered first. Curzon then planned to take up the Straits, capitulations and minorities, on all of which he could expect American support. Meanwhile he minimized Open Door difficulties and actively sought Child's cooperation. As Grew noted in his diary, "he has put his cards down face up with us and means to be friendly. . . ." [21]

Ismet too was anxious to be friends. Though he was backed by a victorious army, his only ally, the Soviet Union, was excluded from the conference except for the Straits discussion. Ismet was well aware of his inexperience and shortcomings as a diplomat. He was faced with an apparently united Allied front and subject to unremitting sneers and scolding remarks from Curzon. He quickly lost control of the agenda. "It is a fine sport," he commented bitterly, "to watch the poor little bird as they pluck out his feathers and clip his wings." In a conversation with Child on the opening day, Djémaleddin Arif Bey intimated that the Turks, though adamant on capitulations and minorities, were more than willing to guarantee protection for American missionary institutions, provide participation in Mosul oil, and clear the way for a commercial treaty.[22]

One might have expected the American delegation to maintain a friendly but reserved attitude toward both sides pending developments. Instead Child came out swinging wildly with Grew cheering him on. Press accounts of the opening session seemingly inspired by the French and British said that the Turks had protested against American participation in the conference. Grew obtained a denial of this from an old colleague on the Turkish delegation. Child lost no time in having a "skirmish" with Curzon, righteously declaring that any misrepresentation of the United States' position would justify his breaking the rule of secrecy and even raise the question of further participation in the conference.[23]

Then on November 25 in the respectful hush following a magnificent peroration by Lord Curzon, Child rose to deliver the first American policy statement. It was a reaffirmation of the Open Door principle condemning Allied zones of influence in the former Ottoman Empire. Child's object was to get the policy on record before discussion of oil questions. Grew, though he toned down some of the more belligerent passages, stood "squarely" behind the statement. It was greeted with amazement, not because, as Child said, it gave "discouragement and doubt to several secret plans around the Conference table," but because of its complete irrelevancy to the business at hand. The press reaction was the opposite of that intended. The statement was interpreted as an endeavor to lay claim to Mosul oil and even worse as tending to throw a monkey wrench into the peace negotiations.[24]

Child, with his horror of becoming entangled in European diplomacy, or, as he put it, getting "snarled up in a hundred coils of war snakes," saw dangerous implications in every move, scrap of gossip, or inspired press report emanating from the Allied camp. He complained of Curzon's "star chamber" procedure in shuffling the agenda, even though American interests were not affected by the switch. He suspected that the Allies were avoiding the minorities issue in order to leave that fight, with its burden of Turkish resentment, to the United States. Grew fully supported Child. He wrote in his diary on November 22 that the Allies "covertly hate us and will do their best . . . to embroil us with the Turks. There is only one thing to do — make the British and French afraid of us, and to that desirable end we are proceeding." Upon reflection he substituted "dislike" for "hate" and crossed out the last sentence. The first version probably represented his feelings of the moment more accurately. The American delegation entered the conference excessively suspicious of the Western powers.[25]

At first, standing off from the Allies meant standing closer to the Turks. Grew betrayed some sympathy for Ismet as the little Turk bore the lash of Curzon's rhetoric. Those "baneful" eyes now registered "nervousness, anxiety, ill-ease." Ismet, Child wrote, "has no complex secrets and tells no lies." The delegation recommended developing closer relations with the Turks, who had no apparent skill and were looking for friends and advisers. That way they might win Turkish confidence, moderate Turkish demands on the Allies, and secure protection of American interests. However, the State Department's reaction was cautious and accordingly on November 29 Child declined to discuss a separate treaty with Ismet on the ground it might embarrass negotiations at the main conference. Grew reported this fact to Curzon and Barrère.[26]

As Curzon's strategy unfolded during early December the agenda was heavily weighted with items on which American and British interests coincided. In obedience to instructions and perhaps somewhat chastened by the reaction to their Open Door statement, the delegation became somewhat more cooperative with the Allies. They gave effective support to Britain and France in subcommittee negotiations on the minorities problem and in plenary session on the Straits question.

The Straits session of December 4 was, as Grew reported, "highly dramatic." To this session the Soviet Union was invited and was represented by the shy, eccentric Georgii Chicherin, who reminded Harold Nicolson of a "golden, but mangy cocker spaniel." Chicherin's objective, since the Soviet Union was then weak and exposed, was to close the Straits to all warships. Curzon's was to open them, and in so doing drive a wedge between the Russians and Turks. He began the discussion by inviting the views of the Black Sea powers, with the result that Rumania, Bulgaria, and Greece lined up publicly against the Soviet Union. He then prodded Ismet to say whether Turkey's views coincided with those of her ally. Ismet, under agonizing pressure not to differ publicly with the only power friendly to Turkey, but aware too that freedom of the Straits was a vital countervailing force to Russian domination, finally conceded a willingness to discuss other proposals besides the Russian. Curzon had driven his wedge. The Americans, suspecting that Ismet might welcome overwhelming opposition to the Russian proposal as an excuse for asserting greater independence, made a statement December 6 supporting freedom of the Straits for both merchant and war ships and demilitarization of the area. Child received the thanks of Curzon, Barrère, and, significantly, Ismet himself.[27]

Cooperation with the Allies was limited and grudging. On December 12 Curzon brought the minorities problem before the full conference. He was no more hopeful of securing guarantees than anyone else, but he did hope to make Turkey uneasy by appealing to world opinion and then induce her to join the League of Nations with its broad umbrella of guarantees, thereby further separating her from the Soviet Union. He had every right to expect American support on minorities. As Secretary Hughes himself said, there was "no issue in which the people of the United States have a more immediate concern." But Child immediately suspected that Curzon planned to use the issue for trading purposes or as a cushion in case the conference broke down. He had no desire to press a hopeless case strongly and allow the Allies to throw the onus of a break on the United States. However, fearful of appearing less sensitive to the plight of the Armenians than the British, he made a statement. It was so vague and general that it gave little comfort to anyone but the Turks.[28]

Meanwhile, Admiral Bristol was making his presence felt. He had arrived late and, aside from warning Child not to accept Turkish promises at their face value, had been content to follow the Ambassador's lead. But the blunt, square-jawed Admiral felt he understood the Turks better than Child or Grew. He shared their view that the Turks were in some respects like children, needing to be reminded of American views again and again. But on the whole he had more respect for them. The new Turk was far different from the old, he kept telling his colleagues. "He has an army and he'll fight. Therefore, we must either accept the Turkish rule . . . or else we must get out and leave him alone, or by influence and reason work out a workable program." Capitulations were dead and the minorities issue only inflamed the Turks. It was pointless to support the Allies, who were selfish and devious anyhow, at the risk of damaging relations with the new Turkey. The reward for standing with Turkey now would be a handsome share for American capital in her future development. He felt that the Turks should be dealt with firmly and respectfully, but frankly, generously, and patiently.[29]

Grew was receptive to the Admiral's arguments. He became convinced that support for the Allies must never be carried to the point where "we . . . sacrifice or impair the good will of the Turks towards us or give them the impression that we are lined up with the Allies." It was important to remember that some day the United States would have to negotiate a treaty with Turkey and would need that goodwill. His advice was "to counsel moderation upon the Turks in every issue, but at the same time to make them feel that we were doing it in their own interests exactly as much as in the interests of the Allies." [30]

By mid-December Grew was willing to go as far as positive cooperation with the Turks on the issue of capitulations. When the subject had first been introduced on December 2, Child had offered hesitant support for the Allies in a statement which Curzon correctly characterized as "rather wobbly." The Turks had remained adamant and on December 17 the American delegation cabled requesting a change of policy. They pointed out that the Allies had in effect abandoned the regime of capitulations and were now only insisting on a substitute arrangement which made liberal concessions to the Turks except in judicial matters. They contended that negotiations had already passed the limit of their instructions. The Allies appeared ready to concede more than the Americans. The situation presented two alternatives, in their view. Either they could adopt a policy of opposition to Turkish demands at every step or they could adopt a conciliatory policy, stimulate Turkish friendliness, offer as bait American capital, and possibly moderate Turkish opposition to some form of transitional juridical regime. They recommended the latter alternative.[31]

On December 21 Ismet announced that Turkey was willing to grant protection to American religious and educational institutions. This had been one of the delegation's major objectives and they had made appropriate representations. Success reinforced the argument for conciliating the Turks and avoiding an open alignment with the Allies. However, the State Department disagreed. On December 22 it cabled rejecting the delegation's recommendation of December 17.[32]

To understand why the Department of State was so unreceptive to the new approach at Lausanne it is necessary to explore the thinking of Allen Dulles, who was responsible for Lausanne policy formulation. Dulles agreed that the new Turkey was radically different from the old and that the Turks could not be bluffed. He too saw great possibilities for American capital in Turkey, but he was less sanguine of the prospects because of the "general fright of making investments in foreign countries." He believed that the only hope for such investment lay in inspiring business confidence by capitulatory guarantees protecting the persons and property of Americans in Turkey. He was not impressed with the "honeyed words" of the Turks without ironclad treaty guarantees, and he doubted the ability of Turkey to accomplish the reforms required if capitulations were scrapped.[33]

With regard to the general position of the delegation at Lausanne, he was disturbed by the lack of unity among the Allies. He saw three possibilities resulting: the United States could drift without agreements, could conclude a separate treaty with Turkey, or could warn the Allies of the dangerous position they were in and come to an agreement with them over certain fundamental points of mutual interest such as minorities, the Straits, and capitulations, with continued Turkish adamancy leading to a boycott. Dulles preferred the third alternative, counting on the threat of economic isolation to bring the Turks around. In the end, he felt, it was not the political favors the United States might grant Turkey at Lausanne that would lead to an understanding, but its real financial ability to assist in the development of Turkey. There was consequently little benefit in gaining Turkish goodwill by giving away important rights.

It is not surprising then that Washington maintained a persistent concern on the issue of capitulations. In its instruction of December 22 the Department of State questioned the prudence of a policy of taking the lead in acquiescing in the abolition of capitulations. This would be taking a very serious responsibility with little evidence that Turkish goodwill depended on it. Concessions by the Allies would be to their own territorial or other advantage in which the United States could not share. If an Allied arrangement embodying a bargain on capitulations were finally rejected by the

Turks, the Allies could return to their former position, while unilateral concessions by the United States would be irreversible. As long as the Allies remained firm, it was to the American interest to remain firm and maintain an attitude of reserve toward the Turks.

Obviously a realignment was indicated for Grew and his colleagues. This was made easier by a stiffening of the Turkish position at Lausanne due in part to the deterioration of the German reparations situation with its consequent strain on Anglo-French unity and in part, the Americans felt, to Russian pressure at Ankara. On December 28 Child issued a strong statement in support of the Allied position on capitulations. On December 30 he issued another statement on minorities which the Turks considered the most offensive one the Americans had made. The delegation's handling of the situation impressed an Armenian lobbyist as having "hit the nail on the head." [34]

The realignment came as something of a relief for Child. He had acted halfheartedly on the recommendation of December 17. When a protest had been called for over the inclusion of the United States in a proposed Straits control commission, he had hesitated and moved only on Grew's insistence. Curzon's and Barrère's displeasure on this occasion had "intensely worried" him and he had suggested a statement supporting some remarks of Curzon's, presumably hoping that this might dispel the disfavor. But Grew had objected strenuously on the ground that alignment of the United States with the Allies and against the Turks would result. Unconsciously perhaps, but perceptibly, Child was drifting into an orbit around Curzon. On December 8 he had described a "warmly friendly" Curzon: "A devil for work they say . . . like a tired child . . . has the mood of a god with influenza." Ultimately, for Child, Curzon would be the only delegate with "stalwart qualities," superior in his contest with Ismet as "a Greek temple against a dish of scrambled eggs." It was not difficult for Child to cooperate with the Allies.[35]

It was not difficult for Grew either. He was cultivating Curzon assiduously. The Foreign Secretary was much struck by Mrs. Grew and engaged her in long conversations. A succession of cozy dinners made him genial and relaxed company. The former Viceroy of India chided Grew for not coming to see him at Simla in 1903 and was pleased as a schoolboy by the Grews' birthday gifts, a copy of *Sport and Travel in the Far East* and a package of his favorite candied fruit, sticky remnants of which adhered to official papers for days. The difference between Grew and Child was that Grew would cross swords with Curzon diplomatically if necessary while cultivating him socially. The career diplomat worried about the disfavor of a Hughes more than that of a Curzon.[36]

The readjustment was not as easy for Bristol. He opposed the new policy of standing closer to the Allies and refused to sign Child's statement on capitulations. Grew had to step in and soothe him down. Near the end of December, Child heard that Bristol had been urging the Turks to reject an Allied proposal on the Straits. Grew suspected that a member of Bristol's staff was the one involved. Bristol denied responsibility, but Child asked him to have no more conversations with the Turks. This restriction rankled with the Admiral because he was on very good terms with Ismet and felt he could be useful. Bored and frustrated, he adopted, in Child's words, "the temper of a minority report." At conference sessions he could barely suppress an impulse to rise and exclaim, "Oh, hell!" and he amused himself by blowing neat smoke rings across the table which now and then lassoed poor old Garroni. He resented what seemed to him the highhanded and secretive way Child was running the delegation. Child on his part had scant respect for Bristol. "When I try to milk the Admiral's intellectual capacity," he told Grew, "all four teats run at once." Everyone rested and exercised too little, ate and drank too much. Tempers frayed as the damp winter fogs curled in from Lake Geneva and the conference dragged on.[37]

On January 14 an explosion occurred. Child had been trying to make Ismet more conciliatory in repeated conversations but had no success. Now he asked Grew to have a try. Grew suggested they consult the Admiral first, whom Child rather bluntly informed of the plan. Bristol kept his silence until Grew returned around midnight when he came into Grew's room and trained his main battery at Child. After four years in Constantinople and presumably understanding the Turks better than either Child or Grew, it infuriated him to be denied access to them. His time had been wasted at Lausanne and he was going back to Constantinople. Grew responded with his utmost tact and spent some time reminding the Admiral how valuable it was to have one man chiefly responsible for policy to keep the delegation from going off on separate lines. He asked the Admiral to sleep on it.

Then Grew went to Child and told him what had happened. Child was for letting the Admiral go and Grew then went to work on *him*, explaining how unwise it would be to let Bristol go with a bad taste in his mouth. He advised Child to sleep on it. He himself spent a thoroughly wakeful night. The next morning is best described by Grew himself:

> Glorious morning — the sun streaming in at our window. The Admiral comes into my room with a springing step. "Well, I've slept on it." Child joins us. "Admiral, I wish you'd go up to Ismet and give him hell," he said. "You know how to talk to him. Give him hell and tell him he's a damn fool." . . . The Admiral says, "That's the idea. I'll do it right away." We all laugh, swap a yarn or two, discuss the situation at the Conference, and adjourn with springy steps and smiling countenances. Glorious morning![38]

January was mostly damp and depressing. On January 4 French troops entered the Ruhr and the Allied front at Lausanne sagged. The Turks were absolutely stubborn and the air was full of rumors of rupture and military preparations. Child, determined to save the conference single-handedly, flitted between Ismet and Curzon with "bright, uplifting ideas." He allowed Grew and Bristol one try each at Ismet. In all these conversations the American position was friendly toward the Turks, but closely aligned with the Allies. Child brought Ismet and Curzon together in his room and joined the latter in warning Ismet that if Lausanne were a failure, "Turkey could look forward to a long period of isolation and no investment." Ismet sought Bristol's support over Mosul, which both the Turks and the British were claiming. The Admiral declined to be drawn into the Mosul controversy and reiterated American adherence to the Open Door. He then enlarged on Turkey's need for providing some satisfactory judicial regime in place of capitulations in order to attract American business. Bristol loyally followed the delegation's policy of "standing off temporarily from the Turks." [39]

Grew had a very important conversation with Ismet on the subject of separate treaty negotiations. The Turks hoped to split the United States from the Allies by offering as bait a separate treaty with special concessions. Riza Nour Bey had told Grew earlier that concessions were on a first come, first served basis. He hoped the United States would not be too late. Grew raised the subject of a separate treaty with Ismet and, when the latter showed immediate interest, Grew told him it depended on Turkey settling her differences with the Allies first. There was no point in hurrying a separate treaty, he wrote Dulles, or in sacrificing legitimate interests, "merely in order to obtain early commercial concessions." The Allies could not have asked for more.[40]

However, they were not particularly grateful. On January 23 Curzon introduced a provocative subject which was to put a severe strain on Anglo-American accord. He stated that the British government recognized the validity of the Turkish Petroleum Company claim. The Americans were especially bitter at Curzon for raising this subject because they had made no representations to the Turks on behalf of American oil interests. The delegation felt compelled, therefore, to reply to Curzon's contention that afternoon. In an extremely awkward and involved statement, Child pointed out the conflict between Curzon's protestations of sympathy for the Open Door and his approval of an exclusive claim. The principle of the Open Door, he concluded, required settlement by arbitration.[41]

Late in January the conference moved toward a climax. Concessions on both sides, particularly the Allied, had narrowed the remaining unsettled questions to capitulations and the economic clauses, in essence the issue of special privileges for foreigners. On these points Ismet was absolutely unyielding. The universal question was, in Grew's words, "How much of his attitude is bluff?" Was he waiting until the final showdown before yielding in order to make the best bargain he could? Or would he leave Lausanne without Turkey's desperately needed peace settlement rather than make further concessions?

The answer really depended on the solution of Grew's riddle on the "inherent nature of the Turk." He was still perplexed. On January 9 he was sure that ". . . the Turks will bluff on every issue up to the last possible moment, with a view to getting the maximum possible advantage out of the conference." Yet two weeks later he was convinced that ". . . the Turk is a child in many respects and must be treated as such . . . he never believes what you say at first. . . ." He remained seized with a Janus-like image of the old and new Turkey: wily carpet dealer and froward child.[42]

Ismet's arguments seemed to make no impression on him. Time and again the Turk insisted that his attitude was not bluff but the core of the Turkish position, as Grew himself testifies. On the opening day Ismet had demanded Turkey's inherent rights to existence and independence, a controversial and threatening speech in Grew's estimation. On November 27 Ismet emphasized to Grew that "the rigidness of his instructions from Angora [Ankara] was most extreme as to points of discussion which touched the independence of Turkey in the control of her own internal affairs." "He talks more in the manner of a military man than a diplomat," commented Grew. "It is complained that we speak too often of Turkish sovereignty," Ismet told the conference on January 6, continuing:

> We represent here a nation which is conscious of its independence. . . . The reason why we have frequently spoken of our sovereignty is that we have been compelled to do so owing to the proposals made to us. . . . The Turkish people has the right, first and foremost, to be regarded like any other nation.

"A drivelling meeting," wrote Grew. Ismet's remarks on Turkish sovereignty "meant literally and exactly nothing." "Sovereignty, sovereignty, sovereignty," said Curzon. It reminded him of a music box.[43]

The first days of February were tense and exciting. The Allies presented the Turks with a draft treaty in the form of an ultimatum, Curzon announcing his intention of leaving February 4. The Turks replied with a counterdraft embodying all points settled at the time. There was a climactic final meeting in Curzon's rooms from which Ismet emerged without having signed. Curzon left for the train. Child, Grew, and Bristol made one last try with Ismet and achieved some concessions. They hurried to the train but it had already left. As the Orient Express pulled out of the station for Paris the

British secretaries anxiously scanned the platform for the hurrying diminutive figure of Ismet coming to sign at the last possible moment. But the Turk was not bluffing.[44]

As Grew settled back into the placid routine at Berne and brought his diary up to date, he tried to figure out why the conference had failed. The chief reason, he felt, was the weakness of the Allied coalition, which he blamed on France. Another reason was Curzon's "browbeating" tactics. Significantly, Curzon "seemed to have no understanding of the Turkish nationalist aspirations." He treated Ismet like "one of his 'natives' in India . . . whereas, as a matter of fact, he was nothing but an equal." [45]

Grew's understanding of non-European diplomacy was deepening, but he still had a way to go. Ismet's diplomacy, which consisted of saying no repeatedly and politely, remained puzzling and irritating. Grew attributed the negativism variously to the fact that Ismet was a military man, that he lacked diplomatic expertise, that he lacked intelligence. "I have no very high opinion of Ismet's intelligence," he wrote. "At times he has seemed dull of comprehension, almost stupid." "Dazed and childish stupidity" characterized the entire Turkish delegation. He still could not fully accept that Ismet's stubbornness faithfully reflected the overpowering, all-embracing, non-negotiable concern of the new Turkey to be treated on a basis of absolute equality. He still tended to discount the force of nationalism in developing countries.[46]

The American delegation had little to show for its efforts. Even on the assumption that the conference would eventually resume, they had not substantially advanced American interests. They had Turkish assurances respecting missionary institutions, for what they were worth. They had helped secure some protection for the Greek minority, but none for the Armenians. They had asserted the Open Door policy, but over American protest the Allies had slipped clauses into the draft treaty which would in effect have validated the Turkish Petroleum Company grant.[47] They had made no headway on capitulations. The extent to which they had created a favorable basis for separate treaty negotiations remained to be seen. Overriding any particular interest of the United States was the concern for peace, and this obviously had not been achieved. Assigned a limited role in the first place, and guided by instructions that tied them closely to Allied diplomacy, the American delegation had little opportunity to improve its position. They were undoubtedly helpful, though not decisive, in interpreting each side to the other, but their small stock of influence was depleted by Child's horror of European entanglements and Bristol's open sympathy for the Turks.

Grew had been friendly and conciliatory from beginning to end. He was the only one of the three who made no enemies. Curzon, who disliked

Child, told the American Ambassador in London that Grew had made an important contribution. He "always seemed to know just the thing to do at every move." [48] Grew played a subordinate role on the delegation loyally and wholeheartedly and was chiefly responsible for maintaining delegation unity. Of the three Americans he proved the most skillful, educable, and useful agent of United States policy.

SIX

Lausanne, Second Phase

NEGOTIATIONS at Lausanne were bound to resume in spite of the breakdown February 4. The break had come over questions relating to the nature of foreign economic and financial influence within Turkey. Agreement had already been reached on the major territorial and strategic issues which threatened peace. The Allies could scarcely balk at further negotiation over profits when peace seemed within reach. They were certainly not inclined to press their demands by force and neither was Turkey. And during the waning winter months there were no untoward events or upset governments to change this disposition.

The Allies did not welcome continued American participation. The United States was excluded from their deliberations and denied information about the circumstances of resumption. Suspecting arrangements injurious to American interests, the Department of State finally notified the secretary general of the conference that an American delegate would be present.[1]

The conference reconvened on April 23, 1923. This time Grew was the only American delegate. The Allies did not return their chief delegates so Child was absent. Bristol was *persona non grata* to the British, and by now the Department of State considered him temperamentally unsuited as a negotiator. He had already begged off attending. Grew was delighted to be in charge. It was "always more fun to run the show alone." With the divided leadership of the first phase gone, he felt free to form a small, happy, efficient staff that worked together and played together. Among them was Fred Dolbeare, his colleague at Vienna and Paris, who sat next to him at all meetings acting as his ears.[2]

American policy of the second phase was essentially no different from that of the first. The Department of State took the same "deep interest" in capitulations. It was unwilling to commit itself on separate treaty negotiations until "further enlightened upon the organization and agenda of the conference." The one significant change in the United States position, not in policy but in circumstance, lay in a new configuration of the interests on which the Open Door policy was based. This resulted from the startling announcement on April 10 that the Grand National Assembly of Turkey had granted a princely concession to the Ottoman-American Development Company.[3]

Seemingly this was good news. The grant, known as the Chester Concession, provided American capital with an enormous opportunity, including the right to build a railroad network covering the entire eastern half of Turkey, as well as rights to construct port facilities, power stations, and pipelines, to sell farm equipment, and to exploit oil and mineral resources. Furthermore, the concession had been obtained by direct negotiation between the company and the Turkish government. The American High Commissioner's office had simply introduced the parties and had exerted no political pressure to secure the grant. The State Department went so far as to call it a "triumph in Turkey of the Open Door policy." [4]

But in fact the Chester Concession created a very "murky" atmosphere for Grew at Lausanne.[5] One of the rail lines was to extend through the heart of Mosul with the company enjoying exclusive right to exploit oil resources up to twenty kilometers from the tracks on each side. This broad forty-kilometer band would have embraced much of the Mosul-Kirkuk oil region which Britain was claiming for Iraq and the Turkish Petroleum Company. In addition one segment of the rail network came in direct conflict with a French concession. These conflicts were sure to exacerbate Grew's relations with the Allies.

Conversely, the Chester Concession implied an awkward identity of interest with Turkey. The Turkish government was undoubtedly aware of the diplomatic as well as economic advantages of the grant. The timing of the award, only days before the second phase began, left little doubt in Lausanne that Turkey's object was to secure American support at the conference. Ismet would probably expect more cooperation from Grew than American interests, particularly capitulations, called for.[6]

The most important result of the Chester Concession for Grew was its effect on the Open Door policy. Far from being a triumph, it seriously weakened that policy. If Mosul were granted to Turkey and if the necessary capital were raised, the resulting economic complex would be so pervasive as to make eastern Turkey and Mosul impenetrable to competition. Now when Grew raised the principle of the Open Door against British exclusiveness in Iraq, he could be charged with hypocritically using the principle to cloak American ambitions for a sphere of influence of her own. Naturally, if the idea that the United States had thrown principles to the winds and teamed up with Turkey in the struggle for Near Eastern oil gained currency at home, where opinion was highly sensitive on the minorities issue, the Administration would be in an embarrassing position.

Grew might have seen the irony of his dilemma if he had known what the State Department knew. There the Chester undertaking offered little hope of success. The company had already failed to exploit a similar grant made in 1909. Then as now, the moving force was Rear Admiral Colby Chester, a man of far greater vision than business sense or means. A bulging file showed that the company was hopelessly mismanaged. Furthermore, the Department was suspecting, as later proved true, that Canadians, not Americans, had a controlling interest. There was even the possibility that British oil interests were using the Canadians to secure the concession in case Mosul went to Turkey. The company required a large amount of capital, three hundred million dollars, but Wall Street regarded the whole proposition as highly speculative. Finally, the Department had taken great pains to ensure that the negotiation then in progress for the entry of powerful American oil interests into the Turkish Petroleum Company would provide adequate Open Door guarantees. Presumably it would much prefer to secure this entry to Mosul oil than the upstart and questionable Chester entry. But to ignore the Chester grant would have meant favoritism, so the Department had to appear perfectly impartial to both.[7]

There was no easy solution to the problem. Grew was instructed to reassert the Open Door principle, to try to prevent the discussion of concessions, to avoid at all costs their inclusion in the treaty, and to advise the settlement of conflicting claims by private negotiation or impartial tribunal.[8]

Thus Grew's main objectives as he faced the second phase were to secure guarantees for the protection of Americans residing in Turkey to replace the capitulations, and to prevent exclusive economic concessions from becoming a part of the treaty. The first required support of the Allies, the second support of the Turks. He could expect the Allies to be hostile and the Turks friendly. To secure his objectives Grew could not play the honest broker of the first phase. He was too deeply involved. Neither could he choose sides. What he needed was bargaining power against both sides. This he found in the *pourparlers* and negotiations for an American-Turkish treaty.

Grew discovered the advantage of separate treaty negotiations during the first weeks of the session when the main issue was capitulations. Since the Allies apparently wished to avoid an immediate clash with the United States over conflicting oil claims, it was to Grew's advantage to cooperate as much as possible with them for the time being. He had in mind active participation in the work of the subcommittees drafting the various agreements for the protection of foreigners in Turkey, with a view to signing separate but identical instruments at the same time the Allies did. This would secure stronger guarantees by strengthening their front and ensure immediate protection for Americans in Turkey. As a sweetener, an act of "good faith," Grew advised starting separate negotiations with the Turks for a treaty of amity and commerce.[9]

He had been encouraged in this direction by Ismet in their first conversation. On April 26 Ismet suggested that an American-Turkish treaty was the natural consequence of enlarged trade opportunities opened up by the Chester Concession. Grew replied that treaty discussions would quickly raise the question of some form of interim regime to replace capitulations, a subject of "the gravest concern" to the United States. Ismet, disappointed, said he had hoped for a relaxation in this viewpoint and warned that the Chester Concession would be looked at with a "cold eye" in Ankara if the United States remained inflexible. But Grew declined for the moment Ismet's invitation to full cooperation.[10]

The requisite authority to begin treaty talks with Ismet was received on May 1. Grew was permitted to begin informal discussions seeking a favorable basis for formal negotiations, but was warned that they must not interfere with Allied negotiations. He must not allow the Turks to "sow discord between you and the Allied delegates." The same evening Ismet tried to do just this. Grew presented his package plan of a convention identical with that of the Allies for the regime of foreigners, and a separate treaty of amity and commerce. Ismet was agreeable but craftily suggested that the American agreements might be concluded more quickly than the Allied ones. Grew was immediately on guard. The American position was "delicate," he said. He was there only as an observer and therefore could not properly sign agreements before the Allies. What if the main conference broke down? Ismet persisted. Then his position might be different, Grew admitted, but he made "all reserves" as to what it then might be, and deplored such an eventuality. They concluded with a discussion of negotiating formalities, Grew skillfully placing responsibility for initiating proposals on the Turks.[11]

Grew informed the Allied delegates of his intentions even before he saw Ismet. Indeed, each side knowing what he said to the other was the source of his leverage. The French and Italian delegates approved, but Sir Horace Rumbold, the British delegate, was very upset. Grew and Rumbold had sealed the British archives in Berlin in 1914, and until now Sir Horace had been as friendly as his frigid demeanor would allow. Grew explained that he would not allow his separate negotiations to hinder the Allies and that the Turkish desire to conclude a separate treaty would be useful in furthering their identical interest on capitulations. Rumbold, who was a shrewd diplomat, warned against a Turkish attempt to divide and conquer. Furthermore, he doubted the propriety of Grew, an observer, participating in subcommittee work. Grew replied that on the contrary he was present in a fully representative capacity. In speaking to Rumbold his capacity was far more representative than he was willing to admit to Ismet the same evening.[12]

Rumbold remained implacably opposed to American participation in subcommittee work, where the detailed negotiation of the convention occurred. Grew now resorted to harsher tactics. During full committee discussion of the regime for foreigners on May 3, Grew stated that he would like to reserve comment. Rumbold accused him of delaying the conference, to which Grew replied that he had no such intention and would comment at the next session. Grew's intention obviously *was* to delay proceedings until given an opportunity to study proposals in their formative stage. The Italian and French delegates supported Grew and Rumbold conceded, sending a secretary to inform Grew he would be welcome on the subcommittee. The following day Grew showed his appreciation and usefulness with a strong statement supporting the Allies which caused a "sharp tilt" with Ismet, the *New York Times* reported. The effect, it continued, was to "bring the United States more deeply into the negotiations, since the Washington Government now stands with the Allies as defied by the Turks." [13]

To protect his position further, Grew sought access to the inner councils of the Allies. He found this in Giulio Montagna, the Italian delegate. Italy had been treated as a poor relation at Versailles and subsequent Near Eastern settlements. She was understandably bitter, and while Mussolini was still generally content to follow Britain's lead, he coveted an independent role in the Near East. This role Montagna was playing expertly. Quiet, experienced, hard-working, and conciliatory, he had already fashioned an important compromise formula. Child's admiration for Mussolini and the fact that both Italy and the United States were have-nots at Lausanne led to close relations between the two delegations during the first phase, which were renewed during the second.[14]

Grew had observed one fact about Montagna that promised to make the relationship even closer now. The Italian was intensely concerned about the future of his diplomatic career under the new Fascist state. In this Grew felt he might be of some assistance to his colleague. On May 6 he thanked Montagna for his cooperation in the subcommittee battle and promised him that American appreciation would reach Mussolini officially through the Italian Ambassador in Washington and informally through Ambassador Child. Montagna was grateful and increasingly informative about Allied plans.[15]

Grew had thus placed himself in a position of actively influencing the conference in behalf of American interests. By being in close touch with Allied-Turkish negotiations through participation in subcommittee work and his relationships with Montagna and Ismet, he was ready to forestall injurious developments and further helpful ones. His separate negotiations with Ismet had the immediate advantage of exerting maximum leverage on capitulations and an insurance value in the event of hostile Allied moves on oil claims.

Influential as he now was, Grew still could not win the judicial guarantees his government sought for Americans in Turkey. In spite of his support of the Allied effort to secure common law protection in such matters as arrest, search, and imprisonment, Turkey refused to admit any law but her own. Rumbold remained cool to Grew's efforts at cooperation. Ismet and the Allies were unwilling to include an American on a proposed panel of foreign judicial advisers.[16]

Failing of success on this issue, Grew was not inclined to hurry his separate negotiations. When word of the *pourparlers* leaked to the press, he denied negotiations had begun, as technically he was able to do. When the Turks formally proposed negotiations, Grew requested modifications in the note. Then he delayed his reply until the receipt of instructions. These he found restricted him for the present to discussion seeking a favorable basis for formal negotiations. The Turks were disappointed. Grew again mentioned his proposal of an American judicial adviser, but again without success.[17]

This backing and filling on capitulations was interrupted May 10 by a serious crisis in the conference. That evening Montagna informed Grew confidentially that Greece was considering an ultimatum to Turkey. As Grew was aware, Greece was deeply involved in the outcome of the conference, not only for the delineation of her eastern frontier, but also for the future of a million Greeks in Turkey. She was humiliated by her recent debacle there and in a fit of political disorder internally. The revolutionary military clique in control at Athens, seeking to bolster its position by recouping Greek prestige abroad, now refused to agree to pay indemnities for destruction caused by Greek troops in Anatolia, and threatened war. Furthermore, Europe was in its own state of jitters. There were cabinet crises in Britain and France and Communist uprisings in the Ruhr. At Lausanne the Russian delegate was murdered and Swiss police took the precaution of confining Ismet to his hotel. Wisely, then, during these tense weeks of mid-May, Grew stopped his maneuvers in support of specific American objectives in order to devote himself wholeheartedly to the preservation of peace.[18]

He made every effort to smooth troubled waters and minimize divisive influences. He told the Allies that he would try to exert moral pressure on Greece by warning Venizelos that resumption of war might cut off refugee relief funds from America, but Montagna felt that Greece did not care that much for the plight of her refugees. Grew told Rumbold that he had not entered into formal negotiations with the Turks and was in no hurry to do so, while he told the Turks that their proposals indicated a satisfactory basis for negotiation did not yet exist.[19]

The solution of the crisis was not primarily Grew's work, however. Part of the credit is Britain's for standing publicly foursquare with her ally to prevent Turkey from taking up the Greek challenge, while privately urging moderation on the Greek government. Part of the credit is France's for suggesting the compromise that was finally accepted, the award to Turkey of Karagatch in the western environs of Adrianople in return for renunciation of indemnities. And a large measure of credit is due Ismet for his courage in accepting this solution with only the reluctant and most tenuous authority of his government.[20]

Grew did play a small part in the solution. A showdown was scheduled for May 26. The night before he had long conversations with Venizelos and Ismet urging acceptance of the compromise. Grew's deep concern was obvious and this undoubtedly contributed to the moral pressure for compromise that was building up about the principals. At the climactic session the following day Ismet squirmed to find a way out "like a fox in a hen coop," but finally agreed to accept the compromise, to the vast relief of everyone. Even Rumbold could not avoid a slight "contraction of the facial muscles which amounted to a smile," while the Serb romped around the room and the Greek and Turk appeared on the verge of embracing. The Secretary of State cabled congratulations for the helpful influence Grew had exerted in resolving the crisis.[21]

This may have been one of those days when Grew, feeling he had earned some relaxation, hired a boat for a row on the lake. The Italian sun transfixed the northern shore of Lake Geneva. The gray damp winter had given way to sparkling spring, and Lausanne, sheltered from the cold north winds, was coming to life again. It was the season, Baedeker advised, of the whey-cure and the grape-cure. Tourists thronged the Place du Port while invalids and convalescents soaked in the warm sun on pension porches. After a meeting such as the one that morning, which reminded Grew of sitting in a dentist's chair, he was alone and quiet at last. From the lake the torture chambers of diplomacy appeared festooned for a carnival with their multicolored flags and gay awnings, islands of pleasure in a verdant sea of rolling lawns and restless shade trees. To east and south rose a magnificent panorama of snow-topped Alps. His Puritan conscience dictated exercise at the oars, but he was enough of a romantic to dabble now and then while the blissful sunlight seeped in.

Grew was not able to relax for long. With the Greek crisis solved the diplomats turned impatiently to the remaining issues. On May 30 the Allies gave up on capitulations. They accepted an arrangement whereby Turkey would allow foreign influence in her judicial system only to the extent of hiring judicial advisers from a panel selected by the Permanent Court at

The Hague. Grew tried once more to get further protections but failed. The capitulations issue was settled for the Allies and by inference for the Americans as well.[22]

Only one issue of importance to the United States remained, the question of oil concessions. Here the United States was opposed to the Allies. Consequently Grew realized there was little more to be gained from the Allied side, and some danger to be anticipated. On the other hand, close relations with the Turks henceforward would provide protection on concessions and progress on the treaty he must ultimately secure. The day the capitulations fight was over Grew told Ismet that a satisfactory basis for formal treaty negotiations finally existed and so informed the Allies. Actually, he had received the necessary authority a week earlier. Now was the time to use it.[23]

He was soon glad he had done so. On June 5, just five days later, Ismet called on Grew to discuss the general situation and specifically to warn Grew that he was under pressure from the Allies to accept a provision confirming concessions made before the war on which work had commenced but which had not been legally validated. He said that this was specifically directed at the Chester Concession and that he might have to yield in the interests of peace. It was the story of the first phase over again. In spite of American protests, the Allies were slipping in a clause validating the old Turkish Petroleum Company concession. Grew's barricade in the drafting subcommittee had been turned; the Allies were now pressing their demands at informal conferences from which Grew was excluded.[24]

He was immediately alert to the danger. First he sought to stiffen Ismet. Was Ismet who had fought so hard for the sovereignty of Turkey now going to abandon the fight? The situation if Turkey yielded, he warned, would react most unfavorably on Turkish-American relations. Ismet then intimated that Grew might wish to exert some pressure on the Allies. But Grew preferred not to be an open partner of Turkey and told Ismet he regarded the question as one to be settled solely between Turkey and the Allies. Grew had no intention of leaving the matter there, however. He told the Allied delegates, each in turn, that he was much disturbed by "press reports" of an article confirming prewar concessions. They were evasive. Rumbold said the article was designed to protect a French company. The French delegate, General Maurice Pellé, said it was only for the purpose of buttressing France's claim for compensation. Montagna argued that the article did not apply to incomplete concessions anyway.[25]

On June 11 Montagna told Grew that Rumbold was pressing Ismet on concessions. The Italian delegate felt he could check him, but only momentarily. Grew leaped to the fray again with a forceful repetition of the case against validating invalid contracts. He warned Montagna that the spirit of American-Allied cooperation might have to end on a sour note if the Allies persisted. He had refused Ismet's request for assistance on concessions, he remarked, leaving the inference that he might no longer remain so impartial.[26]

All to no avail. The next day Montagna reported that the Allies had presented the Turks with draft terms which included the objectionable article validating incomplete contracts. Montagna explained softly that it was only a bargaining move by the French to secure other interests in return for abandoning their concessionary claims. He even urged Grew to persuade Ismet to negotiate on such terms with the French. Grew repeated his warning not to place the United States in open opposition. But he could do little more at this stage than anxiously wait upon developments. He did not dare come into the open until he was sure of Allied intentions, and these were shrouded in the secrecy of private meetings. On June 13 he asked Montagna if he could not be invited to these private meetings. Montagna replied that this would only stir up irritation and Grew had to console himself with a promise to be shown the proposed draft.[27]

The following day Montagna admitted that he had done all he could. It was now up to the United States to carry its own fight. Grew lost no time. Within two hours he saw Pellé and made his most emphatic representations to date. Pellé seemed unsure of the soundness of his position and was quite reasonable. He intimated the clause was intended to cover other interests besides those of the French, obviously those of the British. That evening Grew saw Rumbold, who appeared surprisingly reasonable too. Rumbold attempted to turn the onus of the clause back on the French by denying, so far as he knew, that any British interests were involved. This was a very interesting statement, said Grew. Could he report it to his government? Rumbold, neatly pinned, mumbled something about having to consult first with his expert as he was not fully "*au courant*" on the matter.[28]

It was a day well spent. The following evening Pellé came forth with the proposed draft, which, sure enough, stipulated that contracts and agreements concerning which "all formalities had not been fulfilled" on the opening of war but which had been negotiated or on which work had been begun, would be valid. Furthermore, a British expert called with the information that the obnoxious article did in fact also pertain to the Turkish Petroleum Company. The expert bluntly warned that the clause would not come up in formal meetings so there would be no opportunity to debate it. Here was every indication of an attempted *fait accompli*. At least the Allies had been "smoked out" and Grew was able to report concrete information to Washington the same night.[29]

Grew now held his fire for ten days. He received authority to make a statement, but the timing was left to his discretion. Meanwhile the Department of State instructed American ambassadors in London, Paris, and

Rome to make representations. It probably seemed wise to allow these to have their effect, and also to give the Allies time to work out alternatives. On June 26 Montagna reported that a compromise plan of his own which would eliminate the offensive clause was maturing, and urged Grew to use all his influence. Grew judged that the "right moment" had arrived, and officially informed Montagna then and there, in the latter's capacity as chairman of the committee involved, exactly what the attitude of his government was. The United States opposed any clause which validated concessionary rights that had not been fully validated on the outbreak of war in 1914, meaning the Turkish Petroleum Company concession. He also informed the Allies that he would now have to urge Ismet to reject the clause. Rumbold could only mutter repeatedly, "We must protect our companies." Ismet, last, appeared shaky on the issue. Grew assured him that if only Turkey stood firm she was bound to win in the end. He did not mention the extent of American representations for fear that Ismet would throw the burden of defeating the article on the United States. What he said was enough. Ismet authorized him to inform Washington that he would never yield.[30]

Ten more days passed. Ismet carried the fight while Grew stayed quiet. The Allies yielded an inch, suggesting a change of phrasing, but it was not enough for Grew or the Department of State. The conference remained stuck in sight of its goal.

On July 6 Montagna brought news that Rumbold, in the intimacy of Allied councils, said he was willing to modify the concessions protocol and even drop the troublesome article if necessary. Grew did not pause a moment for self-congratulation but pushed his advantage to the limit. Taking from his pocket a "pretentious-looking document" listing fifteen American objections to the article, he told Montagna that he was fully prepared with regard to the stand he would take if it were not dropped. Though allowing Montagna a peep at his document, he did not, experienced poker player that he was, reveal his hand fully by reading the list. Montagna said "Are you going to read all that?" Grew replied that his statement before the Committee would leave little to the imagination of the public. This "proverbial sword of Damocles" had its effect. Montagna suggested immediately that Grew see Ismet, and implied Grew might tell him that the Allies would not let the article stand in the way of a settlement. Later that same day Montagna reported progress on other remaining issues. Only the smallest margin separated the two sides now, and that margin was concessions.[31]

Ismet might need stiffening, so Grew saw him at midnight. He did indeed. The Turk said he would be in a difficult position if peace depended on the article in question. Grew saw it was time to play high cards. He told Ismet he had "even better reason than before for believing that the Allies would not permit this provision to stand in the way of peace." He would, he told Ismet, make a statement in committee if the article remained in the draft protocol. "It seemed to me wise," he recalled, "to play this important card at this juncture as any indication of weakness on our part would have made an unfortunate impression on Ismet." They parted in good spirits. But for their friendly relations, said Grew, Lausanne would have been another nightmare like Paris.[32]

Ismet resisted stubbornly for six hours the next day, and, as Montagna predicted, the British yielded, suggesting that the experts seek a formula providing compensation for individual companies in place of the validation of incomplete contracts in principle. But one clause of the new article stipulated that Turkey agreed to confirm the "alleged" Turkish Petroleum Company concession. Grew went into action again and Rumbold was forced to yield another grudging inch. The following day Montagna reported that he was urging substitution of the word "rights" for "concession." [33]

The Italian diplomat was embarrassed because Rumbold had said pointedly that one of the Allies had been divulging secrets of their private meetings. Grew knew Rumbold had been suspicious of Montagna at least since May 9 when the British delegate had permitted himself the witticism: "Nowadays the mountain is going to Mohammet." Grew did what he could to cheer up his faithful informer. Rumbold was reported to have said, "If Grew wants information why doesn't he come to us?" The answer was obvious, Grew told Montagna. He had been denied all information, and "if negotiations which directly interested us were carried on in private — 'secret agreements secretly arrived at' — it was my duty to obtain the information in every proper way." Then, to inspire Montagna's confidence further, he showed him part of a letter from Child saying Mussolini was fully aware of his delegate's helpful role.[34]

Montagna's confidence was sufficiently restored to provide Grew with news of every modification in the text, in spite of the fact that Rumbold warned against informing Grew unless he demanded and then only with the maximum delay. On the evening of July 9 the clause read, "The rights granted in 1914 to the Turkish Petroleum Company are valid and maintained." It now appeared so innocuous that Grew, after consulting his staff and Montagna, was inclined to accept it. This he recommended in a telegram to the Department of State which was dispatched early the following day, July 10.[35]

He told the Department that the basis of the Turkish Petroleum Company claim was a letter from Premier Saïd Halim to the British Ambassador outlining the agreement, which was never subsequently ratified by Parliament. With the new wording of the clause, only Turkish Petroleum Company "rights" would be valid and maintained and, since such a letter did not constitute a "right," the clause itself was only surplus verbiage. Though he assured the Department there was still time to object, he personally advised that "it would perhaps be more gracious on our part to acknowledge the British and French endeavor to meet our views by remaining silent when the subject is brought up in committee." He further advised that if the Department still had doubts, American interests would be adequately served by a letter to the principal delegates reserving American rights from injury. Grew had come so far in winning his point that, having the substance of victory, he felt he could grant the losers a gentleman's face-saving way out.

The Department's reply came the following morning, July 11. It was one to make Grew "very sick" with himself. One thousand seven hundred and eight-three words long, divided into six sections, it was severely disapproving. Furthermore, by the use of the first person singular, it was obviously from the hand of none other than Secretary Hughes himself. It was marked "very urgent." [36]

Hughes regarded the clause as meaningless except as an attempt to get confirmation of the Turkish Petroleum Company concession. Grew's contention that the clause would be inoperative for want of recognized rights, "when its plain meaning is to confirm rights, . . . would be difficult and unpleasant to maintain." The United States, Hughes went on, had been objecting to the Turkish Petroleum claim for three years. If now a concession could be erected through the Lausanne Treaty, America's painstakingly formulated and persistently argued Open Door policy would be repudiated. Furthermore, the British would be able to avoid the embarrassment of having to obtain a new grant from the Iraq government (with the result that it would be more difficult for the American oil group to secure an agreement with the Turkish Petroleum Company which explicitly recognized the Open Door principle). Adoption of the clause, the Secretary of State declared, could only be regarded as an "important diplomatic triumph" for Britain. Grew must not be "taken in by Montagna's well-meaning sophistry" and allow such a victory by his own surrender. A mere reservation was not enough. The whole clause must go.

Grew went to work with a will. That same evening he saw Rumbold for an acidulous conversation. Grew made the "strongest possible representations, complaining of being denied the facts and threatening a public statement." He noted in his memo: "I said it would be most unfortunate and disagreeable if I should be obliged to make a statement in Committee on this subject and that I felt it would not look well before the world." Rumbold said he sympathized and fully realized how disagreeable it would be for Grew to make such a statement, to which Grew replied that the disagreeable effect applied not to himself but to others. Rumbold was adamant and promised only to report Grew's representations. He then chided Grew for objecting first to a statement of principle in the validation of concessions and now objecting when the principle was removed and specific companies were provided for. It seemed quite clear to him that the United States all along had specific companies in mind, which Grew denied. The American objection in principle remained, Grew said, whether validation occurred by general statement or by specific guarantees.[37]

For the next week Grew "camped on everybody's trail." He listened sympathetically to Montagna's career problems and cheered up his worn, broken-looking ally Ismet. He passed on to Ismet advance intelligence of every Allied move as reported by Montagna. Thus Ismet learned that the Allies planned to inspire a war of nerves in the press, that they would try to frighten him themselves, that they planned to invite reconsideration of the issue by experts, but that the tone of the invitation was weak, and even that they would drop the article rather than break up the conference.[38]

By the evening of July 15 it was clear that a showdown was near. To give Ismet every ounce of strength for the last battle, Grew told him the United States had made representations at London and Paris and that Ismet would have a "friend" (Montagna) at the meeting the next day, whose views corresponded with their own. The final meeting was a marathon session of seven hours lasting until 2 A.M. on July 17. Ismet received "treatment which would make the third degree in a Harlem police station seem like a club dinner. He had deep circles around his eyes, his hair was standing on end, and he looked completely worn out. . . ." But he withstood the assault and the entire article including the Turkish Petroleum Company validation was dropped from the draft treaty. It was a complete victory for Ismet and Grew. The only unhappy person was Montagna. Ismet praised Britain at the last session but was "sparing and ungenerous" to Italy. Furthermore, Garroni was coming to sign and would take all the credit for Montagna's effort.[39]

The secret agreements were openly arrived at on July 17. Rumbold concluded his round of congratulation on the sour note that he failed to see why a dispute between Britain and Turkey should be interfered with by a third party.[40] But this could not deprive Grew of the sweet feeling of success as he watched the signing of the treaty July 24.

There remained one piece of unfinished business, the separate treaty. Negotiations for a Turkish-American treaty had improved Grew's bargaining power at the main conference, but the treaty in itself was a vital objective of his mission. During May, June, and July experts of the delegations had been quietly defining their positions, but agreement awaited hard bargaining by the principals. To this Grew was now urgently directed by the State Department. Officials in Washington, despairing of the hopeless mismanagement of the Ottoman-American Development Company, were anxious to secure a treaty before the Chester "bubble" burst and the Turks became disillusioned with the United States as an economic partner.[41]

However, Grew's prospects of success had sharply diminished. For Ismet a treaty with the United States was valuable but anticlimactic after his victory on July 24. He was badly worn out and desperately anxious to get home to lead the fight for ratification. His government was disillusioned with prospects of financial assistance from the United States by the failure of the Chester interests to show any signs of exploiting their concession. Most important, while he might have been willing to give Grew more favorable terms earlier, to win him away from the Allies, there was no advantage in this now. Thus Ismet sought a rapid settlement duplicating terms of the Allied treaty.[42]

The difficulty for Grew was that American interests could not be covered by the Allied treaty. While the Allies had aimed primarily at concluding peace, the United States, which had not been at war with Turkey, desired a comprehensive regulation of normal relations, including provisions for consular activities and extradition. Articles of the Allied treaty embodying League of Nations guarantees needed to be changed to meet American susceptibilities. Special American claims and grievances required satisfaction.[43]

It is not surprising then that Grew and Ismet were quickly deadlocked. Rumbold would have found grim satisfaction in the spectacle of Grew "wrangling with Ismet day and night." The Turk was "drunk with success and utterly headstrong — a sort of megalomania." Could not Ismet change the juridical declaration to leave the way open for American advisers? Ismet could not. This was a sore subject in Ankara. Any inclusion of one non-European non-belligerent would open the way to all. Could not the abolition of capitulations be so phrased as not to injure American capitulatory rights in other Asian and African countries? Ismet insisted that any change from the Allied declaration would "injure the form and spirit in which the new Turkey desires to build up her future." Could not the most-favored nation clause be accepted with rephrasing to meet Turkish susceptibilities? No, if Turkey accepted such a clause, other powers would not have to negotiate separate treaties but could ride along on the American treaty. Privileges granted foreigners must be strictly controlled. Why could not Turkey accept the Allied declaration on minorities without its awkward reference to the League? Because, said Ismet, the United States was not otherwise bound by League rulings. Well, would Ismet write a letter acknowledging the general applicability of the minorities declaration? No, said Ismet, this would be a definite engagement.[44]

So it went day after day. Some headway was made. Agreement on a school declaration, on sanitary articles, and on the many details of establishment had already been reached. The Turks were willing to work out a satisfactory formula on the Straits and eventually allowed recognition of the most-favored nation principle, which was Grew's major accomplishment.

But on claims, naturalization, the judicial declaration, capitulations, and minorities, they were completely obstinate.[45]

Ismet appeared so determined and final in his position as early as July 21 that Grew cabled for instructions. Ismet had asked him to report that this was his last word and that he would remain in Lausanne only a few more days. The Department replied with what Grew later called its "famous stampede" cable. The impression conveyed, it read coldly, "is that the Turkish delegate is trying to rush you into assenting to his terms." After demonstrating goodwill as a friendly neutral and not pressing American problems upon the Turks while they negotiated the Allied treaty, the United States found itself confronted with a "sort of ultimatum." "The Government of the United States," the cable continued haughtily, "finds itself obliged to state that it feels no pressing necessity to negotiate under these conditions." However, there would be no objection to continuation of negotiations if Turkey displayed a more conciliatory spirit. Grew communicated much of the substance of this telegram to Ismet on July 24. Ismet said he was sorry for the ill-feeling, excusing himself with the pressing necessity of returning to Ankara, and finally agreed to stay until negotiations were completed.[46]

Grew was now in an agony of indecision as to whether Ismet was bluffing or had truthfully stated his terms. He would finally have to make up his mind about "the inherent nature of the Turk." Ismet had steadily risen in his estimation as the two had worked together. He had become quite fond of him personally. The Turk had a captivating smile and a friendly, courteous manner. Though inclined to be more conciliatory over a bottle of green chartreuse of an evening than at the conference table the following day, he impressed Grew as being essentially honest and straightforward in his dealings. The main conference had shown, above all, that Ismet might be willing to make minor concessions but would never yield his central position that Turkish sovereignty must not be infringed in any way.[47]

Grew finally came to the conviction that Ismet was not bluffing, and that it was essential for the United States to seize this opportunity to make a treaty with Turkey on the latter's terms so that normal intercourse between the two countries could immediately begin on a realistic basis that recognized the changed situation in Turkey. A fresh start was called for.

He therefore took the initiative, and with the reluctant approval of the Department began to concede point after point. It "hurt like thunder to throw overboard so much ballast," but it won him a treaty. That treaty, despite failure of ratification in the Senate, in effect governed relations between Turkey and the United States until he himself, as Ambassador to Turkey, renegotiated most of its provisions in several treaties which the Senate ratified. Grew and Ismet affixed their signatures August 7. Nothing is more striking in showing how far Grew had come in those arduous months than his final judgment on Ismet. He described him now as "Napoleonic — the greatest diplomatist in history. He has played every one of us to a standstill. And he has done it fairly and squarely. . . ." [48]

Grew's diplomacy had not been faultless. He needed stiffening against the final British attempt to validate their oil concession. On the other hand, Washington, still somewhat wedded to the old regime in Turkey, also required instruction. Grew's developing awareness of the force of Turkish nationalism served to make his government more realistic about the basis for future relations with Turkey. The immediate, subjective viewpoint of the diplomatic agent and the broad, detached perspective of his government complemented each other. Throughout, Grew was precise, patient, adroit, and consistent. His efforts to advance particular interests never interfered with the quest for peace. He misled neither side but gained advantage by candor. Given the circumstances, it is difficult to see what more could have been done to advance American interests. Grew's was a craftsmanlike performance.

SEVEN

The Establishment of the American Foreign Service

LAUSANNE showed the value of expert, experienced diplomacy. Grew could argue that the United States needed career ministers and ambassadors to deal with the Ismets, Rumbolds, and Montagnas of postwar diplomacy. In fact, the establishment of diplomacy as a "permanent profession" in the United States had long been his absorbing interest and he was becoming a leading exponent of professionalism among the diplomats.[1] By the time of Lausanne the tide of opinion at home was at last flowing toward a major reorganization of American overseas representation. The following year, 1924, Congress passed the Rogers Act establishing the American Foreign Service. That same year Grew became Under Secretary of State, a position where he could play a major role in setting American diplomacy on a fully professional basis.

Diplomacy did not become a profession overnight, but by degrees over decades. The Foreign Service Act of 1924 was supposed to establish one completely professional civil service out of two quasi-professional organizations, the old Diplomatic and Consular Services, which had different functions, characteristics, and perspectives. General agreement existed in Congress that the amalgamated Service should bear more of the characteristics of the Consular than of the Diplomatic Service. The problem for Grew and the diplomats was to achieve the necessary professional footing without damaging the character of the Diplomatic Service. The crisis helped define a sense of profession that had been developing among them over the years.

This professional feeling developed in part through continuity of experience in diplomacy and the acquisition of skill in its practice. Grew found it difficult to describe diplomacy, to convey, for example, the nature of his contribution at Lausanne. Behind protocol, treaties, notes, and dispatches lay the exercise of intangible qualities such as tact and patience. He was certain, however, that a diplomat needed experience to learn the form and to mature the substance of his art. He had watched the part-time diplomats come and go. He had seen how they depended heavily on their experienced assistants, how they read the minds of foreigners "through a smoked glass" on account of the language handicap, how they lacked a sense of "international proportion," and how they committed unnecessary blunders by ignorance of diplomatic procedure and tactlessness. The distinction developed in his mind that they were amateurs and he, in a sense, was a professional.[2]

He also derived a sense of professionalism from association with European diplomats. The well-established career services of Europe provided him an example of professional diplomacy. In addition, prolonged service in Europe introduced him to the freemasonry of European professionals, who tended to develop a corporate identity apart from their national identity. Grew had a number of things in common with his European colleagues. They had all learned the same ropes, worked up through the ranks the same way, and sported and parleyed together. In terms of educational and social background he was part of the same world. Friendships with foreign diplomats from Cairo days to Lausanne had been one of the most pleasant and useful aspects of his career. It was not difficult to think of himself as one of them, as a professional diplomat.[3]

A third source of Grew's developing sense of professionalism was the Diplomatic Service, "this old Service of ours." Here in his view was an organization that only needed legislative reinforcement to become a full-fledged profession. Expertness already existed: the Service was composed of diplomatic secretaries and a few ministers, all of whom, like himself, had "worked up from the bottom, done the dirty work." Service spirit also existed. Even in Berlin days he had encouraged his fellow secretaries to line their office walls with pictures of their predecessors to inspire a sense of continuity and corporate identity.[4]

Group solidarity had deepened over the years. Though secretaries were scattered all over the world and lacked even a common information bulletin, the Service actually became more closely knit. Expanding needs made frequent transfers necessary and led to appointments to grade rather than post. Whereas from 1867 to 1898 the secretary had only one chance in twelve of shifting posts, by 1914 four out of five had served in more than one mission. Nearly half the prewar secretaryships were in Europe, with the result that by 1913 four-fifths of the secretaries were serving in or had served in Europe. Grew's network of friendships enlarged and stayed intact at the same time. He and his colleagues crisscrossed Europe on business or leave and stopped off to gossip and party together. Europe, after all, was the big stage most of them sought. The prospect of assignment elsewhere made Hugh Gibson feel "as though my spine had been removed by a turkey boning machine." [5]

The war deepened service solidarity. Privations, intense work, and emergencies created intimate "families" in the various missions. Part of Grew's Berlin "family" was enlarged thereafter into a Berne "family" that included Frederick Dolbeare, Allen Dulles, Ellis Dresel, and Hugh Wilson. This group was reunited after the war in Berlin, where Grew used to stop off and visit on his way to and from Copenhagen. Frequent assignment to Washington established a service group in the Department. Several bachelors shared a residence at 1718 H Street, which provided a place to meet and renew acquaintance. The postwar conferences such as Paris and Lausanne, drawing their staffs from the missions in Europe, provided other points of congregation. "The Service would have been far from a congenial career all those years," Grew later recalled, "if it hadn't been for the little group of men who have known each other intimately, and when serving at different posts, have kept up their friendship." Everyone had his own friendships, but the networks interlinked. Furthermore, acquaintanceship and friendship sprang easily from the remarkably similar backgrounds of members of the Diplomatic Service.[6]

Most of them had the same kind of education. One-third of the secretaries serving in Europe between 1898 and 1914 went to Harvard and two-thirds to Harvard, Yale, Princeton, or some foreign university. A large proportion attended private school, particularly St. Paul's, St. Mark's, Groton, and Lawrenceville. Eighty-five percent experienced some form of fashionable education — private school, Ivy League college, or foreign university.[7]

They were virtually without exception well-to-do. Hugh Gibson might talk of "simple homes," but "simple" meant "no butler or footmen." He referred to homes with tradition, "where the boys go to college — the bills are paid — Sunday observed, good books read, and where a standard obtains in respect to private life and public morality." Tradition was liberally interpreted in the United States; wealth and conscience seasoned quickly. Among Grew's friends new fortunes mixed easily with old. Leland Harrison's grandfather started out as an indentured steam fitter and founded a railroad fortune which sent the young heir into diplomacy by way of Eton and Harvard's Porcellian Club. William Phillips, grand-nephew of Wendell Phillips, and Peter Jay, descendant of John Jay, were Harvard classmates of Robert Bliss, whose father made the family money from "Castoria — Children Cry For It." Norman Armour, who joined Grew's staff at Vienna in 1912 after Princeton, was two generations removed from the founders of the Chicago meat-packing fortune. Hugh Wilson, who had tried his father's shirt-making business after Hill School and Yale, could speak of a diplomat understanding "instinctively the social gradations of any cosmopolitan group." [8]

Not the age but the fact of inherited wealth counted. It opened the door to what E. Digby Baltzell calls "a national, inter-city metropolitan upper class" that was emerging at the end of the nineteenth century, a class molded in large part by the common experience of boarding schools and Ivy League colleges.[9]

Service spirit bound the secretaries closely together. In a sense they knew each other before they ever met. The career only deepened and circumscribed existing ties. They possessed a common background, common experience, and a common liking for old wines, proper English, and Savile Row clothing. One amateur ambassador spoke of them grouchily as a "Secretaries' Union." Hugh Wilson preferred to think of them as "a pretty good club." Indeed the Diplomatic Service most nearly resembled a club.[10]

The chief problem facing the diplomats in the postwar years was career insecurity. Ministerships and ambassadorships were still "a fair stamping ground for patronage." Grew was in his early forties, at the height of his powers, yet the prospect of being turned out on the "scrap heap" loomed up with every election. If he were ousted by a political appointee, other professions would be closed on account of his lack of preparation and deafness. In diplomacy deafness was not an insuperable handicap because, he said, so much of the work was on paper and he could usually arrange face-to-face conversations. Business had always been a gloomy alternative. "If you ever hear of me starting in on State Street," he wrote Gibson, "please send flowers as the end will not be far off." If his career was not to be cut off in the prime, the career principle would have to be extended to include chiefs of mission, thus making diplomacy, as he put it, "a permanent profession." [11]

Career insecurity threatened to demoralize the Service in the postwar years. Grew used to keep a list of secretaries, moving each up a peg when a man above retired or was promoted. Between 1904 and 1924 only Gibson, Phillips, himself, and perhaps a dozen others survived to gain missions of their own. Young men of high promise recruited during the war, like Christian Herter, turned elsewhere, and Wall Street beckoned to those who remained. Recruitment lagged, no longer spurred by the expanding horizons of the turn of the century or by the crusading spirit of the war years. Sons of the right homes, graduates of the right colleges, scorned an occupation where ability and hard work promised at best a menial staff rank at four thousand dollars a year, half what the British paid. The State Department discouraged those without private incomes from applying. Only forty-two candidates of disappointing quality took the entrance examination in 1921 and thirty-seven in 1922. Those like Grew who identified their own interests with the larger interests of the Service saw a desperate need for establishing American diplomacy as an attractive career that ultimately allowed for "honor and the satisfaction of public recognition." [12]

The diplomats watched intently as Congress moved toward major reform legislation. Representative John Jacob Rogers introduced the first bill in

January 1919, during the Paris Peace Conference, but it was shunted aside until after the election. The Harding Administration cooperated with Rogers in drafting legislation but took until 1922 deciding what kind of reorganization it wanted, and another year and more passed in developing public support and securing Congressional action. Grew and his colleagues were delighted with the idea of a permanent structure for career diplomacy, with the proposed pay and retirement benefits, and especially with the provision for promotion of the best career officers to ministerial posts. However, they were alarmed by a central feature of reform proposals, the fusion of the Diplomatic and Consular Services into one Foreign Service in which all officers could be assigned equally to consular or diplomatic posts and would be equally eligible for promotion to minister. They feared that their own service would be "totally plundered" by the consuls, in Grew's words, and that they would be reassigned to consular duty.[13]

The consuls viewed reform from a somewhat different perspective. Their service had already been extensively improved. It was career-staffed from clerk to consul general, and boasted a higher pay scale than the Diplomatic Service and a more elaborate personnel system and operating procedures. Nevertheless, consuls still looked forward to old age, as one said, "with fear and trembling" and were eager for the proposed retirement system.[14]

While diplomats regarded amalgamation of the two services as a liability of reform, the consuls considered it an advantage. Joining the two services together would broaden career possibilities and attract better candidates. Some consuls wanted missions of their own. Consul General Robert Skinner could hardly wait for enactment of the Rogers bill to apply for a "proper legation." According to the Director of the Consular Service, only a handful of consuls shared Skinner's ambition, but probably a substantial number were attracted to the idea of trying out diplomacy for a few years, say as economic officers in embassies. More general perhaps was the desire for equality of status with the diplomats. Consuls seemed to have an inferiority complex. They did not enjoy diplomatic immunity and their work was less prestigious. Representative Tom Connally noted a "delicate" point: "Those in the Consular Service desire an enlarged service because the diplomatic secretaries now take social precedence." Classification with diplomats under the all-embracing title of Foreign Service Officer would add dignity to what in many respects was a clerkly occupation.[15]

In securing their objectives, the consuls had a powerful leader in their Director, Wilbur J. Carr. He epitomized the American ideal of self-improvement. From a small-town Ohio and commercial college background he entered the State Department during the Cleveland Administration as a shorthand clerk. He improved every hour, acquiring a mastery of the workings of the Department by day, attending law school at night, practicing French and the violin on Sundays. Carr stayed from one administration to the next, and with effort and knowledge came indispensability and power. More than anyone else he was responsible for reform and improved efficiency in the Consular Service. His name brought "a gleam to every consular eye"; indeed, one consul thought of Carr and not the government as his employer. For years Carr had been in a position to help Congressmen with their constituents' problems of trade and travel. For years he had been testifying on Capitol Hill, patient, self-effacing, expert. He claimed that Foreign Service legislation was drafted in his office. In its final stages a rider was attached creating a fourth Assistant Secretary of State, and it was clearly the intention of Congress that the new officer was to be Wilbur Carr.[16]

Not only did Carr possess influence in Congress which the diplomats could not match, but also he represented a service that enjoyed a far more favorable public image than the Diplomatic Service. Expression of opinion on the subject of American representation abroad displayed a market preference for consuls on two grounds: they more effectively represented American interests in world affairs and they were more representative Americans.[17]

Postwar reformers urged the establishment of a new Foreign Service shaped to serve American interests. A writer in *Outlook* still preferred amateur diplomats "with no other training than courageous American manhood and ideals," but most observers agreed on the necessity of experience. Acceptance of the career principle did not imply approval of European professional diplomacy, however. The prestige consciousness typical of influential Americans during Grew's early career had faded. Hoary prejudices re-emerged: traditional diplomacy was an affair of artifice and subterfuge endangering rather than advancing American interests.

The Return to Normalcy dictated that American diplomacy devote itself to helping American business. According to *Colliers*, an efficient State Department and competent ambassadors were needed "to keep the wheels of American industry turning full time." Arthur Sweetser in *World's Work* argued that the questions of the future concerned solely "the struggle for markets and wealth, in which an efficiently organized foreign service will greatly benefit us." [18] The National Civil Service Reform League pictured a reformed service as the vanguard for trade expansion. Rogers himself claimed that every question of international politics involved a question of business. Powerful business groups actively supported reform on the basis of an amalgamated service, among them the United States, New York, and Chicago chambers of commerce and the National Advertisers Association. Congress felt the pressure. In the debate on the Foreign Service bill Tom Connally became so tired of hearing about improved efficiency and better business that he complained, "the trouble with our foreign service now is that it has got a dollar mark written all over it." The object seemed to be to turn new Foreign Service Officers into "selling agents." [19]

The business orientation of reform sentiment worked to the advantage of the consuls more than the diplomats. The trade argument had won them earlier and more thorough reform in the first decade of the century. Now "keen, highly-trained, and efficient to the last degree," in the words of *Literary Digest,* consuls yielded practical, tangible benefits. Diplomats tended to avoid the common herd, while consuls dealt deeply in the life of the country, Will Irwin pointed out in *Saturday Evening Post.* The diplomat seldom touched business until it became an incident, said Arthur Sweetser in *World's Work;* the consul was his "humble cousin, working on quietly, unspectacularly, winning markets for American merchants." The solution was to remove the "great gulf fixed" between consuls and diplomats by a simple "trick of organization," assigning consuls to diplomatic work.[20]

Criticism of social exclusiveness in the Diplomatic Service also helped the consuls on the issue of amalgamation. Diplomats were twitted as "pink tea types" and "cookie pushers." Some critics distinguished between workers and drones, others discerned a "distinct class" or "caste"; most agreed there were too many precious foplings in American diplomacy. On the other hand, the consuls formed no distinct group. Fewer came from the Northeast; the rural South and West were better represented. Three out of four consuls had attended public schools and only one out of four an Ivy League college. To make American diplomacy representative, salaries would have to be sufficient to support able men without private means. Beginners should be exposed to "fodder for a real eight-hour day" in consulates and the social exclusiveness of diplomacy should be broken down by adding down-to-earth consuls.[21]

Grew was well aware of the jaundiced attitude at home toward diplomats, the conviction, as he put it, that the Diplomatic Service "was instituted for the purpose of permitting the gilded youth of the country to shine in foreign society." He sensed the "blind prejudice" of Congressmen toward diplomats, particularly after the Copenhagen Incident. Recent articles by diplomats only made the image worse. He was nauseated by Norval Richardson's recollection in *Saturday Evening Post* of "pleasurable excitement" in the presence of royalty. Grew frankly admitted the presence of "gay-plumaged birds" in the service, but adamantly opposed intermixture of consuls and diplomats as a solution. Better salaries and assurance of promotion would bring forward the "decent red-blooded men"; better administration would eliminate "the few rotters." [22]

Grew and his friends had no desire whatever to serve in consular posts themselves and thought high diplomatic positions were few enough without opening competition to the much larger Consular Service. If Carr took control, Grew warned, "the little old diplomatic service might just as well go to bye-bye." He also feared that the consuls would "bureaucratize" the whole Foreign Service. They dealt in routine, administrative matters which lent themselves to manuals of operating procedure and reports in triplicate, in short to the impersonal system which free-wheeling individualists of the old Diplomatic Service abhorred.[23]

The question of social fitness for diplomacy was rarely raised explicitly, but snobbishness toward consuls undoubtedly existed. Gibson's picture of a person in a "sweat" was a consul at an embassy dinner. William R. Castle, Jr., a Department officer but close to the diplomats, found consular "standards of civilization" lower, as shown in "sentimentality, . . . a fondness for Y.M.C.A. standards and phraseology." The Consular Service even had "nobility of purpose" as an efficiency criterion. J. (for Joshua) Butler Wright, Lawrenceville and Princeton, spoke of the importance of "breeding." Grew more tactfully referred to "background" and "personal cultivation," Hugh Wilson to "worldliness." Discrimination against consuls could easily follow from such considerations of social fitness for diplomacy. Certainly the consuls sensed discrimination and bitterly resented it. The diplomatic privileges, wrote Nelson Johnson, "ah, there are the almost perfect insulations," making the "career secretariat immune to criticism by the uninitiated." If some of the "white spatters" left the Foreign Service because they did not enjoy associating with the "consular bunch," he could spare them.[24]

More persuasive reasons against interchange of personnel existed. Gibson rejected the equation of business and diplomacy. He pointed out to a House committee that diplomacy was also concerned with other factors which business experience rarely equipped a man to estimate accurately. Grew saw a functional difference between the services. Shifting a diplomat to consular work, he often said, was like trying to make a carpenter into a plumber overnight. Ultimately he came to the conclusion that consular work, by inhibiting imagination and initiative, could be positively harmful preparation for diplomacy.

He groped toward an understanding of the different kinds of mind involved. He believed that intelligent diplomacy required, beyond "mere knowledge," what he called "mentality." He was perhaps trying to say that a diplomat's mind was prehensile, roving, eclectic, a litmus to varying environments, sensitive to mood and nuance. He thought of himself as a bee gathering honey. The consular mind, on the other hand, was a classifying, quantifying, delimiting mind working in the interstices of law and regulations. Craftsmanship in consular work sprang from the "fascination" Carr felt in taking "a collection of facts and applying to them principles of law." Perhaps Grew also sensed a difference of viewpoint: the consul was essentially his government's agent while the diplomat was also an intermediary, an interpreter of another country to his own. Consuls, he would later conclude, were often unfitted for diplomacy by "temperament, personality and outlook." [25]

Much as Grew and his colleagues would have preferred a reformed but separate Diplomatic Service, compromise was their obvious course. In order to make diplomacy an attractive career, a "permanent profession," they would have to get behind the reform movement. At the same time, by cooperating they might influence legislation and administration so as to restrict the amount of intermixture of the two services and in fact keep the old Diplomatic Service relatively intact. They reacted in typical diplomatic fashion to their problem, striving to protect the substance of their interests while yielding in form.

Grew wholeheartedly supported reform and used the popular argument of "business, better business, bigger business." He urged his friends to "get it out of the mind of the public" that the consuls were the only ones who looked after business. Diplomats working at the highest levels of government could also procure dollar benefits. He had no qualms about being thought "infra dig" in selling the idea of diplomacy as a business proposition. He declined to testify before Congress on the ground that those "who talk through their nose and spit on the floor will cut a lot more ice than those who talk like Englishmen." However, he dug examples out of old diaries showing how he had helped business by negotiating favorable settlement of a potash controversy in Germany and by "hammering away" at the Swiss until they lifted a duty on American automobiles. Every visitor to his office was a "potential champion." He converted the vice-president of Equitable Life Insurance Company and stuffed his pockets with material to carry the message to important chambers of commerce. Later, in 1926, he would be informing audiences about a "new diplomacy" that was "eminently practical, business-like and straightforward." The Under Secretary and Assistant Secretaries of State corresponded to vice-presidents in business. Political appointments were an "economic waste." The Foreign Service Act established "a new machine . . . to meet the inevitable law of demand and supply." [26]

In this manner Grew supported the immediate interests of his service, at the cost of reinforcing popular assumptions about diplomacy. The public gained no insight from one of the more experienced practitioners of the art that diplomacy was not simply a business proposition.

In keeping their service substantially intact the diplomats had considerable bargaining leverage. They warned that complete fusion would destroy morale and increase the number of resignations, and they were probably quite right. The Harding Administration was not inclined to weaken its only source of experienced officers, especially when so many of them came from prominent Republican families. Indeed, Charles Evans Hughes made an excellent record of promoting diplomats to ministerial rank. Had he wavered, Phillips, Harrison, and Wright, three of his four principal assistants, were close by to remind him of the interests of the Diplomatic Service. Instead he chose to support a compromise suggested by Carr, whereby officers of both services would be redesignated as Foreign Service Officers under a single examination, rank, pay, and retirement system, but the two services would remain functionally separate. The Rogers Bill establishing the Foreign Service reflected this compromise by not spelling out the terms under which officers of the two services would be interchanged. The struggle between the Diplomatic and Consular Services became an internal one for administrative control of the new system.[27]

The diplomats paid close attention to problems of administrative control. Through correspondence and meetings some eight officers on European service took an active part in discussing reform problems, of whom three, Gibson, Grew, and Wilson, played the most persistent and influential parts.[28] A "Paris Group" met as early as April 1920. At Berlin in 1922 Grew and Gibson met Castle, and according to the last reached "some rather radical conclusions." They recommended that there be a chief of personnel for the forthcoming Foreign Service who would be identified with neither the diplomatic nor the consular branch, an administrator powerful enough presumably to resist Carr's encroachment. That man was to be Castle, as Gibson and Grew suggested to Secretary Hughes shortly after the meeting. Castle, then Chief of Western European Affairs, was ostensibly neutral but in fact was close to the diplomats. "Joe Grew is wonderfully friendly about my being, in the opinion of the service men, really a part of the Service," he wrote. As a descendant of one of the original American grandee families of Hawaii and a classmate of Phillips and Bliss at Harvard, he had impeccable qualifications.[29]

In 1924, as the Rogers Bill neared enactment, a position of crucial importance for protecting the interests of the diplomats became available when William Phillips decided to leave the Under Secretaryship. Gibson, Minister to Poland and a close friend of Secretary of Commerce Herbert Hoover, was a logical successor but pleaded insufficient income, and Hugh Wilson was too junior to be considered. Since Hughes wanted to keep the Under Secretaryship a service post, Grew was an obvious candidate. He simply could not be ignored, Castle observed, adding later, "With Joe here we should not have any fears as to the administration of the Service under the Rogers Bill. . . ." Lausanne had established Grew's reputation and he possessed to an exceptional degree the qualities diplomats admired: background, experience, skill, loyalty, and integrity. He heard from Gibson in late January 1924 that he was being considered. On March 1, after Phillips's strong recommendation, Grew was chosen and accepted with alacrity. He sailed for America on April 5, his last assignment in Europe behind him.[30]

Grew left his family in Europe to finish the school year. He had barely reached Boston when he received the shattering news of the death of his eldest daughter Edith. She had fallen ill with scarlet fever while in Venice on a school sight-seeing trip. Nearly eighteen, she had just passed her university entrance examinations with high marks. She was to have had a coming-out party in America. Now "Didi," his "sweet pea," was gone. Too far away to help and too anguished to wait alone in Boston, he cut short his vacation, reported for duty in Washington, and threw himself into his new job.[31]

He had been "rather appalled at the prospect of the responsibility" of his new post, but he soon learned that responsibility, except during the absence of the Secretary, was the least of his worries.[32] He was in fact hardly more than a glorified administrative assistant to his dominating chief. Charles Evans Hughes was probably the last Secretary of State who could personally manage the nation's foreign affairs. Even with his enormous energy, incisive mind, and ebullient personality, the burden of keeping abreast of world-wide developments was almost too much to bear. He relied heavily on his regional divisions, whose chiefs such as Dulles and Castle were allowed considerable responsibility in policy formulation and reported directly to the Secretary. This direct relationship left the Under Secretary and Assistant Secretaries in an administrative backwash. Hughes expected two things of his Under Secretary, that he take over trivial and routine business, and that he be prepared to step in as Acting Secretary when he, the Secretary, was absent. Thus Grew had no major responsibility except in one area, Foreign Service personnel.[33]

Grew came to office at a crucial moment in the evolution of American diplomacy. The Rogers Bill establishing the Foreign Service became law on May 24, 1924, only a month after his arrival. The Secretary of State was to determine the extent of amalgamation and Old State buzzed with speculation on the outcome.[34]

The Secretary had two plans to choose from. The interests of the diplomats were represented in a plan drafted by Hugh Wilson, who was then on assignment in the Department. It recommended a single personnel chief, as Castle, Gibson, and Grew had agreed in Berlin. The interests of the consuls were represented in a plan drafted by Carr, now an Assistant Secretary of State. He proposed that responsibility for Foreign Service personnel be assigned to a board composed of the Under Secretary and two Assistant Secretaries, assisted by one consular and one diplomatic officer brought back from the field. Also on the board, but not voting, would be a personnel chief and assistant chief, each representing a different branch of the new Service. Since the Assistant Secretaries and Under Secretary could outvote the field representatives, they would possess ultimate control. With Carr one of these, and likely to remain for the forseeable future, the result seemed obvious to Castle: "Everything will lead gently but inevitably toward control by the one man who is permanent."

Hughes chose neither plan. He warned that a chief of personnel reporting directly to the Secretary of State and lacking civil service protection, such as the Wilson plan envisaged, would be fair game for a patronage-minded Secretary, leaving the Foreign Service open to political plunder. He proposed a compromise: a Personnel Board composed of two Assistant Secretaries and the Under Secretary, as in the Carr plan, and also three, instead of two, voting Foreign Service officers, who would form an executive committee of the Board to handle routine administration. Thus the career element would have the same voting power as the Assistant Secretaries and Under Secretary, the element subject to political change.[35]

Castle, undoubtedly bitter over his lost opportunity to be personnel chief, saw no future in the compromise plan since it placed responsibility nowhere and still left Carr in ultimate control through long-term influence in selecting the chairman of the Executive Committee. Carr, less sanguine about his influence, fought the compromise "like a steer." His plan, he said, had been based on years of experience with an organization now "as near perfection as possible." The diplomats had no experience to justify their submitting any plan in the first place. He intimated he would resign rather than share control with a Foreign Service contingent. Grew battled him in meeting after meeting trying to secure adoption of the compromise, but Carr remained adamant. Finally, presumably with Hughes's approval, Grew forced a showdown. On June 5 he sent a memorandum to Carr informing him that the compromise plan had been adopted, and "The Little Father of the Consuls" yielded.[36]

The Hughes compromise worked splendidly for the diplomats. The first Personnel Board was composed of Hugh Wilson and two consuls, forming the Executive Committee, as well as Grew, Chairman, and Assistant Secretaries Wright and Carr. With Carr and the two consuls identified with the consular branch and Grew, Wilson, and Wright identified with the diplomatic, the Board was evenly split. It was in effect two boards, each immune from the other. Since a majority was necessary for effecting an interchange, few were approved. By 1926 only four secretaries, or 3 percent of those engaged in diplomatic work, had shifted to consular work, while only six consuls, or 1 percent of those engaged in consular work had shifted to diplomacy. "Weaving back and forth," said Grew, would not be in the interests of the Service. Separate personnel evaluations, promotion lists, inspectors, in fact separate services were preserved. Carr acquiesced, indeed to the Under Secretary appeared as a "solid rock of support." On the Board everything was going "beautifully," Grew wrote Gibson, but they had made "a very narrow escape from . . . complete bureaucratization."[37]

The Foreign Service was Grew's most important activity as Hughes's

Under Secretary, but he was not left otherwise idle. Hughes told Grew on his first day that they must be "thick as two thieves." The two offices, the Secretary held, must be "spiritually and physically one," but that "one" was well whiskered. Grew was Acting Secretary for seventy-one days in 1924, most of it during Hughes's trip to Europe and the presidential campaign. Whenever possible he prudently followed established policy or deferred decisions until the Secretary's return. As he said, "our chief troubles have been in connection with individual cases rather than large events." [38]

A typical day would begin with the reading of the night's cables, followed by a policy review conference in the Secretary's office and the "machine-gun" questioning of a press conference. A steady stream of callers flowed through Grew's office: a Congressman seeking his son's appointment to a delegation; a man furious with a customs inspector for insulting his daughter; an ambassador complaining that the noise of streetcar reconstruction was keeping him awake at night; another complaining that a Gloria Swanson film intimated that his Queen was born illegitimately; a lady seeking American adherence to an international convention for the free treatment of sailors with venereal disease; and so forth. People with important matters unfortunately often kept away from Grew, Castle noted, because they hesitated to speak of confidential matters loud enough for the deaf Under Secretary to hear.[39]

He would be interrupted at any moment by that "horrible" buzzer summoning him peremptorily to the Secretary's office, there to receive the gist of Hughes's latest conversation or respond to "terrifyingly quick" demands for information and opinion. Castle would hate to be Hughes's Under Secretary "unless I had a mind which worked like lightning." [40]

Around noon there would be temporary repose in a leisurely lunch at the Cosmopolitan Club, followed by more callers and conferences. Appointments had to be made politically and resignations extracted tactfully. Problems to be settled varied from the precedence of diplomats to the prices of pottery, from immigration visas to monument unveilings. The bustle and shuffle continued all day until evening quiet descended on the generous mahogany-paneled offices of Old State and Grew initialed the last outgoing telegram, reached for his homburg, and went home.

The one area outside the Foreign Service in which Grew hoped to make an important contribution as Under Secretary was administration. His concern for efficiency was as strong as in Berlin days. Major reorganization was impossible with the Department's monolithic resistance to change and the Secretary's close management of affairs. "Some day," Grew later reminisced, "I hope our old Department — with all the affection I have for it — can be shattered to bits and remoulded nearer the heart's desire." What he could do, he felt, was improve communications. He tried to make instructions to the field more explicit and ensure that information from the field was forwarded by the more methodical dispatch rather than private letters from chiefs of mission to the Secretary. He argued Hughes into leaving his personal files, those "absolutely essential blocks of information," in the Department when he resigned, and he tactfully managed the transfer of old records to a bureau more accessible to research by historians, who "mould public opinion." He attempted to expedite circulation of papers within the Department, joshing Castle about a dispatch which had lain in the latter's office for nineteen months. But it was a man against a mountain and the State Department felt his impress very little.[41]

No matter how trivial his duties, working so closely with a man of the brilliance and force of Charles Evans Hughes made it a memorable year. It was a sad moment when he went to Union Station on March 7, 1925, to bid good-by to his chief. He had "seldom loved a man so much. . . ." Hughes had recommended him to his successor, Frank B. Kellogg, as "not only a man of great ability but one who has had extended experience." Grew offered his resignation but Kellogg refused to accept it.[42]

The prospect of several more years in the United States encouraged him to buy a house, a $125,000 brick mansion in a wooded ravine flanking Rock Creek Park. He built a library wing where he mounted his game heads and collected his books. Kipling was always handy. There by the fire he could view row after row of sturdily bound diaries and papers, now increasing at the rate of four a year.[43] Twenty years earlier he had paced the streets of Tours trying to decide whether to accept that first appointment in Cairo. From a consular clerk he had risen to the top professional post in diplomacy. He had entered the ranks without examination, one of the last of the amateurs, and now he had become the person chiefly responsible for inaugurating the nation's first fully professional Foreign Service. Grew had come far in twenty years and could look forward to twenty more of fulfillment.

EIGHT

Diplomats and Consuls: A Problem of Integration

WITH Kellogg, Grew's Under Secretaryship went sour. Personality and policy differences led to growing estrangement between the two and increasing isolation of Grew from the inner councils of the Department. Furthermore, Grew's policies for the development of the Foreign Service under the Rogers Act met with mounting criticism from within the Department and from Congress and the public. A series of humiliating reverses in the spring of 1927 left Grew in an untenable position from which his appointment as Ambassador to Turkey came as a welcome relief.

The Secretary and Under Secretary made a curious team. Frank Billings Kellogg grew up on a pioneer Minnesota farm where chores cut schooling to a minimum, but at nineteen he escaped his hard future by entering a law office as clerk. From these humble beginnings he rose in the finest Horatio Alger tradition to become a wealthy lawyer in St. Paul, Theodore Roosevelt's chief prosecutor of the Standard Oil Trust, senator, Ambassador to England, and then Secretary of State. He was short and stocky and his hair at seventy was like "the snow white pad on top of a Georgia cotton bush." [1] "Nervous Nellie," as he was called, had a hot temper, "crusty" humor, and democratic scorn for the softening arts of diplomacy. He was honest, straightforward, and kindly, and worked and worried himself to the point of exhaustion. In spite of their differences, Grew retained an affectionate regard for the old man.[2]

The Secretaryship of Kellogg may be divided into two periods, the first half characterized by bumbling diplomacy, now timid now blustering, the second by hypercautious but more skillfull and at times constructive diplomacy. During the first period American China policy wavered between support of the treaty system in concert with Western powers and unilateral accommodation of the turbulent forces of Chinese nationalism. Pugnacious defense of American oil interests in Mexico and inept meddling in Nicaraguan revolutionary politics aroused a roaring protest in Latin America and at home against Yankee imperialism. Fumbling initiatives in disarmament led nowhere and put added strain on Anglo-American relations. The second period witnessed a dramatic improvement in Latin American relations as a result of the successes of Dwight Morrow in Mexico, Henry Stimson in Nicaragua, and Charles Evans Hughes at Havana; the United States went a step toward accommodating the new China by settlement of the tariff question; Kellogg won his glittering if insubstantial triumph of the Peace Pact. When Grew left Washington at the end of the first period, Kellogg diplomacy was hitting bottom. It would be incorrect, however, to blame Kellogg's troubles on advice he received from Grew, for in fact the Under Secretary had very little influence on policy.

Relations between the two were courteous but never close. Kellogg used to address his former Counselor of Embassy in London as "Fred" but the Under Secretary remained "Mr. Grew." Their working relationship was strained from the beginning. Kellogg would have preferred to choose his own Under Secretary and suggested Dwight Morrow, but President Coolidge apparently decided that the appointment of a Morgan partner would present too inviting a target to critics of Wall Street influence upon foreign policy. Also the President may have preferred to keep an experienced officer such as Grew beside the untried Secretary. "He is a great man to keep the Service as it is, if it is functioning well," observed Kellogg.[3]

In the beginning Grew envisaged a large role for himself. To take the burden from the frail and tremulous Secretary, he started signing telegrams without consulting his chief. However, Kellogg soon took the reins and began formulating policy without even informing Grew, who struggled to stay abreast of developments but fell further and further behind. On the spur of the moment Kellogg would summon him into a policy conference, and ask his opinion. Grew, who needed time and care to "grasp all the threads" of a problem, would make an embarrassed, fumbling reply. Kellogg soon found his advice "useless." Increasingly the Secretary relied on his former law partner Robert Olds, who came into the Department as Assistant Secretary and by 1927 was *de facto* Under Secretary. In such circumstances, taking charge of the Department in the Secretary's absence, which Grew had to do for a total of seventy-six days, was particularly awkward. Excluded from the buzz of diplomatic activity next door, sidetracked into departmental trivia, chilled without the warm sun of Hughes's personality, Grew became profoundly discouraged. He preoccupied himself with Foreign Service reform and lost interest in the rest.[4]

Not that Kellogg would have done better or much differently if he had listened to Grew. Evidence is scanty because of long diary lapses in this period, but such as there is suggests that this top professional adviser's approach to foreign policy was less flexible and imaginative, more rights-minded and stand-pat, than that of Hughes and even to some extent than that of Kellogg. For example, reports from the London Conference in 1924 warned that the British might object to American participation in the proposed Paris conference on reparations. Grew with the President's approval instructed the Ambassador in London, Kellogg at the time, to make a strong reservation if necessary of the American right to participate. Had the Ambassador done this, Hughes said on his return, the London Conference might have broken up. On the question of war debts Grew upheld the popular view epitomized by Coolidge's remark, "They hired the money, didn't they?" He deplored unsettling the "binding power of international obligations," suggested that mandatory payment would push delinquent governments toward financial reform, and pointed out all the United States had done in reducing principal and interest. It was a thoroughly orthodox view.[5]

On occasion Grew could be truculent. When Robert Imbrie, American Vice-Consul in Teheran, was murdered by a Persian mob in July 1924, Grew, Acting Secretary, made a very strong protest, though he managed to deter President Coolidge from sending a warship by pointing out that Teheran was five hundred miles from the sea. By October the Persians had acceded to all American demands except the execution of two of the assailants. Concerned lest American prestige suffer in an area where the nation had important interests, Grew recommended that Hughes call in the Persian Chargé and threaten to break relations. He managed to get Hughes to agree but only with difficulty. The little Chargé was crushed by the awesome Secretary's wrath and the condemned were executed.[6]

Grew advocated a firm hand in Latin American relations. Though the United States subscribed to the principle of withholding recognition from Central American regimes which came to power by unconstitutional means, Hughes had some doubts. He would have preferred to base recognition on prolonged acquiescence by the people to the regime in power rather than on the constitutional formalities by which it arrived in power; it was better to let the Latins "stew in their own juice" than risk the charge of Yankee imperialism. Not so Grew, who upheld the constitutional test. Revolutions were a national sport there, he observed, and if one succeeded others would be tried, but none could succeed without United States recognition. Indeed he went beyond that test and advocated influencing the establishment of regimes which could be recognized. The American Minister to Honduras was to be praised for "bringing about" the election of a president on a constitutional basis. Foreigners, he argued, "look to us to keep the peace and to ensure constitutional government in those countries, and we should be accused of a weak and vacillating policy if we do not do so."

Mexico, the leading troublemaker of Kellogg's day, exhibited "a strain of Oriental shortsightedness": its president must know he could not remain in power without the support of the United States. Grew may have carried no weight with Kellogg but he marched right in step with the querulous Secretary down the path into the Nicaraguan-Mexican imbroglio of early 1927.[7]

On China, Grew found his own difficulty. The years 1925-26 marked one of the most bewildering and anarchic phases of the long Chinese nationalist revolution. In the north the Peking government represented not China but the war lord preponderant at the moment. In the south the Nationalist movement, with Chiang Kai-shek emerging as leader, was just beginning its triumphant march northward. Chinese were united only in their hatred of the tariff and extraterritorial privileges of the foreign barbarians. Foreign powers agreed that some concessions in behalf of Chinese autonomy were necessary, but widely disagreed on what, to whom, and when to concede. Within the State Department counsels were similarly divided. Minister to China John MacMurray advised step-by-step relinquishment in concert with other treaty powers, depending on China's performance in establishing order and protecting remaining foreign rights and interests. Kellogg, anxious to express American sympathy for Chinese aspirations, favored broader, quicker, unilateral initiatives, but was uncertain what kind of Chinese performance to expect in return and how far to go in defending existing rights. Grew found Kellogg's approach attractive at first, praising his "forcible and clean-cut" policies, but found himself in direct opposition to the Secretary over the question of using force in the Taku Incident of March, 1926.[8]

Taku was at the nether end of Peking's lifeline to the sea and thus of acute concern to foreign legations, which were ever mindful of the Boxer Rebellion. Early in March this lifeline was imperiled by a seaborne attack, one thrust of a campaign by Marshal Chang Tso-lin and his allies upon the forces of General Feng Yu-hsiang, who was then in control of Peking. The naval force shelled the Taku forts, blocked the Peiho River leading to Tientsin, and dispatched a landing party which cut the Peking-Mukden railroad. Government forces responded by mining the ship channel and closing the river to all shipping. Alarmed as MacMurray was at this twin threat to American life and property, he also sensed an opportunity for the treaty powers to make a stand in the "rear-guard action" they were being forced to conduct in China. Definitive violation of the Boxer Protocol by both sides, he felt, provided an opportunity for united foreign defense of treaty rights backed up by a display of naval force, without danger of appearing unneutral in the Chinese civil war. He cabled Washington his views and assurance that every effort would be made to explore less drastic possibilities, but he warned that he might have to take a position before receiving a reply.[9]

At the other end was Grew, Acting Secretary while Kellogg was convalescing from the flu in North Carolina. He could restrict the Minister to unilateral or joint action to protect lives and property or he could approve action based on the Boxer Protocol to reopen the lifeline, whether or not foreign lives and property were in imminent danger. Grew's reply was a simple, blanket approval of MacMurray's "attitude," which left the Minister free to use the Protocol if he wished. Undoubtedly Grew felt impelled to back up the expert on the spot. MacMurray was an old friend, a professional diplomat, and a former Chief of the Far Eastern Division whom Grew had strongly recommended for the post. Grew also appears to have believed in the necessity for the more drastic course. "If we hadn't done it," he wrote much later, "the British would have been let down, the Boxer Protocol would have become a dead letter and Peking might have again become endangered." Before cabling he briefed the President, who with his usual monumental indifference to foreign affairs said, "You know more about it than I do; go ahead and I will back you up." [10]

MacMurray had already gone ahead, joining with treaty ministers in charging violation of the Protocol and demanding action "forthwith" to restore communication between Tientsin and the sea. Chinese inaction and the shelling of two Japanese destroyers shortly led the ministers to order a joint naval demonstration with ultimatums to both sides. Then the Chinese bowed and the Peiho again ran unvexed to the sea.[11]

Meanwhile Grew was in trouble. The day after the ultimatums, March 17, ten representatives of American missionary organizations in Peking called on MacMurray to protest this "sudden reversion to gunboat diplomacy." They warned that such a peremptory threat of force over a minor infringement of an outdated protocol would hurt legitimate American interests in China. One of them who was present observed that missionaries were closer to the changing China than the Legation. Arrogant, nagging refusal to give up privileges lowered American prestige among saner Chinese leaders. The British and even the Japanese, it was pointed out, counseled a milder course.[12]

The following day, March 18, as if to prove missionary wisdom, some two thousand students demonstrated against knuckling under to the foreigner and at least seventeen were killed. The missionary protest reached the Secretary's desk by way of parent organizations at home and the American press picked up the theme. Was the United States abandoning Kellogg's policy of "maintaining an independent attitude . . . in Chinese affairs and showing helpfulness to the Chinese, while protecting American interests?" asked a *Washington Post* correspondent.[13]

What did it all mean? the President demanded angrily one morning, brandishing a newspaper at his Acting Secretary. Coolidge was apparently satisfied by a reminder of their previous talk, but Kellogg was not so easy. He returned on March 16 and thundered at Grew, "I understand, Mr.

Secretary, that during my absence you have declared war on China." Kellogg cabled MacMurray his gratification that force had not been necessary, adding in repudiation of Grew's position, "in general it should be our policy not to use force of arms to enforce treaty rights unless such action is necessary in order to protect American lives." [14]

It is very doubtful that Grew in MacMurray's shoes would have handled the Taku problem as truculently. Less willful, he would probably have brought pressure to bear more slowly, shied away from blunt ultimatums, and not allowed himself to outdistance the pack of protocol powers. But he still would probably have used the Protocol. How different the Grew of Lausanne! He went more than halfway to conciliate revolutionary Turkish nationalism but dug in his heels against the same phenomenon in China. Of course Turkey came to Lausanne having already won its full sovereignty by force, united, determined, and oriented toward the West, while China was at a crisis of change, her future orientation very uncertain, and her ability to effect a transition in treaty relations by diplomacy non-existent. It was not a propitious moment for the Lausanne approach.

Grew may have looked at Taku something like this: beyond goodwill there was no concrete advantage in giving up those capital assets of diplomacy, treaty rights; if one right were allowed to become a dead letter, it was only a question of where the next rear-guard action would be fought; short of abandoning the whole structure, which Americans in China were far from wishing, there was little permanent goodwill to be gained and much respect for American willingness to uphold its rights to be lost. It was an orthodox approach, and at least fifteen years out of date so far as China was concerned, even though it solved the immediate problem.

The rigidity in Grew's diplomacy as Under Secretary is largely explained by the difference in environment and scope of diplomacy in the field and in Washington. Grew worked best when he faced a single diplomatic situation which he could probe through his personal relations with the individuals involved. In such a situation he was flexible, constructive, reasonable, and confident. He learned best through people, in this way often intuitively grasping a situation. Such opportunities seldom existed in Washington where events, as he put it, were "kaleidoscopic." On unfamiliar ground he was cautious and literal-minded, sticking by precedents and avoiding experiments. His orthodox view of European debts, his defense of American prestige in Persia, his conception of the United States as policeman of the Caribbean-Central American zone, and his adherence to the Boxer Protocol mark him as a traditionalist and suggest that he remained throughout his Under Secretaryship as unsure of himself as Castle had noticed him to be the first day in office. The diplomacy of cables was not his medium. Grew worked best in the field.[15]

According to MacMurray, years later, Grew's downfall as Under Secretary dated from the Taku Incident.[16] Certainly Olds came more and more to the fore in 1926. He personally handled Nicaraguan and Mexican problems. Whereas Grew seldom initialed telegrams for Kellogg, as he and Phillips had always done for Hughes, by January 1927 Olds was often signing for the Secretary. In February the British Ambassador asked Grew's permission to see Olds to find out if a certain problem could be taken up at a higher level. In March, while Grew was Acting Secretary, President Coolidge wrote Kellogg: "Mr. Olds and I are getting on very well so far trying to take care of the State Department. . . ." Kellogg began offering attractive opportunities in the field, the missions to Japan, Belgium, Canada, and Turkey. Grew turned them down one after another, chiefly because the infant Foreign Service was in an acute crisis.[17]

Grew dealt with problems of Foreign Service reorganization on two levels. All questions pertaining to assignment and promotion of officers below the rank of minister were handled by the Foreign Service Personnel Board, of which he was chairman. In the appointment of chiefs of mission, however, he served in two capacities. He shared in the recommendations which the Board was empowered to make of career officers for ministerial posts. Also, as the Secretary's immediate adviser, he could make recommendations of his own. At both levels Grew encountered difficulties which became critical by the spring of 1927, when his relations with Kellogg were already strained.

The basic issue facing the Personnel Board was the extent to which the consular and diplomatic branches of the new Foreign Service should be amalgamated by interchange of officers. The diplomats favored a minimum of transfer. They argued that only diplomacy could train the diplomat and emphasized in selection and promotion such hard-to-define qualities as tact, adaptability, background, and imagination. Their point of view was represented on the Board by Wright, Wilson, and Grew, but particularly by Grew, who spoke of himself in 1925 as the "Cerberus of the Diplomatic Service." The Under Secretary claimed that Congressman Rogers, who died in 1924, intended transfers to be made with "great discrimination." Grew pointed out that many diplomats would resign before undertaking consular assignments. Furthermore, it was "inexpedient to take men who have chosen a special line of work, and who are trained in it, and bring them over to work of another character." For Grew and the diplomats the presumption was that a man was in the right branch already unless proved otherwise.[18]

Carr was the champion of the consuls. As he said, "[T]he consular branch looks to me to fight its battles and . . . Congress will hold me largely responsible for the enforcement of the Rogers Act." He believed he knew "as well as any man living" what had been in John Jacob Rogers's mind: "The Bill was not only written and rewritten in my office until it took its final form but it became my task to carry the main burden of work in explaining its provisions to the committees of the House and Senate."

Carr agreed with Grew that the purpose of the Act was not a "scrambling" of the two services, but he would not allow a presumption in favor of an officer remaining where he was. The interest of the government was the determining factor, he argued, and that interest made it imperative for a diplomat to have considerable experience in the practical problems of foreign trade with which the consular branch dealt. Furthermore, he and the consuls were of the opinion, which they believed Congress and the public shared, that the old Diplomatic Service was snobbish and unrepresentative and would be improved by an infusion of consuls.

However, Carr was content to achieve his purpose gradually, by "evolutionary" rather than "revolutionary processes." So long as the Board made some progress toward unified procedure, he would cooperate. He and Grew became reasonably compatible. The Under Secretary paid him a graceful and appreciated tribute at a Foreign Service luncheon and, according to Carr, the two discovered a common leaning toward "spiritual, joyous, uplifting religion that demands churches with sunlight in them." [19]

Although the Board did make some progress toward unified procedure, it had no success in effecting a freer interchange of personnel. Early in 1925 it debated the switching of three consuls with three diplomats. Grew finally acquiesced, but at least two of the three diplomats did poorly in their consular assignments. A year later the shortage of diplomats raised the question of further transfers, but Grew was opposed. He preferred to wait for promising men then being trained in the new Foreign Service School.[20]

The continuing separation of the two branches had a significant effect on the relative rates of promotion in the two branches. In 1924 it was agreed that temporarily two promotion lists would be kept, one for the consuls and one for the diplomats, since personnel evaluation on the diplomatic side had been so haphazard that no basis for comparison existed. The Board set up an inspection system, but criteria used by the consular branch were not entirely adopted. The temporary double lists stayed. The unfortunate result was faster promotion of diplomats than of consuls. Heavy pruning of inefficient diplomats together with resignations created more opportunity for promotion among the diplomats. After one year of the Act, 45 of 105 diplomats had been promoted, or 43 percent, and 82 of 288 consuls, or 29 percent. By 1927 the discrepancy was greater. By then, 79 of 120 diplomats had been promoted, or 63 percent, and 135 of 365 consuls, or 37 percent.[21]

Grew and the Board were aware that the system favored the diplomats. As early as December 1924 Castle had worried that the diplomats might overreach themselves "and get a frightfully black eye." In September 1925, responding to a number of complaints from the field over the workings of the Foreign Service, Grew sent one hundred letters to top officers in both branches requesting their views. Skinner, Consul General in London, replied at length, charging a "lawless spirit" in administration of the Act by failure to integrate the two services more thoroughly, and giving figures to show how diplomats had been promoted faster than consuls during the first year. In its reply the Board accepted some of Skinner's recommendations, declared itself satisfied with the limited transfer principle, and took no note of the disproportionate number of diplomatic promotions. Indeed, the only way to have equalized promotions methodically would have been to increase transfers.[22]

The diplomats, far from being pleased with their advantage, complained frequently and bitterly. Some even objected at not being included among those invited to complain! Hugh Gibson called the Board inhuman, arbitrary, and given to playing favorites. Grew stoutly defended the Board and was distressed at the lack of service spirit shown by the diplomats. They constantly complained about their assignments. Of two officers assigned to the important Embassy at Tokyo, one grumbled that it seemed like a demotion and the other worried about the health of his family. Nevertheless, both went. Of two officers assigned to Peking, one resigned to enter law. When the other declined as well, Grew told him he was not practicing what he preached about service spirit, at which the diplomat "looked unutterably pained at my lack of comprehension." Diplomats with private means, accustomed to service largely on their own terms, welcomed the privileges of the new Service but they were slow to accept its responsibilities. They needed disciplining, yet too much of it and they might have all disappeared over the horizon like a herd of high-spirited, pure-bred horses. "I really feel," Grew was compelled to write, "that without a sense of humor on this job one would bust." [23]

Grew's position in the matter of appointments to minister and ambassador was somewhat different from that in promotions within the lower grades. Chiefs of mission were not included in the Foreign Service, the Act providing only that officers of merit might be recommended to the President for promotion to the rank of minister. Grew could participate in the recommendations of the Board, but he also felt free, as the Secretary's principal adviser, to make recommendations of his own.

Grew was deeply interested, almost obsessed, in increasing the number of career chiefs of mission. It was not a question of his own career, for he had already advanced past ministerships, nor was it a question of promoting his friends, for he lost friends. Rather it was his long-standing commitment to a fully professional Service and his conviction that unless the upper grades were opened in substantial numbers to men of ability and ambition, they would not remain in the Service or be attracted to it. He was fond of saying that every private should have a marshal's baton in his knapsack.[24]

As soon as Kellogg had taken office Grew was upon him for service appointments. He pointed out that eleven professionals had been promoted to minister under Hughes and that 634 officers were watching current changes "with the keenest interest." Kellogg managed to equal Hughes's average of three a year and by 1926 increased the number of career ministers to very nearly 50 percent. Unfortunately, five of the six appointments came before February 1926, and only one in the remainder of that year, and four of the six were to steamy Central American republics. Not only did the rate slow down as dissatisfaction within the Service built up, but also Kellogg was uncooperative with the Board. Instead of appointing from the list in the order recommended, he insisted on appointing men well known to him, in one case insisting on an officer whom the Board placed near the end of the list on account of his "snobbishness," and threatening if his wishes were not met to go outside the Service. Faced with a psychology on appointments such as this, Grew often found himself making recommendations at variance with the Board simply to preserve the service principle in appointments.[25]

Grew was equally interested in increasing the number of ambassadorial appointments, for which the Board had no authority to recommend, and frequently interceded with the Secretary to urge appointment of professional diplomats. He was successful in the appointment of Peter Jay, descendant of John Jay and graduate of Eton and Harvard, as Ambassador to Argentina. In this case he had considerable help from Jay's senators. Grew had no qualms whatever in pressing for the appointment. Since no service principle adhered to the rank, the appointment went to the man bringing to bear the strongest pressure, and Grew undoubtedly felt he had as much right to politic for a professional as outsiders did for an amateur. Only by infiltrating ambassadorial ranks with professionals could a service principle be established. However, this was Kellogg's only service appointment to ambassador by the end of 1926, as against four by Hughes.[26]

Further cause of dissatisfaction for Grew was the number of consuls appointed minister, three of the six. Particularly galling was the fact that a consul had received the only appointment in Europe. He was skeptical of the fitness of consuls for the top jobs in diplomacy, but, with the Board equally divided in allegiance, he could not oppose an equal number from each branch being recommended. By November 1926, however, the meager gains for diplomats led him to speak his mind before the Board "very frankly." Consular promotions to minister, he said, should not be made simply by reason of long and faithful service. The only criterion should be competence, and in this respect consuls by their training and experience tended to rely too much on instructions and to use too little initiative. He pointed to one consul appointed minister who failed for this reason. Diplomats, on the other hand, were steadily trained for the work of a minister.

The next list, notwithstanding Grew's statement, contained an equal number of consuls and diplomats, but in subsequent meetings greater attention was paid to the "suavity" and "diplomatic ability" of consuls.[27]

In summary, by November 1926 Grew was convinced there were too few higher promotions of the right kind: too few ministers, too few ambassadors, and too many consuls among those promoted. He was vague about just how many he wanted. He told Foreign Service officers that, while he did not expect that all posts could be filled from the ranks at the moment, he looked forward to the day "in the not too distant future when we should have developed a sufficient number of outstanding officers to justify such a course." His immediate goal was 50 percent, as against the current 40 percent. Stagnation, he warned the Secretary, was setting in in Class I of the Foreign Service, filled with twenty-three men of fifteen to forty years' experience. As he wrote Christian Herter on December 14, 1926: "I fear that this may be a rather crucial time for the Foreign Service and that unless promotions of able Service men to the higher positions are at least equal to the number of political appointments, there will be great discouragement throughout the ranks and that we shall lose some of our best men who are already beginning to question the outlook for the future." A superb opportunity to relieve the situation was at hand: four choice, vacant posts: Argentina, Canada, the Irish Free State, and Hungary.[28]

On November 29, 1926, Grew presented the Secretary with the Personnel Board's recommendations for filling the posts, together with his personal recommendation that Assistant Secretaries Leland Harrison and J. Butler Wright be sent to the field, as they had served a long time in the Department and were getting "stale." The Board's candidates were all unknown to Kellogg except one, and he rejected them all except this one, Frederick Sterling, who had been his Counselor of Embassy in London. Faced with the threat of non-service appointments, Grew took the course he had taken before and personally recommended others within the Service who were known to the secretary. It was not until February that a decision was reached, and the following nine appointments sent to the President: Robert Woods Bliss, Minister to Sweden, as Ambassador to Argentina; Harrison as minister to Sweden; Wright as Minister to Hungary; William Phillips, Ambassador to Belgium, as Minister to Canada; Hugh Gibson, Minister to Switzerland, as Ambassador to Belgium; Hugh Wilson as Minister to Switzerland; Sterling as Minister to the Irish Free State; Francis White and William Castle, in the Department, as Assistant Secretaries of State. After all the shufflings, this list represented a net gain of three service ministerships. Of the nine, six had worked closely with Kellogg and three (Phillips, Gibson, and Bliss) had secure diplomatic reputations and powerful political backing. Grew was triumphant. To Phillips he wrote:

> We are all very much elated over the recognition that has been given to the Foreign Service by recent and impending appointments. . . . A month ago it looked very doubtful if this recognition would be obtained as there was great political pressure for vacant posts, but both the President and the Secretary have come to see not only the necessity of encouraging the Service, but the favorably [sic] effect of such appointments on public opinion and so we have won out all along the line. The effect of all this on the morale of the Service will of course be immense.[29]

Had he stopped to consider just how this slate of nine might appear to Congress and the consuls he would not have been so elated. There was no consul among them. A consul had originally been included with the rest as Minister to Liberia, but he withdrew.[30] Eight of the nine were career diplomats and the ninth, Castle, was closely identified with them. Two of the ministers, Wilson and Wright, were members of the Foreign Service Personnel Board which recommended for minister. Five were graduates of Harvard, two of Yale, and one of Princeton. Nearly all had been active in securing the Diplomatic Service's interest in Foreign Service reorganization. They were all members in good standing of the "club," most of them closely connected by friendships. They all had considerable private incomes. White came from a "fox and hounds" Maryland family. Wright liked to meet dignitaries at Union Station attired as follows: "Bond Street topper, cutaway, tailored in Savile Row, cream-colored gloves and malacca stick." Harrison's haughty manner had already aroused the wrath of The Inquiry and Woodrow Wilson on the way to Paris. Castle had reportedly said that only men with large incomes should be appointed diplomats. Gibson had spoken about homes with "tradition," with or without butlers and footmen. The diplomats had never presented so large and inviting a target.[31]

Grew had been amply forewarned of the criticism that such a slate of appointments would elicit. In June 1925 he had heard rumbles from Capitol Hill about too many high appointments from the Service, and in the fall reported "growlings" that a "small clique" composed of himself, Wright, and Wilson were deciding all such appointments. At the same time he was well aware of complaints from consuls that too many diplomats were being promoted. On December 14, 1926, Congressman Charles Edwards wrote complaining about promotional policies and seeking information. The reply was substantially the same as the one given complaints from within the Service a year earlier.[32]

Finally on February 16, 1927, five days after the big promotion list had been agreed upon, Edwards introduced a resolution in the House of Representatives calling for an investigation of diplomatic appointments. Grew suspected that Edwards and others in Congress were obtaining information from a "poison squad" of three consuls assigned to the Department who went "sneaking up" to Capitol Hill like "contemptible moles." Rumor had it that Carr was involved, but he denied it as "bunk." Whatever the source, it was clear that Congress scented game and was off in full cry.[33]

On March 3 came sensational news that lent substance to rumors, commanded headlines, and focused public attention on the State Department. The *New York Times* reported that three Foreign Service Officers serving in Latin America had resigned, charging that diplomats of wealth and influence were selected for easy berths in overstaffed European posts. One of these three was Lawrence Dennis, First Secretary at Managua, Nicaragua, who, according to the *Washington Post* of March 11, inveighed against "white-spatted cliques utterly unfitted for mental exertion." Such charges, said the *Times*, "promise to lend impetus to unrest in Congress and some parts of the business world over the conduct of the diplomatic service under the new Rogers Act."

Dennis, who figured prominently in "the famous State Department smash of 1927," later turned to writing and became America's leading intellectual Fascist, according to *Life* magazine. A graduate of Exeter and Harvard, he entered diplomacy after World War I and received a series of mostly disagreeable assignments: Rumania, Honduras, Haiti, and Nicaragua. He received no promotion under the Rogers Act, even though as Chargé d'Affaires during the revolution in Nicaragua he had work of great responsibility and delicacy.[34]

Dennis was left in charge at Managua after the United States had refused to recognize Emiliano Chamorro, who came to power by a *coup d'état* in January 1926. Chamorro's government teetered without American blessing and the vice-president under the former regime took the field to regain power. This man, Juan Sacasa, was regarded with a "cold and fishy eye" by Kellogg and Olds, who suspected him of being supplied with guns and Bolshevist propaganda from Mexico. It seemed imperative for a safe constitutional regime to be set up in Nicaragua. On November 2, 1926, Dennis was advised by the Department that if the Congress of Nicaragua were to choose a new president and vice-president, the United States would grant recognition, and if that choice happened to be Adolfo Diaz, a conservative whom Dennis had been strongly advocating, such a choice would be a "wise" one. On November 11, Diaz was chosen, but by January 1927 American marines were landing to keep him in power and Kellogg was facing a storm of criticism from Congress for his intervention. In February 1927 Dennis was recalled, a move interpreted by the *New York Times* as "possibly indicating a desire to facilitate adjustment of the Nicaraguan problem," since he had been accused of "influencing the selection and recognition of Diaz." [35]

Dennis, probably bitter over his distasteful assignments and being made the scapegoat for Kellogg's Nicaraguan policy, not only resigned, attacking

Foreign Service personnel policies, but also let it be known that he had a "mystery document" which purported to show that "in the name of Secretary Kellogg, pressure [was] to be exerted in the election of Adolfo Diaz." Washington denied any such document existed but ordered Dennis to leave ship in Miami and come directly to Washington. The *Washington Post* found State Department officials in a "daze" over the Dennis affair. Some could only "shrug silently and roll their eyes." On March 21 he emerged from a conference with Kellogg, denied the existence of the alleged document, and denied having made any criticisms of the Foreign Service. He was shortly thereafter assigned to the Embassy in Paris, but resigned to enter business. The Department had not, so far as the evidence discloses, ordered Dennis to intervene and secure the election of Diaz, but it had encouraged the event. In any case, the secrecy of its instructions was maintained, but Dennis's reassignment to Paris seemed a tacit admission of the truth of his charges against the Personnel Board.[36]

Meanwhile, a news service feature writer directed public attention at Grew. He pictured Kellogg and Grew as feuding and Grew "doggedly fighting appointment as Ambassador to Turkey. . . ." Grew and Wilson were accused of being heads of an "inner circle of social diplomats which has set the well-to-do diplomats over the hard-working consuls." Coincidentally the specter of the Copenhagen Incident returned. Apparently some member of Congress had asked about it at one of Daisy Borden Harriman's parties, for on March 22, 1927, Grew wrote her a long letter explaining the "wretched affair." Grew confessed in one of the understatements of his career that his job at the moment "was pretty hard sledding from many points of view." [37]

He was in no position to resist Carr now and Carr was ready to act. The champion of the consuls confided to his diary that he hated fighting his colleagues, but could not well do differently. Rogers's widow, Edith Nourse Rogers, was reporting talk among Congressmen of repealing the Foreign Service Act. Another Congressman was warning that recent appointments smacked of "too much exclusive social politics." Carr made up his mind to secure redress for the consuls.[38]

The issue was decided at a climactic night meeting in Wright's home on March 30. Grew opened by saying that he was astonished to learn from figures just compiled that diplomats had been promoted twice as fast as consuls, but suggested that a single list would not have made any difference, since diplomats might have been rated higher. Carr and the consular members replied that actually some diplomats with lower ratings than consuls in the same class had been promoted. The real fault they pointed out was the double promotion lists. Carr raised the question of their legal validity, and Grew wondered why it had not been raised earlier, to which Carr replied that this was because they had assumed the double lists would last only until efficiency records on the diplomatic side were improved. Still fighting, Grew objected to the single list as a "great departure," and suggested they lay the whole problem before Congress.

Wilson then made what Grew later admitted was a most unfortunate remark, given "in a burst of honest frankness — he believed it intensely and thought the time had come to call a spade a spade." It was not simply a question of promotion for diplomats, said Wilson. "They have a higher thought which enures to the good of the Service. They have all felt that they belonged to a pretty good club. That feeling has fostered a healthy *esprit de corps*." The adoption of the single list would end it. Carr thereupon called spades spades himself:

> Congress passed this law with the idea that it would help the consular branch. They did not pass it primarily for the improvement of the diplomatic branch . . . Mr. Rogers said that the bill was calculated to get rid of that something in the diplomatic service which he did not like. He said he would like to send a lot of those young men in the diplomatic branch who thought they were so important to Singapore or some other consular post where they would do some real work. That is the kind of spirit which pushed the bill through Congress. . . .[39]

The diplomats did not have a leg to stand on. Grew suggested that the Board ask the Department's solicitor for a ruling on the single list, and so ended the meeting and the fight. The solicitor ruled for the single list and it was adopted May 2. In reparation for promotions denied under the double lists, forty-four consuls were promoted.[40]

Criticism was by no means assuaged. More resolutions were introduced in Congress. In June Vice-President Charles Dawes warned against appointing too many career diplomats to top posts. Placing small men in high places could inflict incalculable damage in critical times, he said. In October the President was reported as being "bitterly disturbed by incessant attacks upon the Foreign Service," and threatening to step in himself to reform it. He began filling posts from outside. In December the Senate launched an investigation which charged that diplomats on the Personnel Board had promoted their own number faster than consuls and contrived to obtain choice top posts for themselves. The following year legislation was introduced to amend the Foreign Service Act, and was finally passed three years later.[41]

The reorganization was designed to ensure integration and prevent favoritism. Under the new scheme, power over appointments, transfers, and promotions was entirely taken away from Foreign Service Officers and vested in a Personnel Board composed of three Assistant Secretaries, substantially in accordance with Carr's original plan. As chairman of the Board, as well as of the Board of Examiners and the Foreign Service School,

Carr was in a position to shape the Service the way he wanted it, which was the way Congress wanted it too. During the subsequent decade unified procedures were adopted and transfers and dual commissions steadily increased. An invisible gulf remained in the personal relationships of officers of the old services, but so far as law and administration could go, integration was finally accomplished.[42]

The incessant attacks on the Foreign Service throughout 1927 resulted in a significant shift in editorial opinion on professional diplomacy. The *Literary Digest*, with its wide coverage of newspaper editorials, had often in the past described public approval of career appointments, but in March 1927 it reported that recent appointments had met with criticism. In June it found considerable agreement with Dawes's criticisms. The *New York Times* as late as February 1927 had approved career appointments, but in June it agreed with Dawes about the weakness of career diplomats. The same was true of the magazines. The *Outlook*, a steady advocate of reform, also agreed with Dawes that too many career men should not be appointed ministers and ambassadors. The *Nation* had consistently argued for permanency in diplomatic appointments, but in 1927 it was "out of the frying pan and into the fire." Years of agitation, the *Nation* reported, had finally resulted in a permanent Service "only two years ago . . . and behold, there is growing dissatisfaction. . . ." The editorial concluded that "experience shows the career diplomat is too often dull and routinized." *Colliers*, also on the reform bandwagon, got off with Dawes too. "You will never find boldness or imagination in a career diplomat," it warned. Similar shifts of editorial opinion appeared in the *North American Review*, *Harper's*, *World's Work*, and the *Independent*. Perhaps the *Philadelphia Inquirer* summed up the change of opinion best on October 15, 1928, when it said: "The word 'career' possessed honorable meaning up to about two years ago. . . ."[43]

Grew had failed. A minimum of transfer between the branches and double promotion lists had kept the diplomatic branch intact at the cost of indefensible promotional preferment for diplomats. A substantial increase in service chiefs of mission had been achieved, but in such a way as to incur the wrath of Congress and to weaken public support for career diplomacy.

The basic problem was not, as it seemed, one of favoritism but one of integration, of whether there would be two services or one. Grew's overriding concern was to establish professional diplomacy with the acquired skills, experience, spirit, and sense of profession of the old Diplomatic Service. He deeply and sincerely believed that diplomacy was a distinct endeavor requiring distinct qualities and experience. From his point of view the promotions and appointments of 1924-27 were based on ability or seniority or both among the diplomats, and therefore were entirely justified. However, he and the diplomats had not made a convincing public case for separate treatment, and the outsider saw only favoritism and social preferment. In spite of all the debate and discussion that went into Foreign Service reform, one has the depressing sense that the American public was no more, and perhaps less, enlightened about the nature and requirements of diplomatic work at the end of the twenties than at the beginning. As for Grew, his opinion did not change. A year later he judged that the Rogers Act "had been tried in the balance and found wanting." He still preferred two examinations, two promotion lists, and very limited transfer, in short two services.[44]

It was obvious by April 1927 that it had come time for him to go. His acceptance of Kellogg's offer of the Embassy in Turkey provoked new charges from Congress about self-promotion of diplomats, but Kellogg, who was glad to see him go, to be sure, but loyal and kindly too, was undeterred. In July Grew's daughter Lilla married Jay Pierrepont Moffat, a descendant of John Jay and a graduate of Groton and Harvard. Then the family, now only four, boarded the *Leviathan*. Trouble dogged him to the pier. There were reports that an Armenian fanatic might try to assassinate the first American Ambassador to Kemalist Turkey and he had to be accompanied by a bodyguard. Even the Statue of Liberty was shrouded in mist. But Grew with his boundless, boyish optimism could think only of shaking loose the "dry, dry, dust of the old Department," of being able to call his soul his own once more, of the new adventure in an exotic land. Diplomacy, he told a farewell luncheon at the Department, was no bed of roses, but it was the "most splendid, the most exhilarating, the most stimulating, the most satisfying and withal the most useful form of service" he could imagine.[45]

PART THREE

Ambassador to Turkey

(1927 - 1932)

NINE

The Missionary Problem in Turkey

THE Grews left New York July 31, 1927, and arrived in Istanbul on September 18. The trip was a vacation. The crossing to England was smooth, accommodations luxurious, and companions such as Percy Grainger congenial. In London, Grew bought suits in Savile Row, wines for the Embassy at Fortnum and Mason's, hats at Heath's, ties at Beale and Inman's, presents at Asprey's, "and henceforth, oh Lord, lead us not into temptation." Then Paris, Geneva, and Venice.

The family stayed several weeks in Venice, long enough to get sunburned at the Lido and then peel "merrily, like the bell in the Campanile." They took a gondola on the Grand Canal one evening and drifted past softly lighted barges filled with serenaders. He went with Anita to Zermatt for a try at climbing the Matterhorn but had to settle for the Riffelhorn, "a dizzying climb up sheer precipice." The Grews wanted most of all to visit their daughter Edith's grave, which they found marked by a white marble cross shaded by cypresses in a little, walled Protestant cemetery on a lovely island near Venice. They visited this spot of "perfect peacefulness" again and again and eased their loss. It would "never be so hard again." As a memorial they gave five thousand dollars to the British-American Hospital. Then they sailed by way of the Corinth Canal and Athens to their destination.

The American Embassy in Istanbul stood shining white on the heights of Pera. At sunset the view from the terrace was breathtaking. He could see the graceful curve of the Golden Horn, flat calm, a polished sheet of gold trisected by bridges leading over to Stamboul. The ancient city of Constantine rose on low hills behind the Horn, a panorama of crouching mosques and spidery minarets. On the left, above the Seraglio, stood Santa Sophia and the six minarets of Sultan Ahmet on the site of the ancient Palace of Daphne. Straight ahead was the delicate Yeni Jami, mosque of princesses, flanked above and behind by the mosques of Nouri Osmanieh and Sultan

Bayezid II. To the right, crowning a hill, was the massive mosque of Suleiman the Magnificent; beyond in the setting sun, those of Mohammed II and Selim I, each on a hilltop. The city, in deep mauve giving way to gray-black, was sharply etched against a sky that modulated from light green to blue, saffron, rose, and then flaming red. Over Seraglio Point he saw hills rising to the Anatolian Mountains of Asia, above which rose thick clouds touched with fire, turning to shadows resembling a huge fortress in the sky. It was Valhalla, "a sunset of the gods."[1]

Grew must have felt that to be an ambassador in Istanbul was to be an ambassador in a peculiarly evocative and significant sense. The city was a caravanserai of history and prehistory, of cultures, religions, and peoples. With its unique geographical position, it had been the keenly sought prize of mercantile and imperialist ambitions; generations of ambassadors had struggled quietly at the Sublime Porte. Envoys to Suleiman the Magnificent in the sixteenth century found him seated on a low couch covered with exquisite rugs and cushions. They made the deepest bows, came forward to kiss the Sultan's hand, and were led away to dine on a service of silver and gold.[2]

Unfortunately the capital of the Turkish Republic was not at Istanbul but at Ankara in the heart of Anatolia. Thence Grew journeyed a few days after arrival, feeling as though he should be carrying a Turkish Baedecker instead of the credentials of an arriving ambassador. The train was somewhat uncomfortable but the scenery was wild and beautiful. Subsequently he made the fifteen-hour trip more enjoyable by shutting himself in his compartment and changing to comfortable clothes. Fortified with a picnic lunch, a pint of champagne iced in a cracker tin, a fine cigar, and a Flit gun, he would settle down to a good detective story.

He found Ankara bleak, raw, and pretentious. Situated on the desert-like Anatolian plateau a hundred miles from the nearest forest, the capital was hot and dry in summer and bitterly cold in winter. It was past and future Turkey in uncomfortable and uncertain present. Shepherds herded Angora goats down unpaved village streets past monumental buildings being erected to make Ankara the show place of modern Turkey. The Embassy was a rented, two-story villa standing next to what had been a mosquito-infested swamp and might have been a park except that its soil was too salty for anything to grow. Some distance away was the "greener and fresher" suburb of Cankaya where the President lived and most of the diplomatic missions were situating.[3]

Mustafa Kemal received Grew at Cankaya on October 12, 1927. The audience was pinched and formal. Grew, wearing the white tie and tails prescribed for such occasions, made three bows at predetermined spots and gave his speech in English. After formalities and translations, they shook hands and had a minute of polite conversation in Turkish and French, whereupon Grew presented his staff. What impressed him about the President of Turkey were "his curious light grey eyes, his high and prominent cheek bones and his firm, determined mouth and jaw — altogether the face of a fighter." The president remained impassive and unsmiling throughout, "his mouth compressed into a hard, straight line." [4]

In Kemal, Grew confronted one of the outstanding leaders of revolutionary nationalism in the twentieth century. A man of great force and courage, possessed of audacious goals, yet cunning in the acquisition of power and calculating in its use, the President of Turkey was a rare combination of the lion and the fox. The international security which Grew had watched Turkey gain at Lausanne had left Kemal free to consolidate his power at home and start building a viable, homogeneous nation modeled on the West in the ruins of the Ottoman Empire. Already he had severely weakened the forces of traditionalism and orthodoxy by striking at Islamic institutions in Turkey. He had abolished religious schools and courts, dervish orders, and the Caliphate itself. Symbolic of his drive against the old order was his ban of that distinctive mark of a Moslem, the fez. Against the power of Islam he moved a step at a time, but rebellion and conspiracy he cut down ruthlessly. On the constructive side, he was rapidly setting up the apparatus of republican government and adopting Western modes such as the Gregorian calendar, the Swiss civil code, and the international clock. Turkey henceforth would tick according to Greenwich mean time.

The problem was to implant the substance as well as the form of Western society. Kemal was in fact a dictator ruling by control of the Army. Emergency powers and careful selection of candidates for the Grand National Assembly assured him his way with a semblance of constitutionalism. The press was rigidly controlled. The Turkish peasant, though adoring Turkey's warrior leader, had no conception, most often no awareness, of what he was trying to accomplish. Kemal apparently wanted to work toward democracy, but loosening the reins now might slow down reform and alter its nature. He was determined to maintain the pace and orientation of change.

If the substance of modern Western society was lacking in 1927, no challenge existed to its form or progenitor. That October, in a brief calm before new trials, the President delivered a six-day speech before the Grand National Assembly in which he detailed the history of the revolution. Watching from the diplomatic loge on the first morning of the speech was the new American Ambassador.[5]

Unchallenged one-man rule certainly simplified Grew's mission; he was never in doubt where ultimate power lay. Another advantage was that Kemal's faithful lieutenant, Ismet Inönü, was Prime Minister. Grew's friendly adversary of Lausanne days greeted him with the "same pleasant smile and twinkling of the eyes." [6]

Further simplifying Grew's mission was the peaceful bent of Turkish foreign policy. Kemal's overriding aim was to assure the independence and interests of the Republic, not by expansion or truculence, but by winning the confidence and respect of other nations. As Dankwart A. Rustow says, this aim was pursued "with a level-headedness and steadfastness, a sober acceptance of limitations and a shrewd acceptance of opportunities, that are far from characteristic of all nations that have so recently asserted their sovereignty." One by one Turkey was settling the problems left over from Lausanne. The exchange of minorities with Greece was a pathetic task but led to a stabilization of relations between the two countries. Turkey sought friendly accords with her Near Eastern and Mediterranean neighbors and maintained cordial official relations with the Soviet Union. Consular agreements, treaties of commerce and navigation, and non-aggression pacts made for "slow-moving, tedious, and complex" diplomacy, as Rustow notes. Nevertheless, they won Turkey a solid basis for her international relations and the reputation of a peaceful, reliable nation. In the several sunny years between the political and economic crises closing out one world war and those presaging a second, the time of the Kellogg-Briand Pact, the international climate was benevolently disposed.[7]

The firm, central direction and peaceful objectives of Turkish policy and the favorable international climate made Grew's mission easier, but it remained a challenging one. The problem of minorities continued to plague Turkish-American relations. When Grew's Lausanne Treaty was submitted to the Senate, Armenian-Americans organized an aggressive campaign to defeat it, playing on the popular image of the Terrible Turk. The Democrats picked up the issue in the campaign of 1924, denouncing the Administration for bartering American rights and betraying Armenia for the Chester Concession. As Under Secretary, Grew urged support for his treaty but it went to a lingering death. When the Senate finally voted on January 18, 1927, the treaty failed to secure the necessary two-thirds majority by six votes.[8]

This bitter personal defeat for Grew left relations without a treaty basis. American businesses, missions, schools, and colleges had no specific guarantees except those existing on a year-to-year basis through the exchange of diplomatic notes avowing adherence to the principles of international law and the unratified Lausanne agreements. Grew would have to renegotiate a solid treaty basis for relations. He would have to ensure, not only that each American institution in Turkey was properly protected, but that, as each shaped its future during this general crystallization of relations, its activities would strengthen ties between the two countries. He would be building relations from the ground up.

Grew's first preoccupation was to secure confirmation of his appointment as ambassador. His recess appointment was submitted to the Senate in December 1927, where it came under a crossfire of criticism. On the one hand, opponents of the Lausanne Treaty denounced the exchange of notes and ambassadors as an Executive attempt to circumvent the Senate and establish relations on the Lausanne basis without a treaty. On the other hand, Senator Pat Harrison found the nomination a point of departure for his investigation of favoritism in the promotion of diplomats while Grew was chairman of the Personnel Board. Again Grew found it necessary to explain the Copenhagen Incident.[9]

He could do little but worry and wait. The Turks were understandably sensitive to public criticism in America of the exchange of ambassadors. He tried to calm ruffled pride by sending the Foreign Ministry French translations of American press comments that were favorable to resumption of relations. These found their way into the Turkish press and apparently had a quieting effect. After a while criticism died down in the United States. In the Senate it developed that Harrison had no personal objection to Grew and that Borah favored confirmation. Once the personnel investigation was satisfied, the Senate voted to confirm Grew's appointment. However, it had acted in the absence of Senator William H. King of Utah, the prime opponent of the Lausanne Treaty. King protested, the confirmation was withheld from the *Congressional Record*, and a motion of reconsideration was introduced. On April 13, 1927, this was defeated and Grew, having survived several purgatories, finally emerged "in an alleged heaven of national confidence and confirmed ambassadorship." Eleven months after his appointment he could start drawing pay as Ambassador to Turkey.[10]

In January 1928, while Grew was still awaiting confirmation of his appointment, an incident at the American missionary school at Brusa brought about a sharp crisis in American-Turkish relations and threatened the entire future of American educational endeavor in Turkey. American teachers at the school had apparently been proselytizing three Moslem girls. The teachers had prayed with the girls one Easter morning, had talked intimately with them about religion, and had given them the New Testament and religious pamphlets. The missionary work had all been outside school hours, but it had all been recorded in the girls' diaries, which they kept under their pillows. Classmates had stolen the diaries and given them to a disgruntled teacher who passed them on to the Ministry of Public Information.[11]

The incident coincided with the "first ranging shots" of a campaign to replace Arabic script with Roman in Turkey. Kemal and Ismet were also preparing for the formal disestablishment of Islam as the national religion of Turkey. The nation was about to make another surge of modernization and secularization. The evidence from Brusa served that purpose well. It provided an opportunity to dramatize in that citadel of Moslem orthodoxy that the government could be as severe toward Christians as Moslems, that in fact the enemy was not Islam itself, but any influence foreign to the pragmatic, secular, nationalist ethos of Kemalist Turkey. The government accordingly launched an investigation of American schools and a vitriolic press campaign against foreign schools. The moment of silence before meals, no school on Sunday, the singing of "Ave Maria" and "I Would Be True," Bibles in Turkish, even *Silas Marner* and Longman's Dictionary were attacked as evidence of insidious Christian propaganda. The government closed the school at Brusa and announced its intention to prosecute the American teachers involved. The school incident, Grew wrote, was "bad, very bad."[12]

Grew had little sympathy for the missionaries and little hope for the rest of the American schools, but he was deeply anxious about the effect of the incident on American colleges in Turkey, on American public opinion, and on his confirmation by the Senate. Stabilization of Turkish-American relations, his whole mission, depended on how he handled the crisis. Given wide discretion by the Department of State, he determined to lie low at first and wait for the press campaign to subside. "Our position is weak," he wrote, "and an intense nationalistic feeling . . . hard to cope with." The government would ultimately appreciate his having kept out of the row when it was at its height, he argued, and would be more kindly disposed when the time for action was ripe. "The first gleam of light" appeared February 5 when an officially inspired article pointed out that foreign schools were needed until Turkey developed her own system. The following night he took the train to Ankara.[13]

The next day Grew saw the Foreign Minister, Tevfik Rusdu Bey. Tevfik, a voluble little doctor of medicine, had already proved stronger on promise than performance, so Grew tried to be specific in his requests. At the same time, determined to avoid a square-off between the two governments, he was friendly and informal. After describing the mitigating circumstances of the Brusa Incident and the possible repercussions in the United States, he asked for assurance on four points: that an effort would be made to stop the press campaign, that other American institutions would not be prosecuted, that in due time consideration would be given to reopening Brusa, and that the teachers would not be prosecuted. Tevfik was amicable and gave assurances on all points except the last. He gave the impression, however, that if the teachers were convicted, the penalty would be nominal. All things considered, it was a very encouraging talk.[14]

Grew was still not accustomed to the "wild and woolly" diplomacy of the Turkish Foreign Minister. On February 10 Tevfik admitted that he had gone too far in promising to reopen Brusa. Furthermore, the press campaign continued and inspectors hauled down the American flag at another American school and demanded that classes be held on Sundays. Fred F. Goodsell, the representative in Turkey of the American Board of Commissioners for Foreign Missions, was deeply discouraged. He feared that his

Board would close all the schools on the Sunday issue. Washington warned of the incident's "tremendous" news value and reported the first telegrams to Congressmen. Grew decided that another trip to Ankara and stronger representations were in order.[15]

This time Grew felt he needed some immediate, affirmative action to reassure Americans that the Turkish government was not opposed to American schools as such but only to religious instruction. A handsome gesture now would be particularly useful with Senate debate on his confirmation expected any day. Accordingly he suggested to Tevfik that the government permit the opening of two American schools, Talas and Marash, which had been closed since the World War. Goodsell and the Ambassador had been trying to secure their reopening for some time without success. The next day he carried his representations to Ismet as well.[16]

Perhaps he took his case to Kemal himself. He spent the time between his visits to Tevfik and Ismet at an all-night poker party with the President and the Minister of Public Instruction. Whether or not the problem actually came up during the long night, Grew could not resist the image of the American Ambassador gambling with Turkey's rulers for a kitty of missionary schools while champagne flowed freely and the dictator's pet girl friend slept on a nearby couch. Probably a fanciful picture so far as the stakes were concerned, but an appealing one to this fugitive from Puritan Boston.[17]

His representations seemed at first to have some effect. A few days later he was informed that the Ministry of Public Instruction would permit, not Talas and Marash, but two other American schools, Sivas and a vocational section at Merzifoun, to reopen. Grew immediately told the local Associated Press correspondent of this *beau geste* in order to get the advantage of publicity in the United States. It turned out to be a hollow gesture, however, because Sivas was rented to the Ministry of Public Health until 1930, and the government itself had already requested the reopening of Merzifoun. At first Grew thought Sivas had been a mistake: the Minister of Public Instruction "could hardly have been so puerile as to authorize something he knew was impossible of fulfillment." But no mistake had been made and Grew was forced to conclude that he was a victim of pure Machiavellianism. "I have done my best," he wrote at the end of February, "and have met almost complete failure." [18]

He did not give up, however. During March and April the atmosphere improved slowly. The press campaign and investigations ceased. On April 30, after Grew was safely confirmed, the American teachers were convicted and sentenced to three days' confinement in their homes and a nominal fine. Grew reminded Tevfik of his promise again and again, but stayed away from Ankara himself. The Turks yielded inch by grudging inch. On May 11 Tevfik promised to recommend the opening of some other school in place of Sivas. On August 20 the opening of Talas was authorized, but no permit was forthcoming. On September 28 Grew saw Ismet and the next day Tevfik. A phone call elicited the information that Talas should get in touch with the Ministry of Public Instruction. By now thoroughly exasperated, Grew told the Foreign Minister that Talas had been in constant touch with the Ministry and that there was "clearly some incomprehensible misunderstanding." Another phone conversation produced the assurance that the permit would be issued without delay, and this time the promise was kept. The mention of Ismet's name on the phone led Grew to suspect that it was his previous talk with the Prime Minister that finally swung the matter.[19]

Almost a year had passed since Grew made his first representation about reopening of schools, yet in October 1928 he was almost where he had started in November 1927. Talas was reopened but Brusa was closed. The net gain was a vocational section of Merzifoun, asked for by the government itself. Yet his diplomacy had been far from unsuccessful. The pathetic indiscretions of the missionary teachers at Brusa had threatened serious damage to the relations of the two nations. By persistence, patience, and friendliness, by keeping in the background except for timely, informal representations, Grew prevented foreclosure of the American educational effort in Turkey and at the same time kept the way open for negotiating a treaty basis for future relations. He remained constantly aware that the underlying purpose of the Turkish government was severely to restrict and regulate foreign school activity in Turkey, and that no gain was possible except through Turkish goodwill.[20]

The schools crisis of 1927-28 was Grew's most severe but not his only problem involving American educational and missionary activity in Turkey. In 1929 it became apparent that the government might close down American schools and colleges simply by levying a gift tax on their incomes. Grew wrote Tevfik warning him that the tax would close American schools and colleges and arguing that the funds in question were not free gifts in the meaning of Turkish law but operating expenses deriving from investments in the United States.

The issue came to a head in April 1930, when an American college in Istanbul was assessed a gift tax of approximately fifty thousand dollars. Grew promptly went to Ankara and saw Tevfik and then Ismet. Again avoiding a formal, official approach, he appealed for their sympathy and help in a matter affecting, he now emphasized, relations between the two countries. Ismet promised with a smile and a wink that when the matter came before the Council of State he would see that justice was done. In July the Council decided that the tax did not apply to money received by a school or college in a current account from a parent organization. Equally important with saving the particular institution was the fact that the Turkish government had taken a general position favoring prolonged American educational activity in Turkey.[21]

American schools and colleges were a perennial problem for Grew. Now the problem was a tax on teachers' salaries, now delay in permission to build a library, now legal complications over property holding, now insistence that certain courses be taught by Turkish teachers. Listening to the educators' problems made Grew feel like a father confessor to the American colony. He was glad to give advice but preferred to remain in the background himself, letting the institutions deal directly with Ankara. He felt that by saving his ammunition he would be more influential when an important case or crisis arose. Whenever he intervened he warned of the controversy's cost in terms of friendly relations with the United States.[22]

Gradually the situation improved. In 1929 he noted that chauvinism was waning due to Turkey's improving international position and increased domestic security. That year the government approved the conduct of religious exercises for non-Moslems. Early in 1931 a potentially dangerous incident occurred at the American college in Izmir when a young American instructor caught boys cheating and made derogatory remarks about Turkish honesty which were passed on to the authorities. However, nothing serious developed. At the instigation of the Embassy, the teacher was allowed to leave Turkey quietly. When a possibly related press attack opened against the college a few months later, Grew advised forcing a showdown at Ankara by threatening to close the college. When the advice was followed, the government indicated it positively wished the college to remain open. The Turks seemed to be realizing the value of foreign schools while their own system was in its infancy. Problems were handled quietly and constructively. Participants were more confident and casual. Some form of American educational enterprise seemed likely to remain a part of the new Turkey. The question was what kind.[23]

Seeking a constructive approach to the problem led Grew down bypaths unfamiliar to a diplomatist of the old school. It was obvious that the problem was one of cultural nationalism. What the Turks found objectionable was a foreign cultural environment for their impressionable youth. History taught from a foreign point of view, class distinctions engendered by instruction in foreign languages, music, and social manners, the fundamental reorientation of the human being under Christian influence all threatened to turn the young person away from his country and make him dissatisfied with it, in the view of the environmentalists of modern Turkey.[24]

Grew felt that the Turks had a perfect right to develop their own culture or any culture they chose. "When the Turks want our Anglo-Saxon schools to go, they have only to say the word. We can't force them on the country against its will." The only hopeful approach for the Americans was to work in close cooperation with the government, preparing youth for maximum fitness as citizens of the Republic, "totally disregarding religion as such but having in mind that Christian ethics, even if not labelled as such, are the soundest basis for any such training." This approach was perfectly consistent with Grew's own experience. What he remembered of Groton was not bib-and-tucker Episcopalianism but the rugged inculcation of values on the playing field and insistent calls to the service of the nation.[25]

He recognized, however, that it would be very difficult for American educational institutions to adjust to the new approach. Robert College, the citadel of American educational influence in the Near East, was "permeated" with strict, teetotaling, fundamentalist Protestantism. The American colleges tended to remain aloof from Turkish life. Administration was lax, the quality of instruction poor; the older teachers were often narrow and out of step with the times, while the younger were often naïvely idealistic and immature. All in all, Grew concluded, the colleges and schools reflected little credit on the United States and offered little hope for adjustment.[26]

He was sympathetic with the dilemma of Christian educators, most of whom wished to remain in Turkey. Without their Christian mission they saw no use for their institutions, yet most of them acknowledged that proselytizing was impossible. The practice of "unnamed Christianity," that is, quietly leading exemplary Christian lives instead of preaching or teaching Christianity, was a torturing compromise of their commitment to be Christ's witness. As Grew recognized, they often felt compelled to label their ethics as Christian ethics. Often implanting them was "only half the game," only the means to ultimate conversion.[27]

The answer, Grew believed, was a new brand of American educators, men and women who would dig down deeply into the life of Turkey, develop close relations with government officials, and "regard themselves as members of the crew, pulling with the Turks instead of against them, so far as possible setting the pace and rhythm." Those unable to adapt themselves should be recalled and replaced by men and women of broader cultural background.[28]

So seriously did he believe the quality of personnel to affect American prestige that he felt impelled to intervene in the succession to the presidency of Robert College. Dr. Caleb Gates, the president, was near retirement and anxious that his successor carry on his missionary ideals. Grew had an affection for this grand old man of the missionary world, but judged that he had too much "old-time Christian fighting blood." The college seemed to be in a continual tug-of-war with the Turkish government. In 1930 Gates's retirement was postponed for two years, to the disappointment of the government, which had been favorably impressed with the man thought to be his successor. Grew was warned that foreign institutions with a religious bias would be in serious trouble after the expiration of the Lausanne guarantees in 1931. After some hesitation, for disloyalty to Dr. Gates went against the grain, he wrote a frank letter to missionary headquarters in Boston and to the president of Union Theological Seminary urging the choice of a man amenable to the Turkish point of view. Whatever influence these letters may have had, Grew was delighted with the ultimate choice of Dr. Paul Munroe, who in 1932 was appointed head of both Robert College and Istanbul College for Women.[29]

A more congenial medium for communicating his views on American schools and colleges was the commencement speech. He had many such opportunities and he grasped them. He dwelt on the simple virtues he treasured from his own experience: optimism, persistence, patience, faith, strength of body, and loyalty to country. He congratulated the students on living in a period of such exciting progress for their country and he urged them to put their talents to work for Turkey. His object was to preach "patriotism pure and simple in the face of the public clamor against our institutions on the ground that they educate their pupils away from the country." Government officials, to whom he sent copies of the speeches, made their pleasure known.[30]

Easing American educational enterprise in Turkey from the old way to the new was the work of many, but Grew played a significant role. He recognized that the continuation of this potentially valuable work depended entirely on Turkish goodwill. With tact and skill he prevented an exacerbation of the problem and improved the atmosphere for change. He worked steadily to promote a modern approach to American cultural endeavor abroad. Missionary executives themselves applauded his part. Grew had been "most generous and kind and wise," Goodsell wrote the Secretary of State. Goodsell's successor in charge of the Turkey missions made this eloquent testimonial: "I have learned and seen the power of fairness and generosity in Government relationships, leading to a confidence in him and his character that has meant much to all American interests. Again and again, Turkish officials have given me their witness in this regard." [31]

TEN

The Groundwork for Turkish-American Friendship

REPRESENTING American business interests in Turkey was no less difficult than representing American educational institutions. The problems were less politically sensitive but also less manageable. Whether by success or failure, business enterprise could more weightily affect future relations than could cultural endeavors, yet the outlook for trade and investment became less and less promising. Grew was prepared to grant American businessmen the support they had a right to expect, but he was determined not to endanger his overall objective of establishing a permanent foundation for Turkish-American relations. If necessary, trade must wait until diplomacy prepared the way.

American businesses already established in Turkey were in frequent need of Embassy help. Local officials subjected them to arbitrary and confiscatory fines, a form of baksheesh Grew suspected, on top of heavy taxes. Though he often regarded these levies as outrageous, "rank banditry," he moved deliberately. He insisted that the companies first exhaust all other remedies. When he did intercede it was by written communication, not in person. It was important to "reserve our ammunition" and not run in time and again with niggling complaints the way ambassadors did when he was Under Secretary.[1]

In 1931 Washington intimated that he should become more forceful. The Chief of the Near Eastern Division wrote confidentially to suggest that missionaries, and by implication other Americans, should be less apologetic and humble. Instead of taking "every knock they get from the Turks lying down," they should force a showdown. Grew gathered that the Department felt the Turks were "protesting the utmost friendship" but doing little to translate this into "concrete fact." After considerable soul-searching, he concluded that he had done all he profitably could, but for his next business protest he chose the more formal medium of a diplomatic note. This was no more successful. Turkey at the time of his departure seemed "just as full of corruption" as in the old days and a hazardous place to do business.[2]

Grew was even more wary of acting in behalf of American companies seeking new business or investment in Turkey. He was glad to give advice and information. For example, he reassured a representative of American Smelting and Refining Company about the political stability of Turkey, thereby encouraging the company to go ahead with plans for exploitation of a silver mine. He tried to ensure that American firms had the opportunity of bidding for government contracts and he introduced properly accredited company representatives to Ankara officials. Where he drew the line was at endorsement of a company. The dismal failure of the Chester concern to perform on its contract, leading to its annulment in December 1923, was a constant reminder of the danger of involving American prestige too deeply in the fortunes of any particular company.[3]

Shortly after his arrival the case of American Oriental Bankers proved the wisdom of caution. According to its European representative, Marcus Reich, the firm was interested in oil and rail concessions and sought to make a loan to the Turkish government secured by state revenues from monopolies for the establishment of a central bank with a gold reserve of thirty million dollars. Reich asked for Embassy support; Tevfik wanted Embassy advice. The scale of the project roused the interest of the German Ambassador.[4]

Contradictory information immediately put Grew on guard. Reich stated that the contract had been signed and then admitted that it had neither been signed nor approved. He stated that the American Federal Reserve Board had approved flotation of the loan, but the State Department reported that it had not. Grew took the safe course of suggesting to Reich that the company provide the State Department with information on the basis of which the Embassy might receive instructions. For several months the project simmered as Reich sought to convince the Turks of his financial backing and Americans of the near success of his negotiations. The Embassy kept hands off and the Turkish government remained undecided.

It turned out that the firm was even less reputable than the Chester company. The State Department received information that it had a bank balance in only three figures, an office at the address of a goldsmith of doubtful reputation, and a name imitating that of a reliable concern, the American Oriental Banking Corporation. Lewis L. Strauss assured the Department that his firm, Kuhn, Loeb, would have nothing to do with the project. Early in May 1928 Washington sent Grew the "most enlightening" information that the Federal Reserve Board had never even heard of Reich's firm and that the Turkish Ambassador was reporting unfavorably. Grew administered the final coup by warning a prominent Deputy in the Assembly of the importance of Turkey choosing reliable American concerns and advising him to rely on information from his own ambassador. The loan was never consummated.

Meanwhile, in the case of Fox Brothers, which was seeking a railroad construction contract, Grew received information to the effect that the firm was reliable, and he gave both Tevfik and Ismet his personal and unofficial endorsement. Months of delay and dickering followed and the outcome of the Bankers case made him more than ever wary. He declined to endorse the firm in September 1928. He was tired, he wrote, of being informed that contracts were all tied up when in fact they were not. In order to prevent the Turks from placing the blame for the failure of an American company on the United States, the Embassy as a rule should not be involved in the negotiation of a contract.[5]

The only major loan contract signed during Grew's mission was one in which the Embassy was not involved. It went to the biggest international financial adventurer of them all, Ivar Kreuger and his American-Turkish Investment Corporation. Kreuger negotiated a loan of ten million dollars in 1930 with the backing of Lee, Higginson Company of Boston. The Kreuger empire crashed soon thereafter.[6]

Grew's basic problem in representing American business was that Turkey did not inspire confidence as a place to do business and thus attracted only speculators, not well-established firms. Her economy was groping, fettered, and weak. Repairing the destruction of two wars, servicing the remainder of the Ottoman Debt, and buying up foreign concessions drained away her meager capital. The loss of the economically active Greek minority and of oil-rich Mosul further weakened her. Trade failed to generate growth. The capitulatory customs regime did not expire until 1929, preventing Turkey from protecting her infant industries, from raising tariff revenue, and from improving her trade balance by curtailing imports. Shortly after the regime expired, the world depression reduced prices of agricultural products, which constituted the bulk of her exports.[7]

Turkey seemed a poor risk politically as well. Private enterprise became the scapegoat for economic failures and its future seemed dim after the 1929 Crash. Turks turned toward the state, to what they called étatism, as the instrument for economic health and growth. Coincidentally Soviet-Turkish relations improved. Turkish statism, however different from Communism, was bound to scare away American investors.

Doing business in Turkey was slow and uncertain. The whims of local officials, the inertia of a burgeoning bureaucracy, the unfamiliar and untried judicial system, and the habit of baksheesh constantly frustrated vigor and efficiency. Government officials remained highly suspicious of foreign enterprise as a threat to Turkish sovereignty. All the elements seemed to conspire to make the young nation an investment risk.

In spite of the difficulty in securing reliable American investors, Turkey remained interested in financial help from the United States, indeed was increasingly interested as her economy worsened with the onset of the depression. Tevfik told Grew that American money would be welcome because alone of the great powers the United States made no attempt to derive political advantage from loans. He tried to interest Grew in recommending American participation in the settlement of the Ottoman Debt problem, without success. Then in April 1930 Ismet asked Grew to feel out the prospects for a loan of some thirty to fifty million dollars while he was home on leave. Grew sounded out banking acquaintances and reported that it was unlikely the best houses would enter the Turkish field on their own initiative; those that did might not be "the most reputable ones." He advised the Turks to send experts to the United States on a loan mission.[8]

Ismet was slow to move. Julius Klein of the Department of Commerce paid a visit, pronounced himself impressed, and talked encouragingly of a loan, too encouragingly Grew felt. After Klein left, the Ambassador reminded Ismet that, unlike European governments, his own could not pressure banks to loan money. Discussion of a loan was then suspended for nearly a year, a period of protracted negotiations for a Treaty of Residence and Establishment. It is reasonable to suppose that the United States, both in principle and as a bargaining maneuver in treaty negotiations, was not prepared to encourage entry of American capital into Turkey until the conditions under which business might be done there had been regulated.[9]

In September 1931, shortly after the signing of the treaty, Turkey decided to send a loan mission, as Grew had suggested, under Saradjoglou Shukri Bey. Ismet had in mind a loan of from fifty to one hundred million dollars for railroads, port facilities, irrigation projects, and development of cotton production. In his view such projects might be the opening wedge of broad financial and industrial collaboration between the two countries. The Department of Commerce gave the mission its blessing and now Grew put his weight behind a loan proposition. He wrote letters of introduction for the Shukri Bey mission to the Secretaries of State and Treasury, Henry Stimson and Andrew Mellon, and their Under Secretaries, William Castle and Ogden Mills, as well as to bankers Thomas Lamont and John Pierpont Morgan, the last a relative by marriage. He did not often cash in on his relations with Jack Morgan, he wrote, but this seemed a good occasion for doing so. Nevertheless, he worried that Ismet might think that he could "produce the rabbit from the silk hat by a mere flick of the wand,"

and he made a point of not being optimistic. Rightly so, too, because the American depression had not touched bottom and the mission was unsuccessful.[10]

Given the circumstances, it seems doubtful that Grew could have gained significant advantage by more forceful representations. Cautious and conservative by nature, ever mindful of the Chester imbroglio, and after 1929 intimately aware from his shrunken dividend income of the financial catastrophe at home, he felt the game was seldom worth the candle. What he did accomplish was to maintain the attractiveness of an American economic partnership during the "crystallization" of relations in order to induce the Turks to provide a treaty basis that would inspire American confidence and ultimately bring about that partnership.

More often than not Grew's efforts were directed at preventing damage to the Turkish-American relationship, but he found opportunities for positive work in improving public attitudes and he grasped them. Though shy at mixing publicity and negotiation, he was no novice at public relations. Selling war bonds to Western farmers and encouraging Southern businessmen to support a professional Foreign Service provided experience in dealing with people at large. He was keenly aware that public opinion was an inescapable fact of modern diplomacy.

Grew felt that one of the most important tasks of his mission was "to get the achievements, aims, and ideals of the Turkish Republic better known in the United States." He arranged for prominent Americans to meet officials at Ankara so the visitors could return home with the "favorable impressions of modern Turkey which they are perfectly sure to form when they come into contact with such intelligent and sympathetic people as one meets in Government circles." He set up a round of entertainment for Mrs. Lindbergh, the mother of the flier, and gave her a memorandum on modern Turkey. The Lone Eagle never paid a visit, in spite of Grew's hopes, but press clippings from Mrs. Lindbergh showed she had made good use of the memorandum. He was especially solicitous of editors, correspondents, and the occasional senator or representative who came his way. Ivy Lee, the public relations expert, received full-dress treatment, including entertainment and car and guide for sight-seeing. To all Americans he talked enthusiastically about the new Turkey.[11]

Expansion of day-to-day news coverage was equally important. He took care to maintain close relations with regular American correspondents, providing them with background information and news releases and arranging important interviews for them. He worried when the *New York Times* temporarily dropped its Turkey correspondent. The American press seemed already too dependent on correspondents of foreign nationality and foreign press services.[12]

Grew regarded Kemal himself as the best news value in Turkey and urged the government to grant more interviews with him. In 1930 Fox Movietone was given permission to film and record an interview between himself and the President at Cankaya. Here was an opportunity to present the new Turkey vividly to a vast American audience and the setting was prepared with great care. Grew would introduce the President. Kemal would give a message to the American people and then show off his model farm. Unfortunately mooing cows and cackling hens drowned out the voices. Animals of opposite sexes took the occasion "to prove their valor." Worst of all the American Ambassador edged out of the picture "one and seven-eighths inches of the great man's starboard shoulder." The Foreign Ministry suppressed the film.[13]

Grew's best opportunity for influencing Turkish opinion was a non-stop flight of two young Americans from New York to Istanbul in July 1931 that briefly set a long-distance record. To a generation still misty-eyed over Lindbergh, the feat of Russell Boardman and John Polando was exciting news and the Embassy turned itself inside out to welcome the heroes. To Grew they were "ideal representatives of America," the one serious and soft-spoken, the other "a little fox terrier . . . full of humor, tremendously appreciative." Both were spontaneous and unassuming. He shepherded his prizes through ten hectic days of ceremonies including an unprecedented interview with Kemal. Concerned about the allures of Istanbul, he had them closely chaperoned by his staff, gave them "fatherly advice" about "low-class women," warned them their country's honor was at stake, and kept them secluded among the pristine pleasures of the summer Embassy at Yenikeuy. The visit was an unqualified success. The Turks seemed thrilled by the compliment and Grew was sure that his hand was "wonderfully" strengthened.[14]

He recognized that excessive publicity could be dangerous. Too much fanfare over the completion of successful treaty negotiations in 1929 might reinvigorate waning anti-Turkish agitation in the United States. The best program was "to work quietly and steadily without too much of the limelight and to establish a solid basis of respect." Such efforts to mold public opinion as he did make suggest new sensitivity to its importance and awareness of its techniques that make it hard to label him a parchment and petits-fours diplomat.[15]

Grew was determined that the old order of interests in Turkey should give way to a new era of relations. Every activity of his, whether image-building or representing American business or missionary interests, subserved his larger purpose of laying the treaty groundwork for that new era. When complete, his structure consisted essentially of the Treaty of Lausanne, renegotiated and served up to the Senate in two parts, the 1929 Treaty of Commerce and Navigation governing trade relations and the 1931 Treaty of Establishment and Residence governing personal and business rights. Actual negotiation of these treaties was less difficult than reaching the bargaining table.

The year 1928, with the American election, the Brusa Incident, and Grew's confirmation fight, was not a hopeful one in which to submit anything resembling the Lausanne Treaty to the United States Senate. Instead, Grew worked for a renewal of the *modus vivendi* established by the exchange of notes on February 17, 1927. On May 19, 1928, he secured renewal until April 10, 1929, as long as Turkish law allowed. As a sweetener, an indication of desire to enter treaty relations, the United States proposed arbitration and conciliation treaties of the type that Secretary Kellogg was then offering dozens of nations. However, Turkey was determined to double-lock the door against international adjudication of questions such as the Armenian problem, and the State Department was unwilling to modify its general formula sufficiently, so no agreement was reached. The infinitely vague Kellogg-Briand Pact for the renunciation of war fitted the situation better. On January 19, 1929, only three days after the Senate had acted, the Grand National Assembly voted adherence to the peace pact and the two nations at last entered some form of treaty relations.[16]

Gradually Washington and Ankara moved toward a more substantial treaty. On September 29, 1928, Tevfik proposed negotiation of a commercial treaty early the following year, but the lame-duck Coolidge Administration, fearing renewed anti-Turkish agitation, suggested another renewal of the *modus vivendi*. Tevfik rejected a simple renewal and Grew, in a major dispatch, sought to convince his government of the need for proceeding to a treaty. He argued that a brief, simple commercial treaty avoiding all controversial questions could hardly fail to be accepted by the Senate. He pointed out that Turkey had negotiated or was about to negotiate such treaties with all other nations. He emphasized the greater risk of "alienating the present friendly attitude of the Turkish Government . . . through pressing for exceptional machinery to regulate our commercial relations on the ground that we are unwilling to negotiate a formal commercial treaty with the Turkish Republic." He warned that the Turkish government was "intensely sensitive as to its prestige." It had taken one rebuff from the United States and another might evoke grave resentment. The Department commended his tact and skill, accepted his advice, and left the manner of informing Ankara to his discretion. The two governments renewed the *modus vivendi*, this time with the commitment to enter negotiations for a commercial treaty.[17]

The way to the bargaining table was still not clear. In spite of repeated assurances that his object was a simple commercial treaty, Tevfik asked for extension to cover navigation as well. Such an open challenge to critics of the Lausanne Treaty was precisely what Grew hoped to avoid. A 1929 Treaty of Commerce and Navigation would appear as an obvious attempt to replace the 1830 Treaty of Commerce and Navigation, which was a dead letter but which the Senate opposition held to be in force and perfectly adequate for governing relations. Once again Tevfik appeared to have reneged. Grew found it "infuriating to deal with a government whose oral assurances cannot be trusted." In his experience a foreign minister spoke "authoritatively and finally for the Government." Nevertheless, he refused to attribute intentional dishonesty to Tevfik. His underlings might be capable of any Machiavellian maneuver, but the Foreign Minister seemed rather the woolly idealist and amateur, who left details to his crafty experts.[18]

His estimate of Tevfik seems naïve. Each chapter of the protracted treaty discussions of 1928 and 1929 suggests a deliberate policy on the part of the Turkish government to push the United States toward as comprehensive an understanding as possible in order to destroy any remnant of the validity of the old treaty order. Securing American acquiescence by degrees involved deception as to ultimate intent. A number of reasons explain Grew's refusal to accept this element of deception. To begin with, he had a simple faith in human beings and he had gained a basic confidence in Turkish straightforwardness from Ismet at Lausanne. Also, the pledged word was the cement of his diplomacy. He would have found it impossible to proceed except on a basis of good faith. He also believed that manifesting good faith was the best possible way of encouraging good faith. A distinction between Tevfik and his subordinates, in the light of these considerations, was perhaps inevitable. Grew knew that in any case his purpose and Tevfik's were the same, to move their nations closer together.

While puzzling about the intentions of the Turkish government, Grew began to doubt the good faith of his own. Late in May 1929 Under Secretary J. Reuben Clark objected that unconditional most-favored nation treatment, which Tevfik and Grew had agreed would be the rule for the prospective treaty, conflicted with discriminatory weapons in American tariff law. Assistant Secretary Castle and G. Howland Shaw, then Chief of the Near Eastern Division, argued against Clark that the question was theoretical, since the United States was not likely in any event to use such weapons against Turkey, and that repudiation of Grew's pledge might work great harm to American commerce, to say nothing of relations with Turkey. Clark's objection seemed legalistic to Grew when he learned of the dispute, a case of being unable to see the forest for the trees. He felt that repudiation might even require his resignation. However, the disagreement was resolved by Secretary Stimson in favor of Castle and Shaw, and in August 1929 Grew received the necessary powers and provisional text. At last he was down to negotiations.[19]

When Grew announced his readiness September 7, the principal Turkish negotiator, Zekai Bey, said he would be ready in fifteen minutes! They began the following day and soon had clarifications and minor objections disposed of. A week of hard bargaining followed. Zekai refused to allow any distinction between Turkey's treatment of her own vessels and her treatment of foreign vessels. Any distinction reminiscent of the capitulatory era still appeared invidious. Grew understood Turkish sensitivity on the point and withdrew the objectionable phrase, but with one eye on the Senate reinserted it in the minutes, less offensively worded.[20]

He took pains to make the atmosphere conducive to agreement. He sent to Washington copies of the British and French treaties "so that the Department could get an idea of the frame of mind of the Turks." The Department proved invariably cooperative and allowed him wide discretion. He entertained his Turkish opposite and encouraged informal negotiations in French, without stenographers or translators. He was not always conciliatory. In one case where Zekai insisted on a phrase which the Department found objectionable, Grew waited a decent interval without cabling and then told Zekai that his government absolutely refused to accept the phrase in question. Most disagreements were resolved by persuasion or relegation to the minutes.[21]

On September 29, 1929, Grew decided the time had come to stop negotiating. Sizing up his hand, he judged that the United States held the four most important cards in the pack: Turkey needed the American market more than America needed the Turkish market; Turkey needed a treaty to interest American companies and capital in her public works; Turkey wanted the prestige of a treaty with the United States; and finally, Turkey understood the danger of another rebuff by the Senate and would not jeopardize ratification by insisting on unreasonable provisions. He resolved "to stand pat and to offer no compromises." The change of a single comma, he told Zekai, would reopen negotiations "with what eventual result it would be impossible to foresee." Zekai signed the next day.[22]

What Grew obtained was what both governments wanted in the first place, reciprocal, non-discriminatory treatment of their trade. It was a short, relatively simple treaty raising no sore points for the Senate. The chairman of the Foreign Relations Committee, Senator Claude Swanson, consoled himself that it said nothing about giving away capitulatory rights, and, at the strong urging of the Secretary and Under Secretary, agreed to support it. The brief time between signing and submission to the Senate apparently made it difficult to organize opposition and the Senate advised ratification on February 17, 1930.[23]

No serious obstacle other than timing now stood in the way of negotiating another big chunk of the Lausanne Treaty in the form of a Treaty of Residence and Establishment. The Turks proposed a simple, one-article agreement and the State Department agreed in principle. However, the

Department felt that two Turkish treaties in one session was more than Senate traffic would bear, and rather than allow "Turkophobes" time to organize opposition, it preferred to postpone negotiations until the fall of 1930. Tevfik was agreeable.[24]

The Embassy played an equally important role with the Department in formulating the American position on the next treaty. This rare influence is attributable to Grew's successes in Turkey and also to the fact that the immensely capable Shaw was now his Counselor of Embassy. An example of Embassy influence was the problem of discriminatory American immigration law. The Department, trying to prevent conflict between the treaty and the immigration law, finally decided that it was impossible to grant Turkish citizens most-favored nation treatment in admission to the United States. The only solution was to assume that "residence and establishment" did not include entry and sojourn. The Embassy rejoined that Turkey would be upset and might retaliate because such treaties normally included entry and sojourn. The answer was to find a formula which frankly excepted immigration legislation without offending the Turks, and the Embassy found one in the Senate reservation to a similar treaty with Germany. A formula already accepted by a European power would be more palatable to Turkey, and so it was, for Turkey accepted it. The honors in treaty drafting seem clearly to have gone to the Embassy.[25]

Well into the first plenary session on October 18, 1930, a treaty seemed almost in hand. Turkish objections were few and counterproposals reasonable. Then, in Grew's words, the bombshell fell: Zekai proposed an article nullifying all previous treaties. Such a provision would directly contravene the American policy of securing a new treaty structure by never forcing the Senate to repudiate the old. It would wreck the treaty, Grew told Zekai, and was out of the question. Let the capitulations die in peace, he advised.[26]

Formulas to dispose of the 1830 treaty without saying so were exchanged for several weeks without success. Grew referred none of these to Washington, partly, he claimed, to keep them out of official correspondence subject to call by the Senate and partly no doubt to simplify the bargaining until he had a formula he could support. However, the exchanges were revealed by his diary, which went to Castle and the Near Eastern Division. To Grew's embarrassment the legal experts pounced on one Turkish formula which acknowledged the old treaty to be currently in force in order effectively to cancel it. Such an acknowledgment delighted the lawyers because it would assist them in presenting claims for damages incurred during the war and postwar years. Grew was torn between chagrin at having it thought he had "pulled a bull" by rejecting the formula and annoyance at the pettifoggery. "I profoundly hope that the work we are trying to do to build up Turko-American relations in the interests of the many is not eventually going to be damaged in the interests of the few," he wrote Castle. Not for the last time he wondered whether it was wise to circulate his diary.[27]

Further negotiation on the point was unavailing and Grew finally gave up. The two governments' positions were hardening on an issue that needed to be avoided. Adjournment might bring clearer appreciation by both sides of the cost of no agreement as against legalistic satisfactions and perhaps bring forward new and less recalcitrant Turkish negotiators. To allay Turkish fears regarding the American attitude toward capitulations, he presented Ismet a letter emphasizing American awareness of the changed conditions in Turkey and American anxiety to develop treaty relations on the basis of those changed conditions.[28]

This letter contained the germ of the solution. Resumption was postponed until the fall of 1931 to keep treaty signature and Senate consideration close together. Tevfik suggested that a letter such as Grew's, specifying neither the theoretical continuance in force of the 1830 treaty nor the date of its expiration, but recognizing "the changes which have taken place in Turkey," might prove acceptable. Indeed, it did prove acceptable, both to the Turkish Cabinet and the State Department. Anxious to secure his treaty and sure the United States could never do better, Grew now pressed for a conclusion. He told Tevfik time and again that there must be no last-minute changes. Even so, at the last session Zekai threw a fit over alterations he claimed he had not seen. Grew became equally angry and told Zekai that the Foreign Minister himself had approved the texts, that negotiations were closed, that he planned to leave Ankara at seven that evening, and that if he did not have the treaty by then there might be no treaty at all. Grew made his train with the treaty in his pocket.[29]

Actually Zekai and Grew only initialed the treaty August 27, 1931, and kept agreement secret until formal signature October 28, 1931, in order to avoid publicity in the United States. Grew's letter, cleanly separate from the treaty, was withheld from the Assembly by Tevfik to avoid publication. As a result the Senate never saw Grew's disengagement from the old treaty order before advising ratification on May 12, 1932. Earlier Grew had gone to the Senate himself and secured Borah's support with the assurance that he, the Ambassador, "was not trying to put anything over in the way of reviving the Treaty of Lausanne." Some deception was not uncommon in diplomacy after all.[30]

Treaties by themselves do not create friendly relations, but they do provide a concrete manifestation of mutual confidence and mutual interests. They simplify relations by marking out areas of general agreement. They underpin friendship. Laying the groundwork for Turkish-American friendship was the chief aim of Grew's mission. It was "slow and careful work," he said, but added: "What fun it was to have a job where things were not crystallized and where constructive work was possible." Success would not have been possible without favoring conditions, but success might not have been as complete without Grew's contribution, both in what he stood for and what he did.[31]

ELEVEN

Twilight of the Old World

THE abortive treaty negotiations of October and November 1930 kept Grew at Ankara forty-four days, his longest stay at the capital. He averaged only one day in nine there, and at the beginning this seemed more than enough. Going to Ankara "frequently, say once a month, and staying there occasionally for a week or ten days" was neither essential nor agreeable, he wrote Shaw, but he gained acquaintances and made a favorable impression. Other ambassadors would dash up for only a day or two. They talked of building embassies — Sir George Clerk showed plans — but they hoped it would be their successors who occupied them.[1]

In time, living away from the capital became embarrassing. It was "pathetic" how the Turks deplored the shortness of his stays. The government badly wanted Ankara accorded the prestige of ambassadors in residence, and Ismet himself inquired when the United States would build a permanent Embassy there. Grew's stock reply, that it took forty years for the diplomatic corps to move from New York to Washington, sounded hollow when one after another of the powers made the move, leaving him almost the only holdout in Istanbul by 1931.

He had a number of practical reasons for staying at Istanbul. Mrs. Grew suffered from the altitude in the interior and everyone suffered from the heat in summer. The small, temporary Embassy at Ankara was uncomfortable and inadequate for entertaining, and his government had no plans for building a new one. Political intelligence at the capital was meager on account of Kemal's secretive methods, while at Istanbul, Grew was close to the American institutions and businesses whose problems preoccupied him.

Perhaps most important was his conviction that keeping at arm's length from the Turkish government best suited this awkward, transitional phase in relations. A degree of remoteness seemed advisable during the schools crisis and the period of edging toward treaties. Distance seemed to make the heart grow fonder; the Turks were more responsive and impressed when he did visit the capital.

Of course living at Istanbul was far more agreeable. At last he was free from Washington's slogging desk work. Diplomatic activity came in spurts with easy weeks between. In summer he might go to his office only one morning a week. One of the great advantages of the Foreign Service was having "our years of intensive work and then our years of comparative relaxation, with time to enjoy life while we are still young enough to enjoy it." [2]

Life was sweetest at Yenikeuy, a few miles north of Istanbul. Here at water's edge was his summer residence, set among wisteria and roses and crowned by little terraces "where one can rest in the shade of the trees in complete privacy and look out over the lovely Bosporus lying below." Mail and documents were brought out to Yenikeuy to be worked on leisurely at his desk, from which he could watch ships passing up and down the Straits. Gleefully indulging a "marine madness," he kept track of over two thousand of them, identifying them with the aid of Zeiss binoculars and a book of ships and funnels he kept at hand. From his compilations he gained some statistics, probably readily available elsewhere, regarding the national complexion of Black Sea trade, and the not very surprising conclusion that approximately as much shipping entered the Black Sea as emerged. It was frankly a hobby, like collecting stamps. Each ship had a personality, the "aristocrats" being the great, modern, spick-and-span Norwegian tankers.

He grew to love Yenikeuy as no other spot on earth. A "thoroughly athletic day" began at 4:30 A.M. when he rose to see the sunrise and the first batch of ships go by. Then a snooze, swim, and breakfast. Swimming and tennis with intervals of work occupied the long sunny day. The moonlight evenings made an indelible impression, the air soft, his daughters out rowing, people strolling past, his police dog Kim "at the open window with his elbows on the sill, the lighted shirkets and occasionally the lights of a big steamer passing by, Alice on the sofa and the orthophone pouring out that beautiful melody of Tchaikowsky's Fifth Symphony." [3]

At Istanbul he had the world at his doorstep. Winter days were enlivened by boating out to explore cruise liners, from which he emerged, past broadly grinning Turkish police, laden with Listerine, soap, maple syrup, and puffed rice. In summer the family took picnic excursions in the Embassy launch *Heather*, which, not to be outdone by the Royal Yacht Squadron affiliation of the British Ambassador, proudly flew the burgee of the Eastern Yacht Club of Marblehead. In August 1929 the two ambassadors joined forces for a ten-day excursion along the Black Sea littoral of Turkey. They spent the days on the captain's private deck behind the bridge, fanned by sea breezes, watching the unfolding coastline of Mithridates, the Amazons, and Xenophon.

In October 1929, after the worst of the schools crisis and the signature of the commercial treaty, the Grews took a fling in Europe. He tried his luck at Monte Carlo and won five thousand dollars. Then Paris "to make whoopee with a bang." Bedrooms on the Blue Train, clothes to shame "Solomon in all his glory," dining at the Ritz, La Rue's, or Ciro's with Prince this or Baroness that, an "orgy of music" — the trip was a toast to the good life, and a last one, for the stock market crash was just then splintering the dream world of the twenties.

Grew had more than his share of luck. One evening at Monte Carlo he sat through 284 plays without his number coming up once. Then it popped up every few plays and he recouped his losses. Whether there or at the poker table, he seldom lost. Granted his experience and quality, it is hard to ignore the factor of luck in his surviving the quadrennial roulette of diplomatic assignments through eight administrations and forty years.

He did not rest easy about his career while in Turkey. He forecast a Republican victory in 1928, but he had no illusion that the party of Al Smith and Joe Robinson would retain his services. In 1929 the press reassigned him to Berlin, Brussels, Rome, and Latin America, and nominated two successors in Turkey, Louis B. Mayer of Metro-Goldwyn Mayer and John N. Willys, the automobile manufacturer. The speculation was embarrassing and, he felt, hurt his position with the Turkish government. It would be "calamitous" to send a Jew, Mayer, to Turkey under present circumstances, he wrote his brother. Grew told himself that if he were consigned to the "scrap-heap" there were "a thousand things to do," but he very much wanted to stay in Turkey, and he asked several friends, Godfrey Cabot and General "Wild Bill" Donovan, to put in a good word for him with the new President. If move he must, he wrote Castle, he hoped it would be to Berlin. However, Secretary Stimson decided to keep him in Turkey. That was one of the few posts in good hands, he told Grew in June, 1930.[4]

In November 1931 Castle asked Grew if he would like to be considered for the ambassadorship to Japan. He had spent four years in Turkey, his treaty work was complete, and this was the "chance of a lifetime," so the answer was obvious. The appointment was "engineered" by Castle in January 1932. When the Democrats came to power the following year, Grew had the luck to be a new ambassador in Japan instead of an old ambassador in Turkey, to have as President a man who shared Groton, Fly Club, and Harvard *Crimson* experiences, and to have as Under Secretary his old friend William Phillips.

The mission to Turkey was complete, a mission of importance in the history of American foreign relations as well as in understanding Grew's kind of diplomacy. In Turkey he had rare freedom of action for a twentieth century diplomat. As a former Under Secretary, one of the most experienced career diplomats, negotiator of the Lausanne Treaty, and now a nineteen-gun salute ambassador, his advice carried weight in the Near Eastern Division. In Shaw, Grew had a very able and sympathetic junior colleague as division chief during the early, difficult years of the mission. Secretaries Kellogg and Stimson, preoccupied with European, Far Eastern, and Latin American problems, generally let the Embassy and Division work out policy for themselves. Grew was in a position where he could reveal his diplomatic qualities in breadth and depth and cut a broad swath in Turkish-American relations.

The salient characteristic of Grew's diplomacy was its highly personal quality. He found it difficult to make others understand, but his whole career told him that personality and character were vital ingredients of diplomacy. A diplomat might be acting under intelligent instructions and favoring conditions, but unless he could inspire confidence, respect, and, where possible, liking, his success was in doubt. In this conviction he was leading from strength, for he was an unusually attractive and wholesome person.

In his early fifties Grew was as vigorous and arresting in appearance as at forty. "Statuesque," one magazine called him. To *Time* in 1928 he was "John Pierpont Morgan's lithe, athletic and slightly deaf cousin," and again in 1934, on his own feet but decibels the worse for it, the "handsome, deaf United States Ambassador." His hair was parted on the side instead of in the middle and was turning white but the mustache and bushy brows were black, the carriage erect, and the waist so slim the coat he was married in fitted perfectly.[5]

He felt some crimp of age. Tennis singles were too grueling. He had to enjoy feats of athletic prowess vicariously through his daughter Anita, who swam the Bosporus from sea to sea in 1931, her father attending to the gramophone and hot chocolate in the accompanying rowboat. Grew's hearing, sometimes worse, sometimes better, was still a handicap. More frequently he was afflicted with nervous, muscular, and organic disturbances and infections. Doctors advised him to smoke less, drink more water, and take pills. He needed reading glasses, an unfailing indication of age.

He knew his athletic days were numbered, but he was determined to make the best of them. Looking back he confessed it was the athletic rather than the intellectual moments which stood out: "our crew race on the Harlem River, the Harvard-Yale mile run, a ski-run on the Männlichen, and an all-day stalk in Kashmir or Wyoming." [6] Diplomatic victories paled by comparison. He played an avid if "outrageous" game of golf. During the first six months in Japan he tried eleven courses for a low score of 102. One day in 1932 he plowed through eighteen holes of golf, two tennis matches, and a long walk. He was aging but not deteriorating.

The years made him less reserved, more engaging. He would never be one to mix easily with steerage passengers, social parvenus, or Soviet diplomats, but he cultivated a wider variety of people. He could wilt a subordinate, who, forgetting the Ambassador's deafness, spoke softly or indistinctly, but charm a visitor with his pleasant voice, warm, crinkling smile, and direct, simple, kindly manner. It was easy to make good impressions, he noted in 1928, and still more easy to make bad ones. He detested the word propaganda, he wrote Shaw in 1932, because the really important things in life "gradually seep in from personal relationships without active intent." Here spoke Groton and the Somerset Club, but with a difference, for he began: "The Anglo-Saxon is nearly always afraid of slopping over, never realizing that a straightforward, sincere expression of feeling is generally worth its weight in gold." Altogether he seemed a more relaxed, outward-going, and sympathetic personality. "One of the most popular foreigners in Turkey," the *New York Times* called him.[7]

The winning impression made by this sinewy, sunny, stately man was underpinned by qualities which earned him solid respect and trust. His life was patterned out of loyalties and affections, each new twist carrying out the simple, basic design.

He was a devoted husband and father, relishing the shared adventures of his "Swiss Family Grew" and its succession of beloved dogs, Bully, Jimmie, Laddy, Lassie, Danny, Kim, and Sambo. Now the generations were shifting, the last of the older passing with the death of his dear father-in-law, Thomas Sergeant Perry, in 1928 and Mrs. Perry in 1933, and a new generation starting up with the birth of a son to Lilla and J. Pierrepont Moffat in 1932. A second daughter debarked from "the parent ship" when Anita married Vice-Consul Robert English. The "old ship" set out on its last long voyage with only one daughter aboard, and she left in 1933 to marry another Foreign Service Officer, Cecil Lyon. It was a great satisfaction to have all three daughters within the larger family of the Service, but henceforth the intimacy which meant so much to him would have to depend on occasional visits and the exchange of letters and diaries.[8]

For Groton, Harvard, and the Service he held deep, unswerving loyalty. In spite of his bitter disillusionment while Under Secretary with those diplomats who put themselves ahead of the good of the Service, it remained, in his words, his father and his mother, the source of his closest friendships, and the object of his constant concern. It still contained "a lot of good, red-blooded men with plenty of service spirit, willing to play the game." Triumphantly he noted in 1930 that, as he had predicted would happen some day, half of Hoover's ministers and ambassadors were career men. Traveling Congressmen were as likely to hear of the virtues of the Foreign Service as of those of modern Turkey.[9]

The pride of country he felt as a Groton senior in the spring of 1898 was undiminished. Slighting remarks about the United States by foreigners, or cynical ones by Americans, made him furious. "With all her faults, weaknesses, and aberrations," he wrote of his country, "if I became prouder of her, I should bust." Every time his ship passed the Statue of Liberty he would repeat with his daughters the lines of Sir Walter Scott beginning, "Breathes there a man, with soul so dead. . . ." [10]

Root of being was Grew's commanding loyalty to himself, to the kind of man his family, society, and school had made him. The gritty and urbane qualities which he meant by the word gentleman were as fresh and valid as ever. It is true that tolerance and fair-mindedness did not escape the alloy of social bias, nor did modesty that of ambition. Nevertheless, perusal of thousands of pages of his daily record leaves an enduring sense of the determining force of moral values in his career. His commitment to diplomacy was not one for which he would pay the price of losing his individuality. The result was an inner self-sufficiency, an essential honesty and harmony of parts, which William Phillips perhaps had in mind when he said that Grew's outstanding quality as a diplomat was his integrity.[11]

He was a more representative American in 1932 than in, say, 1914. A sight-seer was reported to have said, "The Ambassador is an American all right, but Mrs. Grew doesn't speak like an American at all; she must be an Italian Countess or something." While Grew's qualities of personality and character were not typical of any nation, they were attractive ones for an American representative to have. He deliberately sought a national point of view in world affairs. American diplomacy, he once said, should be the kind where you lay down four aces face up and say, "If you've a royal straight flush you win but I don't think you have." After the fiasco of 1927 he tried to adopt the home-grown style in foreign affairs. He wanted it made perfectly clear that he wore no spats, pushed no cookies, and except when unavoidable went to no teas. Career insecurity undoubtedly was a factor in keeping him in touch. Indeed, Congressional scrutiny of foreign affairs had a pronounced effect on the orientation of this American diplomat.[12]

Grew brought well-seasoned diplomatic skills as well as valuable personal qualities to the task of protecting and advancing American interests. His complete command of diplomatic protocol provided a means of quick entrée into unfamiliar surroundings and of preserving otherwise strained relationships. In presenting his government's views he was sensitive to the whole tonal range of diplomatic communication and adept at striking the right note of emphasis. He was a shrewd, persistent, careful negotiator. Always he strove for precision. In the traditional diplomatic methods he was a superb craftsman.

His weakness lay in the field of intelligence. Reporting internal political developments and foreign affairs in his part of the world was a major responsibility. He brought to the task a well-disciplined, practical mind, a ready supply of common sense, and an admirable clarity of expression, but he lacked intellectual curiosity, a critical viewpoint, and speculative depths. His was a conventional mind.

Reading was not a source of sustained intellectual activity or growth. He still ordered memoirs, biographies, and histories, particularly those relating to his own experience, but he rarely commented on them. He was determined to do more serious reading in Turkey and he claimed to have read 2500 pages in October and 1682 pages in November 1930. Nevertheless, orders for serious books slipped from thirty-five in 1929 to fourteen in 1930 to eight in 1931, while requests for detective stories increased. Reading was mostly for fun and escape.[13]

His diary has little to say about world affairs. *Foreign Affairs* and the London *Times* kept him well informed and the Castle and Moffat diaries were excellent sources of inside information, but his comments were hardly more sophisticated than those of the man in the street. On New Year's Eve, 1930, he asked of the coming year whether the economic situation would get better or worse, whether Germany would default, whether Hitler would win and keep power, whether Congress would modify prohibition, and whether the Japanese would evacuate Manchuria. The depression seemed essentially a psychological problem, rooted in the "pathological" pessimism of the country. Usually he was reluctant to make a diagnosis "too far from the scene." [14]

The fact is that, in spite of nearly three decades in diplomacy, Grew had seldom been required to undertake sustained political reporting. It is illustrative of the episodic involvement of the United States in world affairs that only those months of the Berlin chargéship and the Lausanne Conference, as well as occasional weeks when he was Under Secretary, had elicited maximum intellectual effort from Grew. Most of his career had been spent in humble secretarial or placid ministerial posts. His mind was not severely exercised in intelligence work.

In addition to the cast of his mind and his lack of sustained experience, Grew's assumptions about the role of the United States in world affairs inhibited his intelligence work. He did not see the United States as an integral element of international politics. The Far East and Europe presented important problems, but these were conceived severally and not within a world complex of power or world economy. Thus Europe was a "mess"; the war to end war had "simply led to new formations of hostile camps and . . . sown the seeds of other eventual conflagrations." Europe was not America's problem, however. Its war debts, so prominent a feature of the "mess," must eventually be paid. The American public opposed cancellation and the national government as "trustee" for the property of its citizens had no right to take liberties with it.[15]

Of course the United States could not remain aloof from the world. It must protect specific interests and seek friendly relations with nearly all powers. However, political engagement was not only dangerous and unnecessary, but threatened the cardinal asset of American diplomacy, its devotion to ethical standards in international relations. It was on this ethical ground that he strongly opposed recognition of the Soviet Union in 1933 as a "serious sacrifice of principle and letting down of standards." The United States should never "palliate, by recognition, the things Soviet Russia has done and the things it stands for." His attitude was a curious mixture of Rooseveltian prestige consciousness without the power calculation and Wilsonian idealism without the dynamism. From this point of view a sustained and comprehensive understanding of political developments abroad seemed irrelevant.[16]

The years in Turkey resulted in little strengthening of Grew's capacity for political intelligence work. What he reported of Turkey's foreign policy would be just one more piece in the jigsaw puzzle that Washington must put together. He kept careful track of the settlements and *rapprochements* through which Turkey was methodically improving her security and he watched the Soviet-Turkish connection closely. His sources were the press, Tevfik, and diplomatic colleagues, particularly his warm friend, the British Ambassador Sir George Clerk. He gained much rumor and speculation but little concrete information. His dispatches had something of the academic exercise about them. As he said about the Soviet-Turkish Protocol of 1929, "It cannot in any way affect Turco-American relations." And he was quite right: the foreign policy of Turkey at the time gave very little cause for American concern.[17]

A more exciting assignment was reporting Turkish domestic affairs. The most important event was an experiment in tolerated opposition. In August 1930 Kemal permitted the former Ambassador to France, Fethi Bey, to form a new party, which drew wide support and stimulated much political criticism and discussion. This public enactment of hitherto secret political drama aroused much flutter and clucking in the diplomatic roost. Was this a sincere attempt by Kemal to license opposition and thus carry Turkey a big step toward Western political society, or was it merely window-dressing or a device temporarily to alleviate growing discontent? At first Grew leaned to the idealistic interpretation, then shifted to "more realistic explanations," then returned to his "original theory" that the step was another move in the normal development of Kemal's political idealism. Riots and demonstrations followed, and in November, Kemal dissolved the new party. Even today, in the words of one authority, the "short and unhappy life of the Free Republican Party remains an obscure episode in the history of the Turkish Republic." Grew continued to see glimmerings of democracy the following year, but he was speculative and wishful in what he said. Government by "secret conclave" did not inspire confident forecasting.[18]

Shaw encouraged new departures in political intelligence. He disputed Grew's contention that the Embassy's main task was to provide information, while the Department of State made policy. As Chief of the Near Eastern Division, Shaw encouraged the Embassy to assume a coordinate role in policy and to provide more analysis, interpretation, speculation, and opinion in dispatches, more flour and less wheat. Grew admitted that the Embassy was not "very strong on philosophy," but added, "Turco-American relations are no worse since we took over the job." [19] Nevertheless he reduced quantity and tried to improve quality.

When Shaw went to Turkey as Counselor of Embassy he tried to show what he meant. He encouraged secretaries to undertake extensive, scholarly studies of various aspects of Turkish life such as sport, justice, the younger generation, and modern political and social conceptions. The Embassy soon became a small school of advanced study in Near Eastern affairs. Grew heartily approved of the "new and most healthy atmosphere." It was inspiring "to be thrown into intimate daily contact with a personality and mind such as Howland Shaw possesses." Grew thought that the Counselor's own studies of the Turkish court system, crime, and juvenile delinquency created an exceptionally close and influential position for him with members of the government, broke down suspicion of foreigners, especially foreign diplomats, and helped spread American ideals and methods. Enthusiastic as Grew was, however, he assumed that the plan depended on adequate staff and quiet diplomatic relations. From Tokyo he wrote that depth reporting would be impossible there because all energies went into keeping abreast of current developments. To an old hand like Grew, these new departures were interesting and worthwhile, but a luxury just the same.[20]

Shaw represented the trend in the Department of State toward a more scholarly formulation of foreign policy, based on intensive training of Foreign Service officers in the languages and cultures of exotic but important countries. In this view the best way to determine political trends and policies was to analyze the underlying social, intellectual, and economic currents. Grew was sympathetic, but did not really understand. He admitted that Turkish professors, doctors, businessmen, minority leaders, and religious figures might prove useful to the Embassy, but he argued that their views, though "academically very interesting," would shed little light on the "practical matters" which the Department needed to know. The source of power was Kemal and very little could be learned of his intentions. Shaw would presumably have replied that the choices available to Kemal were limited by ascertainable developments in the society as a whole. The difference was one of generations as well as methods. To Grew the apex of political society had always been the proper, natural focus of diplomatic intelligence.[21]

At bottom the difference was that Grew saw diplomacy less as a question of the mind than the heart. In his view relations between nations were essentially no different than relations between individuals, and were equally dependent on the subjective, intuitive, irrational sources of human behavior. His diplomacy was strongest in the art of bettering those relationships.

The object of his mission to Turkey, and indeed the basic objective of all diplomacy for Grew, was the creation and preservation of friendship between nations. It was a question of "getting Turkey to like America both in theory and practice and trying, here and there, to get America to like Turkey." It was an exasperating task at times. The Turks still seemed afflicted with the "oriental mentality." Zekai Bey must be another of Curzon's "wily Turks." Time and again he was sorely tempted to bang his fist on the table and demand favorable action, he told the French Ambassador, but, he continued, the more he saw of the regime's psychology, the more he realized the uselessness and fallacy of such an attitude. "If you want something from an individual you don't usually begin by shaking your fist in his face," he told himself. Patience, he insisted, was the essential quality of diplomacy in Turkey.[22]

He understood that he must not only treat the Turks as respected and liked equals but must manifestly seem to treat them so. He must subdue bias and preconception because it destroyed the object of diplomacy. "An ambassador who starts prejudiced against the country to which he is accredited," he wrote on the way to Japan, "might just as well pack up and go home." To the task of creating friendship in Turkey, Grew brought not only those qualities which commanded respect and confidence, but also buoyancy, warmth, and great sensitivity for the feelings of others.[23]

In this respect his experience as a diplomat of the old school was a positive assistance. Courtier diplomacy, after all, was not so far removed from popular diplomacy. Both depended partly on mood, impression, form, the irrational and emotional in human conduct. Both were conducted as public spectacles of national and international prestige. None were more sensitive than old school diplomats to the barometer of national prestige, none more devoted and assiduous in ministering to the ego in nationalism. Every curlicue in protocol had as its objective the preservation of unruffled national dignity. To a nation quivering with new-found dignity such as Turkey, Grew's seasoned diplomacy and manifest goodwill were flattering indeed.

From the substantial accomplishments of his mission as well as the many expressions of genuine sorrow by Turkish officials at his departure, he felt he had accomplished his object. Neither before nor afterward did he attain the same completeness of satisfaction in constructive achievement and diplomatic success.

In some respects, however, it was Grew's misfortune to spend nearly five placid years in relatively stable and progressive Turkey. He was insulated from a world of precipitate change, a world where bland assumption about principled conduct in foreign affairs, devoid of power calculations, had less and less meaning. So much of his career had been spent in posts where change seemed unimportant. Prewar Berlin, Vienna, and St. Petersburg looked golden not gilded, and the convulsions of wartime Berlin and peace-making Paris had the air of unreality. Instead ot experiencing the poisonous aftereffects of war in Germany, he had sunny days in Copenhagen and Berne. Stability and order were the norms of his experience, while revolution, social stress, and economic malaise were exceptional.

The Grews sailed for the United States enroute to Japan on March 13, 1932. It was "a hard wrench to pull ourselves away — from a place where we have been happier than in any previous one." One last "sublimely beautiful" view of the Seraglio, the Bosporus, and the Islands, "rising like precious stones from their brilliant blue setting," and he turned to the savage and gloomy world foreshadowed by Manchuria.[24]

PART FOUR

Far Eastern Crises

(1932 - 1938)

TWELVE

The Aftermath of Manchuria

GREW'S career now came abreast of history. The lingering twilight of the old world finally vanished. Subordinate and peripheral diplomatic roles ended. The first of his first generation professionals, he became ambassador to a great power, one of vital interest to the security of his nation. He moved suddenly to the forefront of world affairs at a moment of profound crisis. The year March 1932 to March 1933, from the end of the Turkey mission to the end of the Republican era in the United States, was one of bewildering transition for Grew.

It was a year both of turmoil and stagnancy. The old order passed away numbly as economic indices wandered near historic lows. The dumb frustrations of hunger, idleness, and poverty flared up here and there in suicide, pillage, and riot. Faith in Western political ideals sapped away, ended in Japan, trickled in Germany. In May 1932 the President of France was killed by a crazed White Russian, the fifteenth attempted assassination of the year. A week later the Premier of Japan was shot, and in February 1933 the President-elect of the United States barely escaped a bullet. Ceaseless international conferences left debt, reparation, security, and disarmament questions more intractable than ever. The peace machinery built on the new and hopeful assumptions of 1918 foundered over Manchuria. Then early in 1933 Adolf Hitler came to power, Japan withdrew from the League, and the United States sank into a desperate bank crisis. The new Roosevelt Administration put the nation's ills first. Everywhere the warp and woof of reasoned security unraveled, each nation seeking sufficiency in itself. Presaging a new era, two British physicists discovered that in splitting hydrogen atoms to form helium, energy was created. Pessimists, said the *New York Times*, shudder when they speculate on the possible destructive uses of atomic energy.[1]

The ugly turn in world affairs, with Japan a pace-setting predator nation, only further complicated what at best was a difficult diplomatic mission.

Japan required the most tactful handling.[2] Elsewhere nationalism was jostled by other loyalties and ideals. In Japan it was their supreme expression. Elsewhere it waxed and waned according to economic and social change. In Japan the upswings were sharper, the troughs shallower. Elsewhere it was often artificially imposed. In Japan it derived an organic quality from the tightly knit, homogeneous, insular society. More than most, Japan was a nation with a personality, one of great sensitivity. The extraordinary anxiety attending the individual's relations with society, precisely defined to avoid shame, carried over to his nation's position in a world where his rules did not apply but where respect was equally craved.

Tact was not the least of Grew's diplomatic strengths. Decades of protocol and familiarity with the etiquette of international society would ease his way through the complex formalities of Japanese social and official intercourse. The hierarchical society, titled class, and ceremonial court were entirely familiar. Grew had been bowing before emperors since Hirohito was six years old. This attractive man of obvious goodwill would pay Japanese the compliment of respecting their conventions and through these their nation. After Turkey he was well attuned to national sensitivity, and he could cast his mind back to wartime Germany to catch the deeper reverberations of Japanese nationalism. Insofar as personality — whether national or individual — constituted a problem for his mission, Grew was ideally prepared and suited.

The professional challenge of a Japan mission lay no less in the problem of communication. The Japanese mind confounds the Westerner. It is intuitive, subjective, and emotional in contrast to the rational, analytical bent of the West. Truth seeps in through the senses and is expressed poetically and graphically rather than explicitly and logically. Language suggests but does not reveal meaning. Western diplomats with a common cultural inheritance and a superbly concrete common language, French, find a meeting of minds among themselves relatively easy. In Japan the equivalents often do not exist. Envoys pursue an artistic mind screened by elaborate courtesies and a vague, easily mistranslated language. Precise meaning, so crucial to diplomacy, recedes from their grasp into a gentle Japanese mist.

Grew would find no easy paths to understanding the Japanese. He might, as F. S. C. Northrop suggests, study the classical oriental texts to discover the postulates of the East and then re-examine his own experiences in their light, but he was not scholarly or speculative.[3] Art perhaps offered a more congenial medium of understanding. Grew loved music and was sensitive to beauty in nature. The restraint, harmony, and simplicity of Japanese art would appeal to him. Yet his artistic sensitivity was not like the Japanese. The communion between the viewer and the viewed of the Japanese was absent. The wealth of feeling they bestowed on a leaf, a petal, a stone was lacking. Grew might overcome the barriers to understanding by learning Japanese. At half his age, with fewer responsibilities, a less difficult language, and less international tension he might have tried. Poor Japanese could be more awkward and mischievous than no Japanese at all. He would try to get along with English and an occasional assist from Russian, French, and German.

He had no ready means of solving the problem of communication. The peculiarly Japanese idea, convoluted by abhorrence of saying anything definite or unpleasant, by the usual paraphernalia of politeness, and by the use of the inevitable go-between, would be further weakened by the necessity of translation for Grew, and his own message would be obscured in the opposite direction. Japanese-spoken English was indistinct and particularly difficult for him to hear. More than usually Grew would be aloof and isolated in Japan.

To the problems of Japanese hypersensitivity and unintelligibility was added the difficulty of political diagnosis. The dynamics of Japanese politics have defied systematic analysis. The formal structure of government has scarcely resembled the actual distribution and exercise of power. The government official carried his bundle of social anxieties and obligations to his desk. To avoid loss of face in case of failure he sought to share the burden of decisions as widely as possible. In addition, the punctilios of personal relationship demanded a protective attitude toward his subordinates in return for their loyalty. Not only did he hesitate to overrule them but he felt obliged to be responsive to their ideas. The result was the phenomenon of "rule from below" or *gekokujō*. As *New York Times* correspondent A. M. Rosenthal says, ". . . [D]ecisions in Japan are somehow never actually taken but seem to seep upward in a sort of consensus worked out layer by layer." [4]

The diagnosis of politics was further complicated by factionalism. The Japanese, a clubby people, found unusual strength and comfort in groups formed around common occupations, family ties, friendships, interests, experiences, backgrounds. The result was a myriad of cliques that crisscrossed the formal guidelines of bureaucratic authority. Cohesive yet shadowy, pervasive yet capricious, they were a source of power but also of instability in government. Policy tended to represent a precarious balance of competing pressures. It would seem to the diplomatic observer to move by some divine inspiration, like the wayward palanquin carried by shouting, shoving young men in the Japanese Festival of the Three Protectors.[5]

Grew need not have been totally surprised by the complication of Japanese politics. The old Diplomatic Service had much of the intimacy and common ties of a Japanese clique. Nevertheless, his task would be no more easy for the familiarity. Diffusion of responsibility, rule from below, and cliques had the effect of drawing the dynamics of Japanese politics away from those top officials like the Premier and Foreign Minister with whom he had been accustomed to deal in other countries.

Obviously a Japan mission anytime would pose fresh professional challenges for Grew. The weakening of peaceful presuppositions about world and particularly Far Eastern affairs consequent to the Mukden Incident of September 18, 1931, made these challenges acute. The thirties could not afford diplomatic shadow-boxing in Tokyo.

The Far Eastern crisis was nine months old when Grew took up his mission. While he was completing his patient, constructive treaty-making efforts in Turkey, key officers of the Japanese Kwantung Army were plotting an act of railroad sabotage near Mukden as pretext for the occupation of Manchuria. The Japanese government proved unable to control the officers responsible, and by November 1931 the operation was succeeding brilliantly. In December the League of Nations undertook an investigation, only to be flaunted in January, 1932, by the Kwantung Army's move to the verge of North China. From the time of Grew's appointment in January 1932 to his departure from Turkey in March, Secretary Stimson was skillfully roping the League Covenant, the Kellogg-Briand Pact, and the Nine-Power Treaty respecting the territorial integrity of China into a legal net that, once the facts of Japanese aggression had been established by League investigation, would ensure world condemnation, however Japan might squirm or what little else the world might do. First came the Non-Recognition Doctrine, then the Borah Letter, then, with American prodding, League acceptance of non-recognition. The Secretary's task was easier because Japan became embroiled in full-scale fighting at Shanghai by her admiral on the spot. It was May before she could extricate herself from this unwanted adventure without loss of face. What little hope remained of Sino-Japanese negotiations over Manchuria disappeared in violent public feeling that developed on both sides. Japan stood committed to her Manchurian conquest, the world against it.[6]

Meanwhile Japan experienced an inner crisis. On May 15, 1932, the day the Grews left Washington for San Francisco and the Orient, a band of young naval officers and army cadets assassinated Premier Inukai Ki,* the third prominent victim of violent nationalist agitation that year. In consultations over a successor the Army warned that it would be unable to prevent further violence unless corrupt party government ended. War Minister Araki Sadao did not much care who was made Premier so long as the Army's requests were met.[7] As a result, a compliant non-party government was installed headed by retired Admiral Viscount Saito Makoto. The short and not unpromising life of representative government in Japan came to an end ten days before the *President Coolidge* docked at Yokohama with the

* Japanese names are given in the Japanese style, family names first.

new American Ambassador aboard. From Turkey, a nation moving vigorously toward the West, Grew came to one in a fit of repudiation.

Japan could not be budged from Manchuria except by force, and the Japanese Army had assumed a dominant role in domestic affairs. These were obvious facts. What they portended was most difficult for Grew or anyone else to estimate. He had been "boning up" on Japan in Washington, on the Overland Limited, and during the long transpacific voyage. Ambassador Matsudaira Tsuneo, an old friend, had comfortingly predicted in London that the "pendulum" in Japan would soon swing back to normal, in other words that the military had gone too far, that Japan would come to it senses, and that the moderates would regain control. The notion that the peaceableness and constitutionalism of the twenties still exerted a gravitational pull over events in the thirties would be attractive to Grew. Or one might ignore internal developments and consider Manchuria the limit of forseeable Japanese ambitions. After years of humiliation her pride as a great power had been salved. It had been Japan's "hard luck," Grew noted, to become a great power after the world's open spaces had been appropriated. She had been cheated out of the spoils of victory in the Sino-Japanese and Russo-Japanese wars at the turn of the century. Subsequently the Chinese had repeatedly violated her rights. Now that she had secured Manchuria perhaps she would be content. On the other hand, some held that Japan was incurably expansionistic: first Korea, now Manchuria, then Asia. For the moment it seemed best not to predict or prejudge. An ambassador, he held, must keep a detached and balanced point of view.[8]

It was wise to keep an open mind. The "vast and turgid process" of events in the Far East, so described by George Kennan, defies simple explanation.[9] Optimistic predictions of a return to normalcy were certainly unwarranted. It would have been hard even for a friendly observer at the time to deny that Japan was cutting loose from her immediate past and would be dangerously assertive in the Far East. National ego, military budgets, brute force, propaganda, and authoritarian government were in the ascendency. Democracy, moderation, worldliness, humaneness, reason, and law were in disrepute. Threatening tendencies were at work, countervailing tendencies weak. Japan was in the midst of a major crisis of historical change.

Japan's crisis stemmed from the uneven impact of Western influences. For three generations, since the Meiji Reforms beginning in 1868, Japan had been modeling herself on the West. In institutions and techniques the transformation had been amazingly fast. Western instruments of power — modern, professional military services, sprawling state ministries staffed by career civil servants, a centralized police system, a tightly knit industrial economy, mass communications media — had been assimilated quickly. Western notions of political behavior came more slowly. The Diet lacked ultimate revenue and legislative authority. The Army and Navy, with direct access to the Emperor, could circumvent civilian control and exercised a veto power in cabinet formation by retaining the right to name uniformed officers to the War and Navy portfolios. Civilian leadership, unduly sensitive to criticism, resigned frequently, preventing executive stability.[10] Political parties lacked lower-class support and entertained scandalous relations with the big industrial combines, the zaibatsu. The Western concept of the dignity of the individual, the foundation of democracy, was not widely understood. Yet the Japanese were literate enough, thanks to universal education, and submissive enough by tradition to be easily swayed by propaganda. Japan had acquired Western power but had not developed inhibitions about power.

If Western influence now seems to have been deficient in certain crucial respects, to Japanese at the time it seemed to have gone all too far. Rural Japan decried the grime and rootlessness of factory cities. Traditionalists deplored the venality and self-seeking of Western-style politics. In place of consensus and harmony democracy provided bickering and class dissension. Western individualism seemed to breed disrespect, self-indulgence, and bad manners. Free inquiry only produced a babel of subversive, radical ideas. Japanese seemed on the point of losing their rich cultural heritage, their intricate fabric of family and social responsibility, their sense of community. Japan, many felt, was losing its soul to the West.

The world of the thirties called for a reassertion of Japanese independence. Japan was suffering from the world depression. Collapse of the market for silk and rising Western tariffs against Japanese manufactures were a high price to pay for economic interdependence with the West. Tariff exclusion on top of immigration exclusion and inferior naval ratios attested to the West's scorn for Japan. Now the West, brought low by the depression and itself toying with totalitarian ideologies, appeared not only pernicious but passé. Ominous changes were taking place in the Far East. The Soviet Union after a decade of concentrating on internal development was re-establishing its military forces in Siberia. The Kuomintang had consolidated its position in central China and was exerting increasing pressure against foreign concessions and privileges. Extensive Japanese commercial interests and sensitive strategic interests were threatened. East and West the future seemed to foreclose on Japan. She would find security only in her own resources and energies.

Internal stress and external insecurity produced a violent uspurge of nationalism. The nation already commanded the deepest Japanese feelings. The Emperor, personifying the nation, inspired awe as a descendant of supernatural beings, reverence as the central figure of religion, devotion and a sense of infinite obligation as a father figure, utter obedience as the apex of all hierarchies. Japanese were all siblings around the same hearth, of a proud and potent line. Nationalistic societies were quick to remind any who forgot what it meant to be a Japanese. These spawned increasingly in the twenties, with memberships of every description, from wild-eyed young socialists to beribboned court nobles. Distressed farmers, middle-grade army officers, intellectuals had special groups. Others were mixed. Some were secret and conspiratorial, others open and for discussion. Demagogues and agitators passed among them soliciting funds and disseminating propaganda. Some societies concentrated on external problems, some on internal. They formed, hived, disappeared, re-formed. Much of what they had to say was preposterous. Their total effect was nevertheless important. They created from a host of anxieties one major national crisis. They set Japanese against the world. They undermined the remaining prestige of moderating institutions and squelched minority opinion. They provided the Valhalla-like setting for would-be heroes and crafty opportunists. Their beneficiary was the Japanese Army.[11]

Japan's problems weighed most heavily on the Army. More than any other element of state or society, more than the Navy, the Army stood for traditional Japan. It was not only the undefeated guardian of the realm but also guardian of the Japanese spirit. The soldier was absolutely committed to serve the Emperor and thus the nation. Discipline, sacrifice, and obedience, virtues cherished by every subject, had been honed to their finest edge by the samurai swordsmen of old. To that part of Japan surfeited by foreign influences, the way of the warrior, *bushido*, remained true and unsullied. Largely recruited from and stationed in rural prefectures, soldiers in the ranks were particularly susceptible to the crude and violent nativism that bred on the shriveling rice and silk prices of the early thirties. Peasant and peasant-soldier alike demanded a return to simple, earthy ways. The Army was disgusted with what it took to be weak-kneed foreign policy in the face of Western contempt, Chinese provocation, and Soviet threat. Cooperation with the West meant disarmament, which entailed budget cuts, reductions in force, and premature retirement of officers. The Army felt threatened by the parliamentary criticism and civilian executive control that marked the development of representative institutions in Japan during the twenties. The prestige and power of the Japanese Army was in fact on the wane until the Manchurian Incident.[12]

The Manchurian Incident and the 1932 assassinations gave the Army a central but not a single-minded role in internal and foreign affairs. Here was no mastermind at work or imperialistic conspiracy afoot, but rather a broth of diverse impulses, ambitions, and schemes. The officer corps was the opposite of monolithic. Simple peasant minds at the company level were easily contorted by propaganda into loyally murdering the Emperor's "evil advisers." At the staff and general officer levels more sophisticated

War College minds prevailed, but with every degree of political-mindedness. Hell-for-leather fighters of the *Kodo-ha*, or Imperial Way, mentality demanded immediate action against Japan's enemies abroad, but some of them stood aloof from internal affairs while others plotted fascistic revolution. Subtler minds were prepared to play politics, some shunning direct action at home or abroad in favor of long-term industrial and political mobilization for war, others craftily riding the turbulence to further their own military or political ambitions. The needle of strategic planning swung uncertainly between China proper, Chinese frontier provinces north of the Great Wall flanking the Soviet Union, and the Soviet Union itself. Many argued for consolidating in Manchuria, building a war machine and then deciding. Fundamentals of tactics and supply were in dispute, the traditional school of massed infantry against new concepts of air-and-armor mobility. Assignment, whether to the War Ministry or General Staff with their separate personnel systems, or to the Kwantung Army, a small empire in itself, added institutional points of view to the crazy quilt of clan and clique loyalties and rivalries. The Navy, a shade less turbulent, competed with the Army for prestige and budgets. Nothing was settled, nothing predetermined except trouble.

The essential unpredictability of Japanese affairs at the time of Grew's arrival begged for the professional objectivity he held so important. The danger existed not that he would condemn Japan as a scheming aggressor but that his sanguinary nature and relatively quiet career would lead him to see in lack of aggression abroad and violence internally signs of a return to normalcy. A fundamental change in the power structure of Japan had occurred. The Army was in the saddle. The direction of Japan's ambitions might be undecided, but she was undeniably ambitious. Tokyo in 1932 was a post for the objective pessimist rather than the objective optimist.

In dealing with Japan, Grew possessed few advantages. He could bank on no fund of understanding such as existed between the British and American people. To be sure, America had made a profound impact on Japan. Nearly eighty years earlier, Mrs. Grew's great-granduncle, Commodore Matthew Perry, had opened Japan to the West. Subsequent work by missionaries, educators, and American-trained Japanese imparted what one authority calls a "predominantly American flavor to Japanese Westernization." However, a sense of community does not necessarily develop out of a common affection for baseball. In spite of Japanese borrowings the two people remained strangers, the Japanese stubborn in the spirit of their ways, the Americans massively indifferent to foreign ways. Early cordiality turned to suspicion, resentment, and rivalry. Images of each other became distorted by fantasy and bias: Americans were coarse and self-indulgent, Japanese two-faced and imitative. Immigration legislation of 1924 singled out Japanese as aliens not wanted in the United States even in token numbers.

Grew, Under Secretary at the time, sympathized with the Japanese but felt their resentment would "soon die a natural death." He was to change that opinion.[13]

A more substantial advantage was the common economic interest of the two nations. The United States accounted for a large proportion of Japan's exports as well as imports. It was Japan's chief source of foreign capital and foreign goods, of automobiles, raw materials, oil, and machinery. Americans bought nearly all of Japan's raw silk exports. Trade between the two nations and between each of them and China was mostly in non-competitive items. Depression and high American tariffs severely cut into Japanese exports to the United States, but the potential advantages remained. The trade relationship was one of the few assets in Grew's diplomacy.[14]

The difficulty was that discord between Japan and the United States could not be removed simply by improving trade and friendly feeling. Problems were too fundamental and comprehensive. The emergence of the two nations as primary powers of the Pacific was rapid and simultaneous, a matter of two decades. The sudden arrival of a major industrial nation with a first-class fleet on the opposite side of the ocean created a presumptive security threat to the United States, just as America's immense strength did for Japan. Far Eastern rivalry sharpened security concerns. The United States assumed the role of a Far Eastern power with possessions and rights to protect, a long-standing interest in enlarging its trade with Asia, and a growing attachment to China's self-development along Western lines. In the same period Japan expanded its foothold on the continent, acquiring rights and interests in Manchuria of vital proportions and expanding ambitions, now political and economic, now just economic, elsewhere in China. Japan formulated new strategic axioms and policies for her imperial position, in particular the requirement of naval supremacy in the Western Pacific and a special role in Chinese affairs. Each nation, by protecting and advancing its own Far Eastern position, contradicted or seemed to undermine the position of the other. By the twenties, the Japanese Army and Navy regarded the United States as the most probable enemy, while the American Navy took the same view of Japan.

Accommodation became more and more difficult to achieve. The give-and-take spirit that characterized Japanese-American relations in the time of Theodore Roosevelt gave way with Woodrow Wilson to literal-minded insistence on principles of international conduct. American policy hardened in support of the sovereignty and territorial integrity of China, opposing Japanese encroachment under the Twenty-One Demands and Japanese occupation of Shantung. The ambiguous Lansing-Ishii agreement only papered over the contradiction between American principle and the reality of Japan's special interests in China. Japan accepted the principle of the integrity of China in the Nine-Power Treaty of 1922 but found a loophole in the security clause which seemed to make an exception of its special position. Differences were more intractable and less easily resolved by diplomacy.

At the same time neither nation desired a confrontation. The United States shrank from application of pressure or use of force for a number of reasons, among them the vulnerability, remoteness, and still somewhat speculative nature of its Far Eastern interests and a historic reluctance to engage its power outside the Western Hemisphere. Japan, so long as its fundamental interests were not challenged, was wary of challenging a nation with the resource potential of the United States. At the Washington Conference in 1922 the Pacific powers agreed to limit their navies and exchanged territorial guarantees, thereby reducing tensions, subduing naval rivalry, and achieving a Far Eastern equilibrium. Nevertheless, it was an unstable equilibrium because neither the United States nor Japan was prepared to reduce its commitments, shed its expectations, or compromise its interests, in short to diminish its stature as a Far Eastern power.[15]

Manchuria had the effect of further paralyzing relations. The sour, listless mood of Americans preoccupied with economic tragedy scarcely encouraged vigorous diplomacy, especially in an election year. An Anglo-American diplomatic front had been impossible to establish. President Hoover, preoccupied, gloomy, and at heart a pacifist, had told Grew that Japan must get out of Manchuria but that the United States must not go to war. The President's greatest fear, according to Grew, was the occurrence of some inflammatory incident like the sinking of the *Maine*.[16] Stimson's letter to Senator Borah in February 1932 had pointed out the interrelationship of the Washington treaties. American abnegation in naval building and Western Pacific fortification depended on fulfillment by other parties of their pledges, implicitly Japan's pledge to uphold the territorial integrity of China. The President, who to Stimson possessed not "the slightest element of even the fairest kind of bluff," erased this veiled warning in May 1932 by having Acting Secretary Castle publicly renounce even the use of economic pressure. Grew, who felt he had been deprived of a "useful card," commented that sometimes it was inadvisable to tell the world what the United States was *not* going to do.[17]

One further warning was given, and this the Japanese noticed: the fleet's Scouting Force was directed to remain with the Battle Force on the West Coast after maneuvers instead of returning to the Atlantic. This move might deter the Japanese from attacking American territory, which they had no plans for anyway, but could hardly affect the Far Eastern problem so long as the United States publicly declined to intervene by force. The concentration aroused excitement in Japan at first but then it was discovered that American war preparations were not serious and it only served to inspire further jingoism and justify larger military budgets.[18] All in all it was a bad year for American power plays.[19]

Stimson's arraignment of Japan was the inescapable determinant of Grew's diplomacy. Together, the speeches, notes, letters, and promptings of the Secretary that harrying year constituted a legal seine from which the Japanese could hardly escape. Simply stated his brief ran as follows. The principle of self-denial of aggression had been codified generally in the Kellogg-Briand Pact and specifically for the Far East in the Nine-Power Treaty, which also carried into international law the principles of equal commercial opportunity in, and territorial integrity of, China. The United States as a law-abiding nation signatory to both pacts, as well as in pursuit of its own traditional policy, was obligated not to recognize any arrangement contravening those principles, in particular any Manchurian arrangement by Japan alone, by interested parties, or by anyone else. The League of Nations had before it the Manchurian problem, and the United States would not interfere, prejudge, or prescribe, but the League itself was obliged to countenance no solution in violation of international law, that is, of the two treaties. The League, thus prompted, acknowledged its responsibilities, accepting non-recognition and the applicability of the treaties in question. Stimson thereby managed to interlock the positions of the League and the United States, for the first time creating a world front condemning an act of aggression. Yet his position was thoroughly conversant with traditional American foreign policy. It was an extraordinary feat of diplomatic legerdemain.[20]

The question remains whether it was wise. As often happens in Anglo-American law, Stimson was using precedent to create what amounted to new law. He imparted more acceptance to John Hay's Open Door Notes than had existed. He included Manchuria in China proper where the Washington Conference had not been so precise. He gave a positive force to the Kellogg Pact which the signatories of that vague and well-meaning instrument must never have intended. He directed American policy explicitly and unequivocally against Japanese action in China. It would be very difficult in the future to overturn the Stimson case on aggression, to let bygones be bygones about Manchuria. But he had established a wrong without a remedy. Japan was put beyond the pale, unrepentent and unpunishable, and held the United States responsible. Grew had come upon a situation where problems between the two nations were fundamentally nonnegotiable. He was expected, not so much to build Japanese-American relations as he had Turkish-American, as to concentrate his tact and professional skill on preventing incidents and misunderstandings from dragging the two countries to war.[21]

Grew was most emphatically reminded of the inflamed state of Japanese-American relations throughout his early months in Japan. On June 21, 1932, only a week after the new American Ambassador had presented his credentials to the Emperor, Viscount Ishii Kikujiro made a hostile speech at a luncheon in Grew's honor given by the America-Japan Society. The distinguished statesman, a former special envoy and Ambassador to the United States, seemed to go out of his way not to flatter the guest of honor: the summons to speak had "rudely awakened" him from "leisurely slumber"; he found nothing particularly delicate or difficult about Tokyo and Washington as diplomatic posts. War talk was criminal and absurd, he went on, if only because — an ominous condition — the intelligent people in both countries recognized the folly of exposing their "flesh and bones" in each other's respective spheres of activity, that is, the Western Hemisphere and Far East. In Theodore Roosevelt's day the United States had not opposed Japanese expansion so long as it was peaceful and guaranteed the Open Door. He warned the United States not to do so in the present case. The warning, which reached page one of the *New York Times* the next day, may have been intended for extremists in Japan as much as for those of the Stimson persuasion in the United States.

Ishii's speech could not simply be passed off as ill-mannered. Here in essence was Japan's Asiatic Monroe Doctrine, the guiding rationalization of Japanese foreign policy down to the China War, precursor of the Co-Prosperity Sphere, and Japan's answer to outlawry by the West. Prince Saionji Kimmochi, who did not like Ishii's speech, recognized how the doctrine broke with the past. The last of the Genro, elder statesmen who had superintended their nation's extraordinary rise to power, he attributed Japan's success to cooperation with the leading powers, Britain and the United States. This relationship of mutual interest, he claimed, created a world position for Japan which made easier solution of her problems in the East. By asserting primacy in Asia, Japan would have to "bow before the leaders." Presumably he meant that by withdrawing to her own preserve Japan would be destroying her value to other powers, which in the past had been a source of benefit to Japan in the Far East. Perhaps it took a Saionji to see the implications. Grew, who had difficulty hearing Ishii and was a stranger, did not. He found the tone of the speech inflammatory, but could "hardly take exception to the substance." [22]

Hardly a month went by without added strain to Japanese-American relations. On August 8, 1932, Stimson gave a major address before the Council on Foreign Relations, intended, he confided to his diary, "to support the Kellogg Pact as the fulcrum upon which we will have our issue with Japan." The Pact would provide common ground for the League and the United States to press their case against Japan when the League investigation was complete. Stimson argued a hypothetical case, not naming Japan but referring to Manchuria and using the term aggressor. No mistake whom he was waving his finger at. The *New York Times* saw the speech as an appeal to nations "which united in disapproval of Japan's acts last winter. . . ." According to Stanley K. Hornbeck, Chief of the Far Eastern Division, the speech stood with the Non-Recognition Doctrine and the Borah Letter seeking "crystallization of the public opinion of the world against the present offending power and/or any other. . . ." Not surprisingly the Japanese found the unmistakable implication, and chauvinists in the government sent the volatile press into an anti-American tirade. Grew was called down to steaming Tokyo from his cool mountain retreat but found himself defenseless: the Embassy had received neither official text nor résumé from Washington. By the time the text had come the Foreign Office had closed the issue by describing the speech as a political campaign effort. At least Grew did not have to explain to the Foreign Minister that the Secretary had not really meant what he obviously intended to mean.[23]

In September 1932 and January 1933 occurred two incidents involving American businesses in Japan, one ludicrous, one ugly, and both piling up more popular resentment. In September police accused the Osaka branch of National City Bank of photographic espionage. Under orders from home the branch had been taking pictures of industrial and commercial areas of the city where it had investment interests. That any bank would risk its prestige by sending cameramen into the streets to gather intelligence for a foreign government seemed not ridiculous at all. The press made the most of a delicious spy scare. Then in January two hundred demonstrators involved in a labor dispute with the Singer Sewing Machine Company at Yokohama demolished the company's offices. In spite of warnings by the Embassy the company received no police protection until too late. Warning then came of an attack on the American Consulate, which failed to materialize. Grew even gave some thought to protection of the Embassy. In both the National City and Singer cases he made representations personally to the Minister of Foreign Affairs, who, while not daring to make public apologies, offered suitable amends.[24]

Anti-Americanism was the all-absorbing concern of the Embassy that year. It would subside after an incident only to resurge at slight provocation. The United States seemed to be preying on Japan's nerves. Editorials steadily slammed the United States, especially Stimson. Viscount Kaneko Kentaro spoke at the Harvard Club for nearly ninety minutes itemizing Japan's grievances against America over thirty years. The confidant of Theodore Roosevelt, his face livid with rage, actually shook his fist in Grew's face. On all sides Grew heard the hope expressed that the Scouting Force would return to the Atlantic. The Foreign Office spokesman discovered "reliable" evidence that the American Army was lending noncommissioned officers on active duty to China to fight Japan. An Imperial Prince asked "point-blank" whether it was true that the United States was preparing for war with Japan. The Minister of Foreign Affairs told correspondents that any blunder by Japan might lead to "grave consequences," a term like a hurricane warning to diplomats. The Japanese, it seemed to

Grew, were in a state of high nerves, much like the war psychology he had seen in Germany on the eve of World War I. He was deeply disturbed and perplexed as to what to do.[25]

What course he recommended to his government and what attitude he himself adopted would depend on how he interpreted events in Japan, but he was hesitant to diagnose or predict until more familiar with the situation. To muster more eyes and ears he invited American correspondents to drop in at the Embassy for a chat. Few did at first, but Wilfrid Fleisher, editor of the *Japan Advertiser* was helpful. Grew also had a good Embassy staff of eight officers, chronically reduced by illness, leave, and transfer. Edwin Neville, his Counselor, was a loyal and sound officer of twenty-four years' experience, thoroughly familiar with Japan and highly regarded at the Foreign Office. Presently he was worn out from a nerve-wracking chargéship, his face in continual contortions, and Grew sent him to the hills for a rest. What Neville's dispatches lacked in polish was more than made up by those of Erle Dickover, First Secretary, who was considered the liveliest reporter in the Far East.

It was a good staff, but the Ambassador felt it needed jacking up. He administered encouragement as well as discipline. He asked for information, comments, and suggestions for telegrams. The military, naval, and commercial attachés were called into policy discussions and asked for appraisals. Outlying consulates such as Dairen in Manchuria were ordered to report more fully to the Embassy. Junior officers were given special assignments such as Soviet-Japanese relations. Soon the flow began. Officers took initiative, information accumulated, dispatches rose in volume and quality. By the end of the first year the Far Eastern Division was sending compliments and comparing China reporting unfavorably. In the process Grew was getting his political bearings.[26]

It was obvious to all that the Army was on top in Japan. The more difficult question was, who controlled the Army? The Embassy's answer in the summer of 1932 was that a clique of hotheaded young army officers was in control. They were seen as a dangerous lot, relatively ignorant and stirred to violence easily by chauvinistic and fascistic agitators. They had been responsible for the Manchurian Incident and the recent assassinations. With their champion and spokesman, War Minister Araki, in the driver's seat, there was no telling what they might do next.[27]

It seems now that the Embassy ascribed too much power and influence to these younger officers. "Young officers" is too vague to be very helpful anyway. There was no connection or similarity between, for example, Lieutenant Colonel Ishihara Kanji, the brilliant staff officer who helped plan the Mukden Incident, and the fuzzy-witted young cadet who helped murder Premier Inukai. It would be equally incorrect to equate either of these types with those officers personally associated with Araki, who benefited from his advancement to the post of War Minister. While it is true that Araki was a fighting leader widely admired by infantry line officers, he was not their cat's-paw. Rather he seems to have been performing a delicate balancing act, on the one hand posing as the champion of the varied forces of discontent in the Army, and on the other representing conservative elements both in the high command and in the civilian government who favored restoring discipline in the Army. For a time he was successful. That year and the next plots were uncovered, but no new incidents were perpetrated. Deep cleavages existed in the Army and the government regarding longer-range goals, but sufficient consensus prevailed about immediate objectives — restoration of discipline, larger military budgets, fulfillment and exploitation of the Manchurian conquest — for the Saito-Araki compromise government to hang together for a while.[28]

The Embassy that anxious summer thought the hotheads were still loose and sounded the alarm. The military were absolutely determined to carry out their Manchurian venture, Grew reported, and would fight any power that intervened. The Japanese military machine was preparing for and would welcome war. Like the German military in 1914, they might override all restraining influences. They saw their chief obstacle as the United States. Grew was not prepared to agree that any little incident or indiscretion might lead to war between Japan and the United States, but the "facts of history" required alertness to all possible contingencies. Perhaps he recalled the President's concern about an incident like the sinking of the *Maine*. Such were the warnings of August and September. In early October a slightly different diagnosis of the danger produced a similar warning. The military might act from want of confidence as well as from overconfidence. Should their program appear impeded or likely to fail, "the most dangerous factor" in the situation, that of face, would become involved. Rather than give in to saner elements, they were capable of "plunging the country into any kind of disaster." Such disaster, he confided to his diary but not his dispatch, might include wholesale assassination, revolution or war. Viewed any way, it was a grim outlook.[29]

At such times the professional diplomat lies low, and this is what Grew did. Silence was golden. There was nothing to be gained by "ramming our policy down their throats." In shipboard interviews he talked about Mrs. Grew's relation to Commodore Perry and his book, *Sport and Travel in the Far East* (*Exploitation and Travel in the Far East*, as *Jiji* called it), and thereafter shied away from interviews. His debut before the America-Japan Society, where Ishii spoke with American bluntness, was an exercise in the oriental virtues of calmness, serenity, and philosophy. He said he hoped during his mission to supplement the frail language of the spoken word with an inaudible language, "a sort of X-ray language . . . which perhaps extends less from mind to mind than from heart to heart. . . ."[30]

Grew tried to stay away from the Japanese Foreign Office, as he had from the Turkish Foreign Office during the schools crisis. Formal representations only exacerbated strained relations. In fact any visit to the Foreign Office was likely to be twisted to serve the propaganda of the military. The spokesman of the Foreign Office, Shiratori Toshio, had "associated himself with the group of young military 'fascists' who are in control in Japan today." In the National City Bank affair he called on the Foreign Minister only after visits by a subordinate and by the bank manager had failed to halt the spy scare. Under instructions he protested the Japanese takeover of the Chinese Imperial Maritime Customs at Dairen, Manchuria, but he avoided making representations against Japanese recognition of Manchukuo, although both the British and French ambassadors did. As in Ankara, so in Tokyo, there was an advantage beyond the unbearable summer heat, in being away from the capital. That summer he spent thirty-seven days in the "deliciously refreshing" mountain retreat of Karuizawa, where he could watch butterflies and double-tailed goldfish and swim in an icy, crystal pool fed by a tinkling brook.[31]

Prospects were never hopeless. The thirties were still too young to dispel cozy preconceptions of the twenties and quash Grew's boyish optimism. His crisis dispatches never quite lost sight of the possibility of a return to moderation in Japan. A group he variously described as composed of the "thoughtful," "conservative," "moderate," and "saner" Japanese had no enthusiasm for the ideas and ventures of the militarists. They recognized that Manchuria would be costly and unprofitable and that Japan's internal economic situation was deteriorating. They had serious misgivings as to where the Manchurian venture would lead the country. The moderate element was inarticulate and powerless but was nevertheless "steadily working beneath the surface." It had not yet acted but still might. By avoiding harsh criticism of Japan the United States might at least give it a chance.[32]

With the start of the social season in October, Grew began to hear from the moderates. Debuchi Katsuji, Ambassador to the United States then home on leave, told Grew that the Emperor understood the American position perfectly. The domestic political situation was well in hand and the extreme chauvinists had been compelled to moderate their views. Then came the Ambassador to Italy, Yoshida Shigeru, with assurances that the moderates were stronger than generally believed and would be heard from in due course. Baron Makino Nobuaki, Yoshida's father-in-law, repeated the refrain on several occasions. The seventy-year-old Lord Keeper of the Privy Seal, whom Grew had met at the Paris Peace Conference, emphasized the existing undercurrent of moderate thought. Count Kabayama Aisuke, who acted as an unofficial go-between for the Embassy and prominent Japanese, "spoke along precisely the same lines as Makino." Baron Shidehara Kijuro, former Foreign Minister, whose name was associated with the peaceable foreign policy of the previous decade, paid a call and like Matsudaira spoke of the pendulum action of Japanese politics. One and all sought to convince Grew that the forces of moderation were on the upswing.[33]

Grew was not clear how extensive a group the moderates were, but obviously among these Japanese he had a beginning. They were of a type he knew and understood: gracious, dignified, modest, cultured gentlemen. They were Count Berchtold and Sir George Clerk in a Japanese setting. All had served or studied in the West. He felt at ease with and trusted them. They formed a bridge for him to a still bewildering Japan. How far their influence was felt in Japan he could not know. It was probably not very far in 1932. Viewed in the total configuration of Japanese cliques and coalitions, these Western-oriented Japanese had more prestige than power. A position at court such as Makino's might enable him to influence the course of events here and there, but was as much a liability as a source of strength, the liability being the necessity of not involving the Emperor's prestige in a political reversal. As for the diplomats, Grew well knew that his profession was no source of political strength. Prince Saionji was devoted to Western political ideals, but shepherded his remaining strength for major crises. Clan ties (Makino and Kabayama were of the Satsuma) and zaibatsu connections (Shidehara married the daughter of the founder of Mitsubishi) could be helpful, but again emphasized the derived nature of the moderates' influence. Their hope lay in manipulating cliques and fashioning coalitions among other sources of power — the bureaucracy, political parties, the Navy, the zaibatsu — to counterbalance that of the Army.

Events seemed to prove, nevertheless, that the forces of moderation were gaining strength. Surprisingly General Araki turned cordial. According to Yoshida, the Minister of War was not the fire-eater he was supposed to be. Actually, Grew was told, Araki opposed the chauvinism of the younger army officers and wanted the anti-American press campaign stopped. Grew had himself introduced, and found Araki very pleasant and interested in talking further. By the end of the year Araki was lunching at the Embassy and enjoying conversation with Grew in Russian. Apparently, Grew concluded, the General had found Manchuria a bigger problem than expected and was "singing on a lower note." [34] Furthermore, Araki and Saito seemed to be taking firm steps to prevent further conspiracies and assassinations. On November 5, 1932, police arrested the son of Toyama Mitsuru, a notorious nationalist agitator, for implication in the May 15 Incident. At the same time they nipped in the bud a new plot, this one aimed at Premier Saito. Such firmness seemed proof of the government's growing confidence and authority. The "chauvinistic military hotheads," Grew wrote Stimson, "are less firmly intrenched and are, it is hoped, giving way to a more constructive statesmanship." Kabayama, he recorded in his diary November 8, saw the moderates regaining influence, "and in this I am now beginning to believe he is right. . . ." [35]

The sky seemed to be lightening all around. By December, Grew was dining not only with Araki, but with Kaneko, who had publicly harangued him in the summer, and was "badly rooking" Shiratori, the fiery Foreign Office spokesman, in poker at the Embassy. Shiratori, who now appeared quite human after all, had lost influence, Grew heard. His backer, a political schemer closely connected with the military, Mori Kaku, fell ill and died in December. Whatever the reason — Grew guessed the Emperor may have had some influence — the anti-American press campaign died down. Ambassador Debuchi was ordered back to the United States in spite of presumed military opposition. Economic conditions were improving, easing social conditions and thereby the public temper. At the same time, Grew reported, there was mounting concern at the heavy deficit financing undertaken to meet the cost of the Manchurian venture. He believed that the Japanese were beginning to see the need to ameliorate world hostility to protect the nation's credit standing. So far as Manchuria was concerned, the crisis might have passed. Recognition of Manchukuo on September 15, 1932, appeared to pacify restless elements. The absence of world-wide repercussions gave the military little to grumble about. The press blustered over the Lytton Report, published October 2, but League action promised to be slow and uncertain.[36]

The Japanese seemed encouraged about American policy too. The Foreign Office had to admit that Stimson's speech at Pittsburgh, October 1, was "much more moderate than the one he delivered in August." Makino expressed his pleasure over Castle's speech that month in Cincinnati in which he was reported to have said that prospects were good for a complete understanding between Japan and the United States. Grew doubted the Secretary would agree, but felt the friendly tone did much good. The Japanese were convinced that relations would improve after the November American elections, because Stimson, whom they held chiefly responsible for bad relations, was to be replaced either by Castle if Hoover won, according to rumor, or by a Democratic Secretary of State. A Democratic victory, which they came increasingly to expect, could hardly result in worse relations, and so they were "playing up" to the Democrats in advance, Grew suspected. The accumulation of evidence could not be ignored: a thaw seemed in the making. If all his signals were correct, as Grew fervently hoped they were, the great Manchurian crisis might be passing.[37]

Grew's signals were substantially correct but their meaning escaped him. Japan was seeking a *détente* in the fall of 1932. According to the diary of Baron Harada, secretary to Prince Saionji, the government decided on September 30, to be "as quiet as possible" about the Lytton Report in order to avoid a hostile atmosphere at Geneva when action was under consideration.

As Harada knew, and as Baron Hayashi Gonsuke, Grand Master of Ceremonies, told Grew, the Report's contents were not entirely unfavorable to Japan. The government also decided, Harada learned November 7, that Japan would spend the next two years rearming. The decision whether or not to attack Russia at the end of two years was postponed. In the period of preparation international goodwill was to be maintained, and in particular friendly relations with the United States. The military realized that the United States was an important supplier of raw materials.

Such a policy could gain various supporters, including those who advocated war with Russia, those advocating expansion in a different direction, and those advocating friendly relations with the West. Certainly the moderates supported it, but their capacity to influence the course of events had not increased. Araki had no objection to Debuchi's return to the United States because, as he said, "after returning to Japan and coming to understand the various changed conditions, [he] should not make the same mistakes that he made previously." A proposed trip to the United States by Prince Konoe Fumimaro, the great political hope of the moderates, was canceled by the Army. "If the Army can sway you thus," Harada asked Konoe, "what would you do in case Prince Saionji and the Army differed upon a matter?" [38]

Events of early 1933 shattered Grew's nascent confidence in the influence of the moderates. On January 3 the Kwantung Army edged into North China itself by capturing Shanhaikwan where the Great Wall reaches the sea. Preparations followed to absorb Jehol Province, a strategic wedge of mountainous country between Manchuria and North China. At Geneva wearisome effort at conciliation finally came to an end in mid-February. The League Assembly was advised to censure Japan's actions in Manchuria. On February 24, in the face of overwhelming approval of the censure report by the Assembly, Japan's delegate walked out. Already Japanese columns were on the move into Jehol. By the day Franklin Roosevelt was inaugurated they controlled the western marches of Manchuria and, more ominously, were in position to threaten Peking, less than one hundred miles away, or move upon the inner-Asian flank of the Soviet Union. "Only by leaving the League," said Araki, "can we attain independence and open up a sphere of freedom." [39]

Grew was stunned. He had been complacent about Shanhaikwan: responsibility was hard to assess and the Chinese were "past masters of propaganda." Japanese movement in the Shanhaikwan-Jehol area, presumably protective, had seemed indicated after a Sino-Russian *rapprochement* in December. But with the pendulum swinging toward moderation he had doubted that Japan would secede from the League. "Outstanding men" such as Saito, Saionji, and Finance Minister Takahashi Korekiyo were fighting hard against it. At first the cabinet decision of February 20 that Japan would resign from the League was hard to accept. Possibly it was a last-minute threat to prevent League censure. Finally he admitted he had guessed wrong. "Japan has prepared . . . to destroy her most important link with other countries," he reported, "thereby indicating a fundamental defeat for the moderate elements . . . and the complete supremacy of the military." It was the old story of the military clique threatening internal disorders and the moderates capitulating. Saito, Saionji, "the saner heads," were helpless in the face of this "dictatorship of terrorism." Now, with the situation reverting to that of the previous summer, the Jehol advance wore a grimmer aspect. If Japan went on to Peking, he greatly feared general war: "The outlook could hardly be blacker than it is." [40]

The moderates had never actually staged a showdown. They had, shall we say, intelligently conformed to reality. Harada, scurrying between Saionji, Saito, Shidehara, Takahashi, and Makino, had spun a web of anxieties and wishful thoughts that blurred but did not alter the brute facts. No one was prepared to challenge the Army's contention that Jehol was part of "Manchukuo" and that its conquest was a military decision. At the same time no one in the government, including the Army, wanted an extension of hostilities to the Peking-Tientsin area for fear of full-scale war. Stringent restrictions were imposed on the Kwantung Army.

At Geneva no one was prepared to attempt further conciliation unless Japan accepted Chinese sovereignty over Manchuria, which Japan would never do, and promised not to move on Jehol. Tokyo, seeing no advantage in avoiding condemnation at the moment over Manchuria only to be damned later over Jehol, refused to give assurances. So the inexorable chain of circumstances continued: the end of conciliation, an adverse report, its unanimous adoption, Japan's intolerable position at the League, and her withdrawal. Stimson himself told the Japanese Ambassador that if Japan persisted in her views he saw no other course than for her to get out of the League. The Saito government had always permitted the Army a free hand in what the latter chose to define as "Manchukuo." In return the Army had guaranteed order within Japan. This fundamental arrangement, the Araki-Saito compromise, had governed events ever since Grew had arrived. Swings of the pendulum had occurred only in the minds of those who, like the new Ambassador, hoped for too much.[41]

However Grew's diagnosis might vary from summer to fall to winter, his prescription remained the same: patience and restraint. Month in, month out he remained convinced that Japan would see through her Manchurian venture, whatever the strength of the moderates and the reaction of the world. With Japan willing to risk war and his own country not, he inclined instinctively to velvet-glove diplomacy. "Harsh criticism of Japan, or suggestions of coercion at this juncture," he advised during the summer crisis, "would only serve to strengthen the influence of the rabid chauvinists." The apparent resurgence of the moderates in the fall made little difference. Any hint of force would unite the nation behind the military and overwhelm the moderates, but moral pressure alone "might tend to widen the rift now beginning to be noticed" between them. During the Jehol-League crisis even moral pressure seemed dangerous. Japan's determination was "not modified but only strengthened by the moral obloquy of the rest of the world." Such views were not at all exceptional in Tokyo. That radical concessions by Japan were out of the question, that coercive measures would only strengthen the expansionists, and that restraint and gradual solutions were called for, were axioms for which he claimed the support of the British, French, and Belgian ambassadors as well as the *New York Times, Herald Tribune,* and Associated Press correspondents.[42]

Cautionary advice from Tokyo impressed the President more than the Secretary of State, but by and large the American government followed the policy recommended by its ambassador. Hoover viewed non-recognition less as a means for mobilizing world opinion than of avoiding more positive action. Distraught over the economic crisis and not disposed to go around alone "sticking pins in tigers," he was alarmed by Grew's foreboding dispatch of February 23, 1933, and urged Stimson to make it clear that the United States would not engage in any sanctions except that of public opinion, but Stimson managed to dissuade him.

The Secretary accepted patience and restraint more through force of circumstances than because he saw any value in such a posture. Signs of moderating tendencies from Tokyo during the fall did not call for relaxation of American policy. "Not a bit. Just the reverse. . . . You will not help that breaking of the ice by any sign of weakness," he told Hugh Wilson. Neither was he alarmed by "the various threats that have been floating around to the effect that Japan was in a very hysterical position." They amounted to "diplomatic terrorism." Nevertheless, it was too early for economic pressure and too late, what with the presidential campaign and ensuing political hiatus, for bold public pronouncements like the Borah Letter and the Council on Foreign Relations speech. His design was nearly complete anyway. Discreet prodding proved sufficient to make non-recognition stick with the League. The next step, discriminatory arms embargo legislation, would be for the new Administration to take. Grew was right in sensing a modification at least in procedure on the part of the Secretary. For Henry Stimson, too, the Republican era ended on a note of relative patience and restraint toward Japan.[43]

Grew and Stimson might find themselves in agreement on tactics, but substantively the Ambassador's thinking diverged more and more from his chief's. At first he roundly affirmed Stimson's position. He noted with satisfaction the clarity of American policy, resting as it did on the inviolability of the international peace treaties and the Open Door, and he congratulated Stimson on the "great value and wisdom" of his Council on Foreign Relations speech. However, as he became familiar with the Japanese scene, "practical" considerations gradually eroded his confidence in that approach. Even before arrival he admitted that no treaty which ran counter to the inexorable facts of history and economic necessity could restrain Japan in Manchuria. By end of summer he was sympathizing with the "utter exasperation" of the Japanese over continual violations of their rights in Manchuria by the Chinese, and, ethics aside for the moment, allowing that the Japanese "went ahead to clean up on the perfectly practical theory that offense is the best method of defense." In September he speculated on the difficulty of obtaining the necessary international unanimity for moral ostracism of Japan. In October he recommended friendly gestures and constructive suggestions, "while firmly maintaining our position with regard to the Kellogg Pact, the Nine-Power Treaty and the Open Door." January found him again balancing the ethical against the practical, questioning support of peace treaties to the extent of war, the reverse of what they stood for. "In trying to square theory with fact," he concluded, "we must give predominance to fact." Early in February he saw Japan as a "staunch buffer" against the spread of Bolshevism in China. His hopes were now apparently directed toward chipping away the rough edges of Stimson's policy and registering world disapproval of Japanese expansion as quietly as possible. Stimson of course hoped for precisely the opposite, registering disapproval in order to arouse world opinion to more stringent measures against Japan.[44]

The events of February 1933, culminating in Japan's withdrawal from the League, faced Grew with the question he had been circling the previous months. On February 23, he confided to his diary, "the more one mulls over the whole problem, the more one is inclined to question whether the peace machinery . . . is basically practical." As a Kellogg Pact could not have prevented the United States from going to war with Spain after the sinking of the *Maine*, so treaties would not deter any nation gripped with war psychology, whether legitimately or fraudulently inspired. Furthermore, when covenants were violated the world still remained helpless. Moral ostracism he had already questioned. War would place civilization itself in jeopardy. Breaking relations by itself was futile. An arms embargo, in the case of Japan, would only aid the aggressor. Financial boycott had not deterred Japan. Economic boycott would only lead Japan to aggression elsewhere to obtain needed supplies. Clearly, the treaty structure as well as the whole range of alternatives arising from its transgression led nowhere. The peace machinery "while magnificent in theory is ineffective in practice

. . . like a poultice prescribed for cancer . . . long after the cancer has been allowed to develop." For the moment he had little practical to suggest as a better remedy for the world's ills. The Manchurian crisis had left him a still-bewildered but less complacent diplomat.[45]

THIRTEEN

Understanding Japanese Expansionism

THE Democratic victory in November 1932 forced Grew once again to fight for his job. His position might be less precarious than when the Democrats replaced the Republicans twenty years earlier, but ambassadors in 1933 like secretaries in 1913 had no guarantee of tenure. Naturally he was anxious to remain in Japan: "Every active doctor likes to perform a difficult operation." Retirement in his early fifties, in the midst of the climactic assignment of a thirty-year career, was unthinkable. For once the financial aspect deserved consideration. Grew was a wealthy man. Even at the bottom of the depression, with dividend income severely curtailed and rent from his Washington house reduced by more than half, he met yearly obligations totaling eighteen thousand dollars in allowances for his daughters and nearly three thousand dollars for charity. Still, the times called for prudence. A government salary of $17,500 with free rent, light, heat, and upkeep at the Embassy was not to be sniffed at. Japan had just left the gold standard, reducing by half the value of the yen in terms of the dollar. With prices stable, his salary went twice as far. Aside from personal considerations, he believed without being immodest that Tokyo needed him. If an ambassador were to be not a mere messenger but an interpreter of a foreign people to his own and the reverse, he must be allowed to take root. He needed time to "dig down into the soil" of friendship and acquaintance. He was the seventh American Ambassador to Japan in eleven years and the first professional one. Sometimes, he wrote, "it takes us boys with the white spats to run these jobs right." Tokyo in 1933 seemed obviously such a time.[1]

Franklin D. Roosevelt, Groton '00, Harvard '04, Fly and *Crimson*, would decide the ambassadorship, but Grew, Groton '98, Harvard '02, Fly and *Crimson*, was apprehensive nevertheless. The day after the election he wondered if the President-elect had the courage to resist "party hacks." Suspicion of Roosevelt's motives went far back, certainly to the campaign of 1920, when Grew referred to the vice-presidential candidate's "gutter" politics, and probably back to college days. Then Grew had been the typical club man, wrapped in the Gold Coast side of Harvard and oblivious to the unwashed beyond. Roosevelt was part of this world too ("Frank at least has the proper background of birth and breeding," Grew noted), but he went beyond it, taking exuberant interest in a variety of people and college-wide causes. The club circle would see such enthusiasms as the courting of mere popularity, demeaning to gentlemen. So Grew was led to question whether, beyond astuteness as a politician, the President-elect had "genuine honesty of purpose." Hopefully, the great office would improve him: "Some men, when they get to the presidency, acquire greatness even if they didn't possess it before." In the meantime, Jim Farley would undoubtedly be proposing a "democratic 'statesman' " for Tokyo. Taking nothing for granted, Grew proceeded to wage a campaign to hold his post.[2]

Subtly but unmistakably Grew conveyed his qualifications, wishes, and especially his loyalty to the new Administration. First he sent a "Dear Frank" letter of congratulation. Swallowing doubt, he wrote, "Groton, Harvard, and the Fly are immensely proud and they have good right to be." The new President could count on his wholehearted support and cooperation, whether in official or private life. Then he placed a pro-forma resignation, "in accordance with traditional custom," at Roosevelt's disposal and grimly requested in case of its acceptance appointment as Foreign Service Officer Class I (Counselors of Embassy) until he qualified for a pension in 1934. To the incoming Secretary of State and President-elect went requests for signed photographs to add to his gallery of their distinguished predecessors under whom he had served. If this reminder of his experience failed, he was fortunate in having Billy Phillips back in the Department as Under Secretary, and Grew advised his old friend he wished to stay. Norman Davis, John Davis, and Frank Polk, Democrats prominent in foreign affairs, knew his work and might prove helpful. Mrs. Woodrow Wilson, whom he entertained in Tokyo on the eve of the election, and Colonel House would put in a good word for him. Members of the American colony in Tokyo wanted to help, but he was wary of seeming to start a backfire in his behalf. Proof of loyalty was crucial. Once again he assured the new President of his "desire to be of maximum service to you in carrying out the policies and wishes of your administration. . . ." By now Grew was an old hand at making the transitions required by democratic politics.[3]

Grew was not counting his chickens before they hatched, but there was little cause for concern. True, rumors circulated about candidates for his post. And Roosevelt was known to feel that some senior diplomats had lived abroad too long and lost touch with America. New Dealer Ray Moley sent shivers through the Department with talk of cleaning out all Republicans. There were just as good fish in the sea, said he, as ever came out of it.

However, Grew remembered that "Frank has a useful vein of obstinacy and if he wants us to stay, we'll stay." He winced at the familiarity of a "Dear old Joe" salutation from Hyde Park, but it was a good sign. Newspaper clippings from home reported concern for retention of professional diplomats like himself. Stimson called him a pillar of strength and reported the new leadership's recognition of his success and skill. "A little more taffy while I am alive and a little less epitaphy when I am dead," was Grew's happy comment. Roosevelt, he heard, had reacted favorably to the suggestion of Norman Davis and Colonel House that the triumvirate Gibson, Wilson, and Grew be kept on. "Our excellencies," he chortled, ". . . are mentioned as 'untouchables.'" In fact he was judged the safest of the career chiefs. On March 23, 1933, came final confirmation that the President wished him to carry on in Japan. Tokyo, according to the Democratic National Treasurer, was never an open mission.[4]

Retention of his post was gratifying as a mark of confidence in professional diplomacy. "Isn't it fine the way the President is supporting the career diplomats?" he wrote Norman Armour. Actually Roosevelt remained uncommitted, preferring to experiment. He liked to drive an ill-assorted team to see which horse pulled hardest. Rough equality between career and non-career appointments, his arrangement with Hull, who preferred seasoned personnel, was a typical Rooseveltian solution. Over the years of deepening crisis the career chiefs proved indispensable and their proportion grew to 60 percent by 1939. Veterans of the old Diplomatic Service like Wilson, Gibson, Phillips, MacMurray, Harrison, and Wright kept watch along what Grew saw as America's first line of defense, and imparted to a burgeoning diplomatic establishment some of the values and traditions of the first generation professionals. On the eve of war Grew surveyed the American Foreign Service, at whose birth he had assisted, and judged it had finally reached "full and efficient maturity." [5]

Whatever his earlier opinions, from March 1933 forward, Grew was Roosevelt's ambassador, displaying in voluminous letters and diary never a trace of disloyalty to the President. The alternatives as he saw them were simple: complete loyalty or get out. His attitude was the easier because of growing admiration for the man. He was moved by the inaugural address to utter a "most fervent prayer for Frank's success." The desperate economic crisis seemed to call for a "benevolent dictator." He found the new President's methods "intensely refreshing." With the Administration's Far Eastern policy he could find no fault. Even the New Deal, or at least parts of it, seemed necessary to save the country from revolution. Roosevelt, he wrote his daughter, was playing a "masterly game" of keeping as near the Left as he must but as far from it as he could. Grew's position was secure, his conscience clear. Once again he could turn to the challenges of his mission.[6]

Four relatively calm years followed. Attention shifted from the Far East to the European dictators as they shredded the Versailles and Locarno security systems, to Adowa, Guernica, and the thump of German boots across the Rhine bridges. In Japan violence broke out only once, in the bloody dawn of Febrary 26, 1936. Japanese influence cut deeper into China, not by armed advance, but covertly, by threat, intrigue, and economic subversion. Japan postured and prepared against Russia, but shied away from war. To Western nations, one by one, she offered friendship in return for recognition of her sphere of influence in East Asia. A new current in world affairs set in. Collective security based on world organization, international law, and morality survived only in spectral intonations of the Covenant at Geneva. By twos and threes, with elaborate courtesies and wary intimacies, the powers aligned and realigned to gain immediate security in a totally insecure world. Only one power, the United States, remained aloof, indicating by scarcely a twitch of policy where its interests lay. Force was not yet met by force. It was the time of appeasement, of Hoare-Laval, "time yet for a hundred indecisions,/ And for a hundred visions and revisions. . . ."[7] No waves rocked Grew's boat those years, but a vicious current swept beneath.

These relatively calm years between the Manchurian crisis and the Sino-Japanese War provided Grew leisure to savor the beauty of Japan, learn its ways, and glimpse its mind. He came to know those with whom he dealt and to like and trust not a few. In turn he came to be liked and trusted by Japanese, and in their confidence and affection to find some small point of leverage to steady relations. Above all he developed the conviction that an admirable side of Japan existed. That conviction, sustained in the dark years ahead, was ultimately to prove a precious asset to the two nations.

The means for providing hospitality, and thus meeting Japanese and forming friendships, were readily available at the Embassy. The Grews found it the perfect house: "Not a single con; they're all pros." Newly built to replace the one destroyed in the great earthquake of 1923, it was situated on a hill overlooking the city, but in Tokyo fashion the eye found refreshment within the compound rather than outward over the jumbled rooftops; the bulky Imperial Diet in the distance was no substitute for the graceful minarets of Istanbul. High walls enclosed four buildings, an imposing L-shaped residence on the hillcrest and down below the Chancery flanked by staff dormitories. Gracefully curving Japanese roofs with sharply pointed eaves hung a trifle awkwardly over Roman arches and loggia, but the startlingly white stucco trimmed in black, the azaleas, the "deliciously" green lawns and shrubs, the "little stepping stones through a thick grove of leafy woods," the fountains and pools with tiles of brilliant blue and green, made it all seem as clean, cool, and restful as an oasis.[8]

Easily, handsomely, and under the Grews' management expertly, the

Embassy provided every form of hospitality in the diplomatic repertoire and a few more besides. The residence seemed proof that pinchpenny American representation abroad was a thing of the past. Bronze doors ushered guests into a central hall encircled by a vast polished teak staircase. Close by was a walnut-paneled smoking room where Japanese officials met American correspondents for off-the-record talk over old brandy in big beakers. Occupying the entire right wing was an oval ballroom where Grew showed his Japanese golfing friends Bobby Jones instructional films. He saw them practicing their grip and swing at the buffet supper afterward. Movies such as *Girl of the Golden West*, and *One Night of Love*, always carefully prescreened, as well as home gramophone recordings and jigsaw puzzles helped overcome the difficulty of extended conversation. In the banquet hall to the left of the entrance a white-tie diplomatic dinner for thirty-six might feature leg of wild boar soaked in wine. After dinner in the salon, low lights, deep oriental carpets, big, comfortable chairs, and Mischa Elman playing the violin bespoke the sweet, insidious ways of American influence in the Far East. In warm months entertainment moved outdoors to the terraces, decked in bunting or Japanese lanterns. Almost always Japanese were among the guests, whether by the handful in the "Vultures Club," which met regularly for poker, or by the hundred at garden parties. Occasionally all the guests were Japanese and came in kimono. Grew believed his hospitality was successful; his Japanese guests seemed to "loosen up and enjoy themselves informally at our Embassy as they do at no other." [9]

Apart from Foreign Office officials, whom he would meet anyway, most of the Japanese who came to the Embassy, and who in turn invited him out, may be classified into three groups: naval officers, businessmen, and the court set. What he would learn about Japanese society and politics firsthand from other than diplomatic sources would be learned from these three groups.

Grew saw a great deal more of the Navy than the Army. General Araki was one of the few army officers he met socially. The explanation lay partly in military professional bias. The Japanese Army was modeled on the German Army, the Navy on the British and American navies, so naval officers were more knowledgeable about the United States, and more often spoke English. Through disarmament conferences, naval visits, and China service, Japanese and American officers built up working, and in some cases friendly, relationships. Whereas the Army was concerned with continental rivals and ambitions, the Navy's chief possible contender, and therefore object of closest scrutiny, was the United States, and the same was true in reverse of the American Navy. Grew's naval attaché usually outranked his military attaché. To Grew the naval officers seemed gregarious and cosmopolitan. They were "better mixers" than the Army. Visits by American naval vessels and the comings and goings of naval attachés provided occasions for receptions, dinners, and geisha parties for officers of both navies Embassy. Sitting on the floor for a three-hour geisha affair strained t muscles, but free-flowing hot sake seemed to cement relations marvelo When the vapors wore off a cordial relationship persisted. The broad o look, genial temperament, and knowledge of American power of certa admirals encouraged the Embassy to believe they might exercise a moderating influence on Japanese foreign policy, particularly when, as often happened, they became Premier or Foreign Minister.[10]

More persistent were relations between the Embassy and the Japanese business world; naval and diplomatic personnel shifted from year to year but the same businessmen showed up at the Embassy. Like the admirals they were conversant with the West. A large proportion had been to the United States and a number had lived abroad as students or branch managers. They were presidents, directors, and managers, worldly, conservative men more concerned with the financial than the manufacturing side of affairs, a type Grew was thoroughly familiar with in State Street and Wall Street. All three great zaibatsu were represented on his guest lists and he was a guest at the Mitsui and Sumitomo villas. Aside from the big combines, industries represented were public utilities, insurance, banking, steel, engineering, construction, food processing, automobiles, and shipping. He played golf and poker with several Japanese business friends regularly. The economy of Turkey had been full of problems and uncertainties for him, but that of Japan was mature, had well-established ties with the United States, and represented an asset to his diplomacy. The most effective ambassadors of goodwill, he told the merchants of Osaka, were international traders and industrialists. He told them that the United States was interested in a financially stable and prosperous Japan, and warned that warlike policy was terribly hard on a nation's finances.[11]

Grew regarded his friends in the court circle with esteem and affection to the end, though his confidence in their influence waxed and waned. Beginning with the moderates he met in the fall of 1932, he formed a network of ties with Japanese of their kind. They were more a class than a group, united by title and high birth, mostly standing close to the Throne, and in Grew's eyes sharing a common disposition for peace, order, and Western values.

The thread that led from Grew to most of this network was Count Kabayama, an indefatigable friend of the United States. Too friendly, some felt. One American diplomat called him "an international glad-hander," another "an incorrigible busybody." Grew knew that Kabayama was believed to want to "run" the American Embassy and was perfectly willing to let him think he was doing so. He liked this wispy nobleman with the drooping white mustache. He came to realize that Kabayama was too optimistic, always seeing the rainbow in Japanese-American relations just around the and he was embarrassed by the Count's public admiration for his standing of Japan, which could lead any "hard-boiled Senator" to sus- that he not only understood but supported Japan's aspirations. Still, ayama was a "grand old scout," sincerely helpful and useful. He was a equent visitor, dropping in to help arrange guest lists and ease the Ambassador's way through Japanese formalities. He told Grew he wanted to make the Embassy "cock of the walk" socially. He also came to impart confidences and gossip and take away information Grew wanted to convey discreetly to the Foreign Office. In many ways he was a useful go-between.[12]

More often than not Grew enlarged his circle of acquaintances through Kabayama. Some he saw frequently simply because he liked them. The Matsudairas (he was appointed Imperial Household Minister in 1936) spoke of the Embassy as a second home. Their American-educated daughter was consort to the Emperor's brother, Prince Chichibu, who proved a congenial exception to the "uphill work" of entertaining Imperial Princes. At one party Harada observed Chichibu and Grew conversing "very cordially." They were discussing mountain climbing, the slender Prince having scaled the Matterhorn, while Grew had let well enough alone with the Riffelhorn. Another congenial soul was Prince Tokugawa Iyesato, heir of the last of the Shoguns and sponsor extraordinary of worthwhile causes. Grew who dined at his home found him "as nearly affectionate as that dear old man can be." Count Soejima Michimasa was worthwhile knowing because, unlike most Japanese, he spoke his mind frankly.[13] The Grews were deeply touched by the warm friendship they always found in the home of Maeda Toshinori:

> . . . she, delicate and lovely as an exquisite piece of Dresden China; he, the little Lieutenant General Marquis, making up for his diminutive size by strutting pompously on his heels, but radiating smiles and real friendship and loving his family, his possessions, his golf and his friends no less than his high rank, and proud of the good show he can put on in the perfection of his luncheons and dinners. . . .[14]

Gradually an inner set emerged from the larger circle of Grew's court acquaintances. They invited him for Japanese-style dinners in their homes, occasionally when he was the only foreigner present, and in turn a few of them were usually among Embassy guests. Some were prominent figures. Prince Konoe, of the noblest family next to the Imperial houses, was being groomed as a statesman. He was ultimately a pathetic figure and even then was proving weak and indecisive but he remained the last best hope of the moderates. Harada was one of the best informed men in Japan, his duty as Prince Saionji's secretary being to keep in touch with all political elements. Makino, until he retired from palace office in 1935, took part in the political manuevering to restrain the Army, though he distressed Saionji and

Harada by invoking the assistance of equally dangerous elements. Others of this set were important for putting Grew in touch with prominent businessmen or for keeping him in touch informally with Foreign Office officials. Altogether it was a well-informed and usefully connected, though not intrinsically powerful, group of Japanese.[15]

Here then were the "moderates" as Grew came to know them: the court set, prominent businessmen, and a few admirals. These he referred to variously as the "worthwhile," "best," "better class," or "substantial" Japanese. Those he met at the America-Japan Society and the Tokyo Club were probably not far removed from this type. He knew an occasional editor, news agency chief, politician, professor, and cabinet minister other than foreign, army, and navy ministers and vice-ministers, but the intellectual world, the political parties, and the civil service other than the Foreign Office, were virtually unknown to him personally. The Japan he knew and liked was upper class. On the golf course he found that "the gentlemen are always courteous but the second-class Japanese are not courteous and have no conception of the etiquette of golf." He would probably agree with Hugh Wilson, who served in Japan earlier, in his conclusion: "The Japanese gentleman is one of the most admirable that I have met, the Japanese peasant has to an outstanding degree the virtues of the peasant the world over, the Japanese *petit bourgeois* is a *nouveau* who is hard to bear." There were two Japans, he decided, one alien and threatening, the other familiar and admirable. After attending the funeral of Prince Tokugawa in 1940 he mused:

> After eight years in Japan I had the feeling today of being not outsiders but an intimate part of that group, almost as if the gathering were of old family friends on the Back Bay and not in Tokyo. . . . The Tokugawas, Konoyes, Matsudairas . . . might have been Saltonstalls and Sedgwicks and Peabodys. We knew their positions, their influence and reputations, their personalities and interrelationships as well as those of a similar group in Boston.[16]

The exclusiveness of Grew's own background and experience was not the only reason for his limited spectrum of social acquaintance. Of course these rich and wellborn Japanese were a familiar and congenial type to him. They were also invaluable because they understood the West better than most Japanese, generally by travel or residence abroad, and thus formed a cultural bridge for him to a totally strange society. They also spoke English more distinctly, thanks to residence among English-speaking people, and this was vital for a person hard of hearing like Grew. His deafness was a severe handicap in Japan. The Japanese Ambassador in Washington even regretted it to an official of the Department of State. Japanese like Prince Chichibu, who had studied at Oxford and according to Hugh Wilson spoke

English very precisely, made conversation something more than a strained formality for Grew.[17]

He found venturing beyond these circles difficult. Japanese shied away from close relations with him. He would have liked to play golf and chat at the Club with more of them, but could not help feeling that they were uncomfortable in his presence and might find his efforts to overcome their diffidence embarrassing. East was East and West was West, he decided. Being seen in the company of the American Ambassador could be dangerous. Chauvinists criticized Japanese for being too fond of *keto* (hairy men, or foreigners). In particular *Nippon* castigated Makino for dining at the Grews'. The already limited number of Japanese who circulated among foreigners, more of whom seemed to come to his Embassy than any other, steadily dwindled over the years of rising tension. Even among his Japanese friends reasoned discussion occasionally became impossible and he would slip out. Public attacks on the United States by Kaneko and Araki made them temporarily unwelcome at the Embassy. Grew was the more grateful to those who remained loyal and friendly and turned inward again toward the moderates.[18]

The amount of useful intelligence he could gather by personal acquaintance was limited anyway. With intellectual freedom being extinguished and democratic institutions practically extinct, the thoughts of the intellectual world and the political parties were largely of academic interest. Public opinion was what the controlling elements made it, and was most efficiently evaluated by reading Embassy translations of the vernacular press. Vital information lay hidden away in the great bureaucracies of government, where policy planning and coordination began well below the level at which an ambassador circulated and then passed upward for ratification and compromise. For him personally to cultivate the initiators, bureau and section chiefs, would have been highly unorthodox in this intensely rank-conscious society.[19] Harada, Konoe, Makino, and Yoshida together were probably as familiar with final policy as anyone. Between Embassy staff and their opposite numbers some lateral communication existed in key ministries. A considerable volume of information went the rounds of the diplomatic and press corps, and Grew gathered in a great deal of it with practiced care. This, in addition to staff reports, press summaries, and the confidences of his Japanese friends, constituted the basis of his intelligence work.

Granting the extraordinary difficulty of finding out what was really going on in Japan, the question remains why he did not try harder, why we find neither bold efforts to overcome the difficulty nor despair at his failure to do so. The answer lies in an understanding of his diplomatic method and experience. In the first place, Grew had neither the broad intellectual curiosities, passion for detail, or sophisticated techniques of the modern analyst. He depended more on feel than on fact. He was more interested in what came out the top of the policy-making process than how it worked or what went in the bottom. In the second place, confidences came to him as a byproduct of confidence. Convincing Japanese of his good faith and integrity, and thus of his country's, was crucially important in his diplomacy. To squeeze friends for more information than was freely given, to cajole those who were cool or hostile to the United States, or to fish around for talkative subordinate bureaucrats would have been in his view demeaning, tricky, and out of character for himself and his country. In the third place, the intentions of foreign powers had been of deep concern to him only insofar as they might directly affect his own country. That peace for the United States depended upon peace among all the great powers he had still to learn. Consequently, he would tend to be more interested in gaining intelligence when American-Japanese relations were getting worse, and less interested when they seemed to be improving. Finally, he viewed war not as an object of national policy but as an irrational act. It might come from inflamed feeling arising from an incident or it might be started by some military element "running amok," in either case there being little to learn in advance. These predispositions, then, as well as the difficulty of the task and his personal predilections acted to restrict the range and depth of his intelligence work in Japan.

Grew began his intelligence work for the new Administration in a glum and skeptical mood engendered by Japan's withdrawal from the League. Early in April 1933 he heard the pendulum refrain again. In the company of Kabayama, Makino, Harada, and Yoshida the talk was of periodic cycles of chauvinism and international cooperation. Word directly from the Genro was that a more conciliatory government would soon be installed. Once bitten twice shy, Grew was doubtful. Having taken Manchuria, Japan now was prepared to play by the rules again. Nevertheless, the moderates spoke with conviction. Perhaps the League crisis had been a turning point. After several days' consideration he cabled their remarks with the evaluation that it was idle to predict a change until concrete evidence was forthcoming.[20]

Evidence was forthcoming, namely a halt to Japanese conquest. Though the Kwantung Army plunged on into North China after overrunning Jehol, it stopped short of Peking and on May 31, 1933, agreed to the Tangku Truce establishing a buffer zone south of the Great Wall and north and east of the Chinese capital. With Japanese now proceeding to infiltrate rather than overwhelm North China, the Embassy turned to measuring the force of Japanese expansion in terms of relations with the Soviet Union. Chances of war in this sector seemed to increase in the summer and fall of 1933. Japan's thrust toward Mongolia, her threat to Soviet railroad interests in Manchuria, and the buildup of Soviet Far Eastern strength sharpened a historic rivalry over Northeast Asia. War by 1935 or 1936 was freely predicted. A border clash provoked by young officer fanatics might bring it sooner, Grew believed. Yet no war came. By 1934 he was inclined to doubt both the long-term and immediate prospects of hostilities. He reasoned that Soviet power had deterred Japan, but also that Japanese expansionism had lost force on account of two significant internal developments.[21]

Japan seemed less dangerous, first, because of the emergence of steadier leaders within the Army. Even General Araki, though publicly a fire-eater, displayed in private a streak of sense that led Grew to believe he exerted a restraining influence on the young hotheads. Late in 1933 he took note of officers who enjoyed their power under the existing regime and were loath to disturb it and he remarked on the restraint shown in "Army circles" in the face of Soviet intransigence. Though he neither defined a group nor named individuals, he was beginning to see moderation of a sort in broader terms. The resignation of Araki in January 1934 did not, therefore, have to be viewed as a disaster. His successor as War Minister, General Hayashi Senjūrō, impressed Grew at first as less bellicose and by midyear as a man of "practical sense" and an "influence for peace." Furthermore, there now were "not lacking sane elements" in the Army who saw the dangers in a Soviet conflict and questioned whether the game was worth the candle.

Japan also seemed less threatening on account of the appointment of Hirota Koki as Foreign Minister in September 1933. Hirota was a professional diplomat whose career had roughly paralleled Grew's from entrance in 1906 up the rungs of secretary, bureau chief, and minister to the ambassadorship at Moscow. Unlike Grew he was politically ambitious, having cultivated some of the more reputable nationalists, but convinced the moderates of his desire to resolve Japan's problems by diplomacy rather than force. Trim and energetic at fifty-six, he was a refreshing contrast to the deaf, elderly, reserved Count Uchida Yasuya, his predecessor. Conversation with Uchida had been in platitudes but Hirota greeted Grew warmly, clasped both hands around the American's, and earnestly expressed his desire to improve Japanese-American relations. Grew believed him. Nearly every month until the following spring he reported the peaceful influence of the new Foreign Minister: how he was using his influence with the nationalists "to undermine the position of the chauvinistic military elements," how he had won cabinet assurance that no measures or pronouncements would embarrass his efforts for peace, how his public statement on Soviet-Japanese relations had been restrained and commonsensical, how he was personally responsible for the milder tone of the press, and how the "moderate camp" now controlled the Foreign Office. Grew concluded that the most able efforts were being made for restoration of friendly relations not only with the Soviet Union, but also with Britain, China, and the United States. Though an ardent nationalist, Hirota was trying to establish Japanese leadership in the Far East without provocation or intimidation.[22]

By the spring of 1934 Grew was encouraged to believe that a broad moderating tendency was at work. Attacks on the Army took place in the Diet, press, and cabinet. A revival of exports brought prosperity and a fondness for the *status quo* to the middle classes, while farmers demanded expenditure for relief rather than rearmament. The birth of a Crown Prince in December 1933 removed uncertainty about the succession and increased popular affection for the Emperor. The "highest influences" — the Emperor, the Genro, palace advisers — were pacific. Harada and Makino were optimistic. "A strong group of liberals" had been steadily working behind the scenes and now their influence was being felt more and more. It all represented "the perfectly normal swing of the pendulum as has happened throughout Japanese history," perhaps not all the way back to Shidehara diplomacy, but definitely in that direction.[23] By April 9, 1934, his mechanism of moderation was in good working order again.

No sooner was the pendulum back in action than it broke down. On April 17, 1934, the Foreign Office spokesman, Amō Eiji, disclosed sweeping Japanese Far Eastern intentions that fundamentally challenged the treaty order in the Far East. Basing his remarks on an instruction from Hirota to his Minister in China, Amō stated that Japan had a special mission to keep peace and order in East Asia and would oppose any foreign assistance to China that might encourage resistance to Japan. He specified selling war planes, building air fields, lending military advisers, and negotiating loans of political value (loans which might have the effect of strengthening the Chinese government). It was an informal, almost casual statement, given in Japanese and translated by a newspaperman, but it was front-page news in the West. Governments hastened to learn how authentic and official it was. Cable traffic was so heavy Grew thought of charging Amō with the tolls. Days of explanation and emendation left everyone confused as to who was saying precisely what, but there could be no doubt that Japan was warning the West to keep hands off China. The Amō Doctrine, as it came to be known, was considered in Tokyo the most significant pronouncement of Japanese policy since the Twenty-One Demands, the historic symbol of Japanese expansionism.[24]

Actually Grew's reporting of the previous year had not been as faulty as the revelation of Japanese expansionism in the Amō Doctrine made it seem. Soviet-Japanese relations were improving and the Army was becoming less impulsive. This amelioration did not result from the suppression of young fanatics; the smoldering violence of company-grade officers was always a threat. Instead, the issues of 1933 and 1934 were fought out among high officials nearly all of whom were shocked by the insubordination of 1931 and 1932. What had occurred was an assault upon *Kodo-ha* control of the Army. Araki had encountered severe opposition to his idea of a preventive war on the Soviet Union, both within the Army and in the government. His failure in October 1933 to gain the approval of key ministers for his plans marked his decline. Opposition to *Kodo-ha* also arose from generals, some of them conspirators in 1931, who resented loss of preferment to the Araki clique, as well as from those who deplored the factionalism of both ins and outs. An anti-crisis, anti-faction movement known as the *Tosei-ha,* or Control Group, was emerging, which followed the thinking of General Nagata Tetsuzan that Japan, before making threats, should develop Manchuria, build a modern army, create a war economy, and organize society and government to a high state of readiness for total conflict. The replacement of Araki by Hayashi marked the ascendency of this movement. The decline of Araki permitted a relaxation of tensions and Hirota's effort for an accommodation with the Soviet Union. The military state envisaged by the *Tosei-ha* was hard to square with permanent peace, but at least temporarily the possibility of war in the Far East was lessened. Shadowy as his perception of these developments was, Grew sensed the accommodating trend and correctly ascribed it in part to a new line of thought in the Army, which he mistakenly viewed as stand-pat.[25]

What deceived Grew was not his facts but his thesis. Pressure against continental expansion by the Army was exerted less by Japanese seeking a return to the "normal days of 1921 to 1930," than by expansionists in the Navy and Foreign Ministry oriented in a different direction. Again Grew had not lacked information. He had reported repeatedly and accurately the ambitions of the navy. Though it might be less volatile than the Army, he knew that it was still smarting under the limitations of the 1930 London Conference, which had been imposed by a civilian government on an outraged naval high command. Contrary to Kabayama's assurances that the fleet was completely subservient to retired admirals like Saito, Grew reported in January 1934 the predominance of "fire-eating nationalists" like Admirals Katō Kanji and Suetsugu Nobumasa. He had not known of the Navy's resistance to the Jehol advance, but he appreciated how increased prestige and appropriations attending the Army's success in Manchuria had roused the Navy to seek its own place in the sun. He repeatedly advised Washington of navy pressure for rearmament, and, as preparations began for the 1935 London Conference, of its insistence on parity with the British and American navies. Furthermore, he repeated the warning of the Dutch Minister that if Japan failed to obtain its demands at London, the fleet might take radical action like the Army's in Manchuria and suddenly descend upon Guam. He was not prepared to accept the warning as his own, but the year 1935 should be approached "in all wakefulness." [26]

The large ambitions of the Foreign Ministry revealed by the Amō statement were hardly a surprise. Ishii had asserted Japan's Far Eastern predominance in front of Grew in 1932. Japan's great Imperial Destiny, envisioned as a sphere of influence extending over East Asia, the South Seas, and

Western Pacific was a popular notion, and the Embassy had reported several manifestations of it. On January 11, 1934, the Vice-Minister of Foreign Affairs, Shigemitsu Mamoru, whose thinking more than anyone else's lay behind the Amō Doctrine, told Grew's Counselor of Japan's responsibility for peace and order in the Far East, the words of the Doctrine itself. This "widely held" viewpoint, said the Embassy, bore the corollary that Japan was to be consulted on any question of more than local importance affecting China. Several weeks later Grew noted Japanese suspicions of any extension of influence in Eastern Asia by another power, in this case American aviation assistance to China. Hirota was reported to have said that Japan, "serving as only the cornerstone for the edifice of peace in East Asia, bears the entire burden of responsibilities," and to have suggested a partition of the Pacific into American and Japanese zones. Even friendly Kabayama told Grew that the peace of the world depended on Japan policing the waters of the Far East; America, the Western Hemisphere; and Britain, the Mediterranean and Europe, to which the Ambassador "forebore to make the obvious comments." One wonders why it should have been necessary for Amō to say anything; the statement might have been pieced together from Embassy dispatches.[27]

Grew did not see that the Navy and the Foreign Ministry had a mutual interest. Japanese diplomats were increasingly concerned over Western financial, technical, and military assistance to China. Chiang Kai-shek would never come to terms so long as he could count on such strengthening. The Amō Doctrine was designed to cut this connection. It was also designed to prevent the China problem from arising at the London Conference as it had at the Washington Conference. There would be no need to discuss China along with naval tonnages if Japan's responsibility for peace and order in the Far East were recognized. Large responsibilities required, and were proved by, large means, namely a navy second to none. Undoubtedly popular notions of a great Imperial Destiny facilitated such reasoning, but should not obscure Japan's real dilemma. The Army would not permit giving up positions won by Japan since 1931, yet concessions by China could not but violate the Nine-Power Treaty. Fundamental challenge to the treaty order in the Far East was hard to avoid. Not for the last time, Japan backed into a bigger house, asserting as a solution to a problem the Amō premise, which only enlarged it.

The Amō statement started an important change in Grew's thinking about Japan. His information had not been seriously incomplete. Washington should have been able to form a fairly accurate picture of Japanese affairs on the basis of facts reported by the Embassy. The fault lay with his assumptions, which led him to stress in his evaluation those facts which fit, to the neglect of others. He had wrongly assumed that the peaceableness and order of the twenties were viable alternatives in the thirties, that the moderates had the capacity to reverse the trend, and that the challenge to the *status quo* was largely restricted to young officers in the Army. He now dropped the pendulum theory, but not all the assumptions that made it seem reasonable. Though he was now disposed to see Japanese expansionism as more complicated and powerful than before, he still believed that the trend could be halted by the Japanese themselves. The story of the following two years, from April 1934 to February 1936, is one of the dwindling but not quite the extinction of that remaining faith.

Grew's faith in Hirota was shaken by the Amō statement but came through intact. If the Foreign Minister had authorized such a provocative disclosure, he was either insincere in his policy of improving relations or he was a prisoner of the chauvinists. Neither apparently was the case. Hirota acknowledged as official a milder version of the statement, but assured Grew that Amō had originally spoken without his knowledge or approval and that Japan would take no action in China purposely provocative to other countries or contrary to the terms or spirit of the Nine-Power Pact. The necessity of satisfying both "chauvinists" and "liberals" made his position difficult (his remarks would have to be treated as confidential), but he had the support of the Emperor and the Minister of War and would persevere even to the death. Grew was inclined to rely on his personal impressions and to give foreign ministers the benefit of the doubt. He was convinced of Hirota's sincerity. The words "rang true." He concluded that Shigemitsu had been originally responsible and that reverberations from abroad as well as "pressure from the more conservative elements" had caused the Foreign Ministry militants to recede. Hirota emerged as the "spearhead of the conciliatory forces now articulate." This view did not resolve the Hirota problem at all. If, as Grew wrote June 29, the Japanese government "announced on April 17 a line of policy toward China which it means to follow," what was the Foreign Minister's real standing on that line? Did he seek Japan's special position in the Far East only to the extent that the treaty powers were prepared to accept it, or so far as possible with their acceptance? Grew did not know, but he did believe Hirota was some kind of restraining force.[28]

The successful weathering of a cabinet crisis in June and July 1934 was encouraging evidence of the influence of the moderates. The Saito Cabinet, weakened by scandals, had seemed about to give way to a more aggressive one. The Navy had been more adamant than ever on parity and there had been talk of the appointment of Suetsugu as Navy Minister. While control was being wrested "painfully and by slow degrees" from the military, the die-hards were as unyielding as ever. Japan intended to proceed on her chosen path "irrespective of any other considerations whatever." However, the outcome of the crisis seemed "a victory for the moderates." As Kabayama had predicted, Admiral Okada Keisuke, a moderate like Saito, became Premier. Hayashi and Hirota were to continue, and according to bayama the navy post would soon go to the moderate Admiral Nom Kichisaburo or at least not to Suetsugu. The new Cabinet would purs Saito policies with more force and initiative. Had the United States been able to choose a government in its own interests it could not have done better, said the Count. So the moderates were influential again and the trend was "away from aggressive nationalism." Borrowing an image suggested by the Dutch Minister during the Amō crisis, Grew concluded: "Japanese history has shown that the process of expansion has progressed by waves of violent action succeeded by necessary periods of consolidation and recuperation of the national energies." [29] The swing of the pendulum had given way to the ebb and flow of the wave.

Again events proved him too optimistic. The Okada Cabinet retained the moderate complexion of the Saito government but could not withstand navy pressure for abrogation of the Washington Treaty. Grew knew the Japanese would insist on parity but still had some hopes for the London talks. Yoshida, speaking for Hirota, told him that the Navy might be forced to compromise in the face of a prohibitively expensive arms race if only a solution to the problem of equality could be found. Washington was not impressed, especially when Hirota told Grew shortly after, on September 18, 1934, that Japan would give notice of abrogation by the end of the year anyway. "So the whole Yoshida business was applesauce after all," commented Phillips. "I told you so," said Stanley K. Hornbeck. This "backstage play through Yoshida" reminded Moffat of private assurances received during the Manchurian crisis that civil authorities would moderate the situation if given time. Now the Navy seemed determined to have its way. When Grew reported that Kabayama was suggesting private talks in case the main delegations at London became deadlocked, Moffat intimated that by this "private dickering" the Japanese were trying to take advantage of Grew's more friendly approach to the problem. To Washington the Japanese seemed absolutely rigid. The American public must begin to understand the implications of Japan's new Manifest Destiny.[30]

Grew, listening in through Moffat's diary and letters, would not budge at first. "Backstage play" was a customary way of doing business in Japan. All decisions were reached through a series of compromises, the different groups treating with each other through intermediaries. Kabayama and Yoshida spoke without authority to commit anyone but were in constant touch with and even participated in the councils of those who were in fact shaping policy. Manchuria was not analogous. The military were now in the area of diplomacy, and the diplomats could choose weapons. Confirming Yoshida's story was the report that, if the powers accepted equality in total tonnage, Japan might be prepared to conclude a gentlemen's agreement not to build beyond certain defensive needs. The "liberal elements" might not

: their way at London, Grew advised, but they would probably exert ›re influence than was generally believed.[31]

It soon became apparent that the liberals had no leeway at all. A tacit moratorium on construction in return for parity in principle, the best a backstager could conceivably have offered, was hardly an inducement for the other side to give up the Washington Treaty. The United States might not be prepared to challenge, but was certainly not prepared to underwrite, Japan's new role in the Far East. Inflexible positions taken at London, summarized in telegrams from Washington, dispelled Grew's modest hopes. The Okada Cabinet showed itself "virtually powerless in its efforts to curb the military," not only the Navy over the London talks, but also the Army over its plans to dominate the administration of Manchuria. Contributing to his disillusion was the concurrent oil controversy. The spring and summer of 1934 evidenced a Japanese drive to obtain control of foreign storage, refining, and distribution facilities in the home islands and Manchuria. Informal representations having failed, Grew made a formal protest on December 1, but Hirota's arguments in reply were "specious." Japan seemed determined to defy the Open Door and seek self-sufficiency in a vital war resource. These ominous developments and the charged atmosphere they engendered led the Embassy by year's end to a sobering reappraisal of Japanese tendencies.[32]

In a series of dispatches of December 1934 and February 1935 Grew and his staff undertook intensive studies of Japanese expansionism.[33] One officer concluded that the key to it, as the Japanese saw it, was the absolute necessity of further industrialization. In the Japanese view this development was the only solution to overpopulation, since emigration and colonization had met little success. A steadily improving standard of living, which this hard-working and intelligent people was determined to achieve, could only be gained by economic expansion. Japan, being poor in natural resources, required increasing access to raw materials abroad as well as expanding foreign markets for her goods. These were denied by exclusive trade policies in the West and the West's colonies in the East, resulting in a dangerous frustration of the driving impulse for self-improvement. Another officer viewed the expansionist urge somewhat differently. Throughout history Japan had alternated between periods when foreign influences were welcomed and when they were rejected. Currently the period was exclusivist, manifesting itself in a drive for economic self-sufficiency and in the assertion that Japan was inferior to no power and superior in the Far East. This concern for national prestige was noted in several dispatches. Japanese sensitivity originated in an inferiority complex expressed aggressively in truculence and xenophobia. Whatever the factors responsible for Japanese expansionism, they composed a "highly explosive mixture."

The change in Embassy thinking was more one of emphasis and elaboration than of fresh insights. That Japan was incurably expansionistic wa cliché stuck fast to the minds of foreigners like an old steamer trunk labe On his way to Japan, Grew had speculated on the "irresistible Japanese impulse" to expand. If Japanese expansion was to be viewed as moving in waves toward eventual domination of the Far East, he had stressed the recessive, consolidating phase. As recently as October 1934, alongside his modest hopes for the London talks, lay the question "whether the assimilation first of Korea and then of Manchuria are only the first steps in a definite and perhaps irresistible movement of imperialist expansion." Now he believed they were. It was not simply a question of fanatics in the Army, and the Navy too, who were always "capable of taking the bit in their own teeth and running away with it." Expansionism was broader and deeper, aiming at a "Pax Japonica with eventual complete commercial, and, in the minds of some, eventual political control of East Asia." No effective restraint existed: "The idea that a great body of liberal thought lying just beneath the surface since 1931 would be sufficiently strong to emerge and assume control with a little foreign encouragement is thoroughly mistaken." Deeply devoted as he was to a sympathetic understanding of Japan, Grew was now inclined to stress the aggressive nature of Japanese intentions.[34]

Once again he changed his mind — almost. Each year his hopes had risen in the spring and 1935 was no exception. Japan seemed calm, confident, and prosperous. No adverse consequences resulted from her final withdrawal from the League nor from her notice of abrogation of the naval treaty. Tentative agreement was reached on part of the oil controversy. A sore spot in Soviet-Japanese relations was removed by successful completion of negotiations for the purchase of the Chinese Eastern Railway in Manchuria. Hirota, his prestige enhanced, took another step in his announced policy of conciliation by beginning conversations with the Chinese. By March signs pointed to a Sino-Japanese *rapprochement*. The Foreign Minister was even understood to welcome international assistance to China, Amō Doctrine to the contrary notwithstanding. To the British Ambassador, Hirota appeared to be walking a tightrope between his own conciliatory policies and the demands of the chauvinists. The Netherlands Minister, General J. C. Pabst, saw Hirota's China policy as indicating a drift back to Shidehara diplomacy. Grew had been right in the first place, said the Dutchman: Hirota could not have been responsible for the Amō Doctrine. On April 20 the Foreign Minister told Grew there would never be war while he was in office and that the democratic elements in Japan were steadily getting stronger.[35]

By now Grew had boxed the compass on Hirota. The past December he had classed the Foreign Minister with the righteous but impotent Makino, Saito, Kabayama, Yoshida, and Shidehara. But in February 1935 Hirota's proclamations of friendly intent had cloaked "a purposeful policy of undis-

…ted leadership in the Far East," to be asserted by force of arms if necessary. Now in March and April, Grew joined Pabst and Sir Robert Clive briefly and termed Hirota a "liberal" again. As opposed to "chauvinists" Shigemitsu and Amō, he sincerely desired a restoration of friendly relations with China. Japanese foreign policy was rapidly returning to "Shidehara Diplomacy," the chief principle of which was that of befriending instead of coercing China. This far Grew went in his dispatch, but came back a step or two in his diary: "I do not doubt that Hirota aims at more or less the same goal for Japan as do the reactionaries, but sees the wisdom of trying to reach that goal through international conciliation, slowly and step by step, rather than by force and the mailed fist." By May 1935 he was several steps further back. He had not confirmed Hirota's remark that democratic elements were gaining. Now he interpreted Hirota to mean that his membership in the nationalist society Kokuryukai lent weight to his policies and at the same time restrained the society. American policy should not be predicated on democratic developments in Japan, as Americans understood the term. Hirota had apparently convinced the military that he could achieve their objectives at less cost, without war, and, opportunistic as they were, they were giving him a chance to prove it. "Japanese foreign policy, in fact, maintains a strong arm under his guidance, in spite of his protestations of gentleness." The difference was one of tactics, not objectives.[36]

This time Grew's estimate was confirmed instead of refuted by subsequent developments. In June 1935 pressure from the Tientsin and Kwantung armies forced the Chinese Central Government out of Hopei and Chahar provinces, creating, as in the Tangku Truce, neutral zones for further Japanese economic and political infiltration of North China. Grew's explanation was that the Army disliked Hirota's direct approach to Chiang and took action to maintain its own prestige and power. Manchuria, Jehol, East Hopei, and now Hopei and Chahar: " 'Just one more step' on the forward march," Grew decided, perhaps to be followed by a "resumption of quiescence," lasting no telling how long.[37]

Japan's fundamental urge to expansion, which only war could halt, was now a basic assumption of Grew and he stuck to it. After extended home leave in the latter half of 1935 he made a fresh survey of the Far Eastern scene and his conclusions did not strongly differ from those of the year before. Prosperity persisted in Japan, but also virulent economic nationalism and the drive for markets and resources. Presently, economic expansion was more probable than military expansion. Japan would prepare against the Soviet Union but not attack, accept an uneasy truce but not a reconciliation. The Army, he believed, would consolidate its position in North China through local "autonomous" regimes and similarly extend its influence westward through Inner Mongolia to obtain strategic advantage against the Soviets and Chinese Communists. Sino-Japanese talks offered little hope of agreement, no Chinese government being able to grant *de facto* recognition to the new order in North China. Toward the West, Japan would continue to assert Far Eastern preeminence and naval equality but would try to avoid a naval building race.[38]

He wished to emphasize that he was still of the opinion that no great body of liberal thought lay just beneath the surface ready to emerge and assume control. The liberal element, "if the civilian authorities can be so described," was "precisely as nationalistic and chauvinistic in its aims and purposes as the military element." It differed only in tactics and methods, constantly seeking to restrain the tendency of the military to "slash and cut its way through obstacles." Moderation of this sort existed even in the Army and Navy command, as well as in the court, the cabinet, and, most importantly for Grew, in the person of the Foreign Minister.[39]

Today one can find little to quarrel with in this analysis of 1935. Rigorously applied it would have been a useful criterion of Hirota's diplomatic initiatives. The Foreign Minister was asking, in his own words, for a "small amount of leeway," which he obtained largely by playing off, one against the other, diverse ambitions within the military establishment. He was able to settle the railway controversy and improve relations with the Soviet Union because the Army wished to avoid immediate war and the Navy wished to avoid any war in that direction. He was able to make a start at improving relations with Chiang Kai-shek because the Navy was concerned at the continental thrust of Japanese ambitions and because the Army wished to avoid further military involvement in a southerly direction. At the same time Chiang would have to accept loss of his authority in North China. The Japanese field armies, who looked on Chiang as "a candle flickering in the wind," even sought to discredit this cautious initiative by high-handed pressure tactics in June 1935. At London, Hirota was able to play for time, try for some naval limitation, and seek a political understanding with Britain because of army as well as civilian concern to improve relations with Britain and the United States and avoid a costly naval arms race. But the Navy was insistent on parity and anxious to be free of restrictions, leaving Hirota almost no room to maneuver. Considering his limitations, Hirota displayed considerable virtuosity but himself admitted: "We will expand out utmost [sic] by foreign policy, and when foreign policy arrives at its limits, we will leave the matter to you [the Army and Navy] for disposal."[40]

Grew was still not prepared fully to accept the implications of his broad analysis. After the North China crisis of June 1935 he reported that, according to Kabayama, " a completely reliable source," Okada was in a stronger position than any Prime Minister in recent years. Okada, Saionji, and Makino were said to be in complete control of the situation in North China. Grew also reported Hirota's remark that the relief of a high *Kodo-ha* genal, Mazaki Jinzaburo, was proof of the gradual but effective extension of control over the Army. He was no longer adding personal evaluations confirming what the moderates told him, but he was reporting them and not discrediting them. Late in 1935 the formal London Naval Conference convened in the shadow of Japanese abrogation. The question was whether Japan would break it up. In January 1936 Grew reported that Hirota had "personally and definitely" told him that he had won the contest with the Navy over withdrawal and that at least one member of the delegation would remain at London. The next day the Japanese requested immediate adjournment of the conference. In explaining the "apparent inconsistencies" of the Foreign Minister, Grew reported that Hirota had probably meant his remarks as an expression of hope rather than a confirmation of the facts. That he had been wrong did not mean that the Foreign Office had not influenced the manner of withdrawal. Without the "restraining hand" of Hirota, the delegation would undoubtedly have left the conference in an atmosphere of irritation and returned home in a spirit of bombast. If necessary Grew was prepared to try to prevent the moderates from discrediting themselves.[41]

It is hard to escape the conclusion that Grew even now was allowing the moderates a capacity to change the course of events greater than the modest tactical role he assigned them in overall analysis and than they actually enjoyed. Nothing is clear-cut or self-evident here, not deliberate deception on Hirota's part or gross self-deception on Grew's. Probably both men sincerely hoped, beyond what objective appraisal gave them right to hope, for minimizing conflict of interest between their nations. Probably both men believed in the need for confidence in each other. This was a time when Grew was pondering the great question whether the United States should give up the old treaty order and make a political settlement with Japan. To destroy the credibility of the only individuals who seemed to care what the West thought of Japanese intentions would have been to decide that any arrangement with Japan, indeed any diplomacy at Tokyo, was futile. The inconsistency may also have been due to the inability of Grew to believe what he was learning. His way of looking at events was undergoing profound change. He was being forced as never before to look at "forces" rather than people, to see the hard necessities of national policy formation, and he was having some modest success. At the same time his instincts told him a different story. Words "rang true." Personal reactions refined by thirty years' experience dictated faith and trust where his mind said, "That is not enough." In the topsy-turvy world of the thirties old values persisted alongside new realities.

FOURTEEN

Coping with Japanese Expansionism

VERY early one morning in May 1935, while on a sojourn away from Tokyo, Grew wandered out on the lawn in pajamas to see the view. He was staying at a house perched on a bluff in the hills behind Kobe, which, as one of the busiest ports in the Orient, naturally fascinated him. Now it seemed miles below, with bay, islands, and Inland Sea stretching beyond. He could also see Osaka and the mountains behind Kyoto. Nearby hills were ablaze with wild azaleas. It was a moment to savor: "the morning dew on my bare feet, the clean morning air and the wisps of stray cloud ascending from the deep valley, sunshine, blue sky, freshness, fragrance, harmony." He recalled an early morning on the Bosporus, a sunrise in the Bay of Naples, the clean wind on the bow of a Channel boat, all of them cleansing, reintegrating moments such as he now seldom enjoyed.[1]

The truth was that his mission was a profoundly frustrating and discouraging experience. At the beginning he was determined to be "not merely a messenger but an interpreter . . . of the qualities and ideals, the character and intentions and underlying motives" of the people among whom he lived.[2] With the Turks, experience had led to more complete and confident understanding, but with the Japanese the reverse was true. The more he learned of Japan, the less well he felt he knew it, and the less worthwhile it seemed to try to learn more.

He started out an enthusiastic sight-seer. Nikko was impressive, especially the grove of huge cryptomerias which stood "like stalwart guardians . . . with trickles of sunlight falling through their shade on the vivid red and green and gold of the temples. . . ."[3] But he did not get much further than Nikko, Nara, and Kyoto, the usual tourist haunts of central Honshu. One reason was the constant danger of a crisis. So long as he was in Japan he was in charge and felt it wise to stay within easy reach of the Embassy. Another reason probably was that he could not travel freely like a tourist. In Japan a trip for an ambassador was more a procession than an excursion.

Visiting a silk factory, he was greeted with "The Star-Spangled Banner" played three times over in his honor. Perhaps he believed that the richness and beauty of art, architecture, and countryside had little to tell him of the dark side of the Japanese world he was encountering in the thirties. In any event, his enthusiasm for sight-seeing flagged.

He entered into Japanese life at Tokyo with enthusiasm too. So far as he could with dignity, he did things the Japanese way. At an official function he was to be seen neatly holding cane, top hat, gloves, bowl, and chopsticks, which he willingly learned to use. He found the tea ceremony "delightfully graceful," geisha dinners "gay and highly amusing," and fried eels delicious. On the other hand, the Imperial Duck Hunt, where diplomats fished the hapless creatures out of the water with huge butterfly nets, was not sport at all and Sumo wrestlers with their "tremendous bulging bellies" were ludicrous. The Lion Dance at the Kabuki theater was "tremendously impressive," but the cacophonous music gave him a headache. He nearly froze during a six-hour No play, in which one actor "performed a few slow gyrations and then often went into a coma for half an hour or so." He tried nearly everything once, but seldom went back again. It was all very interesting, but again, perhaps he wondered if it was helpful for understanding the Japan of the thirties.[4]

Most impressive of all his experiences in Japan were ceremonies at the Imperial Palace. He had never seen a court with such "unhurried precision," such "perfect arrangements." At the state luncheon for the Diplomatic Corps it was a thrill to enter the banquet hall behind the Emperor and see "those tremendous lines of gold-encrusted decoration-covered officials bowing with the utmost reverence." He noted the "utmost deference" with which a servant placed a dish on the very edge of the Emperor's table and then slowly pushed it in front of him. At each luncheon guests received special sake cups as mementos. In 1936, as Acting Dean of the Diplomatic Corps with seniority of ten sake cups, Grew had a role to play. He paced up the aisle to the Emperor's table, bowed twice, took two steps forward, took out paper and reading glasses with gloved hands, read a message from the Corps in French, replaced glasses and paper, stepped back, bowed again, and retreated, his every movement keenly watched by hundreds of officials for "the slightest mistake in protocol." In May 1935 Makino told him that there would never be any danger of Fascism or Communism in Japan because the Emperor was supreme and would always have the last word. As he spoke the old nobleman's eyes filled with tears. It was a "momentary revelation of the intensity of their devotion to the Throne." That reverence Grew understood and did not forget.[5]

What struck him with particular force about Japanese reverence for the Emperor was the unique correspondence here between an inner feeling and its outward expression. A profound devotion was revealed in exquisitely performed ritual, fulfilling the gentlemanly ideal of seeming and being, between the manner and the man. Wi. was that, apart from court circles and the unique relations and Emperor, this harmony seemed to exist nowhere else amo "Their traditional politeness," he wrote, "is generally but a vene the case of the well-bred families; that politeness does not c thoughtful consideration of others in any degree." With such discor between appearance and reality, little could be taken at face value.[6]

Translation from appearance to reality seemed a baffling problem. Questions of face were fairly obvious. Fear of loss of face explained why two trucks stood head on, bumper to bumper in a narrow street, their drivers asleep. Shame at loss of face explained why a cyclist grinned as he lay sprawling on the sidewalk after an accident. The constant feeling among Japanese of being "in trouble," of being hemmed in, revealed an inferiority complex which expressed itself in aggressive behavior. At times, in despair, he attributed Japanese contradictions to a stubborn unwillingness to face unpleasant facts, or worse, to deliberate deceit. "The Japanese smile and smile," he would say, "and make unlimited promises, but quietly avoid fulfilling them. . . ." However, the longer he stayed, the more he recognized "how little the Japanese understand American psychology and how little we understand theirs." A great cleavage existed between East and West in mental processes and methods of reaching conclusions. No greater error could be made than to think that because Japanese adopted Western dress, language, and customs, they thought like Westerners. One should never try to measure their reaction by Western yardsticks. A Japanese did not necessarily have his tongue in his cheek when he signed an agreement. When an obligation ran counter to his interests, he interpreted it to suit himself, quite honestly, "according to his own lights and mentality." But then, what *were* those "lights and mentality"? He could never be sure.[7]

Japan artistically, architecturally, and physically offered harmony, order, beauty, and tradition, but revealed little of the mysterious processes that underlay the expansionism of her people. He felt as if he were sitting on a symmetrical but simmering volcano.

When Embassy work permitted he sought escape. Twice a week or so he was to be seen on one or another of Tokyo's golf courses, dressed in knickers and open-necked shirt with sleeves rolled up to the elbows, towering over his Japanese companions like a grandfather over a group of school children. He was known as "The Man with the Strange Putt," a peculiar croquet-like stance he used at short range. Golf was a maddening game but a fine change of pace, and Fujiyama was so "astonishingly beautiful" it was hard to keep his eye on the ball. In summer he stayed in the hills, in touch by phone, but buried in "thick glorious woods." The Grews spent annual leave outside Japan. They had none until the autumn of 1934 when they

[to] visit their daughter and son-in-law. En route their ship [ran into a] devastating typhoon in the Inland Sea which carried away [the ant]enna. Unheard from, they were feared lost. At Dairen they [saw the] "big black war dogs" of the Japanese Navy, some sixty vessels [of the Co]mbined Fleet including the flagship of Admiral Suetsugu. Grew [was not s]ucceeding in getting away from it all.[8]

[Agai]n and again he came back to the baffling problem of understanding [Jap]an, but found no sure guide. Not pattern but paradox emerged. In[sti]nct and reason contradicted each other and both fell short of unfathomable depths of character and psychology peculiar to the Japanese people. The best he could say was that they were predictably dangerous as well as dangerously unpredictable. In any case, the bland assumptions and friendly methods of diplomacy as he had practiced it in Turkey seemed more and more inadequate to the task of protecting his country's interests now. As he became aware of the dimensions of his problem in Japan he cast about for new ways of dealing with it.

It will be recalled that by the end of the Hoover Administration, Grew had lost faith in Stimson's Far Eastern policy. The peace machinery was ineffective in practice. Mobilization of world opinion only made Japan more determined and defiant. His first year as Roosevelt's ambassador gave him no reason to change his opinion. The redirection of Japanese ambitions northward, where no American interests lay in the path, was followed by a seeming return to normal. The pendulum was working. Japan might at least introduce peace and order in Manchuria, Grew argued, and provide a bulwark against Communism. It was time to be realistic and accept existing facts and situations, putting Stimson policies as far in the background as possible.[9]

He was not prepared to abandon the idea of international cooperation for peace. The reliance on traditional neutrality, as advocated by John Bassett Moore, struck him as "folding our hands helplessly." The United States should continue to take part in the slow but steady improvement of international morality. Human conduct had changed for the better in the past and would in the future. Another war would be "utterly devastating." Developments in science enabling "whole cities to be wiped out over night" would make men insist on "saner ways to maintaining the truth than by fighting and dying for it." The current peace machinery was ineffective because it could not be applied early enough, before a problem became aggravated and public passions were aroused. Why not, he suggested in June 1933, set up a Faculty of International Health, a body of farsighted statesmen who would diagnose international ills before the "fever of animosity" developed, and prescribe remedies? He conceded it was a visionary idea, but if nations stuck to the theory of international cooperation for peace, "the practical consummation will come with time, and with absolute certainty." In January 1934 he read an article in *Reader's Digest* entitled "This Mad-House World is Getting Better," and commented, "That's the way to talk." [10]

Whatever Grew's doubts as to their effectiveness, he did not recommend that his government change or abandon the Nine-Power Treaty, the Peace Pact, or the Non-Recognition Doctrine. Any formal departure from established policy must have appeared highly unlikely anyway. Stimson's tightly strung case against Japan made it very difficult to alter the basis of Far Eastern relations without appearing to approve Japanese aggression. Furthermore, Grew worried that his advocacy of friendlier relations with Japan might weaken his standing with his own government. He did not like praise of his work by the Japanese Ambassador in Washington, because it gave the impression he had "swallowed the Japanese point of view hook, bait and sinker." He assured Washington that he was not becoming "imbued with the Japanese atmosphere," and that he "staunchly" supported established policies. Undoubtedly he believed he could be more effective by avoiding frontal assaults on the policies of both governments. The Stimson Doctrine was not a dead letter, he told Ambassador Debuchi, but it was passive not active. The United States had no intention of interfering with Japan's interpretation of her treaty obligations, however much it might disapprove, he told Kabayama. Manchuria and immigration were chronic problems about which the two countries must agree to disagree while they worked to improve relations.[11]

In 1933 and early 1934 Grew put his heart into creating a friendlier climate in Japanese-American relations. The United States, he believed, must stop being Japan's "most popular *bête noir*." He sought to impress on officials that if they wished to improve relations (as they did, on certain terms), they would have to stop anti-American tirades in the Japanese press. At the same time he tried not to magnify the importance of public name-calling. He made representations orally and informally. In order to avoid publicity he saw Hirota at the Minister's residence rather than at the Foreign Office. Most attacks he would not dignify with his attention, but occasionally he had to respond, as when General Araki spoke of the United States and the Soviet Union as "wolves which are sharpening their fangs, and castaway cats showing their teeth for attack." Saving his ammunition for important cases seemed wiser than continual protests, because the Japanese learned that he did not "go off half-cock." The attacks did subside, as both the State Department and Embassy noticed. In August 1934 a remark by a Japanese general which could be construed as insulting to President Roosevelt was published once, but not picked up by the local press at large. While a calmer press was an obvious corollary to Hirota's policy of seeking understanding with Western nations, Grew's friendly warnings undoubtedly made it seem more important, as his patience made it easier to accomplish.[12]

His policy of non-aggravation applied to his own government as well. In January 1934 he was disturbed to hear Stimsonian language from Washington again. To Stanley Hornbeck, American Far Eastern policy was a living thing, sprung from the soil of American ideals and experience, rising straight and fair under the nurture of Secretaries Hay, Hughes, and Stimson. Non-recognition was not abandoned, he told a conference on the Causes and Cure of War. The American people "viewed with disapproval tendencies — where manifested — toward imperialistic angling in troubled waters." He was reported to have referred to "governments made by the sword," though he later denied it. In any case Amō issued a rejoinder and Grew had an incident on his hands. He warned Washington that public reiteration of the Non-Recognition Doctrine would undo his work and make it more difficult for Hirota to carry out his policy of improving relations. The American government's position on Manchuria should be maintained unimpaired, but so far as possible without inflaming public opinion in Japan, by diplomatic conversations rather than by public speeches. The Department agreed, but added waspishly that "neither action nor utterances can be formulated with a view exclusively to ensuring none but pleasant reactions in Japan." The incident was closed by Hirota announcing that Hornbeck's speech was unofficial and incorrectly reported. It was "sometimes best not to pick at chronic sores," Grew wrote Hornbeck.[13]

Actually the Embassy and Washington were substantially in agreement on policy. The Hornbeck speech was illustrative of the Department's groping efforts to strike the right balance between preservation of traditional policies in form and non-aggravation of relations with Japan in practice. The American response to the Amō Doctrine, an *aide-mémoire* delivered by Grew on April 29, 1934, seemed to achieve that purpose. It was slow in coming, bland in tone, and couched in generalities. It asserted the treaty basis of relations with China but mentioned no treaty by name. It pointed out that treaties could only be modified by recognized or agreed-upon procedures and stated the "opinion" of the United States that no nation could make its will conclusive unilaterally where rights and interests of other nations were involved, but it ended with an affirmation of the good neighbor policy. Grew was pleased. The communication had his "full concurrence and admiration." It was "absolutely called for . . . and . . . was expressed with a clarity and moderation which not only puts our Government on precise record, but which will undoubtedly sink into the Japanese consciousness. . . ."[14]

A calmer atmosphere was the necessary condition for the quiet, gradual task of building friendly relations. As always, Grew paid close attention to the small courtesies. He sat down for a nice chat with a Japanese who had requested the honor of bowing before the representative of the nation that had produced Benjamin Franklin. The man nearly fainted when told that the representative's wife was Franklin's great-great-granddaughter. He heard that the Imperial Household was disappointed that so few diplomats attended its concerts of Japanese classical music. They were very boring, but he went anyway, and "little [Marquis] Okubo [Toshikadzu] . . . wagged all over." On the occasion of the birth of the Crown Prince, Grew was the first chief of mission to write in the books of the Emperor and Empress. He did so at 8:15 A.M., an almost indecent ninety-six minutes after the birth. The Japanese, he held, "love to have foreigners show what they consider proper respect to their royalty." Helen Keller's audience proved a problem in this respect. He had to make her understand that she could not "visualize" the Emperor by feeling his face. Visiting American dignitaries had to be induced to make a proper bow to the Emperor instead of giving a terse, democratic nod of the head, as did Philippines High Commissioner Frank Murphy.[15]

Grew had innumerable opportunities for promoting Japanese-American understanding by attendance at public functions. He was used to this wheel-horse aspect of diplomacy, often enjoyed the spectacle of it, and was occasionally deeply moved by impressive displays of feeling. However, in Japan, the unending succession of banquets, visits, meetings, receptions, ceremonies, graduations, inaugurations, and commemorations severely taxed his time and energy. He made thirty-five speeches during his first year in Japan, working as long as ten hours on an important one. Four public addresses, including one by radio to the United States, to celebrate the eightieth anniversary of Perry's treaty with Japan left the streams of inspiration dry. He opened the first Japanese-American football game and threw out the ball for the first professional Japanese-American baseball game. Babe Ruth hit only a "single bingle (hope I have the vernacular correct)," but was "a great deal more effective Ambassador than I could ever be." Grew paraded American sports stars before Japanese cameramen and staged receptions for Japanese and American newsmen to meet visiting boxing, basketball, football, track, and baseball teams, both Filipino and American. Such activities resulted in "prominent and favorable comment in the press," offsetting anti-American propaganda and making "lasting headway," he believed, toward improved feeling about the United States in Japan.[16]

In Japan as in Turkey, Grew proved versatile at publicity, which he regarded as "the most delicate and difficult part of a diplomat's work." He did what he could to broaden news coverage between the two nations, taking an active interest in the bid of Associated Press to replace Reuters in supplying American news to Japan, and putting American correspondents in touch informally with Japanese government officials and business leaders.

e combed his speeches for ambiguities the Japanese press might pounce on, warned an American writer against carping, cynical, or flippant articles about Japan, and encouraged American correspondents to report Japanese expressions of friendly sentiment. He released a presidential message to the Emperor sympathizing over the loss of Japanese fliers bound for the United States, but postponed his own condolences to prolong the favorable publicity. He recognized the value of being well and favorably known himself. When *Nichi Nichi* credited him with the removal of the American fleet to Atlantic waters he archly did not deny it. He was sincerely grateful to a taxicab driver for rescuing his Scottie Sambo from the moat in front of the Imperial Palace, and so was all Tokyo thanks to story and pictures in *Asahi*. Sambo became a celebrity in his own right.[17]

Grew watched over Americans in Japan like a mother hen. He worried about Japanese arrangements for a group of visiting American editors. Good salesmanship dictated "propaganda subtly on the sidelines in personal talks," but he feared that instead the Americans would be exposed to an excess of sight-seeing and speech-making, as they were. He was disappointed that a group of visiting American veterans were mostly former noncommissioned officers with "little background and culture," well below the caliber of the Japanese group whose visit they were returning. In the event, he admitted that they conducted themselves with dignity and won highly favorable attention in Japan. He was furious with Americans in Japan who criticized their own government. Missionaries were particularly at fault. It was one thing to show courtesy and respect to the Japanese, but quite another to toady to them and little short of treason to apologize for one's own country. He told American teachers in Japan it was their duty to help the Japanese understand the United States and give them an "inner grasp" of American motives and incentives. They might explain the great heritage of Western civilization by using as examples Luther, Michelangelo, Shakespeare, Beethoven, Chartres, Rheims, Bayreuth, Westminster Abbey, a Bach cantata, a Brahms symphony, and the Gettysburg Address.[18]

Grew also took a hand in assisting prominent Japanese visitors to the United States. He encouraged informal visits and arranged hospitality in Washington. The idea proved too successful. First-name letters from the President to Japanese acquaintances of Harvard days brought forth an excess of goodwill envoys, including one whom Harada considered something of a hobo. Grew guessed that Hirota meant to "cash in" on these ties as a means of securing direct access to the White House, thereby circumventing a "hard-boiled" State Department, an anti-Japanese Hornbeck, and a Far Eastern Division full of China hands. In any case, he feared that Washington was getting tired of goodwill, so he inspired an editorial in the *Japan Advertiser* suggesting that the idea was being overplayed, let his court friends know, and promoted the next two travelers to "Envoys of Common

Harvard, Class of '02.

An American diplomat in court uniform. Secretary of Embassy Grew and Mrs. Grew at St. Petersburg.

Heinr. Lichte & Co.

First Secretary at Berlin.

Photographia-Presse

The American delegation at Lausanne. Seated, left to right, Admiral Bristol, Ambassador Child, Minister Grew.

F. H. Jullien

With Ismet Inönü and members of the Turkish delegation, Lausanne, 1923.

Ambassador to Turkey. The Foreign Minister of Turkey, Tevfik Rusdu Bey (right), and the Soviet Ambassador, Jacob Souritz (left).

Pacific News and Photo Service

The right, light touch. Seated, Mrs. Grew and Sir Robert Craigie.

The Ambassador presents his condolences to Mrs. Saito on the return of Ambassador Saito's ashes to Japan, 1939.

With Admiral Nimitz at Pearl Harbor, 1944.

Halsman

Ambassador Grew

Sense." Prince Konoe's forthcoming visit was different, however. The heir-apparent to the Genro should be given every opportunity of becoming acquainted with the United States, so Grew felt justified in firing off a broadside of letters to friends in Washington and others such as A. Lawrence Lowell, James B. Conant, Tyler Dennett, Walter Lippmann, Bobby Jones, and Cecil B. De Mille. It is questionable how thorough a grasp of American life Konoe obtained from the deck of a Morgan yacht at the Harvard-Yale crew race, but he returned with what Grew described as the first truthful account of American public opinion on the Far East.[19]

While making strenuous efforts to improve friendly feeling, Grew did not ignore the power factor in diplomacy. He was not averse to applying pressure of the appropriate kind at the appropriate time. In the Taku Incident of 1926 he had been the officer who sanctioned "gunboat diplomacy." He had played the game of diplomatic alignments at Lausanne, maneuvering nimbly from one side to the other to extract maximum advantage for American interests. It is true, coercion had seldom been a factor in his experience, but he was by no means a pacifist.

Calculations of power were never entirely absent during his mission to Japan. The case of Russo-Japanese tensions during the winter of 1933-34 was instructive. At first it appeared that the increase of Soviet Far Eastern strength might precipitate war, but as months passed without conflict it became clear that Japan was held in check by Soviet power. He saw that the Soviets were concentrating a formidable army for the defensive purpose of deterring the Japanese and were succeeding in their aim. He recognized and applauded the hint of power in the actions of his own government. Roosevelt's recognition of the Soviet Union "injected an important psychological element into the situation . . . for regardless of the pacific policy of the United States, American action in the event of a Japanese-Soviet conflict would be to the Japanese an unknown and disturbing factor. . . ." Grew was quite right; the *rapprochement* was a concern. Shigemitsu worried to Harada that the Russians and Americans "may act against us both peaceably and militarily." The President's 1933 program of naval construction also impressed Grew. Roosevelt had "played his cards well: Stimson wrote hostile notes and got nothing but hostility in return; the President said not a word about Manchuria but started building up the fleet and recognized Soviet Russia; as a result he gets an entirely new and more friendly orientation of Japanese policy toward the United States . . . using an unwritten language which the Japanese thoroughly understand." The wise policy was to develop friendly relations and "build up our Navy to the limit," or in other words, said Grew, "Speak softly and carry a big stick." [20]

As *Realpolitik*, the recognition of the Soviet Union might be wise, but personally it was highly distasteful. Up to this point, Grew would probably have agreed with Castle that the influence of the Japanese in the Orient was less to be deplored than that of the Soviets. At the beginning of 1933 he had been "very much against the recognition of Soviet Russia, with all that such action would imply. . . ." Now he had to enter into social relations with the "Bolshies." He even had to attend a reception at the Soviet Embassy on their national holiday. "Imagine congratulating anyone on the success of the Soviet revolution and the future welfare of the Red Flag," he sputtered. "But," he added, "it had to be done." Soviet Ambassador Constantin Yurenev had an "appalling" French accent but proved reasonably intelligent and mannerly. Though Grew never liked or trusted him, the two ambassadors exchanged visits and hospitality, and so far as appearances were concerned their nations stood closer together. One compensation for Grew was buying caviar through the Soviet Embassy at little more than two dollars a pound.[21]

During the first two years of Grew's mission various ways of bringing pressure to bear against Japan were less important than various ways of conciliating Japan. In 1932 all forms of pressure had seemed futile. In 1933 and early 1934 goodwill seemed to be succeeding. Even the Emperor commented on the calmer atmosphere. Grew's patience and hard work for good relations were apparently appreciated and his prestige was high. He was becoming something of a symbol of friendship between the two countries. As Hirota told Harada sometime later, the continued presence of Grew in Japan ensured that "the relationship between the United States and Japan will get better." [22]

The Amō Doctrine was a turning point in Grew's diplomacy. It began an important shift in his thinking about ways of dealing with Japan as well as in his understanding of Japanese expansionism. From April 1934 the outlook darkened for the rest of the year. Talks between Hull and Ambassador Saito Hiroshi in May plainly showed that the United States was not prepared to carry cordiality to the point of bilateral understanding, especially not one granting the proposition asserted by the Foreign Office spokesman. Each month seemed only to reveal how little basis for improved relations existed and how much conflict of interest. Grew came to the conclusion that "American and Japanese policy in the Far East will directly conflict — unless someone puts the helm over hard." The United States must act in ways that would warn and deter Japan.[23]

Now his public activity in behalf of mutual friendship declined. He refused most speech invitations and became dubious of the value of Japanese-American sports events. Talk of understanding and goodwill was "laughable." There was too much "hot air" about friendship and too little "brass tacks" in solving differences. The outcry aroused by Amō served the useful purpose of letting the Japanese know "how we feel about their trying to dictate relations which other countries will have with China." Shaping American policies solely with a view to pleasing the Japanese "will make them more cocky and simply invite aggressive tactics on their part." The President's message to Congress in January 1936, warning Americans to take cognizance of trends toward aggression, was "courageous statesmanship." Senator Key Pittman's inflammatory speech against Japan soon after "should prove that we are not . . . ruled by our peace organizations and women pacifists." Americans in his view were a highly inflammable people. Under certain circumstances they would no more think about the "absurdity and criminality" of war with Japan than about lynching a Negro suspected of rape. The risk of their being aroused was real, despite all talk of "permanent peace, complementary trade, brotherly love and goodwill." It was just as well to let the Japanese know that "fire still exists in what they may believe to be an extinct volcano." [24]

Grew's strong line showed itself in August 1934. The Japanese seemed about to defy the Open Door in Manchuria by discrimination against foreign oil products. American representations had been futile. Failure to back up protests with countervailing measures weakened American prestige, in Grew's opinion. Now he sought a bargaining weapon through some indication of retaliatory measures. It seemed only self-injury for the United States to supply the crude oil with which Manchurian refineries would be able to supplant American refined products. He therefore recommended that Washington together with London consider an embargo on crude oil. The mere call for data on exports might have the desired effect. He argued that whatever the exacerbation of feelings resulting, suppression of contentious issues between the two countries should not be carried to the point of seriously jeopardizing important American policies and interests. This new line from Tokyo amused Minister Johnson in China, who thought his own telegram on the subject should have come from Tokyo while Grew's should have come from Peking. Johnson, an old China hand, could not be accused of being a Japanese sympathizer, but he saw no evidence of Chinese ability to resist Japanese encroachment, and was reluctant to "venture in any physical way" in the Far East. So was Washington reluctant, and Grew was sent back to making more futile representations.[25]

By the end of 1934 Grew's new position was abundantly clear to his government. The studies of Japanese expansionism submitted by the Embassy at this time were accompanied by policy recommendations. In addition, Grew's diary went to Hornbeck and Moffat. In Japan, Grew contended, the compelling factor in all relationships was prestige, and the principal basis of prestige was power. American prestige in Japan had declined because of failure to implement Stimson's representations in regard to Manchuria with positive action. As a result the Japanese had received the impression of American "weakness, irresolution and bluff," and had been led to ignore his own representations and to believe it was possible to secure naval parity. The one nation toward which Japan had modified its policy,

Russia, was the one nation which had devoted itself to building up its defenses. The lesson was clear: either the United States should withdraw gracefully from the Far East or provide firm support for its interests by building up its navy and air force. The Administration appeared to have chosen the second course. The method and manner of day-to-day diplomacy was important, particularly with a hypersensitive nation such as Japan, but vitally important "background" was national preparedness, giving weight to the diplomat's words. The United States should build its navy to treaty strength. In the current naval talks at London, which sought a basis for the forthcoming London Naval Conference of 1935, the United States should insist on maintaining current ratios and refuse to grant parity to Japan, even at the cost of breaking up the talks. If the United States took a strong position, the Japanese, fearing a hopeless arms race, would be likely to "climb down off their high horse." In any event, the risk of Japanese forces running amok was always present and should be covered with adequate strength.[26]

Grew's venture in policy-making was a great success. Warmly received in particular was his dispatch of December 27, 1934, which embodied most of his thinking on the new approach in clear and forceful language. He received a letter of personal appreciation from Hull, who said he had brought the dispatch to the attention of the President and intended to use it with other Administration leaders. Grew had never known a Secretary to write in such flattering terms and he was deeply gratified. Hornbeck in his usual "stiff and impliant style" had been making nearly the same point at the same time, even quoting the same maxim, "Speak softly but carry a big stick." The Far Eastern Chief detected a "community of concept" developing over fundamental principles of policy, and Grew himself was amused to see how their two minds were working alike. Actually, consensus on American Far Eastern policy was mostly about what not to do. The United States would avoid debating, provoking, or challenging Japan. It would acquiesce in, but not assent to, Japanese expansion already undertaken at the expense of China. It would not invoke, but not discard, the Nine-Power Treaty. The one positive element in American policy was the decision to maintain American naval superiority regardless of the consequences. The value of the dispatch of December 27 lay in its reasoned justification of that decision by the officer in the best position to judge the impact of policy on Japan.[27]

Another method of deterring Japan would be an Anglo-American diplomatic front, but this was not easy to establish. Relations between the United States and Great Britain were comparatively poor in 1934. Added to the burden of differences over economic questions was the legacy of suspicion and misunderstanding left over from the Manchurian crisis and earlier failures to coordinate Far Eastern policies. Faced with a resurgent Germany, Britain anxiously was seeking guarantees in the Far East and preferred some kind of naval agreement with Japan in place of the Washington Treaty rather than none at all, as the Americans would have it. Neither nation wished to incur the brunt of Japanese displeasure, so each hesitated to take the initiative in establishing a common front. These strains between the Atlantic powers were felt in Tokyo. In May 1934 Grew reported rumors from press sources that an Anglo-Japanese understanding, possibly an alliance, was in the making. This "perfidious Albion" telegram and subsequent ones of August in the same vein caused considerable anxiety and led to American countermeasures at the London naval talks. In the oil controversy, in spite of their common interest, the British and American ambassadors did not call on Hirota together to make a single protest from a single sheet of paper. Instead, the British were allowed to make the initiatives, and as Grew said, ". . . we have followed up every one of them." [28]

In Grew's opinion the situation called for being close but not too close to the British. He was always on the best terms with British ambassadors in Tokyo, with the "easy-going, gentle, rather vague" Sir Francis Lindley, an acquaintance from Cairo days, as well as with the sound, stolid Sir Robert Clive. On the theory that "it always pays to be as open as possible with a colleague whom one knows and can trust," he regularly exchanged views and information with the British, who occasionally showed him their most confidential telegrams. As the British made a point of keeping all posts well informed, he often obtained a better picture of Anglo-American developments and even of his own government's policy through London than directly from Washington. By February 1935 Japanese intransigence and American pressure had improved Anglo-American cooperation to the point where joint, informal, oral representations on the oil question could be made, though by subordinate officers of the two embassies. Grew approved of a close personal and symbolical relationship. In April 1935 he dined aboard the H.M.S. *Kent*, and was delighted to see the Japanese Navy Minister's look of surprise. It was useful and healthy to have the Stars and Stripes and the Union Jack "entwined, metaphorically, all over Tokyo." On the other hand, he was reluctant to press Anglo-American solidarity too hard. During the North China crisis of June 1935 he canceled an overnight excursion with the British Ambassador for fear of its being wrongly interpreted by the Japanese press.[29]

Grew's accent on power did not preclude compromise. In his view military power provided ultimate protection for vital interests, and together with other forms of pressure created the respect and forbearance that made possible negotiation and settlement of conflicts of interest. There is some evidence that early in 1936 he contemplated a political settlement with Japan that would provide security for important American Far Eastern interests, in return for acceptance of a new *status quo* in the area of Manchuria, Inner Mongolia, and North China. He was obscure and equivocal in discussing such a settlement, but the fact that he did not dismiss the idea differentiated his viewpoint from that of the State Department, which was not prepared to consider any formal abridgment of the treaty order in the Far East.

What gave rise to the discussion was a conversation in London in January 1936 between Sir Robert Craigie of the Foreign Office and roving Ambassador Norman Davis. Sir Robert saw evidence of a Sino-Japanese non-aggression pact in the making, which if consummated would automatically settle the Manchurian question between the two powers directly concerned. In that event, Craigie suggested, the British and Americans might find it advantageous themselves to negotiate a non-aggression pact with the Japanese. This might enable Japan to enter a naval agreement that would preserve the *status quo* and prevent an arms race. Davis passed the suggestion on to Washington which in turn queried the Far Eastern embassies for their opinion. Peking and Washington were cold to the idea, and in London the new Foreign Secretary, Anthony Eden, dismissed it as impractical. Only from Tokyo came an affirmative response, a muffled one at that. Grew sent a telegram and then worried the "confounded" Craigie idea for a month longer. The more he thought about it the more it seemed "utter rot," but he would not let it go. Instead, in a long, tortured dispatch studded with conditional clauses, he presented the idea that the United States should indeed consider entering a political agreement with Japan.[30]

Dispatch number one thousand six hundred and sixty-five (of some six thousand written during the mission) seems designed to be read two ways. One reader, attached to traditional policy, might survey Grew's arguments on behalf of policy reconsideration but note his observation that Japan's conduct in the past did not inspire confidence in any pact concluded with her in the future. This reader would find Grew doubtful that a Sino-Japanese understanding could be reached, since the dominant Japanese military were against binding Japan to peaceful methods and the Chinese could not accept even implied loss of sovereignty over Manchuria and part of North China. Grew also seemed aware that an agreement with Japan would restrict American freedom of action and imply condonation of past aggression. The Ambassador apparently understood that the American government and people were not likely to abandon the principles of world peace for which the United States had struggled for many years. Read this way, Grew's dispatch was properly speculative, as he had been invited to be, but indicated that he was still safely tethered to established policy.

Another reader in a frame of mind to consider change might recall Grew's point in his telegram that arguments against reconsideration of policy were founded more on "the difficulties of adjusting ourselves to new facts and conditions, however unwelcome . . . than upon insuperable obstacles." The new facts and conditions were these: the treaty order in the

Far East was crumbling; Japan would succeed in gaining control of North China whether or not China acknowledged it by pact; no moral or legal methods were effective against Japan, but only force, which China could not and the West would not employ; eventually the United States would face one and only one power in the Far East, Japan, which would bear ever more heavily against American rights and interests with resulting increase of friction and risk of war. In the face of this situation, Grew proposed that the United States "should not neglect carefully to explore every avenue which might lead to some variety of political agreement with Japan. . . ." Recognition of the *status quo* on the Asiatic mainland would be a small price to pay for even limited protection of American interests in the Far East, for lessening the danger of war, for maintaining naval superiority without the cost of a naval construction race, and for preventing a separate Anglo-Japanese understanding.

Grew had to answer the criticism that little value lay in abandoning traditional policy in return for promises respecting Asia mainland interests which the United States could not and would not compel Japan to fulfill. He argued that the Japanese had shown greater respect for bilateral than for multilateral commitments and that a strong American fleet would have a deterrent effect. It was just possible that he had in mind a third inducement to fulfillment, namely Japanese self-interest. Such an argument at least can be constructed from elements scattered about this very confusing dispatch. He stated as a premise that the "principal impelling force" in Japanese expansion was the urge to "consolidate Japan's strategic position against Soviet Russia and thereby to hold Communism in check." To achieve this security, the Japanese would seek "to preserve a *Pax Japonica* in the areas adjacent to their own territory, and to consolidate their control of Manchuria by securing a degree of control over Mongolia and North China." Any arrangement with Japan, he stated elsewhere in the dispatch, "must take into account the fact that the attitude of Soviet Russia is an important consideration in Japanese political calculations."

Now on the assumption that Japan's main concern was directed northward, special meaning attaches to Grew's statement that the only effective course for the United States was to "slow up the Japanese expansionist movement by a series of agreements of limited duration, each of which would be designed to restrain Japan *in one direction or another* [italics added]." Perhaps he meant that just as American recognition of the Soviet Union had helped check northward expansion, an understanding with the United States would appear to the Japanese as protection against the Soviet Union and thus possess inherent, self-enforcing value. It might reduce risk of conflict to the southward, enhance Japanese security in that direction, and keep Japanese attention directed northward and northwestward, away from most American interests. Such containment of Japanese expansion by alternating support between the Soviet Union and Japan is of course classical balance of power diplomacy, in which Grew had received a refresher course from Tyler Dennett's *Theodore Roosevelt and the Russo-Japanese War,* a "most enlightening" book.[31] Admittedly this whole line of reasoning is speculative. All that can be said with assurance is that Grew foresaw increasing conflict of interests between the United States and Japan, interests vital to the latter and peripheral to the former, and turned naturally to a consideration of the resources of diplomacy as a means of avoiding unnecessary war.

Grew's ambivalence and hesitancy about the Craigie proposal reflected deep anxiety that his views and those of his government were diverging. He tried to assure Hornbeck that the Embassy was not defeatist and that it stood by its big-navy position of December, 1934. The Craigie dispatch was not intended as a didactic pronouncement, he wrote, but only "food for reflection." [32] Of course he could point to a wide area of agreement — on the necessity of not aggravating relations with Japan, on the impossibility of challenging Japanese encroachment upon China, on the importance of military preparedness — but different governing assumptions were in fact emerging.

Familiarity with the dynamics of Japanese expansion led Grew to stress the uses of diplomacy and the Department of State to discount them. To those on the scene the diversity of forces competing for control of Japanese policy seemed to provide room for maneuver; skillful diplomacy might bend the direction here or weaken the thrust there. Those at a distance took a simpler view and saw Japan as single-minded, purposeful, and predatory. Agreements not backed with force were worthless, and, since force could not be applied, there was no point in making agreements. From Peking, Johnson expressed a popular view when he responded to the Craigie proposal by saying that he would sooner make a pact with a starving family next door not to steal each other's bread.[33]

The Embassy and Department also began to differ in their views of America's role in the Far East. In spite of the passivity of its policy, the Administration visualized the United States as no less a Far Eastern power in 1936 than it had in 1933. Every Japanese advance or assertion had been crossed with a polite, bland, but sufficient American exception. No agreements had been entered, no promises made, no recognitions extended which in any way repudiated the moral imperatives of American foreign relations. The United States had no "right" to abandon the Open Door or the Nine-Power Treaty because they expressed in concrete form the animating spirit of the nation, it was argued. Naval advantage was to be maintained at all costs. Without it, said the Chief of Naval Operations, "we could exercise no strength in the Far East." Moffat reported the consensus of a White House meeting "that in no circumstances should we indicate any intention either to weaken ourselves in the Orient, to indicate an unwillingness to join issue under certain circumstances or a willingness to allow the Japanese to continue pressing forward without protest on our part." As a last resort Grew was prepared to see the United States accept a lesser role in the Far East to avoid war. The Administration was not yet prepared to face that possibility. Its passivity was tactical, carefully designed to be dropped if circumstances warranted a more active role. Meanwhile, the time for a graceful adjustment of Far Eastern interests was passing.[34]

On the evening of February 25, 1936, the Grews gave a big diplomatic dinner in honor of Viscount Saito. The former Prime Minister, now Lord Keeper of the Privy Seal, had never seen a "talkie," so an after-dinner showing of *Naughty Marietta* was arranged. The kindly old gentleman with his shock of white hair was settled in a comfortable armchair in case he wished to snooze. But Saito was apparently delighted, and some of the ladies moved to tears, by the Victor Herbert music and the singing of Jeanette MacDonald. It was close to midnight before he took his leave and Grew walked him to the door to say goodnight. Some five hours later Saito was shot to death on his bed (thirty-six bullet wounds were counted). The February 26 Incident had begun.[35]

Assassination this time was only the first act of mutiny. Crude and violent nationalism spouted by *Kodo-ha* generals and revolutionary agitators inspired both the May 15, 1932, and February 26, 1936, incidents. Then as now the terrorists were determined to purge Japan of corrupt politicians and capitalists, deliver the Emperor from weak-kneed elder statesmen and admirals, and set the nation again on the path of ancient virtues. The deadly difference now was the participation of twenty-four officers and fifteen hundred troops of the Army's First Division stationed at Tokyo. In the middle of the night assassination parties had fanned out from the barracks through the snow-encrusted city seeking their sleeping victims. Brutally murdered in their beds like Saito were a *Tosei-ha* general (damned because he had succeeded the ousted darling of the *Kodo-ha*, General Mazaki) and Finance Minister Takahashi, regarded by Grew as the "sheet anchor" of Japan's credit system. The Grand Chamberlain, Admiral Suzuki Kantarō, another guest at Grew's party, was wounded but survived. The Genro was whisked to safety. Okada and Makino had hair-raising escapes. The former survived because the mutineers killed his brother-in-law by mistake. He hid two days in the labyrinths of his official residence which was occupied by the killers, and then departed to safety as a mourner in his own funeral procession. Makino was an easy target as he scrambled up a steep slope in back of the burning house he had just fled, but he fell with a wounded helper and the assassins, believing they had scored, decamped.[36]

By 10 A.M. the rebels held key government buildings just west of the Imperial Palace and the Embassy telegraphed a test message that the military had taken partial control of the government.

In the crisis the shattered Cabinet and corps of palace advisers as well as the Army and Navy turned to the Emperor for decision. Hirohito, proving remarkably resolute, ordered immediate suppression of the mutiny and received support from the Navy which concentrated the First Fleet in Tokyo Bay. The Army moved loyal troops into the city and encircled the rebel quarter but was loath to pit soldier against soldier, preferring to talk the rebels into surrender. The ultimate outcome was obvious to all, but as the talks dragged on everyone was uncertain how bloody the last act would be.

The hilltop Embassy made a perfect observation post. With binoculars Grew could pick out rebel soldiers in the Prime Minister's residence, while in the street below stood loyalist barricades. The Japanese-speaking staff went scouting for information which he relayed to Washington every few hours. The authorities advised evacuation because the Embassy would be in the line of fire if fighting broke out, but Grew declined. He feared the demoralizing effect on the foreign colony and judged that his cellars offered sufficient protection for his staff and his little flock of refugees from nearby compounds. The city grimly awaited the outcome. One day passed and another, and finally on the afternoon of February 29 the government made a direct appeal to the rebel ranks, using the radio, leaflets dropped from the air, and a streamer flying from a balloon. The message cleverly combined the command of the Emperor to surrender with offer of pardon and word that "Your fathers and brothers and all the people are praying you to return." Soon they came trickling out and the rebel flag, a tablecloth, was hauled down. Eighty-four hours after the predawn murders the revolt ended. Grew, *protocolaire* as ever, promptly sent a card of condolence to the Okada family and was flabbergasted to receive the supposedly dead Prime Minister's card in return, with thanks!

Even though each historical event is both an ending and a beginning, the February 26 Incident is more significant as an ending. The mutiny had been largely the product of vicious factional strife in the army high command. It will be recalled that 1934 had marked the ascendancy of a neutral group of generals seeking to end factionalism and to ready the economy and society as well as the armed forces for modern total war. From the resignation of Araki to the replacement of Mazaki in July 1935, this *Tosei-ha* group had gradually squeezed out the *Kodo-ha* clique. The victims had fought back and their recriminations had spilled over to the ears of simple-minded, zealous junior officers. In August 1935 an officer who was a protégé of Mazaki stormed into the office of General Nagata, the directing mind of the *Tosei-ha*, and skewered him with a sword. It had been the trial of this officer, Lieutenant Colonel Aizawa Saburo, which roused the passions of the young officers of the First Division and set the stage for revolt. Nagata had been pictured by the defense as the instrument of evil financiers, politicians, and palace advisers. Though Mazaki and company apparently had no direct connection with the revolt, the young officers had hoped to pave the way for a *Kodo-ha* regime of national purification. Now, with the revolt suppressed, factionalism and insubordination could be dealt with effectively. Aizawa and fifteen of the rebel officers were executed. Virtually every senior officer involved in the plotting and rivalry of 1931 to 1936 was retired or barred from headquarters assignment. Factionalism persisted in the Japanese Army, but not the same factions and not such explosive ones.[37]

The first reaction of the Embassy to this dramatic turn of events was one of relief. Lady Clive might refer to "those barbarians, the Japanese," but the bloodless suppression of the revolt impressed Grew as anything but barbarism. As to the future, he was cautiously optimistic. The turbulent element in the Army, as likely to precipitate hostilities abroad as violence at home, had been brought to heel by the "moderate" element, and the incident would probably arouse a healthy revulsion of feeling against the military as a whole. With the "strong, safe" Hirota as Prime Minister and the "distinctly liberal and moderate" Arita Hachiro as Foreign Minister, the outlook was for less jingoism and for calm Japanese-American relations. Hirota would have to conciliate the military, but the slender willow bowed before the storm and survived where the mighty oak was toppled. In any event Japan would be too preoccupied with internal affairs to stir up trouble abroad. He hoped the government would carry through a program of fundamental reform such as it had under consideration. The Embassy held that one of the basic causes of the revolt was the maldistribution of wealth; there was much truth in the rebels' accusation that too great a spread existed between the very rich and the very poor. Only by vigorous measures to improve the welfare of the masses, particularly in rural communities, could future outbreaks be prevented. What Japan needed was a "social and economic New Deal," Grew believed, and Hirota had a historic opportunity to provide it.[38]

The idea of a New Deal for Japan was a novelty in Grew's approach to Japanese internal affairs. For him, stability and order had a diplomatic as well as intrinsic value. War threatened when constituted authority lost control internally, as President McKinley had lost it to public passion in 1898 and the German government to the military in 1914. On coming to Japan he had looked to the court set and the business magnates, the forces of the *status quo* socially and economically, as the natural guarantors of internal peace. His expectation that they would eventually recover power from an unruly Army was disappointed, and they were now "visibly depressed" and out of the picture.[39] Then he had distinguished saner heads among the military (the *Tosei-ha*) who in conjunction with a skillful mediator like Hirota might at least keep Japanese expansion within bounds. These "moderates," having subdued the unruly element in the Army, now represented stability and order, but they could succeed only if they introduced fundamental reform, or in other words altered the *status quo*. What he failed to take into account was that his agents of reform were career servants in the great military and civilian bureaucracies, worlds apart in their experiences and concerns from the distressed peasants and workers whose welfare they were supposed to improve.

At first the government seemed to justify his hopes, though the Army, not Hirota, was riding whip. Insisting on a "progressive, vigorous Cabinet," the Army vetoed the Prime Minister's selection of Yoshida as Foreign Minister because, said Grew, the "liberal" son-in-law of Makino was too closely identified with the old order. While the Hirota Cabinet as a whole seemed to be deliberately procrastinating on reform in order to maintain the *status quo*, the Army, in the Embassy's opinion, was winning popular esteem by severe disciplinary measures against the rebels and by establishing itself as "trustee for fundamental reform." The rebels' fight against "privilege enjoyed by the wealthy, privilege within the Army, privilege close to the Throne, privilege in economic life," might still be won. Grew foresaw increasing adoption of their principles, in particular "Army guided expansion of government control of industry at the expense of private property." Japan's lack of liberal institutions, he argued, should not blind foreigners to the possibility, even probability, of basic political change. It was not the form of government which distinguished Japanese political psychology but "the necessity and authority and rightness of government itself." The constitution defined structure rather than function and would prove adaptable to changing ideas on what the government should bring to the people. At the moment its capacity for action was greater: "From the February 26 Incident, government in Japan emerges strong and the Army emerges strong." [40]

The Army's promise to improve the livelihood of the people turned out to be only a sop to the advocates of reform, and by the end of 1936 the Embassy was admitting that it had not received "even a pretense of fulfillment." Grew had failed to see that what really interested the Army on the domestic front, aside from a huge budget increase, was putting into effect the "national defense state" concept which had so long been agitating its best minds. Generals now in control sought efficient allocation of human and natural resources of the state for total war, with emphasis on economic planning, expansion of heavy industry, and indoctrination of youth. A corollary was suppression of dissent.[41]

These "fascist tendencies," as Grew called them, met with surprising resistance from the political parties. In May 1936 the Embassy saw the Diet acquitting itself creditably as a defender of liberal government against the forces of bureaucracy and militarism. By 1937 protest from the people, though giving no assurance of becoming a check on the military, was nevertheless making itself more strongly felt than any time since 1931, according to the Embassy. In January 1937 vigorous attacks in the House of Representatives played a part in bringing down the Hirota Cabinet, proof to the Embassy of "a more determined effort to resist political dictation by the army than has been attempted in the last 15 years." [42]

A clear picture of the political situation would no sooner emerge than it dissolved. The parties of the Diet possessed no influence at all in the succeeding Cabinet headed by General Hayashi. If army influence was somewhat greater, what direction that influence would take was obscure. The "neutral, controlling group" composed of "saner" generals like Hayashi seemed determined to prevent further factionalism, maintain discipline, and not precipitate hostilities abroad. Toward the Diet the Army would probably adopt a bland and patient attitude to get bigger budgets passed with a minimum of friction. The Cabinet had "less military and fascist leanings than was expected," but perhaps constituted "a short step on the road to some sort of Japanese fascism." The lack of distinctive personalities or cliques gave the new government a relatively innocuous appearance.[43]

Soon the Embassy discerned a new faction and Grew once again was writing of "hard-boiled . . . ultra-nationalists," as opposed to "saner, more level-headed officers." The emerging "Kwantung Army faction," headed by Lieutenant General Itagaki Seishirō had "definite political ideas and definite political danger." It was dedicated to rapid military preparations for war on the Soviet Union, establishment of socialism in Japan on the model of the Manchurian regime, and domination of the Diet by means of an Army-inspired, "monopoly" party, conceived in Japanese terms but in actuality not far different from the Nazi party. The faction had tried to make Itagaki War Minister and Suetsugu Navy Minister in the Hayashi Cabinet and failed because of "fear of the Diet and the Diet's influence on public opinion." Next time, with an army party, it would be invulnerable. Here then was the source of recent disturbing Fascist tendencies.[44]

What the Embassy had in fact touched upon was the Ishihara group with Itagaki as figurehead. State planning and preparation for ultimate war on the Soviet Union were indeed Ishihara objectives, but not his alone. He was the most brilliant and forceful exponent of ideas which predominated in the army high command. Factions developed over who would be in charge of implementation, not over the ideas themselves. Furthermore, the Nazi comparison was unfortunate. A national mass party was proposed, by Hayashi not Ishihara, but was not successfully or vigorously pursued. Unquestionably the national defense state concept involved government control over the individual in a degree abhorrent to Western democracies, but the Fascist analogy tended more to confuse than illuminate Japanese political developments. Whatever the label, the Embassy now saw a tendency toward Army-directed authoritarian government where a year earlier it had seen a tendency toward popular reform. It would soon have to look again. In May 1937, after four months in office, the Hayashi Cabinet fell and Prince Konoe became Prime Minister. Grew decided not to attempt an extensive interpretation of the policies of the new government until they had been disclosed and discussed in the press. Before a new picture emerged, the Marco Polo Bridge Incident occurred.[45]

Reality became ever more elusive as the pace of events quickened. After the February 26 Incident, Grew had been encouraged to believe that Hirota and the Army might introduce basic social and economic reforms that would make Japan more stable and less dangerous. This hope had been disappointed. At least the Diet had come to life with criticism of the government, but his hope for a restoration of popular influence in government had also been disappointed. In fact, a trend to Fascism had appeared, only to be interrupted by the Konoe government, whose course Grew dared not predict.

He and his staff had made a determined and dispassionate effort to understand what was happening in Japan and had gathered some accurate information, particularly about the Army. They understood the anti-faction disposition of the controlling generals and they were at least aware of the national defense state concept if not of its prevalence. They had reflected if not predicted the tendency toward authoritarian government. Yet, the coming and going of cabinets and the conflicting tendencies at work had left them bewildered and uncertain.

In some ways they made their problem more difficult, for example by their habit of viewing Japanese political developments in a Western context. Terms like "socialist," "Fascist," "progressive," and "liberal" bore Western connotations which often blurred Japanese reality. Faith in representative government encouraged excessive hope of the Diet regaining influence. Grew in particular tended to view events in terms of the twin alternatives of moderation and extremism with the result of confusing means with ends or oversimplifying the forces at work. Probably he never did subconsciously rid himself of the old pendulum theory. Still, whatever aberrations the Americans introduced themselves, the fact remains that Japanese developments were becoming increasingly unpredictable. Formal government was more and more a façade behind which the great bureaucracies struggled in obscurity to realize their separate ambitions. National policy decisions resembled treaties between sovereign states. When fighting broke out in China in July 1937, Grew found it impossible to tell whether or not Japan had planned it. "I don't know," he said. "Ask the tourists. It's all guesswork. . . ."[46]

The most discouraging experience of the first half of Grew's Japan mission was the theft of a portion of his diary. Still regularly sending it to his family, he entrusted the excerpt for the last half of December 1936 to a Foreign Service officer returning to his post in China via Tokyo, for delivery to his daughter and her husband Cecil Lyon, who was stationed at the Embassy in Peking. During the night of January 23-24, 1937, on the train somewhere between Seoul, Korea, and Mukden, it was stolen from the officer's unlocked suitcase. Grew was appalled at the breach of confidence and security. The worst disclosure was his report of a conversation with Clive which indicated that the British were advising the Chinese not to overplay their hand with the Japanese. "If Nanking continues to be inflexible," the British were understood to have said, "the result will tend to unite and solidify Japanese public opinion in favor of stronger measures, whereas if Japan's face can be saved by some perhaps unessential concessions, further aggressiveness may be stayed off. . . ." Remarks by the Vice-Minister several weeks later showed that the stolen document containing such information had reached the Foreign Ministry. It was his worst *faux pas* in thirty-three years of service, "and might wreck me yet. . . ." He wanted nothing better than to "slip out and fade away into retirement." [47]

The disclosures may well have been less harmful to Grew's interests than to his feelings. The Japanese probably learned little they did not already know or suspect about British Far Eastern cautionary advice. He believed he had lost face with the Japanese because of uncomplimentary remarks like the entry of December 19 which accused them of bad faith in the oil controversy. Nevertheless, he had already decided that a certain amount of bluntness with them might have a healthy effect. The State Department through Carr held him remiss for not ensuring better care for a highly confidential document, but obviously the person chiefly at fault was the bearer. Henceforth Grew was more careful, sequestering and not circulating confidential portions of his diary, using regular couriers, and admonishing recipients to burn after reading. Personally the theft seems to have hurt very deeply, partly no doubt because the negligence seemed so unprofessional, but chiefly, one suspects, because he could no longer feel easy and secure about confiding in his diary. Not that it had ever been an intimate one, but it had been a way of mulling over information and ideas and testing them out on others. For a partially deaf man such an outlet could be very important. He was a little less in touch, a little more isolated, in an increasingly violent and inexplicable world. He could not get rid of the feeling that his life and work in Tokyo would never again be as happy.

FIFTEEN

The Slide to War in China

AN ambassador must be to some extent an actor. How he looks, talks, dresses, and walks, as much as his official actions, reflect the mood and personality of his country. Ideally his own personality should be almost his representative personality, almost but not entirely. He must also be able to see his own country as others see it and to soak up the personality of the country where he is serving to the point where he can explain it, even in a sense represent it, to his own government. Inevitably then he is a role-player, and while he is in charge the curtain never goes down. Being Ambassador to Japan meant a constant drawing off of physical and emotional reserves. It was not like Switzerland where Grew could in good conscience drop his work and have a lark in the mountains; now he could never really escape the threat of dangerous, unexpected occurrences. It was not like Turkey where he had the satisfaction of seeing relations improve. In Japan the burden of formality, the persistent undercurrent of tension, and the beginnings of a sense of frustration took a steady toll, as did the damp climate and smog of Tokyo. By the spring of 1935 recurrent bronchitis, flu, and deep, persistent tiredness had made him "not so fit nowadays — no energy whatever." Husband and wife both needing a rest and change, they sailed for home July 19, spent seven weeks in New England, seven weeks in Europe, and continued on around the world to Japan. They went home again in 1936, this time for two months.[1]

Going home meant recovering his past and becoming whole again. The North Shore in late summer, New Hampshire in the autumn, Groton, the place still closest to his heart, Paris and memories of old Europe, a steamer to the Far East by way of Colombo, Penang, Singapore, Manila, and Shanghai, the route of his *Wanderjahr* in 1903, when all the world was young and all the trees were green: such experiences, in his familiar phrase, refilled the storage batteries. Richest in continuities and a sense of community with his own was the Harvard Tercentenary in September 1936. Serge

Koussevitsky's rendering of "Fair Harvard," commencing as a quiet hymn and swelling to a gloriously triumphant march, was a thrilling experience, as was the damp but still awesome crowning ceremony in the Yard. As a Marshal of Dignitaries, charged with the Justices of the Supreme Court, Grew sat front row, center. Directly facing him in the seat of honor on the dais was Franklin Roosevelt, something of a crow amid the profusion of academic plumage. The President recognized him, and perhaps grateful to see a loyal face in this coldly polite citadel of the Establishment, or perhaps just in puckish humor at the sight of an officer representing his person shepherding the lions of the Constitution, bellowed a hearty "Hello, Joe" across the intervening twenty yards or so, "somewhat to my embarrassment in front of those thousands of onlookers."

The President radiated strength. Grew made a point of calling at the White House each time he was in Washington and was astonished at the vigor and power of concentration of the Chief Executive, buoyed by his charm and affection, and impressed by the glint of steel showing through his quiet prediction of re-election. In contrast to the "exceedingly vague" Hull, Roosevelt had a detailed grasp of the problems of the Tokyo mission. In October 1936 Grew raised the question of his continuance in Japan, explaining that he was not getting any younger and needed to plan for retirement. The President wanted him to stay for a year or so, not for the rest of his life, and then come back to the Department or take a European mission.[2]

Since gossip had him in line for the Embassy in Berlin, Grew took this opportunity to scotch the idea, saying that he was prejudiced against the Germans, to which the President replied, "So am I." One would think that a professional diplomat would be prepared to serve anywhere, and in fact Hugh Wilson, a Secretary under Grew in wartime Berlin, went to Germany as Ambassador in 1938. But Grew's diplomat, like a lawyer, needed a willingness to believe in the clients he served, and Grew had no room for faith in the Germans, both from experience and on account of their treatment of the Jews. Furthermore, he doubted the Nazis would accept him because of his anti-German speeches of 1918. Regardless of bias, transfer from Japan to Germany must have seemed like jumping from the frying pan into the fire. He would return to Japan, he told the President, but he must have annual home leave for physical and psychological reasons. Roosevelt did not object and on that understanding Grew took up his mission again. He was to come home only once in the next six years.[3]

Grew returned to Tokyo on November 27, 1936, two days after the signing of the Anti-Comintern Pact. This seemingly tenuous but nonetheless ominous link-up between the principal "have-not" powers of Europe and the Far East, Germany and Japan, came as no surprise to the Embassy, nor for that matter to any informed observer; rumors of an agreement had been circulating for some time. Foreign opinion in Tokyo assumed quite rightly that the public undertaking to cooperate against Communism was only the façade for some sort of secret understanding. Grew speculated that it involved exchange of military information and of German arms for Japanese commodities. Actually the parties agreed not to make any separate political understanding with the Soviet Union and to remain each a potential threat to the Soviet Union should the other be menaced or attacked without provocation by their common enemy. This still was a minimal commitment, but it held the promise or threat, depending on how one looked at it, of a closer tie. The significance lay in the establishment of a relationship rather than in its precise nature. As Grew reported, a new orientation had taken place in Japanese policy.[4]

How one viewed this new orientation would depend on how one judged the old. Grew recognized that Soviet-Japanese relations would never be good so long as Japan coveted Mongolia and Siberia and feared Communist penetration, but Hirota's diplomacy had seemed constructive and careful. Now the *modus vivendi* had been "rudely shattered." The Japanese had blundered in incurring unnecessary Soviet hostility. From the Japanese viewpoint, however, Soviet support for Outer Mongolia and for a united Kuomintang-Communist front in China aroused deep concern. The deterrent effect of an alignment with Germany seemed more valuable than any settlement of issues by negotiation. Grew rightly assumed that the Anti-Comintern Pact would result in a deterioration of relations with Great Britain and the democracies, but again the Japanese undoubtedly saw the problem differently. Efforts to secure Western acceptance of Japan's new role in the Far East, a cardinal principle of Hirota diplomacy, had patently failed. Perhaps the German alignment would make Britain more amenable, Hirota told Harada. Of course treaty relations with a power which had just repudiated the Locarno Pact because it had "lost its inner meaning and ceased in practice to exist," as the Nazis put it, were less valuable than an understanding with Great Britain or the United States. Japan stood to lose a great deal by the Anti-Comintern Pact, Prince Saionji believed. But those in control probably did not feel they could be choosy. World power arrangements were changing fast and Japan must grasp security where she found it.[5]

The Anti-Comintern Pact and the events of the succeeding months produced a small but significant shift of emphasis in Grew's way of looking at Japanese foreign affairs. It will be recalled that on the eve of the February 26 Incident he accepted the thesis that Japan's urge to expand was fundamental but he instinctively retained faith in Hirota's ability to guide the movement in safe channels. That faith could not now survive. Grew did not have to make the case against Hirota; the Diet made it for him. Hirota had clearly failed his opportunity to introduce internal reform and he had allowed the Army to dictate, and even through its military attaché at Berlin to negotiate, a blundering treaty. In Grew's judgment Japan had "played her cards unwisely." It was "the old story of dual control of foreign policy wherein the civil authorities of the Government, including the Prime Minister and the Foreign Office, are overridden by the military. . . ." There could be no doubt of the soundness of his assertion a year earlier that the expansionist urge was fundamental. However nebulous internal politics might appear after the fall of the Hirota Cabinet in January 1937, it was obvious that the Army was firmly in the saddle. Moderate generals like Hayashi were still men of the sword and, compared to Hirota, strangers to Grew. The factor of civilian restraint was no longer a significant element in his outlook.[6]

This disillusionment was evident in Grew's reaction to a proposal for the neutralization of the Pacific islands. The idea of a Pacific guarantee had been bobbing up in one form or another ever since Japan's abrogation of the Washington Naval Treaty. Grew's evaluation of the Craigie proposal a year earlier had not ruled out some form of understanding with Japan. Now the President himself proposed that the powers undertake not to fortify their Pacific insular possessions, excluding Hawaii and Singapore, and not to use them as bases in war. The Far Eastern Division spent some seven thousand words fashioning what Roosevelt described as "an argument of defeatism" against the scheme and sent it to Grew for comment. The Ambassador replied at the end of March 1937 that he entirely agreed with the Division's objections to the proposal. Grew's central argument was that Japan could not be trusted to live up to contractual obligations. It seemed foolish to build new peace machinery on the wreckage of the old. Better no agreements at all than treaties that became "scraps of paper," he contended. "If you can't find a rock to build your house on, but only sand, it's much safer not to build a house at all." His advice was to stay out of paper commitments and "keep our powder dry." So long as trustworthy civilian influence was absent fom Japanese decision-making, Grew found little use for negotiation. For once he and Hornbeck were in complete accord.[7]

The premise of expansion did not simplify Grew's task of explaining events in the last half-year of peace. He needed to know when and where and how, but the Japanese themselves could have told him little more than he already knew. Because rivalry of the armed forces made choice within means impossible, Japanese national policy as decided in August 1936 had lumped together diverse objectives that individually were ambitious and in sum grotesque. The Army had gained authority to prepare for inevitable war with the Soviet Union. Though ignorant of the August decision, Grew accepted the Soviet Union as the Army's chief concern and saw war in that direction as the special concern of the Itagaki group. Strong as the Soviets were, he did not consider war imminent. Also, the Navy was authorized to build enough ships to dominate the Western Pacific while the diplomats paved the way for the "Southward Advance" by peaceful expansion of trade in Southeast Asia and the Southwest Pacific. Again, Grew was familiar with the objective and saw the connection of diplomatic and naval policy. He had reported in April 1936: "If important trade routes to the islands to the south of Japan were . . . established, it would be necessary for the Navy to extend its operations further afield for the purpose of protecting these trade routes." Recent allusions to the "Southward Advance" stressed the peaceful aspect, of course. So far as the main North-South routes of advance were concerned, expansionist pressures of 1937 appeared somewhat more threatening but no more concrete than in the several years before. Japanese objectives seemed nebulous, as in fact they were.[8]

As a matter of choice as well as necessity, the Japanese forward movement in China came to a full stop late in 1936. Though a feeling persisted in the Army that all problems in China could and should be settled by force, the generals in control were more preoccupied with the Soviet Union and wished to avoid trouble south of the Great Wall where Japan already had a roomy buffer zone. They ruled out further attempts to detach North China provinces by military threat and intrigue and instituted more rigorous control of the field armies. Grew noticed the new discipline and prudence of the Army, and ascribed these to necessity, to the astonishing new spirit of national unity developing in China in response to Japanese encroachment.

The stiffening of Chinese resistance was indeed the towering fact of late 1936. In November a Mongolian force acting as cat's-paw for the Kwantung Army was decisively defeated by Chinese provincial troops in Suiyuan. In December occurred the Sian Incident, involving the kidnaping of Chiang Kai-shek by a northern war lord, his release apparently through Communist Chinese intervention, and subsequent national rejoicing and enhanced unity. Early in 1937 negotiations began for Kuomintang-Communist collaboration against the Japanese. As incident after incident involving Japanese nationals occurred, it became apparent that the Chinese people themselves were finally "getting their tails up," as Grew put it. It seemed "a very different Eastern Asia from 1932." [9]

In the face of this rising danger Japan seemed to hesitate and draw back. The nation was thunderstruck by China's determination to yield no more, Grew reported. Press and Diet were openly critical of high-handed diplomacy and military bluff. The Hirota government's policy had miscarried with serious loss of face to the Japanese. Then with Hayashi came an improvement. According to Grew, the government now saw the danger and "precisely like a bicyclist suddenly faced with an unexpected steep descent, is trying to back pedal." At first it changed direction too fast. Foreign Minister Sato Naotake rejected "the diplomacy of desperation" and called for friendly and righteous dealing with China, but he infuriated the nationalists and had to recant. However, he was not forced to resign, and as the Hayashi government steadied down in April and May 1937 hope rose for a patient, workmanlike approach to Sino-Japanese problems. Moderate influence seemed more articulate and "possibly more influential" to Grew. One might even think, he said, that the Japanese were returning to Shidehara diplomacy.

This time Grew was determined not to be taken in by appearances. "I do not for a moment . . . delude myself by believing that this new orientation is likely to last very long," he wrote. Since the Army would never relinquish its position in North China, negotiations with the Chinese were unlikely to succeed. After this quiet spell, further consolidation in North China and penetration into Mongolia could be expected. Earlier he had described Japanese expansion in terms of waves. Now to explain the cycle of pause and advance a more precise image used by the Dutch Minister at the time of the Amō Doctrine suggested itself. The movement was "like the incoming tide on the shore: there is a wave of aggression followed by a period of retrocession, as at present, but soon another wave will come which will go farther than its predecessor." It was an image suggestive of the sense of drift the Japanese themselves felt and descriptive of their deeper and deeper incursions on the continent, but it was more accurate as to effects than cause. It implied that a vast central energy impelled Japan outward where in fact the nation was acting more compulsively than impulsively, her foreign policy being drawn this way and that by a profound sense of insecurity and lack of compelling central authority. Grew, finding Japanese power and purpose increasingly incoherent and incomprehensible, turned from cause to effect and found in the successively higher watermarks of Japanese advance the best available guide to the course of events.[10]

July 1937 promised to be no more or less threatening than previous months. The policies of the new Konoe Cabinet had not taken shape. Sino-Japanese negotiations did not look hopeful, but continued. Yoshida was having no success in securing a political agreement at London. Japanese-American relations were at least uneventful. Tokyo was steamy, and Grew decided July 10 to spend a fortnight in the hills. An incident had occurred on the Soviet-Manchurian border and another at a rail junction near Peking, a place called Lukouchiao, but they seemed no more threatening than others recently. He could not believe any of the countries in that part of the world were premeditating war. "Of course we must keep our eyes open," he wrote Hornbeck, "and not be led into a feeling of unjustified security just because these cries of 'wolf, wolf' occur so often." But the situation in Europe seemed much more dangerous at the moment than that in the Far East. With that he left. The Sino-Japanese conflict, beginning at Lukouchiao, or Marco Polo Bridge, was three days old.[11]

It is impossible to say who fired the first shot at Marco Polo Bridge on the night of July 7, 1937. A Japanese company engaged in night maneuvers blundered into a Chinese outpost and skirmishing ensued. Given the broadness with which the Japanese Boxer Protocol force defined its mission of protecting Peking's access to the sea and the new determination of the Chinese to resist Japanese encroachment, some such clash was likely. But contrary to the judgment of the Tokyo War Crimes Trials, this was not another Mukden Incident. From evidence of their troop dispositions and plans it seems clear that the Japanese did not stage the incident as pretext for a new advance. Army Central Headquarters immediately called for a local settlement and the North China command obediently sought to effect one. On July 11 representatives of the Japanese and local Chinese armies signed an agreement without political conditions which disposed of the incident. So far as the authorities on the scene were concerned, Lukouchiao should have been just one more event in a highly peculiar and unstable but not altogether unmanageable Sino-Japanese relationship in North China.[12]

But time had finally run out on local settlements. Lukouchiao was already escalating into a major confrontation between Nanking and Tokyo. Some day, Nelson Johnson had predicted, the Chinese worm would turn, and it did on July 10, when Chiang Kai-shek demanded a review of any local settlement and dispatched four of his divisions toward North China where Central Government troops were barred by previous agreement. Japan accepted the challenge. On July 11, the day the local settlement was arranged, the Konoe Cabinet announced plans for mobilization of three divisions and warned Nanking not to interfere with a local settlement. Grew took one look at the papers the following morning and decided to return to Tokyo.[13]

During the following month the two giants fumbled toward full-scale hostilities. Both governments heavily committed their prestige in strong public statements and continued to move troops into or toward North China. In this impasse the Japanese Army high command was still anxious to avoid war, but subordinate staff officers and the field armies exerted increasing pressure for use of force. At the end of July fighting broke out again. The Japanese cleared the Peking-Tientsin area of local Chinese troops and forced them southward. Following this victory the Konoe Cabinet attempted to negotiate with Nanking, but apparently Chiang Kai-shek had made up his mind to fight. Nationalist divisions were already moving into the neutral zone surrounding Shanghai, upsetting the arrangements which had concluded the Shanghai Incident of 1932. On August 13 fighting broke out in that great city and the Sino-Japanese crisis slipped beyond control.

As the crisis deepened the Embassy strained every nerve to keep abreast of developments. Outgoing telegrams nearly quadrupled in number. Code work became so heavy Grew had to call on the Embassy's student interpreters for help. One code clerk became so practiced he could decipher on sight. The pressure of events left little time or mental energy for analysis and evaluation and the Embassy's reporting in depth suffered. Furthermore, information was harder to come by. It was not simply a problem of wartime secrecy; Japanese were more wary of foreigners. Prince Konoe and Hirota, who was once again Foreign Minister, reduced their contacts to the official minimum, and Grew's friends in the court circle were reluctant to be seen at the Embassy. On his part, Grew had curtailed entertainment ever since the February 26 Incident. He still saw Kabayama, Matsudaira, and Soejima, but they were more useful in conveying his thoughts to others than in bringing news. Something of the old friendliness was gone: Kabayama now seemed to be a sort of propagandist. Crisis made communication more vital but more difficult.[14]

Grew's crisis diplomacy rested mainly on the information he received through four officials. The first two were his military and naval attachés, who retained valuable sources within the service ministries and were "very much on the job" in reporting Japanese troop movements. The third was his new Counselor of Embassy, Eugene H. Dooman, who had arrived just before the crisis. Dooman represented a second generation in American professional diplomacy, combining broad experience with expertise in Japanese affairs. Born in Kobe, fluent in Japanese, he had assisted the American representative at the League Council during the Manchurian crisis and the American delegation at the London Naval Conference in 1935. Delighted to have him, Grew wrote a welcome in the words of Secretary Hughes: "You and I will be thick as thieves." The immediate advantage of Dooman's presence was his intimate acquaintance with Yoshizawa Sejiro, Chief of the American Bureau at the Foreign Office. Such a frank and trusting relationship was a rare asset in the Japan of 1937. Grew's fourth important informant was James L. Dodds, Counselor of the British Embassy. The crisis having caught the British between ambassadors, young Dodds was Chargé, and according to Grew was handling a very difficult assignment with plenty of courage. Welcoming the counsel of the American Ambassador, the British diplomat came so regularly Grew considered him "almost . . . a member of my own staff." However he might disagree with British policy, Grew cooperated wholeheartedly in sharing information and discussing courses of action. For purposes of communication at least, the two embassies were practically one.[15]

The Embassy took nothing for granted these hot and hectic summer weeks, in particular the argument that Japan "engineered" the Marco Polo Bridge Incident.[16] "Indifference to the dangers inherent in a situation where virtually hostile troops are in close juxtaposition, indiscretion in an extraordinary measure, and intolerance of the rights of the Chinese" could properly be charged to the Japanese.[17] However, Grew found no proof that the incident was deliberately instigated. The Japanese Army did not seem ready for a showdown. The window dressing that normally accompanied staged incidents was absent. Indeed, the government seemed to be restraining the public from viewing the incident emotionally. There was no lack of determination on the part of the Japanese. On the contrary, they seemed united behind their leaders in a willingness to fight if necessary. But they had not been looking for a fight just then.

However, as the situation deteriorated in North China, Grew placed an increasing burden of responsibility on the Japanese. On July 16 Dodds brought the Foreign Ministry a proposal from Chiang Kai-shek conveyed through the British Ambassador at Nanking for a military standstill to be followed by arrangements for mutual withdrawal of troops. The Vice-Minister was unresponsive and left the impression that the Foreign Ministry had no control over the military. On July 21, at Grew's suggestion, Dodds conveyed Chiang's concern for a peaceful solution and his warning that China was not bluffing, but again the Foreign Ministry was unresponsive. Grew recognized that to enter negotiations with Nanking the Japanese would have to retreat from their insistence on a local settlement, but felt that their indifference to the standstill proposal threw on them the burden for any further hostilities. On July 22 Hirota told Grew the terms of the July 11 local settlement, which, he said, contained no political conditions. Actually political conditions were unnecessary; the Ho-Umezu Agreement of 1935 had already reduced Chinese sovereignty in the area to a fiction. Nevertheless, promises by local Chinese officials to withdraw troops and suppress anti-Japanese sentiment strengthened Grew's impression of further "whittling away" at Nanking's authority in the North. Japan's determination to effect a settlement on her own terms, her supreme self-confidence, and her continuing military buildup in the affected area seemed aggressive. Grew concluded on July 23 that the military, if they had not planned Lukouchiao, were taking advantage of it to grab another slice of China.

His reading of events was diverging a bit from what appears to have been actually happening. The Konoe government reacted strongly, too strongly, to Nanking's dispatch of troops to North China in the hope of frightening the Chinese into accepting a local settlement which essentially left things as they had been. What seemed like a repetition of the pattern of Japanese advance in North China was in reality a tragically miscalculated maneuver to preserve the *status quo*. However intractable and inflammable Sino-Japanese relations were, the actions of statesmen were still affecting the course of events — for the worse.

On the assumption that Japanese policy from July 8 to July 24 aimed at deeper encroachment on North China, it was not difficult for Grew to explain subsequent hostilities. Japan was obviously anxious to avoid war but her efforts to secure control piece by piece by political maneuver had miscarried, and the military had resorted to force to effect their aims. Perhaps they had not intended to make a further move at that time, he wrote July 27, but the advance had occurred anyway, "willy-nilly." Then Nanking responded by threatening Japanese interests at Shanghai, Japan accepted the challenge, though at first reluctantly, and full-scale war broke out. As events unfolded the pattern became clearer: the war flowed directly from Japanese expansion. Either Japan had to establish complete control over North China or retreat from Manchuria. Hostilities were the "inevitable corollary of the Manchurian conflict." [18] Again and again the word "inevitable" cropped up. In October he saw the invasion of China "just as definitely and inevitably on the army's eventual program as the succeeding waves of the incoming tide, and this is not hindsight on my part because I have constantly talked and written of it in just that metaphor." [19] It was as if he were watching a historical tragedy being played out.

This sense of being a spectator, of watching events over which humans had no control, pervaded Grew's crisis diplomacy. In the beginning, when the problem revolved around the incident itself, he was hopeful that China and Japan themselves might stave off war as they had in the past. When hostilities recurred and widened, diplomacy seemed to bob on the tides of history. The hesitation and dissension that existed within the Japanese government did not show through because the internal configuration of power had grown nebulous and obscure. He assumed that the Army was united, all-powerful, and, once engaged, determined on crushing China. If the two nations really wished to avoid war, they had channels of communication through their own embassies or through the British embassies in Nanking and Tokyo, but the Japanese seemed uninterested. According to the Amō Doctrine they would resent efforts by Western powers to resolve the impasse: "They feel that the western powers have no moral right to interfere in East Asia and acceptance of good offices would constitute an admission of such a right." [20] Western mediation acceptable to Japan would probably carry with it an unwelcome responsibility for terms which further impaired the independence and integrity of China. It was hard to see what could be done in a friendly way.

On the other hand, Grew argued that pressure tactics, in addition to being futile, would be dangerous and destructive. He held that the chief aim of American policy should be to maintain strict neutrality and stay out of the "Far Eastern mess." So far as possible the lives, property, and rights of American citizens should be protected and general humanitarian considerations upheld. The United States should register its position in support of the treaty order. But with respect to forcing Japan to desist, the arguments of 1932 applied. Military force was out of the question: the United States was manifestly unwilling to use it, and in Grew's opinion no American interest in China justified risking war with Japan. Since Japan respected only force, lesser pressures such as characterized Stimsonian diplomacy were futile. The weakness of economic sanctions had been demonstrated in the case of Abyssinia. "Moral thunderbolts" would have as much effect on Japan as "a mild hailstorm in the country." [21] By inciting anger and resentment they might spur the military to further aggression and injury to American interests. In any case, the diplomacy of protest and condemnation as practiced in 1932 could only have the effect of arousing bitterness and suspicion, destroying such Japanese goodwill as he had managed to build up during the previous four years.

In Grew's mind this reservoir of goodwill was no mean asset. He believed that while maintaining strict neutrality the United States should avoid throwing overboard the friendship of either contestant. Since the Japanese were particularly susceptible to manifestations of impartiality and goodwill, an unusual opportunity existed for consolidating relations with Japan, to the point even of overcoming the ill-will generated by the immigration controversy and Stimson's policy. As late as August 13 he hoped for "a genuine as contrasted with a merely theoretical friendship . . . thorough and sound enough to stand without serious injury the periodic knocks which it is bound to experience. . . ." [22] But after the extension of hostilities rising public antipathies and sympathies became harder to ignore. By the end of August he was distinguishing between "sentimental" and "factual" friendship, and emphasizing the practical advantages of consolidating relations. Valuing American goodwill as they did, the Japanese would try the harder to avoid injuring American interests in China. When stalemate or victory made mediation realistic, or if political disorder benefiting only the Communists made it advisable, the Japanese would be disposed to accept American counsel and help, and the United States could without cost play a part in shaping the future of the Far East. Placing the United States in the most favorable position for ultimate peaceful intervention to prevent chaos, Grew argued, had been the chief aim of President Wilson during the first years of the World War.

British policy in July and August convinced Grew of the wisdom of keeping aloof. The British Foreign Office under the energetic leadership of Anthony Eden made an unceasing effort to avert general hostilities. Again and again the British took the initiative in peace-keeping proposals. They explored the chances of good offices and mediation and suggested a scheme for the neutralization of Shanghai with joint foreign guarantee of Japanese nationals. They warned Tokyo of Chinese determination and counseled moderation at Nanking. They urged a stop to troop reinforcement and further fighting. Three times they asked Washington's support for joint efforts. They rang the changes of diplomatic activity short of sanctions, but all to no avail.

Grew viewed these efforts as, worse than futile, inept. Assuming that the British were motivated by the desire to protect their commercial interests in China ("There is not much sentiment or ethical principle involved in international action nowadays, if there ever was."), he was impressed with the "naïveté, if not fatuity," of their attempt to use Anglo-Japanese negotiations at London as a lever to force Japan to employ moderation. The domination of North China would be far more advantageous to Japan than a London agreement removing friction over their respective Chinese interests. The British proposal for a Shanghai guarantee was "ridiculous." Where would the troops be obtained? All this hectoring and harrying could only draw upon Britain the suspicion, irritation, and resentment of the Japanese, and indeed appeared to be doing so. The usual Britisher, he contended, "is generally inclined to overlook the values of finesse." The roles of the Manchurian crisis were reversed. Now Britain had stepped out in front and would, like the United States in 1932, reap her full measure of odium.[23]

Meanwhile the United States was the "fair-haired boy." Washington turned down London's proposals for joint action; an Anglo-American front at Tokyo was out of the question. The United States would make representations parallel with Britain but only on behalf of its citizens and rights in China or preservation of peace. American communications, uniformly polite, impressed on both contestants the vital importance of avoiding hostilities and urged self-restraint and peaceful settlement. The Department of State avoided passing judgment, uttered no threats, made no accusations. Neither would it accept responsibility for settling the controversy, either through mediation or support of the Shanghai guarantee. Hull's public statements of July 16 and August 23 established a theoretical but not a working American interest in the crisis. He believed that the assertion and reassertion of principles of international conduct would edge Americans away from the "slough of isolation." Whatever his object, the Secretary's generalities were impossible to quarrel with. Grew was permitted wide discretion both as to manner and substance of representations and his recommendations were given close attention. Washington's policy had his "complete concurrence and sympathy." The Administration was "playing its cards, or withholding them, with eminent wisdom." The phraseology of Japanese notes, gestures of politeness by diplomatic and uniformed officials, and the absence of critical press comment indicated that the Japanese were genuinely appreciative of the American position. Naturally Grew was delighted: "What a change from 1931 and 1932!"[24]

Even good offices, which involved no formal responsibility for proposals, were tendered only with the utmost care to avoid seeming interference. The British suggested a joint offering on August 3 and Washington asked Grew for comment. He saw little hope for success but agreed because "I should like to feel that history will regard the record of American action in this most critical and pregnant period in Far Eastern affairs as exhaustive, unstintedly helpful, and impartially correct." He and Dodds should approach Hirota separately, however, with himself first to assure the right "light touch." When both embassies received authorization August 10 he made his call, going to the Minister's residence to avoid publicity. He had already prepared the way August 6 by asking Hirota on his own initiative to let him know if he could be of any help. Now, unobtrusively building on this initiative, Grew suggested that the United States act as go-between. Repeating with emphasis, he told Hirota that his approach was informal, confidential, and exploratory. He was only anxious to be as helpful as possible. Hirota received the offer cordially but indicated it was superfluous. The Japanese had already approached Nanking directly, he said, but the United States might help by urging Chiang to counter with a proposal. In reporting the conversation Grew stressed the importance of Nanking's not closing the door to negotiations. Ambassador Johnson was leery of going this far, not wanting to push the Chinese into damaging concessions. On that uncertain note Grew's graceful little minuet was lost in the hurly-burly of fighting around Shanghai.[25]

The great battle for Shanghai made the aloof position of the United States increasingly difficult to maintain. Intense, modern war waged in the heart of this densely inhabited city, which was headquarters for Western interests in China as well as for correspondents and photographers, was bound to have dramatic impact. An American cruiser and passenger ship were bombed and thousands of citizens endangered. The *New York Times* coverage of the Far Eastern crisis jumped from a daily average of one and a quarter to three front-page columns. At the State Department rambling conferences in the Secretary's office went "round and round and round" the myriad problems of protection and neutrality. Moffat, assigned in the Department, noticed "a slight rasping of nerves and considerable physical wear and tear." According to him, the temper of the country was rising fast against Japan. Though the honors for indiscriminate bombing and shelling were shared, most of the victims were Chinese and the fighting was on Chinese soil. The *New York Times* of August 26 printed first photographs of the carnage. Its four-column headline of August 27 reported: JAPANESE FLIERS SHOOT BRITISH ENVOY; LONDON IS CONSIDERING SHARP ACTION; TOKYO MAY SEARCH FOREIGN VESSELS. On page two the Japanese were charged with using poison gas and Prince Konoe was quoted as attaching slight significance to British and American peace efforts and insisting "the first thing needed is to punish the Chinese." In this atmosphere, on the afternoon of

August 27, a long telegram arrived from Tokyo setting forth Grew's policy views, recommending in particular "a special endeavor toward solidifying our relations with Japan." Not surprisingly, it met with an unfavorable reception.[26]

The Embassy's telegram of August 27 precipitated the first open disagreement between Grew and the Roosevelt Administration. He had not intended it that way. Undoubtedly he feared that the extension of hostilities would produce stiffer American policy, as it had in 1932. Furthermore, the British were reported about to renew efforts for joint representations at Tokyo. He hoped that a full exposition of his views might preserve the July–August policy of non-involvement and impartiality. The effect of the telegram, however, was to demonstrate how widely feeling in the Department had diverged from that in the Embassy. To Moffat it was clear that his father-in-law "must be set right as to the way our minds are running in order adequately to present our views in Tokyo." It took six days of drafting by top officials to arrive at just what the disagreement between the Department and the Embassy was, and in establishing this consensus Grew's initiative was useful if for no other reason. Agreement was reached that the fundamental objectives of policy remained non-involvement and protection of the lives, property, and rights of American citizens. Disagreement centered on the question of impartiality.[27]

The Department's reply to Grew was in the first person singular, Hull speaking, and it was stern. What he had to say applied to China as well, but clearly his concern was Japan. Its import was that Japan's course was making an impartial and friendly attitude impossible for the United States. Apparently irked by the very satisfaction which Grew said the Japanese expressed at American policy and sensitive to possible accusations of being pro-Japanese, Hull asserted: "We do not desire that the Japanese shall entertain any impression that this Government looks with less disapproval . . . upon the course which Japan is pursuing than does the British Government or that we condone Japan's course in any sense whatever." American public opinion, he continued, was outraged by the strategy and methods of the Japanese military, which were in direct conflict with principles he himself had enunciated July 16 and August 23. Yet suggestions "quietly and patiently offered" had been ignored. Apparently Japan did not value American friendship. The United States, said Hull, desired no injury to Japan. It would call no names and make no threats. But it would not be guided in its decisions "by being especially solicitous that what we do shall not be displeasing. . . ." If the Japanese wished American goodwill or assistance, "the time for them to show appreciation of our policies and methods . . . is now."[28]

Hull's telegram represented more a disengagement from old policy than adoption of a new one. During the following month the United States drifted toward public disapproval of Japan's course. When the Chinese took their case to the League, Hull was hopeful that placing the controversy in a world forum would promote his principles of peace. He sent an observer, but allowed no hint what action the United States might take and kept carefully in the shadow of League action, neither ahead nor behind. During the month Japanese air attacks shocked a world still innocent of total war. To warn aggressor nations unnamed, to express American revulsion at their violent purposes and deeds, and to counteract further American withdrawal into isolationism by directing attention toward positive yet non-threatening courses of action, Roosevelt delivered his famous Quarantine Speech at Chicago, October 5. It just preceded and helped secure League condemnation of Japan for military operations out of all proportion to the Marco Polo Bridge Incident, unjustifiable on grounds of self-defense, and in contravention of the Nine-Power and Kellogg-Briand Pacts. October 6 the State Department accepted the conclusions of the League, holding Japan's actions "inconsistent" with the Secretary's public statements and the treaties in question. The United States had now accused Japan by name. Britain meanwhile was pressing for a Nine-Power Conference where all agreed the United States would have to be represented. Ahead lay the dismal fiasco of Brussels.[29]

It was fumbling diplomacy at best. The conference powers aimed at a settlement between Japan and China, yet individually or through the League they had judged against Japan and thereby made their auspices unattractive. At the same time, arousing Chinese hopes of intervention made direct settlement between the combatants during the conference period more difficult.[30] What the Administration had in mind regarding positive steps if settlement failed is obscure. It was befogged in its thinking and bewitched by the isolationists. Roosevelt's mind seems to have been toying with the idea of cooperative action by neutral nations to ostracize Japan by breaking relations. No desire or authority existed for economic sanctions. The only positive step Roosevelt was clear about, and the limit of action for Hull, was the mobilization of world opinion against Japan, the direct opposite of the course Grew recommended August 27, and precisely what Stimson's diplomacy ended by doing.

Until his government committed itself to a new position Grew felt free to keep up the argument. He was plainly worried at having "jumped the track." Since 1914 he had never been comfortable opposing feeling back home, which he now saw was running strongly against Japan. At first he tried to minimize the divergence, arguing it was "fairly wide" but not necessarily fundamental, and related to method rather than principle. In a personal letter to Hull of September 15 that was wordy and defensive in tone, he expressed his own outrage at the Japanese program and concurred completely with American moves to date. He said he had no thought of pleasing the Japanese or purchasing their goodwill at the cost of any policy, law, or treaty. But he reiterated his essential argument here and in a more confident and tightly reasoned dispatch of October 2. His point was this: the extent to which a nation at war was willing to listen to representations on behalf of non-combatant interests depended not on considerations of sentiment, principle, law, or ethics, but what it felt was to be gained by paying attention. In his opinion, the Japanese, after carefully balancing the advantages of maintaining and the disadvantages of losing American friendship, would prefer to maintain it and pay attention to American interests, but only just so long as American manner and methods did not arouse their antagonism. With that he rested his case.[31]

The advantage of Grew's low-key diplomacy was that strong representations, when necessary, had greater impact and these were now in order. July and August had been low key. On July 27 he had warned Hirota against a Japanese attack in North China such as might endanger American lives and property, not as the Department put it to the Japanese Embassy against an attack specifically on Peking which by implication could not but endanger foreign and especially American lives with "unfavorable reaction throughout the world." Under an ambiguous instruction that gave him discretion, Grew had spoken a little more softly than Washington. On September 1 he had been less restrained, earnestly appealing against indiscriminate Japanese bombing on humanitarian grounds as well as on account of its effect on Japanese-American relations, and pointing out how the Foreign Minister's responsibility for political relations was paramount to military considerations. Hull had commented: "This is what I have been waiting for days for Grew to do and is just the way I think he should do it."

Now on September 20 the Ambassador forcefully warned against Japanese bombing of Nanking. He laid emphasis on the liability of suspicion, antipathy, and "potential ostracism" Japan was building up, the Foreign Minister's individual responsibility for restraining the military in this connection, and the danger of a serious incident touching American honor like the sinking of the *Maine*. "Nothing was left to Hirota's imagination in the directness and force of my statement's appeal," he informed Washington. He felt it was so strong that a Foreign Minister might have replied, "So you are threatening me with war," but he knew that Hirota wouldn't and he didn't.[32]

Grew's shock at Washington's change of policy early in October was the more severe because of his deep commitment to the policy now apparently repudiated. Building friendly relations had always commanded his best efforts and from the responsiveness of Japanese officials these seemed to be enjoying some success. Wanting to retire before long, he had looked forward to a successful weathering of the crisis as "perhaps a satisfactory climax to a fairly long go of it in the profession of diplomacy." Now his work would be thrown overboard for the "discredited" Stimson approach. He felt like an architect who had seen his edifice "suddenly crumble about his ears," or a doctor who had lost a patient he had worked hard to save. Manchuria, Abyssinia, and Spain had proved to him that moral suasion without a willingness to fight was futile and provocative. "Why, oh why," he wrote, "do we disregard the experience and facts of history which stare us in the face?" The United States had come to a fork in the road and chosen the way that led "potentially to war." [33]

Grew felt defeated. His staff wandered about the Embassy in a bitter, gloomy mood and had to be warned not to criticize the Administration outside the Embassy. He felt the Department had let him down in failing to keep him informed of the rising public temper in America and he was incensed at a report from Moffat that Senator Hiram Johnson considered the Embassy pro-Japanese. He drafted a critical telegram, slept on it, and decided not to send it. It had a complaining tone and criticized a position his government had publicly taken. His conscience was clear on the pro-Japanese charge; there had been no "pussy-footing" in his Embassy and he would not stoop to denial. His recommendations would fall on "stony ground" anyway. For a while he sent few messages to Washington, let his diary lapse, and buried himself in novels, *The Citadel, The Green Light,* and, appropriately, *Gone With the Wind.* When he resumed his diary his comments were so outspoken he withheld an installment from Castle for the first time, on the ground that it was improper to pass criticism to an active worker on the Republican National Committee, even though a trusted friend. The once-incomprehensible words of his father-in-law caught his mood now exactly: "There you see me in my solitary corner growling my impotent maledictions on a deaf world." [34]

This was no frame of mind in which to recognize what in fact was occurring during October, a persistent effort by Japan to settle the conflict. Predominant opinion in the Army still regarded the Soviet Union as the real menace and sought to avoid debilitating involvement in China. Japan's terms were not generous but in view of her military success not unrealistic either. Increased influence in Inner Mongolia, a buffer zone in the Peking-Tientsin area, and another protecting Shanghai interests would satisfy Japan's security requirements. Elsewhere in China it was in Japan's interest for Nanking to preserve order. These and more general terms were communicated by Sir Robert Craigie, the new British Ambassador, who never told Grew of his role. Sir Robert's secrecy may have been imposed by Hirota and may also have been due to his overriding concern to ease Anglo-Japanese tensions arising from the conflict, which outweighed for the moment his government's policy of keeping in step with the Americans. In any case, Chiang proved unreceptive and Craigie's good offices became less attractive because of rising anti-British feeling in Japan. Some other approach was needed.[35]

American assistance would at least have the advantage of minimizing the threat of concerted action by the Brussels powers. Hirota actually preferred the good offices of Britain or the United States for the weight they carried at Nanking, but the Army sought those of Germany and Italy. A compromise agreement of October 22 ruled out any peace role by the Brussels Conference, but permitted Hirota to accept the services of any "unbiased" nation.[36] Indications appeared that the United States was not fully committed to the Stimson approach and might somehow assist. The Roosevelt Administration made it clear that sanctions were not under consideration and that the first business at Brussels would not be arraignment of Japan but settlement of the conflict.[37] According to Harada, when Grew called on October 15 to urge Japan's attendance at Brussels, Hirota said Japan would prefer a direct settlement but would be happy if either Britain or the United States acted as a secret intermediary. If this was said, and if Grew heard it correctly, he did not record or report it. On October 27, when Hirota gave Grew Japan's formal refusal to attend, he explained that other nations could best help by persuading China to negotiate. This seemed a "purely conventional observation" and Grew did not report it. On October 30 Ambassador Yoshida in London was reported to have said that the Japanese Foreign Office had informed Grew and Craigie that Japan wanted to put an end to hostilities and would like to consult with British and American representatives. Grew was "astonished" at Yoshida's statement. The day before, the Germans were reported to be attempting a settlement. After inquiry of the German Counselor of Embassy, who denied it, Grew "nailed this rumor to the mast." But he was deceived. At the very moment the Germans were actively engaged in providing their good offices.[38]

Hirota's approaches to Herbert von Dirksen, the German Ambassador, and to Grew were substantially the same, yet it was the German who proved receptive and not the American. Dirksen was anxious to provide good offices. They would be a means to "extricate us from the difficulties of neutrality." [39] Peace would protect Japan's strength against the Soviet Union, keep Soviet influence out of China, and preserve German interests there. Only peace could reconcile the conflicting enthusiasms of his masters, that of the Nazis for Japan and of the Wilhelmstrasse for China. To Grew good offices meant added difficulties. Washington had told him in no uncertain terms of the comparative unimportance of good relations with Japan. American helpfulness would depend on Japanese worthiness. Tight-lipped, obedient, he was not looking for an opportunity to act. In addition, Dirksen knew the Japanese wanted peace. The Japanese Army, preferring German assistance, had already furnished his military attaché with the principal terms. Grew was unaware of specific Japanese terms. His picture of Japanese internal developments in 1937 was hazy. Lacking a sure grasp of the configuration of politics in the Army and government, he assumed the military were of one mind to crush China. He interpreted Hirota as suggesting American pressure on China to sue for a loser's peace while Japan still lacked decisive victory at Shanghai. Such a role was out of the question, so he attached no particular significance to Hirota's invitation.

By early November, Grew and his staff were thoroughly roused from their October doldrums but still skeptical about peace moves. With the Brussels Conference on the point of convening and Chinese armies weakening at Shanghai, a turning point in the Far Eastern crisis seemed imminent. Press reports and diplomatic cables from Europe indicated a ranging Japanese campaign for peace, yet the talk in Tokyo was of declaration of war, blockade, even an attack on Russia. Grew's military attachés reconstructed the Japanese order of battle from casualty lists and concluded that the Army was concentrating for a decisive blow at Nanking. After sifting through all the contradictory information Grew decided November 6 that, obscure as the situation was, Japanese efforts would be directed primarily toward winning in China, that they anticipated prolonged hostilities, and that the time was still not ripe for peace. Nevertheless he wanted to keep the door open. He and Craigie sent identical telegrams to their governments suggesting that while Anglo-American mediation was impossible because the Japanese would interpret it as pressure, at some future time good offices by a single power, either on its own or representing a small group of powers appointed by the Brussels Conference, might be welcomed. In the meantime the conference should avoid condemnatory action that would preclude such a move. Grew recalled that one reason he had accepted the Japan mission was his conviction that some time he might sway the issue between peace and war. At least he was again on the alert for a chance.[40]

Grew also asked for and received permission to explore once more the thinking of the Foreign Office on the subject of peace, and in fact went considerably beyond this. Perhaps he saw the situation changing faster than he had anticipated. On November 5 Japanese forces landed at Hangchow Bay south of Shanghai, unhinging Chinese defenses in the region. That evening Hugh Byas, highly respected Tokyo correspondent of the *New York Times*, showed the Embassy a dispatch of his suggesting that with their objectives almost in hand the Japanese were creating an atmosphere which presented the United States as the most reliable neutral to pave the way for negotiations. The next day a Hitler offer of mediation was reported but officially denied at Berlin as "premature." A somewhat forlorn Craigie, by the way, had just asked the Foreign Minister whether in view of anti-British feeling the good offices of his government were still acceptable and Hirota, like the looking glass in the fairy tale, had reassured him that Britain was still the most desirable intermediary of all. On November 8 Grew made his move. Dooman in conversation with Yoshizawa suggested that Theodore Roosevelt's role in settling the Russo-Japanese War offered an instructive analogy for the current situation. This parallel had already been drawn in the Byas dispatch and it was a startling one in several respects. The analogy assumed an independent role for the United States, not one in conjunction with the Brussels powers, and it implied that Japan would signify its desire for peace and its terms first, rather than await American pressure on Nanking to seek negotiations. It suggested not just good offices but active mediation. Needless to say, Dooman's approach was secret and unofficial, and for the time being unreported.[41]

Yoshizawa proved unresponsive at first. He said it was Japanese policy not to permit mediation. Military operations in the Yangtze area, he continued, promised to create what the Japanese considered the perfect solution, namely that the Chinese government, after military reverses, propose negotiations. Yoshizawa's disinterest is probably explained by the knowledge that on November 5 Chiang had rejected the Japanese terms transmitted by the Germans. If he was not yet aware of the fact he undoubtedly preferred to wait until he heard. During the following week the conditions for Japan's perfect solution seemed to be approaching almost too quickly. Leaving Shanghai behind, a Japanese army pushed on toward Nanking, sending columns racing for the Yangtze above the Chinese capital to cut off retreat. Meanwhile at Brussels no coercive action had been taken. Politically and militarily China's hopes received disastrous blows. On November 15 Yoshizawa called Dooman back and they discussed how any delay might be fatal because the capture of Nanking would make any settlement of less value and of greater difficulty for Chiang, and no settlement could be considered final without him. Yoshizawa now intimated that the American peace-making role as seen by the Japanese need not necessarily be limited to persuading the Chinese government to enter direct negotiations. Japan would be willing, it developed, to consult with the United States or any other powers with important interests in the Far East, either individually or collectively, but not within a Geneva or Brussels framework. No sooner had Dooman returned and told Grew of this important new development than Hirota's private secretary phoned to ask the Ambassador to call on the Foreign Minister the next morning. Grew's initiative was finally drawing a response.[42]

Next morning the Foreign Minister led off with strong criticism of the Brussels Conference for considering what he understood to be some form of united action against Japan such as a boycott or sanctions. He attacked the United States for reportedly taking the lead in calling the conference and in its proceedings. Then, modulating his approach, Hirota deplored the effect of such American initiative on Japanese opinion. It was particularly unfortunate because, until the President's Quarantine Speech, the United States had been considered the only impartial nation, one capable of playing the role it had played in the Russo-Japanese War. The Chicago speech had only temporarily modified this belief, since the President had subsequently given the impression that the United States was "not so rigid in its attitude as had been feared." Hirota then turned to the question of peace. On account of Japanese military success, the Army had no need to go much further. In her own interests, now was the time for China to bring about peace. He warned that evacuating Nanking would be foolish (In fact that day Chinese officials were beginning the evacuation.), that delay in peace would only further undermine Chiang's position, since some of his generals were already forming an opposition, and that while Japanese terms were reasonable now, they would become drastic if warfare continued. If the United States wished to help, Hirota concluded, it should persuade Nanking to open negotiations with Japan. As soon as the Chinese showed an interest in peace, Japan would send a representative to Shanghai to meet with them.[43]

Hirota's remarks must have been perplexing and disappointing to Grew. Criticism of American policy was an inauspicious introduction to a request for assistance. Failure to repeat Yoshizawa's statement that Japan was prepared to consult seemed in fact a retreat. On the other hand, as Grew noted, Hirota repeated significant points of the Dooman-Yoshizawa conversations, in particular the analogy of Theodore Roosevelt's mediation, and the difficulty of a settlement if Nanking were evacuated.[44] Furthermore, the timing of Hirota's conversation related it to the talks at a lower level. Taking a constructive view, one could argue that the Foreign Minister intended all three conversations to be treated as one. He could be understood as saying that Japan was anxious for a settlement before it was too late and would be receptive to an American offer of good offices made, as in 1905, simultaneously to both belligerents, provided that first the United States showed it was impartial and was acting independently and not as agent of the Brussels Conference.

This would seem to be a reasonable interpretation of Hirota's intent. Certainly Dooman's reference to Roosevelt's mediation in 1905 aroused interest in the Japanese government. Harada, whose business it was to keep track of important developments, heard it this way: "The Councillor [sic] of the American Embassy came . . . to sound out Japan and said: 'During the Russo-Japanese War, both countries accepted at the same time, the conditions presented by the United States with the latter acting as mediator. Would Japan consider anything like that in this Incident?' "[45] Hirota probably did not repeat Yoshizawa's words about consultation for fear of appearing overanxious for peace, a sign of weakness.[46] However, subordinates were more explicit. Suma Yakichiro, Counselor of Embassy in Washington, told Hugh Wilson on November 16 that his government would be ready and willing to entertain suggestions from the United States under certain conditions and Yoshida in London spoke in the same vein. This appears to have been Grew's understanding of Hirota's remarks, though he was very reticent and cautious in commenting on them. He reported that the Foreign Minister went somewhat beyond his government's previous position that other powers could best help by persuading the Chinese to negotiate. It seemed Hirota was "seeking to prepare the ground for consultation with the United States to explore a possible path to peace." He advised Washington that there was "possibly impending" the situation in China he had envisaged earlier, namely a decisive Japanese victory, when the United States might beneficially address itself to both combatants to restore peace and prevent chaos.[47]

The first reaction of the State Department was slightly encouraging. The message Grew was instructed to deliver had a sting in the tail, an expression of "apprehension" about Japanese-American relations, but it sought to allay suspicions of Brussels and American leadership there. Hirota's satisfaction suggested that one of his conditions might have been met. It soon became evident, however, that Washington was unsure whether the Japanese were in fact making a proposition. This was due to the incompleteness of Grew's cabled report of November 16. Though he had included essential points made by Yoshizawa, he had not fully reported the earlier conversations or mentioned Dooman's allusion to the mediation of 1905. He had probably judged that the success of his efforts "to start the ball rolling toward peace" depended on keeping the Embassy's role discreet. Officially at least, Hirota would have to take the initiative in soliciting American good offices and speak for himself, with a minor assist from Yoshizawa. But only as an outgrowth of the Dooman-Yoshizawa conversations did Hirota's remarks seem to invite good offices. Taken alone they seemed weaker and vaguer than his underlings'. As a result the Department invited an elaborate clarification by Grew and Craigie, who by now had joined efforts. At the same time Washington did not rule out the possibility of satisfying Hirota's second condition. As Grew understood the Department's position on November 20, if the Japanese really invited a tender of good offices, "it might not be unwilling to play a part towards peace which would be outside any system of collective security, and that, in my opinion, is a step gained." [48]

Nevertheless an impasse existed, and it was not as it seemed a case of Americans waiting for Japanese to show that they really wanted an offer of good offices and Japanese waiting for Americans to show that they were willing to act independently of the Brussels Conference. Rather it was a question of Americans trying to determine how they could help without condoning a violation of the Nine-Power Treaty. Grew had already made Hirota aware of the "strong distaste" of his government for any role whereby the United States assisted in legitimizing Japanese victory. On November 19 the Department pointed out that the formula for American involvement would have to indicate clearly that no terms of settlement could be recommended to China that were inconsistent with the Treaty. Even the implication that intermediaries were pressing such terms must be avoided. Determined to discover if any opening existed, Grew asked Washington, November 23, "Would we be willing to act . . . merely as a nation having important interests in the Far East and as a friend of both combatants but bearing constantly in mind the provisions of the Nine-Power Treaty and the determination to emphasize or to render compelling those provisions in the formulation of final peace terms?" In other words he was asking if the United States would use its influence to move the parties as close as possible to the kind of peace it wanted. He received no answer. On December 8 Under Secretary Sumner Welles advised the British Ambassador that the only sound position for their countries to take was a "morally secure" one, and on that note the question of American participation in a peace effort simply petered out.[49]

Meanwhile, on December 3 Chiang Kai-shek, his defenses at Nanking collapsing, accepted German good offices and agreed in principle to the Japanese terms he had previously rejected. He was too late. When informed by Dirksen, December 7, Hirota said that recent military successes made it doubtful Japan would still be prepared to negotiate on her original terms. The civilian government and the military were in fact already swinging against a negotiated peace. The public temper was roused by casualties and the prospect of crushing victory to avenge them. On December 14 Japanese troops breached the city wall of the Chinese capital and commenced the appalling Rape of Nanking. Harsher terms, including an indemnity and broader demilitarized zones, were already being formulated. These were presented through the Germans, rejected, explained, rejected again, and sharpened again. On January 14 the Japanese government decided to cease relations with Chiang, to foster an alternative government, and to pursue the war to total victory. Of all the gross miscalculations of that tragic half-year this was the worst.[50]

SIXTEEN

A New Order in East Asia

On Sunday afternoon, December 12, 1937, Japanese naval aviators bombed and sank the U.S.S. *Panay* and several American oil barges in the Yangtze River above Nanking, thereby precipitating a major crisis with the United States. The ungainly but eminently practical gunboat *Panay* was a commissioned vessel in the United States Navy, operating there by treaty right and only trying to stay out of harm's way during the attack on Nanking. Her guns were not manned, she had notified Japanese authorities of her location, and she was emblazoned with American flags painted horizontally across her topdeck awnings. All her officers and many of her crew were wounded, two mortally. Furthermore, the *Panay* was at the moment a floating office of the American Embassy at Nanking, temporarily evacuated on account of the fighting. Aboard were the code section, two Secretaries, one of whom was wounded, and the Assistant Military Attaché. *Panay* was also refuge for foreign correspondents in Nanking, one of whom was mortally wounded, and for a Universal News Reel cameraman who filmed the whole attack. The press, the Foreign Service, and the Navy: three more sensitive targets for an outrage are hardly conceivable.[1]

The resulting crisis would have been worse had the whole story been known at once, but it was three days before survivors could be located and brought to Shanghai. In the interval, with only the bare facts known, the assumption was that *Panay* was the victim of wholly unjustifiable indiscriminate bombing but not of deliberate attack. That assumption made it easier for Washington and Tokyo to move toward a settlement.

Three diplomatic exchanges took place at Tokyo in the interval before the survivors were heard from. The first of these was on Grew's initiative before he had actually heard of the sinking. On Monday morning, December 13, a flight of telegrams from China relayed news that *Panay* had been shelled and forced to move upriver, that contact had been lost with her, and that the Japanese were reported to be under orders to fire on all ships on the river. An incident such as might occur in this situation, touching American honor and rousing American passions, had always been the specter of Grew's Japan mission. He had repeatedly protested against indiscriminate attacks involving foreign lives and property and had specifically warned Hirota against an incident like the sinking of the *Maine*. Now he immediately called on the Foreign Minister, gave him the facts, including the last reported position of *Panay*, and warned again.[2]

It was too late to prevent the attack of course, but Grew's representations may have made the Japanese government aware of the impossibility of avoiding responsibility and thus prompted immediate acceptance of it. That afternoon at 3 P.M. Hirota took the unprecedented step of coming to the Embassy to inform Grew of the sinking and present his government's profound regrets and apologies. He seemed "as genuinely moved as any Japanese is capable of registering emotion." Afterwards Grew courteously saw him to his car and then began planning a hasty packing in case of a break in relations. His mind went back to the *Lusitania* crisis of 1915, but, like Wilson, Roosevelt showed restraint. Twelve hours after Hirota called, when the Japanese Ambassador bore the same message to Hull, the Secretary read him a memorandum from the President expressing the shock of the United States government and suggesting by way of amends the expression of regret and proffer of full compensation as well as guarantee against the recurrence of such an attack. It should be emphasized that so far neither had the United States presented a formal written protest nor Japan a formal written apology, yet the way was open for a settlement of the incident.[3]

The two governments reached formal exchanges December 14. Late that afternoon, while Grew awaited an appointment with Hirota to present the American note of protest, Yoshizawa came to present the Japanese note of apology. The Japanese took full responsibility for the incident, which they described as a mistake, the pilots having been unable to determine the nationality of the ship on account of poor visibility. In all probability the note was intended to meet Roosevelt's conditions, for it promised full indemnification, appropriate measures to deal with those responsible, and strict orders to prevent recurrence. That evening it was Grew's turn. The American note of protest expanded one of Roosevelt's points, asking assurance "that hereafter American nationals, interests and property in China will not be subjected to attack by Japanese armed forces or unlawful interference by any Japanese authorities or forces whatsoever." This was a large order when identification was so difficult and it went considerably beyond the President's requested assurance of no attack similar to that on the *Panay*. Another round of notes would be necessary, but except for this point the controversy was substantially settled a little over two days after the sinking.[4]

As eyewitness accounts and official reports began coming in December 15, Washington took a graver view of the sinking. It appeared that not only had *Panay's* colors been clearly visible and the dive bombers low enough to see them, but also these planes and Japanese army motor launches had machine-gunned survivors in lifeboats and hounded them into the marshes at river's edge. Evidence pointed to a deliberate attempt to sink an American naval vessel, and, most shocking of all, to exterminate witnesses. Coincidentally, the *New York Times* printed a graphic description of the barbarous sequel to the capture of Nanking. The two outrages reinforced each other and confirmed the image of the Japanese invaders as an outlaw band of cutthroats, or as Hull described them to the Japanese Ambassador, December 17, "wild, runaway, half-insane Army and Navy officials." Grew was ordered to apprise the Japanese government of these reports, which, he was to make clear, "raised in acute form" Japanese willingness to discipline the officials responsible as well as to ensure against future attack on American nationals, interests, and property.[5]

The circumstances surrounding the sinking of *Panay* remain obscure, but it is questionable that the attack was deliberate.[6] Far from being out of harm's way, the American gunboat was in the middle of no-man's land. Japanese troops which had reached the Yangtze above her were vigorously seeking to destroy remnants of the Nanking army fleeing upriver by every available craft. The last position of *Panay* had been reported to the Japanese Embassy in Shanghai one hour before the attack, but with units widely scattered and different services involved it is unlikely that the information reached the fliers in time.[7] One of the dive-bomber pilots related in 1953 that he was under orders to attack Chinese transports, and the *Panay* convoy with assorted junks and sampans clustered for safety around it presented a likely target. In the exhilaration and absorption of his first combat mission, he writes, he never noticed the American flags.[8] These may not have been as obvious as has been assumed. The weather was clear but still, and they hung limply. The colors on the topdeck awnings were painted on canvas and were divided into two planes by fore-and-aft ridgepoles. In addition, the first hit, by horizontal bombers flying at seven thousand feet, snapped the foremast which in falling ripped off the forward awning.[9] It is by no means unlikely that the aviators machine-gunned the survivors thinking they were Chinese. The scene on the river was one of utter confusion with Japanese launches firing on Chinese and themselves being fired on by their own airplanes. At first the launches hid from *Panay* thinking her Chinese and then on identification boarded her to render assistance.[10] With bullets whirring in every direction the shocked *Panay* refugees undoubtedly saw themselves sitting on the bull's-eye for every Japanese gun on the river.

The Japanese contended that the disaster had been the result of a series of accidents and not deliberate malice. Their case was argued by the Vice-

Minister of the Navy, Admiral Yamamoto Isoroku, the brilliant officer who was to be Commander-in-Chief of the Combined Fleet at the time of Pearl Harbor. For three hours the evening of December 23 Yamamoto together with army and navy officers who had just conducted on-the-spot investigations presented the facts as they saw them in Grew's study across a floor strewn with maps. The Ambassador, Dooman, and the American military and naval attachés were impressed "with the apparently genuine desire and efforts of both the Army and Navy to get at the undistorted facts." Under instructions not to argue over the "essential undisputed facts" which gave "very definite indication of deliberateness of intent," Grew limited himself to reviewing the actions and attitude of his own government and ended by saying he was still awaiting a reply to the American formal note. This came the following day, Christmas Eve. The Japanese government reiterated the steps it had taken to provide satisfaction, including apology, proffer of indemnity, and measures to prevent recurrence. These last, it now explained, involved navy orders to exercise the greatest caution where third-power vessels were present, even to the point of sacrificing advantage in attacking the Chinese, orders for greater care against "infringement of, or unwarranted interference with, the rights and interests of the United States," greater efforts to identify American interests and nationals, and punishment of naval officers responsible, including the recall of the naval air commander, an especially severe action, Hirota explained, as it meant disgrace for the officer involved. The Army had not entirely, as Moffat put it, "come clean," but otherwise it was hard to see what more the Japanese could have done.[11]

Now Roosevelt moved quickly to close the incident. In spite of American shock and anger over "the whole ghastly tale," the press generally counseled moderation. Indeed the incident brought an upsurge of isolationism. Representative Louis Ludlow was finally able to bring to the floor his resolution calling for a constitutional amendment requiring a national referendum before Congress could declare war. Faced with this challenge to his leadership in foreign affairs, Roosevelt was determined to avoid making risky moves while he marshaled his forces to defeat it, as he was able to do by a narrow margin in January. On Christmas Day, Grew was instructed to inform the Japanese government that the American conditions for a settlement had been satisfied. With respect to "origins, causes and circumstances," each government could rely on its own version. Grew was wreathed in smiles when he called on Hirota with the good news and the Foreign Minister showed tears of relief. On April 22, 1938, the Japanese paid for their error with a check for $2,214,007.36 and the *Panay* Incident was closed.[12]

Grew's relief was mixed with apprehension as to the future. He was profoundly touched by expressions of regret and shame from people of all walks of life who wrote or called at the Embassy. The Japanese were "still a chivalrous people." He hoped that the government had been jolted into realizing the importance of avoiding injury to third powers, but the question remained whether it could restrain the military, and if it did attempt restraint whether the military would not perpetrate another February 26 Incident. The government, it seemed, was between the devil and the deep sea. He doubted that war between the United States and Japan would result from destruction of American interests in China or breach of treaty rights or erosion of principles. Rather the danger lay in open affronts to American sovereignty like the sinking of *Panay*. The patience of the American people, he knew, was not inexhaustible. As a precaution he had leather cases made for his diaries so they could be hurriedly packed and hand-carried aboard ship.[13]

Worst did not come to worst in 1938, though it was the great campaigning year of the Sino-Japanese conflict. The Japanese battled to link up their northern and central armies, drove three hundred miles farther up the Yangtze to capture Hankow, and far to the south descended on Canton, while their bombers ranged far into the vast interior of China. The entire fabric of American interests from treaty port godown to remotest inland mission was exposed to interference, harassment, or destruction. Yet no incident anywhere near as serious as the *Panay* occurred as a result of Japanese operations. One American, a little girl, was killed and her sister and mother wounded in a bombing. Japanese soldiers wounded one American and slapped three, including a Secretary of Embassy. These were Grew's worst cases. The burden of representation lay less in the gravity than in the frequency of incidents. That year cases of injury to American property reached a total of 296. A mission bombed, a university building appropriated, a cargo halted, a flag mutilated, a Chinese employee beaten: protest piled on protest as the Embassy sought apologies, assurances, indemnities, and easements. Grew's task as he conceived it was to make forceful and effective representations with least possible exacerbation of the strain in relations.[14]

He used every means of warning the Japanese government of the rising American temper, which transcended concern for individual cases of protection. Credited in Japanese eyes with a major role in restraining the American government during the *Panay* crisis, he used his prestige to reflect in mien and word the revulsion of the American public at the conduct of the Japanese military. Perhaps he exaggerated the inclination of Americans to act on their feelings, but no opportunity was lost to press home the necessity of avoiding further incidents. In formal representations he spoke "gravely," "in no uncertain terms," and "with the utmost emphasis." He began to adopt a "hard-boiled" posture toward the Japanese as a nation though not toward them as individuals. Among Japanese friends he gave vent to his own shock and anger at "sickening" accounts of the behavior of Japanese troops and used these friends to convey his concern to Prime Minister Konoe. Harada reported the Ambassador as saying that he was "placating" Washington with the argument that the extremist right in Japan was only a passing phenomenon (which of course he wasn't doing at all) and hinting that the contention would be weakened and American policy less restrained if further incidents occurred.[15]

However, in the absence of indications of coercive measures, American public feeling added little weight to Grew's protests. Such effectiveness as they had depended much on his methods. He was undoubtedly relieved at being allowed to handle the less serious cases in a *pro forma* way, that is by sending notes without calling in person and by dealing through subordinates. Where satisfaction was not forthcoming he would keep sending communications on the theory that with the Japanese repetition acted like "the constant dripping of water which finally wears away a stone." His personal representations were the more pointed for being infrequent. In one of the slapping incidents he told Vice-Minister Horinouchi Kensuke he would stay home Sunday waiting for an apology, which he received, he surmised, because Horinouchi knew that anything which kept the Ambassador from his Sunday golf must be serious. Grew almost never lost his temper, so a burst of anger during representations on May 31, 1938, was probably not without intended effect. He would let unresolved cases accumulate and then arrange a major interview with the Foreign Minister for which he would prepare with great care in order to have "every wrinkle of the situation" at his fingertips. At the appointed hour he would present his whole list of unfinished business which impressed by its sheer bulk and use this as the basis for expressions of concern about Japanese-American relations in general.[16]

This vast amount of diplomatic activity for the protection of American lives and property was not without success. Most cases involving indignities and injuries to Americans were settled, as were many other cases negotiated by Japanese and American officials in China. The Japanese government, obviously anxious to minimize its difficulties, regularly instituted investigations, sought to arrange for better identification of American property, and repeatedly issued orders to commanders at the front to pay the greatest attention to the rights and interests of third powers. Nevertheless satisfaction was never complete. New complaints kept arising. Settlement was slow, the case involving the death of the little girl taking over a year. In the bombing cases the Japanese claimed, probably not without some justification, that markings on mission buildings were inadequate, that properties were close to legitimate targets, or that verification was impossible. The United States adhered to the position that Japan was fully responsible whether or not a bombing was accidental. As a result there was always a backlog of cases, a chronic irritation, and a continual expenditure of time and energy. Grew was forever "mopping up." [17]

A more fundamental threat to American interests in China, if less abrasive to public opinion, was Japan's renunciation of the Open Door. The fact became clear by the summer of 1938, which no plea of military necessity could hide, that Japanese were determined to secure a preferred if not predominant position in the economy of China, international treaty or historic policy of the United States to the contrary notwithstanding. Japanese moves all pointed in this direction: non-payment of customs dues, export and import embargoes, erection of monopolies, currency and foreign exchange manipulation, curtailment of business travel and residence, closing of the Yangtze, and interference with international port facilities. Grew's repeated representations in individual cases met with repeated assurances of respect for the principle of equality of opportunity but little modification in practice. By September the Department was considering a comprehensive protest which on October 1, after the Munich crisis, it presented.[18]

Hull's Open Door note of October 1938 lacked the elegance of a Hughes or Stimson missive but was a workmanlike diplomatic instrument nevertheless. It showed precisely how American enterprise was being squeezed out of China in spite of categorical Japanese assurances of protection, and in alarming similarity to the case of Manchuria. It noted the "great and growing disparity" between the treatment accorded American trade by the Japanese and that accorded Japanese trade by the United States under the "letter and spirit" of the Commercial Treaty of 1911. Here was a bare hint of economic retaliation. The note concluded by requesting discontinuance of specific practices in violation of American rights and interests. Throughout it was temperate but pointed.[19]

The note was presented under more auspicious circumstances than intended. As a result of a code garble the word "President" was substituted for "Government of the United States." Perhaps Grew would have questioned the unique reference to the Chief Executive in a telegram which contained "Government of the United States" twelve times had it not been such an opportune moment to use the President's name. Premier Konoe had just temporarily taken over the Foreign Ministry and though not receiving diplomats could hardly refuse to receive a message from the President of the United States. Grew had an opportunity to bring his China problems directly to the attention of the Prime Minister without going over the head of the Foreign Minister. On October 3, after some hesitation, Konoe received Grew privately through the back entrance and the Ambassador presented the gist of the message and left a copy of his remarks. When the garble was straightened out the President approved the use of his name but Grew, his objective accomplished, presented the note at the Foreign Ministry as from the Government not the President, leaving officials there somewhat puzzled. He then blessed the code clerk, and told him to be more careful.[20]

Konoe told Grew, October 3, that assurances already given concerning the Open Door would be "steadfastly maintained," but time was running out for even nominal acceptance of the old order of trade in China. The heart of emerging Japanese policy was the concept of a national defense state based on a Japanese sphere of influence in the Far East providing the markets and raw materials to make her self-sufficient and impregnable to outside attack. With Chinese resources already being exploited in the wake of the advancing armies, the Konoe government was fashioning an administrative mechanism called the China Affairs Board for integrated economic development. The Foreign Ministry, responsible for third-power considerations in China policy, was alloted only a minor role on the Board. Conditions in the fall of 1938 favored public expression of Japanese intentions. In August, Japan settled the disastrous Changkufeng border incident with the Soviet Union, thereby stabilizing the northern frontier. In September the Munich settlement demonstrated the unwillingness of the Western democracies to use force to prevent a change in the *status quo*. At the end of October the capture of Hankow and Canton placed all the great cities of China in Japan's grasp and reduced the Kuomintang almost to a local regime. Japan was now in a position to describe what she wanted and what other powers would be permitted in China. On November 3 Prince Konoe launched Japan's New Order in East Asia.[21]

Konoe's New Order was a curious mid-twentieth-century rationalization of imperialism. What Japan required was a China that ran itself while serving Japan's economic and strategic needs. What Konoe promised was a new oriental civilization based on a political, economic, and cultural symbiosis of the two nations. Only within this higher entity, according with her own race and tradition and purged of Communism, colonialism, and by implication Western influence, could China realize self-determination. Terms for entry into this new era of self-realization were as follows: recognition of Manchukuo, the third element in the bloc; an anti-Comintern agreement; stationing of Japanese troops at specified points in China; designation of Inner Mongolia as a "special anti-Communist area"; freedom of residence and trade for Japanese nationals in the interior of China; and grant of facilities to Japan for development of China's resources especially in North China and Inner Mongolia. As for third powers, provided they accepted the New Order and Japan's option on China's economic assets, their cooperation would be welcomed.[22]

Though Grew had no illusions about the future of the China trade, he was taken aback by such naked reneging on Konoe's explicit assurances. "So much for international commitments," he commented. In all his career he had "never before experienced quite that sort of thing." Glumly he began probing for the explicit meaning of the euphemistic New Order. Four conversations with the new Foreign Minister, Arita Hachiro,[23] one between

Arita and Dooman, and several notes and press statements yielded little substance. Arita made it plain that John Hay's Open Door was history; a new situation existed and it was time to call a spade a spade. He gave virtually no assurances and defended trespass on foreign rights on the grounds of the requirements of military operations or China's development or Japan's strategic and economic needs. At the same time he denied the intention of excluding third powers, appeared reluctant to engage in a duel of diplomatic notes, and encouraged informal exploration of the problem. Grew was undoubtedly right in assuming that the Japanese government was feeling its way toward a definition of permissible third-power economic activity. It was laying hold of what it wanted and insinuating a new legitimacy with as little foreign fuss as possible while keeping a free hand for negotiation of new arrangements. This approach met with absolutely no favor in Washington. On December 31 Grew delivered a note which reasserted the principles of American policy, ruled out unilateral alteration of existing rights, and left on the Japanese the burden of initiating negotiations for a change. By the end of 1938 the Open Door issue was at an impasse.[24]

Eighteen months of war in the Far East had produced a change for the worse in Japanese-American relations, though the two nations were by no means on a collision course. Their small stock of common assumptions and commitments had dwindled in the mid-thirties and they had drifted apart, but they had maintained a profitable commerce and avoided dispute. Nineteen thirty-eight, however, left thorny problems of protection and trade and deep-driven prejudices against the Japanese on the part of the American public. Until now the United States had responded to Japanese actions by appealing to law, treaty, or principle, but the question arose whether such theoretical diplomacy was adequate any longer. Sentiment within and without the State Department favored more positive pressures. In the growing debate over American policy Grew was determined to have his say.

The search for new policy began early in 1938 after the Konoe government cut off peace efforts by declaring its intention of no longer dealing with the Kuomintang. After the proclamation of the New Order the search was pursued more actively into 1939. Grew played a less prominent role than he had in policy formulation during the fall of 1937. The Department of State, fearing its codes were vulnerable (which they were, for Harada quotes an intercepted telegram from Grew and one from Johnson), hesitated to take agents in the field into its confidence except by slow mail. "Afraid of its own shadow," Grew growled when he had to learn of Anglo-American policy discussions through Sir Robert Craigie. Beyond security concern, however, Washington seemed less interested in Grew's opinion, perhaps, as Hornbeck explained with reference to the views of one of his subordinates, because the Embassy supported prevailing policy. The Political Adviser felt that those advocating new attitudes and new steps should be given closer attention because the burden of proof lay on them and because they presented the constructive side of the case. So Grew often felt out of touch with evolving policy and had to peg his arguments on those of Craigie to avoid seeming to advise gratuitously. The curious result as often as not was a policy dialogue between a foreign office and its diplomatic agent conducted as a discussion between agents of different governments.[25]

Fundamental to Grew's policy thinking was the conviction that Japanese were united in their determination to succeed in China. The liberal-moderate elements, which by 1937 had dropped from his calculations as a restraining force, remained feeble throughout 1938. "Alas," he said of Harada, Kabayama, and the rest, "these good men are powerless in the face of the military." He believed that the capitalist class, the zaibatsu, was perhaps more influential but such was the new power of the state that their desires and interests could never be controlling. Not dissension and factionalism but consensus and control characterized Japan at war. He saw a major restructuring of political institutions and the economy under way, designed to win victory in China and place Japan on a permanent war footing. Administrative organs proliferated as the process of concentrating authority kept pace with widening hostilities.

Rationalization, mobilization, integration, and coordination were the key words in Embassy political dispatches. The tide of nationalism finally enveloped the Foreign Office. He recognized that for some years a more parochial type of diplomat had been displacing the Ishiis and Matsudairas, professionals of an older generation who by personality, character, and ideals could "take a high place in any society." Now the Ministry was being reorganized to make it more amenable to control by the dominant elements in the government. This seemed the day of bureaucracy, of machines over men. But the tendency to place political movements in carefully divided categories should be resisted, Grew argued. In spite of similarities between the Japanese and the German and Italian systems, it was unlikely that the national polity of Japan would be altered or personal dictatorship tolerated. Japan was experiencing totalitarianism, if one insisted on using the term, but "totalitarianism *sui generis*." [26]

This was remarkably able reporting. Considering the drain on time and energy from constant representations, and the limitation of sources, it was thorough and accurate, but more important it represented a deeper and soberer awareness of Japanese realities than before. Of course much of the credit is due Dooman and the Secretaries engaged in political and economic affairs, but Grew was the captain of the ship and his leadership is apparent in the consistent Embassy point of view which the varied dispatches of his subordinates produced. His problem, and that of all senior diplomats in the thirties, had been the world's kaleidoscopic and accelerating change in values, assumptions, techniques, and organization. With the best will those reared in calmer days found it next to impossible to keep their way of looking at events abreast of the events themselves. Diplomacy became ever more complex as portents became ever more sinister. However, for about one year the pattern of events in Japan and the Far East ran steady and clear and Grew caught up with reality.

In the Embassy's view, the outward thrust of all the frantic restructuring and mobilization on the home front was a "Pike's Peak or Bust" effort by Japan to realize her objectives in China. The creation of bastions against the Soviet Union and an "enclave" of self-sufficiency in the Far East were matters of vital national interest. No sign of war weariness existed or inclination to accept a settlement cheating the cost in blood and treasure. The Embassy discerned clash of opinion with respect to prosecution of the war: Prince Konoe was understood to advocate a drastic and opportunistic policy to bring peace quickly, while the Army preferred to husband resources and conduct a war of attrition. Also, differences were noted between the government and the military in China over the treatment of foreign rights. But these questions had to do with tactics not objectives, and if anything the swing was to the more drastic course and toward greater indifference toward third powers. However one described it technically, Japan was engaged in a major war and was grimly staking all on winning. Failure would be ruinous and unthinkably humiliating. Such were the realities as Grew saw them behind the "piffle" about a New Order. Even his liberal friends agreed that for Japan there was no road back.[27]

On the basis of his estimate of the Japanese internal situation and objectives in China, though not entirely on that basis, Grew recommended against measures involving direct military or economic pressure. He had nothing to say about breaking diplomatic relations, but for obvious reasons would have opposed it. He was not quite so positive about indirect pressure through financial assistance to China: he opposed it in principle but did not feel qualified to argue the case. His position against direct pressures, as constructed from various communications of 1938 and early 1939, rested on five arguments: that such measures would be subject to misinterpretation, that they would not work or work in time, that they would increase the possibility of war, that the American people opposed war except in defense of American territory, and that American Far Eastern interests did not justify war with Japan.[28]

One difficulty with applying sanctions in the current situation, Grew believed, was the likelihood of misunderstanding. He was not at all sure what Washington meant to accomplish by economic pressure. Hornbeck set the purpose of "compelling Japan to refrain from abuse of American nationals and violation of American rights and other matters in China." What did he mean by "other matters"? It was hard to conceive of accomplishing the limited purpose of protection without materially affecting Japan's basic strategy. Furthermore, the suspicion was likely to arise in the Japanese mind, with its tendency to look behind the given for the true meaning, that the object really was to slow or halt the Japanese advance or to throw Japan out of China. Without some dramatic incident like the *Panay* to pin retaliation on, American pressure would probably be seen as an effort to frustrate Japan's continental expansion. "Japan would think that a conflict with the United States was not to be escaped by less than abandonment of the principal aims in China and peace would not be bought at that price." Indeed, the very object of her China ventures was to make it impossible for other nations to control her destiny by shutting off her trade.

Suppose the American object were in fact to thwart Japan in China and suppose that Japan refused to heed warnings and maximum pressure were applied. Would Japan then be forced to her knees by the brute fact of economic starvation? Not soon enough, in Grew's estimation. Abrogation of the commercial treaty would require six months' notice. Japan would be self-sufficient in food. The loss of trade with Great Britain and the United States would still leave a figure equal to her average foreign trade in the 1916-20 period. The Japanese would not knuckle under to preserve their capitalistic system: its future was already mortgaged against success in China; the capitalist class, which would suffer most, was numerically insignificant; and plans were ready to meet such an emergency through nationalization of industry. Furthermore the Army and Navy would be able to sustain operations from stockpiles of raw materials. It was impossible to estimate the size of these reserves but unsafe to assume they were negligible. The Navy was said to have fuel oil sufficient for three to four years of war steaming. (In July 1941, before American deliveries were halted, the Navy actually had enough for not more than eighteen months.[29]) Above all, Grew deplored the tendency of the sanctionists to base their case on "figures and statistics" alone, ignoring psychological factors. Three years in Berlin during the World War had shown him how little human beings could subsist on if they had the will, and in respect of capacity for self-discipline and self-sacrifice and total emotional commitment to victory the Japanese were in no sense inferior to the Germans.

Grew believed that the application of pressure against Japan would entail an unacceptable risk of war. Economic measures would put Japanese in an ugly mood, reduce the possibility of accommodation, and "cause the gravest risk of serious incidents which, in themselves, might render recourse to force unavoidable." An oil embargo might ultimately lead Japan to attack the Dutch East Indies, he warned the President in the summer of 1939. A naval demonstration would be even more risky. The American battle fleet could not seriously affect Japanese calculations except by moving to a position from which it could threaten Japanese territory, that is by moving to the Western Pacific, yet such a move would in itself pose so grave a threat that the Japanese Navy would forcibly resist it. The throttle of naval deterrence had no intermediate stops. Since every coercive measure involved some risk of war, none should be taken without a willingness to go to war if necessary. As he assessed the temper of the American public, no such willingness existed. It was not unlikely that the Japanese, assessing it the same way, would ignore warnings and call the American bluff. Failure to act in such circumstances would ruin American prestige and influence. Action would probably mean war. Grew was convinced that all measures of a coercive nature would lead the United States into dangerous waters where the American people were not then prepared to go.

Leaving aside the question of public support for a policy of coercion, Grew argued that no sufficient reason existed for war with Japan. One should bear in mind, he said, that American policy aimed at granting independence to the Philippines and when that was accomplished the United States would have no Far Eastern possessions to fight for. Other American interests had not been jeopardized by Japan to the extent that they had been, for example, by Germany in the World War. Japanese pretensions did not present such a threat to civilization as had Germany's. American lives, prestige, and trade had so far suffered less injury. The sinking of the *Panay* was not as grave as that of the *Lusitania*.

He pointed out that on a simple dollars and cents basis the closing of the Open Door did not justify risking war, because trade with Japan was so much greater than with China. He pointed out that in 1937 the United States sold to Japan more than five times what it sold to China and bought twice as much. The favorable trade balance with Japan was itself twice the total value of exports to China, and sales to Japan were increasing at more than twice the average rate. Japan was America's third best customer while China was sixteenth. Japan was fourth best supplier while China was ninth. In fact the total American sales to Japan approximated that to all South America. War would not only be highly unprofitable but would probably destroy the economic system upon which this trade was founded. And he wondered, supposing Japan were defeated, whether the problem of protecting American trading rights in China would not persist, only with China instead of Japan the trespasser.

Grew's foreign policy views in the year of Munich were in substantial agreement with those of Moffat and of Hugh Wilson, who had a brief tour in the Department before going to Germany as Ambassador. These three professionals represented what Moffat described as "the realist school of thought." They had much in common in terms of élitist background, training in the old Diplomatic Service, and extensive European experience. Except for their intense dislike of all things Soviet, they shied away from ideology, abstraction, and emotion in foreign affairs, and concentrated on the tangibles of national power and interest. Inbred caution and absorption in the details of diplomacy made them concerned more with the flow than the direction of events and wary of initiatives. With Sir Harold Nicolson's diplomatist they felt that "time alone is the conciliator . . . [and] mistakes are the only things that are really effective. . . ." They were far from complacent about Germany and Japan but skeptical about committing the United States to the support of French and British diplomacy, which they regarded with suspicion. They argued that so far as the United States had any vital interests outside the Western Hemisphere, these lay in the direction of Europe rather than the Orient. They were working against any change in American Far Eastern policy. Challenging their views from three different but not necessarily incompatible directions were the British, who strove for Anglo-American cooperation against Japan, the idealists, who advocated resistance to Japan on moral grounds, and the China hands of the State Department, who contended that the nation did have vital Far Eastern interests at stake against Japan.[30]

The "realists," believing that nothing short of war would remove the Japanese from China, regarded British proposals for joint action as no less dangerous than coercion by the United States alone. Their own country had no comparable stake in the Far East, not the Imperial prestige, permanent possessions, or huge investments and trade that yielded precious foreign exchange. At the same time they knew that the Royal Navy was concentrated for the protection of the home islands and the Mediterranean and could not spare battleships for the Far East. Such inequality of interests and risks made them highly suspicious of persistent British encouragement of a common front. Wilson saw the British inveigling his nation into an ultimate alignment against Germany by playing on the American weakness for Far Eastern entanglements. Moffat assumed that the United States alone would bear the brunt of a Far Eastern war, so that "once again Great Britain would have somebody to fight her battles for her." Grew thought the British would "always manoevre us out on a limb and then leave us hanging." Heard again was the old metaphor about Americans having to pull British chestnuts out of the fire.[31]

Actually the British did not dare stray far from American Far Eastern policy. They recognized that coercion of Japan was entirely too dangerous without American support and that appeasement might alienate the United States with disastrous consequences in Europe as well as the Far East. Nevertheless, they attempted to protest and negotiate their way out of some of their Far Eastern difficulties and every twist and turn only heightened their unattractiveness to Grew. Their notes were imperious and Craigie only intensified his predicament by repeated personal protests over routine matters. Grew saw no point in attracting Japanese fire by joining

Craigie when in contrast his own infrequent, incisive representations seemed to make the Japanese more amenable. The British performance lacked polish. Once Craigie blundered by authorizing London to announce that the United States had expressed no objection to an Anglo-Japanese agreement over the Chinese customs, when Grew had already told him that the State Department refused to comment on the scheme. Grew smarted under Craigie's criticisms of American policy, a reference to Washington's "armchair statesmen" drawing a heated retort from the American. Though the ambassadors kept in close touch and pooled nearly all their information, Grew remained uneasy that the British would "sell themselves into the Japanese camp." Craigie himself seemed straightforward, but Grew felt it necessary to inquire pointedly about rumors of an Anglo-Japanese dicker in London. He could not escape the feeling that British Far Eastern diplomacy was "inept in all its courses." On all counts — methods, interests, risks — alignment with Britain seemed foolish.[32]

The idealist position was essentially the same one taken by Stimson in the Manchurian crisis and the "realists" were no more impressed by it in 1938 and 1939 than they had been earlier. Most Stimsonians were now chiefly concerned about Germany, but to Dr. Stanley K. Hornbeck the confrontation of good and evil, of law-abiding and lawbreaking nations, of democracy and totalitarianism, was taking place primarily in a Far Eastern context. This veteran of the Paris and Washington conferences and chief specialist on Far Eastern affairs to three Secretaries of State had a tender, possessive feeling about the territorial integrity of China. To the "realists" he represented the "messianic" school of thought, indeed was the epitome of "that all-embracing American conscience." They saw him as a stubborn, sensitive man of intense convictions, given to didactic assertions and a prose style burdened with finicky legalisms like "and/or." To Hornbeck the Japanese threat to American rights and interests was a concrete manifestation of the larger threat to orderly processes posed by aggressor nations. Japan was a "predatory" power in the unshakable grip of militarists who, though less formidable than supposed, were spurred on to conquest after conquest by world timidity. To stop Japan he recommended a comprehensive program of retaliation culminating if necessary in military and economic sanctions. This "diplomatic war plan" involved risk but, he argued, further acquiescence would ultimately lead to war anyway. With such views the "realists" radically disagreed, believing that nothing in international affairs was inevitable and that no abstraction was worth fighting for, but only territory or immense and vital national interests.[33]

Predominant opinion among those Foreign Service and State Department officials who by experience and function were in close touch with China was that the United States did in fact have vital interests at stake in the Far East. As Ambassador Johnson put it, the question was one of saving American not British chestnuts. The difference between Hornbeck and the China hands was really one of emphasis: neither were considerations of power and interest absent from the former's thinking nor concern for orderly procedures and democratic regimes from the latter's. The China hands considered that an independent China was necessary as a balance to Japan and they were concerned that Japan, once having consolidated its hold on China, would move foward against the Philippines as well as British, French, and Dutch possessions in Southeast Asia. At bottom they looked on the United States as a major Far Eastern power and were alarmed at the prospect of Japan establishing a sphere of influence over "everything west of the 180th meridian." Though differing on the possible extent of counterpressure, they agreed that China should be assisted. This concern for the Far Eastern balance of power seemed excessive to Wilson. The specter of Japan dominating the Pacific seemed to be haunting Americans the same way Philip II haunted England: "We see a great power in the making and our political instinct leads us to oppose it." He along with Grew and Moffat believed that on careful examination American interests would be judged minimal and the recommended cure more dangerous than the disease.[34]

The fact that Wilson, Moffat, and Grew opposed any forward policy in the Far East does not prove they were isolationists, at least in the severely introvertive sense of that word in the thirties. They certainly did not consider themselves isolationists, nor did they think the same way. In opposition to the pacifists, they argued for a big fleet because they saw threats to American security and instinctively relied on military power as ballast for their diplomacy. They opposed national self-abnegation, Grew criticizing Senator Gerald Nye and Representative Hamilton Fish for wanting to scrap "our interests, national dignity, and prestige — if not our national honor — in the Far East." They believed that by virtue of its unaligned and uncommitted position the United States might play a modest role in peacekeeping. Even intervention in a European war was not inconceivable. Though Moffat would avoid "at any costs . . . involvement . . . in hostilities anywhere," Wilson held that the nation might as a last resort go to war to save the British Empire, because "the world is a more sympathetic place to exist when we have the British Empire all about it and it would be an obnoxious place if that empire were managed by Germans, Italians or Russians." Grew was more uncertain but wondered in March 1938 whether it would not be wiser to halt an Italo-German bid for world domination while it was still potential rather than actually on America's doorstep. The diplomats were less isolationists than traditionalists, exhibiting the same sense of limited liabilty in world affairs, the same concern for sea power, commerce, and prestige, the same identification with Anglo-Saxon civilization and the world *status quo* that characterized the diplomacy of Republican statesmen at the turn of the century. They had their illusions but they were not blind.[35]

What distinguished these diplomats most sharply from various activists was not complacency about potential threats to the United States but unwillingness to take immediate risks to reduce those threats. Not only Grew's Far Eastern views but his views on the European crisis of 1938 reflected this reluctance. In 1933 he had shared the widely held notion that Hitler at least provided an alternative to Communism in Germany. In 1938 he was no less anti-Communist but now regarded Hitler the more immediate menace, as the megalomaniacal leader of a people easily led into war. His controlling concern, however, was to prevent a war which would probably involve the United States, leave European civilization in ruins, and, of immediate consequence, greatly increase the Far Eastern problem. Of course he might have taken the position that an American guarantee to Britain and France would be the most effective deterrent to Hitler, but aside from the fact that American public opinion ruled out such a commitment, he would oppose it because, in the diplomats' experience, simple confrontations of power conduced to war. Their concern was to avoid the division of the world into hostile camps by keeping power arrangements loose and flexible. Given the failure of collective security and the danger of power alignments, expediency seemed the only alternative. Grew was not particularly hopeful or happy about Chamberlain's appeasement policy as it came into full play in the spring of 1938, but he felt that war postponed might conceivably, by the play of contingencies too complex and remote for him to judge, be war prevented.[36]

Grew was vastly relieved by the Munich agreement but found the path of expediency tortuous. Of course the main justification of appeasement was that it had avoided war. Chamberlain might go down in history as "a great and wise peace-maker" for providing Europe a "breathing spell" it had lacked in 1914. As for the Czechs, who stood near the bottom of Grew's list of worries, he was inclined to rationalize the dismemberment of their republic on the grounds that they had proved oppressive rulers of minorities and that the Versailles settlement was unjust to Germany. Now a "safer and saner" basis for European peace might be laid. On the other hand he did not deny that Hitler had held up Europe at the point of a gun, snatched a valuable prize, and might well be encouraged to try again with less justification. Perhaps in the reprieve ways might be found to circumscribe him. The confusions of expediency disappeared in March 1939, when Hitler overran the rest of Czechoslovakia and reduced European relations to what Grew finally recognized as "a naked computation in the balance of brute force." Now he was encouraged to see "the old British lion . . . stirring uneasily in his serene drowsiness and . . . actually . . . bristling with a slight growl or two. Don't touch that bone (Poland)." [37]

With war fast approaching in Europe and settling interminably over the Far East, decisions pressed ever more insistently on the United States, but the arguments percolating through the State Department still had an academic flavor. Everyone seemed to sense that the Administration could not make major moves. With rearmament just getting under way Roosevelt lacked the strength for strong policy. With the country just awakening from isolationism he hesitated to move too fast. Himself under intense criticism over the court-packing plan, and facing a badly divided Democratic majority and rancorous Republican minority in Congress, he had a major task of political leadership simply to release himself from the iron grip of neutrality legislation. It is true that common understandings were forming which could be rapidly converted into decisions, above all the assignment of stategic priority to Europe. As to the Far East, a broad but hazy conception of American interests prevailed, together with bitter dislike of, and impulse to oppose, Japan. But the ever cautious Hull paid close attention to Grew's warnings of the danger of retaliation. Two small steps were taken, a moral embargo on bombing planes in June 1938 and a $25,000,000 commodity loan to China in December 1938, but these were hints, and the latter move was designed to preserve options rather than commit the United States to oppose Japan. American policy in 1938 and early 1939 remained that of "the eternal question mark," as described by Moffat. Making a virtue of necessity, the Administration sought to keep potential enemies in doubt as to what the United States might do in the event of further aggression.[38]

The policy of keeping Japan guessing suited Grew's purposes well. He was playing the role of broker in unpleasant possibilities, seeking to maintain peace by convincing governments involved of the disadvantages of tougher policy. He tried to convey to his own government his sincere conviction that retaliation would increase the chances of war. At the same time by impressing on the Japanese government the distinct possibility of such retaliation, he hoped to win better treatment of American rights and interests in China. He explained to Japanese that he had always counseled his government to have patience, but like a fireman he needed a free flow of water to do the job.[39] In other words, he needed concrete manifestations of Japanese goodwill. While 1938 proved discouraging in this respect, Grew did not give up hope. So long as the Japanese seemed disposed to negotiate difficulties one by one as they arose, there remained hope of salvaging something from the wreck of American interests in China and of keeping Japanese-American relations on an even keel. Undoubtedly Grew also saw an advantage in holding before the Japanese the possibility of an Anglo-

American front in the Far East. He knew the Japanese watched the comings and goings between the two embassies. So long as these private conferences continued but never quite produced a joint public position, the Japanese might feel some advantage in treating American interests favorably. Grew recognized that leverage in diplomacy lay as much if not more in what governments might do as in what they actually did.

Grew had his reasons, but he sounded drearily negative that year: no on sanctions, no on naval demonstrations, no on denunciation of treaties, no on assistance to China, no on joint action with the British. He considered that war between the United States and Japan would be tragic and absurd but he held no hope of Japan becoming less aggressive or less capable of aggression and he was not prepared to accept appeasement. Viewing the crisis primarily in terms of the Pacific and Far East, he argued that American security would not be vitally affected if Japan succeed in putting the New Order into effect. However, a Japan preponderant in the Far East working with a Germany preponderant in Europe might pose an altogether different problem. By 1939 the sinister possibility of a German-Japanese alliance was working a radical change in Grew's outlook.

PART FIVE

War and Peace in the Pacific

(1939–1945)

SEVENTEEN

The Uses of Diplomacy, 1939

IN the months between Munich and the invasion of Poland the world lived in total insecurity. The Geneva system had long since collapsed. Now Chamberlain's attempt to revive the Locarno system fell before Hitler's driving ambition; peace in their time was to be measured in months not years. Europe divided at the Rhine and the rival blocs reached abroad to secure advantage or at least prevent disadvantage. Regional tensions were transformed into parts of an all-encompassing world crisis. What the Polish Ambassador said in Tokyo concerned Rome and what the British Ambassador said in Moscow concerned Grew. World capitals were caught up in a vast and infinitely complex play for position, yet no alignment, alliance, or system seemed sufficient to deter or protect. Once again man confessed his inability to ensure peace in the human community and accepted the possibility, then the probability, of another great war.

The moment of interlocking between the Far Eastern and European crises occurred for Grew in November 1938 when he learned from Craigie that negotiations were in progress for a strengthening of German-Italian-Japanese ties. Earlier the bonds had not seemed strong: differences of polity and interest had outweighed anti-Communist and totalitarian affinities. Hands off the Far East and disentanglement from Europe were, after all, reverse sides of the same coin. Munich had demonstrated that Japan might take advantage of Europe's distress without risking involvement in Europe's quarrels. At the height of the crisis the Vice-Minister of Foreign Affairs had been at pains to discourage the assumption that in case of war Japan might align itself militarily with Germany. Now, however, Craigie's information and Japan's signature of a new cultural pact with Germany on the anniversary of the Anti-Comintern Pact suggested a broader relationship was developing. Grew observed that increasing authoritarianism in Japan made the Fascist states more attractive. Furthermore, the nations Germany opposed in Europe were the same ones whose interests conflicted with Japan's New Order. Closer association among the *status quo* powers, Britain, France, and the United States, was bound to incline Japan toward the have-not powers, whose Far Eastern interests were negligible. His revised estimate was that Japan was already swinging strongly toward the Axis.[1]

Actually the first moves for a closer relationship took place early in 1938 and an alliance had been under active consideration since that summer. The Japanese Army had proposed a military pact aimed at immobilizing the Soviet Union. With the threat to Manchuria removed the Kwantung Army could be used to bring the China Incident to a close. Hitler, bent on aggression in eastern Europe and less concerned about an already isolated Soviet Union than about Britain and France, had suggested a three-way pact with Italy that could be used against any outside power, not just the Soviet Union. This would have the effect of immobilizing Britain and, through Britain, France, by presenting simultaneous threats in Europe, the Mediterranean, and the Far East. At the time Grew was first hearing talk of an alliance, sharp disagreement was developing within the Japanese government over the broad scope of the German proposal. Prince Konoe's unwillingness to accept the German terms and his failure to terminate the China war led to his resignation January 4, 1939, and the appointment of Baron Hiranuma Kiichiro as Prime Minister. Now the alliance question became acute and for seven months observers were to hear muffled reports of the struggle raging in Tokyo's labyrinths of power.[2]

Grew understood that the issue was whether the agreement should be aimed exclusively against the Soviet Union or against other powers as well. He reported that strong pressure was being exerted by the Germans and by younger army officers in favor of a general alliance and that "important moderate influences" were seeking to prevent Japan from joining the anti-democratic camp. Convinced that the attitude of the American government would have a critical bearing on Japan's decision, Grew decided to throw all his influence into the balance. With Washington's approval he began to campaign actively against the general pact, using his favored method of informal and unofficial approaches. At every opportunity in February, March, and April 1939 he would buttonhole Foreign Ministry officials, prominent journalists, acquaintances in business and court circles, and foreign diplomats to spread the gospel of non-entanglement. He believed it essential to beat the Germans on their own ground of propaganda. This was no time for "pussy-footing."[3]

His intention was not to mislead or threaten the Japanese but to impress them with "cold academic fact and unassailable truths." According to his "thesis," war was imminent in Europe, and the United States would sooner or later be drawn in on the side of Britain and France. American involvement would come not by calculation but by way of incidents which stirred popular passions. Americans, he said again, were the most inflammable people in the world. If Germany and the United States went to war, and Japan were tied to Germany, peace between Japan and the United States would be almost impossible to maintain. In short, Japan would find itself fighting Germany's war with the United States, and fighting a losing one at that. Grew emphasized that war between Japan and the United States would be stupid. No nation, certainly not Germany or Italy, could do more than his own in providing Japan with capital, markets, and resources. Large capacity for friendship existed on both sides. Current difficulties over China could ultimately be overcome. He urged Japanese not to foreclose this bright future relationship by making a foolish liaison now.[4]

Grew's message was all the more persuasive because of initiatives taken by his government which seemed dramatically to confirm both its warning and its promise. On March 1, 1939, the President, on the recommendation of the State Department, offered to send the ashes of late Ambassador Saito Hiroshi home to Japan aboard an American warship. Since Saito had not been Ambassador when he died, having fallen ill and retired some months earlier, it was an unusual gesture. The Japanese, always sensitive to the nuances of relations among nations, and never more so than in this moment of world uncertainty, were immensely gratified. According to Grew they assumed "that a new leaf had been turned in Japanese-American relations and a wave of friendliness for the United States swept over the country." Arrangements for expressing Japanese appreciation soon took the form of a herculean program of welcome for the officers and men of the cruiser bearing Saito's remains. For the State Department this was an embarrassment of riches; Grew was instructed to discourage plans for "general entertainment or social gestures." Gifts were to be politely declined, the ceremonial character of the visit strictly adhered to, and its duration shortened. This sudden caution seemed to Grew like locking the barn door after the horse had been stolen. He had not been consulted about the visit or advised of the Department's thinking. Now he was expected to "reconcile two impossible desiderata: to stop the program and at the same time to avoid embarrassment." On the one hand he risked the constructive effects of the gesture and on the other he was too late to avoid its political repercussions.[5]

As usual Grew worked to enlarge his middle ground by pressing both sides for concessions. Respectfully he pointed out a few plain truths to the Department, namely that radical change in the program would be "fraught with embarrassment," that a political coloration was bound to attach to such an unprecedented gesture at such a critical time, that Japanese gifts were next to impossible to decline politely, and that to the Japanese mind "entertainment after a funeral in no way robs the funeral of its solemnity." Somewhat grudgingly the Department gave way, insisting only that the program be restricted as much as possible without giving offense or causing embarrassment. The task of "harmonizing" these conflicting objectives was left to Grew's discretion. He then proceeded to restrict the scope of the visit, while still allowing the Japanese "some kind of cushion on which to loose their pent-up emotion." Bewildered members of the Japanese welcoming committee were roused from their beds early one Sunday morning to be lectured at the Embassy on the importance of avoiding ballyhoo. A monster public meeting at Meiji stadium, complete with flags, parade, and track meet was shorn of the spectacular and diverted into the soberer surroundings of Waseda University. American correspondents were invited to "tone down" their dispatches to the United States. According to the *New York Times*, Grew's "tactful but inflexible" guidance managed to prevent the visit from becoming engulfed in a wave of national emotion.[6]

The visit went like clockwork. On April 17 the Grews were at dockside for the arrival of the "sinuously graceful" heavy cruiser *Astoria*. Captain Richmond Kelly Turner and a landing party of bluejackets accompanied the massive funeral urn ashore, where the American and Imperial Japanese navies formed a cortege that wound through the streets of Yokohama to the railroad station. After solemn rites in Tokyo the visit became frankly political and social, with exchange of entertainment for the officers and sight-seeing tours and judo demonstrations for the crew. The Embassy's stag dinner attracted War Minister Itagaki, Navy Minister Yonai Mitsumasa, and Foreign Minister Arita, three of the five-member cabinet committee then debating the Axis pact. Grew heard that the Emperor was "filled with emotion" by the visit. On the whole, decorum was maintained, though Captain Turner had to be cautioned not to show a Ritz Brothers comedy film to his Japanese guests aboard ship. Grew was vastly relieved when it was all over: "So now to the *Astoria*, sayonara, for ever and ever, amen." (In 1942 the ship was set afire and sunk by Japanese cruisers off Guadalcanal. Turner came back in command of the amphibious assaults on Iwo Jima and Okinawa.)[7]

Meanwhile, Roosevelt tried to warn aggressors that war in Europe would find the sympathies, interests, and conceivably the economic power of the United States on the side of the democracies. Alarming news came from Europe: on March 14 Hitler incorporated the remainder of Czechoslovakia into the Reich; on March 23 German troops occupied Memel; on March 31 Chamberlain announced his fateful guarantee of Poland; on April 7 Italian forces invaded Albania. Domestic considerations forced the President to move obliquely in establishing the American stake in the outcome of the European crisis. On April 15 he sent a public message to the dictators urging peaceful negotiation and requesting their disclaimer of aggressive intent toward thirty-one European and Near Eastern nations. At the same time he ordered the American fleet, which had been conducting maneuvers in the

Caribbean and was planning to visit the New York World's Fair, to return to San Diego immediately, six weeks early. This move was designed to relieve British concern for their vulnerability in the Far East, which was more glaring as a result of the commitment of their Mediterranean fleet to the protection of Greece against possible attack by Italy. Although Roosevelt's initiatives were inspired more by the situation in Europe than Japan's debate on the Axis pact, they suggested a common purpose among the Atlantic powers as well as intimate naval coordination between Britain and the United States and thereby acted "like a clap of thunder," as the *New York Times* put it, to warn Japan of the dangers involved in too close an association with Germany.[8]

Grew had reason to believe that his representations, reinforced by the *Astoria* visit, the redeployment of the fleet, and the President's *démarche* of April 15, contributed effectively toward keeping Japan out of a general alliance. He had reported the prevailing opinion that Japan would avoid embroilment in a European war and would only consider a strengthening of the Anti-Comintern Pact, but he had been "more or less in the dark" about the shape of the internal struggle. Then on April 16 Baron Harada led him aside at the home of a mutual friend for a private word. The Baron had heard of Grew's concern about Japan entering a general alliance and wished to assure him there was no need for further anxiety. Two days later, at the Navy's dinner in honor of Captain Turner, Admiral Yonai expressed the same thought to Dooman in Japanese. The Minister of the Navy went on to explain that Japanese policy had been decided: the element seeking a tie-up with Germany and Italy had been "suppressed." Japan would not commit itself either to the totalitarian or democratic camps. These assurances, phrased so much alike, were most encouraging. Not only did Grew have the answer he wanted, from the most authoritative source, but also he had proof that Japanese whom he had used to convey his message were close to those actually exercising power.[9]

The alliance question was not to be disposed of so neatly. Persisting rumors of cabinet dissension, intense activity by high officials, and the coming and going of Axis ambassadors suggested that Yonai's assurances had been premature. On April 27 Grew described Japan's decision on the pact as "tentative," and early in May he reported renewed pressure from Germany and Italy as well as from "powerful and sinister" ultra-nationalistic forces within Japan. A closer relationship with the Axis was more attractive because of the opening of Anglo-Soviet conversations, which, even if restricted to Europe, might lead to a "concerting of actions and policies for the protection of common interests in the Far East." He still believed that the government would decide against a general alliance, but it could not afford to alienate the dictators or defy the chauvinists and would probably conclude by offering a mutual defense assistance pact against the Soviet

Union. A strengthening of anti-Soviet ties would give "new expression" to Japan's special relations with Germany without involving danger of war with Britain, France, or the United States. In Grew's opinion Japan would stay in the middle of the road, keeping open ways into both Fascist and democratic camps.[10]

The reality was somewhat different. In spite of the maze of contradictions and ambiguities that characterized inner Cabinet deliberations on the Axis pact in 1939, agreement is evident on the principle of a general alliance. Agreement embraced diverse bureaucratic perspectives, to be sure. While the Army was preoccupied with the continental military advantages of a general alliance, the Navy favored one because inclusion of naval powers among Japan's hypothetical enemies was smart budget strategy and because a diffuse pact would be safer than one which, by concentrating exclusively on the Soviet Union, might hasten continental war. Beyond parochial concerns, moreover, was a common belief that a general alliance would strengthen Japan's diplomatic position on China questions, restraining the democracies and increasing bargaining leverage. Also there was a common concern for security against the Soviet Union, especially after Anglo-Soviet talks began and a border clash at Nomonhan in May led to large-scale fighting along the Manchurian-Mongolian frontier. For a variety of reasons the inner Cabinet was prepared to go far toward meeting Germany's insistence on a pact of unlimited application.[11]

Japan was prepared to go far but not quite all the way. Ministers Yonai and Arita were determined not to involve Japan automatically in a European war. The Navy, dependent on American supplies for rearmament, joined the Foreign Ministry in opposing a pact which might lead to American economic retaliation. Opponents of an unlimited alliance managed to attach hobbling reservations which would limit Japan's military commitment to the case of the Soviet Union and permit Japan to explain the alliance as a strengthening of the Anti-Comintern Pact. Grew heard this explanation repeatedly and believed it. As the struggle continued through seventy meetings of the inner Cabinet, insistent pressure by the Army and by Germany forced Yonai and Arita to give way step by step until Japan was only reserving the right to choose the moment of declaring war in the case of Britain and France. In addition to a military undertaking against the Soviet Union, Japan was prepared to form a diplomatic alignment with Germany against the democracies which would be, at the very least, threatening. Rather than adhering to the middle of the road, as Grew supposed, Japan was willing to put one foot in the Axis camp. The problem was that Germany would allow no reservations, insisting on both feet.[12]

So long as the Hiranuma Cabinet failed to solidify relations with the Axis, it would find advantage in discussing ways of improving Japanese-American relations. Indeed, a clarification of the position of the United States was essential in order to discover how far Japan might safely proceed with Germany. Grew's forthcoming leave in the United States, where he would see the President, provided the occasion for a beginning.

On May 16, 1939, Baron Harada invited Grew, Dooman, and their families to a small farewell luncheon, after which the three men adjourned to another room for a talk. Prince Saionji's secretary began by saying that groups opposed to a political or military connection with the Axis found it difficult to meet the argument that Japan could not afford to remain isolated, because "Germany and Italy are urging Japan 'to come over to their side,' while the democratic nations are turning to Japan a very cold shoulder." If the democracies could indicate that the way was open for restoration of good relations with Japan, the opponents of an Axis alliance would be greatly strengthened. According to Dooman's report of the conversation, Grew replied that peace in China must come first, on terms acceptable to China and the United States. According to Harada's account Grew went further and asked what Japan's terms were. In case the President asked him, what attitude did Japan want the United States to take on the China problem and what should the United States do to "keep in pace" with Japan? Harada said he would arrange for Arita to provide answers, and Grew responded, "Will you do that for me, please?" [13]

Very likely Grew was encouraging a statement of conditions for improving relations. The problem was to elicit terms without officially soliciting them, while permitting the Japanese in their own eyes to act responsively. His solution was to take the initiative privately and continue the conversations officially, so that he could report as Japanese proposals what would otherwise appear as Japanese answers. Grew had used this method in November 1937, when exploring the possibility of mediating the Sino-Japanese War. It was a way "to start the ball rolling toward peace."

The Foreign Minister conversed informally with Dooman the following day and officially with Grew the day after, each conversation being linked successfully with the preceding one, but the yield was discouraging. Arita understood Grew to be seeking assurances that Japan would not act on the Axis alliance until Grew had discussed in Washington the possibility of some American "gesture of welcome" to Japan. Arita was quite prepared to assure the United States that Japan intended to commit itself only with respect to the Soviet Union and otherwise preferred a neutral position. He pointed out, nevertheless, that an Anglo-Soviet alliance might force Japan into closer collaboration with the Axis. Then, should war break out and involve the United States, "the position which Russia might take might conceivably decide whether peace could be maintained between the United States and Japan." Grew's argument for non-entanglement cut both ways.

Arita had very little to say specifically about American rights and interests in China. He was conciliatory in tone but "ambiguous and vague" in substance. In effect he suggested, as he had before and as Japanese statesmen had been suggesting since the turn of the century, that if the United States would only recognize Japan's special requirements there would be plenty of room for the trade of both nations in China. Grew and Dooman were forced to conclude that the Japanese government showed no eagerness to find a way to align itself with the democratic nations.[14]

The same day of his conversation with Arita, Grew went aboard the *Empress of Japan* to sail for home on his first leave in three strenuous years. His feelings as the ship slipped away from the dock are easy to imagine. He planned a leisurely three-week trip by way of Vancouver. At Ottawa he would visit a week with his daughter Anita and her husband Robert English, who was stationed at the Embassy. He would have time to sort out the tangled issues and events of the past months and see what position his government should take.[15]

He could find little satisfaction in recent Japanese treatment of American rights and interests in China. Repeatedly that spring his hopes had risen with seeming improvement in Japanese conduct, only to be dashed by further depredations. In February, Japanese encouraged the belief that restrictions on Yangtze navigation would soon be relaxed but evidence in April pointed to establishment of a Japanese inland shipping monopoly and the river remained closed. In March the Japanese Army courteously handed back the American University at Soochow while systematically looting Tsinghau University at Peking, which was supported by American Boxer indemnity funds. In March the harbor at Tsingtao was reopened and in May the one at Foochow was closed. On April 15 the Japanese declared a willingness to indemnify the parents of the little American girl killed in a bombing raid the previous year and two weeks later the mission where she was killed was bombed again. The frequency of bombing incidents suggested a deliberate attempt to destroy foreign institutions in China. Exchange control and trade restriction were more comprehensive than before. Japanese were elbowing into the administration of foreign concessions at Amoy, Shanghai, and Tientsin. All in all, the New Order was making rapid progress in 1939.[16]

Of equal concern was Japanese acquisition of footholds for expansion in the South China Sea. So long as they did not lay hold of bases south of Formosa, Grew had been willing to go along with the idea that the much-touted "Southward Advance" involved only peaceful economic expansion. Events of early 1939 challenged that assumption. On February 10 the Japanese attacked the Chinese island of Hainan in the Gulf of Tonkin. On March 31 they blanketed within their jurisdiction an ocean area approximately one hundred thousand square miles in size, including the Spratley Islands and untold coral reefs, stretching westward from Palawan in the Philippines to the main shipping lanes rounding the Indo-Chinese peninsula. The Foreign Ministry hastened to explain that the seizure of Hainan was part of the conflict in China and that the annexation of the Spratleys was an economic venture based on valid claims. But with Hainan and possibly next the Paracels guarding the right flank and the vast uncharted area of the Spratleys the left flank, the Japanese were in a position to penetrate deeply into the China Sea with its rich rim of British, French, and Dutch colonies, and endanger the Philippines.[17]

The situation as Grew saw it also wore a more hopeful aspect. Change had taken place internally: the monolithic appearance of Japanese government, which had impressed him so forcefully in 1938, faded away during the long and bitter struggle over the Axis alliance. The desire for peace in China was "increasingly intense." In place of consensus and control he found dissension and indecision. The Army might make its will conclusive on China questions but not on relations with Europe. Surprisingly powerful elements had prevented a total commitment to the Axis and were making "genuine efforts" to improve relations with the United States. Once again moderates weighed in the political balance after being totally absent from his calculations since 1937. The new moderates included business and court acquaintances of old, some of whom now became socially available again. Among them Dooman was careful to distinguish between "congenial, but withal ineffectual" persons of Western orientation and education like Count Kabayama and those like Baron Harada who were closely associated with policy-makers.[18] Now they also included Admiral Yonai, who, speaking for the Navy, added an element of substantive power to the forces of moderation. Astonishingly enough they also appeared to include the reactionary, nationalist Prime Minister, Baron Hiranuma.

The Prime Minister was using Grew's home leave to make a private approach to President Roosevelt. Through Arita he gave Grew a short, suggestive written message to deliver personally to Hull for the attention of the President. Then, after Grew sailed, and without informing Arita, Hiranuma invited Dooman to dine with him alone at home. In an extraordinary three-hour conversation conducted in Japanese the usually taciturn Prime Minister explained his purpose in sending the message and formulated it more precisely.[19]

Simply stated his argument was that the United States and Japan, as powers outside the European circle, had a duty to prevent imminent and catastrophic war in Europe. He explained that Japan was neither democratic nor totalitarian and would ally itself neither with unstable one-man governments like Hitler's nor with thankless partners such as Britain had proved to be during the Anglo-Japanese Alliance. In his view the root of European as well as Far Eastern tensions and the basis for existing sympathy between Japan, Germany, and Italy was the unequal distribution of the world's economic resources. The Occidental powers had denied Japan access to their resources and markets and stiffened Chinese efforts to prejudice Japan's vital economic interests in China. He believed that an improvement in the strategic economic position of the have-not nations might prevent war in Europe as well as enable Japan to ease its terms for peace with China. A solution might be achieved through a world conference where all nations could find "their own proper places." Significantly, Hiranuma was prepared to include the Far Eastern situation among the problems to be discussed. He suggested that the United States sound out Britain and France toward that end and Japan sound out Germany and Italy. If responses were encouraging and if conditions could be agreed upon through normal diplomatic channels, he would be glad to have President Roosevelt call such a conference.

To Dooman the Hiranuma proposal, whatever its merits, was symptomatic of Japan's "groping for security against the gathering storm in Europe." In opposition to Axis enthusiasts the moderates argued that the United States was sure to intervene in a European war and its intervention was sure to defeat the Axis. With the democracies united and triumphant in Europe the outcome for Japan in China was predictable. Therefore, their argument ran, Japan's only security lay in establishing friendly relations with the democracies now by terminating the conflict in China. Dooman believed that the neutral position to which Grew had just predicted Japan would adhere was not a realistic alternative after all. Japan would have to choose either the democratic or totalitarian camp. The choice was not yet made but the moderate forces, if not controlling, were powerful and should not be ignored.[20]

Peace in China was the nub of the problem for both Grew and Dooman. The Far Eastern conflict in isolation had imposed a serious though not intolerable strain on Japanese-American relations, but interacting with the European crisis it raised two grave possibilities, a Southward Advance and a Triple Alliance. To keep Japan on the side of the democracies was the most important objective, and to do so the United States would have to contribute somehow to a solution of Japan's China problem. This line of reasoning led them back to the original conundrum, finding peace terms which would satisfy Japan's requirements, leave enough of China, and take into account the rights, interests, and principles of the United States.

Grew had gained an inkling of what the Japanese would insist on. Arita had said that Japan must retain control of the resources of North China and had spoken of exchange control being permanent there, not elsewhere. However much Grew deplored Japanese methods, he felt that "when they talk about the strategic necessity of controlling the raw materials of North China and of protecting Japan against Soviet Russia and Communism, then they are talking sense which anyone can understand." He had heard these arguments for years and found them by no means repugnant. As he saw the problem now, the United States might have to go further than acquiescence and formally accept Japanese control of Manchuria, Inner Mongolia, and North China in order to bring peace in the Far East.[21]

He wondered if such acceptance was really impossible. The weight of historical tradition was not entirely against it. Reading A. Whitney Griswold's newly published *Far Eastern Policy of the United States,* he noted that John Hay had come to accept Manchuria as not being an integral part of the Chinese Empire and that Theodore Roosevelt had stressed its vital importance to Japan. Explicit American commitment to the territorial and administrative integrity of China dated only from the Nine-Power Treaty. The Japanese had unquestionably violated that treaty but, even so, they had a case. As John MacMurray had pointed out in a memorandum of 1935, which Grew saw in 1937, and as he himself had witnessed during the Taku Incident of 1926, the powers had abandoned the cooperative approach to China problems. They had left Japan to defend its rights with its "own strong arm." The past, it seemed to Grew, was tangled and obscure, and should at least not impose an inflexible course on future action.[22]

He asked himself whether the United States should continue permanently to support the integrity of China "in the face of hard realism."

> And what will be the result in the long run if we do? Would we do so if by compromise we could eventually help to bring about peace? And if by refusing to do so, the war would be indefinitely prolonged? [23]

It is clear that Grew, though not willing explicitly to advocate what in the temper of the time might be regarded as a Far Eastern Munich, was turning his attention more and more to a compromise solution of the China conflict.

He had come some distance from the purely negative attitude of 1938. He did not return home committed to any particular solution or bearing any concrete, official proposal from the Japanese government. Craigie described him as leaving Tokyo more than ever averse to the exercise of pressure against Japan, feeling "that America's most useful role is to use her present stock of influence to prevent any further deterioration in the relations of the democracies with Japan." [24] The difference was one of outlook. Once more there was an opening for the uses of diplomacy: the world crisis provided the necessity and the reactivation of the moderates provided the possibility. He would find out how the chances were at home.

He found that his countrymen did not share his mood. American feeling was rising against Japan as fresh indignities occurred in China. The day Grew called at the White House, June 13, the Japanese blockaded the British and French concessions at Tientsin, erecting a live-wire fence, halting deliveries of milk, and stripping and searching British men and women at the barrier. All foreign concessions in China seemed in jeopardy. On July 6 and 7 the Japanese bombed Chungking, narrowly missing the American gunboat *Tutuila* and the residences of Ambassador Johnson and his Counselor. For a spell the Far East displaced the European crisis as front-page news. Gallup reported that two-thirds of those polled, twice as many as in 1937, favored a boycott of Japanese goods and three out of four an arms embargo against Japan.[25]

The Administration was glacially averse to conciliating Japan. Overriding other considerations was its concern for principle. The chief hope of a return to sanity in world relations, one official argued that year, lay in the commitment of American foreign policy to fundamental principles of orderly procedure in international intercourse. "Surrender or compromise in any given case would act merely as the breaking of a link in a chain which must depend for its strength as a whole upon the strength of its individual parts." [26] The chain stretched back to the Stimson Doctrine and beyond. The United States must not seem to condone aggression or weaken a solemn covenant respecting the territorial and administrative integrity of China. Maintenance of an unimpaired standard for permanent world peace outweighed any short-run gain in manipulating power relations to the advantage of the United States.

Practical considerations weighed as well. Department officials were inclined to discount the importance of the alliance question. The Axis had little to offer that Japan did not already enjoy without the added strain an alliance would impose on relations with America. American mediation of the Sino-Japanese conflict was out of the question. Even if terms acceptable to both governments could be found, an improbable event, and even if they were lived up to by Japanese, an equally improbable event, American mediation would incur the displeasure of both the Chinese and Japanese peoples. Better to let the Japanese Army mire itself deeper in China and lose face. Hornbeck argued that any peace short of total defeat of Japanese aims in China would be temporary, while Joseph Ballantine, Assistant Chief of the Far Eastern Division, allowed that substantial modification might be sufficient. In any case the initiative for conversations must come from the Japanese and be accompanied by concrete demonstration of a change of heart.[27]

The Hiranuma proposition aroused nothing but suspicion. The message Grew delivered was unsigned, unheaded, undated, and apparently unsecret since talk of Japanese-American cooperation for a *détente* in Europe was making the rounds of embassies in Tokyo. Hiranuma's conversation with Dooman being personal and unofficial, the formal initiative would be taken by the United States, leaving Japan in an advantageous bargaining position. Officials could hardly have ignored the fact that such a conference would directly conflict with Administration attempts to repeal the arms embargo as a warning to Germany. A Roosevelt peace move to the democracies alone could not but weaken their will to resist Hitler and so play into the hands of the Axis. Even if taken seriously, a conference of have and have-not powers was bound to result in concessions by the former and what the Administration might conceivably concede in the way of immigration and tariff revision, Congress was not likely to approve.[28]

As usual American aversion to compromise and condonation was accompanied by determination not to provoke Japan. Policy still ran within narrow limits. Military unreadiness and the strategic priority of Europe dictated caution. Congress needed reassurance that the President would not lead the country into foreign entanglements. In July efforts for repeal of the arms embargo collapsed. Without means to deal effectively with the European crisis, Roosevelt and Hull were loath to bring problems with Japan to a head. One after another, positive steps in the Far East were taken up and rejected. The answer to Hiranuma — a negative one — was delayed as long as possible. Hull hoped at least to present another broad-bottom protest, but Grew, from his vacation retreat in New Hampshire, finally dissuaded him, using the familiar arguments that the American position had already been made clear and that another note would only provoke irritation and retaliation. Preventing hostile moves was easier than encouraging friendly ones.[29]

The Administration believed that somehow it must give expression to American indignation over China, if only to prevent Congress from doing so by taking up an arms embargo against Japan. Denying arms to aggressors was more popular with Congress than supplying their victims. Officials feared that passage of such a resolution would be dangerously provocative and its defeat would be interpreted as a sign of weakness. On July 26 the government moved to prevent this dilemma, as well as to stiffen the British who were compromising over Tientsin, encourage the Chinese, clear the way for economic retaliation, and warn Japan clearly but circumspectly. The Japanese were handed the required six months' notice for termination of the Treaty of Commerce of 1911, the legal basis for Japanese-American trade relations. Unless relations substantially improved by January 26, 1940, in accordance with explicitly stated principles, one of the last formal ties would be cut. Japan was invited to consider the capacity of a brooding United States to inflict mortal injury simply by refusing to trade.[30]

The mood of Americans came as a distinct shock to Grew. Uninterruptedly for three years his mind had been working within a medium of ideas, assumptions, and feelings peculiar to Tokyo and he had lost any vivid sense of the climate of opinion at home. Now he was struck by the "steadily hardening" attitude toward Japan not only of his Social Register friends but also of Americans from many walks of life with whom he made a point of chatting — shop clerks, gas station attendants, taxi drivers, and

Pullman passengers. The Administration had strong support in its determination not to be squeezed out of China and in giving notice on the 1911 Treaty. He heard very little of "folding our tents and withdrawing gracefully." On the contrary, the President spoke to him confidently of intercepting the Japanese fleet if it moved southward, of reinforcing Manila and Pearl Harbor, and of holding naval maneuvers in Hawaiian waters. More likely to come from Washington than any "gesture of welcome" was an embargo. The question was not how to improve relations but how to prevent a downward spiral of retaliation and counterretaliation, and the burden of action rested with the Japanese. Some concrete improvement in their treatment of American rights and interests in China must come quickly.[31]

He must switch tactics. Changing the attitude of his own government was impossible. Rather, he would have to change that of the Japanese government, and not with friendly but with hard words. He could not rely on the goodwill of the moderates and had to risk provoking the military. He must administer a stiff shock to Japanese ways of thinking about American policy. He needed to convince them beyond possibility of misapprehension that the United States would not back down and to overcome their dangerous assumption that the American attitude was based only on traditional sympathy for China and "obsolete legal technicalities." Another note would not alter the Diet, but perhaps a candid speech would. The customary welcoming luncheon of the America-Japan Society would provide an influential forum, practically the only one available, and one which Viscount Ishii himself had used for blunt words in 1932. Grew suggested the idea on July 30, four days after notice was given on the 1911 Treaty, and Roosevelt and Hull approved. Officials in the Department drafted a strong, specific indictment which Grew took along to polish on the trip back to Japan.

Hitler invaded Poland September 1. A quarter-century earlier watching nations march to war had been a spine-tingling experience. Now Grew only felt a flattening of spirit. War seemed the chronic disease of civilization. He sailed from San Francisco September 26 and after a glassy-calm crossing took up his mission again October 10. It was a tenuous one now and he had taken the precaution of putting all but his recent diaries into safe storage at Washington.

Grew found Tokyo aghast at the events of the past summer. The notice of treaty abrogation raised the threat of an American embargo. The Nazi-Soviet Pact of August 23, 1939, was a shocking and mortifying alignment of would-be friend and old-time foe. The Japanese responded by suspending Axis negotiations and replacing Hiranuma with retired General Abe Nobuyuki, whose virtue was the lack of any identifiable sympathies and convictions. The previous spring Grew, underestimating the Hiranuma Cabinet's inclination toward the Axis, had described Japan's position as middle-of-the-road. Now that description was entirely accurate. The government was determined to involve itself with neither side in the European conflict and to concentrate on settling the China conflict. The eclipse of army influence in foreign affairs and its concern at possibly being shut off from vital American raw materials gave hope to the moderates for concrete improvement in relations with the United States. This hope was encouraged by the appointment as Foreign Minister of Nomura Kichisaburo, a retired admiral known for his warm feeling toward America and his acquaintanceship with Franklin Roosevelt in Washington during World War I. The Department of State, again preoccupied with neutrality revision, seemed content to let the new trend develop, advising Grew that his primary concern should be "the preservation and strengthening of your wholesome influence with the Japanese Government." Under the circumstances, Grew felt it wise not to be too severe.[32]

He decided to take some of the sting out of his forthcoming America-Japan Society speech. Other avenues were open to present the American viewpoint now: Nomura was sympathetic and Grew's Japanese friends were urging him to talk to General Abe and Prince Konoe. Such informal approaches might accomplish the same purpose without going over the heads of a cabinet already embarrassed with dissident factions in the Army and Foreign Ministry. Furthermore, enunciation of lofty principles about orderly processes seemed like "hurling Jovian thunderbolts from our own comfortable seat" at a people "already up to their necks in war." His staff and Count Kabayama helped whittle down the speech. He excised a major portion consisting of a detailed, point-by-point indictment of Japanese violations of American rights and interests, including bombings, indignities, trade restrictions, and interference with treaty rights, and enumerating American protests made and unanswered. The speech remained an unusually strong one for a diplomat to deliver in the country to which he was accredited, but not nearly as sharp as he had originally intended.[33]

Grew gave his speech before the America-Japan Society on October 19. The audience of two hundred was composed equally of Americans and Japanese. The latter, whose reactions were being scrutinized by Embassy officials, represented Western-oriented business, court, and diplomatic circles. Grew began softly with a graceful compliment to Prince Tokugawa, the ailing president of the Society, and an expression of pleasure at returning "home" to Japan. He sketched a vignette of himself in New Hampshire that Japanese would particularly appreciate, the patriarch surrounded by daughters, sons-in-law, and grandchildren. He praised the Japanese pavilions at the New York World's Fair and the Golden Gate Exposition and referred to Pacific shores feeling the lift of the same tides of friendship. So far, a familiar speech done with finesse.[34]

An ambassador, he went on, "is essentially an interpreter, an interpreter of official and public opinion as they exist in his own country and in the country of his residence." He had tried to make the Japanese picture clear to his countrymen, "with its many sides and many angles," and now he would take advantage of his travels among Americans to describe their attitudes toward Japan. American opinion on the Far East, he explained, was well informed, intelligent, and nearly unanimous. It was a force to be reckoned with. As a friend of Japan and of the members of this Society he must not misstate or obscure it, but present it candidly, "straight from the horse's mouth." The audience listened intently.

It was a fact, he said, that Americans strongly resented Japanese actions in China, and not simply on account of a legalistic view of world affairs, "where one cannot see the woods for the trees." They were motivated by the profound conviction that peace as an interlude between wars was not an environment where civilization could develop or even persist. Peace with them was not a halfway proposition. It meant not merely abstaining from use of force but from any thought of use of force. They believed that the delicate balance of a highly integrated world economy made conflict or the closed door anywhere the concern of all peoples. Was it being "legalistic" then for Americans to practice orderly procedures and urge them on others, "to put to wise and practical use the finer instincts of mankind?" Japanese must disabuse themselves of any such "utterly fallacious conceptions of the American attitude."

Americans knew only too well what was occurring in China. Grew described their anxiety for cherished hopes of an orderly world, their profound shock at indiscriminate bombings, their anger at the menace and indignities to fellow citizens, their rising concern at the destruction and damage to American property and manifold interferences with American rights and interests. The New Order struck them as leaving the Open Door principle "truncated and emasculated" and imposing a closed economy for Japan's benefit over large parts of the continent of Asia. And all these injuries suffered by their nation appeared "*wholly needless*" [35] for the attainment of real security and stability in the Far East.

He stated his thesis carefully: American policy was governed by opinion that was responsive to a concrete situation in China; only if the Japanese considered the facts of that situation and took steps to alter them could Japanese-American relations improve; those relations must improve. He had to plant the idea that unless relations improved they would seriously deteriorate, yet do so without suggestion of an ultimatum or threat. Summoning his skill and experience, he raised the possibility of American economic retaliation by stating the "universal applicability" of his thoughts about the closed door in China. He pointed out the difficulty of any nation avoiding involvement in modern war, the implication being that Japan should not bank on American isolationism. In addition to stating premises and inviting conclusions he conveyed his warning by modulating his delivery. He closed with a plea for stability in a relationship which "*if it can be preserved* [speaking with emphasis], can bring only good to Japan and to the United States of America."

To analyze Grew's argument thus is to risk misunderstanding the impression his speech undoubtedly made on the Japanese present. He realized that to reach them he had to overcome an emotional barrier, a defensiveness to foreign and especially American criticism which would prevent consideration or even cognizance of his argument. He sought to overcome this with courtesy elaborate even for himself but attuned to Japanese sensibilities. He would say, "Forgive me if I very respectfully take issue. . . ." He would interlace hard words with smooth ones and phrase assertions as questions. Again and again he pleaded for, and sought to demonstrate, his own intense commitment to "pure objectivity." Above all he presented himself as a sorrowful though not despairing friend of Japan, working "with all my mind, with all my heart and with all my strength for Japanese-American friendship." In a moving way he tried to convince them that this "precious" relationship was worth preserving. He said he was animated.

> by very deep affection for Japan and by sincere conviction that the real, the fundamental and abiding interests of both countries, call for harmony of thought and action in our relationships. Those who know my sentiments for Japan, developed in happy contacts during the seven years in which I have lived here among you, will realize, I am sure, that my words and my actions are those of a true friend.

The Japanese understood. The unfailing courtesy, the constant faith and goodwill, the proven integrity and sincerity of this man made them willing to accept as fact from him what, in the opinion of one observer,[36] they would accept from no other ambassador. The entire audience, Japanese and American, applauded wholeheartedly.

The American press was nearly unanimous in approval. Home offices of Tokyo correspondents cabled urgently for more details. The *New York Times* carried the story on page one for several days and called the speech "one of the bluntest . . . made by any ambassador in Japan in recent years," raising the superlative next day to "one of the strongest ever made by a diplomat in Japan." Seventy-eight editorials gathered by the Department approved, eight approved with reservations, and only three disapproved. The speech was variously described as "an earful," "a slow-motion thunderbolt," "good, if bitter, medicine," and "bare-knuckle diplomacy." The Japanese were understood to be "dumbfounded," "astounded," "jarred," "rocked." A *Washington Star* cartoon showed Grew shaking his finger at a sinister Japanese soldier with Uncle Sam looking on approvingly.

Actually the "Straight from the Horse's Mouth" Speech, as it was becoming known, had not been exactly straight from the horse's mouth. It seemed so because newspapers emphasized Grew's description of American opinion and translated his hints into plainer language. Nevertheless, if the press was any indication, he had obviously captured better than any official statement how Americans really felt about Japan.[37]

Washington could hardly object. Concern had been expressed by some Far Eastern officials that Grew was missing his chance by whittling down the speech. There should be "no repeat no glossing over" American concerns. In the end the Department had decided to abide by Grew's conclusions. Afterwards the President wrote Grew that he liked the speech and that Hull and he agreed it had been done in the right way at the right time, words reminiscent of those Grew himself had used to describe the representations of Ambassador Gerard at Charleville in 1916.[38]

Grew was in no hurry to carry his message into the streets of Tokyo. He was probably reluctant to risk public controversy until he could judge the reaction of his luncheon audience. Though he released the text of the speech to the American wire services immediately, he withheld it from the local press. He explained that he did so out of courtesy to the government, in order not to seem to go over their heads to the people. He told the Department that "in any case it is shortly to be published in pamphlet form for the members of the America-Japan Society." When he did release the text two days later at the request of the Foreign Ministry the reaction was as anticipated, "keen resentment" mixed with a few encouraging intimations that the American point of view might have merit. More noteworthy, however, was the reaction of the Western-oriented moderates who heard him speak and who might be relied on to pass his message to those in power.[39]

According to informants the speech made a profound impression in these quarters. "Epoch-making," "most courageous," and "splendid" were the comments he heard. The Palace sent for a copy and the Emperor's close advisers as well as the Prime Minister and Foreign Minister were reported to be studying the text in detail. Above all, the Army and Navy were reported impressed. Kabayama said that the War Minister, General Hata Shunroku, and the head of the China Affairs Board, General Yanagawa Heisuke, would cooperate to eliminate specific grievances. However, the Count warned against hoping for immediate settlement of fundamental differences. What could be looked for were steps to remove the emotional tension in Japanese-American relations and clear the atmosphere for discussion of basic issues. The Foreign Ministry was publicly cool to the speech, but Admiral Nomura privately let it be known that he would welcome seeing Grew and would listen sympathetically to whatever the Ambassador might have to say. The inoculation seemed to be "taking." Conditions were right for a direct approach.[40]

The first Grew-Nomura conversation, which took place November 4, 1939, represented the culmination of Grew's efforts to convince the Japanese of the necessity for positive steps on their part to improve relations. He was proceeding on his own initiative and responsiblity without specific instructions from Washington. The significance of the conversation lay not in what he said, for he was repeating what he had said in his speech and in private discussions, but in his saying it to the Foreign Minister, and saying it comprehensively and very plainly.[41]

He began by presenting three unofficial documents. The first was a compilation of all the Embassy's written representations since the China conflict began. It showed that of 382 protests, 256 had not been acknowledged. Of the remainder, many of the replies were unsatisfactory. The second document was a collection of twenty-five statements made to Grew since July 1937, by Japanese Foreign Ministers and Vice-Ministers giving explicit assurances that American rights and interests in China would be respected. The third consisted of unused portions of the recent speech, which had been excised, he explained, in order not to embarrass His Excellency. They showed in a concrete way the difficulties existing between the two countries. Grew asked the Minister to be good enough to read all these documents.

Grew then stated as "objective facts" and "with no other implication" that the coming months might be "critical" in Japanese-American relations and that a "strong demand" existed in the United States for an embargo after the treaty expired. He most earnestly hoped that Japan would take steps promptly which would relieve that pressure. Two which came to mind were, first, cessation of flagrant abuses such as bombing and indignities and, second, advance on the broader issues by reopening of the Yangtze, for example. Grew must have recognized that dropping the barrier on that great avenue to the interior, as had already been suggested in the press, would be dramatic proof of intention to improve relations.[42] These were beginnings only, but they might build confidence for negotiation of fundamental differences.

The Japanese were slow to begin. The Abe government attacked protection problems with relative vigor: bombings and indignities ceased, investigations began, reports piled up, solatiums were paid, properties were evacuated, old protests were answered by the half-dozen. However, an answered note was not a case concluded nor was a sum offered a sum sufficient. Responsibility was hard to define and harder to accept and most replies were unsatisfactory. Less outrageous harassment of Americans continued and at Tientsin increased. Positive steps were not forthcoming at the second Grew-

Nomura conversation December 4. It was difficult for the Japanese to clarify third-power rights on the Yangtze until the Wang Ching-wei regime was established at Nanking, and impossible to set up this semi-autonomous regime until they agreed among themselves and with Wang on its powers. Time was running out on the Japanese-American treaty.[43]

Meanwhile, the United States was displaying a tough and uncompromising mood. With Nomura's assent Grew gave American correspondents an exclusive and detailed account of his November 4 presentation, apparently in the expectation that American press coverage would again reinforce his words. More than underscored, his careful warning of American retaliation was exaggerated into the page-wide headline GREW THREATENS ECONOMIC PRESSURE ON JAPAN in next day's *New York Times,* which described his representations as the strongest action taken by any power to protect its interests in China since the conflict began. Of course Grew immediately denied any such threats, but the impression of American intransigence prevailed. Coincidentally Congress took the first step away from isolationism by repealing the arms embargo, Senator Key Pittman, Chairman of the Foreign Relations Committee, called for an embargo against Japan, and the Navy requested over a billion dollars for new carriers, cruisers, and destroyers.[44]

The State Department was losing no opportuntiy to comment on the insufficiency of Japanese efforts to improve conditions in China. It deplored Japanese publicity to the effect that protection cases were rapidly being settled and pointed out that cases so far adjusted only involved "surface sources of friction" and "little more than touched the fringe of the problem." Under Secretary Welles told the press that Japan was, if anything, adding to frictions. The Department made plain its opposition to the forthcoming Wang Ching-wei regime. Further "Manchukuoizing" of China would "render more difficult rather than . . . facilitate an adjustment of Japanese-American relations." Outstanding difficulties were conceived to be "integral parts of a single larger problem," that of interference with American rights and interests in China. Adjustment of the Yangtze navigation problem, for example, could scarcely be effected without "involving in a fundamental fashion 'basic principles.'" The United States was meeting Japan's halting steps by pointing to the long road of purgatory ahead.[45]

The obstacles in Japanese-American relations might have been less cause for concern had Japan been left with no alternative to improvement of relations with the United States, but in 1939 nations as a rule kept several irons in the fire. Japan's current alternative was a *rapprochement* with the Soviet Union, improbable as that seemed. The two nations were chasms apart and the Soviets were most unlikely to meet Japanese insistence that they stop helping China when Japan's debilitating involvement there was

Russia's prime guarantee of Far Eastern security. Much of the speculation on a tie-up from Japanese, British, French, and Polish sources was undoubtedly tactical, aiming to pressure the United States into a more conciliatory attitude toward Japan. Nevertheless, Grew's information that a minority in the government was actively promoting a political understanding with the Soviets was accurate. Furthermore, Soviet-Japanese relations were improving, with an armistice at Nomonhan, agreement on a border commission, progress on the perennial fisheries problem, arrival of the first Soviet Ambassador in sixteen months, and opening of negotiations for a commercial treaty. As Nomura said December 4, if commerce with the United States should be impaired, Japan would obviously have to seek other commercial channels. Grew was skeptical of a rumored non-aggression pact but admitted that paradoxes were the order of the day. Even a temporary arrangement would enable Japan to divert military resources to China. Earlier the Embassy had ruled out an accommodation; now he advised Washington it seemed less unlikely.[46]

Grew became increasingly concerned at the lack of progress. On the one hand his own government was insisting on a fundamental reorientation of Japanese policies and actions in China as the price for normal commercial relations, while on the other the Japanese were dickering with their arch foe and failing even to take adequate first steps toward improving conditions in China. The Abe government was "floundering" and "groping," subject to the play of "heterogeneous forces . . . pulling in varying directions." Moderates had been influential in preventing an Axis alliance but lacked the force and leadership "to grasp securely the power of directing policy and taking measures in the effective way which alone can bring about good relations." Yoshida came to say that the Prime Minister was profoundly anxious to conciliate the United States but "did not know what to do." Could America at least meet Japan halfway by opening negotiations for a new treaty? Grew had done what he could on the Japanese side. From the end of November onward, he became increasingly preoccupied with what more his own government might do.[47]

Again he tried to view the situation realistically. Japan was united in its determination to retain permanent control at the very least of Manchuria, Inner Mongolia, and North China. Nothing was more "mathematically certain" than that Japan was not going to respect the territorial and administrative integrity of China, then or in the future. So "inextricably bound up with the fabric of the entire nation" was the Army that to await its discrediting or loss of power through prolongation of the China conflict was to await the millennium. Japan could be thrown out of China only by complete defeat and no American measure short of war was likely to bring this defeat. The thesis that Japan ought to be destroyed was no part of his philosophy.

Grew believed that the United States and Japan were entering the most critical period in the history of their relationship. In his view, two paths lay ahead. Following that of intransigence, the United States would insist on Japan restoring conditions reconcilable with the Nine-Power Treaty, Japan would balk, and a treatyless situation would ensue. Then an embargo would set relations on the downward slope of retaliation and counterretaliation leading toward war. The alternative was conciliation. On November 28 he urged Washington to state precisely what had to be done in China to prove Japan's good intentions so negotiations for a new trade agreement could begin. Then, if Japan fulfilled these minimum conditions, an agreement should be completed and ratification or implementation withheld until further steps were taken. By showing a disposition to negotiate, the United States would encourage Japanese who were working for better relations and deprive extremists of the argument that friendship was impossible. It was not a question of abandoning principle. The United States "should and must respect and honor" its commitments under the Nine-Power Treaty, but at the same time it could work to improve relations with Japan and signify a willingness ultimately to reconsider that treaty by orderly processes.

To the argument that the path of conciliation depended on a spirit of cooperation singularly lacking in Japan, Grew would reply that this quality did in fact exist, though until now under the surface. He was speaking not only of business and court circles but of elements controlling Japanese interests in China as well. He noted that many extremists had been removed from higher posts in the Army. War Minister Hata and General Nishio Toshizō, new commander of the armies in China, were known as "level-headed, moderate-minded" men. Grew gained a clue to their attitude in talks with a businessman who headed major industrial enterprises for the Army in China. He was Aikawa Yoshisuke, whom Grew designated "Mr. X" in cables to protect his go-between's confidential role. Aikawa said in essence that the Army knew it needed American financial help in the reconstruction of China and was prepared to provide trading opportunities to get it.[48]

Grew anticipated no sudden dramatic renunciation of Japanese aims in China. Observance of American rights and interests would continue to be governed by expediency not principle. However, conciliation afforded hope of gradual adjustment of some of the more flagrant causes of American complaint and of protection for American nationals and certain tangible interests. How far the trend might carry he could not say, but the door might be kept partly open in China by keeping open the door in Tokyo.

Finally on December 18 Grew's diplomacy drew a response. In their third conversation Nomura said it was the intention of his government to open the Yangtze for navigation in about two months. He made it clear that he now expected the United States to negotiate a new commercial agreement. Again the broad promise and the barest concrete satisfaction, but the statement was at least the beginning of a beginning and Grew felt his government should follow it up. "Obviously we cannot count upon implementation of today's assurance . . . until that step has actually been taken," he cabled, but an uncompromising refusal to negotiate might cause the fall of the government. It had staked its reputation on the decision, according to Debuchi. In a letter to the President and a major dispatch, Grew earnestly recommended the offer of a *modus vivendi* to cover any treatyless period, an opening of negotiations for a new treaty, and a promise to hold an embargo in abeyance. Ratification and implementation of agreements could be withheld until the Yangtze was in fact opened. He emphasized that the United States was "in a position either to direct American-Japanese relations into a progressively healthy channel or to accelerate their movement straight down hill." It was in the American interest to bring the movement toward conciliation in Japan to full vigor rather than to hinder it. There must be no shadow of rebuff, no talk of embargo. The course of realism, of goodwill, and of "resourceful, imaginative, constructive statesmanship" was to encourage the "patent efforts" of Nomura to meet the American position. The resources of diplomacy had not been exhausted. "By nature not a defeatist," he concluded, "I believe those resources may yet win the day." [49]

The United States chose neither conciliation nor, for the moment, intransigence. At the State Department determination not to compromise principle or assist Japanese expansion was stronger than ever. Japanese cabinets were considered fragile and transitory: what the Abe government promised, the next one might not perform. Officials were skeptical of the Nomura proposition. They learned that Japanese authorities in Shanghai were explaining that after reopening of the Yangtze, navigation would still be subject to certain restrictions. Agreement for conditional use of the river might concede a Japanese right to impose restrictions on third-power trade. In return for the specious and paltry Yangtze concession the United States was expected to negotiate a new commercial agreement guaranteeing nondiscrimination in trade and precluding economic pressure. Bargaining with the Japanese seemed ill-advised enough, and on such terms impossible.[50]

American officials believed that the situation did not require concessions. They were not seriously concerned over the possibility of a Soviet-Japanese *rapprochement*. Conflict of interest in that corner was too great and mistrust too deep. Furthermore, they found distasteful the idea that the United States should conciliate one aggressor in order to prevent its alignment with another, Soviet Russia, which at the moment was attacking its little neighbor Finland. Japan seemed in a weak position. Access to resources in Europe was limited by the war and in the United States threatened by embargo. Ambassador Johnson had reported a string of Japanese military reverses in China leading to the conclusion that "Japan has reached the peak of her military effort and that deterioration has begun." Aggression elsewhere in the Far East seemed unlikely while the China imbroglio continued and the outcome of the European war remained uncertain. Officials saw no reason why the United States should pay any price at all for improved relations with Japan.[51]

Instead Washington chose to continue to keep the Japanese guessing. Instructions to Grew stressed fundamentals. The United States would not commit itself to non-discrimination in trade by negotiating a new treaty so long as Japan in fact discriminated against American trade in China. Non-discrimination applied not simply to exchange of goods but in the broadest sense to American nationals and economic and cultural activities in China. The State Department did not rule out a *modus vivendi* but told Grew that any temporary agreement must leave the United States free to impose trade restrictions. The moral embargo on implements of war used in the indiscriminate bombing of civilians was extended to include materials involved in their manufacture, specifically molybdenum and aluminum, and technical know-how relating to the production of high-octane gasoline. The Department was working on ways "to put the screws on the Japanese," in Hornbeck's words, but preferred to apply only a turn at a time. It did not wish to return a categorical negative to Nomura, Grew was told, or discourage Japanese efforts to improve conditions. He could say that the United States welcomed a continuation of the talks and that after the treaty expired discriminatory duties would not be charged at American ports until further instructions. On this day-to-day basis current trade relations would continue. As Grew observed, Japan was put in the position of guessing whether and when the sword would fall.[52]

Grew revealed the American position to Nomura on December 22. The Foreign Minister was "obviously bitterly disappointed, in fact rather crushed by what I told him." For the first time he did not accompany Grew downstairs afterwards. The failure to improve relations with the United States was one of a number of failures, domestic and foreign, leading to the downfall of the Abe government on January 14, 1940. On January 26, 1940, the American-Japanese Treaty of Commerce expired.[53]

Grew did not give up hope. He expected the influence of the moderates to persist in the new Cabinet. The Prime Minister, Admiral Yonai, had been influential in preventing the Axis alliance and was a man of common sense with a grasp of foreign affairs. Grew believed that "quite a lot" could be accomplished in time if the United States helped rather than hindered the "gradual movement toward conciliation" in Japan. It was encouraging that his government had said it was willing to keep talking and had declined for the moment to use its new freedom to engage in economic warfare. This ability to apply pressure might assist Yonai in taking action to improve treatment of American rights and interests. So long as the American threat did not become a reality Grew believed it worthwhile to continue his efforts for conciliation. "Just now," he wrote January 16, "I seem to be fighting two Governments at once. . . . There are unfortunately fire-eaters on both sides of the fence." [54]

In fact the moment for conciliation had already passed. Late in 1939 Japan, finding itself mired in China and isolated in a perilous world, sought to improve relations with its chief supplier and potential antagonist, the United States. Grew hoped to postpone consideration of the fundamental problem, the Japanese presence in China, and to improve the atmosphere by encouraging material improvement in the treatment of American rights and interests there. Using to the full the prestige he had built in Japan and the skill of thirty-five years in diplomacy, he persuaded the Japanese to take the initiative with a concesssion, a highly qualified one but a beginning. However, theoretical diplomacy proved ill-adapted to the bargaining process. Having given notice of treaty abrogation, the United States could only respond with a commitment to some form of commercial agreement which, it believed, would imply acceptance of Japanese presence in China. Such an implication the United States was determined to avoid. In spite of a superb professional performance Grew failed, and his failure injured Japanese-American relations more than the expiration of the treaty. The Japanese were immensely disappointed. They were still determined to avoid war with the United States, but the conviction settled among them that improvement in relations on current terms was impossible.[55] Early in 1940 the search began for alternative solutions to Japan's predicament and was greatly accelerated in May by the German onslaught in the West. Conditions for improving relations would not be as favorable again.

EIGHTEEN

The Politics of Force, 1940

IN May 1940 Grew turned sixty. His face was less sinewy and his hair was nearly white and thinning on top, but he looked slender and loose-limbed to John Hersey who came to write a story about him for *Life*. He seemed gentle and bright-eyed and on account of deafness had the "Cocked, alert expression of a well-trained setter." His mustache and fierce, black, bushy eyebrows belied what Hersey called an "appeasing personality." Diplomacy, Grew was saying, could be reduced to the simple human term, "I want to like you." His charm, Hersey decided, was a blend of handsome bearing, love of sports and music, showmanship, humility, and aristocracy, all ingredients for which Japanese were "temperamental suckers." The more he criticized them, the better they liked him. Through him they would gladly embrace the United States.[1]

War seemed remote in the Embassy compound. Once an air raid drill left Grew in the dark, reading by flashlight. He worried about security and had an American naval technician tap the walls of his office for hidden microphones. Suspecting even a telephone on the hook, he would smother it with a pillow during secret conversations. Outwardly the gracious and orderly life continued. Fresh flowers abounded. Servants pattered about in their formal black kimonos with white eagle crests. In summer Grew took an early morning dip in the pool down the hill by the Chancery. He worked longer and harder than ever before, frequently around the clock and occasionally from near dawn to midnight. When he had a moment he would roll up his sleeves, discard his tie, clamp a pipe in his teeth, and turn to his Corona portable to bring the diary up to date. Keeping the record was a nuisance, but he had done it so long he hated to quit.[2]

Entertaining was both more and less of a chore. The war in China did away with many diplomatic formalities and world tensions most of the rest. The Diplomatic Corps could not even be gathered in the same room. As Dean, Grew recommended inviting the sheep early and the goats late. The

Soviet Ambassador came early, stayed late, and talked to no one, on the theory, Grew surmised, that he also serves who only stands and waits. It was hard to know who was talking to whom. Grew himself broke with the Soviets during the Finnish war. He devised an aunt, "a skinny old thing," whose death excused him from meeting the Germans formally. Dinners were often tense. He exploded at one ambassadress who criticized the United States for sitting out the war. He laughed in the face of the Spanish Minister who was sizzling over America's failure to recognize the Franco regime. British arrangements were inexcusably slapdash. They showed guests a newsreel that turned out to be a German propaganda film. They put on a film of the capture of Benghazi just after the Germans had recaptured it. Diplomatic entertainment was "hell on the head and double hell on the liver." Going out now was a crisis, a bore, or a joke.[3]

"Work, work, work — all work and no play make Joe a dull man," Grew's daughter scribbled on his desk pad, to which he responded in the diary, "Dear me, I must be getting dreadfully morose." Being "profitably busy" was a great satisfaction: "Every professional man likes an opportunity to function at top speed once in a while." But the cable traffic never lessened, the tension never subsided. Grew was stuck with crisis. "Wow" but he was tired. Once he fainted as he rose from his seat. Karuizawa was almost always too far away. Golf, his only sport now, he pursued relentlessly, push-putting as in croquet and swinging as formlessly as "a Fujiyama mist," according to Hersey. A day on the links left him "sunburnt and physically tired but psychologically rested, and that meant much." Even his once-a-week game was occasionally interrupted or canceled. Furthermore, golf was considered frivolous in wartime Japan and the military took over half of his favorite Asaka course. Recreation brought insufficient replenishment and the climate steady depletion. It was a case of "drink, sweat, drink, sweat" through the muggy summers. "We simply drip all day long." Tokyo winters were "thoroughly dangerous." It seemed that the strong wind stirred dust and spread germs. Cold after cold in February and March 1940 left his "old carcass chock block full of poison." "What a life!" he exclaimed.[4]

As the stage of Grew's diplomacy widened his personal world shrank. One senses the constriction in what is absent from his diary. Missing is the sunny curiosity of this description of types coming through a receiving line in 1935:

> . . . the gushers . . . the nervous youths who slump past with one hand in their pockets, the limp handshakes and the bone-cracking ones, the moist and the dry, and above all the sweet young things with the perfectly lovely smiles and the coy expressions which plainly say, "You and I have a delicious secret together, haven't we?"

Less often come the bits of nonsense such as the 1936 entry about the "intimate — though perfectly respectable — relations" he instantly established with an Austrian beauty at a diplomatic luncheon when, on learning her nationality, he murmured in his best Viennese accent, "*Gemütliches Wien, du Stadt meiner Träume.*" Family joking is rarer. Early in 1937 his wife wrote, describing her first airplane flight, that it gave her a curious feeling but that her companion loved it "because they gave us gum to chew," and he replied that he had played golf and the Swiss Minister loved it "because they gave us nuts to eat afterwards." The diary of the mid-thirties confessed an urge to get up and dance when he heard a tearing "Blue Danube" at a concert, sought to capture the beauty of cherry-blossom time in Tokyo, enthused over new hobbies, but such evidence that the world was fresh and fun dwindled at the decade's end. Life became less experimental and adventurous, more dreary and disciplined. It was like a school, he wrote his daughters in 1941. The cycle was complete: Boston and Groton to Kipling and the world and back again.[5]

Recreation became more of a solitary affair. Lacking the sociable and sporting pursuits of earlier days and missions, he continued to enjoy detective stories and crossword puzzles. The new rage was Double-Crostics, for the solving of which he collected no less than fourteen reference volumes. Dinner and a movie on the roof of the Imperial Hotel was a cool way to spend a summer evening. Films provided a convenient if not entirely satisfying form of escape. Mickey Rooney's "heavy middle-West accent" queered the role of Puck in *Midsummer Night's Dream*, *Gunga Din* was a poor imitation of the Kipling original, and *Mr. Smith Goes to Washington* gave the Japanese the unfortunate impression that Congress was corrupt. Good music over short-wave radio was a solace. Of an evening he would turn out the lights, settle himself in a comfortable chair, and let the sound sink in.[6]

So much had changed. He would savor a wine and be reminded of Rüdesheimer 1897 and the cementing of Danish-American friendship at Copenhagen. Such days and such wines, he mused, would never return. He felt the crimp of age and crisis and watched the erosion of manners and civility. With the spread of war mankind seemed to be reverting to the jungle. It was a different world, passing into the care of a "hard-headed, sometimes hard-boiled, generation." [7]

Yet it was his world too, he insisted. He would not be among those "who sit on the shore and try like King Canute to wave back the tide" of change. Hard as it was to depart from the "pleasant byways of the past," the times required extraordinary political measures and Franklin Roosevelt, in spite of his muddling and juggling, deserved full credit for awareness of the fact. Grew supposed that as a member of the so-called "moneyed aristocracy" he would be called disloyal to his caste, but at least, he added, "I have a glimmer of conception that the day of the Tories is over. . . ." [8]

If not the outlook and position, at least the values of his generation and class carried over. He wrote his daughter about the bringing up of children, in particular his grandson and namesake who was four months old and already put down for Groton. Consideration for others was a primary concern of life, he advised, and "mighty good doctrine to plant while the planting is good, slowly but steadily, in every little issue that arises." "Gentle but firm" was the watchword. The roots of his conviction, thus planted in genteel Victorian Boston, remained as strong as ever. Underlying thought and sentiment, never abstracted, systematized, or contemplated, but forming the core of being, his simple faiths were a staunch anchor in a dark world. They were the "impulse and intuition" on which he said 80 percent of his actions had been taken. They explain his dogged optimism, his determination, as he put it, to see a swan in every goose. Current world chaos represented only a temporary retrogression for the "forces of progress." We had expected too much and neglected the spiritual side of life. But the "all-time curve" of the "collective good of mankind" was upward. This was no time for cynicism, indifference, or despair, he told graduates of the American School of Tokyo. "Let us get down into the arena and take part with all the force and stamina, all the determination and character that we possess." He would find it very hard to continue in any line in which he did not have "the faith that can move mountains." [9]

While all his strength and purpose were devoted to his task in Tokyo, his heart turned increasingly homeward. America seemed better than ever. Current politics were an Elysian field compared to the days of James G. Blaine, whose biography he was reading. The American system and institutions had come safely through the depression. The nation had developed a "hard-headed citizenry, apart from the conservative rich," which kept government from heeling too far toward radicalism or reaction. The radio was improving American taste in music and knowledge of world affairs. News was "drilled, without active effort" into the consciousness of the people, arousing their interest in periodicals and books. At home in the summer of 1939 he found Americans surprisingly enlightened and mature about foreign policy. They seemed less likely to be swept off their feet by incidents like the *Maine*. However, they were not decadent. They had not lost their "unconquerable spirit" to fight for their rights, or their enduring beliefs, or their "abundant and spontaneous charity." He recalled Kingsley's lines from *The Water Babies:*

When all the world is old, lad,
And all the trees are brown;

And all the sport is stale, lad,
And all the wheels run down:
Creep home, and take your place there,
The spent and maimed among:
God grant you find one face there
You loved when all was young.

The wheels had not run down yet, he insisted, and the old place was as warm as ever, warmer even, but that line about creeping home was "poignant." Spiritually he was inward bound.[10]

America reciprocated his affection. Grew was by now probably the best known and best liked Roosevelt ambassador. A. Whitney Griswold ranked him with Benjamin Franklin, Thomas Jefferson, John Quincy Adams, William H. Seward, Hamilton Fish, Charles Evans Hughes, Dwight Morrow, Amory Houghton, Sumner Welles, and Cordell Hull. He was *Fortune*'s "archetypical" American diplomat, a "walking argument" for the superiority of the professional over the amateur. To the *Minneapolis Tribune* and *Philadelphia Inquirer* he was just the right man for the post, to the *Washington Star* one of America's "ace" diplomats. He was on the cover of *Time* and featured in *Life, Christian Science Monitor*, and the *New York Times*. Celebrity collectors sought him out. In Hollywood Cecil B. DeMille showed him *Captains Courageous* in the making and introduced him to Myrna Loy ("We came, we saw — and were utterly conquered.") Paulette Goddard ("scintillating"), and Freddy Bartholomew ("a simple and charming lad"). "Say," said the manicurist at the Copley-Plaza, recognizing him from pictures, "you're doing a swell job in Japan." Most important of all, Harvard offered him an honorary degree in 1941. Heartbroken at being unable to return and accept it, he asked for a postponement.[11]

Grew had established a thoroughly satisfactory rapport with his countrymen. Where he had seemed unrepresentative to the Congressional delegation at Copenhagen in 1921 and to critics of the Foreign Service in 1927, he was now the *Inquirer*'s "sturdy Ambassador." The press was delighted with the forthrightness of his speeches. The *Louisville Courier-Journal* applauded him for discarding the mysterious, subtle ways of diplomacy. The *Denver Post* contrasted his "bluntness and frankness" with the tendency of old-school diplomats to beat about the bush, the Topeka *Capital* his "direct" diplomacy with the circumlocutions of the State Department. All the while Grew was appearing marvelously tactful and subtle to the Japanese. He had projected two contrary images of himself, each of which served his diplomacy and neither of which was entirely out of character for him.[12]

Grew had served his government for thirty-six years, longer than anyone else then in the Foreign Service except for one consul general. He longed for a change of atmosphere and fully intended Japan to be his last assignment, but he could not in good conscience retire yet. The President was "delighted" with his work, writing, "More power to your pen, your voice and your diplomatic personality (whatever that may mean)." Grew in turn, in spite of differences with the State Department, believed that Rooseveltian foreign policy was "wise, sound, and beyond substantial reproach." It was certainly preferable to Republican isolationism.[13] He would stay as long as he was wanted. Furthermore, he felt a professional obligation to remain as long as the patient was sick and there was hope of a cure. Of course success would be a satisfying climax to his career, but more than that, his departure would be taken as a sign of deterioration in relations. His continuance in Tokyo represented the possibility of reconciliation. He was a hostage for peace.

For Grew the possibility of reconciliation never entirely disappeared, but in 1940 his hope was reduced to the barest flicker. Germany's victory in the West and siege of Britain posed serious threats to American security directly across the Atlantic and indirectly by way of the Far East. New and tempting alternatives for the achievement of basic national objectives upset the internal balance of forces in Japan and brought about a new orientation. Grew's conception of the formulation, modes, and implications of Japanese foreign policy, as well as of the necessary response of the United States to the new situation, underwent radical readjustment.

The readjustment was slow and painful. During the last months of the "phony war" Grew continued to believe that conditions were favorable for accommodation. He noted signs of popular disenchantment with the New Order. According to informants, not only methods but fundamental Japanese aims were being called into question. Even certain army leaders were said to recognize that Japan could never achieve economic security by means that incurred the hostility of the great commercial powers. Realization was spreading that peace in China would come not through puppet regimes and exclusive economic practices but by seeking Western cooperation, dealing with Chiang, and offering terms of equality. Here was evidence of a return to sanity and realism. The Embassy discerned "a gradual but unmistakable budding of a more moderate trend and policy in Japan."[14]

Hopes were not matched by deeds and the early months of 1940 were barren of accomplishment. Beyond continuing to urge Washington not to rebuff the encouraging trend in Japan there was little Grew felt he could do. He was alarmed by talk of an embargo in the United States. "Mr. Stimson and his satellites" dangerously underestimated the attendant risk of war. However, the Administration stuck to its policy of giving neither provocation nor concessions. To every Japanese visitor Grew reiterated the necessity for concrete improvement in the treatment of American rights and interests in China, and he believed his words were conveyed to those in power, but without result. The Yangtze offer lapsed, conversations were discontinued, and in April bombings and harassment increased. Anxiety aroused among Japanese by his impending annual leave of absence at least served to put him in touch with Foreign Minister Arita. In spite of Grew's categorical denial, rumors persisted he was actually resigning in despair. He kept the question of leave open and finally Arita accepted an invitation to the Embassy April 26 on grounds of Grew's alleged early departure and begged him to stay. Grew sounded appropriately discouraged about the prospects for constructive work in Tokyo and further talks were arranged for the coming visit of High Commissioner to the Philippines, Francis Sayre.[15]

Sayre came to Tokyo for a social visit and to discuss the problem of Japanese immigration to the Philippines. He also came with information from Dr. J. Leighton Stuart, president of Yenching University at Peking, that Chiang Kai-shek, with whom Stuart had talked, would under certain conditions welcome President Roosevelt's mediation of the Sino-Japanese conflict. Sayre wished to convey this information privately to Arita, and Grew, believing it might stimulate Japanese peace thinking, approved. Sayre had four conversations with Arita between May 1 and 6 which aroused much speculation in the press and diplomatic quarters. According to Harada, whose home was used for a secret meeting, Arita told him that Sayre went so far as to say the President "intended to intervene if Japan would only consent." After consulting the Prime Minister and War Minister, Arita discouraged the idea of mediation but suggested instead that Sayre might work behind the scenes to bring together representatives of Chiang and of the Japanese Army at Hong Kong. However, the State Department, on being advised of the exchange, instructed Sayre and Grew to have nothing to do with indirect or secret approaches between Japanese and Chinese authorities. Washington had "no thought . . . that Sayre should or would embark upon discussions with Japanese officials of any subject of high policy," and was at a loss to understand why he did so. Particularly deplorable was "the development of approach and necessary rejection." Sayre promptly withdrew, leaving the Japanese puzzled by the whole affair. "The Japanese Government complied with Sayre's suggestions," Arita told Harada, "but this time, they [the Americans] were the ones who declined." [16]

The unstated assumption of Grew and probably most people during the "phony war" was that the outcome in Europe would be either deadlock or victory for the democracies. A German victory was not seriously contemplated. The corollary of course was that Far Eastern problems could be worked out separately. Moderate tendencies in Japan could be allowed to ripen and disillusionment with the China venture deepen. "Time, I believe, will play into our hands," Grew wrote April 10, "if we allow nature to take its course unhindered by us." Even as this was written Nazi troops were storming across Norway. At first Grew thought the Germans had made a possibly fatal blunder by carrying the war outside Europe where Britain controlled the seas. The shocking power of the German Army did not become fully apparent until the invasion of France and the Low Countries beginning May 10, just after Sayre's departure. Grew was stunned by the "appalling developments" of May and June. He sickened at the thought of German tanks streaming through familiar, quiet French villages. Words were insufficient to convey his feelings. When Paris fell Mrs. Grew sent a bouquet of red, white, and blue flowers to the French Embassy.[17]

The conquest of Holland and France and the beleaguerment of Britain presented Japan with alluring opportunities for advancing a solution of the China problem, displacing Western influence in East and Southeast Asia, and attaining economic self-sufficiency by forcing open colonial sources of raw materials. Indeed, as Japanese noted with mounting anxiety, unless they joined the Axis soon, they might have no say in Hitler's disposition of Europe's colonies in the Far East. Craigie warned that the Germans, whose prestige in Tokyo had shot up, were doing all in their power to foster the impression of American intransigence, as indeed they were. Grew was profoundly thankful he had not gone home on leave. Had he "left the field to the Germans by default and not even tried to influence the situation," he would have never forgiven himself. In his view the rise of the moderates had been cut short, but the pro-German elements had by no means won out yet. A teetering balance of forces existed such that "a little extra weight in one of the scales is sufficient to swing the issue." More pessimistic but equally concerned, Hull also wished to prevail on the Japanese not to "gallop off on a wild horse." Provided with an opening for conversations by indications that Arita misunderstood the American attitude, Grew began another search for a basis of understanding.[18]

The format of the Grew-Arita conversations, June 10–July 11, 1940, was different from that of the Grew-Nomura conversations. Earlier the Department had left Grew the initiative and contented itself with the role of naysayer. Now the American position was formulated in all detail at Washington. According to Herbert Feis, drafting officers made the circuit of the Department, "taking on clauses at each stop." Over the course of the five conversations a barrage of instructions totaling some five thousand words went out to Tokyo. They were in the form of suggestions with comments invited, but the determination of the Department to maintain sentence-by-sentence control was manifest in the frequent use of phrases like "I desire" and "it is essential" as well as Hornbeck's favorite device of underscoring for emphasis (telegraphically "China repeat China"). Grew's role was essentially that of arranging the presentation of the Department's arguments and acting as agent for the transmission of the voluminous documentation.[19]

The conversations were different too in their concentration on general and long-range problems. The State Department advised Grew to formulate his "whole approach . . . in broad, not in specific, terms." He must convince the Japanese that their choice lay between the way of respect for law, order, justice, free trade, international cooperation, territorial integrity, and national sovereignty and the way of force, interference in internal affairs of other countries, trade restrictions, preferential systems, and economic autarchy. Should Japan join the United States in the path of righteousness, then specific problems could be worked out easily enough and economic benefits would flow from the large credit capacity of the United States and the complementary character of Japanese-American trade. Should Japan incline toward the Axis, however, she should consider the rapidly growing military capacity of the United States. Under no circumstances must the inference be allowed that the United States government or its Ambassador was "leaning toward a procedure of compromise or abandonment." [20]

China problems looked considerably different from the new perspective. With Nomura, Grew had directed attention toward solution of concrete issues involving American lives and property to pave the way for consideration of fundamental problems involving treaties and principles. The State Department had accepted progress on tangibles as the route toward improved relations, though it had not been satisfied with the degree of improvement accomplished or envisaged and had insisted that any progress must be in accord with fundamental principles. Now cessation of bombings, indignities, depredations, and interferences "must precede any positive steps looking toward the restoring of friendly relations," and was *not alone* "capable of opening the way." Japan must also renounce force as an instrument of national policy. The root problem, not only in China but in general, was the "desire on the part of Japan's effective leaders to extend and expand Japan's political authority at the expense of other nations, in disregard of law and of agreements, and by force." [21]

An understanding under such terms was exceedingly unlikely. At the first conversation Arita inquired whether the American government had any "suggestions of a concrete nature." He probed for American interest in providing good offices for a settlement of the China conflict, the subject of the Sayre-Arita talks, and in concluding a commercial *modus vivendi*, the concern of the Grew-Nomura talks. When Grew brushed these aside and escalated the level of discussion to generalities, the Foreign Minister countered with generalities himself. He talked of immigration restriction, colonial preferences, high tariffs, special conditions, special relationships, and special geographic regions. Grounds for American complaint in China could not be removed so long as hostilities continued and not entirely when they ceased. Furthermore, he asserted, the absence of a commercial treaty was in itself an obstacle to the improvement of relations. Grew saw that the talks had become "a mere debating match." "The vicious circle is complete and how to break it is a puzzle which taxes the imagination." [22]

He offered no comment on his instructions and carried them out to the letter. Finally on July 11, in response to a more than routine request for his views and judgment, he replied that the Department's presentation was "irrefutably sound" but that when the Axis was tempting Japan with the golden opportunity presented by events in Europe, talk of principle was not likely by itself to affect Japanese policy. Specific steps were needed, such as he had recommended the previous December. The Department asked what Japan might do to match an American offer to negotiate a *modus vivendi* and new commercial treaty. His reply July 14 indicates his sense of futility. He suggested the type of action the moderates might have taken had they gained firm control of the government: a declaration of willingness to deal with Chiang Kai-shek, a renunciation of the Amō Doctrine, a compatible definition of the New Order. Two days later the Yonai Cabinet, which had been tottering for several weeks, fell.[23]

The American position in the Grew-Arita talks cannot be understood in terms of earlier context, dialogue, or formulas. Out of the confusion and fear produced in Washington by the cataclysmic events of May and June 1940 there emerged a determination to aid Britain with all means short of war and consistent with continental defense requirements. Defense production targets were raised beyond all previous conception, in the case of planes to fifty thousand a year. Now, peace in China, even on the best of terms, would not remove and might in fact increase threats to American security elsewhere. The *status quo* in the entire Far East, particularly in the colonies of Southeast Asia, assumed decisive importance, to assure control of their vital raw materials and to bolster Britain's position. Fearful that Japan might pounce, the President ordered the fleet to remain on Hawaiian station following maneuvers. Otherwise severely limited in concrete measures he might take, Roosevelt emphasized in his Charlottesville speech of June 10 the world-wide stakes, the resolve, and the ideological commitment of the United States. The nation was overwhelmingly convinced, he said, that victory for the "gods of force and hate" would endanger democracy in the Western world and equally that American sympathies lay with "those nations that are giving their life blood in combat against these forces." [24]

The Grew-Arita conversations must be viewed within this developing comprehensive ideological framework. Only thus can the emphasis on values and underlying national roles and objectives and the avoidance of specific cases be understood. Grew's instructions did not rule out agreement and in fact included a proposal for a joint guarantee of the Pacific possessions of European belligerents, but there was no expectation of a comprehensive understanding. The intent was to warn, to exhort, to explain, to make a record, perhaps to delay by parleying. Serious negotiation involving give-and-take bargaining was not envisaged.

Arita no less than Nomura would have welcomed an understanding with the United States that afforded some assurance against an embargo and assisted in settling the China conflict with due provision for Japan's interests. The difference was that Nomura had searched for steps that might begin to satisfy the Americans while Arita took no initiative and pursued an opportunistic course. The Yonai Cabinet applied pressure against Britain and France to remove their China garrisons and seal off Chiang Kai-shek's supply routes through Burma and Indo-China. It took steps toward stabilization of relations with the Soviet Union and closer relations with the Axis and sought economic advantages in the Dutch East Indies and political influence in Thailand. East Asia and the South Seas, said Arita in a radio broadcast June 29, were geographically, historically, racially, and economically destined for unity "under a single sphere." Their future was "a matter of grave concern to Japan in view of her mission and responsibility as the stabilizing force in East Asia." To be sure, he was determined to prevent a military alliance with Germany and to avoid dangerously antagonizing the United States. Contrary to American fears, a descent on the Dutch East Indies was not contemplated. Nevertheless, Grew in his stubborn optimism had carried the strength of the moderates past its day. The balance was already swinging against the democracies, though not fast enough for Yonai's critics. The Japanese, in no mood to concede, hoped for a softening of American policy on account of European concerns, but the Grew-Arita conversations indicated, if anything, a hardening.[25]

The difference between the Yonai Cabinet and its successor, the second Konoe Cabinet, related more to tempo and method than direction. In the summer of 1940 Japanese were seized with the conviction that momentous changes in the world order were occurring and that unless their nation grasped opportunities it would fall by the wayside as a great power. The Yonai government seemed irresolute and supine. The times called for boldness, decision, and action. Only pressure and force succeeded, as Germany had so stunningly demonstrated. It was in this mood that the Konoe government reformulated policy.

Konoe policy developed along three main lines. First, the Cabinet planned more thorough internal restructuring to harness the nation's energies for total war. Second, it decided to hasten the Southward Advance and solution of the China conflict in order to achieve political hegemony and economic invulnerability in the Far East. Third, it determined to play the world power game hard and fast to secure acceptance of, or at least protection for, Japan's Greater East Asia sphere. Decisiveness should not be mistaken for decision, however. Interservice haggling and hedging persisted. Despite grandiose definitions of Japan's new role, the government was uncertain what risks it was ultimately prepared to accept to achieve its ends. It was imperative and sufficient to act now.

Internal reform along totalitarian lines was the first part of Konoe's program that became apparent. His "New Structure" carried beyond the economic planning and control which were at the heart of the national defense state concept. He started a mass movement, directed and subsidized by the government, to promote political harmony in the nation. The American Embassy conceded that dictatorship by an individual or party was foreign to Japanese experience, but pointed out that the Imperial Rule Assistance Association, as it was called, was in fact a monopoly political organization in the pattern of the dictatorships. Service to the state was to be the guiding ethical principle of society and police were already busy "cracking down hard" on dissenters, Grew noted. He commented on the Konoe government's spartan and puritanical regimentation of everyday life. It frowned on "lightheartedness, bright colors, fun, sport, and general gaiety." Golf was for stamina: no caddies, no trophies. That struck home! Foreign Minister Matsuoka Yosuke was "amazingly frank" about the government's intentions. Totalitarianism would unquestionably defeat democracy and rule the world, he told an American correspondent. In Japan, Fascism would develop by the people's will, not concentration camps, he added. From all accounts a powerful trend toward national socialism was under way. In spite of Japanese differences, the new regime had all the earmarks of totalitarianism and the "impelling force" behind it was the same as that behind Nazism and Fascism, namely "the necessity of unifying the total energies of the people to meet the requirements of the occasion." In Grew's mind the ideological identification of Japan with the Axis was substantially complete by early September.[26]

The expansion of Japanese influence and control within the Greater East Asia sphere, the second part of the Konoe program, was well advertised. Grew was entirely correct in assuming, however, that they would move "with some degree of caution and that high pressure diplomacy will probably precede each step." In other words, there would be no sudden surprises. At navy insistence the government had determined to proceed for the time being only so far as not to provoke hostilities with Britain or the United States. An attack on the Dutch East Indies seemed too dangerous and after some Japanese bluster and Dutch stubbornness a period of drawn-out negotiations ensued. French Indo-China was more immediately important and conditions more favorable. Where the United States had expressed a direct economic interest in the East Indies as well as a general concern for the *status quo* and orderly processes, it mentioned only general concerns in regard to Indo-China.[27] The Japanese threatened force and the French, without assurance of support, finally gave way and agreed in principle to grant troop transit rights in Tonkin as well as recognition of Japan's preponderance in the Far East. The Foreign Ministry took nearly six weeks to answer Grew's mild representations and then did so in a sloppy, rude statement penciled in Japanese.[28]

China problems had less dynamite than the Southward Advance but more spark. Beginning with the collapse in Europe, Japanese authorities and agencies sharpened their pressure on the Western position in China. A measure of their new confidence, propaganda hitherto directed against one country at a time now attacked Britain and the United States together. A campaign of intimidation began, with acts of terrorism, arrest of correspondents, press vituperation, street demonstrations, and arrogant protests. Grew feared the "wild men" were at work engineering incidents and magnifying them. In August a dangerous situation arose in Shanghai over the question of policing a vital sector of the International Settlement about to be vacated by British troops called home. The United States government had taken the position that new arrangements should be worked out with Japanese approval, but the American Marine Commander, Colonel De Witt Peck, who believed in maintaining a united front "because we are all Whites here," secured Shanghai Defense Council authority over Japanese objections to send in his own troops and the State Department backed him up. Under instructions Grew informed the Japanese of his government's approval of the plan and its hope that they would accept it at least until final arrangements could be made. The Foreign Ministry not only strongly objected but informed Grew that such a move would be opposed by Japanese forces. The State Department promptly backed away from a showdown, agreeing not to move troops before an understanding had been reached. "Ah," said the Japanese negotiator at Shanghai, patting his tummy with an air of relief.[29]

Negotiation of the Shanghai Defense Sector controversy quickly reached an impasse and became an issue involving fundamentals. The Japanese had the entire advantage. They proposed leaving the situation as it was, neither side replacing the British but the Shanghai Volunteer Corps being left with the responsibility. That way they would have taken one nibble out of the Western position and be set for another. They were not in the least impressed with American arguments. Finally on August 23 Grew was pleased to see the State Department show its teeth. He was to tell the Japanese that, failing an equitable agreement and in view of Japanese insistence on paramountcy in China and cumulative interferences with American rights and interests, the United States might have to reconsider its policy and examine anew the many benefits extended to Japanese nationals and commerce in the United States with a view to making treatment "more nearly reciprocal." The Japanese replied September 4 that they were at a loss to understand why the United States was making "threats" over an issue of such trivial importance. Not "threats," Grew insisted, but a "logical reciprocal adjustment of relations." Then September 12 it was Matsuoka's turn to say that if American forces moved, Japanese forces would also move and "a serious clash which might lead to war would then be inevitable." He took issue with nearly every American point and Grew left with "a reluctant sense of complete frustration." It was now a question of "grave basic principles" and "high policy." In Grew's opinion the time had come to begin the readjustment of relations on a gradual and progressive basis, that is, to turn the screws on Japanese trade.[30]

The Shanghai Defense Sector controversy served to bring Grew's policy prescriptions abreast of his rapidly changing appreciation of the situation. At first he had been cautious about the Konoe Cabinet, forecasting no abrupt, drastic, or irrevocable changes of policy and admitting only that his efforts for conciliation had been "checked." However, the embracing of totalitarian reform, the acceleration of the Southward Advance, and the scaling presumption of Japanese authorities in China were unmistakable evidence of a new trend. The time of teetering had passed. Even his influential Japanese friends, "who used to come to help us appraise the situation have evidently lost hope, because they come no longer." Militarist and extremist elements, intoxicated by German victories, saw their golden opportunity to pursue expansion unhampered by the democracies. Japan was bending its course toward the totalitarian camp. It was a "predatory Power" like Germany, Italy, and Russia, suppressing "all moral and ethical sense . . . frankly and unashamedly opportunist, seeking at every turn to profit by the weakness of others." He believed he had laid at least a foundation for improved relations under Yonai, but now it was gone. A typhoon could not have more effectively swept it away.[31]

When Grew began his mission in 1932 he believed that war between Japan and the United States would be stupid and unnecessary. Now, over three thousand telegrams and nearly five thousand dispatches later, he came at last to accept that it might be necessary and justifiable. He did not reach that conclusion by way of injury to American interests in China; his valuation of them had not changed. He was newly concerned about American territorial and economic interests in the Pacific and American prestige in the Far East, the marrow of the entire American position. "Unless we propose to pull out of the Far East entirely," he commented on the Shanghai question, "we shall have to put our foot down somewhere, and I think this is the time and occasion to do it." [32] His concern for that position, however, stemmed less from its intrinsic importance to the United States than from its importance relative to the security of the British Empire.

All his life, even during the First World War, Grew and his countrymen had taken for granted the existence of the British Empire. That had been a condition of life apart from which one calculated American interests. Perhaps lately there had been uneasiness at British weakening, a wish for more Curzon and less Craigie in British diplomacy. But only with cross-Channel invasion imminent was the value of Britain to the United States fully appreciated. Anglo-Saxon to the core, Grew felt a strong tug of cultural affinity. He saw the English-speaking way of life imperiled. More shattering was the realization that England and the British fleet at the moment provided America's principal defense against Hitler's Europe. The era of free security was over. "Whatever way we look at it," Grew wrote his cousin, "they are fighting our battles." The new logic of security dictated that since the continued existence of Great Britain and the British fleet were vital to the security of the United States and since the British Empire and Commonwealth sustained the home island, then Australia, New Zealand, Singapore, the Malay Barrier, and the Imperial lifelines must be held. The United States would have to protect the *status quo* in the Pacific, Grew decided, even to the point of war with Japan.[33]

He recognized that altered circumstances required altered policy but not that his previous policy had been wrong. Ideological and emotional currents were running strong at home. Articles and editorials sent on by the Department were nearly unanimous in advocating a policy of firmness against Japan and often branding as appeasers those like Walter Lippmann who had been advocating a settlement. Grew was extremely sensitive to the charge and used his diary extensively, though not his official correspondence, for self-justification. He "utterly" dissociated himself from the ugly connotation of the word appeasement, insisting that his recommendations of the previous December had not involved expediency, weakness, defeatism, or surrender of principle. He would always believe, he said, that in the circumstances then applying the offer of a *modus vivendi* and promise to negotiate a treaty might well have "jolted Japan into healthy channels." But, he added with an unaccustomed touch of bitterness, the offer was never made, the incentive never given. His arguments were persuasive, though not new. Their repetition and defensive tone suggest that the patent unpopularity of conciliation in America was a hastening factor, once circumstances began changing, in Grew's reversal of method.[34]

The obvious response was counterpressure. That method had been implicit in American policy since July 1939 and was becoming steadily more explicit. The era of moral embargo ended July 2, 1940, when Congress gave the President export control over all weapons of war and machinery and materials for producing them. Roosevelt promptly swept broad categories of strategic materials under a licensing system and on July 31 prohibited the export of aviation gasoline outside the Western Hemisphere. With the Shanghai controversy the Department seemed on the verge of retaliation, indeed was now left with little choice but to retaliate. The American public was receptive to firmness and the Japanese in their current seizure seemed impressed by nothing else. On September 12, the day of his hopeless conversation with Matsuoka over Shanghai, Grew sent a major policy analysis and recommendation to Washington. Since his previous recommendations, arguing against the use of coercive measures, had been the "red light" kind, he labeled this one his "green light" telegram, and so it became known. He considered it then perhaps the most important message of his mission. It was certainly one of the most important.[35]

The "green light" telegram described the changed circumstances in Japan and the changed interests of the United States. It deliberated over the relative risks and advantages of a "laissez-faire" policy and a strong policy. A strong policy risked countermeasures by the Japanese government or, more likely , some unauthorized, "do or die" stroke by the Army or Navy. The possibility of war attendant inevitably upon firmness must be squarely faced, but the greater risk lay in permitting Japan's encroachment upon vital interests, which would occur "in precise ratio to the strength of her conviction that the American people would not permit . . . [American] power to be used." "Force or the display of force" alone could prevent predatory powers from attaining their objectives. He recommended that the United States deter Japan from altering the *status quo* in the Pacific by the gradual, progressive application of countermeasures. He did not say specifically what these should be, but the implication was clear that he had in mind an embargo program.

On the line between conciliation and force the center of gravity of Grew's diplomacy had been toward conciliation, but force politics was neither strange nor inconsistent to him. In the fall of 1934 the exclusion of American oil interests from Manchuria had prompted him to recommend an oil embargo. "Suppression of contentious issues," he had said then, "should not be carried to a point where important American policies and interests become seriously jeopardized." In the last analysis, he continued in December 1934, Japanese respected the rights of foreigners "only when they are confronted with superior force or the certitude of retaliation." All along he had favored a large navy as ballast for diplomacy. Grew's current reversal was tactical; his object remained the same. He did not contemplate driving Japan out of China because that would probably involve war. "We can tolerate her occupation of China for the time being just as we have tolerated it for the past three years." He did not want to see Japan reduced to a second- or third-rate power. The United States needed a strong Japan. He believed that if the line could be held in the Pacific until and if Britain won in Europe, Japan's current opportunism and arrogance would be impossible to maintain and then the uses of diplomacy could once again be directed toward a comprehensive and equitable adjustment of Far Eastern problems.[36]

The third part of the Konoe program had not been revealed when Grew sent the "green light" message. It involved a bold re-entry of Japan into world power politics to secure acceptance of her Greater East Asia sphere. It was inspired by anxiety not to miss the historic opportunity afforded by revolutionary disturbances in the world order to attain long-term sufficiency and security. It was characterized by acceptance of force as the dominant element in power arrangements, political and military commitments as the main source of leverage, and heightened risk of war the inevitable consequence. The major instrument of that attempt was to be a strengthening of ties with the Axis.

The trend toward the Axis was clear, but Grew did not anticipate an outright alliance. The pattern of the Southward Advance suggested that Prince Konoe, reflecting the attitude of the Emperor and his advisers, was exercising some control over the extremists and moving with caution. Japan would advance in the time, place, and manner it was safe to advance, keeping a watchful eye on the reaction of other powers. No "definitive and irrevocable" commitments to the Axis would be undertaken until the outcome of the Battle of Britain was clear. In the "green light" telegram Grew was more confident, noting a dawning realization that Germany might not defeat Britain after all. Furthermore, the Japanese seemed impressed with the two-ocean navy program, the destroyers-for-bases deal, and rumors of eventual American use of Singapore. It was true that these measures furnished arguments for the expansionists but they also emphasized the potential danger of positive action by the United States and Britain or the United States alone. He believed that, in balance, American firmness would breed caution regarding ties with the Axis.[37]

When the "green light" telegram went off, negotiations were already well advanced in Tokyo for a political and military alliance between Germany, Italy, and Japan. Grew knew the Germans were after an alliance and had no intention of leaving them a clear field. He liked the German Ambassador General Eugen Ott, and as late as January 1940 had enjoyed an informal dinner and music at the German Embassy. But in diplomacy as contrasted with music he accepted that the two were "steadily working against each other." Grew took every occasion to warn the Japanese not to become the tail to Germany's kite. He expatiated on German ambitions in the Far East, the worthlessness of Hitler's promises, and the practical impossibility of effective German support. Reports were encouraging. The Germans were said to be overplaying their hand, irritating the Japanese with their efforts to influence domestic politics and embroil the nation with Britain and the United States. Concern was expressed over the Far Eastern implications of a German victory. Nevertheless, reports of German pressure persisted. By September 19 Grew had to admit that some deal was not impossible. That same day a Liaison Conference approved the alliance. Count Kabayama called and for the first time did not predict the rainbow around the corner. Instead he said, "Something is rotten in the state of Denmark." Even so, Grew thought his friend was referring to domestic difficulties. The following day, according to reliable and, as it proved, accurate information, the Emperor approved the alliance. Grew was still not sure until the Tripartite Pact was signed at Berlin September 27, 1940.[38]

The events of the spring and summer had exhausted Grew's capacity for surprise, but he certainly was chagrined. He was the Harvard man after a Yale victory. What stung more than losing to the Germans was his well-documented forecast that the alliance would not occur. Complaint, rare for him, was an indication of his embarrassment. Surely the Embassies in Berlin and Rome had provided information by which to measure and correct his own, he grumbled, but the Department had not taken him into its confidence "even to an infinitesimal degree." He had been left "shooting from the dark into the dark." As a matter of fact, Berlin and Rome had been even more in the dark than Tokyo. Paucity of information was not Grew's fault. The negotiations had been conducted in the utmost secrecy. Few Japanese dared to come to the Embassy any more on account of police intimidation and friends were scarcer in the Foreign Office on account of Matsuoka's clean sweep of pro-Western diplomats.[39] His mistake lay in forecasting Japanese policy on his own assumptions rather than on those, foolish as they might appear, which guided the new leaders of Japan and made the alliance seem to them both logical and highly advantageous.

Grew would not dream of gambling on a British defeat. On September 6, in the fury of the Battle of Britain, he quoted in his diary the lines of Lord Dunsany:

> *They do well to wait,*
> *Who watch like wolves about the gate,*
> *For to fight England is like fighting Fate.*

The Konoe government, on the contrary, took a British defeat to be imminent and hastened to secure the commitment of the master power of Europe before it disposed of Europe's colonies by itself. The alliance provided German recognition of a broadly defined Japanese Greater East Asia sphere which included the colonies of Holland, France, Britain, and Portugal. Furthermore, it provided solidarity with Germany that the Japanese believed would impress and restrain the Soviet Union, and by way of the Nazi-Soviet Pact it opened an avenue to Moscow for stabilizing relations to the northward so that the China Incident could be closed and the Southward Advance pursued unhampered. Germany might also prove helpful in mediating with Chiang Kai-shek. Such a friend seemed eminently worth having to an isolated Japan in a wildly swinging world.[40]

The Pact also provided for mutual political, economic, and military assistance should one of the signatories be attacked by a power which, according to the specifications, could only be the United States. The thought of abandoning American interests in the Pacific in the face of threat could not have been further from Grew's "green light" mentality. Precisely to the contrary, the Japanese considered the military commitment a logical device for keeping the United States closeted in its own hemisphere, fearful that intervention either in Europe or the Far East might bring war in both directions. Examining the text, Grew could see how preoccupying the United States in the Pacific might assist Germany, but Japan seemed to be only begging trouble by allying with a power which posed the more immediate threat to American security. He suspected a secret understanding limiting Japan's liability in case of war in the Atlantic and he was substantially correct. In order to win the approval of the Navy, which had opposed a military commitment and was sensitive to the risk of war, Matsuoka had fashioned the assistance provisions less explicitly than Germany desired and had secured a letter from the German Ambassador allowing Japan considerable discretion in determining the occasion and means of assistance. The alliance was more a political than a war instrument. The Konoe government reasoned that Japan might reap the advantage of deterrence and still, if her assumptions proved wrong, escape fatal involvement.[41]

In any event, Grew concluded, Japan would now proceed more confidently with the Southward Advance and be more susceptible to Germany's aggressive stimulation. The alliance project seemed terribly risky and therefore irresponsible, and the Konoe government the less respectable. The reasoning of the "green light" message was reinforced. Japan was not only a predatory power but "a member of a team or system" of predatory powers respecting force and force alone. His heart was heavy as he closed the September diary: "This is not the Japan I have known and loved." [42]

The Tripartite Pact had some of its intended effect on the United States. Perhaps it did seem only a surfacing of ripe and evil purpose, but it lent urgency to Secretary Hull's stubborn caution in dealing with Japan's thrusts southward. The problem of the moment was Indo-China, where the French were being forced to concede in fact what they had already conceded in principle, namely Japanese air and army presence in Tonkin. Activists in the Roosevelt Cabinet called for an oil embargo, but Hull, referring to Grew's telegram of September 20 giving first reports of the coming alliance, warned of provoking hostilities. The President chose instead the milder but still hurtful countermeasure of an embargo on iron and steel scrap. Still minimizing risk, the Administration further demonstrated its concern and displeasure by extending another commodity loan to China and calling for the repatriation of Americans in the Orient. Further than that Roosevelt would not go in the final weeks of his third-term campaign.[43]

It was a case of checkmate. German victory had created a yawning power vacuum in Southeast Asia. There the interests of Japan and the United States, hitherto contingent, derivative, or theoretical, became primary. Control of the area or denial of control to the other nation became a vital concern. As one, both nations, steeped in suspicion and jaded about conciliation, were seized with a bristling, fang-bearing instinct to oppose. They began warily by adopting programs of pressure to compel respect for their interests without war and came quickly to an impasse which provided a fragile security in mutual deterrence. Meanwhile Grew's role shrank, but his official and private records richly portray the momentous shift from the uses of diplomacy to the politics of force.

NINETEEN

The Extremities of Peace

BY October 1940 Grew had a number of reasons to suppose his mission was coming to an end. A Republican victory in November would provide an appropriate moment for retirement. If Roosevelt won a third term, one could expect measures against Germany or Japan leading probably to a break in relations, possibly to war. "Taking time and events by the forelock," he emptied his vault, destroyed years of accumulated "junk," and shipped home sixty-seven parcels of correspondence and papers by diplomatic pouch and six cases of bound periodicals by freight. That effort prompted thoughts of retirement. He would take a leisurely cruise to the West Indies and Latin America, then settle in Washington and summer in New Hampshire. He would be hard-boiled about requests to serve as president of this or that charitable organization, but appointment as Overseer of Harvard, if it came his way, he could not refuse. All he needed was a small work room with a multitude of shelves for his papers, his beloved Corona, blocks of paper, a jar of good tobacco, a bottle of better whiskey, and he would be "up and at" his long-delayed diplomatic memoirs.[1]

The more his career edged toward history the more he contemplated it as history. He planned to leave his papers and diary to Harvard where in due time some "enterprising student" could separate the wheat from the chaff. He was more than ever sure that those in a position "to watch the wheels go around from the inside" had a responsibility to keep a full and accurate report of their observations. More than a record was involved, however. He could not resist the temptation figuratively to look over the student's shoulder, pointing to what was important, explaining, amplifying, justifying. He had the keenest sensitivity about his place in history. Perhaps there would be no crowning achievement to his carefully nurtured career and the last chapter would have to be characterized, in the phrase of Sir Nevile Henderson, "Failure of a Mission." He wanted it clear, however, that failure would not be his fault, that he had done all he possibly could and was a victim of uncontrollable circumstances. On September 21, 1940, just after the "green light" telegram, he began an off-hours account of his mission as Dispatch Number 5000, summarizing Embassy activities and correspondence over the eight years and providing "future students" with references to pertinent telegrams and dispatches.[2]

To contemplate the end of his mission was one thing, to quit another. Grew embraced America's emerging internationalism, its moral certitude and its hard-nosed realism. Hitlerism must be eradicated and Japanese militarism discredited. Yes, "Give an aggressor an inch, he takes twenty miles." Since the continued existence of Britain was vital to the United States, it was "perfect rot" to quibble over the destroyers-for-bases deal. Furthermore, it was morally wrong to stand idly by while Britain defended civilization alone. He was pleased to note Walter Lippmann's shift of opinion paralleling his own and deplored the bitter-end isolationism of his old friend Castle. He wanted henceforth to be known as a hard-liner, with Hull, Hornbeck, and Admiral Thomas C. Hart. In step with the developing consensus, he was not ready for declaring war, but he was prepared to risk it, and after Lend-Lease, that "monumental act," he would consider the nation for practical purposes already at war with Germany.[3]

Much as he admired Wendell Willkie, Grew valued the Republican contender chiefly as insurance against isolationism in case of a Roosevelt defeat. He considered the President "precisely the right man in the right place at the right time," with the courage, determination, vision, experience, and prestige to prepare the nation for the hazards ahead. "Thank God for Roosevelt" was his reaction to the great "fireside chat" of December 29, 1940, with its granite-like assurance that the Axis would not win this war. Grew reread the speech until he practically memorized it. In such a time, he wrote, "none of us can pull out from service of some kind." When the President passed word that he was eminently satisfied with Grew's services, the question was decided. He would continue for "another four years — maybe."[4]

Meanwhile, the Greater East Asia sphere was making little if any progress toward reality. The Southward Advance mostly marked time, the Dutch spinning out negotiations at Batavia. The vast menace of a Soviet-Tripartite grouping remained a matter of speculation. Tokyo found Moscow preoccupied with Berlin and Berlin no help in moving Moscow. As a matter of fact, Soviet-German relations were deteriorating and Hitler was turning his thoughts to an attack on Russia. Matsuoka attempted direct dealings with Chungking, failed, and settled for a basic treaty with Wang Ching-wei which made solution of the China Incident even more remote. Soviet aid to China continued, Britain reopened the Burma Road, and the United States granted Chiang Kai-shek a hundred-million-dollar loan, the largest yet. The American fleet remained at Pearl Harbor, trade restrictions increased item by item, always stopping short of oil, and the introduction of Lend-Lease dramatically demonstrated Roosevelt's commitment to Britain. Matsuoka's many-sided diplomatic offensive stalled on all fronts. However, what was in fact a persisting equilibrium did not seem so to one living through the waning months of 1940. To Grew it was a time of mounting uncertainty and danger, the more so on account of the bizarre diplomacy of Foreign Minister Matsuoka Yosuke.[5]

At the beginning of the Konoe government, Matsuoka provided a refreshing contrast to his predecessor Arita. It was a new experience to deal with a Foreign Minister who spoke fairly idiomatic English, who now and then asked him in for "a cup of tea" and private chat, whom he could even telephone directly! The two became quite chummy before the Tripartite Pact and Grew was willing at least to report the soon-discredited rumor that Matsuoka opposed it. Admittedly, Matsuoka set one's head spinning with his interminable, woolly, disjointed discourses. His volubility was exceeded in Grew's experience only by that of Tevfik Rusdu Bey. Nevertheless, a dialogue that was 95 percent Matsuoka and 5 percent Grew was better than none at all. It was also true that Matsuoka could be unpleasant, with his ostentatious shuddering over the prospect of war and his reference to Anglo-Saxon smugness. However, the nastiness was accompanied by an "unstudied naïveté," a constant willingness to amend and retract when offense was taken, and an occasional astonishing admission of Japanese wrongdoing. Matsuoka stressed his desire for peace and Japanese-American cooperation and his determination to improve the treatment of American rights and interests in China. For a start, Grew was prepared to accept him as "patently straightforward and sincere according to his own lights" and give him a chance.[6]

As time went on it became increasingly difficult to place any favorable construction whatsoever on Matsuoka's motives. His comprehensive reply of December 17, 1940, to Grew's representations in behalf of American rights and interests in China bristled with "argumentation by denial and counter allegation," clearly revealing the new spirit of "toughness" and "assertiveness" of the Japanese government. "Not one line" of the eleven-page statement struck Grew as showing a disposition to alleviate conditions. Matsuoka's public blustering, which had seemed perhaps a naïve attempt to influence the American election, continued thereafter and became intolerable in his abrasive America-Japan Society speech of December 19, 1940. "We must think big and act big," he adjured. Grew responded wryly, "Let us say of nations as of men: 'By their fruits ye shall know them.' " By year's end every facet of Matsuoka diplomacy glinted menacingly to Grew. The Greater East Asia sphere would be established "in so far as possible" peacefully and with "least possible" change in the *status quo*. The Tripartite Pact was the "pivot" of Japan's foreign policy and would command her entire loyalty, whatever the fortunes of her allies. The United States might provoke war by sending a powerful squadron to Singapore as well as by entering the European conflict. Matsuoka gave the impression of a nation determined to achieve its objectives at all cost and that was precisely the impression he sought to create.[7]

It was not an impression that entirely suited Grew's information. He had contrary reports of dissension and hesitancy. He took for a fact that Prince Konoe had fought the alliance project (actually he had favored it) and now could scarcely hide his chagrin. He understood the Emperor was unhappy with the Pact, business wholly opposed, and the public unenthusiastic. He noted that the Navy was beginning again to exert its influence for moderation. High naval officers were reported to have persuaded Admiral Nomura to accept the ambassadorship to Washington and were remarkably friendly toward his own Embassy. He also noted general discontent with totalitarian reform and anxiety at the stiff attitude of the United States. Certain Japanese were known to be working for the overthrow of Matsuoka. Dissatisfaction with the position Japan found itself in was "rife" and "may well gather strength." Meanwhile the Southward Advance marked time.[8]

The problem was whether to accept the Matsuoka image of a nation on the warpath or a more complex and shadowy picture involving elements of caution, indecision, dissension, and sensitivity to how other powers acted and reacted. The latter was the more difficult to accept and the closer to reality. Grew was worried about his inconsistency during the past year, in particular his tendency to underrate the forces of expansion. Having already adopted the image of Japan as a predatory power, he was reluctant to abandon it. Also he undoubtedly considered it dangerous not to take a Foreign Minister at his word. Furthermore, deeply committed as he was to the defense of the *status quo*, he may have overreacted to Matsuoka's challenge. In any case, he accepted that the militarists were in full control and the moderates inarticulate and powerless. The pendulum cliché was back in use: he anticipated a further swing toward extremism if Konoe fell, involving a military dictatorship or even "a sort of revival of the shogunate." The image that prevailed in his mind at the beginning of 1941 was the one so ardently fostered by Matsuoka.[9]

"We are getting ready, steadily, for the ultimate showdown," Grew wrote on Armistice Day, 1940. In January and February 1941 that showdown seemed imminent. A petty war had broken out at the strategic center of Southeast Asia, between Thailand and French Indo-China over Mekong River borderlands. On January 18 Japan, deeply attracted by what might be gained through mediation, demanded that the French agree to a truce on pain of Japanese occupation of southern Indo-China. The French submitted and on February 7 Thai-French treaty negotiations began at Tokyo. This intervention with its attendant naval march-pasts in the South China Sea and the Gulf of Siam aroused deep concern in Western quarters. Japan's price for mediation might be, at the least, air and naval bases in southern Indo-China, at most, bases on the western side of the Gulf of Siam, opening the way to Burma, the Indian Ocean, and the investment of Singapore.[10]

For some weeks the American Embassy had been noting straws in the wind pointing southward. Craigie had it that Germans in Tokyo were predicting an attack southward in February to knock out the British Empire in conjunction with a German invasion of England. Then came a report of a Japanese landing force off Singora on the Kra Isthmus near Malaya. The Southward Advance seemed to be gaining mass and speed. Grew assumed that following "conservative strategy" the Japanese would wait until Germany defeated England but felt he had to reckon with the "present headstrong do or die spirit" of the militarists. The outlook had "never been darker," he wrote February 1. In this mood he passed on to Washington the "fantastic" rumor picked up by his Peruvian colleague that the Japanese were planning an all-out surprise attack on Pearl Harbor.[11]

Somehow Japan must be deterred from advancing on Singapore. The "green light" message had answered the question "why" but not "how" and "when." Grew was wary of explicit action recommendations. His views on policy must be reconstructed from stray diary comments and tangential telegrams over the last quarter of 1940 and the first quarter of 1941. He was certainly convinced that words alone were not enough. He had been "cultivating a very warlike psychology" and taking every opportunity to convey American determination and convictions, but Japanese who were impressionable were powerless and those in power had closed minds. "Firm but patient" tightening of trade restrictions and stepped-up aid to China suited the nibbling advance, but not the great leaps forward he feared now. Yet an oil embargo might "upset the whole kettle," driving Japan southward. The British had been urging the sending of an American naval squadron to Singapore. Some such show of strength, with all the risk it would entail, seemed ultimately the only alternative: "At a given point, if the southward advance proceeds, we must without any question send a substantial part of our fleet into Asian waters, presumably to Manila, if not to Singapore itself." [12]

Early in February 1941 Grew was on the point of recommending a naval demonstration in the Far East including the possibility of a visit to Singapore. He had a telegram drafted but delayed sending it pending the arrival of Dooman, who was returning from furlough in the United States. The evening of the Counselor's return February 6, a meeting was held in the Ambassador's study. Several officers argued in favor of sending the telegram as drafted, but Lieutenant Colonel Harry I. Cresswell, the

Military Attaché, was opposed, on the ground that his intelligence did not indicate a major Japanese move was impending. Dooman considered the rumors of a landing on the Kra Isthmus a British device to involve the United States in war with Germany by way of Japan and pointed out that the dispatch of a few cruisers would not provide a credible deterrent, while Japan would not tolerate the presence of major American fleet elements in the South China Sea. In other words, far from deterring, the Singapore venture risked war, and he knew from firsthand experience in Washington that senior American naval officers agreed. Grew was impressed with the arguments of Cresswell and Dooman to the point of striking out the reference to Singapore and the telegram went forward.[13]

The result was a telegram that recommended nothing in particular. It set forth the reports indicating an acceleration of the Southward Advance, the arguments for the critical importance of holding Singapore, and the danger of half-measures. The question was not whether to call a halt in the advance but when, it continued. Having marched to water's edge, the telegram only dipped a toe. "Increased American naval concentration in the Far East" would entail risk of war, which must be faced, but greater was the risk of quiescence. "The moment decisive action should be taken," the telegram concluded, "if it is ever to be taken, appears to us to be approaching." Lord Halifax, British Ambassador in Washington, when shown this telegram by the President, commented that the analysis was clear and forceful but that it had not suggested a solution. Grew maintained that the nature of measures to be taken was not within the competence of the Embassy to determine.[14]

The Embassy did take one positive step, but not by design. On February 14 Dooman called on the Vice-Minister of Foreign Affairs to pay his respects. Ohashi Chuichi, who bore his chief's truculence without knowing when to put it off, was so irritating Dooman finally "let him have it" in fluent Japanese. Entirely on his own initiative he lectured the Vice-Minister on the ABC's of American security, British survival, and the integrity of British Empire communications. He warned that if Japan, either by direct action or by placing herself in a menacing position, should jeopardize those communications, "she would have to expect to come into conflict with the United States." Ohashi, shocked into silence, finally asked, "Do you mean to say that if Japan were to attack Singapore there would be war with the United States?" Dooman replied, "The logic of the situation would inevitably raise that question." The conversation then moved to easier ground and ended. The next caller found the Vice-Minister "agitated and distrait."[15]

Meanwhile the crisis boiled over onto the front pages. Australian troops and planes moved into Malaya, the Dutch called their shipping in the Far East into neutral ports, and Americans were warned again to come home from the Orient. Predictions of grave impending events, of a "swift push," a "lightning stroke," emanated from London, Melbourne, and Batavia. The result of these manifestations of concern was described by Hugh Byas in the *New York Times* as a "painless showdown." President Roosevelt eased tension by saying publicly he did not think a new war likely. Matsuoka and Ohashi delivered numerous protestations of innocence and it became increasingly evident that Japanese intentions were for the moment confined to Indo-China. On February 18 Grew reported a relaxation in the crisis atmosphere of Tokyo. The British Admiralty had apparently "got the wind up" and sounded the alarm prematurely. "Some circles, perhaps with justice, are very, very jittery these days," he added. On February 20 Churchill informed Roosevelt that he had better news about Japan. On February 26, when the "February War Scare" had subsided, Grew felt free to report more explicitly the warning Dooman had given Ohashi February 14, and to tell Matsuoka the following day that everything Dooman had said had his approval. Superfluous to say, Grew wrote a friend, this was "one hell of a life." [16]

It had been a somewhat artificial crisis. The Japanese, moving when and where they could without war, sought facilities in Thailand and Indo-China preliminary to a possible major advance on British and Dutch colonies. The British were apprehensive of an immediate attack on their territory, but they undoubtedly also saw the value of assuming this to be the Japanese intention. By responding as if a war crisis actually did exist, they might deter Japan's preliminary moves. For the time being they succeeded, the Japanese stepping back and stipulating for neutralization of Indo-China and Thailand against third powers but not for bases. The United States declined a major role in British countermeasures. Though Roosevelt considered Singapore important, he was more concerned to provide direct assistance to Britain against Hitler and wished particularly to avoid dangerous involvement in the Pacific while the Lend-Lease battle raged in Congress. "Our problem being one of defense, we cannot lay down hard-and-fast plans," he wrote Grew, January 21. Dooman's spur-of-the-moment warning was the most positive American move and undoubtedly contributed to the growing Japanese conviction that Britain and America were inseparable.[17]

Grew at first was receptive to the exaggerated view of the threat because he believed the defense of Singapore was vital and because he was assuming that Japanese militarists had control and were set on unlimited conquest. Beginning February 6, he shifted position as he became aware the crisis was partly artificial, Japanese policy ambiguous, and his own government's position less than heroic. Furthermore, a course of action depending on projected analysis, a bold and risky course, was not congenial to a diplomat whose approach was more subjective than intellectual and who was profoundly conservative and conciliatory by nature. Force politics was not Grew's strong suit.

March was a month of marking time. The February crisis seemed to have made Japan pause. After weeks of the most acute anxiety over the worsening of relations with the United States the atmosphere in Tokyo was more relaxed. The press took a milder, defensive tone and the government moved hesitantly and cautiously. Roosevelt's refusal to be intimidated by the Triple Alliance, his determination to continue assistance to Britain while keeping a weather eye cocked on the Pacific, was having a marked effect. Also the German invasion of England failed to materialize. Grew's fears of uninhibited, unlimited advance and of the power of the pro-Axis elements subsided slightly, though he kept constantly in mind the possibility of the military creating an incident or launching an outlaw attack. He assumed that Singapore and the Indies remained Japan's goals but once again he anticipated a nibbling advance with "intermittent periods of digging in and watching for the effects abroad." War as a deliberate act of government seemed less likely provided the United States remained firm and the European war did not take a serious turn for the worse.[18]

The prime event of the following month was the Russo-Japanese Neutrality Pact signed by Matsuoka on April 13, 1941, at Moscow. Any change in the Soviet position naturally aroused intense interest, not least at the American Embassy in Tokyo. At first Grew anticipated an easing of Japan's China problem. The Pact apparently violated the Soviet-Chinese Non-Aggression Pact of 1937 and it sanctioned a derogation of Chinese sovereignty by providing for Soviet recognition of Manchukuo in return for Japanese recognition of the Mongolian People's Republic. Moscow seemed to have established a second and contradictory point of departure for its Far Eastern policy, which, if developed, might cause a drift away from Chungking. The mere fact of the agreement would tend to exacerbate current dissension between Chiang Kai-shek and the Chinese Communists. However, the Japanese seemed to gain little satisfaction. Already by May they were finding on "cold examination" that the text was silent on Soviet assistance to China and that American aid only increased. The government was stressing the need to strengthen the Nanking puppet regime and to prosecute the war on Chiang vigorously. Japan's longed-for settlement seemed as remote as ever.[19]

So far as Japan's relations with Germany were concerned, Grew found the Neutrality Pact no reason for discouragement. True, it tended to reinforce and extend the fence-sitting role of the Soviet Union and in that sense was a success for the Triplice. On the other hand, it was a negative, limited, last-minute affair, aimed less at defining common interests than at creating an effect on third powers. In the case of the Soviet Union it substantiated accumulating evidence of a deterioration in relations with Germany, leading Grew to the conclusion April 22 that a German-Soviet war was eventually "almost inevitable." A telegram from the Embassy at Moscow, repeated to Tokyo, went further to suggest that the Neutrality Pact evidenced a desire on the part of Japan, in the face of the growing possibility of Germany becoming involved at the same time with the Soviet Union and the United States, to limit its obligations under the Tripartite Pact. In any event the great threat of a Soviet-Tripartite grouping had not materialized. Germany had proved no help along the route to Moscow.

Grew recognized the danger of the Neutrality Pact stimulating and supporting the extremists in the vigorous prosecution of the Southward Advance, particularly at a time of British reverses in the Eastern Mediterranean, and he noted that southern policy became markedly more aggressive in tone. Nevertheless, he tended to discount the practical benefits of the Pact in this respect. So long as Japanese-American relations were bad, as they were bound to be when Japan required strategic materials which the United States denied or threatened to deny, Japan's relations with the Soviet Union, always the reciprocal of relations with the United States, would improve. Even without the Neutrality Pact Japan enjoyed some protection to the north in the fact that Germany would hardly allow the Soviet Union to profit from Japan's difficulties and thereby defeat the main purpose of the Tripartite Pact, which was the containment of the United States. However, the Embassy had all along maintained and continued to maintain that Moscow and Tokyo could never achieve any substantial community of interest. Grew would go further and argue that any pact by any power with the Soviet Union was "very risky and shortsighted procedure," and he believed that many Japanese fully agreed. "There are indications," he wrote April 17, "that the complete confidence which would impel a southward advance is not yet felt with regard to the northern neighbor." All in all, his characterization of Japanese policy as cautious and hesitant was confirmed by the Neutrality Pact.

That view was encouraged while Matsuoka was abroad by a significant change in the complexion of the Konoe government. Entering the Cabinet in April were two acquaintances of Grew's, Ogura Masatsune, head of the giant Sumitomo zaibatsu and president of the America-Japan Society at Osaka, and the "sound and sensible" Admiral Toyoda Teijiro. Grew attributed these moves to Home Minister Hiranuma whom he considered now "the most important influence in the Government." The ultraconservative, insular Hiranuma could be expected to exert a healthy influence against adventurism and foreign political and ideological attachments. He would lend strength to the notoriously weak-willed Konoe in bridling the militarists. Dooman picked up the threads of the relationship he had established with Hiranuma in 1939 and repeated for the Home Minister the warning he had given Ohashi, February 14. The return information was encouraging. Hiranuma let it be known that the primary preoccupation of the government was to fulfill the Emperor's wish that the Axis alliance be used as an instrument of peace and that the Cabinet had decided the day after the signing of the Neutrality Pact to pursue the Southward Advance only by peaceful means so long as the United States did not resort to drastic economic pressure or naval dispositions. Grew believed that the Hiranuma faction was perhaps a countervailing power to Matsuoka and the militarists. Again the Japanese scene was complex, "a mass of heterogeneous forces pulling in all directions." Japan would be likely to wait upon events in Europe.[20]

Several swallows do not make a summer, as Grew knew only too well. Early in April a letter from Hornbeck apparently brought the first word that private and semi-official efforts were under way in America by a group of Japanese and Americans, including Catholic missionaries Bishop James E. Walsh and Father James M. Drought, to work out a basis for negotiation of differences between the two countries. Then on April 25 Grew learned that Hull was willing to discuss the group's proposal provided Ambassador Nomura submitted it officially and it conformed to certain well-known principles of American policy. The Department was skeptical of success. Early in May, Grew heard talk of some approach being made by Tokyo and skepticism among Japanese. They were concerned that the United States would insist on Japan clearing out of China entirely, or try to make Japan publicly desert its ally, or scheme to remove the risk of war in the Pacific only to turn on Japan after Germany was defeated. Grew was heartened to hear talk of negotiation again but considered it too early to expect results. A major obstacle was that according to his information Prince Konoe expected to leave direction of negotiations in the hands of Matsuoka.[21]

Matsuoka was still in charge, but not comfortably. His journey to Moscow as well as Berlin and Rome had been splendid personal publicity, but the Neutrality Pact was small recompense for months of arduous diplomacy. His various initiatives, far from reinforcing one another and solidifying the Greater East Asia sphere, had only increased the strains and contradictions of Japan's position. He returned to find the Cabinet anxious about the extension of American naval patrolling in the Atlantic. Convoying might be next, leading to war with Germany. The Walsh-Drought draft understanding, which Nomura had transmitted with the implication that it was a proposal of the American government, inspired hope that the United States might assist in a China settlement that still allowed a special position for Japan in North China. Finding the government intent on pursuing the Washington conversations, Matsuoka stiffened the draft.

He redrafted the European provisions, which would have in effect nullified the Tripartite Pact, so as to inhibit American assistance to Britain against Germany and reassert Japan's obligations under the Pact. He hoped to make any Pacific settlement conform to the spirit of the alliance. However, he was forced to release Japan's "reply" May 12, before fully consulting with the Axis partners. Then Ambassador Ott delivered Germany's warning that "the American proposal for a secret understanding" was a Roosevelt device for dividing the allies while he involved the United States in the European conflict through a series of unneutral acts that placed the onus for war on Germany. Matsuoka should give a "brutally frank demonstration" that, whatever America might do, Japan would stand by her ally. To Ott, Matsuoka's redraft seemed to breathe "an atmosphere from which even the mildest criticism of America's unneutral conduct is excluded." Thus discomfited, and still coughing badly from a bout of bronchitis, the Foreign Minister had his first conversation with Grew since his return from abroad.[22]

At this conversation May 14 Grew found Matsuoka more "caustic and bellicose" than ever before. The objects of the Foreign Minister's wrath were the American neutrality patrol and the possibility of convoying ships to Britain. Hitler's "patience and generosity" had been tried severely, he warned. If German submarines sank American ships and were then attacked by American naval vessels, he would consider America the aggressor. This act of aggression would call for deliberations under the Tripartite Pact which he felt sure would lead to war between Japan and the United States. The "manly, decent, and reasonable" course for the United States was to declare war openly on Germany instead of engaging in acts of war under cover of neutrality.[23]

Grew did not have to report Matsuoka's insulting adjectives. The Foreign Minister withdrew them on Grew's angry complaint and wrote a letter explaining that he had spoken as a "quasi-American," not as Foreign Minister, and meant to say "discreet" instead of "decent." Earlier in their relationship Grew would probably have closed the incident there in order to keep strains to a minimum, but not this time. He reported the conversation in all detail and made sure other members of the Japanese government received an accurate account of it. The difference now was his belief that Matsuoka's warning did not represent the view of the Cabinet as a whole, and this belief was confirmed by reports from the Navy Minister and Privy Seal. However, the Foreign Minister was so tightly bound to pro-Axis policy that he did represent a major obstacle in the path of negotiations. It was not for an ambassador to work the downfall of a foreign minister, but Grew would not hinder this one from creating difficulties for himself. The episode probably did add strain to Matsuoka's relations with his cabinet colleagues but it served his purpose too: he showed Grew's letter deploring the Minister's "grave and far-reaching" remarks to the German Ambassador as proof of a "brutally frank demonstration."[24] Then he invited Grew in for a sip of tea to express surprise at learning by way of Nomura and Hull that he had intimidated the American Ambassador. He explained that his words might have been bellicose but his heart and thoughts were peaceful.

By the end of May, Grew's appreciation of the Japanese scene was radically different from that at the beginning of the year. Matsuoka and the extremists were not to be wished away, but the dynamic factors were those working against the Axis orientation. What caught his attention was growing awareness that neither Allied nor German victory would bring the longed-for solution of the China conflict or guarantee fulfillment of Japan's larger East Asian ambitions. The cabinet reconstruction and the recent "emasculation" of Konoe's totalitarian party pointed to disenchantment with Axis ideology. American rearmament and determination had aroused deep concern over the possibility of war with the United States. According to his reports the predominant influences in the government — the Emperor, the Prime Minister, the majority of the Cabinet and the Navy — would make every effort to find an interpretation that would release Japan from the obligations of the Tripartite Pact if this could be done without sacrificing honor or losing face. He would not report a decisive change in internal power arrangements but the momentary trend was in favor of the moderates. Japan's course was as unpredictable as it was malleable. It would be highly sensitive to events in Europe and to the course of American policy.[25]

Grew was in this frame of mind when finally at the end of May he was invited to comment on the Hull-Nomura talks. The Department had left him practically in the dark, being in no hurry to communicate before the Japanese took an official interest and sending the key documents the slow way by pouch to preserve secrecy. Grew nad received documents relating to the initiation of the talks but not the Japanese "reply" of May 12. His assignment was relatively easy. He was not asked to comment on the provisions specifically and he could see from Hull's memoranda and a Department counterdraft to the Walsh-Drought proposal that the American position was a well-protected one. Nor was he asked whether the Japanese were likely at the moment to agree to such terms, an unlikely event so long as Matsuoka was Foreign Minister. The Department wanted to know whether, if a settlement were reached, the Japanese were likely to implement it and whether it was wise for the United States to enter such commitments. His answer was that the Japanese government would not sign any agreement without the approval of the armed services and he believed that the War and Navy Ministers favored some such settlement. In any case, it appeared that the commitments on the American side were mostly "abstentious and negative" while those of the Japanese were positive, and accordingly the United States risked little by failure of implementation. The greater risk was a progressive deterioration of relations leading to war. Japanese policy, as he had explained, was malleable. Proceeding with negotiations would help create conditions favorable for a settlement and the fact of agreement would encourage fulfillment. That was the creative role of diplomacy.[26]

By June 1941 then "green light" mentality had all but disappeared. The protection of Singapore and the Indies was no less important but Grew doubted the likelihood of an attack. On June 6 the Netherlands East Indies government, after months of stubborn resistance to Japanese demands, delivered its final reply virtually rejecting them. The question now was whether the Japanese would make an armed descent on the oil-rich islands. Matsuoka of course was still powerful and extremists and Nazis were said to be pressuring him for strong action. They were known to be encouraged by the recent dispatch of one-quarter of the American battleship force from Pearl Harbor to the Atlantic. However, Grew decided it was more likely that the government would stay its hand and continue high-pressure diplomacy. An attack southward would be perilous while the China conflict continued. If the decision were deliberated by the Cabinet, he had little doubt that "moderate and restraining influences" would prevail, or else the Cabinet would fall. He was against warning the Japanese that an attack would involve his own government and against writing a letter to the President advocating a "positive demonstration of force." He explained to Hornbeck, who had suggested such a letter, that in the months since the February 7 telegram with its talk of a naval demonstration, "the chances of a Japanese attack on Singapore or the Netherlands East Indies — to put it conservatively — have not increased." The United States must prepare for all eventualities. Another Manchurian or *Panay* Incident was always possible, as he had warned time and again, but he believed that war would not come through any "carefully calculated and deliberated policy." [27]

In the early hours of June 22, 1941, Hitler sent one hundred and twenty divisions hurtling eastward in a supreme gamble to conquer Russia before winter. If Hitler had invaded Hell, Churchill would have at least made a favorable reference to the Devil, but not Grew, not yet. He was immensely relieved but too taken with the Bolshevik incubus and disgust for the Nazi-Soviet Pact and the assault on Finland to find sympathy for Hitler's latest victim. His first reaction was: "Let the Nazis and the Communists so weaken each other that the democracies will soon gain the upper hand or at least will be released from their dire peril." Remembering Napoleon, he thought the respite might be a long one.[28]

The immediate question was whether Japan would join her ally against

Russia. Days of intense deliberation followed, culminating in an auspicious Imperial Conference July 2. Finding the vector of decision among the scattering rumors and limp official statements was "wholly speculative," but Grew's hypothesis of caution and hesitancy worked well and he became increasingly sure Japan would not move north. He noted that far from inspiring Tripartite harmony the new war was causing surprise, dismay, and uncertainty in Tokyo. Japanese were questioning Germany's good faith and suspecting German designs in the Far East. He accepted — correctly — that Japan's Tripartite policy had been predicated on German-Soviet peace, so that once again, as with the Nazi-Soviet Pact of 1939, Germany had played false with Japan's expectations. Officials confirmed the impression of Tripartite disunity. Matsuoka told Craigie that Japan's liberty of action was not impaired either by her pact with Germany or that with Russia and Prince Konoe said Japan could reconcile both pacts. Grew heard reports of accentuated tension between the Matsuoka and Hiranuma factions, which made an all-out decision difficult to reach. The evidence suggested that Japan would "simply get good and ready and then sit on the fence until the outcome in Russia is clear." [29]

Tripartite disunity could only benefit the United States. Prince Konoe gave an American newsman an interpretation of the alliance obligations that seemed much more defensive and less pugnacious than before and his comments to Grew's informants showed a "strong desire, if not determination, to avoid conflict with the United States." On June 27 Grew anticipated "adjustments of personnel" for failure to read German intentions correctly and the resignation of the Konoe Cabinet July 16 and its reconstitution without Matsuoka fulfilled his expectation. Japanese were saying how wise the withdrawal from Europe of the thirties had been and how foolish Matsuoka's entanglement. With the Hiranuma faction predominant Japan would favor an independent course. So far as possible, the Tripartite Pact would be interpreted to avoid being dragged into any American war with Hitler.[30]

Grew was not expecting any Japanese moves in the direction of Singapore and the Indies. His view July 2 was that the Imperial Conference decisions probably would "restrict and not enlarge the chances of conflict with the United States as the result of Japanese initiatives." Yet during the second and third weeks of July signs pointed more and more toward resumption of the Southward Advance through acquisition of bases in southern Indo-China which would threaten the entire Singapore-Batavia-Manila arc. Grew tried to reconcile his thesis of Japanese inaction with the accumulating evidence but he was neither clear nor convincing. On July 6 he reported "with some degree of assurance" that "a positive and dynamic policy creating new commitments and involvements" was unlikely. The alleged Indo-China plan might be only a German suggestion aimed at getting Japan to divert America from Europe, or more obscurely, "an attempt to rationalize and put into concrete form such German desires." Troop mobilization in Japan prompted him on July 17 to choose as the most likely objective, not an attack north or south, but a "knockout blow" in China, with acquisition of bases in Indo-China, "fairly close to the heart of unoccupied China," a subsidiary move. He wrote in his diary: "I cannot believe that Japan will be so foolish as to start another major war with Great Britain, and to risk war with the United States, by attacking Singapore or the East Indies. . . . " By now, however, the arrow pointed straight south and Grew was frankly bewildered. "In my long experience in Japan," he wrote, "there has never been a time when greater difficulty has been encountered in . . . presenting seasoned views and estimates of Japanese policy." He would "make no pretensions at being able to predict the future course of events in this area." [31]

The Imperial Conference decision to move into southern Indo-China was as usual a point of intersection for diverse and contradictory aims and perspectives in the Japanese government. It was a preemptive move. Should Hitler fulfill his aims, as seemed not improbable considering British reverses in the Eastern Mediterranean and the swift, massive German advance in Russia, Japan would be positioned quickly to achieve her East Asian ambitions. Should the Americans impose all-out sanctions, a not unlikely event in view of the steady tightening of trade restrictions and an oil embargo from East Coast and Gulf ports announced June 20, and remain adamant about a settlement, as they appeared to be in the stiff Hull note of June 21, Japan would be set to attain imperial self-sufficiency by force. The decision represented a more positive approach to the problem of securing oil, negotiations with the Dutch having failed. Yet in the twisted context of Japanese decision-making, southern Indo-China was also the moderate option, displacing the attack on Russia Matsuoka and the Germans were urging, completing a penetration already under way rather than opening a new one. It seemed the relatively safe course while Russia was engaged with Germany, and the United States, having reduced its Pacific fleet, was preoccupied in the Atlantic. The democracies had not drawn the line in Indo-China. Having decided, the Japanese put brutal pressure on Vichy and secured naval and air bases at the southern end of the Indo-Chinese peninsula. On July 24 forty thousand Japanese troops moved in. Grew recognized that the bases agreement constituted a new threat to Singapore and "very distinctly increased the risk of eventual war with the United States." [32]

President Roosevelt and select advisers had no difficulty reading Japanese intentions because American cryptanalysts had recently broken the most secret Japanese diplomatic code. "Magic" intercepts dating from July 2 starkly revealed Japanese designs on southern Indo-China. In response

Roosevelt issued oblique warnings, proposed a neutralization scheme for Indo-China, and then took control of Japanese assets. Apparently he intended a flexible program presenting the new Konoe government inducement, threat, and a little time before applying stringent pressure. If this was his intention, he acted too late, after the Japanese were fully committed. In the absence of any change of course, the American government applied pressure. With every commercial transaction now requiring separate approval and the weight of bureaucracy on the side of denial and delay, trade soon practically ceased. The United States like Japan had played out the politics of force.[33]

Grew did not read Japanese intentions correctly in July 1941. Reports of Japanese designs in southern Indo-China did not fit his characterization of Japanese policy as cautious and hesitant. Yet at the beginning of the year he had credited reports that Japan was heading across the Gulf of Siam toward Singapore and the Indian Ocean. Both the underestimation and the overestimation of Japanese expansionism arose from his conception of Japan's relationship to Germany.

Hitler's victory in Europe in the spring of 1940 and the Tripartite Pact were cumulative shocks to Grew. At first he overreacted: Japan, dominated by pro-Axis militarists, was bound up with Germany in a scheme of world conquest. The Axis connection both represented and stimulated the forces of expansion. Gradually over the next months this monolithic view was replaced by the familiar extremist-moderate dichotomy, with Matsuoka and army elements representing the German attachment and unrestrained expansion. Prince Konoe, the Hiranuma faction, the Navy, and the court represented non-involvement, caution, and conservatism. Until the February War Scare the extremists predominated but during the spring and early summer of 1941 the failures of Matsuoka diplomacy, the Hull-Nomura conversations, the Russo-German war, and the patent efforts of prominent Japanese to minimize alliance obligations encouraged the view that a moderate trend was under way. His estimate of the Southward Advance, whether at the beginning of the year or in July, depended on how he happened to be viewing German-Japanese relations. In his mind, as the Axis infection subsided, so did the disease of expansionism. Actually Japanese expansionism owed very little to the Tripartite Pact. As Grew might have said earlier, the Southward Advance was *sui generis.*

Grew was dismayed by the events of late July 1941. When the new Foreign Secretary, Admiral Toyoda, gave the usual "flimsy" explanations and assurances, Grew bitterly recounted how again and again and again Foreign Ministers had given him assurances which the Army had made worthless. "How could my Government or myself accept any promises whatever from any Japanese Government?" Then on July 30 a Japanese bomb barely missed the stern of the gunboat *Tutuila* at Chungking. Eight yards closer and another *Panay* Incident would have occurred. The American freezing order caused astonishment and bitter resentment in Japan. The vicious circle of retaliation and counterretaliation was complete. It was difficult for Grew to see how the "down-grade movement" could be arrested short of its obvious conclusion, war.[34]

Grew's hopelessness and sense of drift were short-lived, however. Taking a second look, he decided that the move into southern Indo-China was not necessarily a prelude to further Japanese aggression. He might not have to abandon his characterization of Japanese policy as cautious and independent after all. It was significant that the move was "conceived and already set on foot" while Matsuoka was Foreign Minister. Given a government composed of "various discordant groups which in varying degrees . . . must be given considerable ration in the formulation of policy," the project should be understood as the necessary ration of the Axis element. Now that Matsuoka had been ostentatiously dropped and the "Nazi-Fascist tinge" removed from the Cabinet, that ration would be smaller. All his reports indicated that ties with Germany were weakening. The "honest, frank and communicative" Toyoda was a refreshing contrast to Matsuoka. Grew thought he liked him better than any Foreign Minister he had ever dealt with. He concluded that the Indo-China move did not fairly represent the "more conservative and cautious policy" of the reconstructed Konoe government. The idea of a swing toward moderation had been so strongly reinforced in his mind by the events of the spring and the dropping of Matsuoka that the contradictory evidence of the Indo-China advance could not dislodge it.[35]

Furthermore diplomacy was still functioning and Grew was determined to keep it going. On July 26 he repeated for Toyoda what Hull told Nomura, that in view of the Indo-China advance no basis seemed to exist for pursuing the Washington conversations. But Grew added that he was reluctant to leave an "atmosphere of defeatism" and he urged Toyoda to do his best to prevent further deterioration in relations. The next day Grew received the President's neutralization scheme for Indo-China and, though it was Sunday and he had no authority from Washington, he secured an appointment to make certain the Foreign Minister understood the proposal. To his amazement Toyoda was ignorant of it, Ambassador Nomura apparently having failed to grasp its significance, and Grew thereupon explained it and urged it with all the force he could muster in what he considered perhaps the strongest representations he had ever made. He added on his own authority that acceptance of the President's proposal might lead to a new basis for continuing the Washington conversations. On August 6 Nomura presented a Japanese proposal which was conceived as an answer to the President's and this, though "lacking in responsiveness," served at least to keep open communication. The freezing of Japanese assets had worsened relations but it also seemed to be having a healthy effect. Grew guessed that the Japanese as usual had miscalculated the severity of the American reaction to their move. Stringent economic pressure had forced them "very quickly to take stock of the potential situation" and positive, he might almost say frantic, efforts began to bring about a *rapprochement* with the United States.[36]

Prince Konoe was in fact prepared to make a supreme effort for an understanding with the United States. The Japanese had indeed miscalculated the severity of the American reaction. The stoppage of trade, particularly oil, presented the appalling prospect of slow immobilization of Japan's land, sea, and air forces. A sense of finality settled over the Japanese consciousness: their nation would have to solve its problems with the United States or resort to war. War might ultimately be necessary, but it was a desperate alternative. It offered no sure supply of oil, what with the prospective destruction of the East Indian oil fields and American submarine attacks on Japanese shipping. The United States appeared indestructible and its rapidly growing war potential unmatchable. Worse still, the German campaign in Russia was lagging. Stalemate would make a Hitler victory doubtful and immensely increase Japan's problems. Each day the German alliance lost leverage, each day cost twelve thousand tons of irreplaceable oil. Japan must strike to the heart of its difficulties with the United States and find out if a settlement was possible before too late.

In spite of the rigidity of the American position, a settlement had not been proven impossible. The United States held that the Nine-Power Treaty was not immutable provided it were changed by peaceful processes. If the two heads of government could get together, bypass their bureaucracies, cut through formulas, and in confidence and familiarity discover their "true intentions," the worst might be avoided. If they failed, at least no stone would have been left unturned. Konoe noted that after Chamberlain's failure at Munich the British entered war with the greater determination. On August 4 he took up one of the Walsh-Drought proposals of the previous spring, that he meet with President Roosevelt at Honolulu. After receiving the backing of key ministers, he had Nomura approach Hull and then Roosevelt, after the President returned from his Atlantic Conference with Churchill. The same day that Nomura saw the President, August 18 Tokyo time, Foreign Minister Toyoda took up the proposal with Grew.[37]

The gravity and care with which Toyoda presented Konoe's proposal for a leader's meeting was a far cry from the posturing of the Matsuoka period. Grew was forewarned that the interview would be of the greatest importance and that if Prince Konoe's efforts for peace failed, no other Japanese statesman could succeed. As it was an insufferably hot and humid day, Foreign Minister and Ambassador worked in shirtsleeves and swabbed themselves with cold wet towels. Though Toyoda spoke English, he used an interpreter and Grew took down every word on foolscap. The Minister made no effort to conceal the seriousness of the situation. He reviewed the rocky course of recent Japanese-American diplomacy in detail and then came to the Konoe proposition. He pointed out that it was unprecedented for a Japanese Prime Minister to go abroad and Konoe's determination to do so reflected the "strongest desire to save the civilization of the world from ruin." The occasion called for the highest statesmanship on both sides. He asked Grew's cooperation as one who had made a sincere effort for "nine long years" to improve Japanese-American relations. He ended by stressing the importance of absolute secrecy. The conversation lasted two and a half hours, Grew's longest with any Foreign Minister. He then wrote his memorandum, had Dooman take it back to Toyoda for checking, and worked long past midnight on his report. The code room did not close until dawn.[38]

Grew felt swept into the mainstream of diplomacy again. Since the Grew-Nomura conversations, diplomacy had been practically non-existent at Tokyo. He had been given only a minor role in the Hull-Nomura conversations. The Japanese had to go to the Americans because they were the ones who more and more needed a settlement and because only in Washington could they circumvent what they regarded as State Department obstructionism by working through other parts of the American government. Admiral Nomura was friendly with the President and in touch with the American Navy. The Walsh-Drought group had a channel to the President through Postmaster General Frank Walker. Perhaps the Japanese also accepted that Grew, for all his efforts, did not have decisive influence with his government. He had not been able to match Nomura's Yangtze concession of December 1939. Of the Washington conversations Grew received delayed reports and few clues to his government's thinking. His own policy telegrams were like "shying pebbles into the dark." He was in a security cul-de-sac. Both the Japanese and the State Department explained that they did not take him into confidence because of the vulnerability of American codes and when the State Department gained an authentic source of information through "Magic" it was probably the less inclined to prime its Tokyo Embassy. One of Grew's best lines of communication was the British who, on the reasonable assumption that good intelligence depends on full exchange of information and views, passed around their missions a great deal about American policy thinking which Grew considered "infra dig" to be learning from foreigners. In any event, he was now again in touch with high diplomacy and possessed a function, and he was exhilarated.[39]

The idea of a leader's meeting was immensely appealing to Grew. In a sense it was an unprofessional reaction. The function of diplomacy is to discover areas of agreement in confidence without involving national prestige, a function difficult to perform when heads of government themselves negotiate. The procedure begs agreement for the sake of agreement without a meeting of minds and lends itself to imprecision, haste, ambiguity, and confusion. Surely the former Secretary of the American delegation to the Paris Peace Conference understood the dangers of leaders' meetings! But of course Grew's concept of professionalism did not rule out enthusiasm for such a project at all. Precisionist that he was, diplomacy was for him essentially a matter of personal relationships, the intercourse of nations being governed best by the code of gentlemanly conduct. Diplomacy retained an aristocratic flavor. Konoe Fumimaro was a descendant of the most ancient and distinguished family in Japan after the Imperial Houses and Franklin D. Roosevelt came from as distinguished a family as his equalitarian society would suffer. It would be unthinkable to Grew that face-to-face meetings over several days between these two gentlemen would not generate more understanding than a decade of turgid and sterile bureaucratic diplomacy.

The project touched Grew's romanticism at a number of points. He had invariably characterized Prince Konoe as weak-willed before but now he stressed the Premier's "courageous determination to override the extremists" and, in the face of assassination threats, to sacrifice his life if necessary. Perhaps some polishing of a tarnished reputation was involved here, but also faith in human perfectibility. The Prince bore a heavy responsibility for Japan's predicament, but now perceived the "fundamental error" of the Tripartite Alliance and was "courageously working to find a way out." His effort should be met with "magnanimity." It was a drama of morality: waywardness, suffering, repentence, forgiveness.[40]

It was also epic history. A successful summit conference averting war would be a decisive moment in history. It would be a supreme act of individualism, a triumph of personality, character, and faith in human progress over the brute, impersonal forces of the world. He would be in attendance, traveling aboard Prince Konoe's ship the *Nitta Maru*, he could imagine. Here perhaps — and the thought must have been tantalizing — was the crowning moment of a mission, a career, the perfect last chapter.

Grew sought to convey in his telegrams on the proposed leaders' meeting that this was the climactic moment in Japanese-American relations. He emphasized that an extraordinary opportunity existed. After the fall of the Yonai Cabinet the year before, the moderates had been powerless and diplomacy in eclipse until a combination of American firmness and world developments such as the Russo-German war had discredited the extremists. Now the embargo was bringing Japan near the end of the tether. The "green light" approach had worked. Japanese expansionism had been checked and moderate elements had come to the top. Under the Konoe-Toyoda regime the pendulum was positioned for diplomacy again.[41]

However, time was of the essence. He warned against complacency in case of delay or rejection. The Japanese would never capitulate in the face of foreign pressure. The growing conviction that differences with the United States could never be settled peacefully, along with the steady throttling of their economy, would create a psychology of despair which in Japan "leads characteristically to a do-or-die reaction." He was not precise about the result. At first he predicted a cabinet reconstruction "with a view to placing the future destiny of the nation in the hands of the army and navy for an all-out do-or-die effort to extend Japan's hegemony over all of 'Greater East Asia' entailing the inevitability of war with the United States." Later he wrote of a progressive deterioration of relations involving reprisals and counterreprisals, incidents, inflamed public opinion, and a disinclination to avoid war. In either case, if this opportunity were lost, the route led straight downhill. The possibility of overcoming "growing counsels of despair" lessened each day. It was vital to "bring these efforts to a head before they lose the force of their initial impetus." He urged with all the force at his command, "for the sake of avoiding the obviously growing possibility of an utterly futile war . . . that this Japanese proposal not be turned aside without very prayerful consideration."

His government must not insist on clear-cut, treaty-like commitments as conditions for a meeting. The Japanese government had to be abstract and equivocal in written exchanges because Matsuoka followers in the Foreign Office might inform the Germans. What he did not say but undoubtedly had in mind was the fact that Prince Konoe needed proof of American sincerity and flexibility before he could give explicit undertakings. Grew believed Konoe was prepared to pay well nevertheless. He would probably make far-reaching concessions with respect to China and the eventual withdrawal of Japanese forces from Indo-China and would satisfy the President of Japan's withdrawal in fact, if not in name, from the Tripartite Pact. The very entering of formal negotiations with the United States would reduce it to a dead letter. The very proposing of a meeting, when failure would be disastrous, suggested a degree of confidence in satisfying American demands. The vital point was to place confidence in the good faith and sincerity of Prince Konoe and his associates.

He warned against expecting an abrupt reorientation of Japanese policy. The results of the meeting "might be not wholly favorable and at best, gradual in materializing." Failure of implementation was a risk, but less than that of failure of agreement. The United States would retain its capacity to exert economic pressure and could relax that pressure step by step with Japanese fulfillment of terms. The Americans had the long-term advantage. A British victory against Hitler would "automatically solve many problems." A Pacific settlement would facilitate the defeat of Hitler. Meanwhile, acceptance of the Konoe proposal would in itself improve prospects for implementation. American policy had already "rendered the political soil of Japan hospitable to the sowing of new seeds which, if carefully planted and nourished," might lead to the regeneration of thought he had anticipated in the "green light" telegram. In other words, given that American policy and Japanese politics were bound to interact, a confidence-building approach strengthening the hand of the moderates would positively assist in establishing the conditions favorable to a realization of American objectives. That was what he had consistently meant by constructive conciliation. That was the creative role of diplomacy.

Meanwhile in August the Japanese press daily hammered on the theme of encirclement. From Tokyo's point of view, America's military preparations in the Philippines and stepped-up aid to China, as well as American-British-Dutch joint naval planning and identical sanctions, seemed like ever-tightening chains. Pressure intensified in August while Konoe was trying to arrange a leaders' meeting. The United States encouraged the Thais to resist Japanese encroachment, dispatched Flying Fortresses to the Philippines, announced a military mission to China, and named an aid mission to Moscow. The President scored "compromisers and appeasers" at home and abroad and called for naked force to meet naked force. Churchill sent more RAF units to Singapore and warned Japan to stop or face an Anglo-American coalition. The Japanese were particularly incensed over American oil shipments to Vladivostok, feeling as they did about oil like fish in a shrinking pond. Grew hoped the tankers at least would take a more northerly route so as not to sail under the noses of the Japanese. The American government denied encirclement, stressed its defensive intent, and labeled the Japanese protest as "preposterous." The shipments, fueling the war against Hitler, went forward.[42]

On August 28, with Japanese feeling in this hypertensive state, Ambassador Nomura delivered a message from Prince Konoe to President Roosevelt and announced that fact to White House reporters when he emerged. The next day's *New York Herald Tribune* headline was TOKYO BID FOR U.S. ACCORD. The *Times* said: WIDE TALK IN VIEW. Then the *Tribune* speculated on a Roosevelt-Konoe meeting and American radio broadcasts spoke of Japan surrendering to the United States. Nomura's indiscretion was impossible to suppress in Japan and Grew watched helplessly as Tokyo newspapers "poured fuel on the extremist fires," accusing the government of kowtowing to American pressure. Toyoda, who was known to be appalled by his ambassador's *faux pas*, pleaded for secrecy and tried to parry the searching questions of the German Ambassador. The Foreign Ministry appealed to Grew for a prompt decision in favor of the meeting and announcement of its date, before the Prince's effort was wrecked by premature publicity. Grew seconded the appeal and suggested that the Administration give the American press and radio a "leader" to counterbalance the efforts of the extremists in Tokyo. Could not the President in his Labor Day speech stress the concrete benefits that would accrue to Japan from a change of course? The President's next major speech at least was silent on Japan, but the Administration was not yet prepared to agree to a meeting and not prepared publicly to encourage the idea of accord.[43]

In spite of harassing circumstances the Konoe government made persistent efforts to bring Roosevelt to a Pacific meeting. On August 17 the President mixed receptiveness to a meeting with a warning against further aggression. He urged Japan to aim for economic security through peaceful cooperation under the principle of equality of opportunity and invited a clarification of Japanese intentions. Konoe was anxious to avoid preliminary discussions but had to respond. On August 28 Nomura made his inauspicious call at the White House to deliver a cordial letter from Konoe urging a meeting and a statement from his government which the Americans had intercepted in its original and stronger version with a gloss. The gist of the message with explanations was that Japan had two crucial problems, settlement of the China Incident and securing a sufficiency of resources, on which her military presence in Indo-China and its ultimate withdrawal depended. Toward resolving the resource problem Japan desired American acceptance of her East Asian sphere, which would be characterized by good neighborliness, economic leadership, and responsibility for ensuring strict equality of economic opportunity after Japan's vital needs were met, not by domination, threat, or use of force. The implication was clear that in any case progress toward stability in the Pacific depended on relaxation of American economic pressure. The Konoe government skirted the intractable problem of conditions for peace in China, probably hoping that easing the immediate issues, the Southward Advance and the freezing of assets, would improve the atmosphere and pave the way for a China solution.[44]

Cordell Hull and his Far Eastern advisers were determined to bring the China problem forward. They had been cool to the idea of a leaders' meeting and were cooler still when they saw how Japanese generalities, as usual, left wide discretion in application. Their suspicions probably leaped at the sight of discrepancies between Nomura's instructions and his delivered documents, in particular proof in the intercepts that Japan was still attached to the idea of a "Greater East Asia Co-Prosperity Sphere." Noticing that Japanese withdrawal from Indo-China would come only after conclusion of the China Incident, they asked how discussion of China terms could be excluded. Hull convinced the President that further development of Japanese intentions was necessary before agreement to a leaders' meeting and he was responsible for setting forth the American position to Nomura the evening of August 28 and September 3. First, the United States requested assurance that Japan "earnestly" stood for Hull's four basic principles: respect for territorial integrity and sovereignty, non-interference in internal affairs, equality of commercial opportunity, and peaceful procedures. In particular the Japanese would please clarify their position on abandoning a policy of force and conquest. Second, the United States would discuss the matter fully with the British, Chinese, and Dutch. Third, the United States raised the unresolved questions of the previous spring, namely trade discrimination in China, stationing of Japanese troops in North China and Inner Monogolia, and Japan's relations with the Axis. The China question, said Hull, was "pivotal." In his view a leaders' meeting would serve to ratify agreements previously reached. By September 3, so far as Hull was concerned, the discussions had substantially become a continuation of those of the previous spring.[45]

The Japanese response of September 4-6, through Grew, reflected their unwillingness to become involved in the details of the China problem, but their desire to go as far as possible to meet Hull's conditions for a meeting. Prince Konoe told Grew personally, with Dooman present to interpret, that he "conclusively and wholeheartedly" agreed with the four principles of peace. The government offered a military standstill agreement for Southeast Asia, Japan undertaking not to move southward and the United States agreeing to halt its military buildup in the Far East. Japan of course had nothing to say about American consultation with the Chinese, but it was not willing at this time to reveal its precise terms for a China settlement and it expected the United States to stop helping the Chinese while the belligerents arranged peace. On the unresolved questions, Japan would undertake not to interfere with American economic activities in China "so long as pursued on an equitable basis," to withdraw its forces from China as soon as possible after a peace agreement in accordance with the terms of that agreement, and to define its relation to the Axis defensively and independently. Japan counted on reciprocal commitments with respect to procurement of resources on a non-discriminatory basis in Southeast Asia and resumption of normal trade relations.[46]

Discussions that were complicated enough now tangled on a well intentioned move by Nomura. September 4, about the time Toyoda was giving Grew a brief outline of the kind of bargain that might be struck at a leaders' meeting, Nomura took it upon himself to hand Hull a detailed Japanese draft agreement he had been holding back since July, a tag-ender of the April-May-June exchanges. He probably thought that a return to the old format was the quickest, simplest way of satisfying the Secretary. Perhaps it was, but now the State Department had two Japanese proposals, entirely different in form and ill-matched in substance, and it took a week for diplomats in Tokyo and Washington to straighten out, in Dooman's words, "what the position of the Japanese Government was, say as of September 4." This was only the latest example of Nomura's inexpertness as a diplomat. Grew had all "too much evidence," shared by the Foreign Ministry, that the Embassy in Washington was "half the time asleep at the switch."

The American Ambassador might after all become the principal intermediary. Toyoda said he would prefer to have further conversations conducted in Tokyo, and on September 6 Prince Konoe invited Grew to dine to convey his personal assurances for Hull respecting the four principles and the Prince's ability to carry out an agreement reached at a leaders' meeting. That was a dramatic moment: official license plates removed for secrecy, servants sent away, and three hours of talk with the man he had tried so often to see and on whom so much depended. It was only a moment, however. The Department preferred to keep the definitive conversations in Washington, explaining that the President was taking a close interest. Perhaps it was also aware that by keeping Japanese communications strung out, "Magic" would be more revealing. However, while Washington spoke through Nomura, Tokyo continued to speak through Grew, and the two governments never seemed to be talking to each other. Conciliators like Grew and Nomura spent all their time clarifying.[47]

By September 6 Konoe's original project was in pieces. He had hoped to reveal to the Americans only enough of the Japanese position to encourage a leaders' meeting. Now the Japanese position hung awkwardly between the agenda Konoe wanted and the draft treaty Hull wanted. From September 6 to September 25, members of the Department's Far Eastern Division and the Tokyo Embassy conducted a critique of Japanese proposals and statements designed to eliminate discrepancies between what the Japanese had said in Washington and Tokyo and between what they had said August 28 and September 4-6. They also searched out every detail of the Japanese position on a comprehensive settlement. It was tedious diplomacy. So complex and fragile did the structure of explanation become that the Japanese Embassy in Washington decided not to deliver certain documents for fear another discrepancy would bring it all tumbling down. Nevertheless, the probe was successful, revealing the current Japanese peace terms for China and attitude on the Open Door. On September 25 it was only a matter of convenience for Toyoda to give Grew a comprehensive draft understanding tidying up the ill-assorted exchanges of the past weeks in the same format as the Hull-Nomura conversations of the previous spring.[48]

The Japanese draft understanding of September 25 followed the outline proposal of September 4 in calling for restoration of normal trade relations between the two nations, virtual nullification of the Tripartite Pact as a factor in their relations, neutralization of Southeast Asia by territorial guarantees, a military standstill, Japanese withdrawal from Indo-China after peace in China, and equal access to resources in the area. On the basis of Japan's terms, the United States would use its good offices to bring Sino-Japanese peace, halting assistance to Chungking while efforts were in progress. Japan's terms envisaged restoration of China, less Manchuria, under a Wang-Chiang coalition, with provision for stationing of Japanese troops and naval forces in certain areas. The principle of non-discrimination in trade was admitted, but with it, as often in the past, the principle of special relations between Japan and China deriving from geographical propinquity. Japan would have a position more equal than the rest in China's economic future, one buttressed by garrisons. In essence, Japan was offering the United States peace in the Pacific, permitting full concentration against Germany. In return Japan gained a great deal: peace in China, with the long-sought preferred position underwritten by a great power, American approval for access to the resources of Southeast Asia, insulation from the European war, and resumption of trade and peace with the United States.[49]

Meanwhile Grew continued, he said, to work and think and pray in a constructive spirit. He was more than ever impressed that Japanese-American relations were coming to the final turning point. It was a time for superlatives: the longest conversation, one of his longest telegrams, "the most important cable [reporting his conversation with Prince Konoe, September 6] to go from his hand since the start of his diplomatic career." Again and again he warned his government that time was short. He sent along every scrap of evidence indicating moderate influence and control. In telegrams of September 4, 6, and 29 and in a personal letter to the President of September 22 he urged the course of constructive conciliation. Above all, he urged against insisting on detailed, clear-cut commitments before a meeting. The Japanese mentality could not bring itself to express in concise, unambiguous language the commitments Prince Konoe was prepared to make at a meeting. The leaders' meeting itself should not be expected to produce a complete settlement. The conciliation process was evolutionary, gathering momentum with each accomplishment. By adopting it the United States stood to gain its basic objectives without war. The manifest sincerity of Prince Konoe, the favoring moderate trend, the provisional acceptance of American basic principles, and the concrete expectation of a solution of the Tripartite problem were reasons enough, with an act of faith, to make a beginning. Peace was worth the try. He spoke to the American colony in Tokyo early in October about his efforts:

> We who are working could never look forward to our eventual evening of life with any clear conscience and with any hope of achieving that "peace which passeth all understanding" if we failed to exert every ounce of deeply thoughtful effort during these times of crisis where great issues can sometimes be swayed by individual exertions.[50]

In the one hundred and tenth month of Grew's mission faith and reason would not suffice. The vital ingredient was confidence, which circumstances tended to suffocate rather than inspire. Grew needed to convince his government that the moderates had the ballast to begin a fundamental reorientation of Japanese policy, but his advices could give the opposite impression. If the issue of war and peace wavered in the balance and each day's delay weakened the chances of conciliation, then the Konoe regime's control over the extremists must be fragile indeed. On August 28 Grew wrote Hornbeck that all his confidential papers had been sent home except what could be destroyed in five minutes. On September 20 he passed on a report of an unsuccessful attempt on the life of Prince Konoe. Baron Hiranuma had been wounded by assassins August 14 and Grew, knowing he was on various death lists, took to carrying a pistol. He felt a little silly and "wild West" but had no intention of being carved up by sword-wielders without "a reasonable attempt at repartee." This was a peculiar climate for constructive statesmanship.[51]

At the same time Grew moved with professional rigor to leave the Japanese under no misapprehension whatever as to the American viewpoint. A Department press résumé received August 10 showed an "almost unanimous and very insistent demand for a firmer American stand in the Far East." So his moderate friends received much argumentation of the "straight from the horse's mouth" and "green light" variety. Was it not the breaking of the Nine-Power Treaty that started the long line of international wrongdoing by certain nations? How could his government believe any assurance by any Japanese government? How could it accept a Far Eastern order where Japan exercised her interests to the exclusion of American? On the basis of Hull's four principles, "and, I fear, only on such a basis," could there be good relations between the two countries. At the Foreign Ministry, Grew carried out his instructions to the letter, all the while fearing that each question pinning down the Japanese position in advance of a leaders' meeting reduced the chances of a meeting, and that by asking, for example, precisely in which direction Japan would be obliged not to attack "without any justifiable reason" his government was manifesting lack of confidence in Japanese sincerity. Yet the moderates needed every ounce of strengthening he could give them. Here was an implosion of the diplomat's dual representational roles, destroying the spirit of conciliation.[52]

The case for conciliation would have been more convincing if Grew had shown concretely how the positions of the two governments might be reconciled. At first, say from August 17 to September 4, a precise negotiating scheme did not seem called for because he believed the Japanese would be doing all the conceding. Once Japan had given satisfactory proof of her intentions, the United States could relax economic pressure, a concession entirely within American power to give and take away again in case Japan failed to live up to her promises. When the China question was brought forward, however, the problem became much more difficult. If the

United States disapproved the Japanese terms for peace with China and refused its good offices and suspension of assistance to China, the leaders' meeting would not materialize. Grew had no idea whether his government was at all flexible on conditions for a meeting — he was feeling very much the pawn and messenger boy — but so long as Washington did not reject Konoe's idea or the Japanese proposals, a chance for conciliation existed, and he was determined to pursue every chance. Assuming that the question remained open, he faced the problem of making an official recommendation for accepting or somehow ameliorating the Japanese terms for a China settlement.[53]

Grew faced a dilemma. He was a realist and moral relativist. He accepted the moral axioms of American policy as unquestionable and some Japanese presence in China as inevitable, but he believed that with time, patience, goodwill, and skillful diplomacy a tolerable approximation of ideal and reality was possible and that the quest for it was better than war. However, his approach depended on avoiding a confrontation between what was right and what was practical. A formal compromise of principle was no less repugnant to him than to Secretary Hull or Hornbeck, particularly now that his moral commitment was edged with emotional intensity by the struggle against Hitler. Once the State Department had insisted on Japanese specifications and the Japanese had presented them, a confrontation could not be avoided. Somehow, in a way phraseology could not conceal, the United States would have to urge the Chinese to bargain on terms that would result in some impairment of Chinese sovereignty and qualification of the Open Door if it wanted a leaders' meeting. Much as he wanted a meeting, Grew could not recommend negotiation of the Japanese position.

Furthermore, Grew had no desire whatever to leave himself open to the charge of appeasement. A letter from Hornbeck full of excerpts from Grew's letters and telegrams of the "green light" period suggested that he was already giving the impression of "advocating so-called 'appeasement' in contradistinction to my former recommendations for a strong policy." Appeasement was a tainted word he used only to deny absolutely its applicability to what he proposed. His approach was that of "constructive conciliation," he insisted. Even so, the bogey of appeasement remained. The Department said that a unilateral concession it had made to the Japanese in the matter of repatriation ships seemed to be in line with the course the Embassy had been advocating in matters of high policy. Grew commented: "Appeasement. Is that what the Department thinks I have been advocating?" How completely he seemed to be misunderstood. He had a feeling that his opinions were "not particularly welcome nowadays." [54]

On the one hand, a recommendation involving concessions at China's expense was repugnant to Grew. On the other hand, one involving rejection of the Japanese terms or protraction of the preliminary conversations would close the door to conciliation. Grew chose neither alternative but instead pointed out that Japanese paper proposals were equivocal, abstract, and in this case premature. He insisted that they did not represent the position Prince Konoe would take at a leaders' meeting nor the ultimate result of the process of conciliation. The United States would have to place

> a reasonable amount of confidence . . . in the professed sincerity of intention and good faith of Prince Konoe and his supporters to mould Japan's future policy upon the basic principles they are ready to accept and then to adopt measures which gradually but loyally implement those principles, with it understood that the United States will implement its own commitments *pari passu* with the steps which Japan takes. . . .[55]

The State Department's attitude toward a leaders' meeting progressed from cool to frigid. It never did reply to the Japanese in the sense of offering counterproposals or stating minimum conditions for a meeting. Late in September it received reports that Japanese troops in Indo-China were persecuting the inhabitants and demanding more barracks and air fields. Once again Japanese actions contradicted their words. Finally on October 2, after weeks of probing and criticizing, Hull delivered a summary view of Japanese proposals which brought discussions to a head. It was an utterly discouraging document. The United States, it said, was disappointed that the Japanese proposals disclosed divergence in the concepts of the two governments and served to narrow and qualify unnecessarily the application of principles that formed the basis of conversations. The proposals offered no resolution of the problems of trade discrimination and stationing of troops in China. It suggested that the Japanese government might "give further study to the question of possible additional clarification of its position" in regard to the European war.[56]

Japanese officials found the statement preceptive, argumentative, and entirely unhelpful. To many it appeared that their government had been trapped into revealing its hand while the American government refused to lay its cards on the table. They were embarrassed by its reference to Konoe's secret assurance of wholehearted subscription to Hull's four principles, as given to Grew September 6. Toyoda withdrew from that exposed position by saying that the assurance had been given privately and that what Konoe had really said was that he subscribed to the principles as principles, but that adjustments would be required in application. So far as the Third Konoe Cabinet was concerned, Hull's statement was conclusive and it resigned October 16. The alternative of peace lingered on but the idea of a leaders' meeting was dead.[57]

TWENTY

Japan as Enemy

PERHAPS a leaders' meeting would have averted war. F. C. Jones in his authoritative study of Japanese expansion suggests that a partial agreement was possible. Roosevelt might have undertaken to relax sanctions in return for Konoe giving up the Southward Advance and making a dead letter of the Axis alliance. The two of them might have agreed to disagree about their respective sets of principles and left the China problem aside until a decisive turn in the European war made conclusive decisions on the future of the Far East possible. Perhaps so, but that was not the kind of leaders' meeting Grew had in mind. In August, when the Konoe project was fresh and unencumbered, he believed that Konoe would "appeal for American cooperation in bringing the China affair to a close and would probably be prepared to give far-reaching undertakings in that connection, involving also the eventual withdrawal of Japanese forces from Indo-China." In other words, Grew had in mind a settlement restricted as to detail, but not as to issue. He looked for a comprehensive understanding not a *modus vivendi*. He did not consider the details of a China settlement crucially important because he believed that once the conciliation process began, the details would take care of themselves. Konoe seemed to have reversed the Japanese course so fundamentally, in ways so obviously in the American interest, that American conditions were bound to be satisfied in the long run if the impetus of the trend were maintained. Whereas he did not grapple with the China problem in September because it seemed too forbidding, he ignored it in August because it did not seem a major obstacle.[1]

Grew tended to a more hopeful view of things than circumstances warranted and his optimism of August was reinforced by his habit of viewing Japanese developments in terms of swings between moderation and extremism represented by the pendulum image. This way of describing internal power arrangements in Japan and predicting armed expansion or peaceful diplomacy had proved unhelpful during the early years of his mission because the pendulum was always stuck at the extremist-expansionist terminal and he had dropped it by 1937. However, the struggle over the German alliance in the spring of 1939 seemed to restore the internal dynamic. Following the Nazi-Soviet Pact came a moderate period under the Abe and Yonai Cabinets, succeeded by an extremist period under the Second Konoe Cabinet and Matsuoka. In the spring of 1941, with Matsuoka's failures and signs of strain in the Tripartite relationship, the trend turned once more toward moderation, wobbled a moment with the advance in southern Indo-China, and then went forward with increasing momentum under the Third Konoe Cabinet. The values attached in Grew's mind to a moderate swing were very substantial. It meant that men dedicated to peaceful, humane conduct in international relations were in ascendant power. Credibility and honor, the essentials of diplomacy, existed once more. Therefore, in his mind, a pronounced moderate swing culminating in Konoe's unprecedented gesture placed the intractable problems of Japanese-American discussions in an entirely new light and rendered them capable of solution.

As before, the pendulum image was misleading. Japan was indeed hypersensitive to world developments, but reacted less by internal shifts of power or by changing her requirements than by changing her methods of satisfying her requirements. The Army was no less influential and no less determined to achieve its basic objectives in China. The Navy, which Grew persisted in seeing as an influence for moderation, had become quite the reverse. Staff officers urged the Southward Advance as the only way to secure a guaranteed source of fuel for the fleet, accepted the inevitability of war with the United States as a result, and were swinging their superiors to the same view.[2] Retired officers in senior statesman or diplomatic roles like Yonai, Nomura, and Toyoda were not representative of their service. The Army and Navy conceived Japan's role as a great power to mean preponderance in the Far East with control of an inner strategic zone on the mainland comprising North China, Inner Mongolia and Manchuria, dominance of the Western Pacific, and access to resources in the area to assure imperial self-sufficiency. To retain that position they would fight the United States.

The moderates of August and September 1941, no less than the Army and Navy, desired economic invulnerability and East Asian leadership for Japan. However, they were more subtle, flexible, patient, and wary. The Greater East Asian sphere as they saw it did not necessarily require political domination and the Nine-Power Treaty order just might be negotiable. They would say to the military, "If we could end the China war while keeping what Japan really wanted, a preferred economic position, and gain access to American and Southeast Asian resources while avoiding a suicidal war with the United States, Japan would forfeit nothing that time and toil could not eventually secure." To the Americans they would say: "We believe in the *status quo* and territorial integrity, but a nation must act when its very existence is threatened, as is ours by want of resources. The German alliance need not stand in the way of peace in the Pacific. We need peace in China, need your help in securing it, and need your cooperation in the reconstruction and development of China. We believe in equality of economic opportunity but China bulks larger in our world than in yours and we cannot be blind to what occurs there." So they argued and would argue. The moderates were not wielders of power or representatives of a contradictory point of view. Their methods were radically different from Matsuoka's but not their aims. They were not a force in their own right as Grew thought they were. They were essentially brokers of power and ideas.

Konoe gained approval to try for a leaders' meeting, but with a time limit and without authority to promise total evacuation of China. Some idea of the amount of oil the armed forces expected in case of a settlement can be gained from the fact that the Liaison Conference of November 22 decided that if the United States accepted Japan's conditions, Japan would require that the United States guarantee an annual quota of 3,500,000 tons from the United States and 2,000,000 tons from the Dutch East Indies, or the same amount Japan imported during the year of immense stockpiling before the embargo.[3] Japan was prepared to make concessions but it is doubtful that Grew appreciated their limitation or the extent of the concessions Japan expected in return.

The United States was not in a mood for concessions. American public opinion, sentimental about China, hostile to Japan, determined to stand firm against aggressors, is one reason. The importance of keeping faith with friendly powers, evidence of Japanese preparations for further expansion, staggering resource and production requirements as set by the Victory Program, and the tendency to underrate the danger of war with Japan are others.[4] Most obvious to Grew was the reason of principle. From nearly a decade in Japan he knew as well as anyone the importance attached to equality of commercial opportunity, non-disturbance of the *status quo*, non-interference in internal affairs, and territorial integrity. The United States had tolerated much and acquiesced in much since 1931 but never, year after year, note after note, had it in the slightest degree formally approved Japanese action in derogation of the policies established and nurtured by Secretaries Hay, Bryan, Hughes, Stimson, and Hull. By 1941 the burden of the clean record was overpoweringly against any settlement short of Japanese capitulation.

The probability of success for a broad-front approach to Japanese-American problems was very small by August 1941 and less than Grew supposed it to be. Whether or not he would have done better to use his influence for a stopgap agreement that avoided China problems or a broader agreement that temporarily accepted Japanese control of part of China are matters of speculation. In any case, his concern was less with the kind of solution than arriving at a solution. He believed that the process of conciliation afforded an honorable and realistic approach to peace, that war would be senseless and dangerous, and that his function as a diplomat was to try for reconciliation so long as peace existed, however irreconcilable the differences appeared to be.

The argument for "constructive conciliation" was neither proved nor disproved during Grew's mission to Japan. If the prospect for success was small by the time of the Third Konoe Cabinet, it was greater at the time of the Grew-Nomura talks in 1939. A mediated settlement in China was by no means hopeless in 1937. Opportunities arose time and again for the United States to lend a hand for peace in the Far East and to reach limited, practical agreements with Japan establishing confidence and the habit of negotiation and settlement. Certainly Grew's approach seems more imaginative, positive, and resilient than that of his government. In that decade and earlier the United States might have at least manifested a greater awareness of the very real problems of Japanese security and economic well-being, might have provided profitable, reasonable, honorable alternatives to the use of force and to Imperial isolation, might have above all indicated the very great importance to the United States and the Western world of a nation with the drive and skill and culture and extraordinary sensitivity to the world environment of Japan. That respect Grew never failed to show. His mission was a failure, but not a failure of his own making or of professional diplomacy as he conceived it.

The collapse of the Konoe project did not necessarily spell war, at least not immediately. Prince Konoe urged Grew not to be discouraged and not to discourage his government. Japanese friends tried to wear away the boots-and-spurs image of the new Cabinet of General Tōjō Hideki. They ticked off the moderating factors and related the Emperor's concern for peace. It all seemed familiar, but Grew admitted he had been wrong about a military dictatorship taking over if Konoe failed and agreed that Tōjō was the man to make the Army accept a settlement. The Washington conversations resumed and while they lasted time was gained. "Why on earth rush headlong into war?" he asked October 19. The Japanese problem would solve itself when Hitler was defeated. So he passed on to Washington as encouraging a picture as he could, if only to counteract the assumption of American press and radio that the Tōjō Cabinet meant new aggression. But he was discouraged. Reaching an agreement now would be "little short of miraculous," hard to imagine in the near future "if ever," "in the lap of the gods." He could not avoid the conviction that with the passing of Konoe the outlook for peace was "far less favorable than it was before." [5]

Grew had borne constantly in mind the danger of war in case peace efforts failed but he had taken it as a hypothetical danger so long as conversations continued. From the end of October he began to worry that not the fact of conversations but their progress was decisive. On October 29 he heard reliable reports of elaborate plans for an army-navy attack on Thailand. On October 30 he had his first conversation with the new Foreign Minister Tōgō Shigenori. The grim and "ultrareserved" Tōgō warned that the deterioration in Japanese-American relations was "fraught with the gravest dangers" and that the Washington talks must be brought to a successful conclusion without delay. The Foreign Minister was even more chilling in his talks with the British Ambassador. Craigie reported Tōgō as saying that time was now a very important factor and that further deterioration in the situation "might necessitate an extension of Japan's military measures." Craigie felt that there might be less time left than he thought for solutions. Determined not to let his government "get into war with Japan through any possible misconception of what the Japanese, especially the Japanese army, are capable of doing, contrary to all logic and sanity," Grew composed a war warning.[6]

The purpose of Grew's telegram of November 3 was to warn Washington against assuming that continuance of economic pressure would force the collapse of Japan as a militaristic power without war and without resolution of the peace talks. Again he pointed out that the Japanese temper could not be measured by American standards of logic. The Japanese would not yield to foreign pressure. Japan's "capacity to rush headlong into a suicidal struggle with the United States" must not be underestimated, nor her "obvious preparations to implement a program of war if her peace program fails." If that program failed, the pendulum would reverse and swing even further toward extremism than before. In that event he foresaw an "all-out, do or die attempt, actually risking national hara-kiri, to make Japan impervious to economic embargoes abroad." Those who felt the Japanese temper and psychology from day to day recognized that such an attempt was not only possible but probable. "Action by Japan which might render unavoidable an armed conflict with the United States may come with dangerous and dramatic suddenness." He did not mean to imply that the Administration was pursuing an undeliberated policy or to recommend "for a single moment" any compromise of principle, but the United States government must decide whether war with Japan was justified by American national objectives, policies, and needs. In short, the emerging alternative to settlement was war, the United States must make a positive decision whether it wanted war, and it must decide quickly if it had not decided already because "the sands are running fast." [7]

The succeeding two weeks only confirmed Grew's sense of urgency. As the Embassy Commercial Attaché reported, the Ambassador concurring, Japan's economic plight made a choice between war or agreement with the United States necessary "in the very near future." Yoshida confessed his fear that a breakdown of the conversations would bring "drastic and fateful results." A pessimistic Tōgō was understood to be shocked at the failure of Washington to understand the need for speed. In the Foreign Minister's view the conversations were already negotiations and these were in the final stage. Craigie reported him as saying that a conclusion was necessary in a week or ten days. Grew warned the Department November 12 that dragging out the talks indefinitely might accelerate the all-out reaction discussed in his November 3 telegram. He could not be sure that Japan had presented her final terms and he was at a loss to say when and where an attack might occur. Rumors of troop concentrations and dates and directions of attack abounded. The best indicator of potential Japanese military action, he pointed out, was the state of progress of the Washington conversations. November 17 he directed the Department's attention to the great importance of guarding against sudden Japanese military and naval action outside the China theater, exploiting the advantage of surprise. He warned his government not to count on the Embassy to provide prior information since strict security precautions made it impossible for his officers including the military attachés to gather reliable intelligence. He concluded: "Therefore, the United States Government is advised, from an abundance of caution, to discount as much as possible the likelihood of the Embassy's ability to give substantial warning." There was little more he could say, either about peace or about war. When this telegram went off the last echelons of the Pearl Harbor Striking Force were slipping out of Kure naval base on the Inland Sea and making for a final rendezvous at Tankan Bay in the Kuriles.[8]

Actually the Japanese had accepted the alternatives as being war or settlement since the Imperial Conference September 6, the day Grew dined with Konoe. The difficulty lay in establishing a consensus on fighting or compromising. Typically they decided to keep working for a settlement while preparing for war and set a deadline for final decision. As long as the impasse continued the final decision was postponable, but the lateness of the season for attack, the relentless economic squeeze, and the lack of progress in discussions steadily hardened a decision for war. Tōjō's deadline was November 25, extended to November 29. The Japanese knew they were in the final round and so by November 20 did the Americans, thanks to "Magic." Both sides turned to consideration of partial, stopgap proposals, the Japanese presenting one and the Americans drafting several. Even on that basis crucial differences remained: the question of stopping American aid to China while Sino-Japanese peace talks were under way; the amount of oil the United States would supply; the timing of Japan's withdrawal from Indo-China. At the last moment, the Administration backed away from the *modus vivendi* idea in the face of violent Chinese objections, tepid British approval, and mounting evidence of Japanese aggressive purpose furnished by "Magic." Instead, Hull presented a proposal November 26 that was comprehensive, uncompromising, and entirely unresponsive to all Japanese drafts. Though providing for an unfreezing of assets and negotiation of a trade agreement, it called for the evacuation by Japan of Indo-China and China, presumably including Manchuria, in other words a reversal to the *status quo* of 1931. The document served to clear the record for the Americans and to convince the Japanese beyond all doubt that settlement was impossible. On December 1 an Imperial Conference ratified the decision for war and the following day Admiral Yamamoto confirmed the order to attack Pearl Harbor.[9]

For Grew the last days of peace were ritualistic. The Tokyo Embassy played no part in the Japanese-American diplomacy of late November. His advice was neither asked nor given. He was not informed of the various *modus vivendi* proposals until after the Hull note of November 26, and he did not comment on them. He assumed the United States was on the verge of war with Germany. On October 27, after the torpedoing of the destroyer *Kearny* in the Atlantic, the President had warned "the shooting has started," and Grew had commented, "There we go, and I'm all for it." He knew his Japanese friends were dismayed by Hull's proposal of November 26, but, in a burst of sheer wishful thinking, he registered support of it. He described it as "a broad-gauge objective proposal of the highest statesmanship, offering to Japan in effect the very desiderata for which she has ostensibly been fighting and a reasonable and peaceful way of achieving her constantly publicized needs." He argued fervently in support of the proposal at the Tokyo Club, one of the few places he could meet Japanese any more. Lacking means of practical assistance and rational hope, lacking even a desire to compromise, he seemed to be trying to resuscitate diplomacy by an act of will. Vague warnings of a break came from Washington, but he packed nothing. On November 29 he wrote in his diary that his mission had survived many critical days and would surmount this crisis, "I still firmly believe." On December 5 he wrote a friend in the State Department, "I am still hopeful that we may be successful." [10]

Late in the evening of December 7, Tokyo time, the Embassy received a message from President Roosevelt for communication to the Emperor. It contained a polite but pointed warning against hostile action in Southeast Asia and an offer for the neutralization of Indo-China. Grew urgently arranged a midnight meeting with Tōgō, at which he requested an audience with the Emperor at the earliest possible moment. Tōgō said he would present the request to the Throne and Grew returned to the Embassy and went to bed. The message was delivered to the Emperor at 3 A.M., about twenty minutes before the attack on Pearl Harbor began. At 7 A.M. Grew awakened to a request for him to come and see the Foreign Minister at once. He dressed hurriedly and reached the Foreign Ministry at seven-thirty. The imperturbable Tōgō received him at once in formal attire, slapped a document on the table with a gesture of finality, and made a short oral statement as a reply from the Emperor to the President. The document, which served as the Emperor's written reply, was Japan's notice breaking off conversations. Nomura had already delivered it to Hull, but, on account of another muddle, not before the attack was launched. The Minister side-stepped Grew's argument for an Imperial audience, thanked him for his efforts in behalf of Japanese-American friendship, and saw him down to his car. Grew returned to the Embassy intending to change clothes for a game of golf, only to hear first news that Japan and his country were in armed conflict. He would not believe it until it was confirmed. Soon police locked the Embassy gates and at 11 A.M. an official of the Foreign Ministry delivered notice that a state of war existed.[11]

Grew had warned against war, in fact against sudden war, and he had planned against it by shipping home private papers and destroying duplicate code books, but even so, the fact of war, of attack on American territory close to home, was a terrible surprise. Only when the news had been confirmed did he order the destruction of codes, confidential files, seals, and fee stamps. Two officers locked themselves in the code room, sloshed water on the floor, and set the secret material blazing in a half-dozen iron wastebaskets. In the midst of the burning, Japanese radio experts came looking for short-wave sets and asked to inspect the code-room vault, but they took an American word of honor none were in there and went away. Papers burned all day in every fireplace and outside, and the air became thick with floating ash. At dusk the garage courtyard looked like an inferno with fires burning in every direction. No one was permitted to leave the compound, with the result that about one hundred officials and Japanese employees squeezed into makeshift sleeping quarters in the Residence, Chancery, and apartments. The ex-Embassy's only communication with the outside world was through a Foreign Office clerk assigned as liaison. That evening Ambassador and Mrs. Grew had the entire staff in for drinks and then the shocked and exhausted little American colony settled down for its first night of internment. Never before, Grew mused, except for Austria-Hungary in 1917, had a nation declared war on the United States. He had been in Vienna at the time, and in Berlin too. Surely he was the only American diplomat to superintend the closing of three missions due to war.[12]

He and his staff were interned from December 8 to June 25, 1942. They were bitterly critical of their confinement. It was "incarceration" not internment. They were treated as "prisoners, if not criminal prisoners," contrary to all civilized diplomatic usage. Policemen patrolled inside the compound, snooping about the Residence, strutting into the Chancery. Petty officialdom ruled, with its literal-mindedness and swollen sense of importance. The most ordinary transaction with the city, even getting clothes from homes outside the compound, involved an infinity of consultation and negotiation. During the winter months they "nearly froze" for lack of fuel, and they felt crowded, marooned in a sea of hostility, anxious about their repatriation, which was repeatedly postponed, humiliated by American military reverses, and simply bored. On the other hand, they always had enough food, and after a few weeks enough fresh food. They were never subjected to brutality, serious deprivation, or gross indignity. Life was by no means pleasant but it was not intolerable.

Being an embassy gave them advantages besides diplomatic status over other American internees. They were already a community, "a well-united and co-operative group, and a congenial one," in Grew's words, with a system of authority and rank, yet with civilian flexibility. A central commissary purchased food and meted it out to separate messes. Eating arrangements were both hierarchical and equalitarian, Foreign Service Officers and attachés being assigned to the Ambassador's table, but swapping places freely with other tables. The charwomen having been discharged, secretaries of embassy formed sweeping gangs to keep the Chancery clean. As diplomats familiar with Japanese ways they had the patience and know-how to make the best of their forlorn bargaining position and won some improvement in their treatment. Hymn-singing and caroling, toasts and tournaments, the constant practice of their well-developed art of sociability, relieved tedium and preserved *esprit de corps*. They even set up a Greater East Asia Co-Prosperity Golf Course inside the compound, a nine-hole, 422-yard, pitch-and-putt affair with the swimming pool and reflecting pond only the most obvious hazards. One hole offered the choice of a dog-leg around an apartment or a pitch over it. Window breakage, Grew was relieved to note, was minimal. Grew vetoed a dance as flaunting conviviality in the face of authorities, but Christmas was complete with turkeys, plum puddings in flaming brandy, a Santa Claus, and Grew himself at the piano. They played bridge or poker, waited, read, packed, and waited some more.

Time passed "not unpleasantly" for Grew, with a little work, a lot of reading, regular exercise and poker. Yet he had an ashen feeling. On Memorial Day he told his fellow internees that he had been at leisure to "survey the ruins of a life's work, as an architect might regard, after earthquake and fire, the ruins of a great building which he had conceived and had endeavored to erect, pier by pier and stone by stone. . . ." Bataan, Corregidor, Singapore: each black month brought fresh Japanese conquests. The Greater East Asia Sphere became a reality, from Assam to Wake and Kiska to the Coral Sea. He had "not an iota of doubt" of eventual victory. That was a matter of "fundamental instinctive conviction." But the cost of rolling back the Japanese Empire and destroying Japanese militarism was terrible to contemplate. Had it all been necessary? What if the leaders had met? The questions itched and festered during the months of waiting. Why had the President encouraged a leaders' meeting August 28, a month after the Indo-China advance, and then given no further encouragement? Because of "quibbling over formulas"? "Was the transcendent importance to our country of preserving peace to depend on the utterly futile effort to find satisfactory formulas?" Why hadn't the President made that speech telling the Japanese about the concrete benefits of a settlement? Why had the November 26 note, with "an egregious error of timing," been delivered too late to do any good? Why not in August or September? These questions were all subsidiary to the central one, "whether, compatible with our national interests and without sacrificing any point of principle, war with Japan could have been avoided." He was certain it could have been.[13]

He decided to answer the question in the form of a final political report on his mission. That way he could go on record with a confirmation and justification of his position. That way, life being a school for progress, his experience might provide guidance for the future through the medium of history. That way put the days of internment to constructive use. He quoted George Meredith: "And if I drink oblivion for a day, so shorten I the stature of my soul." So he gathered the memoranda and telegrams of the period of the Third Konoe Cabinet and recapitulated the arguments for a leaders' meeting: the plight of Japan at the time, the choice of peace or war, Konoe's recognition of the danger, his attempt to reverse course, his support in the Army, Navy, Cabinet, and Palace, the new opening for diplomacy, the need for prompt action, the value of a dramatic gesture, the American interest in a settlement. The main thrust of his case was the same, but it derived force and cogency from being collected in one place and from being removed from the uncertainties of pre-Pearl Harbor days. In other words, retrospectively his argument was more convincing than it had been in August and September 1941.[14]

Now, after Pearl Harbor, he gave the China problem positive treatment. He argued that what China needed most was peace. According to the Japanese terms, she would have obtained most of her desiderata immediately and all later. The retention of Japanese garrisons in North China and Inner Mongolia would have been only a "face-saving expedient." In fact, foreign garrisons had only been international practice, he added, adopting Toyoda's argument. He contended that any commitment on interrupting aid to China would have been contingent on Japan's proving beyond doubt her intention and ability to implement her commitments. How Japan was to give the necessary proof before China was brought around to accepting peace he did not say. In any case, the argument that agreement with Japan would not involve "selling China down the river" was easier to make now than in September 1941.[15]

The "lessons of history" taught by his experience of a decade in Japan were significant nonetheless. A nation could no longer isolate itself from world affairs and the United States had rightly and inevitably shown concern in situations where war threatened. However, he contended, the right to intervene morally or physically carried with it an obligation to show equal concern for the root causes of conflict. As long as the United States manifested indifference to the conditions giving rise to wars and followed policies exclusively for the protection and furtherance of its own interests — he had in mind the whole range of diplomatic, political, and legislative policies and actions — just so long would it fail to employ its limitless strength toward the development of civilization and its own welfare and avoid the "dissipation of lives and wealth in useless wars." History, experience well learned, might still recover value from the "lost opportunities of the past." [16]

After torturing delays the Embassy group and some of the other Americans in Japan boarded the exchange ship *Asama Maru* on June 18, 1942. They waited in Yokohama harbor another week while final arrangements dragged on. Last impressions of Japan starkly presented the contradictory sides of Japanese behavior that had plagued him from the beginning. Early one morning while they were at anchor, up in the bow of the ship, three elderly American missionaries gave him a realistic demonstration of the water cure as it had been practiced on them. They explained how the victim was bound knees-to-neck, how as much as six big buckets of water were poured down his throat, and how the cure was repeated in one case six times over. On the other hand, he recalled the courtesies of Japanese friends during the internment, the kind notes, the cheese, the oranges, the turkeys, the flowers. He carried away the image of two Japans, the dark side dominant but the light side not quite forgotten.[17]

At 1 A.M. on June 25, ten years and nineteen days after his mission began, he awoke sensing that something was happening. He looked out the porthole and saw a piece of wood moving slowly past and then another moving faster. He was finally homeward bound. The ship picked up other contingents at Hong Kong and Saigon, sailed out of Japan's China Sea at the Sunda Strait, and headed west across the Indian Ocean. At Lourenço Marques in Mozambique on the southeast coast of Africa the *Asama Maru* met the *Gripsholm* and the ships exchanged passengers. Nomura invited Grew to visit but he declined, knowing the press would have played up the meeting. He passed Nomura on the way to town one day but only tipped his hat. "There was really nothing else to be done." The *Gripsholm* turned about, rounded the Cape of Good Hope, stopped a day in Rio de Janeiro where Mrs. Grew left to join her daughter in Chile, and sailed into

New York August 25. That passing of the Statue of Liberty was inexpressibly moving. Grew was first off the ship, smiling and mum to reporters, and went straight to Washington to report.

Grew had an hour and a half with Hull on the day of his arrival. He did not keep a record of the conversation, but it can be inferred that the main subject was the Ambassador's final political report dealing with the leaders' meeting question. Grew apparently presented the gist of the report and Hull then asked, "If you thought so strongly, why didn't you board a plane and come to tell us?" The thought that he had not conveyed his strong feeling in favor of a meeting must have shaken Grew. He wondered if the Secretary had even seen his "For the Secretary and Under Secretary Only" telegrams. Actually, there is no reason to suppose that Hull did not see them or that Grew could have gained more success in person than at a distance. In any case, the Secretary asked him to destroy the report. Grew explained to one of his former staff members: "This is not a moment to bring forward controversial issues. Our entire effort must now be devoted to winning the war, forgetting the past and looking forward to a victorious future." The "lessons of history" would have to wait.[18]

The question of employment for the former Ambassador to Japan was settled quickly and easily. He was determined to do his part in the war, but he did not want to enter the line of command at the State Department. He looked on his career as a closed book and he was anxious to be free of routine. In any case, a close working relationship between himself and Hull at this stage is hard to imagine. Strengthening the home front by speech-making, as he had in 1917-18, was the obvious assignment. He was well known and well versed in public speaking. Having just emerged from the midst of the enemy, he was the object of intense curiosity. A radio broadcast he made soon after arrival elicited a pile of correspondence to make the Washington Monument blush for shame, he told Castle. What he had to say about Japan after ten years there as Ambassador would be, so to speak, "straight from the horse's mouth." In particular he might serve to overcome the "wishful thinking, unfounded optimism and smug complacency" of the American public toward Japan, the idea that once Germany was defeated Japan would be a pushover. Accordingly, Grew was appointed Special Assistant to the Secretary of State, placing him in effect on detached service to bring the war against Japan home to Americans in any way he saw fit. The Office of War Information proved helpful in arranging speaking tours, writing speech drafts, and suggesting points that needed to be driven home, but for the most part he himself determined what was said. Between engagements he worked in his handsome home on the edge of Rock Creek Park, which he had not occupied for fifteen years. Awakening to the birds chirping in the glorious trees and breakfast on the terrace put life in something like its proper proportions again.[19]

Moments of quiet were rare. He was nearly always "storming up and down the country," swinging twice through the South and once through the West, touching Canada twice, and taking innumerable excursions to the Midwest and Northeast. He gave nine speeches in one sixty-hour stint, and two hundred and fifty in the year after his return from Japan. He spoke at Town Hall and Carnegie Hall, at the Tavern Club and a tank arsenal, to nurses' aides and investment bankers. He received invitations from the infinite variety of professional, business, patriotic, social, educational, and charitable organizations through which Americans formulate their public attitudes. He preferred small influential groups or public rallies, frequently broadcasted, with as many as ten thousand attending on one occasion. His large collection of clippings indicates that he was an immensely popular speaker and that his message carried. "Record crowd listens with fascination," said the *Detroit Free Press* February 9, 1943. He would read from a short prepared text and then talk "intimately, off-the-record and man-to-man" about his experiences in Japan.[20]

Grew's message was that Americans must accept the necessity of totally defeating Japan, that this would require a long, bloody war, and that it could be accomplished only by unity, sacrifice, hard work, and determination on the home front. It was a propaganda message, exaggerating by emphasis, and occasionally altering the substance of his earlier views, but it suited the belligerent mood in which he returned home and the way Japan would look with the pendulum positioned at the far point of extremism. The real enemy, he told his audiences, was the formidable Japanese military machine. It was formidable because of its ruthless, fanatical, coldly calculating leaders who had plotted conquest since 1931 and planned to bomb and invade the United States, because of its tough, experienced, do-or-die soldiers, because of its mastery of the Far East with all the resources necessary for modern war and interior lines of communication, and because of its control of a docile, regimented, frugal, skilled people, prepared to make every sacrifice for Emperor and homeland. He warned against a Japanese peace offensive, launched perhaps by setting up a puppet liberal cabinet, aiming to lull the United Nations into leaving the military in control of some of its holdings and its power. Such a "jujitsu" peace would only be an armed truce. Already the enemy was digging in and would be ever harder to dislodge. Security, freedom, permanent peace, and humanitarian values required battle now and with ever increasing intensity until the utter defeat and discrediting of the Japanese military machine.[21]

In spite of stern language bringing headlines like GREW EXCORIATES JAP

MURDERERS, he never called for the extermination or destruction of the Japanese nation. His aim was always military defeat and reconstruction. He was careful to distinguish implicitly if not explicitly between the Japanese people and Japanese militarism. "The average Japanese," he wrote Elmer Davis, October 12, 1942, "is a gentle, courteous, friendly, beauty-loving person and it is only when he is dragged into the maw of the military machine that he becomes brutalized and is capable of the horrible deeds carried out during the rape of Nanking and elsewhere." Once the military machine was defeated and discredited, once the "cancer of militarism" was cut out, the United States and the United Nations would find "liberal elements" to constitute the nucleus of authority in the new Japan. However, the theme of moderation was barely represented in his speeches of the first ten months. In his radio broadcast August 30, 1942, he spoke of Japanese friends he "admired, respected, and loved," but thereafter, probably because critics found the reference to good Japanese anticlimactical and confusing, he spoke only of moderates who had not wanted war, had not started war, were powerless, and would fight to the last for Emperor and country. Nevertheless, he was careful not to paint too black a picture. The very qualities that made Japan formidable as an enemy were qualities which, in other circumstances, could not only be respected but admired. He reserved his harshest terms like "bestiality," "ruthlessness," and "rapaciousness" for the military, particularly the military police. After one venture into atrocity stories just after his return, he referred to them without details. He did not use the word "Jap" except in quotations. His image of the Japanese enemy was harsh but not inflexible.[22]

Beginning with a speech May 20, 1943, there was a significant modulation in Grew's themes. The qualities and capacities of the foe were no less formidable, the road to Tokyo would be no less long and bloody, the need utterly to defeat and eradicate Japanese militarism was no less great, but he devoted less time to these themes. Now he began to differentiate the people of Japan from the military and to make them recognizable as human beings. They were not "racially bad," not "wolves in human form." They exhibited "a very human kind of prejudice." Other peoples had been obsessed with ideas more cruel and bestial than those infecting Japan. He noted the honor in which Japanese used to hold the United States and their friendliness, courtesy, and loyalty to Americans. They had been caught in the military machine and now were fighting to preserve their enslavement. Their civilian leaders had been tricked into preparing aggression when they thought they were planning against war. Japan had been conquered from within. After defeat change would have to come from within; it could not be imposed. Whatever was found healthy in the Japanese body politic should be preserved. One could not uproot an ancient tree and expect it to grow again, but if the trunk and roots were healthy and the rotten branches ruthlessly cut away, the remaining branches and foliage could with care achieve regeneration. He was confident in the great powers of regeneration of the Japanese people. He could foresee some day, somehow, another chance for the Japanese and American peoples to understand one another. "With no militarism or feudal propaganda on their side, and with no touch, however faint, of arrogance or superiority on ours, we shall be able to meet on common ground. . . ." [23]

On December 29, 1943, in a speech before the Illinois Educational Association, Grew warmed to the theme of peace. It was a plea for tolerance and statesmanship in dealing with a defeated Japan. He chipped away at the common prejudice expressed in the saying, "The only good Jap is a dead Jap," at the common assumption that Japanese were "a barbarous, tricky, brutal mass that we can have no truck with, ever again." Japanese, he argued, could be led to peaceful ways if given hope for the future. They must have something better to look forward to than being fenced in and left to "stew in their own juice," as some suggested. He visualized reconstruction in a "helpful, cooperative, common-sense spirit . . . with emphasis laid upon what the Japanese would have to gain by playing the game with the rest of the world. . . ." He dwelt on the theme of indigenous growth and change according to Japanese traditions as opposed to the imposition of ready-made Western reforms. For example, some favored eliminating Shintoism because as a cult it had been used by the military to stress the virtues of war and instill subservience. The evil as Grew saw it was not the cult, but military influence and power. Once that was destroyed, Emperor homage and ancestor worship did not seem objectionable, indeed under a peace-seeking ruler could be an asset. In conclusion he quoted the authority on Japan, Sir George Sansom, as contemplating the development in Japan under favorable conditions of "a more modern and democratic type of constitutional monarchy." [24]

Grew gave no explanation for his shirt from war to peace themes beginning in May 1943. Undoubtedly saturation was a problem: having said it would be a long, hard war at two hundred and fifty places, the marginal utility of saying it again was small. By mid-1943 rousing the public to superhuman efforts was not so important because war production was in high gear. Another reason is obvious from the content. He feared that Americans were so vindictive toward Japan that they would demand a Carthaginian peace. The end of the war was a long way off but with American forces beginning to inch forward in New Guinea, the Solomons, and the Gilberts, it was not too early to instill the thought of a peaceful, prosperous, stable postwar Japan. The future of Japan in a territorial sense was already the subject of high-level discussion and agreement at Moscow, Teheran, and Cairo and detailed planning was under way in postwar policy committees of the State Department.[25]

One further reason suggests itself, though it cannot be substantiated. Grew may have been talking to the Japanese moderates as well as the American public. Many of his speeches were published in the *Department of State Bulletin*, which Japanese could obtain without difficulty. In Tokyo something like a peace conspiracy was developing among the Jūshin, or ex-Premiers, and Palace advisers. They scored their first success in April 1943, the month before Grew's speeches began changing, with the appointment of Shigemitsu as Foreign Minister. It had been Shigemitsu who informed Grew in September 1941 of the Emperor's interest in a *rapprochement* with the United States and who was among those sending presents to Grew during internment. Whatever Grew said would be listened to carefully because he was a known quantity and each speech would be compared with the one before. It seems not unreasonable to suppose that the new approach was meant to encourage the moderates by giving them hope for the future once Japan was totally defeated, thereby strengthening their hand against Tōjō and the military.[26]

Grew was "roundly damned," he said, for the Chicago speech. A *New York Times* editorial, criticizing him by name, suggested that the Emperor institution was not a fit subject for public debate in time of war. Anything resembling defense of Shinto or the Emperor seemed out of place when Americans were fighting against everything these stood for.[27] However, *Times* to the contrary, the question could not be ignored. The United States as principal belligerent could not avoid deciding what kind of Japan it would work for, and the Emperor question was central to that decision. The Chicago speech contributed to a developing debate within the community of scholars, writers, and policy-makers concerned with Far Eastern affairs. Grew more than anyone represented the school of mild, in the sense of selective, reform. Opposed were those who argued for root-and-branch reconstruction.

The radical reformers argued that Japan even under a reformed Emperor system would still be an unresolved and dangerous problem for the rest of the world. In their view the institution had become inextricably bound up with pernicious dogma sanctifying aggression and withering the shoots of individual political and moral responsibility. Some would argue further that the institution served an oligarchy of landlords, zaibatsu, and military which found a mutuality of interest in depression of the working classes and imperialism and used the Emperor as a device for maintaining authority and perpetuating their power. Generally the radicals held that the institution of the Emperor had been too thoroughly associated in the past with the forces of aggression and reaction to encourage the development of attitudes and institutions characteristic of a democratic and peaceful way of life. Abolishing State Shinto was not enough; the institution of the Emperor must be entirely discredited and discarded.[28]

In Grew's mind, the question was not how much of the old Japan had to be destroyed but how much could be saved. He was clear that the institution of the Emperor as distinct from the incumbent Hirohito, whom he could not see continuing after the war, would provide a stabilizing influence, a "cornerstone" for the Japan of the future. The Emperor represented authority, which could be just as well used by the United Nations for efficient occupation, implementation of reform, and inauguration of a new order of international cooperation as it had been used by the military for aggression. The excrescences of state religion would fall away naturally if not openly attacked. Grew's main concern was preservation of order. Unlike the radical reformers, he did not see Japan swelling with suppressed democratic or proto-democratic sentiment. Rather Japanese were easily led, like sheep. Destruction of the symbol and modes of authority would create a chaotic situation ripe for would-be dictators and Communists. As to goals for Japan, he was vague. He approved of the breakup of the zaibatsu and agrarian reform. He had recommended a New Deal for Japan in 1936 and did so again now. However, it is doubtful that he envisaged any profound change in the social structure. He probably assumed leadership by moderates of the type he knew, who, he wrote in May 1944, were "the best one can find in any country in point of character and outlook." Some leveling up and leveling down economically, something of the old "gentle and cultural life," and a rebirth of Shidehara diplomacy: Grew was not breaking new paths of thought at sixty-four.[29]

These were Grew's private opinions; publicly he declined to debate. He claimed that his Chicago speech was incorrectly and incompletely reported and that he had spoken as an individual and not officially. In an interview with *New York Times* correspondent Bertram Hulen published February 2, 1944, he expressed his "fiery rage" at reports of Japanese atrocities. His next speech in the State Department *Bulletin* was a warning against complaceny and premature peace moves. The Chicago venture had been discouraging. Anything said in favor of the Emperor was anathema to the American people, he wrote an old friend. In a memorandum to Hull of April 1944 he wandered from his subject a moment to say that sometimes it was in the nation's best interests to lead rather than follow public opinion. He added that he often had wished for such leadership during his mission in Japan and was "prepared at any time to elaborate this thought." [30]

Instead of debating, he approached the problem of moderate peace obliquely. In the spring of 1944 *Ten Years in Japan* appeared, a book consisting mainly of excerpts from his diary together with important speeches and incidental correspondence. It is not a reliable document for historians. Representing only a small fraction of the vast bulk of his papers, it is seldom comprehensive on any given subject or event, though it does give the flavor of his diplomacy and the main lines of his thought. It suffers from the disadvantages of near-contemporaneous publication on a highly sensitive subject. Within passages selected, Grew cut the text for reasons of security and protection of sources in addition to irrelevancy. He also excised indiscreet remarks that would be embarrassing to himself or wounding to colleagues or countrymen, as well as criticism of American policy and rationalization of Japanese actions. Regarding his diary as his personal property, he felt free to pick and choose for publication, even without giving signs indicating changes had been made, though he did give appropriate warning in the Foreword. Occasionally, where he felt the text was valuable but personally embarrassing or unclear, he added or substituted but in only one case did he alter the original meaning of a passage relating to diplomacy by doing so. In 1934 the Dutch Minister had warned that the Japanese Navy might descend on Guam and Grew had commented in the diary, "I do not think that such an insane step is likely. . . ." In *Ten Years* he added the word "now."[31] The book was not intended to be his last word in print. The memoirs and the case for a leaders' meeting would have to await peace and retirement. This was a quick dipping into the historical record mainly for a specific diplomatic purpose.

What emerged was a compact, colorful narrative, aiming, he explained to his former First Secretary at Tokyo, to break down the wall of American prejudice toward Japanese that strongly resembled the prejudice toward Germans in World War I. In his opinion such attitudes led to harsh and temporary peace. The material selected balanced the beauty and delicacy of Japan against its chauvinism and brutality. The story conveyed his sense of the depth and genuineness of Japanese feeling about the Emperor, and told of the Emperor's evident concern for good relations with the United States and the sincere but futile efforts of the moderates to curb the military. It was a warm, personal account, telling of money, equivalent to twenty cents, sent by little boys of Meguro for California earthquake victims and the near-destruction of his dog Sambo in the moat of the Imperial Palace and heroic rescue by a taxi driver. Coincidentally appeared a *National Geographic* article on Japan seeking to accomplish pictorially what Grew said in accompanying words and in the book.[32]

The reviews of *Ten Years* were mostly favorable, Grew being credited with making the best of a hopeless assignment in Japan. Some dissented, however, criticizing his aristocratic and big-business connections in Japan. T. A. Bisson, who had taken him to task for favoring retention of the Emperor, likened Grew's mission to Nevile Henderson's and China to Czechoslovakia. War with Japan could have been averted, not by Grew's method of pouring oil on troubled waters, but by early and uncompromising resistance to aggressors. The public liked the book and it rose to second place on the *New York Times* best-seller list in June and July, behind Catherine Drinker Bowen's *Yankee from Olympus,* fading in August perhaps because of a switch in interest to Europe with its great post-invasion battles. Americans who read it could hardly have avoided the impression that simple generalization about the enemy was impossible and that victory would find much of the old Japan that was promising to work with.[33]

Henceforth Grew pursued his peace concerns from the inside. On May 1, 1944, he replaced Hornbeck as Director of the Office of Far Eastern Affairs. The shift to a policy assignment did not bring him into active participation in policy-making, however. He spent most of his time on other work, negotiating civil aviation treaties and attending the Dumbarton Oaks Conference as a member of the American delegation, while Joseph Ballantine, the Deputy Director, ran the Office. Nevertheless, Grew was now in a position to oversee work of the Inter-Divisional Area Committee on the Far East, the postwar planning group that concerned him most. On that committee the so-called "Japan crowd" was well represented. They included, by Grew's account, Dooman, Ballantine, and Erle Dickover, formerly his First Secretary in Tokyo. Also from the Tokyo Embassy were Frank S. Williams, his former Commercial Attaché, and Robert A. Fearey, his former private secretary. On a committee numbering thirteen to sixteen representing eight or ten divisions of the Department, a minority of five or six with common ties and purpose can exercise considerable influence.[34]

On May 9, 1944, the Inter-Divisional Committee recommended in effect that the Emperor be kept. It did so in a curious roundabout fashion suggesting unresolved internal disagreement. It did not really respond to the questions put to it respecting the status of the Emperor, insisting that the answer depended on the Japanese, the United Nations, and the American public. The Committee noted that China and increasingly the American public seemed to prefer abolition of the institution. However, the report proceeded to assume that continuance was desired and useful. Under those circumstances, the Emperor should be kept in seclusion under protective custody with access to personal advisers. All powers of civil administration would be in the hands of the United Nations theater commander who might exercise his authority with respect to civil administration through the Emperor, permitting use of only such Imperial functions as related to delegation of administrative duties. That way the theater commander would in effect rule the people through their Emperor and civil servants. Occupation authorities should take no action implying recognition of the Japanese concept that the Emperor was different from or superior to other temporal rulers, that he was sacrosanct or indispensable. Grew seems to have had the balance of opinion at the divisional level on the side of keeping the institution, but not to the point of recommending that it be kept.[35]

On November 21, 1944, the Hull era finally came to a close with the resignation of the ailing Secretary of State. The President wanted a successor who would accept White House direction of foreign policy but who had the organizing ability to bring the State Department into the twentieth century. He chose Edward Stettinius, a man of warmth and energy with a dazzling career in big business and wartime government. Stettinius needed an experienced diplomat at his side to run ordinary business and prevent *faux pas* and he offered the Under Secretaryship to Grew. Grew had no desire to go through another 1927 again. Running an embassy and "coordinating the warring elements in a government department" were as different as day and night, he had explained to his old chief James Gerard, who had been importunately promoting him for the office in 1943. Nevertheless, Grew accepted out of a sense of duty and because he had come to like "Ed" Stettinius immensely when the latter was Under Secretary and worked comfortably with him. Undoubtedly Grew recognized the opportunity of gaining influence in the Japan settlement. Perhaps he also relished the thought of seeing Old State churn with reform.[36]

Grew's nomination was reported to the Senate floor December 6, 1944, and ran into opposition. Senator Joseph Guffey read into the record an editorial from the *Philadelphia Record* attacking Grew for advocating "doing business with Hirohito" and for connections in Japan reminiscent of the Cliveden Set. The editorial noted that he had been sharply criticized as Under Secretary in the days of Coolidge. Again 1927! A handful of liberal and independent senators joined Guffey and a restive Senate recommitted the nomination together with a slate of Assistant Secretaries. Appearing before the Foreign Relations Committee again, Grew gave the usual denials and explanations about his Emperor position and then used an interesting analogy. The Emperor was like a queen bee, he said, administered to and venerated by the hive. With momentous decision impending, the hive vibrated and suddenly the queen was thrust forth and the hive followed her to a new home. "It was not the queen which made the decision; yet if one were to remove the queen from the swarm the hive would disintegrate." We should wait and see about the Emperor, he concluded. He might save us from having to control indefinitely a disintegrating community of seventy million.[37]

Actually the delay was less on account of Grew than the list of appointments he headed, which included Nelson A. Rockefeller and William L. Clayton, a rich cotton broker. With a Secretary of State who was formerly head of United States Steel and son of a Morgan partner and these two Assistant Secretaries, Senator "Happy" Chandler wondered if the poor folks had won the election after all. It was more a scuffle than a fight.

The White House applied pressure and the nominations went sailing through December 19, Grew's margin of 66 to 7 topping the rest. Nevertheless, the stigma of wealth had been attached along with appeasement and "soft peace." He had stepped into what was essentially a political role on the peace question and was finding it difficult to slip back into professional anonymity again.[38]

The enthusiasm of Stettinius was infectious. Efficient command of State seemed a simple matter the way he described it. Desks clean, routine systematized, the Secretary and Under Secretary would have time "just to sit and think." If one of them were tired, he could go away a week or ten days for a rest. That vision must have seemed ironic to Grew in succeeding months. The Secretary left for Yalta in January 1945, went directly from there to a conference in Mexico City, and soon after left again for the United Nations Conference at San Francisco. Grew was Acting Secretary nearly half the time from December 20 to April 24 and all the time from April 24 to the swearing in of a new Secretary July 3, 1945. These were months of vast consequence, bringing the death of Franklin Roosevelt, V-E Day, and Okinawa, the last battle before invasion of the home islands. With one war concluding and another reaching its climax, the problems before the American government were staggering in variety and magnitude, yet its capacity for planning and decision was at a low point. With the strength of one President fading and the grip of his successor unsure, State lacked its accustomed political direction from the White House. With personnel and organization undergoing radical change and many principal officers absent at conferences, the Department lacked coherency. It was a time of hiatus, confusion, and appalling responsibility for Grew.[39]

The story of Grew's second Under Secretaryship is obscure. He had stopped keeping a personal record since he left Japan. Such official records for 1945 as are available relate more to the great conferences than to the officials who stayed home. Records where he is involved rarely indicate his personal initiative or point of view. He did not enjoy power in his own right but as a stand-in. To the forceful personalities who dominated the scene he must have seemed rather quaint. In Cabinet one day he was presenting a survey of the world situation that he had obviously taken some pride and care in preparing, but before he had finished President Truman interposed a remark and switched the discussion to domestic affairs.[40]

Grew moved carefully and deferentially. He kept in touch with Stettinius and every morning at nine-thirty consulted the Secretary's Staff Committee, composed of the principal officers in the Department. He seldom took a position without first establishing consensus in that committee and he appears to have seldom taken action without first consulting President Truman. The fact that on one visit to the White House he took up and received decision on fourteen items in fifteen minutes suggests not only that the President was a prompt decision-maker but also that Grew was taking up matters with him that a Secretary would ordinarily decide for himself. On matters of high strategic policy Grew consulted laterally with Secretaries James Forrestal and Henry Stimson in the State-War-Navy Coordinating Committee (SWINK) which met every Tuesday. In that group the influence of Stimson was predominant. Grew's role as Acting Secretary was that of coordinator, in the circumstances a useful if not heroic function.[41]

He worked harder than ever before, six and often seven days a week, from eight until past seven in the evening. He would come home, his wife said, looking like a piece of Gorgonzola cheese, only to work on into the night. In April he had a painful gallstone attack. A decision on surgery was postponed but hung over him. At least deafness was no longer a severe handicap. He took to wearing a hearing aid that picked up sounds he had never heard before. Another advantage was having Billy Phillips by his side. His old friend heard of his predicament and offered to help out. Together the two professionals, with experience totaling eighty-odd years, agents of an unremembered past, sought to smooth the transition to a new age of American diplomacy.[42]

On one subject, surrender terms for Japan, Grew clearly did take the initiative. So long as great battles remained to be fought his concern about the Emperor institution had been long-range and somewhat hypothetical, but now each month made the question more immediate and acute. Late in 1944 he visited Admiral Chester Nimitz at Pearl Harbor and presumably saw the plans for Iwo Jima and Okinawa. He was pleased to report to Stettinius that Nimitz agreed about the importance of the Emperor not only in preventing chaos but also in bringing about peace. Surrender by "some" Japanese government, Grew wrote in April 1945, would be no guarantee that millions of Japanese soldiers throughout East Asia would lay down their arms. The one thing that might prevent a costly mopping up was an Imperial Rescript, sacred to all Japanese, ordering the Japanese armies to give up. That Rescript would hardly be forthcoming so long as the Emperor had every reason to suppose it meant abolishing the Throne as well. All evidence available to Grew indicated that the Japanese masses wished to retain the institution. Prisoners of war who were collaborating in psychological warfare insisted in every known instance on not being required to say anything derogatory of the Emperor. Polls of civilian internees on Saipan and elsewhere were overwhelmingly in favor of retaining him. Every practical, humane, and reasonable argument seemed to beg for declaring that the Japanese could keep their Emperor after surrender if they wanted to.[43]

However, any such declaration was bound to conflict with unconditional surrender, the formula which had governed Allied war effort and maintained Allied unity since the Casablanca Conference in January 1943. Grew's attitude toward unconditional surrender was ambivalent. On the one hand he found it "difficult to conceive that any Japanese government, or any Japanese faction, will ever surrender unconditionally," but at the same time he declared the importance of unconditional surrender as a means of bringing home to the Japanese their utter defeat, thus destroying the militaristic psychology. Any retreat from the formula would indicate lack of determination. Once again, as in the case of the contradiction between the independence of China and the Japanese stipulation for retaining garrisons there, he denied the existence of a problem in order to circumvent it. He made a distinction between terms and treatment: insisting on surrender without terms, he said, did not conflict with telling the Japanese beforehand what treatment they might expect after surrender. The fact remained, nevertheless, whatever Grew might say, that any restriction of the freedom of the occupation authority stated as an inducement to surrender would qualify that surrender.[44]

By the end of May 1945 Grew felt that some positive step by the United States to induce surrender was urgently necessary. The President's public statement May 8 that unconditional surrender did not mean extermination or enslavement opened the way to more precise definition of what it did not mean. Fighting in Europe had ended and redeployment of American forces was under way. Planning was complete for over 700,000 troops to invade the home island of Kyushu in November. Bitter fighting in progress on Okinawa suggested that the cost would be high. Meanwhile B-29's were reducing Japanese cities to rubble and ashes. May 27 headlines in the *Washington Post* read: TOKYO "SCORCHED TO GROUND"; IMPERIAL PALACES DEVASTATED. Bomber crews reported that "walls of fire" from eight thousand tons of incendiaries were "sweeping upon the imperial palace compound." This seemed to Grew the right psychological moment to encourage surrender. It must have seemed the last moment as well, if the Emperor were to play a part.[45]

Developments within Japan were encouraging. In April 1945 Admiral Suzuki Kantarō became Premier. The former Grand Chamberlain had been a guest at the Embassy the evening before the February 26 Incident and had been among those wounded by assassins the next day. His credentials as a moderate were well established. Reports from neutral capitals indicated, if not authorized peace moves, at least a waxing interest in peace. Military authorities in Japan betrayed their concern by threatening to deal drastically with anyone agitating for peace. The military still retained control, Grew acknowledged, but added, "we feel certain that the issue of surrender or destruction will sooner or later be debated, if it is not now being debated, within the innermost recesses of the Japanese political structure." He feared American demands for the abolition of the emperorship would be uppermost in the minds of civilian members of the government. By removing their apprehension Japan might be coaxed into total surrender before the bloody final act.[46]

Another concern of Grew that may have related to the surrender question was the threat of Soviet Russia. During the spring of 1945 the Cold War mentality was fast gripping American policy-makers, especially the staunchly anti-Communist Acting Secretary. Grew watched country after country in eastern Europe come under Soviet domination or influence. In May, Tito of Yugoslavia moved to take over the strategic port of Trieste, precipitating an acute crisis in which Grew recommended firmness. He had no doubt that Tito was acting as the cat's-paw of the Russians. At Yalta the Soviet Union had confirmed its intention of entering the war against Japan about three months after the defeat of Germany and that clock was ticking. On May 12 Grew raised the question with Forrestal and Stimson of reopening the Yalta accords on the Far East at the forthcoming Big Three meeting (Potsdam) to obtain more specific Soviet guarantees. He asked whether a Soviet demand for participation in the occupation of Japan should be granted and whether such occupation would "adversely affect our long term policy for the future treatment of Japan." May 19, at the height of the Trieste crisis, he spent a sleepless night and at dawn set down his thoughts in a private memo which he read to associates and then locked away. In it he took an alarmed view of Soviet ambitions, seeing them as extending across Europe and East Asia. The war against the Axis, necessary as it was, had resulted in transferring totalitarian dictatorship and power from Germany and Japan to the Soviet Union, which would become an equally grave danger to the United States. Once Russia entered the Far Eastern war her influence would expand until finally both China and Japan would slip into her orbit. "A future war with Soviet Russia," Grew wrote, "is as certain as anything in the world is certain." After the setting up of the United Nations, American policy toward Russia should "immediately stiffen, all along the line." [47]

The true relationship between Grew's surrender policy and his concurrent concern over Soviet ambitions cannot be established from available documents. Indeed, it may be impossible to establish since Grew would be reluctant to make a record of the connection while the Soviet Union, officially at least, remained a partner. Furthermore, the argument for a definition of the treatment Japan might expect did not need to rest on the Soviet problem since the anticipated cost of invasion and mounting Japanese interest in peace provided, at least in Grew's view, adequate justification. It is reasonable to assume that, given his evident alarm about the Russians, the idea of ending the war with Japan before they entered it was very much in his mind and lent urgency to the question of inducing surrender.

Grew took the initiative by recommending to President Truman that he include in his forthcoming speech to Congress on the progress of the war a statement aimed specially at the Japanese nation. He made his recommendation personally to Truman at the White House May 28, 1945, the other person present being Judge Samuel Rosenman, Special Counsel to the President. Grew argued that the object of the war, the blotting out of Japan's military machine and cult, must be thoroughly accomplished, but with least possible cost in lives. Any step rendering it easier for Japan to surrender unconditionally now should be carefully considered. He continued: "If some indication can now be given the Japanese that they themselves, when once thoroughly defeated and rendered impotent to wage war in the future, will be permitted to determine their own political structure, they will be afforded a method of saving face without which surrender will be highly unlikely." He pointed out that even Chiang Kai-shek had said that a defeated and penitent Japan should be permitted to determine its own political future. Then he reiterated his arguments for preserving the Emperor institution and submitted a draft statement for inclusion in the President's speech. According to Grew, Truman replied that his own thoughts were "following the same line." He asked the Acting Secretary to consult the Secretaries of War and Navy, as well as Admiral Ernest J. King and General George C. Marshall and report back.[48]

Grew did so the following day. Stimson, Forrestal, and Marshall (King was absent) "liked the idea but for military reasons they wanted another couple of months before acting," Grew wrote in October 1945. Not to be put off for military reasons, he tried the President again June 15, 16, and 18. He pointed out that another opportune moment for a statement was approaching with the imminent fall of Okinawa. He advised the President to tell the Japanese that after rehabilitation they would not only "be permitted to determine for themselves their future political structure," but also allowed to retain a peacetime economy sufficient to enable them "to work their way back into the family of nations." The statement should in any case be made before the invasion of the home islands because the casualties sustained in that fighting would so harden American opinion that the only alternative would be to let matters take their course "until the bitter end." The President was inclined to wait until the Big Three meeting. Grew argued there was no reason why the United States, having borne the brunt of the fighting, could not act alone. The President decided to wait and Grew finally accepted that "there was of course nothing more to be done. . . ."[49]

From May 28 to June 18 Grew, assisted and supported by the Japan experts in the State Department, took the initiative in pressing for clarification of the treatment Japan might expect in defeat in order to bring prompt surrender. Meanwhile, the decision on the invasion of Kyushu was concluded and understanding was reached that atomic weapons would be used if the July test proved successful. The military program for the defeat of Japan seemed well established. What was lacking in the view of Secretary Stimson was a political program that might translate enormous American military advantages and certain victory into achievement of American objectives economically, that is without invasion, perhaps without the bomb as well. He had in mind a political offensive closely timed to military action. Warning of destruction, coupled with the kind of inducement Grew had been suggesting, should be tried first, followed if necessary by use of the bomb giving awesome meaning to the warning. If this program did not work, invasion would have to follow. Stimson's politico-military approach assumed the probability of having to administer further shocks to the enemy as well as further encouragement about the future, while Grew's exclusively political approach assumed that military force already applied was enough and only further encouragement was necessary. Stimson began moving to the front at a meeting of the Joint Chiefs, and the service Secretaries with the President June 18. He had the backing at least of Forrestal, King, and Admiral William Leahy and he gained the interest of the President. Thus encouraged, the Secretary of War threw his immense prestige into the development of his approach and the initiative passed from Grew to him.[50]

Stimson, with the full support of Forrestal and Grew, marshaled the arguments in favor of a warning to Japan, which he drew up in impressive array in a memorandum he handed the President July 2. At the same time a drafting committee under the direction of his Assistant Secretary, John J. McCloy, with Dooman and Ballantine representing the State Department, worked on the text of the warning. Their final draft was in the form of a joint proclamation, as the President insisted, to be issued by the United States, Great Britain, China, and, if then a belligerent, the Soviet Union. The key paragraph, Number 12, stated that the occupying forces would withdraw when their objectives were accomplished and "a peacefully inclined, responsible government of a character representative of the Japanese people" had been established "in accordance with the freely expressed will of the Japanese people." It continued:

> This may include a constitutional monarchy under the present dynasty if the peace-loving nations can be convinced of the genuine determination of such a government to follow policies of peace which will render impossible the future development of aggressive militarism in Japan.[51]

In delivering the draft proclamation to the President, Stimson explained that it was not a final document approved by the Secretaries of State and Navy or the Joint Chiefs, but only something put on paper to suggest how a warning such as they had in mind would appear. His caution can be explained by the fact that there was no Secretary of State to approve the draft, the resignation of Stettinius having been accepted June 27. The new Secretary, James F. Byrnes, was named June 30 and took office July 3. It would have been neither responsible nor politic for Stimson or Grew to move to an official recommendation without the approval of Byrnes. Gaining that approval was up to Grew, and on July 3 the initiative passed back to him.[52]

The explicit allowance for the retention of the Emperor institution encountered serious difficulty in the State Department. Grew's Japan policy had never carried the Department and opposition was now strongly represented in the Secretary's Staff Committee by Assistant Secretaries Archibald MacLeish and Dean Acheson. Critics argued that clarification of unconditional surrender which in fact satisfied Japan's irreducible terms would be conditional surrender. They also presented the familiar argument that retention of the Emperor institution would mean perpetuation of the power of feudal, reactionary groups in Japan that were responsible for imperialism and aggression. Unable to satisfy his critics, Grew had to proceed without the backing of his own Department. Cordell Hull, ever the barometer of Congressional sentiment, whom Byrnes consulted by phone, said that the Emperor stipulation seemed "too much like appeasement." Later, in a message to Byrnes forwarded by Grew, Hull added that failure of the assurance to effect surrender would lead to "terrible political repercussions" in the United States. The political sensitivity of the question was obvious from a Gallup Poll reported on the front page of the *Washington Post* June 29. It showed that 33 percent of those polled favored executing Hirohito, 37 percent favored putting him on trial, imprisoning him for life, or exiling him, and only 7 percent favored leaving him alone or using him as a puppet. Grew tried to interest the new Secretary in the proclamation and gave him a copy of it, but found him preoccupied. On July 6, three days after taking office, a non-committal Byrnes departed for Potsdam.[53]

The scene shifted to Potsdam and Stimson followed through. Plans synchronized perfectly. The atomic device tested successfully in the New Mexico desert July 16. The first bomb would be dropped between August 1 and 10. That news gave Truman his "cue" for a warning that was issued from Potsdam, July 26, by the United States, Great Britain, and China. The Potsdam Proclamation generally followed Stimson's draft except for one crucial deletion, the assurance about the Emperor in Paragraph 12. Concern over the domestic repercussions of changing course too fast was a major factor with Truman and Byrnes in avoiding explicit assurance on the Emperor, as was undoubtedly the feeling that political risk did not have to be taken now that the military alternative to invasion seemed so promising. However, without specific assurance about the Throne the peace party in Japan was unable to bring about a decision for surrender. The Suzuki government chose to ignore the Proclamation and gave the impression of rejecting it. The warning having failed, sanctions were applied at Hiroshima and Nagasaki, August 6 and 9, and on the latter date the Soviet Union attacked in Manchuria. In spite of these cataclysmic shocks, surrender hung in the balance until the Emperor for once inserted his immense influence in the decision-making process. Japan accepted the Potsdam Proclamation, August 10, on the one condition that it did not "comprise any demand which prejudices the prerogatives of His Majesty as a Sovereign Ruler." [54]

Byrnes began composing a reply on the morning of August 10, Washington time, using a draft prepared by his Special Assistant Benjamin Cohen. The Japan experts were not invited, but asked to come anyway. Herbert Feis gives this account: "Grew, mastering his personal pride, opened the door between his office and Byrnes' and said, 'Mr. Secretary, if you are working on the Japanese note I believe I and some others could be helpful.' He and Dooman were then reluctantly admitted into the discussion." Several of their suggestions, of an undisclosed nature, were accepted but their advice not to humiliate the Emperor by insisting that he personally sign the surrender document was "firmly rejected." When the British made the same suggestion it was accepted. The American note went a small step further on the Emperor question, stating that his authority and that of the Japanese government would be subject to the Allied Supreme Commander. At least that statement could be interpreted to mean that the institution would not be eradicated. The peace party, placing the best possible construction on the Proclamation and the American note, and with a second powerful intervention by the Emperor, forced through an acceptance and the Pacific War ended August 14.[55]

The slights Grew suffered could not detract from the satisfaction he felt at the outcome. He would always be glad he had taken the position that the Emperor should be "kept on ice," he wrote in October 1945. He regarded his May 28 initiative at the White House as the beginning of the Potsdam Proclamation which emerged "just about as I had envisaged" and "greatly helped" to end the war. Stimson had been "splendid through it all." However, time cast the events of that hectic summer in a different light. In a 1947 article in *Harper's*, Stimson stressed his own very considerable role in bringing about the Proclamation and the importance of the atomic bomb in effecting surrender. Grew received only passing mention and was pained. He wrote Stimson suggesting that the history of the surrender "might be somewhat pieced out by a few further facts." Gently he pointed out that "the almost unique position you enjoy before the American people gives any statement of yours a conclusive character and crystallizes history. . . ." He said he had long insisted that surrender would be highly unlikely without a public undertaking by the President that it "would not mean the elimination of the present dynasty if the Japanese people desired its retention." He added that as early as May he had recommended such a statement to the President and he pointed out that such a commitment had been implicit but not explicit in Paragraph 12. Postwar evidence convinced him that even in May the Japanese were surrender-minded. An explicit statement at that time might well have set in motion the process of surrender before the atomic bomb was used and before the Russians entered the war.[56]

The only reasonable conclusion to be drawn from the evidence available is that Grew did not make a recommendation to the President in May or June for a statement that explicitly assured the Japanese on the Emperor question. No such draft statement has been found.[57] On the contrary, his contemporary references to the draft statement suggest an implicit assurance, to the effect that the Japanese would be allowed to determine their own future political structure.[58]

The cautious, veiled mode is the one Grew would be likely to adopt in the draft statement. It accorded with his stand-in position as Acting Secretary, his sensitivity to the charge of mollycoddling cliques around the Throne, and his public position that "the problem should be left fluid." A unilateral statement that even seemed to grant a condition would have been a dangerous move. Note that Stimson's explicit reference to the Emperor was tied to ability to deliver atomic weapons and Truman's interest in a statement to developments at the Big Three meeting. As much as Grew wanted the war ended before Russian entry, he could not deny from the perspective of May and June that such entry might be invaluable. By rousing Russian suspicions of a separate peace, as they had been roused in March and April over the surrender of the German Army in Italy, the United States would place Japan in a position to play off the powers against each other, as in fact Japan tried to do in July by seeking Russian mediation. A unilateral statement that was unobjectionable to all concerned would have to be an expression of commonly held purpose. The hope of choosing their own form of government was, after all, no more than the Atlantic Charter promised all peoples of the world.[59]

Grew recommended in May about the same degree of assurance on the Emperor that the Potsdam Proclamation finally offered. It is true "political structure" is somewhat more suggestive of the emperorship than "government," but in neither case was the dynasty or the Emperor specifically mentioned. An implicit assurance was no more likely to be effective in May or June than it proved to be from July 26 to the date of Hiroshima.

The likely explanation for Grew's error in 1947 is that he confused a later draft that was explicit on the Emperor with the earlier one that was not. He was very clear in his mind that on May 28 he had argued at length before the President the importance of letting the Japanese know they could retain the Emperor, as he had. Moreover, he considered that he had been primarily responsible for making his government aware of the importance of the institution in the surrender and the postwar settlement, as he had. Furthermore, almost alone he had kept alive before the public in months of profound hatred of Japan and under bitter criticism against himself a view of the enemy that was rational and humane and made conceivable an eventual accommodation. For his efforts toward peace in war he felt he deserved credit, as indeed he did.

With the end of the war Grew had a variety of reasons for retiring. He was aware that Byrnes wanted a change sooner or later. "I saw the handwriting on the wall and would not and could not have stayed," he wrote Castle. The two were not compatible and Grew was something of a liability. He was publicly identified as favoring a "soft" peace and was being described in liberal journals like the *Nation* as an appeaser and a reactionary. Drew Pearson had him "the spearhead of the Hirohito clique." Weightier opinion was calling for greater policy-making and administrative ability at the Under Secretary and Assistant Secretary level. Byrnes suggested that he go to Japan as General MacArthur's political adviser, but Grew doubted that the General wanted any advice and found distasteful the idea of returning to Tokyo as a conqueror. The idea of sitting awhile "in innocuous desuetude" was appealing. Above all was the sense of an ending, of his work closing and new and very different problems beginning. He was sixty-five and had served his government forty-one years. It was enough. On August 15, the day after the surrender of Japan, Grew submitted his resignation and the following day, in a friendly and gracious letter, the President accepted it.[60]

Epilogue
(1945 – 1965)

Epilogue

ONE chore remained before he was free. At the end of November 1945 he testified at length before the Congressional committee investigating the Pearl Harbor attack. Republicans on the committee probed for evidence and opinion to use against the Administration. They were particularly interested in obtaining his diary which according to the Foreword to *Ten Years* consisted of thirteen large typewritten volumes for the Japan mission. Grew resisted, claiming that it was private, that it was a "sort of sketchbook" containing raw material for his reports but not considered, confirmed opinion, and that the determining material, after all, was his official correspondence, which was already available to the committee. There was talk of a subpoena, but Grew stood his ground and the matter was not pursued. He wrote his brother that he would go to jail before delivering it up. Grew's testimony added little to the historical record. The Congressmen asked the wrong questions and spent their time chasing hares. It was impossible for them to reconstruct the tangled diplomacy of 1941, particularly in the partisan spirit in which the inquiry was conducted. Grew fenced questions with considerable skill and stood loyally by the Administration. His own view of events on the eve of Pearl Harbor would have to wait some more.[1]

Grew finally told his story in 1952 with the publication of *Turbulent Era, A Diplomatic Record of Forty Years,* a work in two volumes totaling over fifteen hundred pages. It is a composite memoir presenting Grew in four distinct relationships to experience. The bulk of the book consists of his writings contemporaneous with events, including diary, letters, and official papers, selected and edited with insight and craftsmanship by Professor Walter Johnson, then of the Department of History at the University of Chicago, assisted by Nancy Harvison Hooker. *Turbulent Era* is also partly autobiographical, presenting Grew's latter-day recollections of his youth and early career. In addition, important chapters were written by himself shortly after the events they describe, providing a narrative based on private and official papers while the events were still relatively fresh in his memory. In this category is the history of his Japan mission begun in the fall of 1940, which he had carried from 1932 to 1938. Finally, two portions of *Turbulent Era* are essentially argumentative, giving his interpretation of diplomacy on the eve of war in 1941 and of the surrender in 1945 and justifying the positions he took on those great events.[2]

In *Turbulent Era,* Grew was more than ever sure he had been right in 1941 and 1945. Writing at the time of Korea, he must have found the world incomprehensible and unacceptable. It was a time of subversion at home and revolution abroad. Russia had exploded an atomic device and China had turned Communist. Americans were fighting in the Far East again. History seemed to be regressing instead of progressing. Casting back across Hiroshima and Pearl Harbor, he saw two wrong turns where he had recommended alternate courses of action. A leaders' meeting in 1941 might have averted a profoundly destructive war. Assuring the Japanese about the Emperor might have ended the war before Hiroshima and Russian entrance. If his advice had been followed, how different the course of events might have been!

So it seemed looking backward, yet the past as it was and the past as it is remembered can never be the same. His memory of wanting alternatives to the courses taken was compelling. Dimmer were the contradictory views, the anxieties, and the desperate uncertainty of prediction in and about Japan. Less apparent in retrospect were the limitations of his role.

Grew was a sensitive, imaginative, and articulate observer of Japan. He realized the determining influence of public opinion in modern diplomacy and to an unusual degree for a civil servant he was prepared to go outside official channels to improve the climate of his diplomacy. His official policy recommendations were at times extraordinarily perceptive and generally displayed a high level of cogency and objectivity. In the last analysis, however, he conceived his role to be that of working out solutions from given terms more than of redefining those terms. Essentially he was the loyal and efficient middleman and agent. He hesitated to press his policy differences too hard or too far. His recommendations of 1941 and 1945 lacked explicitness, avoided controversy, and failed to carry his estimates to their logical conclusions.

Grew's limited role is hardly surprising. His "appeasing personality," to use John Hersey's words, was a strength in conciliation but a weakness in policy debate, which called for assertiveness, even combativeness. Not particularly inclined to the life of the mind to begin with, he seldom found sustained, rigorous analysis necessary before the Japan mission and was not confident in his judgments. At the same time, career insecurity induced a habit of caution in his relations with the State Department and President.

His long residence abroad and socially élite background set him apart from most Americans and left him vulnerable to the criticism of being an unrepresentative American. Feeling isolated from his own country, he was the less inclined to break from the cover of prevailing attitudes at home. These were heavily weighted with moral imperatives during the interwar years, with deadening effect on policy discussion. And the growing complexity of world affairs made it difficult for anyone not at the center of the intelligence network in Washington to argue policy on an equal footing. What is surprising is how often and persuasively, when circumstances allowed dissent, he managed to escape his limitations.

To recognize the limitations of Grew's role is not to deny the importance of his objective or his efforts. His object was peace through diplomacy. He did not deny the importance of military power, but he had a jealous regard for the virtues of his own profession. For the most part he considered the Army and Navy as unmentionable assets. It was vital, but sufficient, that they should exist in strength. The creative role of diplomacy lay beyond the application of power, in the patient building of confidence and understanding, the sober assaying of interests, the grasp of foreign mentality, the sure conduct of intergovernmental business, and flowing from all these efforts, the reconciliation of differences through negotiation in good faith. It was an approach that enjoyed real success only in Turkey and that became less and less possible to apply. However, he believed that in the long run it was the only practical, humane, and rational way to resolve conflicts of interest among nations. He would go further and say it was not sufficient to let diplomacy happen. It required courage, faith, and a beginning.

He made one exception to the rule. He saw no value in engaging in diplomacy with Communist nations. Communism, in his view, made diplomacy impossible. He held that view from the time of the Russian Revolution and maintained it into retirement. In 1953 he joined with Herbert Hoover and others in sponsoring a petition to the President against the admission of Red China to the United Nations. The petition ultimately gained over a million signatures.[3]

Grew was a successful man in the sense that he managed to achieve a full career in diplomacy, no mean feat, and to rise to the top of his profession. Though he had limitations of mind and outlook as well as role, and never secured the crowning success he longed for, he was an immensely valuable public servant. Career diplomacy in the modern world provides few opportunities for greatness, but he had a moment of greatness when, in the midst of the fantasy and hatred of war, he presented a realistic and objective view of the Japanese enemy to prepare the public mind for peace and ultimate reconciliation. His essential concern was peace, both as a way and an end. If he made few successful endings, he never ceased to look for or make beginnings. Considered as a whole, it was a satisfying life, noble in endeavor, rich in experience, challenging, developing, extending the strong qualities in him.

The most cherished token of esteem for his public services was an honorary degree from Harvard which was conferred in June 1943, on the same day as his election to the presidency of the Harvard Alumni Association. He lived quietly in retirement, spending most of the year in Washington and summers in New England. Mrs. Grew died in 1959. He passed some more frail years at Manchester-by-the-Sea, Massachusetts, gradually receded from the world, and gently passed from it on May 25, 1965, two days before his eighty-fifth birthday.

Notes

ABBREVIATIONS IN NOTES

TE	*Turbulent Era*
TY	*Ten Years in Japan*
FR	*Foreign Relations*
SDA	State Department Archives
DGFP-D	*Documents on German Foreign Policy,* Series D
DBFP	*Documents on British Foreign Policy*
PHA	*Pearl Harbor Attack* Hearings

PREFACE

1. Joseph C. Grew, *Turbulent Era, A Diplomatic Record of Forty Years,* 1904-1945, ed. Walter Johnson (2 vols.; Cambridge, Mass., 1952). Hereafter cited as TE.

1. THE MAKING OF A DIPLOMAT

1. New England Historic Genealogical Society, *New England Historical and Genealogical Register,* 1911 (l-li), 1921 (lxv); *Boston Evening Transcript,* January 20, 1916, November 28, 1924.
2. William Phillips, *Ventures in Diplomacy* (Boston, 1952), 4-5; TE, I, 5.
3. Diary, October 27, 1921; Grew to Lilla Cabot Perry (his mother-in-law), December 6, 1914. Unless otherwise indicated, all citations are from the Grew Papers.
4. Conversation, Grew with author, December 31, 1958; Diary, September 2, 1922.
5. *Groton School Catalog,* 1892-93; Editorial, *The Grotonian* (school magazine), January, 1896, 57. On Groton in Grew's day: Frank B. Freidel, *Franklin D. Roosevelt: The Apprenticeship* (Boston, 1952), Chap. 3; George Biddle, "As I Remember Groton School," *Harper's,* CLXXIX (August 1939), 298; *Groton School Catalog,* 1892-98; *The Grotonian,* 1892-98; Groton School, *Groton School,* 1884-1912 (Groton, 1913).
6. Diary, July 20, 1930; Grew to Rev. Endicott Peabody, July 11, 1933; George Santayana, *The Last Puritan* (New York, 1936), 404.
7. Speech at Groton Alumni Dinner, April 21, 1925.
8. *The Grotonian,* May 1893, 111.
9. *Ibid.,* June 1897, 154, May 1898, 141.
10. Address to Class of 1929, September 26, 1925.
11. *Ibid.*
12. Diary, August 1-19, 1934; Grew to H. Sturgis Grew, Jr., October 31, 1921.
13. Grew to Dr. William L. Smith, September 29, 1911, to Dr. Isaiah Bowman, July 11, 1919. On his round-the-world trip: Joseph C. Grew, *Sport and Travel in the Far East* (Boston, 1910); Diary, November 22, 1931.
14. Grew to Mrs. Waller, November 19, 1931 (in Correspondence, 1932).
15. TE, I, 7; Hugh Wilson, *Education of a Diplomat* (New York, 1938), 2-4.
16. Grew to author, February 17, 1959; Harold Jefferson Coolidge and Robert Howard Lord, *Archibald Cary Coolidge, Life and Letters* (Boston, 1932), 43-49.
17. Richard Hofstadter, *The Age of Reform* (New York, 1956), 139, 165-67; Phillips,

Ventures in Diplomacy, 7; Phillips, conversation with author, November 17, 1958.

18. TE, I, 8. Material for the remainder of this chapter, unless otherwise cited, is drawn from: TE, I, Chaps. 1-7; Speech at Farewell Luncheon of the Foreign Service Association, June 16, 1927; Diary, November 15, 1932.
19. Diary, January 4, 1929. On Thomas Sergeant Perry: Edwin Arlington Robinson, ed., *Selections From the Letters of Thomas Sergeant Perry* (New York, 1929).
20. On Grew's deafness: Diary, September 13–October 11, 1934; Grew to Dr. Charles Heath, June 26, 1912, to Thomas Sergeant Perry (hereafter cited as Perry), April 6, 1914, to his wife, October 25, 1920, to Dr. Bordley, May 3, 1932. Speech, June 16, 1927.
21. *The Nation*, LXX (May 24, 1900), 394. On nineteenth-century diplomatic and consular organization and early reforms: J. Rives Childs, *The American Foreign Service* (New York, 1948), 5-11; Graham H. Stuart, *The Department of State* (New York, 1949), Chaps. 13-18; Warren Frederick Ilchman, *Professional Diplomacy in the United States*, 1779-1939 (Chicago, 1961), Chaps. 1-2.
22. U. S. Congress, House of Representatives, *Report of the Honorable Herbert H. D. Peirce on Inspection of United States Consulates in the Orient*, House Document No. 665, 59th Cong., 1st Sess. (Washington, 1906), *passim.*
23. The periodical literature of the period 1890-1914 contains scores of articles condemning diplomatic and consular practice and recommending professional status, adequate pay, and official residences. A few examples are: William F. Wharton, "Reform in the Consular Service," *North American Review*, CLVIII (April 1894), 412-22; Henry White, "Consular Reforms," *ibid.*, CLIX (December 1894), 711-21; Henry A. Garfield, "The Business Man and the Consular Service," *Century*, LX (June 1900), 268-71; E. L. Godkin, "Ambassadors," *The Nation*, LVI (April 6, 1893), 246-47; Editorial, *Independent*, LXIII (September 5, 1907), 580-2; Herbert H. D. Peirce, "Our Diplomatic and Consular Service," *Arena*, XVII (May 1897), 909-21.
24. Diplomatic Service lists in Department of State, *Register of the Department of State*, 1898-1906.
25. Theodore Roosevelt to Maria Longworth Storer, January 9, 1905, *Letters of Theodore Roosevelt*, 1858-1919, eds. Elting E. Morison, *et al.* (8 vols.; Cambridge, Mass., 1951-54), IV, 1095-96.
26. Alfred L. P. Dennis, "The Foreign Service of the United States," *North American Review*, CCXIX (February 1924), 178.
27. Harold Nicolson, *Diplomacy* (New York, 1939), 204-5.
28. Grew to Perry, February 27, 1923; TE, I, 53; George Kennan, *Russia Leaves the War* (Princeton, N. J., 1956), 3.
29. TE, I, 131; Herbert Hoover, *Memoirs . . . Years of Adventure*, 1874-1920 (New York, 1951), 135.
30. Diary, January 1913; Grew to his mother, November 26, 1909, March 2, 1913. The description of Mrs. Grew is Hugh Wilson's (*Education of a Diplomat*, 165).
31. Grew to his mother, March 7, 1910. On courtier diplomacy: Nicolson, *Diplomacy*, 64.
32. John Bassett Moore, "American Diplomacy: Its Influence and Tendencies," *Harper's Monthly Magazine*, CXI (October 1905), 695; Mark Twain, "Diplomatic Pay and Clothes," 1899, reprinted in *Forum*, XCV (March 1936), 137.
33. Editorial, *Independent*, LXIV (April 2, 1908), 762-63; Robert Lee Henry, "Official Homes for Our Diplomats," *ibid.*, LXXV (August 14, 1913), 377-78; "Dollars and Diplomacy — Poll of the Press," *Outlook*, CIII (April 5, 1913), 756-59; "The Ambassadorship Muddle," *Nation*, LXXXVI (April 2, 1908), 298.
34. Grew to Davies and Son, November 7, 1912, to Irwin Laughlin, November 8, 1912, June 27, September 2, 1913, to Ulysses Grant-Smith, October 21, 1912, to Charles Wilson, November 6, 1913.
35. Grew to his mother, February 6, 1910, February 22, 1914, to Perry, June 9, 1911.
36. Grew to his mother, November 26, 1909, January 29, 1911; Wilson, *Education of a Diplomat*, 90-91.

37. Grew to Willing Spencer, October 15, 1911.
38. Grew to the Secretary of State, October 16, 1916, to his mother, December 12, 1912.
39. Diary, November 27, 1909, January 23, 1914, March 11, 1915; Grew to Margaret Perry, November 27, 1909, to Mrs. Charles Heath, June 26, 1912.
40. Grew to Perry, October 17, 1910; TE, I, 131.
41. Department of State, *Papers Relating to the Foreign Relations of the United States* (hereafter cited as *FR*), 1908-14.
42. Footnote by Grew, TE, I, 100.
43. Diary, February 6, 1914; Grew to Ulysses Grant-Smith, April 10, 1915, to Ambassador F. C. Penfield, July 15, 1915; Spencer Borden to Secretary of State Philander Knox, November 4, 1911, File 123 G 861/88, State Department Archives, National Archives, Washington, D.C.
44. Grew to Charles B. Curtis, September 21, 1912; TE, I, 93.
45. TE, I, 112-14; Stuart, *Department of State*, 205-7, 212-20.
46. Grew to Charles B. Curtis, January 7, 1910, to Edgar Wells, November 3, 1910.
47. Grew to Charles B. Curtis, September 28, 1910, to General John J. Pershing, April 21, 1922.
48. Grew to Arthur Orr, April 2, 1910, to B. F. Stevens & Brown, Ltd., April 16, 1910; Theodore Roosevelt to Ambassador David Jayne Hill, March 24, 1910, to G. O. Trevelyan, October 1, 1911, Morison, ed., *Roosevelt Letters*, VII, 61, 392; TE, I, 66, fn. 9.
49. Grew to Theodore Roosevelt, February 17, 1911, to Irwin Laughlin, February 12, 1912.
50. Grew to his mother, July 22, November 8, 1912, to Basil Miles, December 20, 1912, telegram to Perry, February 18, 1913, telegram to Representative Andrew J. Peters, February 18, 1913, to Randolph Grew, February 25, 1913, to Norman Armour, February 9, 1914, to Henry White, December 9, 1914; TE, I, 106.
51. Grew to Perry, March 9, 1914.
52. Grew to his mother, July 14, 27, 1914, to Roland Harvey, July 14, 1914; Gerard to Secretary of State (hereafter cited as SecState), July 27, 1914, FR, 1914, *War Supplement*, 16.

2. WARTIME BERLIN

1. James W. Gerard, *My Four Years in Germany* (New York, 1917), Chap. 9 and photographs facing pages 20, 30, 136, 148; TE, I, Chap. 8.
2. Grew to Edward Bell, September 1, 1914.
3. Diary, August 8, 1914 (On second thought he crossed out his reference to the "Yellow Peril."); footnote by Grew, TE, I, 144.
4. Grew to John V. A. MacMurray, May 11, 1912, to Basil Miles, October 21, 1912, to John G. A. Leishman, December 24, 1912, to Roland B. Harvey, March 11, 1914; House to Wilson, May 29, 1914, Charles Seymour, *The Intimate Papers of Colonel House* (4 vols.; Boston, 1926-28), I, 248-49; On Rumbold: see for example Rumbold to Sir Edward Grey, July 11, 1914, *British Documents on the Origins of the War, 1898-1914*, eds. G. P. Gooch and Harold Temperley (11 vols.; London, 1926), XI, 36; also Franklin L. Ford, "Three Observers in Berlin: Rumbold, Dodd, and François-Poncet," *The Diplomats, 1919-1939*, eds. Gordon A. Craig and Felix Gilbert (Princeton, 1953), 438-40.
5. Grew to Perry, December 6, 1914, to his mother, January 8, 29, 1915; TE, I, 157-60, 164-65.
6. Grew to his mother, September 2, 1914, to Boylston Beal, November 17, 1914, to Henry Grew, December 28, 1914.
7. Diary, June 10, 1915; TE, I, 152-55.
8. Diary, March 5, 1915; Grew to Endicott Peabody, February 18, 1915, to Roger Pierce, April 18, 1916, to Archibald C. Coolidge, August 21, 1916, to William Phillips, June 20, August 18, 1916, to Hugh Wilson, February 12, 1918.

9. Diary, March 2, August 3, 1915; Grew to Willing Spencer, April 7, 1915.
10. Kennan, *Russia Leaves the War*, 396; Kennan, *The Decision to Intervene* (Princeton, 1958), 338.
11. Grew to Irwin Laughlin, July 29, 1915, to Franz H. Krebs, July 15, 1916.
12. Diary, July 3, 1915; Grew to William Phillips, August 1, 1916.
13. Kennan, *Russia Leaves the War*, 117.
14. Diary, February 18, 1914; James W. Gerard, *My First Eighty-Three Years in America* (New York, 1951), 24, 35.
15. Dairy, July 23, 1915; Wilson quoted in Arthur Link, *Wilson the Diplomatist* (Baltimore, 1957), 26. For Gerard's correspondence see *FR*, *The Lansing Papers*, 1914-1920, I, 664-700.
16. Diary, February 26, March 5, May 29, September 25, 1915, July 8, 1916; Grew to his mother, December 7, 1914, to Perry, August 23, 1916; TE, I, 288-93; Gerard, *My Four Years in Germany*. For Gerard's side of two such incidents see Gerard to Colonel House, December 29, 1914, Private Papers of E. M. House, Yale University Library, New Haven, Conn.
17. TE, I, 240.
18. Grew to his mother, December 7, 1914.
19. Diary, April 13, 1915, August 25, 1916; Grew to George Chamberlain, November 26, 1915, to William Phillips, March 12, 1915, February 22, 1916, to his mother, June 16, 1915; Gerard to House, May 10, 1916, House Papers.
20. Diary, July 13-24, 1914; Grew to his mother, August 17, 1915, January 31, 1916, to House, June 22, 1915, to Phillips, November 8, 1915, to Lanier Winslow, June 14, 1916; House to Grew, July 8, 1915, House Papers. On House's control of personnel see for example House to Phillips, March 10, 1916, House Papers.
21. Grew to Gerard, May 30, June 5, 1916; House to Phillips, March 10, 1916, Phillips to House, March 14, May 31, September 23, 1916, House to Lansing, September 17, 1916, Lansing to House, September 19, 1916, House Papers.
22. Grew to his mother, October 31, 1916.
23. Evelyn, Princess Blücher, *An English Wife in Berlin* (New York, 1920), 50, 165; TE, I, 190, 193.
24. Grew to his mother, October 31, 1916.
25. On the Belgian deportations issue: TE, I, Chap. 12; Arthur S. Link, *Wilson: Campaigns for Progressivism and Peace, 1916-1917* (Princeton, 1965), 194-96.
26. TE, I, 255-56.
27. House Diary, November 15, 1916, House Papers; Lansing to Wilson, November 15, 21, 1916, *FR*, *Lansing Papers*, I, 40-42, 44.
28. As quoted in Ray Stannard Baker, *Woodrow Wilson, Life and Letters* (8 vols.; New York, 1940), VI, 343; House Diary, November 27, 1916, House Papers.
29. SecState to Grew, November 29, 1916, *FR*, 1916, *War Supplement*, 70-71.
30. TE, I, 259.
31. Cf. Karl E. Birnbaum, *Peace Moves and U-Boat Warfare* (Stockholm, 1958), 367. Birnbaum accepts Bethmann's somewhat different account of Grew's remarks. According to the Chancellor's memorandum of December 5, Grew said only that the President noted with deepest interest "what your Excellency was good enough to say to me" November 22, not that the President noted "the evident distress and disappointment of the Chancellor that nothing had come of his intimations about peace." The memorandum is printed in *Official German Documents Relating to the World War*, translated under the supervision of the Carnegie Foundation (2 vols.; New York, 1923), II, 1305-6. According to the Bethmann account then, Grew did not, as he claimed (TE, I, 260), deliver the message verbatim. Nevertheless, it is more likely that the omission was in the Chancellor's account rather than in Grew's remarks. Birnbaum himself shows (*Peace Moves*, 198-200, 218-34) that Bethmann was anxious for an American initiative at the time of the November 22 conversation, but that by December 5 he had become skeptical of its materializing soon enough and for a number of reasons was leaning toward the other alternative

of his "double-track" policy, that of a Central Powers peace move. Given this shift, the American recollection of the mood of November 22 would have been embarrassing. While he did not wish to discourage an American peace move, he would not wish to appear within the German government as actively soliciting one. Therefore, it probably seemed prudent to remain silent in the record about his earlier "distress and disappointment."

32. Speech to the Women's Club, Istanbul, Turkey, March 2, 1929.
33. Grew to Cyril Wynne, November 17, 1933, to his mother, December 26, 1916; Charles Seymour review of *FR*, *1916*, *War Supplement*, in *American Historical Review*, XXXVI (April 1931), 623-25. For Grew's dispatches see especially: Grew to SecState, *FR*, *1916*, *War Supplement*, October 16 (300-305), October 17 (61-64), October 17 (305-7), November 7 (314-18), December 21 (129-38). In the House Papers is a dispatch of Grew's of December 1, 1916, passed on to House with a notation by the President, "I knew you would like to see this." On the reception of Grew's dispatches: House Diary, October 13, 1916, and Phillips to House, October 11, 17, 1916, House Papers; House to Grew, November 13, 1916, and Phillips to Grew, October 31, 1916, Grew Papers.
34. Grew to Rear Admiral Walter Gherardi, February 14, 1931; TE, I, 257-58.
35. Grew to Phillips, October 10, 1916; Grew to SecState, October 16, December 21, 1916, *FR*, *1916*, *War Supplement*, 304, 137-38.
36. Grew to SecState, October 14, 20, 1916, *FR*, *1916*, *War Supplement*, 296-97; Ernest R. May, *The World War and American Isolation*, 1914-1917 (Cambridge, Mass., 1959), 293-301, 364; Birnbaum, *Peace Moves*, Chaps. 5-8.
37. Grew to his mother, December 26, 1916, March 16, 1917; Phillips to Grew, November 24, 1916, December 23, 1916, Lansing to Grew, December 29, 1916, Grew Papers; House to Grew, January 17, 1917, House Papers.
38. Grafton W. Minot, "A Brief Account of the Recent Departure of the American Mission from Berlin," Grew Papers, 1917.
39. TE, I, 308.
40. Grew to Perry, February 25, 1917, to Ulysses Grant-Smith, April 17, 1917.
41. Grew to Ellis Dresel, May 23, 1917; TE, I, 327-30.
42. List of Speeches, 1917-18, Grew Papers, 1918; Grew to Perry, February 23, 1918, to his mother, February 7, 22, March 17, 1918, to Phillips, February 27, 1918.
43. Speech entitled "Why Germany Must Be Defeated," Grew Papers, 1918; *Milwaukee Journal*, February 7, 1918.
44. Grew to Gerard, April 27, 1915.
45. Grew to his mother, February 7, 1918, to Phillips, February 27, 1918, to Lithgow Osborne, March 20, 1918; Kennan, *Decision to Intervene*, 5-8.

3. THE PARIS PEACE CONFERENCE

1. Grew to Perry, August 24, October 2, 1917; *House Intimate Papers*, III, 169; Baker, *Wilson*, VII, 254, 275; Lawrence E. Gelfand, *The Inquiry; American Preparations for Peace*, 1917-1919 (New Haven, Conn., 1963), 25-27.
2. Grew to Archibald C. Coolidge, December 24, 1917, to Lithgow Osborne, March 20, 1918. On Bullitt: Grew to Ulysses Grant-Smith, August 19, 1916, to Phillips, January 14, 1918.
3. Gordon Auchincloss Diary, October 13, 1918, House Diary, October 22, 1918, House Papers; TE, I, 335.
4. Grew to his wife, October 18-25, November 6, 10, 1918; Auchincloss Diary, October 26, 1918, House Papers; Baker, *Wilson*, VIII, 565; TE, I, 343-47, 355. On the Paris Peace Conference, unless otherwise cited: TE, I, Chaps. 14, 15.
5. Grew to Boylston Beal, February 10, 1920, to Lansing, April 14, 1921; Chart of Organization of American Commission, *FR*, *1919*, *The Paris Peace Conference*, XI, facing p. 550.
6. House Diary, December 3, 14, 1918, December 20, 1919, Auchincloss Diary, No-

vember 11, 12, 1918, House Papers; House to SecState, November 11, 1918, and SecState to House, November 13, 1918 (2 telegrams), *FR, Paris*, I, 122, 123, 158.

7. Auchincloss to Vance McCormick, November 28, 1918, House Papers.
8. Auchincloss Diary, November 14, 23, 1918, House Papers.
9. On the setting up of the Commission in Paris: *FR, Paris*, I, 122-23, 178-80, 194-96; *ibid.*, XI, 497-501, 537-47, 557-67.
10. House Diary, December 14, 1918, House Papers; SecState to House, November 13, 1918, *FR, Paris*, I, 158; TE, I, 366; Gelfand, *Inquiry*, 161-62, 169. Grew felt Herbert O. Yardley's description of diplomats in *The American Black Chamber* (Indianapolis, Ind., 1931) was a perfect portrait of Harrison (Diary, July 13-27, 1931). Yardley described the diplomats with whom he worked, Harrison among them, as "good-natured, jolly, smartly-dressed figures, strutting around with affected European mannerisms" (p. 19). For Wilson's dislike of this type of diplomat, see Link, *Wilson the Diplomatist*, 24-25.
11. House Diary, December 14, 16, 1918.
12. House Diary, February 23, December 20, 1919, Auchincloss Diary, December 6, 1918; List of personnel attached to House [n.d.], House Papers.
13. Auchincloss Diary, December 15, 1918, January 18, 1919, House Papers.
14. James T. Shotwell, *At the Paris Peace Conference* (New York, 1937), 16-17.
15. Bowman to Beer, Day, *et al.*, December 20, 1918, and S. E. Mezes to Grew, December 21, 1918, *FR, Paris*, I, 208-9.
16. Grew to Acting SecState, December 7, 1918; *ibid.*, 179-80; Minutes of Commissioners' Meeting, February 21, 1919, *ibid.*, XI, 64.
17. House Diary, February 23, 1919, House Papers; Memorandum by Bliss [n.d.], *FR, Paris*, I, 186; Memorandum by Bowman [n.d.], and Memorandum on The Personnel of the Commission, May 1919, *ibid.*, XI, 501-3, 559; Minutes of Commissioners' Meetings, January 31, February 1, 1919, *ibid.*, 4, 8.
18. Auchincloss Diary, December 8, 1918, House Papers; Phillips to Grew, December 19, 1918, and Grew to Phillips, December 23, 1918, *FR, Paris*, I, 181, 188-89; Memorandum on the Personnel of the Commission, May 1919, *ibid.*, XI, 559.
19. Diary, January 9, 1919; Minutes of Commissioners' Meeting, February 13, 1919, *FR, Paris*, XI, 37; Margaret L. Coit, *Mr. Baruch* (Boston, 1957), 227.
20. Grew to Hugh Gibson, January 18, 1920.
21. Shotwell, *At Paris*, 381; TE, I, 394.
22. Shotwell, *At Paris*, 91.
23. Grew to Dresel, November 7, 1918; House to SecState, November 21, 1918, and Acting SecState to Commission, December 19, 1918, *FR, Paris*, I, 199-200, 207-8; Dresel to Grew [n.d.], *ibid.*, XI, 495-96; Memoranda on Composition and Functions of the Commission, May 1, 1919, and Organization of the Commission, August 1, 1919, *ibid.*, 553-54, 627.
24. Grew to Herter, December 24, 1918; Hugh Wilson, *Diplomat Between Wars* (New York, 1941), 74-75.
25. On Grew's search for a mission: Grew to Phillips, June 3, 1919, to Edward Bell, July 3, 1919, to House, October 6, 1919; Frank Polk to Lansing, March 11, 1919, Henry White to Lansing, November 15, 1919, Polk to Grew, December 9, 1919, Grew Papers; Phillips to Lansing, May 2, 1919, Grew to Phillips, June 3, 1919, Henry White to SecState, November 5, 1919, File 123 G 861/170, 172, 190, State Department Archives.

4. MINISTER GREW

1. Material for this chapter, unless otherwise cited, is taken from Grew's Diary for 1920 and 1921 and TE, I, Chaps. 16 and 17.
2. Grew to Dewitt C. Poole, July 21, 1921, to Robert W. Bliss, May 10, 1920; TE, I, 425.
3. Grew to his brother Randolph, April 14, 1920.

4. Grew to Perry, March 26, 1921.
5. Phillips, *Ventures in Diplomacy*, 106-8.
6. Diary, July 4, 5, 1921; Grew to Perry, September 25, 1921, April 13, 1922.
7. Diary, June 23, 1921; Grew to his wife, May 11, 1921.
8. Grew to Robert W. Bliss, May 10, 1920, to his mother, March 28, 1921.
9. Diary, March 25, 1922; Speech at Harvard Reunion, June 19, 1922.
10. Grew to Dresel, January 28, 1920; clipping in Diary, *Fenille D'Avis Neuchatel* (Switzerland), November 2, 1921. See also clippings in Diary with translations: *Politiken* (Denmark), June 2, 1920; *La Tribune de Lausanne* (Switzerland), November 2, 1921; *Journal du Jura* (Switzerland), November 3, 1921.
11. Grew's book orders to B. F. Stevens & Brown, Ltd., London, Brentano's, Paris, and Old Corner Book Store, Boston, 1910-24.
12. Diary, June 22, 1921; Grew to Norman Armour, March 4, 1920, to his mother, October 18, 1919; to his brother Randolph, March 31, 1920.
13. Grew to Franklin D. Roosevelt, November 1, 1920, to Dresel, January 1, 1921, February 28, 1920, to his mother, March 3, 1920.
14. Grew to Perry, April 24, 1922; Wilson, *Diplomat Between Wars*, 49.
15. Diary, June 14, 1920; Grew to Robert W. Bliss, August 18, 1920, to Perry, March 26, 1921, to William R. Castle, Jr., May 17, 1920, to his mother, September 24, 1919; Speech at Harvard Reunion, June 19, 1922.
16. On the Copenhagen Incident: Diary, August 21, 1921; Grew to William R. Castle, Jr., November 28, 1921, to Marion Letcher, August 26, September 1, 1921, to Ulysses Grant-Smith, December 5, 9, 1921, to Perry, September 25, 1921; Ulysses Grant-Smith to Under Secretary Henry Fletcher, November 1, 1921, File 123 G 861/248, State Department Archives.
17. On Robinson: Joseph Alsop, Jr., and Turner Catledge, "Joe Robinson, the New Deal's Old Reliable," *Saturday Evening Post*, CCIX (September 26, 1936), 74. On Britten: *Outlook*, CLI (February 13, 1929), 258; *Nation*, CXXXIII (September 2, 1931), 228.
18. On the problem of confirmation: Diary, April 8–May 14, 1932; Grew to T. Hart Anderson, Jr., July 20, 1922, to Perry, August 25, 1921, to Henry Fletcher, October 2, 1922, to Marion Letcher, August 28, 1923, to G. Howland Shaw (telegram), March 29, 1928, to Irwin Laughlin, March 31, 1916; Footnote by Grew, TE, I, 435-36.
19. Grew to Hugh Gibson, February 17, 1925, to Arthur Bliss Lane, June 12, July 19, 1922; Diary of Willam R. Castle, Jr., November 9, 1922, at the time of research in Mr. Castle's possession, now at Harvard University Library.
20. Diary, November 1, 1921; Grew to Phillips, April 10, May 18, 1922; Speech at Foreign Service Officers' School, October 27, 1926. On Grew's Berlin speech: Major General Henry T. Allen, *My Rhineland Journal* (Cambridge, Mass., 1923), 452.
21. Grew to William R. Castle, Jr., November 28, 1921, to Leland Harrison, January 10, 1922.
22. *Literary Digest*, LXXIV (September 23, 1922), 14.
23. Grew to Leland Harrison, January 10, 1922, to Phillips, May 31, 1922.
24. Diary, November 26, 1921; Grew to Gilchrist, November 21, 28, December 2, 1921, to William R. Castle, Jr., July 29, 1922; Conversation, author with Huntington Gilchrist, August 30, 1959.
25. Diary, December 23-31, 1921, April 27, September 12, 1922.
26. Diary, October 7, 1922; Grew to Leland Harrison, September 25, November 10, 1922, to Boylston Beal, November 10, 1922, to Phillips, May 18, 1922; Conversation, Grew with Sweetser, May 12, 1922, with Agustín Edwards, September 27, 1922; TE, I, 458.
27. Diary, September 11, 1922; Grew to Arthur Bliss Lane, July 11, 1922; TE, I, 464.
28. Grew to Lieutenant Commander Hugo W. Koehler, April 18, 1922.
29. Diary, March 29, 1924; Grew to Perry, November 16, 1921, to William R. Castle, Jr., September 10, 1923.

30. Grew to William R. Castle, Jr., October 14, 1923, to Leland Harrison, August 10, 1923, to S. C. G. Watkins, May 24, 1923.
31. On the background of arms traffic control: Grew to Phillips, September 29, 1922; *FR*, 1920, I, 180-201; *FR*, 1922, I, 543-56; *FR*, 1923, I, 34-46; League of Nations, *Report of the Temporary Mixed Commission for the Reduction of Armaments*, Document A.16.1924.IX (Geneva, 1924), 1-7; Manley O. Hudson, "America and Arms Traffic," *New York Times Magazine*, February 17, 1924; F. P. Walters, *A History of the League of Nations* (Oxford, England, 1952), 218-25.
32. Charles Evans Hughes, "The Foreign Policy of the United States," Speech of November 30, 1923, *Current History*, XIX (January 1924), 575-83. Sir Eric Drummond pointed out to Grew the need for control in view of Turkish use of French war surplus arms against the Greeks (Grew to Phillips, September 29, 1922).
33. Hughes to President Warren Harding, August 2, 1922, *FR*, 1922, I, 553.
34. SecState to Grew, February 2, 1924, *FR*, 1924, I, 19.
35. On the Commission meeting: Diary, February 4-8, 1924; *FR*, 1924, I, 17-30; *New York Times*, February 5-10, 1924; Footnote by Grew, TE, I, 606-7.
36. George Slocombe, *A Mirror to Geneva* (London, 1937), 109.
37. Grew to SecState, February 6, 1924, *FR*, 1924, I, 26.
38. SecState to Grew, February 7, 1924, *ibid.*, 27-28.
39. Grew to Hugh Gibson, February 14, 1924, to William R. Castle, Jr., February 21, 1924.
40. Sweetser to Leland Harrison, February 8, 1924, Leland Harrison Papers, Library of Congress, Washington, D.C.

5. THE LAUSANNE CONFERENCE

1. Bernard Lewis, *The Emergence of Modern Turkey* (London, 1961), 234-49; George Lenczowski, *The Middle East in World Affairs* (Ithaca, N.Y., 1952), 98-107; Roderic H. Davison, "Turkish Diplomacy from Mudros to Lausanne," Craig and Gilbert, *The Diplomats*, 172-209; Harry N. Howard, *The Partition of Turkey; A Diplomatic History*, 1913-1923 (Norman, Okla., 1931).
2. Diary, November 20, 1922. On Grew at Lausanne: Diary, November 1922–July 1923; TE, I, Chaps. 18-21.
3. SecState to Ambassador in France, October 27, 1922, to Ambassador in Italy, November 15, 1922, *FR*, 1923, II, 888, 899. On the American role at Lausanne: Files 711.672/, 767.68119/, 867.602/, State Department Archives (hereafter cited as SDA); *FR*, 1923, II, 879-1172; John A. DeNovo, *American Interests and Policies in the Middle East*, 1900-1939 (Minneapolis, Minn., 1963), Chap. 5; Laurence Evans, *United States Policy and the Partition of Turkey*, 1914-1924 (Baltimore, Md., 1965), Chap. 14.
4. On Bristol: Diary, January 22, 1923; Bristol War Diary and Correspondence, Mark L. Bristol Papers, Library of Congress, Washington, D.C.
5. Richard Washburn Child, *A Diplomat Looks at Europe* (New York, 1925), 6. On Child: Grew to William R. Castle, Jr., February 24, 1923, to Perry, March 30, 1923; Mrs. R. W. Child to her parents-in-law, April 27, 1923, Richard Washburn Child Papers, Library of Congress; Child to Hughes, February 10, 1923, File 767.68119/836, SDA.
6. SecState to Ambassador in France, October 27, 1922, *FR*, 1923, II, 886-88.
7. On Capitulations: Dulles to Bristol, December 28, 1922, Bristol Papers; Lucius E. Thayer, "Capitulations of the Ottoman Empire and the Question of Their Abrogation as It Affects the United States," *American Journal of International Law*, XVII (April 1923), 207-33; Philip Marshall Brown, "Capitulations," *Foreign Affairs*, I (June 15, 1923), 71-81.
8. Howard Morley Sachar, "The United States and Turkey, 1914-1927" (doctoral dissertation, Harvard University, 1953), 24-27.
9. On the oil controversy: Files 867.602 ot81/ and 890g.6363/, SDA; *FR*,1920, II, 649-75, *FR*, 1921, II, 80-94, *FR*, 1922, II, 333-52, 966-83, *FR*, 1923, II, 240-64,

1198-1252; John A. DeNovo, "Petroleum and American Diplomacy in the Near East, 1908-1928" (doctoral dissertation, Yale University, 1948); DeNovo, "The Movement for an Aggressive American Oil Policy Abroad, 1918-1920," *American Historical Review*, LXI (July 1956), 854-76; DeNovo, *American Interests*, 167-96; Edward M. Earle, "The Turkish Petroleum Company — A Study in Oleaginous Diplomacy," *Political Science Quarterly*, XXXIX (June 1924), 265-79.

10. SecState to Special Mission at Lausanne (hereafter cited as Lausanne), November 27, 1922, File 890g.6363/156, SDA.
11. Memorandum by Dulles, November 17, 1922, File 867.4016/926, SDA; Acting SecState to Ambassador in France, November 1, 1922, *FR*, 1922, II, 947-49.
12. Bristol War Diary, December 6, 1922, Bristol Papers; Dulles to Dresel, June 27, 1921, Ellis Loring Dresel Papers, Harvard University Library, Cambridge, Mass.; Memorandum by Dulles, August 3, 1923, File 711.672/183, SDA; Child, *Diplomat*, 103; TE, I, 497.
13. SecState to Lausane, December 3, 1922, *FR*, 1923, II, 912-13; *The Times* (London), September-October 1922. Other interests of minor importance were: "Claims for Damages," "International Financial Control," and "Archeological Research."
14. Hughes to President Harding, October 24, 1922, File 767.68119/62A, SDA; SecState to Ambassador in France, October 27, 1922, *FR*, 1923, II, 886.
15. On Curzon: Harold Nicolson, *Curzon: The Last Phase*, 1919-1925 (Boston, 1934); Earl of Ronaldshay, *The Life of Lord Curzon* (3 vols.; London, 1928), III, 325-33. Nicolson's *Curzon* has been invaluable on the conference setting and proceedings and the British role.
16. Diary, November 21, 1922; Nicolson, *Curzon*, 46, 285, 303, 320.
17. Nicolson, *Curzon*, 309. On Ismet: Robert Strassler, "Ismet Inönü, Turkish Leader" (Senior honors thesis, Harvard University, 1959).
18. Dairy, November 21, 1922; TE, I, 489, 493, 512.
19. Diary, January 22, 29, 1923; Grew to Phillips, January 10, 1923; *TE*, I, 526, 553. For similar views see: Child to Hughes, February 10, 1923, File 767.68119/836, SDA; Bristol to Dulles, January 29, 1923, Bristol Papers; Great Britain, *Lausanne Conference on Near Eastern Affairs*, 1922-1923*: Recordings of Proceedings and Draft Terms*, Turkey No. 1, Cmd. 1814 (London, 1923) (hereafter cited as *Lausanne Proceedings*), 435.
20. Nicolson, *Curzon*, 52-53, 282, 324.
21. Conversation with Sir Horace Rumbold, November 19, 1922; TE, I, 496; Nicholson, *Curzon*, 292-93.
22. Lausanne to SecState, November 22, 1922, *FR*, 1923, II, 900-902; TE, I, 526. Ismet is quoted in Grace Ellison, *An Englishwoman in Angora* (New York, n.d.), 298.
23. Diary, November 22, 1922; Child, *Diplomat*, 89-90.
24. Diary, November 25, 1922; Child, *Diplomat*, 93-94; Nicolson, *Curzon*, 296-97; TE, I, 500-501; Lausanne to SecState, November 25, 1922 (2 telegrams), *FR*, 1923, II, 904-6.
25. Lausanne to SecState, November 23, December 1, 1922, File 767.68119/184,228, SDA; Child, *Diplomat*, 12.
26. Diary, November 22, 29, 1922; Lausanne to SecState, November 22, 1922, and SecState to Lausanne, November 27, 1922, File 767.68119/174, SDA; Child, *Diplomat*, 94-96.
27. Nicolson, *Curzon*, 307-11; TE, I, 504-10. On Chicherin and Soviet diplomacy of the period: Kennan, *Decision to Intervene*, 297-98; Theodore H. Von Laue, "Soviet Diplomacy: G. V. Chicherin, Peoples Commissar for Foreign Affairs, 1918-1930," in Craig and Gilbert, *Diplomats*, 234-81.
28. Lausanne to SecState, December 13, 1922, File 767.68119 T&M/14, SDA; Lausanne to SecState, December 13, 1922, and SecState to Lausanne, December 14, 1922, *FR*, 1923, II, 920-23; Bristol War Diary, December 13, 16, 1922, Bristol Papers; Child, *Diplomat*, 103-7; Nicolson, *Curzon*, 315.
29. Bristol War Diary, November 30, 1922, Bristol Papers. On Bristol's views: Diary,

January 22, 1923; Bristol War Diary, December 11, 1922, January 26, 1923, Bristol Papers; Bristol to Dulles, January 19, 29, March 26, July 28, 1923, Bristol Papers.

30. TE, I, 517.
31. *Lausanne Proceedings,* 470; Lausanne to SecState, December 17, 1922, *FR,* 1923, II, 925-27; TE, I, 503.
32. Lausanne to SecState, December 21, 1922, and SecState to Lausanne, December 22, 1922, *FR,* 1923, II, 931-33.
33. Dulles to Bristol, December 28, 1922, January 10, 1923; Bristol Papers; Memorandum by Dulles, December 4, 1922, File 767.68119/375, SDA.
34. Lausanne to SecState, *FR,* 1923, II, December 26, 1922 (935-36), December 28, 1922 (936-38), December 30, 1922 (940-41), January 1, 1923 (941-42); TE, I, 522-25, 542; Child, *Diplomat,* 113.
35. Child to Hughes, February 10, 1923, File 767.68119/836, SDA; TE, I, 516-18; Child, *Diplomat,* 102, 117, 118. See also *ibid.,* 95, 99, 108.
36. Diary, December 21-31, 1922, January 16, 1923; Grew to his mother, January 11, 1923; Bristol War Diary, November 26–December 30, 1922, January 9, 1923,
37. Diary, December 21-31, 1922, January 14, 27, 1923; Grew to his mother, February 11, 1923; Bristol War Diary, November 26 — December 30, 1922, January 9, 1923, Bristol Papers; Child to Hughes, February 10, 1923, File 767.68119/836, SDA; TE, I, 503-04.
38. Diary, January 15, 1923. On the January 14 Incident: Diary, January 14-15, 1923; Bristol War Diary, January 14, 1923, Bristol Papers.
39. Bristol War Diary, January 17, 30, 1923, Bristol Papers; Child, *Diplomat,* 112-13, 118; Nicolson, *Curzon,* 314, 320; TE, I, 537-38.
40. Diary, January 14, 1923; Grew to Dulles, January 15, 1923; TE, I, 521-22, 534-35.
41. Diary, January 9, 1923; Bristol War Diary, January 23, 24, 1923, Bristol Papers; *Lausanne Proceedings,* 360-61; Lausanne to SecState, January 24, 1923, *FR,* 1923, II, 957-58.
42. Diary, January 22, 1923; TE, I, 526, 534, 536.
43. Diary, January 6, 1923; *Lausanne Proceedings,* 4, 514; TE, I, 489, 502, 525.
44. On the last days: Bristol War Diary, February 4, 1923, Bristol Papers; Nicolson, *Curzon,* 550-55; TE, I, 543-55.
45. TE, I, 553-54.
46. Diary, February 2, 4, 1923; Jay Pierrepont Moffat, "Turkish History, 1918-1923," File 867.00/2062½, SDA.
47. Lausanne to SecState, February 6, 1923, with comments by Stanley K. Hornbeck, File 767.68119/447, SDA; Lausanne to SecState, February 7, 1923, *FR,* 1923, II, 968.
48. Grew to his mother, March 21, 1923.

6. LAUSANNE, SECOND PHASE

1. Ambassador in France to SecState, April 6, 1923, File 767.68119/513, SDA; Memorandum by Dulles, April 4, 1923, *FR,* 1923, II, 974-80; SecState to Grew, April 7, 19, 1923, *ibid.,* 980-86.
2. Ambassador in France to SecState, April 12, 1923, and Child to Hughes, February 10, 1923, File 767.68119/536, 836, SDA; Bristol to SecState, March 30, 1923, File 767.68119 P43/83, SDA; Grew to his mother, May 7, 1923, to Perry, May 14, 1923, to J. Butler Wright, August 25, 1923, to Mrs. W. J. Holt, June 17, 1925.
3. SecState to Grew, April 19, 1923, *FR,* 1923, II, 981-86.
4. SecState to Bristol, April 20, 1923, *ibid.,* 1207. The possibility exists that Vice-Consul Robert Imbrie at Ankara took a more active role in negotiations than merely introducing the parties. See Rear Admiral Colby Chester to Hughes, July 22, 1924, File 123 Im 1/121, and Bristol to SecState, October 27, 1923, File 867.602 ot81/420, SDA. On the Chester Concession: File 867.602 ot81/, SDA; *FR,* 1922, II, 966-83, *FR,* 1923, II, 1198-1252; Bristol War Diary, 1922-23, Bristol Papers; De-

Novo, *American Interests*, Chap. 7. The terms of the concession are in Ottoman-American Development Company to Hughes, July 25, 1923, *FR*, 1923, II, 1215-41.
5. Grew to Perry, May 14, 1923.
6. J. Pierrepont Moffat, "Turkish History, 1918-1923," File 867.00/2062½, and *London Daily Telegraph*, April 24, 1923, clipping in File 867.602 ot81/299, SDA.
7. Memorandum by Mr. Starrett, Office of the Economic Adviser, February 28, 1923, File 867.602 ot81/257, SDA; SecState to Grew, May 4, 1923, and Acting SecState to Bristol, September 17, 1923, *FR*, 1923, II, 1210-12, 1243; Robert L. Daniel, "The Armenian Question and American-Turkish Relations, 1914-1927," *Mississippi Valley Historical Review*, XLVI (September 1959), 270, fn. 62.
8. SecState to Ambassador in France, April 13, 1922, *FR*, 1923, II, 1201-2 and fn. 56; SecState to Grew, April 19, May 2, May 4, 1923, *ibid.*, 983-84, 1209-10, 1211.
9. Diary, April 21, 1923; Conversations with Giulio Montagna, April 30, 1923, and General Maurice Pellé, May 1, 1923; Grew to SecState, April 29, 1923, and May 5, 1923, *FR*, 1923, II, 993-94, 1002.
10. Grew to SecState, April 27, 1923, *ibid.*, 990-91.
11. Conversation with Ismet, May 1, 1923, 10 P.M.; SecState to Grew, April 30, 1923, *FR*, 1923, II, 996.
12. Conversation with Rumbold, May 1, 1923, 2:30 P.M.; TE, I, 571-72.
13. Conversation with Rumbold, May 1, 1923, 9 P.M.; Grew to SecState, May 4, 1923, File 767.68119 E/11, SDA; Grew to SecState, May 4, 1923 (2 telegrams), *FR*, 1923, II, 1000-1002; *New York Times*, May 5, 1923. Grew's original statement that he would comment at the next session (*procès-verbal* in File 767.68119 E/, SDA) was altered in ink to a simple reservation for comment at a later date if he wished. Presumably the change was made after Grew's tactic succeeded.
14. Conversation with Montagna, April 30, 1923; TE, I, 557; H. Stuart Hughes, "The Early Diplomacy of Italian Fascism: 1922-1932," Craig and Gilbert, *Diplomats*, 210-33. The "Montagna Formula" was ultimately the basis for agreement on the judicial regime of foreigners in Turkey.
15. Conversation with Montagna, May 6, 1923, 10:30 P.M. The State Department did express its appreciation to the Italian government (SecState to Grew, May 4, 1923, File 711.672/35, SDA).
16. Conversations with Rumbold, May 9, 1923, 3 P.M., with Ismet, 5 P.M., and Montagna, midnight, May 10, 1923; Grew to SecState, May 4, 1923, *FR*, 1923, II, 1001-2.
17. Conversations with Mr. Dosch-Fleurot, reporter of *New York World*, 3:30 P.M., and Montagna, 6 P.M., May 8, 1923, with Hussein Bey, May 4, 5, 1923, with Ismet, May 10, 1923, 5 P.M.
18. *New York Times*, May 1923; TE, I, 573-74.
19. Conversations with Montagna, May 15, 1923, 10 P.M., with Pellé, May 17, 1923, 11 A.M., with Rumbold, May 16, 1923, 2:30 P.M., with Hussein Bey, May 18, 1923.
20. Strassler, "Ismet," 62-70; TE, I, 574-75.
21. Conversations with Rumbold, Montagna, Venizelos, and Ismet, May 25, 1923; Speech to American consular officials at Interlaken, September 2, 1923; SecState to Grew, May 28, 1923, File 767.68119 F/18, SDA; TE, I, 578.
22. Conversation with Ismet, May 31, 1923, 3:30 P.M.; Grew to SecState, May 31, June 1, 1923, *FR*, 1923, II, 1012-14.
23. Conversation with Ismet, May 31, 1923, 3:30 P.M.; SecState to Grew, May 24, 1923, *FR*, 1923, II, 1069-70.
24. Conversation with Ismet, June 5, 1923; Department of State to British Embassy, March 31, 1923, and Memorandum by Dulles, May 11, 1923, *FR*, 1923, II, 972-74, 1005-9.
25. Conversations with Ismet, June 5, 1923, with Rumbold, 2:30 P.M., and Pellé, 5:30 P.M., June 6, 1923, with Montagna, June 7, 1923, 3 P.M.
26. Conversation with Montagna, June 11, 1923, 3 P.M.
27. Conversations with Montagna, June 12, 1923, 2:30 P.M., June 13, 1923, 2 P.M.; TE, I, 579.

28. Conversations with Montagna, 2:30 P.M., Pellé, 4 P.M., Rumbold, 10 P.M., June 14, 1923.
29. Conversations with Pellé, 5:30 P.M., Mr. Payne, 9:15 P.M., June 15, 1923; Grew to SecState, June 16, 1923, File 867.602/86, SDA; Grew to SecState, June 16, 1923, *FR*, 1923, II, 1021-22.
30. Conversations with Montagna, 3 P.M., Rumbold, 7 P.M., Ismet, 11 P.M., June 26, 1923; SecState to Grew, June 16, 1923, File 867.602/85, SDA; SecState to Ambassador in France, June 23, 1923, and Grew to SecState, June 27, 1923, *FR*, 1923, II, 1023-25, 1025-26.
31. Conversations with Montagna, 4 P.M. and 9:30 P.M., July 6, 1923; TE, I, 581-82.
32. Conversation with Ismet, July 6, 1923, 11:15 P.M.
33. Conversations with Montagna, 11 P.M. and 2 P.M., July 7, 1923, July 8, 1923, 8:30 P.M., July 9, 1923, 2:45 P.M., with Ismet, July 8, 1923, 4:15 P.M.
34. Conversations with Montagna, July 9, 1923, 2:45 P.M., with Rumbold, May 9, 1923, 10 P.M.
35. Grew to SecState, July 10, 1923, File 867.602/101, SDA.
36. Grew to Dulles, September 12, 1923; SecState to Grew, July 10, 1923, *FR*, 1923, II, 1030-34.
37. Conversation with Rumbold, July 11, 1923, 11:30 P.M.
38. Conversations with Montagna, July 12, 14, 15, 1923, with Ismet, July 13, 14, 15, 1923; TE, I, 583.
39. Conversations with Ismet, July 15, 1923, 10:30 P.M., and Montagna, July 17, 1923, 11:30 P.M.; Grew to SecState, July 17, 1923, *FR*, 1923, II, 1035-36; TE, I, 584.
40. Grew to SecState, July 17, 1923, *FR*, 1923, II, 1038.
41. Memorandum by Dulles, June 26, 1923, File 867.602 ot81/378, SDA; SecState to Grew, July 10, 1923, *FR*, 1923, II, 1101-02.
42. Grew to Hughes, August 6, 1923, to his mother, August 19, 1923; Bristol to F. Lamott Belin, July 23, 1923, Bristol Papers; Grew to SecState, July 21, 1923, *FR*, 1923, II, 1105-06; Bristol to SecState, July 24, August 23, 1923, *ibid.*, 1119, 1241-42.
43. State Department instructions, January 18, June 3-26, 1923, *FR*, 1923, II, 1045-46, 1085-97.
44. Grew to his mother, July 30, 1923; Conversations with Ismet, July 20, 1923, 11 A.M., July 21, 1923, 5:30 P.M.; Grew to SecState, July 21, 22, 1923, *FR*, 1923, II, 1105-13.
45. Grew to Hughes, August 6, 1923, to Dulles, September 12, 1923.
46. Grew to Dulles, September 12, 1923; Conversation with Ismet, July 24, 1923, 10 P.M.; Grew to SecState and SecState to Grew, July 22, 1923, *FR*, 1923, II, 1107-16.
47. Grew to his mother, August 19, 1923.
48. Grew to Perry, August 2, 1923, to Elbert Baldwin, August 15, 1923, to Dulles, September 12, 1923. On the points conceded: *FR*, 1923, II, 1116-37.

7. THE ESTABLISHMENT OF THE AMERICAN FOREIGN SERVICE

1. TE, I, 114.
2. Grew to Hugh Gibson, November 12, 1923.
3. Harold Nicolson, *The Evolution of Diplomacy* (New York, 1962), 102; TE, I, 23.
4. Grew to Charles Curtis, January 7, 1910, to John W. Garrett, October 18, 1919.
5. Hugh Gibson to Dresel, September 1, 1921, Dresel Papers; Diplomatic Service lists in Department of State, *Register of the Department of State*, 1867-1914; Ilchman, *Professional Diplomacy*, 127-30. Grew declined an ambassadorship in South America in 1922 (Grew to his wife, July 13, 1922).
6. Grew to Dolbeare, February 29, 1928. On service "families": Grew to Wilson, Gibson, J. Butler Wright, and Ulysses Grant-Smith, 1919-25, Grew Papers; Dresel-Gibson and Dresel-Dolbeare correspondence, 1920-21, Dresel Papers; Hugh Wilson, *Diplomat Between Wars, passim*; *The Moffat Papers: Selections From The Diplo-*

matic Journals of Jay Pierrepont Moffat, 1919-1943, ed. Nancy Harvison Hooker (Cambridge, Mass., 1956), Chap. 1. William Phillips (interview with author, November 17, 1958) deplored the disappearance of a "family feeling" in the Foreign Service.

7. Department of State, *Register*, 1917; *Who's Who in America*. Twenty-eight out of thirty who listed their secondary education had attended private schools, but those who attend private schools would be more likely to specify their secondary education than those who attended public school, so the proportion is probably excessive. Ilchman (*Professional Diplomacy*, 170), working with secretaries recruited between 1914 and 1922, found that 72.3 percent had attended residential private secondary schools.
8. *Hugh Gibson, 1883-1954; Extracts from His Letters and Anecdotes from His Friends*, ed. Perrin C. Galpin (New York, 1956), 97; Hugh Wilson, *Diplomacy as a Career* (Cambridge, Mass., 1941), 33; E. Digby Baltzell, *Philadelphia Gentlemen, The Making of a National Upper Class* (Glencoe, Ill., 1958), 183-84; Drew Pearson and Robert S. Allen, *Washington Merry-Go-Round* (New York, 1931), 139-55.
9. Baltzell, *Philadelphia Gentlemen*, 16.
10. Ambassador Brand Whitlock, as quoted in Ilchman, *Professional Diplomacy*, 137-38. Wilson used the term "club" at a meeting of the Foreign Service Personnel Board in 1927. See Minutes of Foreign Service Personnel Board, March 30, 1927, Grew Papers; Grew to Phillips, November 14, 1927, to G. Howland Shaw, October 19, 1927; G. Howland Shaw, "The American Foreign Service," *Foreign Affairs*, XIV (January 1936), 327.
11. Grew to Perry, March 9, 1914, to his mother, June 26, 1919, to Gibson, September 15, 1922; TE, I, 386.
12. Grew to Gibson, September 15, 1922; Speech at Foreign Service Officers' Luncheon, May 3, 1926; Frank Polk to Lansing, March 11, 1919, Grew Papers; Representative John Jacob Rogers, "Are Changes Provided by the Rogers Bill Necessary?" *Congressional Digest*, III (January 1924), 124; Statement by Secretary of State Hughes, U.S. Congress, House of Representatives, Foreign Affairs Committee, *Foreign Service of the United States* (Hearings on H.R. 17 and H.R. 6357), 68th Cong., 1st Sess. (Washington, D.C., 1923), 57; TE, I, 385-86, 412; Ilchman, *Professional Diplomacy*, Chap. 4, *passim;* Wilson, *Diplomacy as a Career*, 2.
13. Grew to Perry, November 13, 1924. On the development of Foreign Service legislation: Ilchman, *Profesional Diplomacy*, Chap. 4. The text of the final Rogers Bill is in Childs, *Foreign Service*, Appendix A.
14. Consul John W. Dye to Wilbur J. Carr, May 16, 1924, Wilbur J. Carr Papers, Library of Congress, Washington, D.C.; Consul M. L. Myers to Nelson T. Johnson, April 7, 1923, Nelson T. Johnson Papers, Library of Congress, Washington, D.C.
15. Skinner to Carr, June 26, 1924, and Carr Diary, November 5, 1923, Carr Papers; *Congressional Record*, 67th Cong., 4th Sess., 3147 (February 6, 1923); Ilchman, *Professional Diplomacy*, 150.
16. On Carr: Stewart McMillan to Carr, August 21, 1924, and other consuls to Carr, 1924, and Carr Diary, particularly January 27, 1901, December 10, 1902, October 19, 1919, March 23, 29, 1920, April 10, 1925, April 6, 1927, Carr Papers; "The Little Father of the Consuls," *Saturday Evening Post*, CXCV (January 27, 1923), 26. Congress on Carr: Remarks of Representatives Otis Wingo and John Jacob Rogers, *Congressional Record*, 68th Cong., 1st Sess., 8823-24 (May 17, 1924).
17. Discussion of attitudes toward Foreign Service reform in this chapter is based on examination of all the articles on consular and diplomatic representation appearing in the periodical press from 1893 to 1928, a total of some two hundred and fifty. The following periodicals were represented: *American Review of Reviews, Arena, Atlantic Monthly, Century Magazine, Chautauquan, Colliers, Commonweal, Congressional Digest, Current History, Foreign Affairs, Forum, Harper's Monthly, Harper's Weekly, Independent, Literary Digest, Nation, New Republic, North American Review, Outlook, Overland Monthly, Saturday Evening Post, World Today,*

and *World's Work*. For a more detailed exposition of attitudes using many of the same sources and reaching substantially the same conclusions see Ilchman, *Professional Diplomacy*, Chapter 4.

18. William T. Ellis, "Frank Words on the 'Trained' Diplomat," *Outlook*, CXXVII (March 9, 1921), 383; *Colliers*, LXVII (March 26, 1921), 7; Arthur Sweetser, "Why the State Department Should Be Reorganized," *World's Work*, XXIX (March 1920), 514. Also: Andrew Ten Eyck, "Uncle Sam's Tin Halo," *ibid.*, CXXVII (February 16, 1921), 251-53; Nicholas Roosevelt, "Removals From the Diplomatic Service," *ibid.* (March 9, 1921), 382; Maurice Francis Egan, "Your Move Mr. Harding," "Our Extraordinary Envoys," "More Business in Diplomacy," "Telling the Diplomatic Truth," *Colliers* (LXVII, February 5, 1921, 11) (LXVII, March 26, 1921, 7-8) (LXIX, February 4, 1922, 9) (LXX, September 9, 1922, 15-16); Herbert Corey, "He Has Jobs for Rising Young Men," *ibid.*, LXXII (November 3, 1923), 14; Will Irwin, "Business in Diplomacy," *Saturday Evening Post*, CXCIII (August 14, 1920), 30; Norval Richardson, "My Diplomatic Education," *ibid.*, CXCV (February 10, 1923), 8-9; *ibid.* (March 3, 1923), 24-25; *ibid.* (March 17, 1923), 20-21; *ibid.* (March 31, 1923), 14-15; Breckenridge Long, "Stories of State," *Independent*, CI (February 7, 1920), 202-03; W. J. Carr, "To Bring Our Foreign Service Up to Date," *ibid.*, CV (February 26, 1921), 207; "Praise For Harding's Diplomats," *Literary Digest*, LXXIV (September 2, 1922), 16; William Phillips, "Cleaning Our Diplomatic House," *Forum*, LXIII (August 14, 1920), 164-72; "Reorganizing The State Department," *World's Work*, XXXVIII (August 1919), 350-51; "Definite Proposals to Improve Our Diplomatic Service," *ibid.*, XLV (February 1923), 355-57; "The United States Developing a Real Diplomatic Service," *ibid.*, XLVI (August 1923), 349-50; "Representation Allowances for Ambasadors," *ibid.*, XLVIII (May 1924), 16; "When Diplomats Write Ads," *New Republic*, XXXV (July 11, 1923), 167-68.
19. Ilchman, *Professional Diplomacy*, 154, 155, 173, 181; *Congressional Record*, 68th Cong., 1st Sess., 7573 (April 30, 1924), also *ibid.*, 67th Cong. 4th Sess., 3143, 3159, 3165 (February 6, 1923).
20. "The Yankee Consul, New Style, on the Job," *Literary Digest*, LXVIII (January 29, 1921), 60; Irwin, "Business in Diplomacy," 30, 69; Sweetser, "Why The State Department Should Be Reorganized," 514-15.
21. John J. Rogers and Tom Connally, "Are Changes Provided by the Rogers Bill Necessary," *Congressional Digest*, III (January 1924), 124-25; "The Last Refuge of the Spoilsmen," *Atlantic*, CXIII (April 1914), 433-45; Mark Sullivan, "A Quiet Reform in Our Foreign Service," *World's Work*, LI (November 1925), 46; Norval Richardson, "My Diplomatic Education," *Saturday Evening Post*, CXCVI (September 8, 1923), 69; Footnote 18 articles by Sweetser (515), Egan ("Your Move, Mr. Harding," 27), Corey (14), Irwin (29-30, 69), *World's Work* ("Representation Allowances for Ambassadors"), *New Republic* (168); *Congressional Record*, 67th Cong., 4th Sess. (February 6, 1923), 3145, 3159, and 68th Cong., 1st Sess. (April 30, 1924), 7572, 7580. On backgrounds of consuls: Ilchman, *Professional Diplomacy*, 164, 172.
22. Grew to Perry, March 30, 1923, January 19, 1924; TE, I, 410, 435. The Richardson articles are cited in Footnote 18.
23. Grew to Gibson, February 20, 1923; Statement by Hugh Gibson, *Foreign Service Hearings*, 21; Shaw, "American Foreign Service," 327; TE, I, 619; Ilchman, *Professional Diplomacy*, 149, 151.
24. Grew to Francis Peabody, December 30, 1925; Speech at Foreign Service Officers' School, April 20, 1925; Minutes of Foreign Service Personnel Board, June 13, 1925, Grew Papers; Gibson to Grew, July 2, 1924, Harrison Papers; Castle Diary, December 2, 1924; Statement by J. Butler Wright, *Foreign Service Hearings*, 52 (for reaction to Wright's use of "breeding" in testimony see *Congressional Record*, 68th Cong., 1st Sess., April 30, 1924, 7565); Johnson to N. B. Stewart, May 28, 1924, Johnson Papers; Wilson, *Diplomacy as a Career*, 33.
25. Grew to Albert Ruddock, December 11, 1919, to Robert W. Bliss, May 10, 1920

(likeness to a bee), to Senator Frank B. Willis, May 14, 1926 ("mere knowledge"); Memorandum, November 2, 1926; Carr Diary, November 26, 1924, Carr Papers; Statement by Gibson, *Foreign Service Hearings*, 41-42; Shaw, "American Foreign Service," 325. "Mentality" as in: "It was agreed that some one with poise and mentality and background is needed by Ambassador Bancroft [at Tokyo]" (Minutes of the Foreign Service Personnel Board, June 13, 1925, Grew Papers).

26. Grew on business diplomacy: Grew to Gibson, January 18, 1920, March 20 and 23, 1923, November 12, 1923, to John W. Garrett, October 18, 1919, to J. Butler Wright, September 15, 1919, to Jefferson Caffery, February 10, 1920, to Ulysses Grant-Smith, May 3, 1919; Diary, January 5, 1920, May 4, 1922; Radio Speech, February 24, 1926; TE, I, 410; Castle Diary, April 19, 1922; Dresel to Godfrey L. Cabot, November 22, 1921, Dresel Papers; Ilchman, *Professional Diplomacy*, 152.
27. Carr Diary, September 1, 1921, Carr Papers; Ilchman, *Professional Diplomacy*, 157-61.
28. The three were singled out as the best diplomats by Castle (Diary, December 7, 1922). The others were Sterling, Wright, Harrison, Dresel, and Grant-Smith. Frederick Sterling, Grew's companion at 1718 H Street in 1917, apparently participated only in the 1920 Paris discussions. He was assigned to Peru in 1921. Harrison and Wright participated at Paris before assignment to the Department. Though Wright was deeply involved in Foreign Service legislation as Director of the Diplomatic Service, he was believed to be too amenable (Grew to Gibson, October 15, November 3, 1923; Castle Diary, November 2, 1923, May 8, 1924). Harrison's papers give no indication he played a prominent role in the Department; if he did he was very circumspect about it. Castle noted Harrison supported Carr on the fourth assistant secretaryship (Diary, May 19, 1924). Dresel participated in the Berlin meetings but lost his post and left diplomacy. Ulysses Grant-Smith and Lewis Einstein corresponded on the problem but apparently did not join the meetings or help shape plans. Einstein was probably too negative in his views (Ilchman, *Professional Diplomacy*, 180-81).
29. On the meetings: Wilson to Representative Rogers, April 7, 1920, Grew Papers; Grew to Ulysses Grant-Smith, April 15, 1920, to Gibson, December 22, 1920, to Bliss, September 30, 1921. On Castle as personnel chief: Castle Diary, October 21, November 11, 1922, December 28, 1922; Grew to Gibson, February 20, 1923, to Hughes, February 18, 1923, to Castle, February 24, 1923; Gibson to Hughes, January 17, 1923, Charles Evans Hughes Papers, Library cf Congress, Washington, D.C. On Castle: Robert Ferrell, *American Diplomacy in the Great Depression* (New Haven, Conn., 1957), 38.
30. Grew to Perry, February 13, 1924, to Gibson, February 14, 1924; Diary, March 1, 1924; Castle Diary, November 23, 1922, January 19, 1923, January 29, 30, 1924; interview, author with William Phillips, November 17, 1958; Herbert Hoover, *The Memoirs of Herbert Hoover; The Years of Adventure*, 1874-1920 (New York, 1951), 206-7; Merlo J. Pusey, *Charles Evans Hughes* (2 vols.; New York, 1951), II, 412-13.
31. Grew to his children, April 5, 1924; Diary, January 1, March 13, April 14, 1924.
32. Diary, March 1, 1924.
33. Diary, October 21, 1924; Castle Diary, September 29, 1924; Pusey, *Hughes*, II, 412.
34. Castle Diary, May 23, 1924.
35. On the struggle for administrative control: Diary, May 13 to June 6, 1924, parts of which are in TE, I, 619-21; Castle Diary, May, June, 1924; Memorandum, Castle to Grew, May 14, 1924, Grew Papers. A copy of the Carr Plan (Memorandum to Phillips, January 14, 1924) is in the Harrison Papers.
36. Grew to Gibson, June 5, July 1, 1924; Memorandum, Grew to Carr, June 5, 1924.
37. Grew to Gibson, June 5, 11, July 1, August 8, 1924; Diary, June 21, 1924; Minutes of Foreign Service Personnel Board Meetings, June 23-26, 1924, Grew Papers; TE, I, 699; Department of State, *Register*, 1926, Ilchman, *Professional Diplomacy*, 191; Wilson, *Diplomat Between Wars*, 171.
38. Diary, December 19, 1924; Grew to Gibson, October 1, 1924; Memorandum [n.d.],

1924; Memorandum, Grew to Hughes, August 12, 1924; interview author with Phillips, November 17, 1958; TE, I, 615.

39. Based on Diary, Conversations, Memoranda, Letters, 1924-25. Castle Diary, July 15, 1924.
40. Phillips described the buzzer as "horrible" (interview with author, November 17, 1958). Castle Diary, February 13, 1924.
41. Diary, December 20, 1932; Grew to Gibson, April 6, 1925; Memoranda, Grew to Chief of Index Bureau, June 5, 1925, to Castle, September 30, 1926.
42. Diary, February 27, 1925; Hughes to Kellogg, January 23, 1925, Hughes Papers; TE, I, 650.
43. Grew to his wife, August 14, 21, 1925.

8. DIPLOMATS AND CONSULS: A PROBLEM OF INTEGRATION

1. As quoted in David Bryn-Jones, *Frank B. Kellogg, A Biography* (New York, 1937), 59.
2. On Kellogg: Carr Diary, June 17, 1926, Carr Papers; Bryn-Jones, *Kellogg*; L. Ethan Ellis, *Frank B. Kellogg and American Foreign Relations, 1925-1929* (New Brunswick, N.J., 1961), 6-10; Robert H. Ferrell, *Peace in Their Time; The Origins of the Kellogg-Briand Pact* (New Haven, Conn., 1952), 79-80; Wilson, *Diplomat Between Wars*, 174-75. For Grew's views: Diary, March 7, 1925, November 20, December 22, 1937; TE, I, 652-53.
3. Kellogg to Frederick Sterling, April 25, 1925, July 8, 1926, Frank B. Kellogg Papers, Minnesota Historical Society, St. Paul, Minn.; Bryn-Jones, *Kellogg*, 166-67; Ellis, *Kellogg*, 10, fn. 15.
4. Memorandum, Grew to Leland Harrison, May 12, 1925 (routing memoranda of the Secretary's conversations through the Under Secretary's office), Harrison Papers; Diary, March 7, 1925; TE, I, 651-53, 705. Ellis, *Kellogg*, 10, has the Secretary using the adjective "useless."
5. Diary, August 13, 1924; Grew to Francis Peabody, September 21, 1926.
6. File 123 Imb/, SDA; Diary, July 26, 29, October 21, 28, 1924.
7. Diary, September 25, October 2, 10, December 19, 1924, February 1, 1926; Memorandum to the Secretary, April 1, 1926; TE, I, 634, 636-38; Dexter Perkins, *History of the Monroe Doctrine* (Boston, 1955), 332-35; Ellis, *Kellogg*, Chaps. 2, 3.
8. Grew to Henry Fletcher, July 8, 1925, to E. L. Dresel, July 14, 1925; TE, I, 656-61; Dorothy Borg, *American Policy and the Chinese Revolution, 1925-1928* (New York, 1947), 1-67, especially p. 60; Ellis, *Kellogg*, Chap. 5.
9. MacMurray to SecState, March 9, 1926, *FR*, 1926, I, 595-96; File 893.00/7139-7166, SDA; Arnold J. Toynbee, *Survey of International Affairs, 1926* (Oxford, 1928), 249-54; H. G. W. Woodhead, ed., *The China Year Book, 1926-27* (Tientsin, n.d.), 1029-33.
10. Reconstruction of Grew's role in the Taku Incident is difficult owing to diary lapse virtually throughout 1926 and his confused memory of the event. His diary of November 20, 1937, records a conversation in Tokyo with MacMurray about the incident which he dated at Christmas-time, 1926 (TE, I, 690). His confusion possibly arose from the fact that again, late in December 1926, he was faced with a decision respecting the use of force, this time at Shanghai. In the Shanghai case, however, Grew prudently postponed a reply until after the Secretary's return (File 893.00/7960, State Department Archives). A further problem arises from the vagueness of Grew's cable which read simply: "Attitude proposed by you in paragraph 3 is approved." MacMurray's third paragraph had outlined his views on the utility of the Protocol but so far as action was concerned made no mention of the Protocol but only use of naval forces to enforce a demand that both sides "refrain from action dangerous to foreign life and property in connection with the port of Tientsin." It is hard to be sure what Grew's word "attitude" was intended to cover. However, in a letter to MacMurray of March 25, 1926, only a few days after the incident was over, Grew wrote that failure to take action would have "entailed far

more serious consequences than the action contemplated," suggesting that he originally had in mind possible use of the Protocol. The cable was initialed by Nelson Johnson, Chief of the Far Eastern Division, and has on it in Grew's hand "approved by the President" (File 893.00/7166, State Department Archives). On MacMurray's appointment: Kellogg to Hughes, March 24, 1925, Kellogg Papers; Conversation with Hughes, May 21, 1924, Grew Papers.

11. MacMurray telegrams to Secretary of State, March 10-18, *FR*, 1926, I, 596-602.
12. Roger Greene to Nelson Johnson, April 7, 1926, Nelson Trusler Johnson Papers, Library of Congress, Washington, D.C. The British Minister had been instructed that armed force was to be used only as a last resort to safeguard foreigners in the areas affected (Toynbee, *Survey*, 1926, 254, fn. 1). The Japanese seemed happy to let the United States take the onus of leadership (MacMurray to SecState, March 15, 1926, and SecState to MacMurray, March 19, 1926, File 893.00/7181, 7211a, SDA).
13. *Washington Post*, March 25, 1926. On the American reaction: *Washington Post*, March 16-25, 1926; *Washington Star*, March 11-22; 1926; File 893.00/7191-7226, SDA.
14. SecState to MacMurray, March 19, 1926, *FR*, 1926, I, 603-4; Diary, November 20, 1937.
15. Diary, July 15-23, 1924; Castle Diary, April 18, 1924.
16. Diary, November 20, 1937.
17. On Olds's signing see File 817.00/, State Department Archives. Conversations with Sir Esme Howard, February 28, March 3, 1927; Grew to Arthur Bliss Lane, February 23, 1927, to Alexander Kirk, July 15, 1927; Diary, November 20, 1937; Coolidge to Kellogg, March 1, 1927, Kellogg Papers; Perkins, *Monroe Doctrine*, 336.
18. Diary, May 15, 1925 ("Cerberus"); Grew to Peter Jay, May 24, 1926; Memorandum, October 17, 1925; Minutes of Foreign Service Personnel Board (hereafter cited as FSPB), March 21, 1925, Grew Papers (all FSPB Minutes citations are from the Grew Papers). Differing viewpoints on fitness are well exemplified in the relative weighting of oral and written examinations. Carr felt it was very dangerous to rely too heavily on a judgment of intangibles such as an oral examination provided, while Grew regarded the oral as a "far better criterion" of fitness than the written. Katherine Crane, *Mr. Carr of State, Forty-Seven Years in the Department of State* (New York, 1960), 107-12; Grew Memorandum, October 5, 1925.
19. Carr Diary, May 3, September 29, 1926, and Memorandum by Carr to Grew, November 12, 1925, Carr Papers; Consul N. B. Stewart to Nelson T. Johnson, June 19, 1924, Johnson Papers; Skinner to Grew, October 8, 1925, File 120.1/151, SDA; Crane, *Carr*, 283-84.
20. FSPB Minutes, March 21, 1925, May 5, 1927; Grew Memorandum, September 30, 1925; Grew to Orme Wilson, October 13, 1926, to Peter Jay, May 24, 1926; Carr Diary, May 7, 1926, Carr Papers; interview, author with William Phillips, November 17, 1958; Crane, *Carr*, 282.
21. Diary, October 11, 1924; Grew to Gibson, June 11, 1924, to Dolbeare, October 1, 1924; Memorandum, March 29, 1927; Wilson, *Diplomat Between Wars*, 167-71. The figures are in: Skinner to Grew, October 8, 1925, File 120.1/151, SDA; FSPB Minutes, May 2, 1927; U.S. Congress, Senate, Committee on Foreign Relations, *Reorganization and Improvement of the Foreign Service*, Senate Report No. 1069, 70th Cong., 1st Sess. (Washington, D.C., 1928), 3; Ilchman, *Professional Diplomacy*, 191.
22. Castle Diary, December 2, 1924; Skinner to Grew, October 8, 1925, with FSPB comments, File 120.1/151, SDA. Grew's letters to the one hundred officers, September 7-14, 1925, are in Correspondence, 1925.
23. Grew to Warren Robbins, October 19, 1925, to Gibson, September 12, October 14, 1925, to Henry Fletcher, June 25, 1925, to Phillips, November 14, 1927; Memoranda, March 7, October 10, 1925; FSPB Minutes, August 4, 1925, December 16, 1926.

24. Grew to Edward Clark, April 19, 1927.
25. Diary, March 20, 1928; Grew to Alanson Houghton, February 18, 1926, to Castle, June 20, 1928; Memoranda for Kellogg, March 12, 1925, November 29, 1926; Memorandum, April 25, 1927; FSPB Minutes, March 15, 1927. Of the five ministers Kellogg appointed before February 1926, three had worked under him in the Department and a fourth had been Consul General in London while he was Ambassador.
26. Diary, January 5, 1925; Grew to DeLancey K. Jay, February 2, 1925; Memoranda, [n.d.] 1925, April 25, 1927; Memoranda for Kellogg, [n.d.] 1925, January 29, March 10, 12, 13, September 12, 1925.
27. Memorandum, November 2, 1926; Memorandum for Hughes, December 30, 1924; Memorandum for Kellogg, November 29, 1926; FSPB Minutes, November 4, 1926, January 11, 1927.
28. Memorandum for Kellogg, November 29, 1926; Grew to editor of *Foreign Service Journal*, December 14, 1926, to Perry, June 25, 1925, to Dresel, September 8, 1925.
29. Grew to Phillips, February 14, 1927. Diary, March 20, 1928; Memoranda for Kellogg, November 29, 1926, February 7, 1927; Memorandum for Hengstler, February 7, 1927; Memorandum for Carr, February 12, 1927; Kellogg to Sterling March 26, September 10, 1925, to Coolidge, June 23, 1925, Kellogg Papers.
30. Conversation with Consul James G. Carter, February 15, 1927.
31. Gibson attended Pomona College, California but did not graduate, and then went to the École Libre des Sciences Politiques. Wilson and White graduated from Yale, Wright from Princeton, and the rest from Harvard. All except Bliss and White were active in Foreign Service reform. Bliss, from his correspondence with Grew, was keenly interested, but it is not clear what part he took. On Wright and White: Pearson and Allen, *Washington Merry-Go-Round*, 145, 155. On Castle: Carr Diary, March 5, 1923, as quoted in Crane, *Carr*, 261.
32. Grew to Perry, June 25, 1925, to Dresel, September 8, 1925; Memorandum January 10, 1927; Ilchman, *Professional Diplomacy*, 193-94.
33. Grew to Castle, June 6, 1928; Diary, September 7, 1931; Carr Diary, February 24, 1927.
34. Pearson and Allen, *Washington Merry-Go-Round*, 142, On Dennis: Arthur M. Schlesinger, Jr., *The Politics of Upheaval* (Boston, 1960), 74-78; *Life*, January 20, 1941.
35. SecState to Dennis, November 2, 1926, *FR*, 1926, II, 803-4; *New York Times*, February 9, 1927. On the Nicaraguan imbroglio: Isaac Cox, *Nicaragua and the United States* (Boston, 1927); Perkins, *Monroe Doctrine*, 336.
36. *New York Times*, March 12, 13, 22, 1927; *Washington Post*, March 11, 1927. On March 12 the Department requested the Legation to investigate and verify a report that a document existed signed by the Secretary containing private instructions to bring about the election of Diaz and to place the document in the Legation "strongbox" for safekeeping and eventual destruction. The Department considered any such document to be a forgery designed to compromise the Legation and the Department. On March 17 the Legation replied that no such document existed. Acting Secretary Grew to Minister Eberhardt, March 12, 1927, and Eberhardt to SecState, March 17, 1927, File 817.00/4668, SDA; *Washington Post*, March 15, 1927.
37. Grew to Arthur Bliss Lane, April 16, 1927; Frederick Maryland *News*, March 18, 19, 1927, clipping in Grew Papers; TE, I, 698-99.
38. Carr Diary, March 17, 25, 26, 1927, Carr Papers.
39. Grew to G. Howland Shaw, October 19, 1927; FSPB Minutes, March 30, 1927.
40. Grew to Arthur Bliss Lane, May 3, 1927; FSPB Minutes, May 2, 1927; Carr Diary, April 6, 1927.
41. *Literary Digest*, XCIII (June 25, 1927), 14; *Washington Star*, October 23, 1927; *Philadelphia Inquirer*, October 6, 1928; U.S. Congress, Senate, Committee on Foreign Relations, *Reorganization and Improvement of the Foreign Service*, Report No.

1069, 70th Cong., 1st Sess. (Washington, 1928); Crane, *Carr*, 287. A copy of Dawes's speech at the University of St. Louis Commencement, June 7, 1927, is in the Kellogg Papers, Box 22.

42. Crane, *Carr*, 305; Ilchman, *Professional Diplomacy*, 198-201.
43. *Literary Digest*, XLVII (September 27, 1913), 513; LXXIV (September 2, 1922), 16; LXXXII (August 2, 1924), 18; LXXXV (April 4, 1925), 13; XCII (March 26, 1927), 11; XCIII (June 25, 1927), 14. *New York Times*, February 4, June 9, 1927. *Outlook*, LXXXV (January 26, 1907), 211-15; XCII (May 15, 1909), 93; CVI (March 7, 1914), 523-24, 533-38; CXXVI (December 20, 1920), 724-27; CXLV (March 2, 1927), 259; CXLVI (June 22, 1927), 236. *Nation*, LVI (April 6, 1893), 246-47; LXXXIX (October 28, 1909), 398; XCVII (December 18, 1913), 582; CXXV (July 6, 1927), 5. *Colliers*, *LXXX* (July 16, 1927), 38.
44. Diary, March 20, 1928.
45. Grew to Alexander Kirk, July 15, 1927; Speech at Farewell Luncheon of Foreign Service Officers Association, June 17, 1927; TE, II, 707-11.

9. THE MISSIONARY PROBLEM IN TURKEY

1. Diary, November 8, 1927; H. G. Dwight, *Constantinople Old and New* (New York, 1915); Edwin A. Grosvenor, *Constantinople* (2 vols.; Boston, 1895). On Grew's first impressions of Turkey: Diary, September-November 1927.
2. Roger Bigelow Merriman, *Suleiman The Magnificent, 1520-1566* (Cambridge, Mass., 1944), 177, 195.
3. Grace Ellison, *Turkey Today* (London, n.d.), 47-60; Sir David Kelly, *The Ruling Few* (London, 1952), 316-17.
4. Diary, October 12, 1927.
5. On Kemalist reform: Lewis, *Emergence of Modern Turkey*, Chap. 8; Kemal H. Karpat, *Turkey's Politics; The Transition to a Multi-Party System* (Princeton, 1959), Chap. 2. TE, II, 733-36.
6. TE, II, 733.
7. Dankwart A. Rustow, "The Foreign Policy of the Turkish Republic," Roy C. Macrides, ed., *Foreign Policy in World Politics* (Englewood Cliffs, N.J., 1958), 298-99.
8. Robert L. Daniel, "The Armenian Question and American-Turkish Relations, 1914-1927," *Mississippi Valley Historical Review*, XLVI (September 1959), 268-73. On Grew's efforts in behalf of the treaty: Grew to Bishop Lawrence, April 17, 1926, to Senator Borah, April 26, 1926; Memorandum to Secretary of State, November 18, 1926.
9. Grew to his brother Randolph, January 6, 1928, to G. Howland Shaw, March 26, April 1, 1928; SecState to Grew, December 21, 1927, File 123G 861/322a, SDA; *New York Times*, December 1, 1927; TE, II, 747-48.
10. Diary, December 6, 1927; Grew to Admiral Bristol, December 23, 1927, to Hugh Wilson, February 23, 1928, to Castle, March 24, 1928; SecState to Grew, February 4, 1928, Grew Papers; Memorandum by Carr, March 13, 1928, Carr Papers; *Congressional Record*, 70th Cong., 1st Sess., 6029 (April 6, 1928), 6142-43 (April 10, 1928); *New York Times*, April 8, 1928; TE, II, 747-52, 772.
11. On the Brusa (modern: Bursa) Incident: File 367.1164/, SDA; *FR*, 1928, III, 964-81; TE, II, Chap. 26; Karpat, *Turkey's Politics*, 61, fn. 82. On the background of the schools controversy: A. J. Toynbee and K. P. Kirkwood, *Turkey* (London, 1926), 244-51.
12. Grew to G. Howland Shaw, February 1, 1928; Lewis, *Emergence of Modern Turkey*, 270-71, 406-10; Karpat, *Turkey's Politics*, 60-61.
13. Diary, February 1, 1928; Grew to G. Howland Shaw, February 1, 1928; Conversations with Fred Field Goodsell, February 2, 1928, and Hussein Bey, January 31, 1928; TE, II, 758-59.
14. *Ibid.*, 759-62.

15. Diary, January 31, 1928; Conversations with Goodsell, February 13, 1928, and Tevfik, February 20, 1928; SecState to Grew, February 14, 1928, *FR*, 1928, III, 972.
16. Conversation with Tevfik, February 20, 1928; TE, II, 766-67. On Grew's previous efforts to reopen the schools: Diary, November 2, 20, December 6, 1927, February 8, 1928; Grew to G. Howland Shaw, November 9, December 17, 1927; Conversations with Goodsell, October 5, November 5, 1927, January 20, 1928; *FR*, 1927, 804-12; TE, II, 746-47.
17. To General William J. Donovan he wrote February 26, 1928: "I got the Minister of Public Instruction into a game the other night and the next day two American schools were authorized to reopen. . . ." This is crossed out on his copy. See also: TE, II, 764-67.
18. Diary, February 29, 1928; TE, II, 767, 770.
19. Diary, May 11, 19, August 20, 27, September 6, 22, 1928; Conversation with Tevfik, April 19, 1928; TE, II, 773-74, 794-95.
20. Grew to G. Howland Shaw, December 17, 1927.
21. On the tax question: Diary, March 19, December 24, 1929, April 2, 1930; Grew to Wallace Murray, August 17, 1931; *FR*, 1930, III, 873-79; TE, II, 843, 852-55, 858.
22. Diary, January 15-25, August 10-31, September 14, 1931; Grew to Wallace Murray, August 17, 1931.
23. Diary, January 15, 1930, January 15-25, February 27, June 10, 16, 1931; Conversations with Ismet, April 9, 1929, and Tevfik, February 16, 1931; File 367.1164/141, 144, 147, SDA; TE, II, 811-14.
24. Grew to Goodsell, July 29, 1930; Grew to SecState, July 28, 1930, File 367.1164/134, SDA; TE, II, 780-83.
25. Diary, September 4, 1931; Grew to Wallace Murray, August 17, 1931.
26. Grew to Goodsell, July 29, 1930, to Dr. Paul Monroe, May 9, 1932; Grew to SecState, July 28, 1920, and June 29, 1931, File 367.1164/134,155, SDA.
27. Diary, January 22, 1928, July 13-27, December 10, 1931; Grew to Wallace Murray, August 17, 1931; Memorandum by Wallace Murray, July 29, 1931, File 367.1164/157, SDA.
28. Grew to Dr. Paul Monroe, May 9, 1932.
29. Diary, April 17, July 14, 30, August 18, September 4, October 17, 1930, September 14, 1931, February 16, 1932; Grew to Goodsell, July 29, October 20, 1930, to Dr. Henry S. Coffin, November 18, 1930, to Miss Eleanor Burns, June 16, 1932; Conversation with Gates, December 30, 1930; File 367.1164/135, 165, SDA.
30. Diary, June 8, 19, 1928, June 13, 16, 1931; Speech at Robert College, June 13, 1931.
31. Address by Luther R. Fowle, March 11, 1932, Grew Papers; TE, II, 755.

10. THE GROUNDWORK FOR TURKISH-AMERICAN FRIENDSHIP

1. Diary, January 25, April 15, August 26, 1930; Conversation with Russell H. Kuhn, January 3, 1930.
2. Diary, August 10-24, 1931, February 9, 1932; Grew to Wallace Murray, August 17, 1931.
3. Diary, September 7, December 7, 11, 18, 1928, February 1, 1930. On the collapse of the Chester Concession: DeNovo, *American Interests*, 226-27.
4. On the American Oriental Bankers case: Diary, January 22, February 2, April 25–May 21, 1928; Conversations with Marcus Reich, January 31, 1928, with Tevfik, January 10, 1928, with Count Nadolny, German Ambassador, January 4, February 13, April 18, 1928; Conversation, Julian Gillespie, American Commercial Attaché, with Reich, February 11, 1928; File 867.51 American Oriental Bankers Corporation/14, 23, 24½, SDA.
5. On the Fox Brothers case: Diary, February 10, April 25, 27, May 14, September 22, 1928; Conversations with Tevfik, January 10, February 20, September 29, 1928,

with Ismet, February 21, 1928. See also: Diary, April 18, 1928, June 19–July 3, 1929; Grew to G. Howland Shaw, April 21, 1928.

6. Z. Y. Hershlag, *Turkey: An Economy in Transition* (The Hague, n.d. preface dated 1958), 121-22.
7. On the unfavorable business climate in Turkey: *Ibid.*, Chaps, 2-4, 7, 8; Lewis, *Emergence of Turkey*, 275-82; Karpat, *Turkey's Politics*, 84-85.
8. Diary, March 20, 1930; Conversations with Tevfik, April 22, March 3, 23, July 24, 1930, with Ismet, April 2, 22, 1930; Grew to Wallace Murray, March 24, 1930.
9. Diary, November 8, 1930; Conversations with Ismet, July 26, November 27, 1930.
10. Diary, September 22, 23, October 1, 5, 1931; Grew to J. P. Morgan, October 5, 1931; DeNovo, *American Interests*, 266.
11. Diary, July 27–August 11, September 25, 1928, January 8, March 23, September 14, October 1, 1929, February 7, 1930, October 14, 1931; Conversation with Tevfik, January 5, 1929; Grew to Sheldon Crosby, February 9, 1929; Ivy Lee to Secretary Kellogg, December 10, 1928; File 123G 861/341, SDA.
12. Diary, January 31, 1928, February 21, 1929, August 27, September 26, 1930, February 16, 1932; Conversation with Tevfik, April 22, 1930.
13. Diary, September 6, 15, October 26, November 6, 11, December 1-15, 1930; Grew to Jefferson Patterson, January 26, 1931.
14. Diary July 27–August 10, 1931.
15. Grew to Sheldon Crosby, October 27, 1929.
16. SecState to Grew, March 23, 1928, *FR*, 1928, III, 940. On renewal of the *modus vivendi* in 1928: (text) *FR*, 1927, III, 794-99; *FR*, 1928, III, 950-64. On negotiation of the arbitration and conciliation treaties: Diary, August 20, 1928; Conversations with Tevfik, July 2, August 21, September 29, December 12, 1928, January 5, 1929; *FR*, 1928, III, 940-50; Ellis, *Kellogg*, 222-23. On the Kellogg Pact: Diary, August 20, 1928; Conversations with Tevfik, August 21, 25, September 7, 1928; Ellis, *Kellogg*, 209; TE, II, 797.
17. Conversations with Tevfik, February 17, March 21, April 4, 1929; SecState to Grew, December 26, 1928, *FR*, 1928, III, 962-64; Grew to SecState, February 25, 1929, and SecState to Grew, March 18, 1929, *FR*, 1929, 803-8, 809; *ibid.*, 810-20; TE, II, 799, 805-10.
18. Diary, February 29, 1928, April 2, 9, 1929.
19. Diary, August 21, 1928; Grew to Shaw, June 19, 1929; Memoranda to the Secretary of State by Castle, May 24, 1929, and Clark, May 25, 1929, File 611.6731/138, SDA.
20. Diary, September 7-10, 1929; *FR*, 1929, III 821-42; TE, II, 834.
21. Diary, September 14–October 3, 1929; Grew to Shaw, June 5, 1929; TE, II, 836-37.
22. TE, II, 835.
23. Grew to Shaw, October 12, 1939; Memoranda by Wallace Murray, January 7, 1930, File 711.672 (1929)/11½, and February 18, 1932, File 711.679 Residence and Establishment/84, SDA.
24. Grew to Wallace Murray, January 6, March 12, 24, 1930; Conversation with Tevfik, March 23, 1930; File 711.679 Residence and Establishment/4,5,24,38, SDA; *FR*, 1930, III, 852-55.
25. *Ibid.*, 855-63.
26. Diary, October 18, 1930.
27. Diary, October 18-27, November 22, 1930; Grew to Castle, January 14, 1931; SecState to Grew, November 21, 1930, *FR*, 1930, III, 869-70.
28. Diary November 5-24, 1930; Conversation with Ismet, November 27, 1930; *FR*, 1930, III, 864-72.
29. Diary, May 28, 29, June 29–July 13, 1931; Conversations with Tevfik, January 11, May 7, July 6, 1931; Grew to Stimson, January 27, 1931; Grew to SecState, November 17, 1930, *FR*, 1930, III, 868; *FR*, 1931, II, 1037-44; TE, II, 904-5.
30. Diary, November 20, 1931; Grew to Shaw, May 7, 1932; Conversation with Tevfik, December 2, 1931.
31. Grew to Arthur Bliss Lane, May 24, 1932.

11. TWILIGHT OF THE OLD WORLD

1. On the question of residence at Ankara: Diary, December 12, 1927, January 3, 1928, February 19, July 30–August 12, 1929, January 15, March 22, November 18, 1930, January 26, 1931; Grew to Shaw, January 18, 1928, June 5, 1929, to Jefferson Patterson, January 26, 1931, to William Chilton, September 28, 1931; TE, II, 752. On the basis of yearly compilations in his diary, Grew spent a total of 178 days at Ankara.
2. Diary, August 20, 1928; Grew to Castle, January 16, 1929, to Sheldon Crosby, October 27, 1929.
3. Diary, November 24, 1929. On Yenikeuy, Istanbul, and travels: Diary, February 13, March 5, September 23, 1928, July 3-17, August 27–September 6, November 7-24, 1929, February 27–April 8, June 26, July 13-27, October 13, 1931; Grew to his daughter Lilla, May 14, 1928, to Shaw, June 27, 1929, to his brother Henry, September 6, 29, 1930; TE, II, 814-28, 858-59.
4. On Grew's career: Diary, September 15, October 15, 1928, February 20, 1929, June 16, 1930; Grew to Cabot, July 9, 1928, January 17, 1929, to Castle, March 13, 1929, April 8, 1933, to Donovan, February 5, 1929, to his brother Henry, February 22, 1929, to Moffat, March 12, 30, 1929, December 30, 1931, to Shaw, July 17, 1929; *New York Times*, February 1, 1929, *Washington Evening Star*, February 1, 2, 1929, *Washington Star*, July 10, 1929, *Brooklyn Eagle*, December 27, 1929, *Boston Transcript*, July 11, 1929, *Providence Journal*, July 11, 1929 (clippings in Diary, 1929); TE, II, 909-10.
5. Diary, March 8, 1933; *Town and Country*, August 15, 1928; *Time*, August 15, 1928, May 7, 1934.
6. Diary, September 15, 1928. On the Bosporus swim: Diary, September 12, 1931; TE, II, 899-903. On golf: Diary, April 8, 1928, August 21, September 6, 1931, August 27–September 9, 1932; Grew to J. M. Nye, December 13, 1932.
7. Diary, February 9, April 23, 1928; Grew to Shaw, March 15, 1932; *New York Times*, January 24, 1932.
8. Diary, December 26, 1929, April 8–May 14, 1932; Grew to Lady Agnes Durham, May 24, 1932.
9. Diary, February 27, 1930; Grew to Arthur Bliss Lane, May 24, 1932.
10. Diary, February 5, 1929, July 11, 1934; Grew to Perry, November 16, 1921; TE, II, 711.
11. Interview, author with William Phillips, November 17, 1958.
12. Diary, February 11, 14, 1928, March 8, 1929; Speech to Harvard Class of 1902, June 19, 1922.
13. Diary, November 1, 30, 1930; Grew to Old Corner Book Store and B. F. Stevens and Brown, Ltd., 1924-34.
14. Diary, June 23, 1931, December 4, 1934; Grew to Hugh Wilson, December 26, 1930, to Moffat, October 21, 1931.
15. Diary, April 23, 1928 [n.d.], 1932; Grew to Nicholas Roosevelt, December 31, 1930.
16. Diary, October 21, 1933.
17. TE, II, 842.
18. On the experiment in tolerated opposition: Diary, August 8, September 17, 21, 24, 1930; Grew to Stimson, August 25, September 8, 1930; TE, II, 862-74; Lewis, *Emergence of Modern Turkey*, 274-75.
19. Diary, January 15, 1930; Grew to Shaw, September 10, 25, December 29, 1928; TE, II, 847.
20. Diary, August 16, November 30, 1930, June 20, 1931; Grew to Castle, January 14, 1931, to Burton Berry, November 12, 1932.
21. Diary, January 15, 1930; Grew to Shaw, September 10, 1928; TE, II, 850-51.
22. Diary, August 17, 1928, December 4, 1931 [n.d.], 1932; Grew to Walter Gherardi, February 14, 1931, to Wallace Murray, February 2, 1932, to Castle, January 16, 1929, to Arthur Bliss Lane, May 24, 1932.

23. Diary, May 14-18, 1932.
24. TE, II, 918.

12. THE AFTERMATH OF MANCHURIA

1. Arnold Toynbee, *Survey of International Affairs*, 1932, (London, 1933), 1; *New York Times*, May 8, 1932.
2. The following discussion of the problems a diplomat faced in Japan is based on Edwin O. Reischauer, *The United States and Japan* (Cambridge, Mass., 1957), Part III; Fosco Maraini, *Meeting With Japan*, tr. Eric Mosbacher (New York, 1960); Nobutaka Ike, *Japanese Politics* (New York, 1957), Part I; F. S. C. Northrop, *The Meeting of East and West* (New York, 1950), 315-22; Ruth Benedict, *The Chrysanthemum and the Sword* (Boston, 1946); Yale Candee Maxon, *Control of Japanese Foreign Policy, A Study in Civil-Military Rivalry*, 1930-1945 (Berkeley, 1957), Chaps. 1-3; James Buckley Crowley, "Japan's China Policy, 1931-1938: A Study of the Role of the Military in the Determination of Foreign Policy," unpublished doctoral dissertation, University of Michigan, 1959.
3. Northrop, *Meeting of East and West*, 321.
4. *New York Times*, June 25, 1963. For an analysis of Japanese foreign policy emphasizing the role of *gekokujō*, see Maxon, *Control of Japanese Foreign Policy*.
5. Maraini, *Meeting With Japan*, 42; Robert J. C. Butow, *Tojo and the Coming of the War* (Princeton, N.J., 1961), 61.
6. On Japanese internal and foreign developments I am particularly indebted to Crowley's persuasive analysis in "Japan's China Policy." On events of 1931-32: Crowley, Chaps. 1-2; Butow, *Tojo*, Chaps. 2-3; Maxon, *Control of Japanese Foreign Policy*, Chap. 4; Hugh Byas, *Government By Assassination* (New York, 1942), Part 1; Richard Storry, *The Double Patriots, A Study of Japanese Nationalism* (Boston, n.d. [1957?]), Chaps. 3-5.
7. Diary of Kido Kōichi, May 21, 1932, Library of Congress microfilm, reel WT 5. Except in citations of secondary works, Japanese names are given in the Japanese style, family names first. Japanese authors' names are cited as printed, as a rule in the English style.
8. Diary, March 30, April 8–May 18, 1932.
9. George F. Kennan, *American Diplomacy*, 1900-1950 (Chicago, 1951), 49.
10. See Saionji-Harada Memoirs, Library of Congress microfilm, reel SP 49, *passim*.
11. On Japanese nationalism: Storry, *Double Patriots*, Chaps. 1-5.
12. On the Japanese Army: Crowley, "Japan's China Policy."
13. Reischauer, *United States and Japan*, 15; Diary, June 17, 1924.
14. William L. Neumann, *America Encounters Japan; From Perry to MacArthur* (Baltimore, 1963), 221-23.
15. On Japanese-American relations before September, 1931: Kennan, *American Diplomacy*, Chaps. 2-3; Raymond A. Esthus, "The Changing Concept of the Open Door, 1899-1910," *Mississippi Valley Historical Review*, XLVI (December 1959), 435-54; Edward H. Zabriskie, *American-Russian Rivalry in the Far East: A Study in Diplomacy and Power Politics*, 1895-1914 (Philadelphia, 1946); Howard K. Beale, *Theodore Roosevelt and the Rise of America to World Power* (Baltimore, 1956), 157-58, Chap. 5; Burton F. Beers, *Vain Endeavor, Robert Lansing's Attempt to End the American-Japanese Rivalry* (Durham, N.C., 1962); Sadao Asada, "Japan's 'Special Interests' and the Washington Conference," *American Historical Review*, LXVII (October 1961), 62-70; Gerald E. Wheeler, *Prelude to Pearl Harbor, The United States Navy and the Far East*, 1921-1931 (Columbia, Mo., 1963).
16. Diary, April 8–May 14, 1932.
17. Stimson Diary, January 26, 1932, as quoted in Robert H. Ferrell, *American Diplomacy in the Great Depression* (New Haven, Conn., 1957), 186; Henry L. Stimson and McGeorge Bundy, *On Active Service in Peace and War* (2 vols.; New York, 1947), I, 252; Armin Rappaport, *Henry L. Stimson and Japan*, 1931-1933 (Chicago, 1963), 159-60.

18. Stimson and Bundy, *On Active Service*, I, 245, states that on Stimson's suggestion the fleet was left at Hawaii after its regular mid-February maneuvers instead of returning to its West Coast bases and that it was "probably useful in restraining the more flagrantly headlong Japanese militarists." Stimson's *Far Eastern Crisis; Recollections and Observations* (New York, 1936), 138, states that the fleet remained in the "neighborhood" of Hawaii and was not dispersed or sent back to the Atlantic, that the possibility of an attack on the Philippines existed, and that the fleet "exercised a steadying effect." However, according to the *New York Times* (April 14, 21, December 1, 1932), the concentration consisted of retaining the Atlantic-based Scouting Force with the West Coast Battle Force on the West Coast, not at Hawaii, though elements of the combined fleet may have visited Hawaii briefly for maneuvers. In diplomatic documents of the year the concentration is invariably referred to as the Atlantic force joining the Pacific force in the Pacific, not the entire fleet moving to Hawaii. On this point and on Japanese reaction to the concentration, see *FR*, 1932, IV, 197-98, 289, 302, 325-26, 345, 719. There is no evidence of Japanese plans to attack American territory in 1932. See also Rappaport, *Stimson*, 161-62.
19. A hint by Thomas W. Lamont of J. P. Morgan that Japan might have difficulty borrowing money in New York unless further military operations ceased may have had some effect in limiting the Shanghai Incident. Lamont gave this warning to the Financial Attaché of the Japanese Embassy in Washington after a phone call from President Hoover, the Attaché reported to the Finance Minister in Tokyo. The Finance Minister was concerned and Baron Harada Kumao, secretary to Prince Saionji Kimmochi, reported the telegram in full in his diary. Saionji-Harada Memoirs, reel SP 49, 244-47 (February 16, 1932), Library of Congress microfilm. Possibly Hoover's message was conveyed by Castle, a confidant of the President, who had discussed Japanese credit with Lamont a week before the Attaché's report. Lamont assured Castle that New York would lend no money to Japan at that time. *FR*, 1932, III, 92-93.
20. On Stimson's diplomacy: Stimson and Bundy, *On Active Service*, I, Chap. 9; Elting E. Morison, *Turmoil and Tradition, A Study of the Life and Times of Henry L. Stimson* (Boston, 1960), Chap. 21; Ferrell, *American Diplomacy*, Chaps. 8-11; Richard Current, *Secretary Stimson, A Study in Statecraft* (New Brunswick, N.J., 1954), Chaps. 4-5; Rappaport, *Stimson*.
21. Castle spoke of the critical importance of having a man of tact such as Grew in the Tokyo Embassy. Speech to Rotary Club of Chicago, September 20, 1932, copy in Nelson T. Johnson Papers.
22. On the Ishii speech, text in Diary, June 21, 1932; *New York Times*, June 22, 1932; Saionji-Harada Memoirs, reel SP 49, 378, 443-44 (July 9, October 8, 1932).
23. Stimson Diary, as quoted in Current, *Secretary Stimson*, 108; *New York Times*, August 8-11, 1932; Hornbeck to Nelson T. Johnson, November 14, 1932, Johnson Papers; Grew to SecState, August 10, 1932, *FR*, 1932, IV, 198-99; Grew to SecState August 13, 1932, *FR*, *Japan*, 1931-1941, I, 99; Diary, August 15, 1932. The text of the speech is in *FR*, 1932, I, 575-83. Its receipt was delayed by garbled transmission (Diary, August 15, 1932). Stimson knew on the basis of reports from Grew in July of conversations with the American member of the Lytton Commission, General Frank McCoy, that the Commission report would be unfavorable to the Japanese case for self-defense and self-determination with regard to Manchuria (Grew to SecState, July 16, 1932, *FR*, 1932, IV, 149-50).
24. On the National City Bank Incident: Diary, September 10, 16, 18, 1932, January 18–February 10, 1933; Joseph C. Grew, *Ten Years in Japan* (New York, 1944), 41-45, hereafter cited as TY; Grew to SecState, September 10, 1932, *FR*, 1932, IV, 240-41. On the Singer Incident: Diary, January 18–February 10, 1933; TE, II, 937-38; *FR*, 1933, III, 716-17.
25. Diary, October 7, 1932; TE, II, 931, 934, 936; TY, 31, 39-40, 49; *FR*, *Japan*, I, 99-100; *FR*, 1932, IV, 240-41, 706-15, 715-20; *FR*, 1933, III, 195-96, 700-702.

26. Diary, 1932-34, *passim;* Nelson T. Johnson to Stanley K. Hornbeck, June 29, 1933, Nelson Johnson Papers; Grew to Castle, July 8, 1932.
27. Grew to Hugh Wilson, July 21, 1932; Diary, September 16, 1932; Grew to SecState, July 15, June 30, 1932, *FR*, 1932, IV, 148, 697-98; Grew to SecState, August 13, 1932, *FR*, *Japan*, 1931-41, I, 99-100.
28. James Crowley, "Japan's China Policy," 110-19, 173-202; Saionji-Harada Memoirs, reel 49, 391-92 (July 30, 1932).
29. Grew to SecState, August 13, September 3, 1932, *FR*, *Japan*, 1931-1941, I, 99-100, 102; Grew to SecState, August 26, October 8, *FR*, 1932, IV, 702-3, 718; Diary, September 16, 1932.
30. Grew to SecState, September 10, 1932, *FR*, 1932, IV, 242; TY, 7, 9, 13, 22-27, 49, 50.
31. Grew to SecState, July 7, 22, 28, 1932, *FR*, 1932, IV, 133, 179, 700-702; TY, 13, 31, 42; Diary, June-October, 1932.
32. Grew to SecState August 13, 1932, *FR*, *Japan*, 1931-41, I, 100; Grew to SecState, July 15, September 10, October 8, 1932, *FR*, 1932, IV, 148, 242, 717-19.
33. Diary October 7, 18, 24, 31, November 1, 7, 1932.
34. Diary, November 1, 5, 8, December 25, 1932. A few months later a traveling American found Araki "thoughtful and studious . . . polite and friendly" (Major General William Crozier to Nelson Johnson, May 6, 1933, Nelson Johnson Papers).
35. Diary, November 7, 8, 1932; Grew to SecState, November 17, December 3, 1932, *FR*, 1932, IV, 720-24, 726. Storry. *Double Patriots*, 120-21.
36. Diary, September 22, 28, December 7, 13, 1932; TY, 52, 58; Grew to SecState, October 8, November 15, 28, December 3, *FR*, 1932, IV, 717-18, 344, 372-73, 726-27.
37. Diary, October 31, 1932; TY, 55; Grew to SecState, October 10, 1932, *FR*, 1932, IV, 294. Grew was correct regarding Japanese expectations of a Democratic victory. Debuchi was reporting that the Democrats would probably win, and further that the United States had no intention of waging war on Japan (Saionji-Harada Memoirs, reel 49, 445, October 8, 1932). Jay Pierrepont Moffat, Grew's son-in-law and Chief of the Western European Affairs Division of the State Department, considered a Stimson speech of that month "safe and sane" (Moffat Diary, October 1, 1932, Jay Pierrepont Moffat Papers, Harvard University Library, Cambridge, Mass.).
38. Saionji-Harada Memoirs, reel 49, 440 (October 1), 453 (October 22), 464 (November 5), 469-70 (November 10), 475 (November 16), 478-79 (December 6).
39. Saionji-Harada Memoirs, 520 (February 9, 1933).
40. Diary, January 3, 4, January 27–February 10, 1933; Grew to SecState, February 20, 23, 1933, *FR*, 1931-1941, I, 109-11; TY, 75-76.
41. Saionji-Harada Memoirs, reel 49, 492-539 (December 26, 1932–February 28, 1933); Minister in Switzerland (Hugh Wilson) to SecState, February 9, 13, 14, 1933, *FR*, 1933, III, 161-64, 174-80; Memorandum of Secretary of State, January 5, 1933, *FR*, *Japan*, 1931-1941, I, 107-8; Crowley, "Japan's China Policy," 120-26.
42. Diary, November 28, 1932; Grew to SecState, September 10, November 28, December 3, 1932, *FR*, 1932, IV, 242, 372-73, 727-28; Grew to SecState, February 23, 1933, *FR*, *Japan*, 1931-1941, I, 110.
43. Grew to Moffat, January 14, 1933; Memorandum of telephone conversation between Secretary of State and Ray Atherton, January 13, 1933, *FR*, 1933, III, 55-56; President Hoover to Secretary of State, February 24, 1933, *ibid.*, 209-10; Memorandum of telephone conversation between Secretary of State and Hugh Wilson, December 15, 1932, *FR*, 1932, IV, 427; SecState to Grew, November 3, 1932, *ibid.*, 325-26; Hoover, *Memoirs*, 1920-1933, 366.
44. Diary, May 14-18, August 27–September 9, September 16, 1932, January 27–February 10, 1933; Grew to Moffat, January 14, 1933; Grew to SecState, September 10, October 8, 1932, *FR*, 1932, IV, 242-43, 719.
45. Diary, February 23, 1933, most of which is in TY, 78-80.

13. UNDERSTANDING JAPANESE EXPANSIONISM

1. Grew to Margaret Perry, February 13, 1932, to his brother Randolph, August 19, 1933, November 21, 1935, to J. M. Nye, December 13, 1932; Diary, August 26, November 9, 1932, March 9-23, 1933; Speech to Japan Society of Boston, April 27, 1932.
2. Diary, November 9, 1932; Grew to Gibson, February 16, 1933, to his brother Henry, February 3, 1933; Freidel, *Roosevelt: The Apprenticeship*, 52-66, especially footnote p. 57.
3. Diary, November 6, 9, December 13, 1932, March 7, 1933; Grew to FDR, November 12, December 5, 1932, February 25, 1933, to Gibson, January 28, 1932, to Wilbur Carr, December 5, 1932, to his brother Henry, February 3, 1933, to Cordell Hull, February 25, 1933, to Hugh Wilson, March 7, 1933, to Phillips, March 10, 1933; Moffat Diary, December 12, 1932, Moffat Papers.
4. Diary, January 13-26, February 17, March 24–April 7, 1933; Clippings, 1932; Grew to Gibson, February 3, 18, 1933; Moffat Diary, March 6, October 11, 1933, and Moffat to Hugh Wilson, January 31, 1933, Moffat Papers; TY, 55, 83.
5. Diary, August 1, 1940; Grew to Norman Armour, September 11, 1933, to Hugh Gibson, February 2, 1934, April 28, 1938; *The Memoirs of Cordell Hull* (2 vols.; New York, 1948), I, 180-83; Ilchman, *Professional Diplomacy*, 212-13.
6. Diary, March 1-5, 1933, March 18, 1935; Grew to his daughter Lilla Moffat, December 29, 1934, to Castle, July 30, 1934, to Lithgow Osborne, April 24, 1933, to Rev. Endicott Peobody, March 7, 1933.
7. T. S. Eliot, "The Love Song of J. Alfred Prufrock," *Collected Poems, 1909-1935* (New York, 1936), 12.
8. Diary, June 6, 7, 1932, May 6, 1933; *Japan Advertiser*, December 6, 1931, clipping in Grew Papers; photographs in TY and TE.
9. Diary, April 3, 1936. On entertainment at the Embassy; *Japan Advertiser*, December 6, 1931, clipping in Grew Papers, 1932; Diary, February 20, and October 12, 1933, May 12, 1934, January 16-31, 1937; TY, 28-29, 37.
10. Admirals in touch with the Embassy socially included: Takahashi Sankichi, Takeshita Isamu, Yamamoto Isoroku, Osumi Mineo, Tosu Tamaki, Nagano Osami, Nomura Kichisaburo (Foreign Minister), Saito Makoto, Okada Keisuke and Yonai Mitsumasa (the last three Premiers). Diary, April 13, June 2-5, September 18, 1933, January 31, 1934, February 27, April 18, 1939; Grew to SecState, June 27, 1935, *FR*, 1935, III, 862-63; TY, 93-94, 279-81; Butow, *Tojo*, Chap. 1.
11. Identifiable business acquaintances of Grew are: Mitsui Hachiroemon (president, Mitsui), Ogura Masatsune (Sumitomo), Imamura Sakio (Sumitomo), Tajima Shigeji (Mitsui), Kawasaki Hajime (insurance, banking), Godo Takuo (president, Showa Steel), Isshiki Toraji (director, Japan Steel), Aikawa Geisuke (president, Nissan Motorcar Co.), Kadono Chokiuro (vice-president, Okura zaibatsu), Kushida Manzo (president, Mitsubishi Bank), Baron Ito Bunkichi (president, Nippon Mining Co.), Fukai Eigo (vice-president, Bank of Japan), Okubo Toshikata (manager, Yokohama Specie Bank), Asano Ryozo (Asano zaibatsu), Komatsu Takashi (Asano), Tamura Keizo (fisheries, canning), Murayama Takeshi (manager, food company), Ishida Teiji (shipping), Oshima Kenzo (Sumitomo), Murata Shozo (president, *Osaka Shosen Kaisha*). Seventeen of these twenty had been to the United States or Europe. Speech at Osaka, November 22, 1932; Diary, November 19-23, 1932, February 14, 22, April 6, 1933, January 1-6, April 3, 4, 7, May 11, 1934, March 7, 1935, July 7, 1936, January 9, June 9, 1937, May 11, 1939; *The Who's Who in Japan* (1930-1931) and (1937), ed. Kamesaka Tsunesaburo (Tokyo, n.d. and 1937).
12. Diary, September 9, November 7, 1932, September 18, December 21, 1933, July 5, 1935, January 18, 1936, December 18, 1939, March 4, 1940, October 21, 1941; Willys Peck to Stanley K. Hornbeck, February 24, 1936, Nelson Johnson Papers; Moffat to Norman Davis, September 19, 1934, Moffat Papers.

13. On Chichibu: Diary, September 10, 1932, December 23, 1933, May 4, 1934; Grew to his daughter Anita, May 13, 1938; Saionji-Harada Memoirs, reel 50, 876 (May 4, 1934). Palace advisers were concerned that Chichibu, a major in the Army, was lending his ear to young officer radicals, but apparently he gave them no encouragement: Saionji-Harada Memoirs, reel 50, 1730-31 (March 12-19, 1937); Kido Diary, February 28, 1936; Storry, *Double Patriots,* 113 and fn. 1. Also Diary, February 21, 1933, July 20, 1933, February 8, 1939.
14. Diary, May 23, 1941.
15. The set included: Konoe, Harada, Makino, Maeda, Soejima, Kabayama, his son-in-law Shirasu Jiro, and Yoshida (compiled from Grew's guest lists in Diary, 1932-39). On Konoe: G. R. Storry, "Konoye Fumimaro, 'The Last of the Fujiwara,'" G. F. Hudson, ed., *St. Antony's Papers,* Number 7, Far Eastern Affairs Number 2 (Carbondale, Ill., 1960); Saionji-Harada Memoirs, reel 49, 478-79 (December 6, 1932), reel 50, 880 (May 16, 1934), 1433-34 (March 14, 1936); Butow, *Tojo,* 134. On Makino: Saionji-Harada Memoirs, reel 50, 777 (January 15, 1934), 807-8 (February 14, 1934), 881-82 (May 22, 1934). Others Grew saw frequently included: Ishii, Hayashi, Baron Matsui Keishiro, Viscount Inouye Keijiro, Marquis Okubo Toshikadzu, Viscount Matsudaira Yoshitami. Shidehara came to the Embassy only once, and then by mistake (Diary, April 4, 1935). Diplomats included in this society, aside from the Foreign Minister, Vice-Minister, and American bureau chief, were: Kishi Kuramatsu, Secretary to the Foreign Minister, ex-Ambassadors Yoshizawa Kenkichi, Obata Torikichi, and Debuchi.
16. Diary, June 11, 1940 (also, with substitution of "in Boston" for "on the Back Bay," TY, 320). Diary, September 19, 1932, March 21, April 6, 1934, March 22, 1935, October 4, 1937; Wilson, *Diplomat Between Wars,* 141.
17. Diary, November 27, 1933; Wilbur J. Carr Diary, May 21, 1933, Carr Papers; Wilson, *Diplomat Between Wars,* 189; TY, 15-17, 51.
18. Diary, August 25, November 16, 1932, January 20, 1934, January 22–February 1, 1935, October 23, 25, 1939; TY, 93.
19. The American bureau chiefs in the Foreign Ministry and in Naval Intelligence were approachable, but that was part of their job.
20. Diary, April 3, 10, 13, 15, 1933; Grew to SecState, April 15, 1933, *FR,* 1933, III, 275-76. The message from Saionji was undoubtedly delivered by Harada who had had just returned from seeing him. Saionji-Harada Memoirs, reel 49, 578-80 (April 16, 1933).
21. This account of Grew's estimates of Soviet-Japanese relations, of moderating tendencies in the Army, of the influence of Hirota Koki, and of the generally improving picture internally is based on his following dispatches and telegrams to the Secretary of State: *FR,* 1933, III, July 18 (372-73), (letter to Under Secretary Phillips) October 6 (421-24), October 11 (710-11), October 20 (434-38), October 23 (440-41), November 18 (458-63), December 12 (479-83), December 14 (713-15); *FR,* 1934, III, January 11 (631-33), January 23 (15-16), January 26 (18-22), February 8 (32-36), March 8 (66-69), March 23 (85-88), April 6 (644-48), July 2 (207). Also Diary, January 11, 21, March 16, 23, April 3, 6, 1934; Grew to Nelson Johnson, April 9, 1934; TY, 95-96, 98-99, 115-21; TE, II, 945, 949-50; David J. Dallin, *Soviet Russia and the Far East* (New Haven, Conn., 1948), Chap. 1. Grew gave his private secretary, J. Graham Parsons, the task of reporting on Soviet-Japanese relations, but of course reviewed his dispatches and was responsible for them.
22. See dispatches and telegrams cited above. Also: Diary, July 7, December 19, 1932, April 29, 1933; TY, 99; Saionji-Harada Memoirs, reel 49, 694 (September 25, 1933), 702 (October 2, 1933), 704 (October 9, 1933); Storry, *Double Patriots,* 48, 149.
23. Grew to Nelson Johnson, April 9, 1934.
24. On the Amō Doctrine: Diary, April 17-29, 1934; Grew to Hornbeck, April 28, June 29, 1934; *FR, Japan,* 1931-1941, I, 223-32; *FR,* 1934, III, 112-64; Arnold J. Toyn-

bee, *Survey of International Affairs, 1934* (London, 1935), 646-59; Wilfrid Fleisher, *Volcanic Isle* (Garden City, N. Y., 1941), 259-62.

25. The common postwar interpretation was that the *Tosei-ha* opposed war on the Soviet Union because they favored war on China, a thesis which James Crowley has convincingly disproved. Rather, consensus seems to have prevailed that Russia was the chief threat and that Japan should make the most of opportunities in North China but try to avoid full-scale war with China. Differences were over timing and method rather than objective. Crowley, "Japan's China Policy," Chaps. 3 and 4. On the army factional fight I am indebted to Mr. Ikuhiko Hata for his kind assistance.

26. Diary, April 13, 1933, January 8, 1934; Grew to SecState, September 15, 1933, *FR*, *Japan*, 1931-1941, I, 249-53; Grew to SecState, December 12, 1933, *FR*, 1933, III, 479-83; Grew to SecState, January 22, 1934, *FR*, 1934, I, 217-20; Grew to SecState, February 1, 1934, *FR*, 1934, III, 23; Saionji-Harada Memoirs, reel 49, 545 (March 8, 1933), 650-51 (August 3, 1933), 707 (October 14, 1933); Crowley, "Japan's China Policy," 126-34; Takehiko Yoshihashi, *Conspiracy at Mukden; The Rise of The Japanese Military* (New Haven, Conn., 1963), 61-79.

27. Diary, November 21, 1933; Grew to SecState, *FR*, 1934, III, January 11 (2-3), 22 (13), February 8 (26-29), 21 (44-46), March 9 (638-39), April 6 (643-44); Saionji-Harada Memoirs, reel 49, 862 (April 27, 1934); Crowley, "Japan's China Policy," 126-34.

28. Grew to Hull, May 2, 1934, to Hornbeck, June 29, 1934; Grew to SecState, April 25, 1934, *FR*, *Japan*, 1931-1941, I, 227-28; to SecState, May 4, 1934, *FR*, 1934, III, 160-62; to Consul at Geneva, May 17, 1934, *ibid.*, 181-85.

29. Grew to SecState, July 2, 1934, *FR*, 1934, III, 207-8. Diary, April 24, June 29, July 6, July 30, 1934; Grew's dispatches and telegrams: *FR*, 1934, I, June 14 (255-57), June 22 (270-71), and *FR*, 1934, III, May 17 (183), July 2 (204-8), July 5 (667-71), July 6 (671-72).

30. Diary, September 17, 19, 1934; Moffat Diary, September 18, 19, October 17, 24, 1934, Moffat to Grew, September 17, 1934, to Norman Davis, September 13, 19, 1934, Moffat Papers; Saionji-Harada Memoirs, 945-89 (July 20–August 29, 1934), 1004 (September 13, 1934); Grew's dispatches, *FR*, 1934, I, June 14 (255-57), June 22 (270-71), September 11 (306), September 13 (307), and *FR*, *Japan*, 1931-1941, I, September 15 (249-51), September 18 (253-54).

31. Grew to SecState, October 17, 1934, *FR*, 1934, I, 309-11.

32. Diary, November 13, 27, December 1, 4, 8-31, 1934; Grew to Paul D. Cravath, January 21, 1935. On the naval talks: Grew to SecState, December 13, 1934, *FR*, 1934, I, 408-11; SecState to Grew, October 31 and November 22, 1934, *FR*, *Japan*, 1931-1941, I, 257-62; Grew to SecState, October 20, 1934, *FR*, 1934, III, 294-96. On the oil controversy: *FR*, *Japan*, 1931-1941, I, 130-46; *FR*, 1934, III, 699-774, especially Grew to SecState, December 1, 1934, 773-74.

33. Diary, January 7, 1935; Grew to SecState, December 27, 1934, *FR*, 1935, III, 821-29; Grew to SecState, February 6, *ibid.*, 843-52; Grew to SecState, December 11, 1934, *FR*, 1934, III, 684-87.

34. Grew to SecState, December 27, 1934, *FR*, 1935, III, 821-29; Diary, September 13–October 11, 1934, January 26, 1935; TY, 3.

35. Diary, February 28, March 5, 16, April 10, 1935; Grew's dispatches and telegrams: *FR*. 1935, III, February 7 (45-49), March 2 (67-68), March 19 (560-63), March 22 (88-89), April 5 (106-11), April 13 (896), April 16 (898-900), April 20 (119-20).

36. Diary, March 22, 1935; Grew's dispatches: *FR*, 1935, III, December 27, 1934 (826), February 7, 1935 (45-49), March 22, 1935 (88-89), April 20, 1935 (119-20), May 3, 1935 (148-51).

37. Diary, June 13, 1935; Grew to SecState, June 14, 1935, *FR*, 1935, III, 244-48.

38. Diary, December 18, 1935, January 6, 7, February 10, 1936; Grew to SecState, January 7 and February 7, 1936, *FR*, 1936, IV, 706-18 and 44.

39. Grew to SecState, January 25, 1936, *ibid.*, 25-28. Considered by Grew as moderates in the Navy were Admirals Nomura, Nagano, Nakamura Ryozo, and Kobayashi Seizo (Grew to SecState, June 27, 1935, *FR*, 1935, III, 862-63).
40. Saionji-Harada Memoirs, reel 49, 987-88 (August 29, 1934); reel 50, 1248 (May 31, 1935); reel 49, 710 (October 14, 1933). This account of Hirota's problems is based on the Saionji-Harada Memoirs, reel 49, pages 649-51, 684-85, 704, 724, 945-89, 992, and reel 50, pages 1050, 1066, 1089-95, 1175, 1225, 1245-48, 1258, 1294, 1359. Also Kido Diary, May 30, 1935, and Crowley, "Japan's China Policy," Chap. 3.
41. Diary, July 5, 1935, January 13, 1936. Grew's dispatches and telegrams: *FR*, 1935, I, July 23, 1935 (79-80); *FR*, 1935, III, June 29, 1935 (283-84), July 16, 1935 314); *FR*, 1936, I, January 13, 1936 (32); *FR*, 1936, IV, January 25, 1936 (26-27); *FR*, *Japan*, 1931-1941, I, January 12, 1936 (290-91). Norman Davis (London) to SecState, January 14, 1936, *ibid.*, 291-92.

14. COPING WITH JAPANESE EXPANSIONISM

1. Diary, May 19, 1935.
2. Speech to Japan Society of Boston, April 27, 1932.
3. TY, 54.
4. Diary, November 8, 1932, March 19, 1933; TY, 20-21, 56-58, 82, 110-11; *Japan Advertiser*, May 19, 1936, clipping in Grew Papers.
5. Diary, November 3, 8, 1932, April 29, 1933, January 5, 1936; TY, 155-56, 162, 181.
6. TY, 207.
7. Diary, December 17, 22, 1934, January 13, March 17–April 1, 1935, April 14, 1936; TY, 60, 84, 88.
8. On the Peking trip (Diary, September 20–October 3, 1934) he stayed with Minister Johnson and had extensive conversations with diplomats, but noted very little beyond sight-seeing in his Diary.
9. Diary, November 2-14, 1933; Grew to Luther Fowle, April 12, 1933.
10. Diary, June 5, July 25–September 11, November 2-14, 1933, January 19, 1934; TY, 88-91; John Bassett Moore, "An Appeal to Reason," *Foreign Affairs*, XI (July 1933), 547-88; Robert A. Divine, *The Illusion of Neutrality* (Chicago, 1962), 21.
11. Diary, January 27–February 10, November 21, 1933, January 29, 1934; Grew to Hornbeck, February 8, 1934; Grew to SecState, January 22, 1934, *FR*, 1934, III, 7.
12. Diary, May 10, 1933; Grew to Castle, February 27, 1934; Grew to SecState, *FR*, 1933, III, April 21 (700-702), May 8 (306-7), May 24 (344-46), August 14 (388-91); Grew to SecState, October 3, 1933, *FR*, *Japan*, 1931-1941, I, 123-24; *FR*, 1934, III, 677-79.
13. Hornbeck to Grew, February 24, 1934, copy in Nelson Johnson Papers, including text of speech. Hornbeck explained that the phrase, "governments made by the sword," which was not in the original release of the speech, was the mistake of an inexperienced Associated Press correspondent who was formerly his student. Diary, January 22, 1934; Grew to Hornbeck, February 8, 1934; Hornbeck to Frank Lockhart, June 27, 1933, copy in Nelson Johnson Papers; Grew to SecState and SecState to Grew, January 22, 1934, *FR*, 1934, III, 6-8; *ibid.*, 16-18.
14. SecState to Grew, April 28, 1934, *FR*, *Japan*, 1931-1941, I, 231-32; Grew to SecState, May 4, 1934, *FR*, 1934, III, 163; TY, 133-34. On American policy and the Amō Doctrine: Dorothy Borg, *The United States and the Far Eastern Crisis of 1933-1938* (Cambridge, Mass., 1964), 75-92.
15. Diary, March 16, October 23, 1933, December 13, 1934, May 22, 1936, April 16, 1937; Grew to SecState, January 11, 1934, *FR*, 1934, III, 633.
16. On Babe Ruth, Diary, November 5, 1934; TY, 144. Grew to SecState, June 8, 1933, *FR*, 1933, III, 702-3, and May 4, 1934, *FR*, 1934, III, 649-50.
17. Diary, January 22, 1933. On Sambo: TY, 112-13, 117.

18. On the editors: Diary, September 19, October 12-24, 1934. On the veterans: Diary, April 25, 27, May 16, 1936. On American missionaries and educators: Speech to Annual Conference of Foreign Teachers in Japan, April 1, 1933; Diary, March 20, April 1, 1933, March 16, 1934, April 21, July 9, 1935.
19. Diary, December 20, 23, 1933, March 29–May 13, 1934, June 13, 1934; Conversation with Hirota, October 27, 1933; Grew to Hornbeck, March 30, 1934, to Hull, April 26, 1934; Saionji-Harada Memoirs, reel 49, 795 (January 8, 1934); TE, II, 948-49, 962-63.
20. Diary, November 18, 30, 1933, January 8, 1934; Grew to SecState, September 29, 1933, *FR*, 1933, III, 413, 415, November 18, 1933, *ibid.*, 461-62, February 8, 1934, *FR*, 1934, III, 34; Saionji-Harada Memoirs, reel 49, 719 (October 24, 1933).
21. Diary, January 13-26, November 20, 1933, January 10, November 7, 1934, December 23, 1935, December 8, 1936, April 16, May 15, 1937; Grew to Romasheff, Chief Accountant of the Soviet Embassy, January 27, 1934; Castle to Johnson, January 27, 1936, Nelson Johnson Papers.
22. Diary, February 23, April 2, 1934; Saionji-Harada Memoirs, reel 50, 1322 (September 27, 1935); *FR*, *Japan*, 1931-1941, I, 127-29.
23. Grew to Consul at Geneva, May 17, 1934, *FR*, 1934, III, 185. On the Hull-Saito talks: *ibid.*, III, 650-62; Borg, *Far Eastern Crisis*, 92-99.
24. Diary, April 22, 23, October 23, November 27, 1934, January 10-21, June 16, 1935, February 11, 1936; TY, 154, 163.
25. Grew to SecState, August 20, November 27, 1934, *FR*, 1934, III, 721-22, 769; SecState to Grew, October 31, 1934, *ibid.*, 752; Johnson to Hornbeck, August 23, 1934, Nelson Johnson Papers.
26. Diary, October 11, November 13, 27, December 4, 1934; Grew to SecState, December 29, 1934, *FR*, 1934, III, 687-90, and December 27, 1934, *FR*, 1935, III, 821-29.
27. Diary, February 14, 1935; Hornbeck to Johnson, January 17, 1934, and Memorandum by Hornbeck, April 13, 1935, Nelson Johnson Papers; Moffat Diary (Hornbeck's style), July 3-4, 1934; Grew to SecState, December 27, 1934, *FR*, 1935, III, 821-29; Memorandum by Hornbeck, January 3, 1935, *ibid.*, 829-37; SecState to Grew, January 21, 1935, *ibid.*, 842; Borg, *Far Eastern Crisis*, Chap. 3. On the decision to maintain American naval superiority: Moffat Diary, September 26, 1934, recording a meeting between Hull, Phillips, Hornbeck, Moffat, the Assistant Secretary of the Navy, the Chief of Naval Operations, and others; Moffat Diary, October 3, 1934, including a memorandum of a conversation at the White House attended by the President, Hull, Chief of Naval Operations, Norman Davis, and Moffat.
28. On Anglo-American relations generally and with respect to the London naval talks: Moffat-Davis correspondence, 1934, Moffat to Grew, December 29, 1934, Moffat Diary, October-November 1934 and Hornbeck to Ray Atherton (London), June 5, 1934 (copy), Moffat Papers; *FR*, 1934, I, 216-405; Borg, *Far Eastern Crisis*, 102-11. On Grew and the rumored Anglo-Japanese understanding: Diary, May 23, August 1-19, 1934; Conversations with Sir Robert Clive (August 30, September 13, 1934) and General J. C. Pabst (September 17, 1934); Moffat Diary, May 28, August 21, 1934; SecState to Ambassador in France, May 24, 1934 (based on Grew to SecState, May 23, 1934), *FR*, 1934, I, 238-39; Grew to SecState, August 22, 23, 1934, *ibid.*, III, 250-51. On Grew and oil representations: Dairy, December 4, 1934; *FR*, 1934, III, 699-799.
29. Diary, July 13, 1932, January 6, October 25, 1933, November 22, December 4, 1934, January 24, February 19, April 26, June 10, 1935, June 16, July 2, 1936, January 16-31, March 1-18, 1937. On Grew's persistent complaints of lack of information from Washington: Diary, July 16, December 20, 1932, January 7, 1933, March 4, 1935; Grew to Moffat, June 1, 1934.
30. Diary, January 9, 20, February 7, 1936; Grew to SecState, January 9, February 7, 1936 (Dispatch No. 1665), *FR*, 1936, IV, 7-8, 42-49; *ibid.*, 1-6; *ibid.*, I, 24-27.
31. Diary, July 15-31, 1934.
32. Grew to Hornbeck, January 24, February 7, 1936.

33. Memorandum by Hornbeck, January 16, 1936, *FR*, 1936, I, 37; Johnson to SecState, January 15, 1936, *FR*, 1936, IV, 13.
34. Memorandum by Hornbeck, April 13, 1935; Moffat Diary, September 26, 1934, and Memorandum of Conversation at the White House in Moffat Diary, October 3, 1934, Moffat Papers. On American Far Eastern policy generally: Hornbeck-Johnson correspondence in Johnson papers, Moffat papers, and Dorothy Borg, *Far Eastern Crisis*. Miss Borg demonstrates that policy was passive but that acquiescence did not imply assent. I would only emphasize the determination of the Administration not be a prisoner of its passivity.
35. On the February 26 Incident: Diary, March 1, 1936; TY, 169-78; TE, II, 987-94; Butow, *Tojo*, 63-70; Storry, *Double Patriots*, Chap. 8; Fleisher, *Volcanic Isle*, Chap. 3; Byas, *Government by Assassination*, Chap. 9; *FR*, 1936, IV, 719-56.
36. This is the Byas version (*Government by Assassination*, 122). The story heard by Grew at the time was that Makino's lovely granddaughter shielded the old man with her kimono and the soldiers were too deeply moved by this act of courage to fire (TY, 175).
37. Crowley, "Japan's China Policy," Chap. 4.
38. Diary, March 18, April 3, 12, 1936; Grew to Hornbeck, March 6, 1936, to Nelson Johnson, March 25, 1936, to Colonel E. M. House, May 21, 1936; Roger Greene to Nelson Johnson (reporting a conversation with Grew), April 13, 1936, Nelson Johnson Papers; Grew to SecState, *FR*, 1936, IV, February 29 (734), March 5 742-46), March 6 (749-50, 755), March 9 (759), March 19 (762-66); TY, 174, 176-78.
39. Diary, April 26, 1936.
40. Grew to Hornbeck, August 6, 1936; Grew to SecState, *FR*, 1936, IV, March 7 (756-59), May 14 (769-72), July 18 (779-81); TY, 178.
41. TY, 199; Storry, *Double Patriots*, 196, 204-5; Crowley, "Japan's China Policy," 245-6.
42. Diary, January 1, 1937; Grew to Hornbeck, January 9, 1937; Grew to SecState, May 29, 1936, *FR*, 1936, IV, 773-76; Grew to SecState, January 22, 27, 1937, *FR*, 1937, IV, 703-5; TY, 198-200.
43. Grew to Hugh Wilson, May 13, 1937; Grew to SecState, January 30, February 6, 1937, *FR*, 1937, IV, 705-9. In negotiations preceding the formation of the Hayashi Cabinet, Ugaki Kazushige, a popular, retired general, had attempted to form a cabinet but failed because of army opposition. In his letter to Hugh Wilson, Grew accurately explained why: Ugaki had been head of one of the older factions, and the "neutrol, controlling group" were determined to rid the Army of such political and factional methods. See Crowley, "Japan's China Policy," 239-40.
44. Grew to Hugh Wilson, May 13, 1937; Grew to SecState, February 18, 1937, *FR*, 1937, IV, 710-14.
45. On Ishihara: Crowley, "Japan's China Policy," Chap. 5. The similarity of information in the Embassy's dispatch of February 18 and in Harada's diary entry of February 10 suggests that the Embassy had good sources of information on the faction, though it failed to identify Ishihara (Saionji-Harada Memoirs, reel 50, 1700-1708). On the national mass party: Storry, *Double Patriots*, 212-13. Grew to SecState, June 4, 1937, *FR*, 1937, IV, 718.
46. TY, 212.
47. On the stolen diary: Diary, December 16-31, 1936, January 16-31, February 1, 1937; Grew to Hornbeck, February 9, 13, May 14, 1937, to his daughter Elsie (Mrs. Cecil Lyon), January 22, 1937, to Cecil Lyon, February 2, October 1, 1937, to his daughter Anita (Mrs. Robert English), April 4, 1937, to his brother Henry, May 13, 1938, to Frank P. Lockhart, February 3, 1937, to Boylston Beal, April 4, 1937.

15. THE SLIDE TO WAR ON CHINA

1. On his health: Diary, February 7 and April 15, 1935. On his travels: Diary July 19–December 16, 1935, August 28–November 18, 1936.

2. Diary, August 4-5, 1935, October 20-23, 1936.
3. Diary, February 23, 1934, October 23, 1936; Grew to Neville, December 29, 1936, to Castle, March 1, 1937.
4. On Embassy forecasting of an agreement: *FR*, 1936, I, 390-92, 397-98; *ibid.*, IV, 93; Chargé Erle Dickover to Hornbeck, September 18, November 14, 1936, Grew Papers. On Grew's reaction: Diary, November 27, 28, December 4, 8, 1936; Grew to SecState, December 4, 18, 1936, *FR*, 1936, I, 404-5, 119; Grew to SecState, December 16, 1936, *ibid.*, IV, 426-28; TY, 191-98. On the Pact: Ernst L. Presseisen, *Germany and Japan: A Study in Totalitarian Diplomacy*, 1933-1941 (The Hague, 1958), Chap. 4, and text of secret protocol, p. 328.
5. Report of a Privy Council Investigation of the Japanese-German Pact held November 13 and 18, 1936, Document 1105 A, Exhibit 484, Tokyo War Crimes Trials Collection, Harvard University Law School Library; Saionji-Harada Memoirs, reel 50, 1626 (November 18, 1936), 1641-42 (December 4, 1936); Presseisen, *Germany and Japan*, 104-5; Dallin, *Soviet Russia and the Far East*, 25-27, 67; Borg, *Far Eastern Crisis*, 207-17; German Memorandum of March 7, 1936, as quoted in Arnold J. Toynbee, ed., *Survey of International Affairs*, 1936 (Oxford, 1937), 264.
6. Grew to SecState, December 9, 1936, *FR*, 1936, IV, 408-9; TY, 192-96.
7. Grew to Hornbeck, March 31, 1937; Department of State Draft Memorandum, February 16, 1937, Hornbeck to Grew, February 26, 1937, and Memorandum by Roosevelt, March 1, 1937, *FR*, 1937, III, 954-74; Borg, *Far Eastern Crisis*, 244-48. Grew's argument was more fully developed in Diary, May 24, 1937, and Grew to SecState, May 28, 1937, *FR*, 1937, III, 979-82.
8. On the northward orientation: Grew to Castle, January 26, 1937; Grew to SecState, December 16, 1936, *FR*, 1936, IV, 428. On the Southward Advance: Diary, April 30, May 20, 1936; Grew to SecState, April 30, 1936, *FR*, 1936, IV, 133; Grew to SecState, January 1, May 11, 1937, *FR*, 1937, III, 10, 86. This interpretation of the August 7-11, 1936, decisions of the Five Ministers Conference is based on Crowley, "Japan's China Policy," 246-50.
9. Grew on Japan's China problem, 1937: Diary, January 1, February 23, March 1-31, 1937; Grew to Hugh Wilson, May 13, 1937; Grew to SecState, *FR*, 1937, III, January 1 (2-5), February 25 (29-31), March 5 (34-35), March 11, 12, 13 (39-44), March 17 (48-52), May 14 (96-100), June 24 (118-21). Crowley, "Japan's China Policy," 242-45; Borg, *Far Eastern Crisis*, 218-34; F. C. Jones, *Japan's New Order in East Asia; Its Rise and Fall*, 1937-1945 (Oxford, 1954), 22.
10. Grew to Hugh Wilson, May 13, 1937; TY, 206-7.
11. Grew to Hornbeck, July 10, 1937.
12. On the crisis of July 1937: James B. Crowley, "A Reconsideration of the Marco Polo Bridge Incident," *The Journal of Asian Studies*, XXII (May 1963), 277-91; Jones, *Japan's New Order*, Chap. 2.
13. Diary, July 12, 1937; Johnson to F. M. Dearing, October 12, 1935, Nelson Johnson Papers.
14. Diary, June-December 1937, *passim.*
15. On the attachés: Diary, August 3, 1937; On Dooman: Diary, May 22, 1937, Grew to Dooman, February 9, 1937, to Hornbeck, June 22, 1936; *Register of the Department of State*, 1944. On Dodds: Diary, July 15-23, 1937.
16. The following account of the diplomacy of the Far Eastern crisis is based mainly on the dispatches, instructions, and memoranda in *FR*, 1937, III, 128-848. On Grew's understanding, of particular importance are: Diary, July 14, 22, 27, 29, August 10, 13, 27, September 26–October 10, 1937; Grew to SecState, *FR*, 1937, III, July 14 (165-66), July 22 (243-44), July 23 (251-53), August 6 (345-48), August 27 (485-88), September 15 (525-30), October 8 (590-93).
17. Grew to SecState, July 23, 1937, *ibid.*, 251-52.
18. Grew to SecState, August 27, 1937, *ibid.*, 485-86.
19. Diary, September 26–October 10, 1937.
20. Diary, July 14, 1937.
21. TY, 221.

22. Diary, August 13, 1937.
23. Diary, July 14, 28, August 7, 14, 20, 22, 1937; Grew to SecState, August 6, 1937, *FR*, 1937, III, 345-48.
24. Diary, July 14, 22, 28, August 13, 1937; Grew to SecState, July 31, 1937, *FR*, 1937, III, 305; Statement by Hull, July 16, 1937, and Press Release by Department of State, August 23, 1937, *FR*, *Japan*, 1931-1941, I, 325-26, 355-57; Borg, *Far Eastern Crisis*, Chap. 10.
25. Diary, August 6, 7, 10, 1937; Grew to SecState, August 6 and 10, FR, 1937, III, 337, 340-41, 368-69; Johnson to SecState, August 12, *ibid*., 385-86; Memorandum by Grew, August 10, 1937, *FR*, *Japan*, 1931-1941, I, 339-41; *FR*, 1937, III, 319-20, 328-29, 353, 387-88.
26. Moffat Diary, August 27–September 1, 1937, Moffat Papers; Grew to SecState, August 27, 1937, *FR*, 1937, III, 485-88; *New York Times*, July 8–September 1, 1937. The *New York Times* devoted a daily average of thirty front-page column inches to the crisis during the two weeks before August 14 and seventy-four column inches during the two weeks after. Using microfilm, a full column measured slightly less than twenty-four inches. A page contains eight columns.
27. Diary, August 27, 1937; Moffat Diary, August 27–September 1, 1937, Moffat Papers.
28. Moffat Diary, August 27, 1937, Moffat Papers; SecState to Grew, September 2, 1937, *FR*, 1937, III, 505-8
29. On State Department policy and the Quarantine Speech: Borg, *Far Eastern Crisis*, Chaps. 12 and 13. "Statement by President Roosevelt, October 5, 1937, in Chicago," Stephen Heald, ed., *Documents on International Affairs* (London, 1939), 582-87; *Moffat Papers*, 150-55.
30. Jones, *Japan's New Order*, 55.
31. Diary, September 2, 1937; Grew to SecState, September 15, 1937, October 2, 1937, *FR*, 1937, III, 525-30, 574-77.
32. Diary, September 20, 1937; Moffat Diary, September 1, 1937, Moffat Papers; SecState to Grew, July 27, and Grew to SecState, July 28, 1937, *FR*, 1937, IV, 238-41; SecState to Grew, July 27, 29, 1937, *ibid*., III, 275-76, 297; Grew to SecState, September 1, 20, 1937, *ibid*., 504-5, 535-36.
33. Diary, August 13, September 26–October 10, 1937; Grew to Mrs. S. V. R. Crosby, November 2, 1937.
34. Diary, September 26–October 10, October 30, November 4, 1937; Grew to Castle, October 28, December 9, 1937.
35. Borg, *Far Eastern Crisis*, Chap. 15; Jones, *Japan's New Order*, 56-62; Crowley, "Japan's China Policy," 285-93.
36. Borg, *Far Eastern Crisis*, 456-57.
37. *Ibid*., 383-86; Statement by Roosevelt, October 19, 1937, Heald, ed., *Documents on International Affairs*, 1937, 591.
38. Diary, October 30, 1937; Saionji-Harada Memoirs, reel 50, 1909 (October 25, 1937); Acting SecState to Nelson Johnson and Grew to SecState, October 29, 30, 1937, *FR*, 1937, III, 648-49; Grew to SecState, November 18, 1937, *ibid*., 688; Grew to SecState, October 15, October 27, November 1, 1937, *ibid*., IV, 80, 112, 134-35; Acting SecState to Grew, October 31, 1937, *ibid*., 128-29.
39. As quoted in Carl E. Schorske, "Two German Ambassadors: Dirksen and Schulenberg," Craig and Gilbert, eds., *The Diplomats*, 1919-1939, 480. On German good offices: *Documents on German Foreign Policy*, 1918-1945 (Washington, 1949), Series D (hereafter cited as *DGFP-D*), I, 769-820; Presseisen, *Germany and Japan*, 124-42.
40. Diary, October 30, November 1, 5, 11, 1937; Grew to SecState, November 2, 6, 1937, *FR*, 1937, III, 653-54, 662-65; Grew to SecState, October 30, 1937, *ibid*., IV, 122-23, 124-25; *ibid*., III, 648-49, 652, 660; *ibid*., IV, 118, 128-29, 134, 136-37. On progress of the fighting: *New York Times*, October–December, 1937; Toynbee, ed., *Survey of International Relations*, 1937, I, 213-25.
41. Grew to SecState, October 30, 1937, *FR*, 1937, IV, 122-23; Grew to SecState, November 6, 1937, *ibid*., III, 662-63; Saionji-Harada Memoirs, reel 50, 1923 (No-

vember 18, 1937) (Craigie); *New York Times*, November 4, 1937 (Byas dispatch); *ibid.*, November 5-6, 1937 (Hitler mediation). Grew's full report of the Dooman-Yoshizawa conversations was contained in a dispatch sent by mail which arrived in Washington December 16 (Grew to SecState, November 18, 1937, *FR*, 1937, III, 690-97). On Theodore Roosevelt's role in 1905: Beal, *Theodore Roosevelt*, 268-314.

42. Diary, November 15, 1937; Grew to SecState, November 18, 1937, *FR*, 1937, III, 690-97; German Ambassador in China to German Foreign Ministry, November 5, 1937, *DGFP-D*, I, 780-81.
43. Grew to SecState, November 16, 1937, *FR*, 1937, IV, 189-93.
44. Diary, November 16, 1937.
45. Saionji-Harada Memoirs, reel 50, 1928 (November 18, 1937).
46. It was stipulated in the Japanese interministerial agreement of October 22 that Japan's disposition for peace should not be revealed too quickly or too obviously for fear of creating the impression of weakness (Borg, *Far Eastern Crisis*, 457).
47. Grew to SecState, November 16, 1937, *FR*, 1937, IV, 192; Memorandum by Hugh Wilson, November 16, 1937, *ibid.*, 194-96; Grew to SecState, November 18, 1937, *ibid.*, III, 687; TY, 225-26. Grew told the Department on November 18 (*FR*, 1937, III, 688) that he had "received no impression that he [Hirota] was soliciting an offer of good offices." Of course, officially Hirota wasn't; he was revealing a receptivity to an offer of good offices. Grew explained in another dispatch the same day that the Japanese would not be likely to answer the question as to whether they wanted good offices until the conditions Hirota had laid down were met (*ibid.*, 697).
48. Diary, November 20, 1937; Grew to SecState, November 18, 1937, *FR*, 1937, III, 687-88, 695-96; SecState to Grew, November 19, 1937, *ibid.*, 699-700; SecState to Grew and Grew to SecState, November 16, 18, 1937, *ibid.*, IV, 196-97, 210-11; TY, 227-29.
49. Diary, November 20, 1937; Grew to SecState and SecState to Grew, November 18, 19, 23, 1937, *FR*, 1937, III, 696-97, 699-701, 714-15; Memoranda by Hugh Wilson, November 28, 1937, and Welles, December 8, 1937, *ibid.*, 727-28, 776; Grew to SecState, November 16, 1937, *ibid.*, IV, 192; Memorandum by Moffat, December 2, 1937, *ibid.*, 233-35.
50. German Ambassador in China to German Foreign Ministry, December 3, 1937, and Dirksen to Foreign Ministry, December 7, 1937, *DGFP-D*, I, 787-89, 799; Crowley, "Japan's China Policy," 293-308; Borg, *Far Eastern Crisis*, 474-81; Jones, *Japan's New Order*, 62-70.

16. A NEW ORDER IN EAST ASIA

1. On the sinking of the *Panay*: *FR*, *Japan*, 1931-1941, I, 517-63; *FR*, 1937, IV, 485-520; *New York Times*, December 13, 1937–January 2, 1938; TY, 232-40; Samuel Eliot Morison, *The Rising Sun in the Pacific*, 1931–*April*, 1942, Vol. III of *The History of United States Naval Operations in World War II* (15 vols.; Boston, 1948-62), 16-18; Borg, *Far Eastern Crisis*, Chap. 16.
2. Grew to SecState, December 13, 1937, *FR*, *Japan*, 1931-1941, I, 520; Grew to SecState, December 13, 1937, *FR*, 1937, IV, 497-98; *ibid.*, 485-88; TY, 232-33.
3. Grew to SecState and Memorandum by SecState, December 13, 1937, *FR*, *Japan*, 1931-1941, I, 521-23; TY, 233, 234. 3 P.M., December 13, Tokyo time, was 1 A.M., December 13, Washington time. Hull saw Saito, the Japanese Ambassador, at 1 P.M., December 13.
4. SecState to Grew and Grew to SecState, December 13, 14, *FR*, *Japan*, 1931-1941, I, 523-26.
5. SecState to Grew, December 16, 1937, and Memorandum by SecState, December 17, 1937, *FR*, *Japan*, 1931-1941, I, 527, 529-30; Commander in Chief United States Asiatic Fleet to Chief of Naval Operations, December 15, 1937, *FR*, 1937, IV, 501-2; *New York Times*, December 16-23, 1937.

6. It is generally accepted that the air attack on *Panay* originated in the febrile mind of Colonel Hashimoto Kingoro, commander of an artillery regiment in the area. Hashimoto was responsble for the shelling of the British gunboat H.M.S. *Ladybird* the same day *Panay* was sunk. A notorious ultra-nationalist plotter and agitator, he is supposed to have hoped that by provoking war with the Western democracies he could further plans for a military dictatorship at home. Information relating to Hashimoto's responsibility was furnished to *New York Times* correspondent Hallett Abend by none other than General Matsui Iwane, commander of the Japanese Central China Army, and appeared in the *New York Times* December 20, under the four-column headline COLONEL HASHIMOTO ORDERED PANAY FIRING (Navy Department to Department of State, n.d., received December 20, 1937, *FR*, 1937, IV, 513). Nevertheless, this evidence is not entirely satisfactory for the following reasons: (1) On the morning of December 12 a British naval officer protested the shelling of *Ladybird* personally to Hashimoto at Wuhu, some twenty-five miles upriver from the last position of *Panay*, where she had only just anchored after moving thirteen miles upriver that morning (Toynbee, ed., *Survey*, 1937, I, 310; *FR*, 1937, IV, 486-87). It seems unlikely that Hashimoto could have known of *Panay* or where she was. (2) It is unlikely that the Japanese had developed tactical air power to the point where a regimental commander could call down a naval air strike. More likely the order originated in General Matsui's headquarters on the erroneous assumption that foreign vessels were either near Nanking or Wuhu but not in between. *Panay* had moved upriver twice in the twenty-four hours before her sinking (*ibid.*, 485-86). (3) If the error had in fact been Matsui's, Hashimoto, who was well known for his political activities, was implicated in the February 26 Incident, and was already in trouble for the shelling of *Ladybird*, would be a likely scapegoat. On Hashimoto's involvement: Morison, *Rising Sun*, 16-18; Storry, *Double Patriots*, 227-28; Jones, *Japan's New Order*, 130-31.
7. Consul General at Shanghai to SecState, December 13, 1937, *FR*, 1937, IV, 491.
8. Okumiya Masatake, "How The *Panay* Was Sunk," *United States Naval Institute Proceedings*, LXXIX (June 1953), 587-96.
9. On the flags: *FR*, *Japan*, *1931-1941*, I, 534-35, 543; *New York Times*, December 18, 1937, and photographs December 29, 30, 1937, and January 2, 1938.
10. On the launches: Grew to SecState, December 20, 1937, *FR*, *Japan*, 1931-1941, I, 531; *New York Times*, December 21, 24, 1937.
11. SecState to Grew, December 16, and Grew to SecState, December 23, 24, 1937, *FR*, *Japan*, 1931-1941, I, 527, 547-48, 549-51; SecState to Grew, December 22, 1937, *FR*, 1937, IV, 516-17; Moffat Diary, December 20, 1937, Moffat Papers; TY, 237-39; Saionji-Harada Memoirs, reel 50, 1985-86 (December 27, 1937).
12. SecState to Grew, December 25, 1937, and Grew to SecState, April 22, 1938, *FR*, *Japan*, 1931-1941, I, 551-52, 563; *New York Times*, December 18, 1937; TY, 240; Borg, *Far Eastern Crisis*, 501-3; Divine, *Illusion of Neutrality*, 219-21.
13. Diary, February 10, 1938; TY, 236, 240.
14. On protection cases in 1938: *FR*, 1938, IV, 214-558; *FR*, *Japan*, 1931-1941, I, 564-641. Most serious were the Nyhus, Scovel, Thomson, Allison, and Massie cases. The case total (1937 and 1938) is in Memorandum by Grew, December 26, 1938, *ibid.*, 632.
15. Diary, January, February, June, July, October, 1938, no day (Grew at this time began regularly giving monthly summaries of events in his diary, so there is often no day of the month given); Saionji-Harada Memoirs, reel 51, 2323 (November 4, 1938, which date is incorrectly given as October 4, 1938); *ibid.*, 2340 (November 11, 1938); *FR*, *Japan*, 1931-1941, I, 566-67, 577, 596, 611-19, 627; TY, 249-50.
16. Diary, January, February, May, June [n.d.], 1938, June 28, 1938; Memorandum by Grew, May 31, 1938, *FR*, *Japan*, 1931-1941, I, 594-95; Grew to Foreign Minister Ugaki, July 4, 1938, *ibid.*, 611-19; Grew to Foreign Minister Arita, December 22, 1938, and Memorandum by Grew, December 26, 1938, *ibid.*, 630-32; Grew to *SecState*, January 6, 1938, *ibid.*, 735; SecState to Grew, February 18, 1938, *FR*, 1938, IV, 273-74.

17. Diary, August [n.d.], 1938. Phoebe Nyhus, age three, was killed October 24, 1938, and the Nyhus case was settled November 27, 1939 (*FR*, 1939, IV, 408).
18. On Japanese interference with American treaty rights and equality of commercial opportunity to October 1, 1938: *FR*, *Japan*, 1931-1941, I, 729-45, 757-81; *FR*, 1938, III, 211-13, 279; *ibid.*, IV, 1-47.
19. SecState to Grew, October 1, 1938, *ibid.*, 48-53.
20. Diary, October [n.d.], 1938; Memorandum and Oral Statement by Grew, October 3, 1938 and Grew Note to Konoe, October 6, 1938, *FR*, *Japan*, 1931-1941, I, 781-90; Grew to SecState, October 3, 1938, Acting SecState to Grew, October 5, 1938, and Grew to SecState, October 6, 1938, *FR*, 1938, IV, 53-55, 56-57, 59; TY, 263-66.
21. Toynbee, ed., *Survey*, 1938, I, 493-502; Maxon, *Control of Japanese Foreign Policy*, 135; Jones, *Japan's New Order*, 85-87, 135-37; David J. Lu, *From Marco Polo Bridge to Pearl Harbor; Japan's Entry Into World War II* (Washington, D.C., 1961), 39.
22. Statement by the Japanese Government and Radio Speech by Konoe, November 3, 1938, and Statement by Konoe, December 22, 1938, *FR*, *Japan*, 1931-1941, I, 477-83.
23. Hirota resigned in May 1938 and was succeeded by Ugaki Kazushige who resigned in September.
24. Diary, October–December, 1938; Grew to Debuchi Katsuji, December 19, 1938; Grew's dispatches and telegrams, *FR*, 1938, IV, November 7, (80-82), November 16, (86-87), November 19, (93-95), December 20 (106-7), December 23 (110-13); Arita to Grew, November 14, 18, 1938, *FR*, *Japan*, 1931-1941, I, 795-800; Memorandum by Dooman, November 19, 1938, *ibid.*, 801-6; Memoranda by Grew, November 21, December 8, 26, 1938, *ibid.*, 806-8, 813-14, 818-20; Grew to Arita, December 30, 1938, *ibid.*, 820-26.
25. Diary, December [n.d.], 1938, February 21, March [n.d.], 1939; Saionji-Harada Memoirs, reel 51, 2333-34, 2344 (November 4, 11, 1938); Grew to SecState and Acting SecState to Grew, April 21, 1938, *FR*, 1938, III, 155; Grew to SecState, January 7, 31, March 15, 1939, *FR*, 1939, III, 478-81, 497-500, 519-21; Memorandum by Hornbeck, February 25, 1939, *ibid.*, 511-12.
26. Diary, February [n.d.], October 29, 1938, February 23, 1939; Grew to SecState, May 16, December 1, 2, 1938, *FR*, 1938, III, 168-70, 400, 405; Grew to SecState, May 2, October 4, November 1, 1938, *ibid.*, IV, 596-600, 604-7, 607-9; Grew to SecState, January 7, 1939, *FR*, 1939, III, 481.
27. Diary, June [n.d.], 1938, May 18, 1939; Grew to Hornbeck, April 17, 1938, to Admiral H. E. Yarnell, August 12, 1938; Grew to SecState, April 11, August 2, October 28, November 1, 1938, *FR*, 1938, III, 138-39, 250-51, 349, 354; Grew to SecState, January 7, 1939, *FR*, 1939, III, 481.
28. Diary, May 18, 1939; Grew to Admiral H. E. Yarnell, August 12, 1938, to Hornbeck, March 17, April 12, 1938; Conversations with Craigie, January 7, 10, 1938; Grew to SecState, December 1, 1938, *FR*, 1938, III, 400-402; Grew to SecState, October 18, 1938, *ibid.*, IV, 67-72; Grew to Craigie and enclosure, December 7, 1938, *ibid.*, 99-102; Grew to SecState, January 7, 31, March 15, 1939, *FR*, 1939, III, 478-81, 497-500, 519-21; Memorandum by Grew, March 13, 1939, *ibid.*, 516-19; TE, II, 1211-12.
29. Butow, *Tojo*, 234.
30. Moffat Diary, January 31, 1938; extracts from the diary of Hugh Wilson in Hugh R. Wilson [Jr.], *Disarmament and the Cold War in the Thirties* (New York, 1963), 58-76; Harold Nicolson, *The Evolution of Diplomacy* (New York, 1962), 106.
31. Diary, October 14, 1937; Moffat Diary, November 5, 6, 1938; *Moffat Papers*, 154; Wilson, *Disarmament*, 64, 67, 72; Grew to SecState, December 1, 1938, *FR*, 1938, III, 402, and October 15, 1938, *FR*, 1938, IV, 70-71.
32. Diary, February, March, April, August, November [n.d.], 1938, June 25, 1938, January 13, April 12, May 18, 1939; Grew to SecState, February 12, September 9, November 19, December 20, 1938, *FR*, 1938, III, 84, 282, 386-87, 422-24; Grew

to SecState, October 15, 1938, *ibid.*, IV, 70-72; Grew to SecState, May 17, 1939, *FR*, 1939, III, 407. On British policy: E. L. Woodward and Rohan Butler, eds., *Documents on British Foreign Policy*, 1919-1939 (hereafter cited as *DBFP*), 3rd Series, VIII (London, 1955), Documents 11, 45, 52, 64, 118, 128, 131, 138, 207, 208, 276, 279, 288, 290, 304, 308, 330, 338, 433, 479, and Appendix I.

33. Diary, May 5, 1939; Moffat Diary, January 31, February 10, November 5-6, 1938; Wilson, *Disarmament*, 66, 73; Hornbeck Memoranda, November 14, December 22, 1938, *FR*, 1938, III, 572-74, 425-27, and January 25, February 11, 1939, *FR*, 1939, III, 489-90, 506-7.
34. The China hands included, besides Ambassador Johnson, John Carter Vincent and Walter A. Adams of the Far Eastern Division. Maxwell Hamilton, Chief of the Division, had served in China and was close to Hornbeck's point of view but was more cautious about action to be taken. On the other hand, officers of the Division who had served in Japan were closer to the Tokyo Embassy's point of view and advocated watchful waiting. See Hornbeck Memorandum, February 25, 1939, *FR*, 1939, III, 507-12 and Hamilton Memorandum, October 10, 1938, *FR*, 1938, IV, 62-65. Memoranda by John Carter Vincent, July 23, 1938, *ibid.*, III, 234-37, and January 20, 1939, *FR*, 1939, III, 483-85; Nelson Johnson to President Roosevelt, February 27, 1939, *ibid.*, 512-14; Wilson, *Disarmament*, 66-67.
35. Diary, December 22, 1937; Grew to Hornbeck, March 17, 1938; *Moffat Papers*, 183; Wilson, *Disarmament*, 63, 68, 73, 75.
36. Diary, December 28, 1933, February [n.d.], 1938; Grew to Ellery Sedgwick, March 18, 1938; *Moffat Papers*, 183; Wilson, *Disarmament*, 65, 75.
37. Diary, September [n.d.], 1938, February [n.d.], April [n.d.], 1939; Grew to Mrs. S. V. R. Crosby, October 2, 1938; TY, 274-75.
38. *Moffat Papers*, 194; *Hull Memoirs*, I, 567-71, 636-39; William L. Langer and S. Everett Gleason, *The Challenge to Isolation* (2 vols.; New York, 1964), I 32-53. On the commodity loan: *FR*, 1938, III, 568 ff.
39. Grew to Debuchi Katsuji, December 19, 1938.

17. THE USES OF DIPLOMACY

1. Diary, September 1938; Grew to SecState, *FR*, 1938, III, September 20 (296-97), September 27 (298-99), October 10 (314-15), November 26 (396), December 2 (403-6). Craigie's information came from London (Halifax to Craigie, November 18, 1938, *DBFP*, 3rd Series, VIII, No. 254).
2. On the alliance negotiations: Saionji-Harada Memoirs, reel 51, 2405-2555 (January 5–June 15, 1939); Presseisen, *Germany and Japan*, Chap. 7; Jones, *Japan's New Order*, Chap. 4; Lu, *From Marco Polo Bridge*, Chap. 4; Frank William Iklé, *German-Japanese Relations*, 1936-1940 (New York, 1956), Part Four.
3. Diary, February 21, February [n.d.], April 5, 15, 16, 26, 1939; Grew to SecState, February 8, 14, 1939, *FR*, 1939, III, 6-7, 11-12.
4. Diary, April 15, 16, 1939; TY, 282-83; TE, II, 1209-10.
5. On the visit of U.S.S. *Astoria:* Diary, March, April, 1939; File 701.9411/1094-1186, SDA; TY, 275-81; *FR*, 1939, IV, 455-62; Hull, *Memoirs*, I, 629.
6. *New York Times*, April 17, 1939.
7. Diary, April 24, 25, May 4, 1939; *New York Times*, April 17, 1939; Samuel Eliot Morison, *The Struggle for Guadalcanal, August, 1942–February, 1943*, Vol. V of *United States Naval Operations in World War II*, 44, 57-58.
8. Ambassador Bullitt to SecState, April 11, 1939, File 740.00/770, SDA; *New York Times*, April 18, 1939, also April 10-26, 1939; Langer and Gleason, *Challenge to Isolation*, I, 75-90, 103-5.
9. Diary, February, March, April [n.d.], April 16, 1939; Grew to SecState, April 20, 1939, *FR*, 1939, III, 22; TY, 280-81.
10. Grew to SecState, April 27, May 5, 8, 1939, *FR*, 1939, III, 26-32.
11. Lu, *Marco Polo Bridge*, 45-48. On the Nomonhan Incident: *New York Times*, May 24, 1964, reporting observance of the anniversary of the incident, which, ac-

cording to Harrison Salisbury, involved some five hundred Soviet tanks and five hundred Soviet planes.

12. After the Nazi-Soviet Pact and the interruption of German-Japanese negotiations, Dooman received more accurate information regarding the extent of the government's inclination toward Germany's demands. See Dooman to SecState, September 12, 1939, *FR*, 1939, III, 64-65.
13. Saionji-Harada Memoirs, reel 51, 2529-30 (May 23, 1939); Dooman to SecState, June 7, 1939, U.S. Congress, *Pearl Harbor Attack; Hearings Before the Joint Committee on the Investigation of the Pearl Harbor Attack* (hereafter cited as *PHA*), 79th Cong., 2nd Sess. (Washington, 1946), part 20, 4144-48.
14. *Ibid.*; Diary, May 18, 1939; Grew to SecState, May 18, 1939, *FR*, *Japan*, 1931-41, II, 1-5.
15. Diary, May 18, 19, 1939.
16. Diary, February 23, 1939; *FR*, 1939, III, 355-56, 360-63, 371, 375-76, 387, 395-96, 399-401, 781-86; *ibid.*, IV, 35, 111, 300, 307-9, 315-16; *FR*, *Japan*, 1931-1941, I, 642-48, 834-37, 841.
17. Grew to SecState, February 18, May 17, 1938, *FR*, 1938, III, 98, 170-72; Grew to SecState, February 10, 17, March 31, 1939, *FR*, 1939, III, 103-4, 110-11; Japanese Embassy to Department of State and Secretary of State to Japanese Ambassador, March 31, May 17, 1939, *FR*, *Japan*, 1931-1941, II, 278-81.
18. Diary, January 15, April 12, 27, 1939; Dooman to SecState, June 7, 1939, *PHA*, Part 20, 4145-46.
19. *Ibid.*, 4150-61; Grew to SecState, May 18, 1939, *FR*, *Japan*, 1931-1941, II, 1; Saionji-Harada Memoirs, reel 51, 2540-41, 2543 (May 31, June 6, 1939).
20. Dooman to SecState, June 7, 1939, *PHA*, Part 20, 4144-45, 4161-64; Dooman to SecState, May 26, 1939, *FR*, 1939, III, 40-42.
21. Diary, May 18, 1939.
22. The references to Griswold's *Far Eastern Policy* (New York, 1938) are in an off-the-record speech entitled "The Horrid World We Live In," a draft of which is in Diary, 1939. The speech was intended for American audiences. During his leave he spoke to Washington newsmen, the Institute of Pacific Relations, the Harvard Class of '02, and several small groups. The draft also quoted from John MacMurray's memorandum entitled "Developments Affecting American Policy in the Far East," November 1, 1935, a copy of which is in Diary, 1937.
23. Diary, May 18, 1939.
24. Craigie to Sir A. Cadogan, May 23, 1939, *DBFP*, 3rd Series, IX, Document 107.
25. *New York Times*, May 1–July 10, 1939. The poll was reported June 16. From May 1 to June 15 Far Eastern news appeared on the front page on the average once every four days and never with as much space as one column. In the period June 15-30 it was on the front page every day but one, with two- and three-column headlines more often than not and with a daily average of one and a half columns of space.
26. Memorandum by Laurence E. Salisbury, November 29, 1939, *FR*, 1939, III, 123.
27. Memoranda by Ballantine, April 11, May 24, June 7, 1939, Files 893.014/231, 894.00/856, 793.94119/557, SDA; Memorandum by Hornbeck, May 11, 1939, *FR*, 1939, III, 34-37.
28. Memorandum by Ballantine, June 7, 1939, File 793.94119/557, SDA; Memoranda by Maxwell Hamilton and Joseph Ballantine, June 13 and May 22, 1939, *PHA*, part 20, 4133-34; SecState to Dooman, August 4, 1939, *ibid.*, 4200-4201; Hull, *Memoirs*, I, 631; Langer and Gleason, *Challenge to Isolation*, I, 151-52.
29. Langer and Gleason, *Challenge to Isolation*, I, 136-57.
30. *Ibid.*, 157-59; Hull, *Memoirs*, I, 635-38.
31. On Grew's "Straight From the Horse's Mouth" Speech and its background: Diary, August 28, September 12, October, 1939; TY, 288-89, 294-99; TE, II, 1211-15; Langer and Gleason, *Challenge to Isolation*, I, 291-302.
32. On political developments in Japan: Dooman dispatches and telegrams, September 12, 25, 1939, *FR*, 1939, III, 64-69, 582-83, August 28, September 12, 1939, *ibid.*,

IV, 447, 449-54; Saionji-Harada Memoirs, reel 51, 2617, 2619, 2623, 2631, 2641, 2670, 2671 (September 1–October 19, 1939); Lu, *Marco Polo Bridge*, 59-60. SecState to Grew, October 7, 1939, *FR*, 1939, III, 584; Ambassador Eugen Ott to Foreign Ministry, October 16, 24, 1939, Documents 264, 293, *DGFP-D*, VIII, 298-303, 335-36.

33. Diary, October 13, 15, 19, 1939; Grew to SecState, October 16, 1939, *FR*, 1939, III, 584-85. The excised portions, gathered into a twelve-page document, are in Diary, 1939.
34. *FR*, *Japan*, 1931-1941, II, 19-29 (text).
35. All italics are Grew's.
36. Hugh Byas, *New York Times*, October 22, 1939.
37. On American reaction to the speech: Diary, October 19, 21, December 3, 1939; SecState to Grew, October 26, 1939, File 123G 861/828, SDA; *New York Times*, October 19-23, 1939; clippings in Grew Papers (*Washington Star*, October 22, 1939, *Louisville Courier-Journal*, October 21, 1939, *Dallas News*, October 21, 1939, *Philadelphia Bulletin*, October 21, 1939); TE, II, 1214.
38. Draft Instruction and Memorandum by Joseph Jones, October 16, 1939, File 123G 861/814-15, SDA; SecState to Grew, October 18, 1939, *FR*, 1939, III, 587; TE, II, 1213, fn. 11.
39. Grew to SecState, October 31, November 7, 1939, and Memorandum by Cabot Coville, December 7, 1939, File 123G 861/831, 855, SDA; Grew to SecState, October 19, 1939, *FR*, 1939, III, 588; TE, II, 1215.
40. Grew to SecState, October 19, 23, 1939, *FR*, 1939, III, 587-89; Grew to SecState, October 23, 1939, *FR*, *Japan*, 1931-1941, II, 29-30; TY, 297-98.
41. On the November 4, Conversation: Diary, October 23 and October [n.d.], 1939; Grew to SecState, November 6, 1939, File 711.94/1363, SDA; SecState to Grew, October 24, 1939, and Grew to SecState, November 4, 1939, *FR*, 1939, III, 590, 593-95; Memorandum by Grew, November 4, 1939, *FR*, *Japan*, 1931-1941, II, 31-34.
42. Grew to SecState, October 30, 1939, *FR*, 1939, III, 592; *New York Times*, October 23, 1939.
43. Diary, November 6, 1939; Saionji-Harada Memoirs, reel 51, 2707 (December 10, 1939); Memorandum by Maxwell Hamilton, December 2, 1939, File 711.94/1386, SDA; Grew to SecState, November 1, 8, 27, 1939, *FR*, 1939, III, 310-11, 595-96, 600-601; Grew to SecState, November 6, 29, 1939, *ibid.*, IV, 403, 411-12; SecState to Grew, November 28, December 8, 1939, *ibid.*, 410-11, 418; Grew to SecState, December 4, 1939, Memorandum by Dooman, December 6, 1939, *FR*, *Japan*, 1931-1941, II, 40-42, 43-46; *New York Times*, November 1, 7, 11, 21, 22, 24, 1939; Lu, *From Marco Polo Bridge*, 89-93.
44. Diary, November 5, 1939; Grew to SecState, November 8, 28, 1939, *FR*, 1939, III, 595-96, 602-3; State Department Press Release, November 4, 1939, *FR*, *Japan*, 1931-1941, II, 34; *New York Times*, November 4, 5, 7, 8, 26, 1939.
45. Memorandum by Maxwell Hamilton, November 14, 1939, and SecState to Grew, December 8, 1939, *FR*, *Japan*, 1931-1941, I, 857-58, 671; SecState to Grew, November 13, December 8, 1939, *ibid.*, II, 34-35, 46-48; SecState to Grew, December 8, 1939, *FR*, 1939, IV, 418; *Hull Memoirs*, I, 724-27; *New York Times*, November 26, 1939.
46. Diary, October [n.d.], November 27, 1939; Saionji-Harada Memoirs, reel 51, 2630, 2646, 2687 (September 11, October 2, November 27, 1939); Dooman to SecState, September 18, 1939, Grew to SecState, November 27, 28, 1939, *FR*, 1939, III, 71-73, 83-86, 602-4. On Soviet-Japanese relations: *ibid.*, 51-102, 247, 261-62, 319-21; Langer and Gleason, *Challenge to Isolation*, I, 294-95, 305-6; Lu, *From Marco Polo Bridge*, 67; Jones, *Japan's New Order*, 185-87.
47. Diary, November [n.d.], 21, 29, December 4, 18, 1939; Grew to SecState, November 21, 1939, *FR*, 1939, III, 597-98. The statement of Grew's position below is based on the following telegrams and dispatch: November 27, 28, December 1, 18, 1939, *FR*, 1939, III, 600-613, 622-23.

48. Grew to SecState, November 21, 1939, *FR*, 1939, III, 596-97. See also Grew to Cameron Forbes, February 19, 1940.
49. Diary, December 19, 1939; Grew to SecState, December 18, 1939, *FR*, *Japan*, 1931-1941, II, 48-51; Grew to SecState, December 1 (dispatch), December 18, 20, 1939, *FR*, *Japan*, III, 604-13, 619-20, 622, 624-25. The dispatch of December 1 went forward in the pouch December 23 (Grew to SecState, January 5, 1940, *FR*, 1940, IV, 256). It was identical to diary excerpts which he mailed to the President under cover of a letter dated December 21 (*FR*, 1939, III, 604, fn. 18). According to Grew (TY, 313), these were excerpts from the diary written and dated December 1. The question then arises why he waited so long to send them and the dispatch based on them. The reasonable explanation seems to be that between December 1 and December 18 the Japanese took no positive steps such as would justify a detailed statement of his views and recommendations to his government. Nomura's December 18 proposal satisfied him, and though Washington's immediate response was negative, it did not entirely rule out a *modus vivendi* and invited his comments. (SecState to Grew, December 18, 1939, *FR*, 1939, III, 620; SecState to Grew, December 20, 1939, *FR*, *Japan*, 1931-1941, II, 193-94). The moment undoubtedly seemed opportune to forward a complete statement of his position as it stood in his diary, both to the President and in a dispatch to the Department. Sending at the end of December a statement of views dated December 1 would have the added advantage of emphasizing the degree to which the Japanese were in fact fulfilling the program he had outlined in his diary at the beginning of the month.
50. SecState to Grew, November 18, 1939, File 711.94/1347A, SDA; Memorandum by State Department, undated, copies of which were delivered to the French and British ambassadors on December 2 and 6, 1939, *FR*, 1939, III, 92-94; SecState to Ambassador in France, December 23, 1939, *ibid.*, 101; Consul General in Shanghai to SecState, December 19, 1939, *ibid.*, 795; Department of State to British Embassy, January 2, 1940, *ibid.*, 799-800; Langer and Gleason, *Challenge to Isolation*, I, 303-11.
51. Memorandum by Laurence Salisbury, November 29, 1939, with comment by Hornbeck, December 5, 1939, File 794.00/163, SDA; Memorandum by State Department, undated, *FR*, 1939, III, 92-95; Johnson to SecState, October 17, 1939, *ibid.*, 286-88; Memorandum by Welles, November 21, 1939, *ibid.*, 321-23; Memorandum by Hull, December 15, 1939, *ibid.*, 98-99.
52. Diary, January [n.d.], 1940; SecState to Grew, December 18, 20, 21, 1939, *FR*, *Japan*, 1931-1941, II, 190-95; Department of State Press Releases, December 15, 20, 1939, *ibid.*, 202-4; John Morton Blum, *From the Morgenthau Diaries; Years of Urgency*, 1938-1941 (Boston, 1965), 127.
53. Diary, December 22, 1939; Lu, *From Marco Polo Bridge*, 66-69.
54. Diary, December 22, 1939, January [n.d.], 1940; Grew to George D. Andrews, January 16, 1940, to Franklin D. Roosevelt, January 16, 1940.
55. For example see the remarks of Ikeda Seihin, former Finance Minister, in Saionji-Harada Memoirs, reel 51, 2720-21 (January 10, 2940). Also Ambassador Eugen Ott to Foreign Ministry, December 31, 1939, Document 496, *DGFP-D*, VIII, 585-86.

18. THE POLITICS OF FORCE

1. John Hersey, "Joseph Grew, Ambassador to Japan," *Life*, July 15, 1940.
2. Diary, August 12, 13, September 15, 25, 1937, October 10, November 27, 1939, February [n.d.] 1940; Grey to Margaret Perry, January 20, 1938.
3. Diary, February 10, 1938, March 14, December 2, 1939, March 31, April 2, May 15, June 18, September 30, December 27, 1940, April 24, 1941.
4. Diary, July 26, 1932, August 14, 15, 22, December 8, 1937, August [n.d.], October 31, November [n.d.], 1938, February 12, 1939, February 2, 12, March 31, July 12, August [n.d.], September 22, 1940; Grew to Mrs. S. V. R. Crosby, October 2,

1938; Hersey, "Joseph Grew," *Life*, July 15, 1940; TY, 217, 327-28, 346, 373.

5. Diary, February 22, April 2-15, October 18, December 10, 31, 1935, April 22, 1936, January 1-15, 1937, February 9, 1938; Grew to his daughters Anita and Elsie, July 28, September 3, 1941.
6. Diary, March 4, 1936, May 11, 1938, November 30, December 12, 1939, September 18, October 26, 1941.
7. Diary, May 2, 27, December 22, 1935.
8. Diary [n.d.], 1941.
9. Diary, June 18, December 30, 1940; Grew to his daughter Anita, June 9, September 21, 1937, July 28, 1941, to Arthur Hugh Frazier, August 8, 1940; Address to American Association of Kobe, November 23, 1939, to American School in Tokyo, June 18, 1940.
10. Diary, December 4, 1934, April 15, 1936, March 31, 1938; Address to American Association of Kobe, November 23, 1939.
11. Diary, November 4-6, 1936, June 24, 1939, September 6, 1940; Grew to Jerome Greene, Secretary of the Harvard Corporation, April 7, 1941; Address to the American Association of Kobe, November 23, 1939; *Philadelphia Inquirer*, *Minneapolis Tribune*, *Washington Star*, December 20, 1940; *Christian Science Monitor*, July 20, 1940; *New York Times Magazine*, November 12, 1938; *Time*, November 12, 1934, *Life*, July 15, 1940; "Their Excellencies, Our Ambassadors," *Fortune*, IX (April, 1934), 108-22; A. Whitney Griswold, "Our Policy in the Far East," *Harper's*, CLXXXI (August 1940), 267.
12. *Philadelphia Inquirer*, *Atlanta Journal*, and *Denver Post*, December 20, 1940; *Louisville Courier-Journal* and Topeka *Capital*, December 21, 1940. See also *Milwaukee Post*, Fargo *Forum*, Knoxville *Journal*, December 21, 1940, *Boston Herald*, December 22, 1940, Lynchburg, Virginia, *News*, December 23, 1940, *St. Louis Globe-Democrat*, December 25, 1940. All citations of newspapers in this and the preceding footnote are from clippings in the Grew Papers.
13. Diary, July 19, 1938, June 13, 1939, February 14, 19, June 10, 28, 1940; Grew to Lilla and Pierrepont Moffat, June 10, 1940, to Anita English, February 7, 1940.
14. Diary, March 26-29, April [n.d.], April 10, 1940; Grew to Hornbeck, January 31, 1940; Grew's telegrams to SecState, *FR*, 1940, IV, January 5 (255-56), February 3 (282-84), March 18 (962), April 2 (311-12), April 17 (318), May 17 (333), June 3 (338-40), 1940; TY, 314.
15. Diary, January 23–April 26, 1940; Grew to Hornbeck, January 31, 1940, to his daughter Elsie, May 9, 1940; Grew to SecState, April 23, 1940, *FR*, 1940, IV, 852-53, 870; Henry L. Stimson Letter to the Editor, *New York Times*, January 11, 1940; *New York Times*, March 12, 22, 1940; TY, 314-318.
16. Evidence at hand is insufficient to explain this curious episode. It is hard to believe that Sayre would have raised the possibility of Roosevelt's mediation, even in the most cautious manner, or Grew approved it, without some intimation of the President's approval, but no such authorization has been found in the State Department Archives, the Roosevelt Papers, or the Grew Papers. Roosevelt possessed the same information as Sayre in a letter from Stuart which was acknowledged routinely through the State Department (Dr. J. Leighton Stuart at Hong Kong to President Roosevelt, April 10, 1940, *FR*, 1940, IV, 315-16 and File 793.94119/632, SDA). According to the Director of the Franklin D. Roosevelt Library there is no communication in the Roosevelt-Sayre correspondence concerning possible mediation of the Sino-Japanese War nor any additional correspondence on the subject in the Roosevelt-Stuart correspondence (Elizabeth Drewry, Director, to author, June 15, 1965). Grew to Hull, May 15, 1940, and to Sayre, November 30, 1940; Grew to SecState, May 3, 4, 6, 1940, *FR*, 1940, IV, 322-25, 328-30; Acting SecState and SecState to Grew, May 4, 8, 1940, *ibid.*, 327-28 330; Memorandum by R. Walton Moore to Hull, June 7, 1940, quoting a letter from Sayre of May 21, 1940, File 711.94/1566, SDA; Saionji-Harada Memoirs, reel 51, 2819-25 (May 11, 1940); Ambassador in Japan to German Foreign Ministry, May 10, 1940, Document 233, *DGFP-D*, IX, 321-24; *New York Times*, May 2-8, 1940.

17. Diary, April 9, May 24, 1940; Grew to Arthur Hugh Frazier, August 8, 1940; TY, 314, 319.
18. Grew to Hornbeck, June 10, 1940; Conversation with Craigie, May 31, 1940; SecState to Grew, May 30, 1940, Grew to SecState, June 3, 1940, SecState to Grew, June 4, 1940, *FR*, 1940, IV, 336-38, 338-42, 345-46; German Embassy Tokyo to Foreign Ministry, May 10, June 12, 1940, Documents 219, 418, *DGFP-D*, IX, 310-11, 551-53; Hull, *Memoirs*, I, 895; TY, 319; Langer and Gleason, *Challenge to Isolation*, II, 591-92.
19. The memoranda and notes relating to the Grew-Arita conversations are in *FR*, *Japan*, 1931-1941, II, 67-100, the instructions and dispatches in *FR*, 1940, IV, 336-47, 353-56, 381-87, 398-400. Feis, *Road to Pearl Harbor*, 61.
20. SecState to Grew, June 4, 1940, *FR*, 1940, IV, 346.
21. Oral Statement by Grew to Arita, June 10, 1940, *FR*, *Japan*, 1931-1941, II, 71-73; SecState to Grew, June 4, 15, 1940, *FR*, 1940, IV, 345-46, 355-56.
22. Memorandum by Grew, June 10, 1940, Grew to SecState, June 12, 1940, Oral Statement by Arita to Grew, June 28, 1940 *FR*, *Japan*, 1931-1941, II, 70, 79, 90-91; TY, 321.
23. SecState to Grew, July 4, 12, 1940, *FR*, 1940, IV, 386-87, 401; Grew to SecState, April 2, July 11, 14, 1940, *ibid.*, 312, 398-400, 401.
24. As quoted in Langer and Gleason, *Challenge to Isolation*, II, 516. *Ibid.*, Chaps. 14, 15.
25. Saionji-Harada Memoirs, reel 51, 2829-30, 2852 (May 22–June 28, 1940); Grew to SecState, June 29, 1940 (text of Arita's radio broadcast), *FR*, *Japan*, 1931-1941, II, 93-94; Jones, *Japan's New Order*, 163-68, 187-190, 221-25, 233, 238-43; Lu, *From Marco Polo Bridge*, 69-77; Presseisen, *Germany and Japan*, 237-47.
26. Diary, July 21, 1940; Grew to SecState, July 21, September 5, 1940, *FR*, 1940, IV, 966-67, 974-77; Statement by Japanese Government, August 1, 1940, *FR*, *Japan*, 1931-1941, II, 108-11; TY, 327-28; Lu, *From Marco Polo Bridge*, 101-5.
27. Compare State Department Press Release, April 17, 1940, and Acting SecState to Grew, August 6, 1940, *FR*, *Japan*, 1931-1941, II, 282, 290.
28. Diary, September 14, 1940; Saionji-Harada Memoirs, reel 51, 2892-95 (August 19, 1940); Memorandum by Grew, September 14, 1940, *FR*, *Japan*, 1931-1941, II, 293-94; Grew to SecState, September 3, 1940, *FR*, 1940, IV, 94-95; Lu, *From Marco Polo Bridge*, 142-43, 148-49; Jones, *Japan's New Order*, 224-29, 241-44.
29. On the growing tension in China: Diary, July [n.d.], 1940; *FR*, *Japan*, 1931-1941, I, 862-71; *ibid.*, II, 101-8; *FR*, 1940, IV, 408-13 736-62, *passim*. On the Shanghai Defense Sector question: Department of State to Department of the Navy, June 27, 1940, *ibid.*, 747; Consul General at Shanghai to SecState, June 27, August 12, 20, 1940; *ibid.*, 750, 762-63, 779; Acting SecState to Grew and Grew to SecState, August 17, 18, 1940, *ibid.*, 767-70; *ibid.*, 764-68.
30. Diary, September, 1940; SecState to Grew, August 23, 1940, *FR*, 1940, IV, 791; Grew to SecState, September 4, 6, 12, 1940, *ibid.*, 798, 807, 812-14; *ibid.*, 770-810.
31. Diary, July [n.d.], 1940; Grew to SecState, July 23, September 12, 21, 1940, *FR*, 1940, IV, 967-69, 599-603, 421; TY, 324-25.
32. Diary, August 25, 1940.
33. Diary, July 12, August 31, 1940; Grew to Boylston Beal, May 14, 1940; TE, II, 1227-29.
34. Diary, July [n.d.], 1940 (TY, 324-26 has only part of the diary entry on the subject), September [n.d.], 1940; clippings in Grew Papers. For a sample of press criticism of a settlement with Japan see: Memorandum attributed to S. K. Hornbeck, July 16, 1940, Exhibit No. 96, *PHA*, part 16, 1998-2006.
35. Diary, September [n.d.], 1940; Grew to SecState, September 12, 1940 ("green light" telegram), *FR*, 1940, IV, 599-603 and TE, II, 1224-29. On export controls: *FR*, *Japan*, 1931-1941, II, 211-18.
36. Diary, September [n.d.], September 30, 1940; Grew to SecState, August 20, December 29, 1934, *FR*, 1934, III, 722, 689; TE, II, 1232.

37. Diary, July [n.d.], 1940; Grew to SecState, July 23, 1940, *FR*, 1940, IV, 969.
38. Diary, January 27, August 23, September 19, September [n.d.], 1940; Grew to Moffat, September 1, 1940; Grew to SecState, September 16, 19, 20, 1940, *FR*, 1940, I, 646-48; Grew to SecState, September 12, 1940, *ibid.*, IV, 601; TY, 329-30, 332-33.
39. Diary, August 23, September [n.d.], October 2, 1940; Grew to Maxwell Hamilton, September 28, 1940, and Hamilton to Grew, November 2, 1940, *FR*, 1940, I, 652-53, 672; TY, 339.
40. On the Tripartite Pact: Paul W. Schroeder, *The Axis Alliance and Japanese-American Relations*, 1941 (Ithaca, N.Y., 1958), 116-25; William L. Langer and S. Everett Gleason, *The Undeclared War*, 1940-1941 (New York, 1953), 21-32; Presseisen, *Germany and Japan*, Chap. 9; Lu, *From Marco Polo Bridge*, Chap. 8; Jones, *Japan's New Order*, 193-202; Butow, *Tojo*, 160-82.
41. Diary, October 7, 1940; Grew to SecState, October 7, 12, 1940. *FR*, 1940, I, 663, 666; Grew to SecState, September 29, 1940, *FR, Japan*, 1931-1941, II, 169-71; TY, 333-34.
42. Diary, September 30, 1940; Grew to Roy Howard, November 8, 1940; TY, 340.
43. Grew to SecState, September 20, 1940, *FR*, 1940, I, 648; Blum, ed., *From The Morgenthau Diaries*, II, 359-60; Jones, *Japan's New Order*, 228-31; Langer and Gleason, *Undeclared War*, 16-21, 33-38; Feis, *Road to Pearl Harbor*, Chap. 14.

19. THE EXTREMITIES OF PEACE

1. Diary, October 24, November 14, 1940; Grew to George A. Morlock, August 7, 1940; Nathaniel P. Davis to Somerset A. Owen, November 19, 1940, File, 123G 861/923, SDA.
2. Diary, September 21, November 14, 1940; Grew to his daughter Anita, July 23, 1940; Grew to Bertram Lippincott and Roland Morris, May 21, 1940; Grew to SecState, September 21, 1940, *FR*, 1940, IV, 421-22.
3. Diary, October 15, 24, 31, November 30, November [n.d.], 1940, March 30, 1941; Grew to Theodore Walser, June 3, 1941; TY, 358.
4. Diary, June 10, 28, October 24, December 30, 1940, January 5, January [n.d.], 1941; TY, 319, 357-58, 377-78.
5. Grew to SecState, November 11, 1940, *FR*, 1940, I, 672-73, and November 16, 1940, *ibid.*, IV, 434-36; Jones, *Japan's New Order*, 202-10, 244-45; Langer and Gleason, *Undeclared War*, 119-46, 290-319; Lu, *From Marco Polo Bridge*, 124-30. On American trade restrictions: *FR, Japan*, 1931-1941, II, 228-63.
6. Diary, September 16, October 5, 24, October [n.d.], 1940; Grew to SecState, August 26, October 7, 1940, *FR*, 1940, I, 643-45, 663; Grew to SecState, May 27, 1941, *FR*, 1941, IV, 234-38; Grew to SecState, September 29, 1940, *FR, Japan*, 1931-1941, II, 170; TY, 322, 326, 328-29, 332, 344-45, 351, 353, 374.
7. Diary, October 5, 24, November 11, December 24, 1940; Grew to Cabot Coville, November 22, 1940; Oral Statement by Matsuoka, December 17, 1940, *FR, Japan*, 1931-1941, I, 895-99; Addresses by Matsuoka and Grew, December 19, 1940, *ibid.*, II, 123-30; Grew to SecState, November 11, 1940, *FR*, 1940, I, 673; Grew to SecState, December 19, 1940, *ibid.*, IV, 561; TY, 341-43, 349, 366. The diary entry in TY, 366 should be December 19, 1940, instead of January 18, 1941.
8. Diary, September 27, October 3, 1940; Grew to SecState, October 2, 7, 1940, *FR*, 1940, I, 657-59, 662-64; Grew to SecState, December 7 (two telegrams), 24, 1940, *ibid.*, IV, 459, 461-63, 981-84.
9. TY, 349-50, 358-60.
10. Diary, November 11, 1940; Lu, *From Marco Polo Bridge*, 144-48; Jones, *Japan's New Order*, 232-37.
11. Diary, January 3, 12, 31, 1941; Grew to SecState, January 30, 31, 1941, *FR*, 1941, IV, 18-20; Grew to SecState, January 12, February 7, 1941, *ibid.*, V, 13-14, 62-63; TY, 369. Rumors of prosecution of the Southward Advance prior to January,

1941: Diary, November [n.d.], November 25, 26, December 12, 1940; *FR*, 1940, IV, 161, 192, 223. The Grew Papers do not disclose any further information respecting the origin of the Pearl Harbor attack rumor, which Grew reported January 27, 1941 (*FR*, *Japan*, 1931-1941, II, 133). The rumor was entered routinely in his diary on the same date.

12. Diary, October 15, November 11, December 24, 1940, January 3, 22, February [n.d.], 1941; Grew to Thomas Lamont, December 26, 1940, to his daughter Lilla, February 16, 1941; Grew to President Roosevelt, December 14, 1940, to SecState, October 11, 1940 (two telegrams), *FR*, 1940, IV, 469-71, 541, 937. The reference to sending the fleet to Asian waters is in Diary, March 30, 1941.
13. I am indebted to Mr. Dooman for this account of the meeting (letters to author, July 18, 31, 1965).
14. Diary, February 19, 1941; Grew to SecState, February 7, 1941, *FR*, 1941, V, 62-64.
15. Mr. Dooman to author, July 14, 1965; Grew to SecState, February 26, 1941, *FR*, *Japan*, 1931-1941, II, 137-43.
16. The key phrases of the February 14 telegram reporting Dooman's conversation are: "idle to assume that the United States would remain indifferent" and "might well lead to the most serious consequences" (Grew to SecState, February 14, 1941, *FR*, 1941, IV, 37-39). Compare with phrases reported February 26, in preceding paragraph. Diary, February 17, 18, 1941; Grew to Alexander Kirk, February 25, 1941; Grew to SecState, February 18, 27, 1941, *FR*, 1941, IV, 43-45, 53-54; Grew to SecState, February 17, 22, 24, 1941, *ibid*., V, 80-81, 84-85, 89-91; Churchill to Roosevelt, February 20, 1941, *ibid*., 83; *New York Times*, February 1-24, 1941.
17. TY, 363; Langer and Gleason, *Undeclared War*, 311-31; *The Memoirs of Anthony Eden, Earl of Avon: The Reckoning* (Boston, 1965), 354-59.
18. Diary, March 20, 30, 1941; Grew to Sir Francis Lindley, March 12, 1941, to Hornbeck, February 25, 1941; Grew to SecState, March 11, April 7, 1941, *FR*, 1941, IV, 69, 129-30; Grew to SecState, March 13, 19, 1941, *ibid*., V, 109-11, 114-15; TY, 378-79.
19. On the Neutrality Pact and its effects: Diary, February 22, April [n.d.], April 22, 1941; Grew's telegrams and dispatches, *FR*, 1941, IV, February 16 (909-10), February 27 (914), March 5 (58-60), April 14 (945-47), April 18 (958-59), April 21 (961-65); *ibid*., V, April 17 (131), May 10 (499-501), May 15 (503-4); TY, 380-84.
20. Diary, April 15, 1941; Grew to Castle, May 8, 1941; Grew to SecState, April 7 (two telegrams), 10, 18, 1941, *FR*, 1941, IV, 128-30, 140, 958-59; TY, 379.
21. Diary, May 6, 1941; Hornbeck to Grew, March 15, 1941, *FR*, 1941, IV, 80-81; SecState to Grew and Grew to SecState, April 25, May 6, 1941, *ibid*., 163, 178. Colonel Iwakuro Hideo of the Army General Staff, who participated in the Walsh-Drought effort, called at the Embassy in February before leaving for Washington as special adviser to Nomura but he talked about "maintaining an equilibrium until prospects appeared of a basic solution being found" (Grew to SecState, February 27, 1941, *ibid*., 53). On Japanese-American discussions in Washington during the spring of 1941: Langer and Gleason, *Undeclared War*, 314-15, 464-85; Robert J. C. Butow, "The Hull-Nomura Conversations: A Fundamental Misconception," *American Historical Review*, LXV (July 1960), 822-36; Lu, *From Marco Polo Bridge*, 159-73; Feis, *Road to Pearl Harbor*, Chaps. 22, 24, 25.
22. Proposal Presented to the Department of State Through the Medium of Private American and Japanese Individuals, April 9, 1941, and Draft Proposal Handed by the Japanese Ambassador to the Secretary of State, May 12, 1941, *FR*, *Japan*, 1931-1941, II, 398-402, 420-25; German Foreign Ministry to Embassy in Japan, May 11, 1941, and Ambassador in Japan to Foreign Ministry, May 13, 14, 1941, Documents 496, 507, 512, *DGFP-D*, XII, 777-80, 794, 806-10.
23. On the May 14, conversation: Grew to SecState, May 14, 1941, *FR*, *Japan*, 1931-1941, II, 145-48; Grew to SecState, *FR*, 1941, IV, May 14 (188), May 15 (189-90), May 16 (194-95), May 17 (199-200), May 19 (202-3), May 19 (204-6), May 27 (234-38).

24. Ambassador in Japan to German Foreign Ministry, May 15, 1941, Document 516, *DGFP-D*, XII, 818-19.
25. Diary, June 4, 1941; Grew to SecState, *FR, 1941*, IV, May 13 (187), May 16 (194-95), May 21 (207), May 26 (228-31).
26. Hornbeck to Grew, March 15, May 2, 1941, *FR, 1941*, IV, 80-81, 173-74; SecState to Grew, April 24, May 24, 26, 1941, *ibid.*, 163, 224, 228; Grew to SecState, May 27, 1941, *ibid.*, 231-32. The Walsh-Drought group's original proposal (*FR, Japan, 1931-1941*, II, 398-402), Hull's memoranda of conversations with Nomura April 14 and 16 launching the proposal (*ibid.*, 402-10), and the Department's revision (*FR, 1941*, IV, 159-61) were mailed May 2 and apparently reached Grew May 27 (see line 2, Grew to SecState, May 26, 1941, *ibid.*, 228, and fn. 99, *ibid.*). The Department sent Grew a copy of the Japanese "reply" on May 14, (*ibid.*, 189).
27. Diary, June 10, 16, 1941; Grew to Hornbeck, June 13, 1941; Grew to SecState, June 10, 1941, *FR, 1941*, IV, 264-65; Grew to SecState, June 15, 18, 1941, *ibid.*, V, 176, 181-82.
28. Diary, June [n.d.], June 22, 1941; Winston Churchill, *The Grand Alliance* (Boston, 1950), 370.
29. Diary, June [n.d.], 1941; Grew's telegrams, June 23–July 17, 1941, *FR, 1941*, IV, 979-1010.
30. Grew to SecState, *FR, 1941*, IV, June 27 (987-89), July 2 (991-93), July 6 (999-1001, July 18 (326-28).
31. Diary, July 13, 1941; Grew to SecState, July 2, 6, 17, 1941, *FR, 1941*, IV, 993, 999-1001, 1007; Grew to SecState, July 16, 22, 1941, *ibid.*, V, 210, 222-23. The last sentence of paragraph 4 of Grew's telegram of July 22 (*ibid.*, V, 223) should read "I nevertheless do not alter the opinion . . ." instead of "I nevertheless alter the opinion . . ." See diary excerpt for that day (TE, II, 1348) reading: "In passing this information on to the Department I said that I had no reason to alter my previous opinion. . . ." The original of the telegram received reads the way it is printed in *Foreign Relations* (File 740.0011 P.W./276, State Department Archives), so the corruption must have occurred somewhere in transmission.
32. Jones, *Japan's New Order*, 257-63; Lu, *From Marco Polo Bridge*, Chap. 12; Langer and Gleason, *Undeclared War*, 625-45.
33. Memoranda by Acting Secretary of State, July 21, 23, 24, 1941, *FR, Japan, 1931-1941*, II, 520-30; Feis, *Road to Pearl Harbor*, Chaps. 29-31; Langer and Gleason, *Undeclared War*, 645-62.
34. Diary, July [n.d.], 1941; Grew to SecState, July 26, 1941, *FR, 1941*, IV, 344; Acting SecState to Grew, July 30, 1941, *FR, Japan, 1931-1941*, I, 719-20; Memorandum by Grew, July 26, 1941, *ibid.*, II, 532-34.
35. Diary, July 18, August [n.d.], 1941; Grew to SecState, July 19, 23, August 30, 1941, *FR, 1941*, IV, 332, 336-38, 416; TY, 413, 417.
36. Diary, August [n.d.], 1941; Memoranda by Grew, July 26, 27, 1941, *FR, Japan, 1931-1941*, II, 532-37; *ibid.*, 546-53; TY, 411-12.
37. Kido Diary, August 7, 1941; Memoirs of Prince Konoe, Exhibit No. 173, *PHA*, part 20, 3999-4001; Feis, *Road to Pearl Harbor*, Chap. 32.
38. Diary, August 18, 1941; Memoranda by Dooman and Grew, August 18, 1941, *FR, Japan, 1931-1941*, II, 559-64; TY, 416-21.
39. Diary, October 1, 1940, January 23, September 30, 1941; Grew to SecState, July 10, 1941, Acting SecState to Grew, July 11, 1941, Grew to SecState, August 7, 1941, *FR, 1941*, IV, 299-300, 304-6, 364-65.
40. Grew to SecState, August 19, 29, 30, 1941, *FR, 1941*, IV, 382-83, 409, 416-17. On Konoe, see for example Grew to SecState, January 13, 1939, *FR, 1939*, III, 3.
41. Grew's telegrams on the leaders' meeting: *FR, 1941*, IV, August 19 (382-84), August 27 (397-98), August 30 (416-18), September 29 (483-89), September 30 (489-90); *FR, Japan, 1931-1941*, II, August 18 (565).
42. Grew to SecState, August 22, 27, 29, 1941, *FR, 1941*, IV, 391, 400, 408-9; SecState to Grew, August 23, 25, 1941, *ibid.*, 391-92, 394; Memorandum by Hull, August 27, 1941, *FR, Japan, 1931-1941*, II, 569-70; "Magic" intercepts, Nomura to Tokyo,

August 18, 19, 1941, *PHA*, part 17, 2753-55; *New York Times* August 22-28, September 2, 4, 1941; Langer and Gleason, *Undeclared War*, 709-13; Butow, *Tojo*, 245.

43. Diary, October [n.d.], 1941; Memoranda by Grew, August 29, 30, September 3, 1941, *FR*, *Japan*, 1931-1941, II, 579-83, 586-87; Grew to SecState, August 29, 30, September 6, 1941, *FR*, *1941*, IV, 409, 418, 429; "Magic" intercepts, Tokyo to Nomura, August 29, 1941, *PHA*, part 17, 2797-2799, and Tokyo to Nomura, September 3, 1941, *ibid.*, part 12, 25; Ambassador in Japan to German Foreign Ministry, August 29, 30, 1941, *DGFP-D*, XIII, 410-11, 414-15; *New York Times*, August 29, September 12, 13, 1941; TE, II, 1324, fn. 59 quoting *Herald Tribune*; Langer and Gleason, *Undeclared War*, 703-4; Jones, *Japan's New Order*, 286; Lu, *From Marco Polo Bridge*, 198-99.

44. Memoranda and documents exchanged at White House, August 17 and 28, 1941, *FR*, *Japan*, 1931-1941, II, 556-59, 571-75; Foreign Ministry to Nomura, August 26, 28, 1941, *PHA*, part 17, 2779-93. The original text (*ibid.*, 2779-88) is badly reproduced photographically in *Pearl Harbor Attack*, but can be read except for a few words.

45. Memoranda by Hull and Documents Handed to Nomura, August 28, September 3, 1941, *FR*, *Japan*, 1931-1941, II, 576-79, 588-92; Memorandum by Ballantine, August 28, 1941, *FR*, *1941*, IV, 403-5; Hull, *Memoirs*, II, 1024; Langer and Gleason, *Undeclared War*, 704-6.

46. Memorandum by Grew, September 6, 1941, and Draft Proposal Handed by Nomura to Hull, September 6, 1941 (the same one handed to Grew by Toyoda September 4), *FR*, *Japan*, 1931-1941, II, 604, 608-9.

47. Diary, August 7, September 6, 1941; Memoranda by Grew, September 5, 6, 13, 1941, *FR*, *Japan*, 1931-1941, II, 602, 604-6, 621; Statement Handed by Nomura to Hull, September 4, 1941 (cf. Draft Proposal, *ibid.*, 608), *ibid.*, 597-601; Memorandum by Dooman, September 18, 1941, *ibid.*, 626; SecState to Grew, September 9, 1941, *FR*, *1941*, IV, 434; "Magic" intercept, Nomura to Foreign Ministry, September 17, 1941, *PHA*, part 17, 28; Konoe Memoirs, *PHA*, part 20, 4003; Lu, *Marco Polo Bridge*, 199-200.

48. *FR*, *1941*, IV, 428-29, 449-50, 470-77, 481-82; *FR*, *Japan*, 1931-1941, II, 610-36; "Magic" intercepts, Nomura to Foreign Ministry, September 27, 29, 1941, *PHA*, part 12, 36, 41.

49. Japanese Proposals Submitted to Grew, September 25, 1941, *FR*, *Japan*, 1931-1941, II, 637-40.

50. Address to American Association of Tokyo, October 8, 1941. The superlative about his report of his conversation with Konoe September 6 (*FR*, *Japan*, 1931-1941, II, 604-6) was recalled by Konoe (Memoirs, *PHA*, part 20, 4006), not by Grew. Undoubtedly there was some tactical inflation of adjective here but Grew was obviously impressed by the Prince's assurances. The evidence of moderate influence and control: reports of the Emperor's concern and initiative in a leaders' meeting (Memorandum by Grew, September 17, 1941, *FR*, *Japan*, 1931-1941, II, 624-25), of the playing down of Tripartite anniversary celebrations (Grew to SecState, October 1, 1941, *FR*, *1941*, IV, 492), of the general support, even in military circles, for a leaders' meeting noted even by reactionary sources (*ibid.*), of the establishment of a unified military command directly responsible to the Emperor as a means of controlling expansionist, extremist elements (Grew to SecState, September 12, 1941, *ibid.*, 445-47). Comments by Grew on his Memoranda of Conversations, September 4, 5, 1941, *FR*, *Japan*, 1931-1941, II, 594-95, 601-3; Grew to SecState, September 19, 29, 30, 1941, *FR*, *1941*, IV, 463-64, 483-89, 489-90; Grew to Roosevelt, September 22, 1941, *ibid.*, 468-69; TY, 444-47.

51. Grew to SecState, September 20, 1941, *FR*, *1941*, IV, 464; TY, 459; Jones, *Japan's New Order*, 286, fn. 4.

52. Diary, August 10, 1941; Grew to Count Soejima, September 1, 1941, TE, II, 1233-43; Proposed Instructions to Nomura Handed by Toyoda to Grew, September 13, 1941, *FR*, *Japan*, 1931-1941, II, 623.

53. Diary, September 30, 1941; Grew to Craigie, September 5, 1941, in Diary, September [n.d.], 1941; Grew to SecState August 19, 1941, *FR*, *1941*, IV, 382-83.
54. Diary, September 30, October 13, 1941; Grew to Craigie, September 5, 1941, in Diary, September [n.d.], 1941.
55. Grew to SecState, September 29, 1941, *FR*, *Japan*, 1931-1941, II, 650. Grew to SecState, September 4, 5, 1941, *ibid*., 594-95, 601-3.
56. Oral Statement Handed by Hull to Nomura, October 2, 1941, *FR*, *Japan*, 1931-1941, II, 656-61; Memorandum by Hornbeck, October 2, 1941, *FR*, *1941*, IV, 493-94; Consul at Saigon to SecState, September 27, 1941, Grew to SecState, September 30, 1941, and SecState to Grew, October 2, 1941, *ibid*., V, 296, 299-300, 304-5.
57. Memorandum by Grew, October 7, 1941, *FR*, *Japan*, 1931-1941, II, 663-64; Grew to SecState, October 7, 1941, *FR*, *1941*, IV, 500-1; Lu, *From Marco Polo Bridge*, 207-10. For what Konoe said September 6, I have chosen to accept Dooman's translation as paraphrased ("Prince Konoe, and consequently the Government of Japan, conclusively and wholeheartedly agree with the four principles. . . .") rather than Konoe's version after his resignation (". . . I said that they were splendid as principles but when it came down to actual application a variety of problems arose.") because of Grew's positiveness of the accuracy of his report, Dooman's fluency in Japanese, the fact that he recorded the conversation the same evening, and the fact that after October 2 it was embarrassing for Konoe to have said what he did (Memoranda by Grew, September 6, October 7, 1941, *FR*, *Japan*, 1931-1941, II, 604, 664; Konoe Memoirs, *PHA*, part 20, 4005).

20. JAPAN AS ENEMY

1. Grew to SecState, August 19, 1941, *FR*, *1941*, IV, 382-83; Jones, *Japan's New Order*, 459.
2. Akira Iriye, "Japanese Imperialism and Aggression: Reconsiderations. II," *The Journal of Asian Studies*, XXIII (November 1963), 110; Lu, *From Marco Polo Bridge*, 189.
3. Lu, *From Marco Polo Bridge*, 225. Japan imported 37,960,000 barrels of crude and refined oil in the year ending March 31, 1941, a figure equal to 5,516,524 tons (Morison, *Rising Sun in the Pacific*, 63 and 63 fn. 37).
4. Memoranda by Hornbeck, August 27, 30, September 2, 5, 1941, *FR*, *1941*, IV, 398-99, 412-16, 419, 425-28; Memoranda by Ballantine, September 23, 25, *ibid*., 470-75, 478-80; Langer and Gleason, *Undeclared War*, 707-9, 738-41, Feis, *Road to Pearl Harbor*, 273-77; Schroeder, *Axis Alliance*, Chap. 8.
5. Diary, October [n.d.], October 17, 19, 25, 1941; Grew to SecState, October 20, 26, 1941, *FR*, *1941*, IV, 541-43, 553-54; Memorandum by Dooman, October 17, 1941, and Konoe to Grew, October 16, 1941, *FR*, *Japan*, 1931-1941, II, 689-92; Memorandum by Grew, October 25, 1941, *ibid*., 697-98; TY, 456-63.
6. Diary, October 29–November 3, 1941; Memorandum by Grew, October 30, 1941, *FR*, *Japan*, 1931-1941, II, 699-700; Grew to SecState, November 1, 1941, *FR*, *1941*, IV, 563-64; TY, 465-66.
7. Grew to SecState, November 3, 1941, *FR*, *Japan*, 1931-1941, II, 701-4.
8. Diary, November 15, 1941; Memoranda by Grew, November 7, 10, 12 (two), *FR*, *Japan*, 1931-1941, II, 705-6, 710-14, 719-22; Grew to SecState, November 17, 1941, *ibid*., 743-44; Grew to SecState, November 6, 13 (two), 1941, *FR*, *1941*, IV, 570-72, 587-88, 589-91; Morison, *Rising Sun in the Pacific*, 88.
9. Draft Proposal (Plan B) Handed by Nomura to Hull, November 20, 1941, Document Handed by Hull to Nomura, November 26, 1941, *FR*, *Japan*, 1931-1941, II, 755-56, 768-70; Americans *modus vivendi* drafts and draft suggestions, *FR*, *1941*, IV, 626, 627, 635-37, 642-44, 661-64; Langer and Gleason, *Undeclared War*, Chaps. 26, 27; Jones, *Japan's New Order*, Chaps. 9, 10; Lu, *From Marco Polo Bridge*, Chaps. 13, 14.
10. Diary, October 28, November 29, 1941; Grew to James C. Dunn, December 5,

1941; SecState to Grew, November 28, 1941 (two telegrams), Grew to SecState, December 1, 5, 1941, *FR*, 1941, IV, 682, 683-84, 707, 720-21; SecState to Grew, November 22, 1941, *ibid.*, V, 443; TY, 483-85.

11. All times are Tokyo time. The attack took place at 3:30 A.M., December 8, Tokyo time, 7:50 A.M., December 7, Honolulu time, and 1:20 P.M., December 7, Washington time. The telegram containing the message for the Emperor was held up ten and a half hours in Tokyo, apparently as a result of an Army-inspired slow-up on delivery of telegrams (Butow, *Tojo*, 396-98). It is difficult to see how prompt delivery could have made any difference. Diary, December 8, 1941; President Roosevelt to Emperor Hirohito, December 6, 1941, *FR, Japan*, 1931-1941, II, 784-86; TY, 486-93; TE, II, 1249-53; Butow, *Tojo*, 378-96.
12. On the internment: Diary, December 1941–June 1942; TY, 493-538; *Life*, September 7, 1942.
13. Grew to F. D. Roosevelt, August 14, 1942 (not sent); TY, 528-32.
14. Grew to F. D. Roosevelt, August 14, 1942 (not sent). In two instances Grew's letter to Roosevelt of 1942 differed from the record of August-September 1941. First, he said, "Prince Konoe . . . told me with unquestionable sincerity that he was prepared at that meeting to accept the American terms whatever they might be." Possibly the Prince did use these words to convince Grew of his sincerity but did not allow him to report them. In any case, Grew did not report them in his memorandum of the September 6 conversation (*FR, Japan*, 1931-1941, II, 604-6). Second, Grew said in the letter to the President of August 1942 that the Emperor "actually instructed the chiefs of the Army and Navy that they were to avoid war with the United States." This is putting somewhat more bluntly a report of October 26, 1941, which, regardless of its validity, could not have influenced American deliberations on the Konoe project, he having resigned October 16 (Grew to SecState, October 26, 1941, *FR*, 1941, IV, 553-54.) Neither of these pieces of evidence is included in Grew's final presentation of the case for a leaders' meeting ("Pearl Harbor From the Perspective of Ten Years," TE, II, Chap. 34).
15. Grew to F. D. Roosevelt, August 14, 1942 (not sent); Memorandum by Grew, September 22, 1941, *FR, Japan*, 1931-1941, II, 632.
16. TY, 516-17; TE, II, 1371-72.
17. On the voyage home: TE, II, 1377-80; TY, 533-35; *New York Times*, August 26, 1942.
18. Grew had also written a letter to the President dated August 14, 1942, aboard the *Gripsholm* presenting the gist of his final political report and enclosing a copy of it. This letter was not sent and is in the Grew Papers. In the margin of the letter, beside a reference to the final report, are the words "destroyed at Mr. Hull's request" in Grew's handwriting. To his former staff member James Espy, Grew wrote on January 15, 1943, ". . . that celebrated despatch which I was working on in Tokyo has not yet been filed and probably never will be. . . ." What Grew apparently did was to file the covering letter and documents with a brief final report, after excising the original report. See Dispatch No. 6018, February 19, 1942, Grew Papers, from which pages 13-146 have been eliminated. According to the gist of the original in the letter to the President, the argument is substantially the same one he made in TE, II, Chap. 34, "Pearl Harbor From the Perspective of Ten Years."
19. Grew to his daughter Anita, September 2, 1942, to Castle September 2, 1942, to Robert Blakely, October 22, 1942, to Sir Henry Chilton, March 20, 1943, to John Cudahy, August 6, 1943, to Elmer Davis, September 25, October 12, 1942.
20. Grew to Paul Linebarger, September 28, 1942, to Elmer Davis, October 12, 1942, to Sir Henry Chilton, March 20, 1943, to Baron Albert de Bassompierre, November 24, 1944; miscellaneous correspondence relating to speeches, 1942, 1943; clippings, 1942, 1943.
21. Grew's addresses, August 30, 1942–April 27, 1943, *The Department of State Bulletin*, VII (July-December 1942), 719-23, 758-68, 777-78, 797-804, 845-50, 865-75, 915-25, 945-47, 993-98, 1018-22; VIII (January-June 1943), 22-27, 49-55, 123-29,

150-53, 166-69, 205-8, 272-74, 365-69. On the "jujitsu" peace see for example *ibid.*, 54.

22. Grew to G. William Gahagan, December 11, 1942, to Maxwell Hamilton, September 27, 1942, to Sir Henry Chilton, March 20, 1943; *Washington Times Herald*, April 23, 1943 (clipping in Grew Papers); TY, 535.
23. *The Department of State Bulletin*, VII (January-June 1943), 439-42, 482-87, 591-94; IX (July-December 1943), 126-28, 345-47.
24. *The Department of State Bulletin*, X (January-June 1944), 8-20.
25. Frederick S. Dunn, *Peace-making and the Settlement with Japan* (Princeton, 1963), Chap. 2.
26. Diary, December 31, 1941; Grew to SecState, September 18, 1941, *FR*, 1941, IV, 457; F. C. Jones, *Japan's New Order*, 422-23.
27. Grew to Sir Robert Clive, June 28, 1944; *New York Times*, January 2, 1944.
28. *New York Times*, February 2, 1944; T. A. Bisson, "The Price of Peace For Japan," *Pacific Affairs*, XVII (March 1944), 5-25; (Anonymous) "The Future of Japan: A Canadian View," *loc. cit.* (June 1944), 194-203; William C. Johnstone, "The Hot Springs Conference," *Far Eastern Survey*, XIV (January 31, 1945), 16-17.
29. He did not refer to the problem of Communism in postwar Japan until October 1945. Although the problem undoubtedly seemed greater by then, it seems safe to assume he had it in mind in 1944 as well. Grew to Erle Dickover, January 19, 1944, to Edward Adams, November 4, 1944, to Miss Marion Talbot, May 15, 1944, to Hornbeck, September 30, 1943, to Thomas H. Johnson, October 12, 1944, to Dr. J. Gordon Holdcroft, August 4, 1945, to Max Bishop, October 19, 1945, to Admiral J. W. Shafroth, October 18, 1945, to Nelson Newton, September 9, 1945; TE, II, 1408-15.
30. Grew to Erle Dickover, January 19, 1944, to Sir Robert Clive, June 28, 1944; Memorandum to Hull, April [n.d.], 1944; *The Department of State Bulletin*, X (January-June 1944), 219-23.
31. TY, 147.
32. Grew to Edward Crocker, June 17, 1944; Grew, "Japan and the Pacific," *National Geographic Magazine*, LXXXV (April 1944), 385-414.
33. Nathaniel Peffer, "Ambassador Grew's Story," *New York Times Book Review*, May 14, 1944; Henry C. Wolfe, "Failure of an American Mission," *Saturday Review of Literature*, XXVII (May 13, 1944), 7; A. Whitney Griswold, "Headstone to History," *Far Eastern Survey*, XIII (August 23, 1944), 163-64; *New Yorker*, XX (June 3, 1944), 77-78 (critical); T. A. Bisson, "Ambassador Grew's Mission," *The Nation*, CLVIII (June 3, 1944), 654-55.
34. Grew to his daughter Elsie, September 30, 1945; Memoranda of the Inter-Divisional Committee, *FR*, 1944, V, 1198-1285; TE, II, 1383.
35. Memorandum Prepared in the War and Navy Departments, February 18, 1944, *FR*, 1944, V, 1192, items d) and i); Memorandum of the Inter-Divisional Committee, May 9, 1944, *ibid.*, 1250-55.
36. Grew to James Gerard, August 30, 1943; Richard L. Walker, "E. R. Stettinius, Jr.," *The American Secretaries of State and Their Diplomacy*, Robert H. Ferrell and Samuel Flagg Bemis, eds., XIV, 4-10; Walter Johnson, "Edward R. Stettinius, Jr.," *An Uncertain Tradition; American Secretaries of State in the Twentieth Century*, Norman A. Graebner, ed., 210-214; TE, II, 1383-86.
37. *Congressional Record*, 78th Cong., 2nd Sess., XC, 8900, 8903, 8908 (December 6, 1944); Statement by Grew before Senate Foreign Relations Committee, December 15, 1944, *The Department of State Bulletin*, XI (December 17, 1944), 762-63.
38. *Congressional Record*, 78th Cong., 2nd Sess., XC, 8901 (December 6, 1944); Walker, "Stettinius," 20-21.
39. TE, II, 1384; Winston Churchill, *Triumph and Tragedy* (Boston, Massachusetts, 1953), 455-56. The problem of coordinating policy within the Department in 1945 is illustrated by the fact that all the geographic divisions except the Latin

American ones reported through their respective offices to one Assistant Secretary, James C. Dunn, who was absent both at Yalta and San Francisco. See Tables of Organization of the Department, December 20, 1944, and May 1, 1945, *Department of State Bulletin,* XI (December 17, 1944), 794-96, and XII (May 13, 1945), 898-99.

40. TE, II, 1517-19.
41. Grew to Stettinius, February 5, 1945, to Cecil Lyon, May 2, 1945.
42. Grew to A. E. Bateson, December 19, 1945, to Dr. Lorrin A. Shephard, December 19, 1945; TE, II, 1385; Phillips, *Ventures in Diplomacy*, 457.
43. Memorandum for Stettinius, January 3, 1945; TE, II, 1420-21.
44. Grew to Vera Micheles Dean, August 9, 1943, to Rev. Ernest Caldecott, July 20, 1945.
45. TE, II, 1422, 1425; Herbert Feis, *Japan Subdued; The Atomic Bomb and the End of the War in the Pacific* (Princeton, 1961), 7.
46. Diary, March 1, 1936; Grew to Lieutenant General Robert C. Richardson, Jr., May 25, 1945; Robert J. C. Butow, *Japan's Decision to Surrender* (Stanford, California, 1954), 54-57, 103-11, especially p. 56 fn. 80 and p. 105.
47. TE, II, Chaps. 37, 38, especially pp. 1445-46, 1456, 1479, 1481; Louis Morton, "The Decision to Use the Atomic Bomb," *Foreign Affairs,* XXXV (January 1957), 342.
48. TE, II, 1423, 1428-31.
49. Grew to Admiral J. F. Shafroth, October 18, 1945; TE, II, 1434-37; Feis, *Japan Subdued*, 18-22. In 1950 (TE, II, 1424) Grew explained the military reasons for delay as follows: "It later appeared that the fighting on Okinawa was still going on, and it was felt that such a declaration as I proposed would be interpreted by the Japanese as a confession of weakness." However, this was Stimson's explanation in 1947 (Stimson and Bundy, *On Active Service*, II, 628), not Grew's in 1945. By May 29 American forces on Okinawa had captured Naha and Shuri Castle and the end could hardly have seemed "another couple of months" away. More likely the military reason for delay was related to the testing of an atomic device in July and to the readiness of an atomic weapon thereafter. Grew knew of atomic progress (Feis, *Japan Subdued*, 19, fn. 7) and probably understood the real military reason for delay. There is no evidence, however, that he pressed for an early declaration in order to avoid use of atomic weapons. Later he argued that avoiding their use would have been a beneficial result (TE, II, 1426), but at the time, in May and June, his view seems to have been that prospects were sufficiently promising for inducing surrender without further military sanctions whatever their nature.
50. Stimson to Truman, July 2, 1945, and Enclosure 1, *FR, Conference of Berlin (Potsdam)*, 1945 (hereafter cited as *FR, Potsdam*), I, Document 592, 888-92; *The Forrestal Diaries*, ed. Walter Millis (New York, 1951), 69-71; Stimson and Bundy, *On Active Service*, II, 624, 628-29; Morton, "Decision to Use the Atomic Bomb," 337-41, 344-46; Feis, *Japan Subdued*, 11, 22-25.
51. Minutes of a Meeting of the Committee of Three, June 26, 1945, Document 591, *FR, Potsdam*, I, 887-88; Stimson to Truman, July 2, 1945, and Enclosure 1, Document 592, *ibid.*, 888-92; United States Delegation Working Paper (Draft Proclamation) [n.d.], Document 594, *ibid.*, 899. The text of Paragraph 12 given here is from a revision of the draft Stimson submitted to Truman (Stimson to Truman, July 2, 1945, Enclosure 2, Document 592, *ibid.*, 893-94) which clarified but did not alter the meaning or explicitness of the July 2 version of this paragraph.
52. Stimson to Truman, July 2, 1945, *ibid.*, 888-89.
53. MacLeish to Byrnes, July 6, 1945, Document 593, *ibid.*, 895-97; Minutes of the 153rd Meeting of the Secretary's Staff Committee, July 7, 1945, Document 595, *ibid.*, 900-901; Grew to Byrnes, July 16, 1945, Document 1237, *ibid.*, II, 1267; Hull, *Memoirs*, II, 1593-94; TE, II, 1424.
54. Stimson to Truman, July 16, 1945, Enclosure, and fn. 6, Document 1236, *FR, Potsdam*, II, 1265-67; Stimson to Truman, July 20, 1945, fn. 3, Document 1241, *ibid.*, 1272; Acting Chairman of Interim Committee to Stimson, July 23, 1945,

Document 1312, *ibid.*, 1374; Stimson and Bundy, *On Active Service*, II, 626; Butow, *Japan's Decision*, 140-81 and Appendix C (Potsdam Proclamation), 243-44.

55. Feis, *Japan Subdued*, 121, fn. 9a, 122; Butow, *Japan's Decision*, Chap. 9.
56. Grew to Admiral J. F. Shafroth, October 18, 1945, to Max Bishop, October 19, 28, 1945, to Stimson (copy), February 12, 1947; Henry L. Stimson, "The Decision to Use the Atomic Bomb," *Harper's*, CXCIV (February 1947), 97-107. Most of the letter to Stimson is in TE, II, 1421-28. Stimson's made amends regarding Grew's role, though disagreeing with his position, in Stimson and Bundy, *On Active Service*, II, 626-30.
57. The draft statement that follows after Grew's memorandum of the May 28 meeting in *Turbulent Era* (II, 1431-34) is erroneously identified as "Completed in Department of State, May, 1945." It is clearly a product of the drafting committee set up June 26 to prepare the statement Stimson delivered to the President July 2 (see Document 594, fn. 1, *FR*, *Potsdam*, I, 897; Feis, *Japan Subdued*, 18, fn. 4). The editors of *Foreign Relations* have located a document which they judge to be a Department of State draft statement of May 1945 (*ibid.*; File 740.0011 EW/5-3145) and which the author has seen. It consists of three papers, in carbon, stapled together, without initials, heading, indication of origin, or date. The top paper is a memorandum proposing and arguing for a public statement and is a longer draft of Document 589, *FR*, *Potsdam*, I, 884. The second paper is a note saying that the attached draft statement, the third paper, was nearly identical with one prepared by Dooman and approved by Grew. In the third paper, the draft statement itself, the pertinent part is as follows:

    If the Japanese by surrendering now were left in the fullness of time to determine for themselves their future political structure, they would not be permitted to make a travesty of the principle set forth in the Atlantic Charter that nations shall be allowed to choose their own form of government. It is we who will judge whether the institutions they propose to maintain for the eradication of militarism and tyranny will conduce to the observance by Japan of its international obligations and to furthering common peace and security.

    Compare with Grew's memorandum of his conversation with the President May 28 (TE, II, 1429): "If some indication can now be given the Japanese that they themselves . . . will be permitted to determine their own future political structure. . . ." The original of the third paper seems to have been the draft statement Grew handed the President May 28. Needless to say, it is not explicit about the Emperor. Some of the language and much of the substance carried into the Stimson drafts, probably through Dooman's work on the combined drafting committee, so the draft in *Turbulent Era* is a third- or fourth-generation offspring of the May 28 draft. This relationship may account for Grew's recollection in 1947 that he gave Byrnes on July 6, 1945, the draft he had shown the President (TE, II, 1424).
58. TE, II, 1429, 1434, 1435, 1523; Grew to Max Bishop, October 19, 1945 ("I explained to the President that we must tell the Japanese more definitely what unconditional surrender would mean and what it would not mean and that the Japanese people must be allowed to choose their eventual form of government."). Truman says that Grew spoke to him late in May "about issuing a proclamation that would urge the Japanese to surrender but would assure them that we would permit the Emperor to remain as head of the state." Harry S. Truman, *Year of Decisions* (*Memoirs*, Vol. I; New York, 1955), 416. However, Truman does not make the distinction between explicit and implicit assurances and he is undoubtedly referring to the intended effect of the statement rather than to its wording.
59. Statement by Grew before Senate Foreign Relations Committee, December 15, 1944, *The Department of State Bulletin*, XI (December 17, 1944), 763; Butow, *Japan's Decision*, Chap. 6; Winston Churchill, *Triumph and Tragedy* (Cambridge, Mass., 1953), Chap. 7.
60. Grew to his daughter Elsie, September 2, 1945, to Harry Grew, August 21, 1945, to Phillips, August 17, 1945, to Castle, September 5, 1945; *Washington Post*, May 31,

June 30, August 14, 17, 1945; *Nation*, CLXI (July 14, 1945), 23, 25-32; TE, II, Chap. 41.

EPILOGUE

1. Grew to Harry Grew, December 3, 1945, to William D. Mitchell, November 12, 1945; testimony of Grew, *PHA*, part 2, 560-603, 615-773, especially 695-98.
2. On the diplomacy of 1941: TE, II, Chap. 34. On the surrender: *ibid.*, 1406-08, 1421-28.
3. *Time*, October 19, 1953 (text of the petition).

Bibliography

THE principal source of this study was the Papers of Joseph C. Grew at the Houghton Library, Harvard University. The bulk of the papers is a series designated LETTERS, which consists of 123 volumes arranged chronologically from 1909 to 1945. Except as specified below, this series includes Grew's diary, correspondence, memoranda of conversations, and newspaper clippings, each classification generally bound separately within any given year. The diary for 1941 is not bound and is filed separately as PERSONAL NOTES. Beginning with 1932, CONVERSATIONS are bound as a separate series (7 vols.), and beginning with 1941, CLIPPINGS are boxed and designated as a separate series (14 boxes). SPEECHES, 1904-45, are a separate series (4 vols., 5 boxes). The collection also includes several folders of miscellaneous material.

Several collections besides the Grew Papers proved indispensable in detailing the course of Foreign Service development. Especially valuable were the Wilbur J. Carr Papers, Library of Congress, Washington, D.C., including his diary, correspondence, and memoranda, and the diary of William R. Castle, Jr., for the years 1919-27. The Castle Diary, which was examined when it was in Mr. Castle's possession, is now deposited at the Houghton Library, Harvard. Other collections bearing on Foreign Service development were the Papers of Jay Pierrepont Moffat and Ellis Loring Dresel, both at the Houghton Library, and correspondence in the Nelson Trusler Johnson and Leland Harrison Papers, both at the Library of Congress.

Useful for Grew's career during World War I and the organization of the American delegation at Paris were the Private Papers of Colonel Edward M. House, Yale University Library, in particular his diary and correspondence with Grew, Lansing, Gerard, and Phillips. Also useful were the diary and correspondence of House's son-in-law, Gordon Auchincloss, in the same collection. The war diary and correspondence in the Papers of Mark L. Bristol, Library of Congress, Washington, D.C., established the viewpoint of Grew's colleague at Lausanne. The Moffat Diary in the Moffat Papers proved immensely helpful in describing the Washington viewpoint during Grew's Japan mission. Also helpful for the Japan mission were the

Johnson Papers. Of incidental value to this study were the Papers of Richard Washburn Child and Charles Evans Hughes at the Library of Congress and of Frank Billings Kellogg at the Minnesota Historical Society, St. Paul, Minnesota.

Two translated Japanese sources were used, the Saionji-Harada Memoirs and the Diary of Marquis Kido Kōichi. The former source, a diary kept by Prince Saionji's well-informed secretary, Baron Harada, is a document of the first importance for the inner history of the Japanese government in the 1930's. It was particularly useful because of Harada's contacts with Grew. The translations used were exhibits of the International Military Tribunal for the Far East in the Library of Congress microfilm series, "Checklist of Archives in the Japanese Ministry of Foreign Affairs, 1868-1945," reels SP49-51 (Saionji-Harada) and WT5 (Kido).

The State Department Archives (National Archives, Washington, D.C.) were used extensively for the Lausanne Conference and the principal subjects which occupied Grew as Ambassador to Turkey. They were occasionally helpful for Foreign Service development and Grew's Under Secretaryship, 1924-27. For the Japan mission the Archives were used selectively, since the Grew Papers provide a record of all his communications and since the volumes on the Far East in the *Foreign Relations* series proved to be an extensive and well-chosen collection of documents. The Archives for 1943 and after are not open to research.

PUBLISHED DOCUMENTS

Documents on German Foreign Policy, 1918-1945: From the Archives of the German Foreign Ministry, Series D. 13 vols. Washington, D.C., 1949-64. Vols. I, IX, XII, XIII.

Great Britain. *Documents on British Foreign Policy*, 1919-1939, 3rd Series. E. L. Woodward and Rohan Butler, eds. 9 vols. London, 1949-55. Vols. VIII, IX.

———, *Lausanne Conference on Near Eastern Affairs, 1922-1923: Records of Proceedings and Draft Terms of Peace*. Cmd. 1814. London, 1923.

League of Nations. *Report of the Temporary Mixed Commission for the Reduction of Armaments*. Document A.16.IX. Geneva, 1924.

Royal Institute of International Affairs. *Documents on International Affairs, 1937*. Stephen Heald, ed. London, 1939.

United States Congress. *Congressional Record*, 67th Cong. 4th Sess., 68th Cong. 1st Sess., 70th Cong. 1st Sess., 78th Cong. 2nd Sess. Washington, D.C., 1923, 1924, 1927, 1944.

———, Joint Committee on the Investigation of the Pearl Harbor Attack. *Hearings Before the Joint Committee on the Investigation of the Pearl Harbor Attack*. 79th Cong. 2nd Sess. 39 parts. Washington, D.C., 1946. Parts, 2, 12, 16, 17, 20.

———, House of Representatives, Foreign Affairs Committee. *The Foreign Service of the United States*. Hearings on H.R. 17 and H.R. 6357. 68th Cong. 1st Sess. Washington, D.C., 1923.

———, House of Representatives. *Report of the Honorable Herbert H. D. Peirce on Inspection of United States Consulates in the Orient*. House Document No. 665. 59th Cong. 1st Sess. Washington, D.C., 1906.

———, Senate, Committee on Foreign Relations. *Reorganization and Improvement of the Foreign Service*. Senate Report No. 1069. 70th Cong. 1st Sess. Washington, D.C., 1928.

United States Department of State. *Register*. For the years 1867-1945.

———, *The Department of State Bulletin*. Vols. VII-XII. Washington, D.C., 1942-45.

———, *Papers Relating to the Foreign Relations of the United States*. Beginning in 1932 the title changed to *Foreign Relations of the United States: Diplomatic Papers*. All were printed in Washington, D.C.

1908 (1912)
1909 (1914)
1910 (1915)
1911 (1918)
1912 (1919)
1913 (1920)
1914 (1922)
1914 *Supplement: The World War* (1928)
1916 *Supplement: The World War* (1929)
1919: *The Paris Peace Conference* (13 vols. 1942-47), Vols. I, XI
The Lansing Papers, 1914-1920 (2 vols. 1939-40)
1920 (3 vols. 1935-36), Vols. I, II
1921 (2 vols. 1936), Vol. II
1922 (2 vols. 1938)
1923 (2 vols. 1938)
1924 (2 vols. 1939), Vol. I
1926 (2 vols. 1941)
1927 (3 vols. 1942), Vol. III
1928 (3 vols. 1942-43), Vol. III
1929 (3 vols. 1943-44), Vol. III
1930 (3 vols. 1945), Vol. III
1931 (3 vols. 1946), Vol. II
1932 (5 vols. 1947-48), Vols. III, IV
1933 (5 vols. 1949-52), Vol. III
1934 (5 vols. 1950-52), Vols. I, III
1935 (4 vols. 1952-53), Vols. I, III
1936 (5 vols., 1953-54), Vols. I, IV
1937 (5 vols. 1954), Vols. III, IV
1938 (5 vols. 1954-56), Vols. III, IV
1939 (5 vols., 1955-57), Vols. III, IV
1940 (5 vols. 1955-61), Vols. I, IV
1941 (7 vols. 1956-63), Vols. IV, V
1944 (1965), Vol. V
Japan, 1931-1941 (2 vols. 1943)
Conference of Berlin (Potsdam), 1945 (2 vols. 1960)

MEMOIRS, AUTOBIOGRAPHIES, PUBLISHED PAPERS

Baker, Ray Stannard. *Woodrow Wilson, Life and Letters*. 8 vols. Garden City, New York, 1927-39. Vols. VI-VIII.

Blum, John Morton. *From the Morgenthau Diaries: Years of Urgency, 1938-1941*. Boston, 1965.

Child, Richard Washburn. *A Diplomat Looks at Europe*. New York, 1925.

Coolidge, Harold Jefferson, and Robert Howard Lord. *Archibald Cary Coolidge, Life and Letters*. Boston, 1932.

Galpin, Perrin C., ed. *Hugh Gibson, 1883-1954: Extracts from His Letters and Anecdotes from His Friends*. New York, 1956.

Gerard, James W. *My First Eighty-three Years in America*. New York, 1951.

———. *My Four Years in Germany*. New York, 1917.

Grew, Joseph C. *Sport and Travel in the Far East*, Boston, 1910.

———. *Ten Years in Japan: A Contemporary Record Drawn from the Diaries and Private and Official Papers of Joseph C. Grew, United States Ambassador to Japan, 1932-1942*. New York, 1944.

———. *Turbulent Era: A Diplomatic Record of Forty Years, 1904-1945*. Edited by Walter Johnson assisted by Nancy Harvison Hooker. 2 vols. Boston, 1952.

Hooker, Nancy Harvison, ed. *The Moffat Papers: Selections from the Diplomatic Journals of Jay Pierrepont Moffat, 1919-1943*. Cambridge, Massachusetts, 1956.

Hoover, Herbert. *The Memoirs of Herbert Hoover: The Cabinet and the Presidency, 1920-1933*. New York, 1951.

Hull, Cordell. *The Memoirs of Cordell Hull*. 2 vols. New York, 1948.

Millis, Walter, ed. *The Forrestal Diaries*. New York, 1951.

Morison, Elting E. *et al.*, eds., *Letters of Theodore Roosevelt, 1858-1919*. 8 vols. Cambridge, Masschusetts, 1951-54. Vols. IV, VII.

Phillips, William. *Ventures in Diplomacy*. Boston, 1952.
Robinson, Edward Arlington, ed. *Selections from the Letters of Thomas Sergeant Perry*. New York, 1929.
Seymour, Charles. *The Intimate Papers of Colonel House*. 4 vols. Boston, 1926-28. Vols. III, IV.
Shotwell, James T. *At the Paris Peace Conference*. New York, 1937.
Stimson, Henry L. *Far Eastern Crisis: Recollections and Observations*. New York, 1936.
———, and McGeorge Bundy. *On Active Service in Peace and War*. 2 vols. New York, 1947.
Truman, Harry S. *Memoirs: Year of Decisions*. Garden City, New York, 1955.
Wilson, Hugh. *Diplomat Between Wars*. New York, 1941.
———. *Education of a Diplomat*. New York, 1938.
Wilson, Hugh R., Jr. *Disarmament and the Cold War in the Thirties*. New York, 1963.

A NOTE ON OTHER SOURCES

Interviews were chiefly useful for background information and for gaining a grasp of the personalities involved. The author interviewed the following persons besides Mr. Grew: William R. Castle, Jr.; Huntington Gilchrist, Grew's intermediary with the League of Nations; Joseph C. Green, formerly chairman of the Board of Examiners of the Foreign Service; William Phillips; and G. Howland Shaw, Grew's Counselor of Embassy in Turkey. In addition he corresponded with Grew's Counselor of Embassy in Japan, Eugene R. Dooman.

No useful purpose would be served by including in this bibliography the miscellaneous newspapers and periodicals used. They are appropriately cited in the Notes. The periodicals used to establish public attitudes toward Foreign Service development are cited comprehensively in the Notes to Chapters 1, 7, and 8. The one newspaper used extensively was the *New York Times*.

Similarly, no useful purpose would be served by furnishing a complete bibliography of secondary works and articles. Again, they have been appropriately cited in the Notes, which include a number of topical notes covering works used for background on particular subjects as they arise. Secondary works of particular value to this study are grouped by phases of Grew's career in the following section.

SELECTED SECONDARY WORKS AND ARTICLES

I. BACKGROUND AND EARLY CAREER

Birnbaum, Karl E. *Peace Moves and U-Boat Warfare: A Study of Imperial Germany's Policy Toward the United States, April 18, 1916–January 9, 1917*. Stockholm, 1958.
Freidel, Frank B. *Franklin D. Roosevelt: The Apprenticeship*. Boston, 1952.
Kennan, George F. *Russia Leaves the War*. Princeton, New Jersey, 1956.
———. *The Decision to Intervene*. Princeton. New Jersey, 1958.
Link, Arthur S. *Wilson: Campaigns for Progressivism and Peace, 1916-1917*. Princeton, New Jersey, 1965.
May, Ernest R. *The World War and American Isolation, 1914-1917*. Cambridge, Massachusetts, 1959.

II. DEVELOPMENT OF THE FOREIGN SERVICE

Baltzell, E. Digby. *Philadelphia Gentlemen: The Making of a National Upper Class*. Glencoe, Illinois, 1958.
Cambon, Jules. *The Diplomatist*. London, 1931.
Childs, J. Rives. *The American Foreign Service*. New York, 1948.
Crane, Katherine. *Mr. Carr of State: Forty-seven Years in the Department of State*. New York, 1960.
Ellis, L. Ethan. *Frank B. Kellogg and American Foreign Relations, 1925-1929*. New Brunswick, New Jersey, 1961.

Hulen, Bertram. *Inside the Department of State*. New York, 1939.
Ilchman, Warren Frederick. *Professional Diplomacy in the United States, 1779-1939: A Study in Administrative History*. Chicago, 1961.
McCamy, James L. *The Administration of American Foreign Affairs*. New York, 1950.
Nicolson, Harold. *Diplomacy*. New York, 1939.
———. *The Evolution of Diplomacy* (first published as *The Evolution of Diplomatic Method*). Collier: New York, 1962.
Pearson, Drew, and Robert S. Allen. *Washington Merry-Go-Round*. New York, 1931.
Shaw, G. Howland. "The American Foreign Service," *Foreign Affairs*, XIV (January 1936), 323-333.
Stuart, Graham H. *The Department of State*. New York, 1949.
Webster, Sir Charles. *The Art and Practice of Diplomacy*. London, 1961.
Wilson, Hugh. *Diplomacy as a Career*. Cambridge, Massachusetts, 1941.

III. LAUSANNE AND THE MISSION TO TURKEY

Craig, Gordon A., and Felix Gilbert, eds., *The Diplomats, 1919-1939*. Princeton, New Jersey, 1953.
DeNovo, John A. *American Interests and Policies in the Middle East, 1900-1939*. Minneapolis, Minnesota, 1963.
Hershlag, Z. Y. *Turkey: An Economy in Transition*. The Hague, n.d. [1958?].
Howard, Harry N. *The Partition of Turkey: A Diplomatic History, 1919-1923*. Norman, Oklahoma, 1931.
Karpat, Kemal H. *Turkey's Politics: The Transition to a Multi-Party System*. Princeton, New Jersey, 1959.
Lewis, Bernard. *The Emergence of Modern Turkey*. London, 1961.
Nicolson, Harold. *Curzon: The Last Phase, 1919-1925*. Boston, 1934.
Rustow, Dankwart A. "The Foreign Policy of the Turkish Republic," in Roy C. Macrides, ed., *Foreign Policy in World Politics*. Englewood Cliffs, New Jersey, 1958.
Sachar, Howard Morely. "The United States and Turkey, 1914-1927." Doctoral dissertation, Harvard University, 1953.
Strassler, Robert. "Ismet Inönü, Turkish Leader." Senior honors thesis, Harvard University, 1959.
Toynbee, A. J., and K. P. Kirkwood. *Turkey*. London, 1926.

IV. THE JAPAN MISSION

Borg, Dorothy. *The United States and the Far Eastern Crisis of 1933-1938: From the Manchurian Incident Through the Initial Stage of the Undeclared Sino-Japanese War*. Cambridge, Massachusetts, 1964.
Butow, Robert J. C. "The Hull-Nomura Conversations: A Fundamental Misconception," *American Historical Review*, LXV (July 1960), 822-836.
———. *Tojo and the Coming of the War*. Princeton, New Jersey, 1961.
Byas, Hugh. *Government by Assassination*. New York, 1942.
Crowley, James Buckley. "Japan's China Policy, 1931-1938: A Study of the Role of the Military in the Determination of Foreign Policy." Doctoral dissertation, University of Michigan, 1959.
———. "A Reconsideration of the Marco Polo Bridge Incident," *Journal of Asian Studies*, XXII (May 1963), 277-291.
Divine, Robert A. *The Illusion of Neutrality*. Chicago, 1962.
Feis, Herbert. *The Road to Pearl Harbor*. Princeton, New Jersey, 1950.
Ferrell, Robert H. *American Diplomacy in the Great Depression: Hoover-Stimson Foreign Policy, 1929-1933*. New Haven, Connecticut, 1957.
Iklé, Frank William. *German-Japanese Relations, 1936-1940*. New York, 1956.
Iriye, Akira. "Japanese Imperialism and Aggression: Reconsiderations. II," *Journal of Asian Studies*, XXIII (November 1963), 103-113.
Jones, F. C. *Japan's New Order in East Asia: Its Rise and Fall, 1937-1945*. Oxford, 1954.
Langer, William L., and S. Everett Gleason. *The Challenge to Isolation: The World*

Crisis of 1937-1940 and American Foreign Policy. 2 vols. Harper & Row: New York, 1964.

———. *The Undeclared War, 1940-1941: The World Crisis and American Foreign Policy*. New York, 1953.

Lu, David J. *From Marco Polo Bridge to Pearl Harbor: Japan's Entry into World War II*. Washington, D.C., 1961.

Maxon, Yale Candee. *Control of Japanese Foreign Policy: A Study in Civil-Military Relations, 1930-1945*. Berkeley, California, 1957.

Morison, Elting E. *Turmoil and Tradition: A Study of the Life and Times of Henry L. Stimson*. Cambridge, Massachusetts, 1960.

Morison, Samuel Eliot. *The Rising Sun in the Pacific*. Vol. III in *The History of United States Naval Operations in World War II*. 15 vols. Boston, 1948-62.

Neumann, William L. *America Encounters Japan: From Perry to MacArthur*. Baltimore, 1963.

Okumiya, Masatake. "How the *Panay* Was Sunk," *United States Naval Institute Proceedings*, LXXIX (June 1953), 587-596.

Presseisen, Ernst L. *Germany and Japan: A Study in Totalitarian Diplomacy, 1933-1941*. The Hague, 1958.

Rappaport, Armin. *Henry L. Stimson and Japan, 1931-1933*. Chicago, 1963.

Royal Institute of International Affairs. *Survey of International Affairs*. For the years 1932-37. London and Oxford, 1933-38.

Storry, Richard. *The Double Patriots: A Study in Japanese Nationalism*. Boston, n.d. [1956?]

Wheeler, Gerald. *Prelude to Pearl Harbor: The United States Navy and the Far East, 1921-1931*. Columbia, Missouri, n.d.

V. JAPAN'S SURRENDER

Butow, Robert J. C. *Japan's Decision to Surrender*. Stanford, California, 1954.

Feis, Herbert. *Japan Subdued: The Atomic Bomb and the End of the War in the Pacific*. Princeton, New Jersey, 1961.

Morton, Louis. "The Decision to Use the Atomic Bomb," *Foreign Affairs*, XXXV (January 1957), 334-353.

Index